DOCUMENTS OF AMERICAN REALISM AND NATURALISM

DOCUMENTS
OF
AMERICAN
REALISM
AND
NATURALISM

Edited by
DONALD PIZER

SOUTHERN ILLINOIS UNIVERSITY PRESS
Carbondale and Edwardsville

Library of Congress Cataloging-in-Publication Data

Documents of American realism and naturalism / edited by Donald
Pizer.
    p. cm.
   Includes bibliographical references and index.
   1. American fiction—History and criticism.   2. Naturalism in
literature.   3. Realism in literature.   I. Pizer, Donald.
PS374.N29D63   1998
813.009′12—dc21   97-20787
ISBN 0-8093-2096-7 (cloth : alk. paper)   CIP

To the group of dedicated humanists who during my years as an undergraduate and graduate student at the University of California, Los Angeles, helped introduce me to the methods and ideals of literary scholarship: Bradford Booth, Lily Bess Campbell, Vinton Dearing, Hugh Dick, John Espy, Majl Ewing, Robert Falk, Edward N. Hooker, Leon Howard, Paul Jorgensen, John Loftis, William Matthews, Ada Nisbet, Hugh Swedenberg

CONTENTS

PREFACE

My study of late nineteenth-century American realism and naturalism has often led me to George J. Becker's *Documents of Modern Literary Realism*, a collection of critical texts bearing on the movements that he published in 1963. Becker's edition, however, contains only a few selections that deal specifically with American realism and naturalism. It therefore occurred to me that a companion volume, collecting the major critical discussions of late nineteenth-century American realism and naturalism from the beginnings of the movements to the present, would be a comparable boon to scholars and critics of the period.

The importance and usefulness of a volume of this kind are supported by two tendencies in recent criticism. First, the return of academic criticism to historical and cultural studies has prompted a major revival of interest in American literature of the late nineteenth century. By my own rough count, at least twenty-five books devoted entirely to the period have been published since the early 1980s; many more works are in part concerned with it. In addition, it has been increasingly recognized that the terms "realism" and "naturalism" as they have been employed in American criticism since the 1880s are far more complex than is implied by their conventional formulaic definitions. Literary criticism, it is now understood, is a significant form of cultural discourse in its own right and thus embeds the terms in intellectual, moral, and social contexts richly suggestive of the underlying values of the moment in which they appear. Few critics and scholars now seek to derive from the fiction and criticism of American realism and naturalism all-encompassing definitions of these movements, but many are absorbed in the ways in which the cultural baggage accompanying critical discussions of the terms express the preoccupations and beliefs of specific historical moments.

It should be clear, however, in relation to the contemporary desire to establish the worth of writing by previously neglected women, minority, and ethnic authors during the premodern periods of American literature, that until very recently *criticism* of American realism and naturalism was written almost exclusively by white males about white males. Thus, except for critical essays published within the last decade, *Documents of American Realism and Naturalism* does not include commentary on what was earlier believed to be "minor" or "marginal" writing. The collection, in short, is principally an act of historical recovery; it seeks to reflect not what should have occupied the critical interest of the periods it covers but what indeed did occupy that interest.

The principal criterion for inclusion in *Documents of American Realism and Naturalism* is the extent to which the selection reflects the ongoing debate about the nature and value of late nineteenth- and early twentieth-century American realism and naturalism. I have tried to include the most often cited discussions, from those by William Dean Howells, Henry James, and Frank Norris in the late nineteenth century to those by V. L. Parrington, Malcolm Cowley, and Lionel Trilling in the early twentieth. But I have also included many essays that are less often referred to and that in a number of instances have never been collected, since these provide the full context for the critical discussion of the movements. For scholarly criticism since World War II, I have sought to provide selections that reflect the major academic tendencies in the study of late nineteenth-century American fiction. Inevitably, given the prominence of William Dean Howells and Theodore Dreiser in their own times, many of the essays in the late nineteenth-century phase of the collection are devoted to Howells and many in the early twentieth to Dreiser. But I have included essays centering on these figures only when they also contain a more general approach to the nature of realism or naturalism.

The organization of the book tracks the history of the discussion of the movements. The first two phases (Part One) comprise material devoted largely to polemical attack or defense. This period is divided to reflect the shift in focus from Howells and realism during the late nineteenth century to Dreiser and naturalism in the post–World War I period. And since World War II (Part Two), almost all significant writing about the movements has been scholarly and academic. I have attempted in the introductions to these three phases to suggest some of the principal issues present in the critical discussion of realism and naturalism in each period.

I would like to thank Sandra Haro and Shirley Shiman for their help in the preparation of the manuscript, the Tulane University Council on Research for its aid in paying for permissions, and James D. Simmons of Southern Illinois University Press for his support of the project in its various stages.

Portions of the introduction to Part One, "The Late Nineteenth and Early Twentieth Centuries, 1874–1914," are reprinted from my essay " 'True Art Speaks Plainly': Theodore Dreiser and the Late Nineteenth-Century Debate over Realism and Naturalism," *Nineteenth-Century Prose* 23 (Fall 1996): 76–89. Reprinted by permission of *Nineteenth-Century Prose*.

EDITORIAL NOTE

With few exceptions, essays or chapters from books are reprinted in full. Omitted material is indicated by a line of asterisks in the text. All notes are those of the original authors. Texts and notes are reprinted without normalization of spelling or punctuation, except that obvious typographical errors are silently corrected.

Headnotes are provided to offer basic information about the life and career of the author of the selection and, when pertinent, its critical context. The textual footnote for each selection indicates its initial appearance, its first reprinting when there has been one, and the source of the text reprinted in this volume.

PART ONE

The Critical Debate, 1874–1950

THE LATE NINETEENTH AND EARLY TWENTIETH CENTURIES, 1874–1914

INTRODUCTION

The critical debate from the mid-1870s to the outbreak of World War I over the nature and value of realism and naturalism seldom included discussion of the formal characteristics of these modes of expression—of specific devices of narrative technique, for example, or of prose style. Nor were critics who participated in the debate able to achieve the distance evident in René Wellek's 1963 definition of realism as "the objective representation of contemporary social reality,"[1] in which the terms "objective" and "social reality" are of course problematical but suggest nevertheless that Wellek is seeking a neutral terrain of critical discourse. Rather, the debate was conducted principally within an arena deeply colored by controversial and polemicized social and cultural issues, a field of action that in its mix of anger, fear, and hope approximates Stephen Crane's notion of a Civil War battlefield. The questions that occupied critics on both sides of the debate were often ostensibly about such general issues as representing life truly, as in William Dean Howells's call for fiction to exhibit a "fidelity to experience and probability of motive" (74).* But the underlying and compelling questions were usually both more practical and social: What kind of society do I wish for America, and do realism and naturalism contribute to the achievement of that society? The debate was therefore conducted largely by means of a coded diction in which ideas about people as social, ethical, and above all sexual beings were expressed in terms heavily inflected by cultural values.

The social dimension of the late nineteenth-century debate over realism is usefully revealed in William Dean Howells's famous grasshopper passage in his December 1887

---

*Here and elsewhere in the introductions to the sections of this book, references to quoted material that is reprinted in this volume are to page numbers in this volume.

Harper's Monthly "Editor's Study" column. Howells offers as an example of the life that should occupy the novelist not an "ideal," "heroic," and "impassioned" grasshopper, the "good old romantic . . . grasshopper" of earlier fiction, but rather a grasshopper above all "commonplace" in its attributes (85). In defense of this substitution, Howells employs a rhetoric of democratic egalitarianism. The young writer attempting to describe everyday life (that is, real grasshoppers), he states, is "made to feel guilty of something low and unworthy" by those who stand "apart from experience in an attitude of imagined superiority." The "common, average man," however, will eventually come to see that the commonplace grasshopper is the true grasshopper, despite the effort of "some sweet elderly lady or excellent gentleman" to sustain the conventional artificial grasshopper as a model of fictional excellence (85).

The grasshopper section as a whole contains an underlying web of reference to other value systems, especially to those centering on science (as I will discuss shortly), but much of its considerable rhetorical energy, as in the passage just quoted, is devoted to establishing a linkage between traditional democratic ideals and literary realism. The grasshopper symbol itself semi-farcically satirizes the desire for the heroic and ideal by the Dickensian and more-than-slightly aristocratic figures of the sweet old lady and excellent gentleman, while the positive stress on the average and everyday exploits a century of Jeffersonian and Jacksonian democratic faith in the good sense, vigor, and moral insight of the common person.

Howells in his own fiction was no doubt deficient in achieving the goals implied by this rhetoric,[2] as were indeed most of the contemporary writers whom he praised for their realistic rendering of American life. But he is nevertheless successful, in this passage and elsewhere in his "Editor's Study" columns, in establishing the premise that the beliefs of a person of refinement and culture—that is, a figure who is the product of an upper middle-class world—are suspect. Implicit in this suspicion is a corollary belief—one that will emerge more fully and openly in the 1890s both in Howells's own criticism and in the defense of Howellsian realism by others—that a support of the status quo in literary matters by those in a position of social power is inseparable from a desire to avoid social change itself. Howells indeed looks forward to this association toward the close of his December 1887 column when he notes that the horror exhibited by many proponents of the older romanticism when exposed to the new realism "is matched only by the frenzy of the *Saturday Review* [a conservative British journal] in defending the British aristocracy" (86). Without referring directly to late nineteenth-century social conditions, Howells has nevertheless introduced in the context of a defense of a realistic aesthetic the basic underlying emotions in the emerging debate over social justice in America: the fear engendered by an empowered lower class, the anger stimulated by the obstacle to reform present in an entrenched and obdurate upper class.

Howells also notes in his grasshopper passage that proponents of realism will often find themselves in the position of "one to be avoided" (86), a formulaic phrase of social distaste reflecting a class bias that runs powerfully through much of the debate over realism. Thus, in 1884 Charles Dudley Warner, after noting the propensity of realistic fiction to examine the "seamy" side of life, declares that the realistic novel "force[s] us to sup with unwholesome company" (41). Hamilton Wright Mabie echoes this dining-room criterion of literary acceptability when he remarks in 1885 that realism is "crowding the world of fiction with commonplace people; people whom one would positively avoid coming into contact with in real life" (64). And as late as 1893 Maurice Thompson could note that "we find that in fiction and poetry we are hobnobbing with persons with whom we could not in real life bear a moment's interview" (126). In opposition to these evocations of beleaguered gentlemen fending off undesirable companions, defenders of realism offered a counterimage of democratic equality and comradeship. George Pellew, Thomas Sergeant Perry, and Hamlin Garland all associated realism with "a democratization of literature," as Pellew put it in 1891.[3] As Garland boldly stated in 1894, in language revealing his full awareness of the conventional prejudices associated with the issue, the realist or veritist "discerns nobility among his street companions" (155), unlike the romanticist, who is "essentially aristocratic" (156).

Garland, in his discovery of nobility in the commonplace and of a linkage between the romantic and the aristocratic, was not merely seeking to draw upon the late nineteenth-century remnants of an Emersonian and Whitmanesque idealism. He was also, as his essay "Productive Conditions of American Literature" makes clear, attempting to identify realism as a force contributing to the achievement of social progress. Garland's conflation of social justice and veritism (his coinage for a form of Howellsian realism) characterizes as well the arguments in defense of realism by H. H. Boyesen and Clarence Darrow during the 1890s. Again, as with Howells's grasshopper metaphor, the issue for literary criticism as a discourse in this union of realism and social progress is not whether the specific works of American fiction these writers were defending betray a reform ideal by unconsciously reflecting a middle class ethos. The significance of the criticism itself is that its writers perceived themselves, and were perceived by others, as encouraging by their support of realism a fuller application of the ideals of social justice in specific social areas. When William Roscoe Thayer, for example, used the term "anarchy" in 1894 in connection with realism (164), he was consciously drawing upon this pervasive perception in order to elicit a negative response to the social implications of realism.

The association between attacks on realism and a class-based rhetoric of social distaste and fear is rendered explicitly in Theodore Dreiser's short essay of 1903, "True Art Speaks Plainly." Dreiser states that those who dismiss portrayals of life as it is are in fact seeking to avoid

> the disturbing and destroying of their own little theories concerning life, which in some cases may be nothing more than a quiet acceptance of things as they are without any regard to the well-being of the future. Life for them is made up of a variety of interesting but immutable forms and any attempt either to picture any of the wretched results of modern social conditions or to assail the critical defenders of the same is naturally looked upon with contempt or aversion. (180)

Dreiser in this passsage lays bare the major issues in the attack on realism. At its core this assault assumes the superiority of one class over another in order to dismiss efforts to ameliorate social injustice and thereby achieve a greater measure of social equality. Dreiser thus posits a conflict between defenders of the "immutable," whose faith in the unchanging includes both literary expression and class divisions, and those committed to a new and truthful delineation of contemporary social evils and the "well-being of the future." His essay reveals fully how the late nineteenth-century debate over realism—because realism as a literary mode was sited in the most popular literary form of the day, the novel, and because its subject matter was above all social life—provided in its various stages a major forum for the expression of deeply held social beliefs.

In addition to their engagement in the principal social issue of their time, almost all participants in the late nineteenth-century debate over realism and naturalism introduced an ethical dimension into their analysis of the advantages and disadvantages of the modes. Broadly speaking, critics tended to endorse either one or the other of two general beliefs about moral truth—that it was best derived from such analogues of the scientific method as verifiability and objectivity, or that it lay in the heart and soul of man. The first, as in Howells's example of a real grasshopper examined by a scientist,[4] was closely allied to the method and themes of realism, the second was a resource of the romantic or traditional writer of fiction.

These underlying moral positions are well revealed in Thomas Sergeant Perry's 1882 study of Howells's recent novels and in William Roscoe Thayer's 1894 defense of the new romanticism in fiction. Perry states:

> Just as the scientific spirit digs the ground from beneath superstition, so does its fellow-worker, realism, tend to prick the bubble of abstract types. Realism is the tool of the democratic spirit, the modern spirit by means of which the truth is elicited, and Mr. Howells' realism is untiring.[5]

For Thayer, however,

> The lamp of Art differs from the lamp of Science; confound not their uses. Think not by machine or tool, which is material, to discover the secret of the heart of man, who is spiritual. The Real includes the Ideal; but the Real without the Ideal is as the body without life. (166)

Perry believes that man is similar to other objects in nature; if he is to be delineated truthfully he must be studied as one studies other natural phenomena. To do so will ally science and literary realism in dispelling both traditional "superstition" about man's special origin and conventional beliefs about his ideal capacities, as embodied in the "abstract types" of popular romantic fiction. Perry, in this reliance on a rhetoric associated with a faith that science can play a major role in intellectual and social progress (his references to the "democratic spirit" and "modern spirit" are instructive here), thus provides a sanitized version of Zola's more openly atheistic call for the novelist to pursue an "experimental method" analogous to that of the scientific investigator. Thayer, on the other hand, begins with a dualistic rather than monistic premise. Man and nature are two entities and therefore different methods must be employed to examine each. To study human experience by "material" means is to miss the distinctive essence of life, the spirit of man. In an obvious allusion to the traditional language of Christian dualism, Thayer announces that the Real (the body) without the Ideal (the soul) is "the body without life."

At the center of the debate over realism (and later naturalism) there lay a not uncommon nineteenth-century conflict between religious faith and doubt, a conflict that was seldom introduced openly but that nevertheless underlies a good deal of the language in which the debate was conducted. Much of the diction that pertained on its surface to such literary matters as characterization, plot, and tone also pointed to an author's presumed religious beliefs—to his faith or doubt in a divine creator who provided man with a soul as well as a body and thus with a capacity to aspire to a life of ideal fulfillment. The criticism of those defending a romantic aesthetic is filled with a phraseology conveying the essential religiosity of fiction that meets this standard. Such terms as "idealization of nature" (33) and "reality of the spirit" (108) and above all a constant call for the dominance of "imagination" and the "beautiful" suggest the nature of this coding. Realism, moreover, is attacked as a literature of the "external" (64), the "photographic" (165), and the "epidermal" (160).

Some critics, indeed, did occasionally allude openly to the Christian dualism underlying much of this ostensibly literary discourse. Richard Watson Gilder notes that while strands of the real and ideal are often united in a work of art, "It is the ideal side of art and of life that makes [the real] worth while, and raises mankind ever higher above the beasts" (113). And even less obliquely and far more angrily, Maurice Thompson characterizes realism as "unholy" (123) and Hamilton Wright Mabie finds it to be "practical atheism applied to art" (67).

In counterattack, proponents of realism almost universally used a rhetoric dependent—as in the 1880s statements by Howells and Perry which I have already discussed—on terms and analogies suggesting the ethical value for a modern, democratic society of a literature which was "scientific" in spirit and method. Wary of attacking religious faith directly, most early defenders of realism relied on the general association of scientific inquiry with anticlerical beliefs to imply the largely pragmatic ethical values of the doable, workable, and unharmful that they wished their readers to identify with realism. It was only Clarence Darrow, a professed agnostic, who stated a belief no doubt held by many defenders of realism—that opponents of the form were guilty of "religious prejudice" (136).

Late nineteenth-century critics of realism and naturalism not only reflected in their commentary the significant ethical and social conflicts of their time but exhibited as well a more fully conscious and thus often far more violently expressed concern about the issue of sexuality in fiction. Indeed, with some notable exceptions, critics of all persuasions shared in varying degrees the late Victorian unease over the depiction of sexual desire and its consequences in a literature destined for a largely middle-class audience. It was not until the close of the century that the widely supported ban on the representation of man's sexual nature was openly and concertedly challenged.

Earlier, however, critics strongly opposed to the fictional depiction of sexual desire and of premarital and adulterous relationships often relied on the charge that the preoccupation of the realist with this kind of material revealed his greed, his obsessive interest in the sexual, or some mix of the two. Charles Dudley Warner suggests the tone of this form of attack in his remark that overt sexuality in fiction exposes the novelist's "morbid mind" (39), a sentiment echoed by Hamilton Wright Mabie's discovery of a "moral pathology" (66) in realism. Critics who combined a defense of the conventional romance with a deep suspicion of the presumed stress on the sexual in the realistic novel frequently used a diction that associated the sexual in fiction with the gutter or sickroom. Such terms as "physiological" (66), "filth" (109), and "coarseness" (126) thus carry a considerable ideological load. Here, in the area of the sexual, the critic appears to be saying, is the full degradation implied by the lowering of social and ethical barriers inherent in an acceptance of realism. Reading a realistic novel, we find ourselves in the brothel and operating room. To critics of this school, the explicit sexuality of much of Zola's fiction joined with more than a touch of literary xenophobia to confirm the "pornographic" impulse of realism in general. William Roscoe Thayer summed up this tendency when he labeled Zola "the arch-priest of the obscene rites of French Realism" (159) who above all satisfied a "pornographic appetite" (161).

Even such staunch defenders of realism as William Dean Howells and Hamlin Garland refused to countenance the presence of the sexual in fiction and used Zola's work as a touchstone of what they wished American realists to eschew. There are no doubt personal reasons of some consequence for the acceptance by these writers of a principle of propriety that violated the social and ethical beliefs that they upheld in other areas of fictional representation. After all, it might be argued, a scientist observing a commonplace grasshopper would describe its sexual behavior. But ah, Howells and Garland might reply, a grasshopper functions in a natural world while man is also a social being and thereby a product of both animal and social evolution. The American novelist, they would claim, in his representation of American social life is depicting, insofar as sexual behavior is concerned, forms of behavior that are different from and better than those that prevailed in earlier societies. As Howells explained at considerable length in his "Editor's Study" column on "Propriety in Fiction," American social interaction is now largely free of the open expression of sexuality, and, as he puts it, "the manners of the novel have been improving with those of its readers" (88).

Moreover, Howells accepts the limitations imposed upon the novelist by an audience consisting largely of young women. Whereas the European-born H. H. Boyesen chafes at this "Iron Madonna" of propriety "who strangles in her fond embrace the American novelist,"[6] Howells's beliefs suggest the far more amiable image of a middle-class parlor where civilized men and women engage in civilized discussion. Howells thus proposes a code of silence in sexual matters that, despite his effort to associate it with social evolution, differs little in effect from the icon of the youthful feminine soul exploited by Richard Watson Gilder and William Roscoe Thayer to prop up their defense of a conventional romantic fiction. Whatever the commitment by such defenders of realism as Howells and Garland to the "modern" ideal of scientific objectivity, they shared with almost all critics of the day an acceptance of a traditional ethical dualism in which man's sexuality was associated negatively with his animal past and was therefore a retrogressive element when found either in society or fiction.

Henry James is a notable exception to this widespread endorsement during the 1880s and early 1890s by critics of all persuasions of a code of fictional propriety. In his 1884 essay on "The Art of Fiction," James does initially seem to support such familiar defenses of this code as the necessary constraints placed on the writer of fiction in "Protestant" countries, the significant role played by the "young person" in determining the content of fiction, and the unacceptability of much of Zola's work. But toward the end of the essay James reveals his true colors. Relying on the principle of the organic nature of the artwork that he had used throughout the essay to attack Walter Besant's simplistic and mechanistic notion of the novel form, James challenges the conventional identification of the subject matter of a work of fiction with its morality. A writer of integrity and intelligence, he argues, will produce an ethical novel whatever its subject. While taking care not to advocate openly a more explicit or extensive depiction of the sexual, James nevertheless vigorously defends the serious novelist's right to explore this or any other conventionally suspect area of experience.

In support of this ideal of artistic freedom, James states that "the deepest quality of a work of art will always be the quality of mind of the producer. In proportion as that intelligence is fine will the novel, the picture, the statue partake of the substance of beauty and truth" (58). James is here seeking to claim for the "intelligent" novelist a ground long available to workers in the other arts. Just as the painter and the sculptor can devote themselves to studies of the nude and create works of truth and beauty, so the writer of fiction, it is implied, can represent the analogue of the nude in a social context, the sexual, and achieve a similar effect. The convention of nudity in pictorial art was, indeed, to attract the attention of many later commentators on the issue of fictional propriety. Howells, in contrast to James, noted in 1888 that he had "no desire to deal with nakedness, as sculptors and painters freely do" (88). Maurice Thompson, no ally of Howells's in most matters, commented in 1892 that while nakedness might be appropriate in a Greek statue because it reflected the ethos of Greek life, it was thoroughly unsuitable as a model for contemporary American artistic expression (128). Clarence Darrow, on the other hand, attached nudity in art not to discarded social mores but to the beauty found in nature, a beauty offensive to conventional religionists but powerfully ethical in its own right (135).

The criticism of Darrow, Garland, and Thayer in the early 1890s participates in the debate over sexuality in fiction in terms established during the 1880s. That is, the issue is pursued almost entirely in its social context: Is the depiction of sexuality in fiction appropriate to the conditions of late nineteenth-century American society? At the turn of the century, however, several younger commentators on the problem, who were themselves novelists eager to break new ground in fiction, returned discussion of the issue to the more elemental Howellsian question sidestepped by Howells himself: Is a fiction lacking this dimension true to experience? Thus, Frank Norris, as he worked toward a definition of naturalism as a form of romance, rejects Howells's idea of the commonplace as too circumscribed by the "well behaved and ordinary and bourgeois" (168). Rather, the novelist must explore the turmoil of the inner life, "the unplumbed depths of the human heart," where he will find, among other "problems of life," "the mystery of sex" (174).

In a similar vein, Theodore Dreiser admonishes that "the sum and substance of literary as well as social morality" is "to tell the truth" (179). Dreiser thus recasts James's belief in an organic union of the ethical and aesthetic into a more explicit demand that the novelist free himself from restraints governing the depiction of sexuality. "The extent of all reality is the realm of the author's pen," Dreiser states, "and a true picture of life, honestly and reverentially set down, is both moral and artistic whether it offends the conventions or not" (180). "True art" must therefore "speak plainly" about sex if we are to achieve social progress is Dreiser's bold message:

> The influence of intellectual ignorance and physical and moral greed upon personal virtue produces the chief tragedies of the age, and yet the objection to the discussion of the sex question is so great as to almost prevent the handling of the theme entirely.
>
> Immoral! Immoral! Under this cloak hide the vices of wealth as well as the vast unspoken blackness of poverty and ignorance; and between them must walk the little novelist, choosing neither truth nor beauty, but some half-conceived phase of life that bears no honest relationship to either the whole of nature or to man. (180)

Norris and Dreiser have thus turned the tables on the principal arguments of earlier defenders of propriety in fiction. The depiction of sexuality in a novel does not imply a writer's preoccupation with the base character of man but rather an effort to render his tragic nature. And its presence does not signify a retrogression to an earlier stage of social evolution but rather a desire to engage the sexual because it is an area of experience inseparable from issues of social justice and progress.

Although the late nineteenth-century debate over realism was characterized throughout its history by an interest in the social, ethical, and sexual implications of arguments for or against realism, it also contained distinctive phases or moments as it moved from its initial stages in the 1870s to the first decade of the twentieth century.

Realism as a term entered American critical discourse slowly and with a European coloration. During the high point of the debate over realism in France, from 1830 to 1870, the term appears only occasionally in American writing, and then usually in connection with landscape painting. By the 1870s, however, it begins to appear more frequently in American literary criticism, though usually in relation to French and Russian fiction.[7] At this early stage in the history of the term in American commentary, discussion occurred largely within the parameters established by French polemics of the previous generation—that realism should be defended because it sought to render accurately contemporary social life, or that it could be attacked because it substituted a scientific method and its associated gross physicality for the beautiful and the ideal in art.[8]

George Parsons Lathrop's "The Novel and Its Future" and Charles Dudley Warner's "Modern Fiction," though separated by almost ten years, represent these two conventional poles in the debate over realism as they become domesticated within the American scene during the 1870s and 1880s. Lathrop, whose essay was published in the *Atlantic Monthly* when Howells was an editor of the journal, shared with Howells an enthusiasm for Hippolyte Taine's emphasis on the writer's need to be responsive to the conditions of his time.[9] Much current fiction lacked this quality, Lathrop argues, because of its commitment to a Victorian "theatricality"—that is, a Dickensian mix of the sentimental and melodramatic. The novel of the future, on the other hand, would resemble the fiction of such an exemplar of the "analytical" school of realism as Turgenev. It would stress character over plot, would seek to portray objectively a wide range of social life, and would especially attempt to render "the moral value of the familiar" (31). To Warner, however, the analytic method and an interest in "the worst phases of social life" (36) produced only dull novels of a debased social and ethical character.

Lathrop and Warner thus lay out much of the ground for the more widespread and intense argument over realism which was to follow. Indeed, by the mid-1880s, even Henry James, who avoided the use of the term realism in his criticism, nevertheless indirectly alluded to many of the issues in the debate in a number of his essays of the period. In his 1884 "The Art of Fiction" and his 1886 essay on Howells,[10] for example, James not only pays homage to such criteria of realism as the need for all fiction to possess an "air of reality" and to exhibit a "solidity of specification" (52) but also finds in his and Howells's fiction in particular the qualities associated with the fulfillment of a realistic aesthetic. James praises Howells above all for his commitment to the depiction of commonplace American life,[11] and he devotes a good deal of high-spirited energy in "The Art of Fiction" to a defense of his own emphasis on "psychological reasons" (56) in the portrayal of behavior. And without overtly rebutting the frequent attack on realism as photographic and thus lacking imagination, James offers, in the anecdote of the woman novelist's observation of a French Protestant family at prayer, an aesthetic of creativity that stresses both the source of a writer's knowledge in immediate experience and the role of the imagination in developing and reshaping that knowledge.

These early discussions of realism were sporadic and also unfocused in the sense that realism itself was seldom the principal subject. But with the onset of Howells's "Editor's Study" columns in *Harper's Monthly* in January 1886 (the column was to appear until early 1892) and with the increasing association of Howells's own novels of the 1880s with realism, the debate began to occupy a dominant place in American criticism of the period. Howells's open attack on romantic fiction and his defense and practice of realism provided, far more than did James's indirectly expressed critical beliefs and complex fictional method, the basis for a close and full-scale examination of the implications of realism for American life and literature. As early as mid-1886,

Howells's role as the foremost spokesman of realism was sufficiently a matter of public awareness for James Lane Allen to note facetiously in a New York newspaper essay that "the man who cannot 'criticize Howells' nowadays isn't respectable. He's a pariah—a pale shade—a nonentity" (101).

Despite its comic intent, Allen's remark captures the centrality of Howells's role in the debate over realism from approximately the early 1880s to the mid-1890s.[12] The chronological markers of his position as primary touchstone of the movement in America are his much noted and derided statement in his 1882 essay on James that "the art of fiction has . . . become a finer art in our day than it was with Dickens and Thackeray"[13] and William Roscoe Thayer's comment in his 1895 "The New Story-Tellers and the Doom of Realism" that "perhaps no higher compliment can be paid to Mr. Howells than to state that those who undertake to write about Realism in America will inevitably find themselves dealing with it as though it were his private property, instead of with the doctrines and assertions of a system" (164). This undisputed centrality of Howells's ideas about realism in his own time has several explanations, not least of which is Howells's own energy in disseminating his beliefs through his activities and writing as editor, critic, and novelist. But perhaps the principal reason can be found in the combined attraction and repulsion of Howells's ideas for his largely middle-class audience.

I have already noted several ways in which Howells's ideas can be viewed as accommodations to conventional assumptions of his time. Howells's underlying belief that science and democracy were the sources of America's greatness might serve well in an Independence Day oration if science and democracy were interpreted (as they commonly would be) primarily in terms of their practical and material advantages. And Howells's notion that the commonplace in fiction is the product and analogue of the scientific and democratic was consciously tilted by him toward a rejection of such elements disturbing to a middle-class audience as sensationalism, sexuality, and (in the early days of his ascendancy) social reform. The question, then, is, given Howells's seeming capitulation to class expectations, why the great furor and anger engendered by his critical ideas?

The answer lies in the threat that Howells's deepest values represented for conventional late nineteenth-century belief and the instinctive recognition by many of his readers of this threat. At the core of Howells's ideas is above all an evolutionary interpretation of human experience. As Howells and his followers repeated again and again, life changes and the principle of change engages every aspect of life, including the social, ethical, and literary. Of course, many of Howells's attackers also accepted progressive change as a principle in human affairs—that the nineteenth century, for example, was superior in its accomplishments to earlier centuries. But Howells's ideas about change, as I suggested earlier, contained deep strains of doubt about the permanence of what many Americans would hold to be fundamental and eternal beliefs about God, man, and society. A conventional late nineteenth-century middle-class American could hold that Americans had created a far better society than any that had previously existed and have beliefs about the immediate presence of God in man's affairs, the eternal soul of man, and the propriety of class divisions that differed little from traditional ideas in these areas. Howells, because his deepest sympathies were toward agnosticism, toward a dismissal of ideal constructs, and toward social justice, inspired concern and resistance. Indeed, it is probable that the intensity of the attack on Howells in his own time arose from a sense of betrayal. Here, his critics seem to be saying, is someone who is obviously one of us and yet is seeking to undermine the values and ideals we live by.

Although conflation of Howells's critical ideas and fictional practice into the general issue of realism characterizes most critical commentary about realism during the late 1880s and early 1890s, it is useful to recognize that this common tendency contains three distinctive yet overlapping phases: an opening salvo of argument and counter-argument following the publication of *The Rise of Silas Lapham* in 1885 and the appearance of Howells's early "Editor's Study" columns; an even more vitriolic polemic stage in the early 1890s as Howells's social ideas came into greater clarity and prominence; and the presence throughout the late 1880s and early 1890s of an association of Howells's ideas about realism with local color fiction.

Hamilton Wright Mabie's 1885 essay-review of *The Rise of Silas Lapham* sets the stage for the more concerted attack on Howells that was to come once the "Editor's Study" began to appear the following year. Howells's fiction, for Mabie, though it displays adequate workmanship, lacks "warmth" and a "vital spark" (62), deficiencies attributable to Howells's acceptance of the realist premise that life is to be depicted analytically and with "dispassionate and scientific impartiality" (63). Both Howells's fiction and the critical ideas underlying it, Mabie concludes, reveal his "paralysis of the finer feelings and higher aspirations" (64). Howells and Zola are thus similar in their "denial of the spiritual side of life" (68).

Mabie's critique sounds the notes that were to appear frequently in negative evaluations of Howells over the next decade, as in Richard Watson Gilder's 1887 essay on "Certain Tendencies in Current Fiction." Gilder praises Howells's fictional craftmanship and critical sincerity but finds him lacking in a vital and irreplaceable attribute, a soul. To note, as did Gilder and many other critics, that Howells's conception of realism omitted a role either for the imagination or for the "ideal side of art and of life" (113) was, as I suggested earlier, to play the trump card of implying the incompatibility of a realistic aesthetic and religious faith. It is thus no wonder that George Pellew, in his 1888 defense of Howellsian realism, "The New Battle of the Books," not only vigorously restates Howells's basic association of realism with scientific advance and social progress but also seeks to respond to the common charge that realism fails to include a place for the imagination and the ideal. With something of the stridency of a youthful disciple (Pellew was twenty years younger than Howells), he declares that "human sympathy has broadened, society has become more democratic; a scientific study of history has shown the interdependence of all men, the comparative unimportance of exceptional men, and the all-importance of the commonplace individuals who form the mass of a people . . . " (119). This greater emphasis on the common and the mass, Pellew goes on to argue pointedly, is not irreconcilable with a belief in the imagination and the ideal. The imagination is the means by which the writer grasps, from external evidence, what is in the heart of man, and the heart has the capacity to believe in the ideal. A commitment to the Howellsian requirement that realism exhibit "probability of motive" includes an acceptance of the need for penetrating insight into human nature and of the presence of varied beliefs and values within a psyche.

Whatever civility accompanied the debate over realism during the 1880s—as in James Lane Allen's and Richard Watson Gilder's acknowledgment of Howells's competence and good will—evaporated in the more turbulent literary and social climate of the 1890s. Zola's immense fictional edifice, the twenty-volume Rougon-Macquart series, was increasingly both available in English translation and highly regarded by "advanced" critics in America and abroad,[14] circumstances which for many conservative critics demanded an even more concerted mud-slinging attack on his work and on that of other European writers who appeared to be following in his steps in depicting the previously forbidden. Moreover, a western agricultural decline in the late 1880s had by the early 1890s developed into a full-scale national economic depression accompanied by much social turmoil. This more volatile literary and social climate combined with the more urgent demand by Howells and others that fiction play a major role in furthering social reform to raise the level of the debate over realism to the boiling point.

Maurice Thompson's *The Ethics of Literary Art* of 1893 and Clarence Darrow's "Realism in Literature and Art" of the same year reveal the guerilla-fighting[15] character and tone of the early 1890s debate over realism. For Thompson, the work of Ibsen, Tolstoy, Flaubert, Hardy, and above all Zola "utter the cry of our civilization's lowest and most belated element" (126). Thompson expresses his appeal to every class, religious, and sexual bias available to the critic of realism in a pulpit rhetoric of great intensity. To feminine readers of *Hedda Gabler* he cries, "Woman, you have taken Ibsen's arm and have gone with him into vile company and have been delighted with the novelty of it. The smack of hell is sweet to your lips, as it was to those of new-made Eve" (129). For Darrow, on the other hand, the great figures of late nineteenth-century fiction and drama—almost entirely the same writers named by Thompson—are the end product of a century of literary and social progress. No longer blinded by religious and social prejudice, they deal with life honestly, including "the passions and affections as they are" (139). And to depict life honestly, Darrow argues, is to write as a social moralist, since the realist's dramatization of the great gulf between the rich and the poor is implicitly a call to social action. As was true of Howells's fiction and criticism of the early 1890s, Darrow's socialist ideals deeply inform his defense of realism.

Hamlin Garland's 1894 "Productive Conditions of American Literature" and William Roscoe Thayer's 1895 "The New Story-Tellers and the Doom of Realism" participate in the equally bitter argument of the period on the relationship of realism to the future of American writing. Garland believes that the way ahead lies in the pursuit of "veritism," his coinage for a Howellsian realism which is both regionally focused and socially committed. The veritist "fires [his readers] with exultant and awakened humanitarian religion" (154). Unlike the class-ridden and woman-degrading romantic novelist, the veritist of the future is one who stands for individuality and freedom; who puts woman on an equality with man, making her a human being; who stands for a pure man as well as a pure woman; who stands for an altruistic and free state where involuntary poverty does not exist; who teaches the danger and degradation of lust and greed, and who inculcates a love for all who live, teaching justice and equal rights. . . . (154)

In the face of Garland's prophecy, William Roscoe Thayer and Hamilton Wright Mabie (in his "Two Eternal Types of Fiction" of 1895)[16] cite the actuality of the recent surge into popularity of such novelists writing in a romantic vein as Hall Caine, George Du Maurier, James Barrie, F. Marion Crawford, Arthur Conan Doyle, and Robert Louis Stevenson. The success of these figures, they argue, demonstrates both the eternal hold of romantic art and the limitations and ephemeralness of the realistic. At the conclusion of his essay, in which he cites every conventional objection to realism, including its damning ethical flaw of depicting a woman's sexuality, Thayer contemptuosly announces the "knell" (165) of realism with a confidence born out of occupying the moral high ground and supported by a knowledge of the immense sales of popular romantic fiction.

Garland's stress in his essay on the local color roots of veritism or realism (an emphasis also present in his 1894 manifesto, *Crumbling Idols*) constitutes a basic weakness in the defense of realism by American proponents of the movement, a weakness defined as well by the scanty presence of American authors in Darrow's list of major realists. It had become evident by the 1890s that few great exemplars of realism had emerged in America. Aside from his most fervent admirers, Howells's work was considered engaging but lacking in intensity; James's interest in European upper-class life was difficult to reconcile with a notion of the commonplace; and Twain was held to be a great humorist but not a serious artist. As a result, those who argued for the inherent strength and eventual dominance of realism could present as evidence either a group of European writers, many of whom were suspect to some of their American supporters because of their overconcern with the sexual, or a large number of lesser American authors who produced a regionally based fiction only loosely related to a realistic aesthetic. Thus Garland, after proclaiming the desirability of a bold new realism to be achieved largely through the pursuit of the local in subject and theme, cites as examples of this method the work of Mary Wilkins Freeman, Alice French, Joseph Kirkland, and Mary Noailles Murfree. And H. H. Boyesen, digging even deeper into the barrel of minor regionalists of the period, identifies Edgar Fawcett, Thomas Bailey Aldrich, and Thomas Nelson Page as among those whose work in local color marks the "progressive" realism of American fiction.[17]

Another major detrimental effect of the almost axiomatic linking of realism and local color in the 1890s arises from the disparity between the actual nature of local color fiction and the tenets of realism.[18] James Lane Allen anticipated this issue in 1886 in his essay "Realism and Romance" when he gently chided Howells and his followers for noting disturbing elements of the "odd" and "picturesque" (101) in southern fiction. Writers in the South, Allen argues, include material of this kind not out of a stubborn disinclination to heed the dictates of Howellsian realism but because they in fact find them in southern life. There may indeed be no relationship, Allen implies, between southern local color and a Howellsian conception of realism. By the mid-1890s, however, as is clear from Boyesen's "The Progressive Realism of American Fiction" and Garland's "Productive Conditions of American Literature," proponents of realism had fully capitulated to the attraction of bolstering their cause by joining it to the widespread acceptance and popularity of local color. But in attempting to absorb into a realistic credo such widely divergent regional writers as, for example, George Washington Cable and Harold Frederic, Garland and Boyesen were unable to do justice either to the distinctive charactertistics of these writers or to the distinctive literary impulses within specific areas of the country, neither of which could be comfortably reconciled to a Howellsian ideal of realism. Local color, in brief, lacked both quality and coherence, and the attempt, stemming from Howells's own early efforts in the "Editor's Study" and continued by others in the 1890s, to yoke it to realism deeply compromised the legitimacy of a realistic aesthetic.

Frank Norris's attempt to construct a workable definition of naturalism at the turn of the century derives not from Zola's *The Experimental Novel* (a work he nowhere mentions) but from his response both to the declining vitality in the late 1890s of realism as literary idea and fictional expression and to the great popularity of the meretricious romantic novel. Howellsian realism, to Norris, was a fiction of surface behavior and conventional ideas (as was indeed true of much local color fiction) and was therefore bankrupt both as a concept and as a fictional method. And romantic fiction of the kind championed by Maurice Thompson and William Roscoe Thayer was guilty of a socially irresponsible catering to the lowest level of popular taste. What is needed, Norris proclaimed, is a fiction that violates every canon of Howells's beliefs (except for a commitment to portray accurately contemporary experience) as it seeks to dramatize the violent and extraordinary both in social life and in man's interior landscape in order to render a large-scale interpretation of the human condition as a whole. Norris's grandiose ideas, though sketchily proposed and expressed in part to defend his own fiction, nevertheless anticipate and contribute to the reformulation of the American debate over realism that was to occur in the twentieth century. He has shifted the general debate to the more specific area of naturalism. And in couching a definition of naturalism that uses Zola as the principal exemplar of the naturalist novelist but that is essentially non-Zolaesque in its avoidance of a deterministic philosophy he also introduces a central crux in later efforts to describe and define late nineteenth-century American naturalism.

NOTES

1. René Wellek, "The Concept of Realism in Literary Scholarship," *Concepts of Criticism* (New Haven: Yale UP, 1963), 240–41.

2. Michael Davitt Bell devotes much energy to making this point in his *The Problem of American Realism: Studies in the Cultural History of a Literary Idea* (Chicago: U of Chicago P, 1993).

3. George Pellew, "Ten Years of American Literature," *Critic* 18 (17 January 1891): 29.

4. Howells's implicit comparison between the scientist and the realist occurs in his December 1887 "Editor's Study" passage on real grasshoppers when he comments that the young writer attempting to depict a real grasshopper "is approached in the spirit of the wretched pedantry into which learning, much or little, always decays when it withdraws itself and stands apart from experience in an attitude of imagined superiority and which would say with the same confidence to the scientist: 'I see that you are looking at a grasshopper . . . ' " (85).

5. Thomas Sergeant Perry, "William Dean Howells," *Century* 23 (March 1882): 683.

6. H. H. Boyesen, "Why We Have No Great Novelists," *Forum* 2 (February 1887): 619. See also Leonard Lutwack, "The Iron Madonna and American Criticism in the Genteel Era," *Modern Language Quarterly* 15 (1954): 343–48.

7. See Robert Falk, "The Rise of Realism, 1871–1891," in *Transitions in American Literary History*, ed. H. H. Clark (Durham: Duke UP, 1953), 401. The best general account of the period remains Falk's "The Literary Criticism of the Genteel Decades: 1870–1900," in *The Development of American Literary Criticism*, ed. Floyd Stovall (Chapel Hill: U of North Carolina P, 1955), 113–57. But see also John W. Rathbun and H. H. Clark, *American Literary Criticism, 1860–1905* (Boston: Twayne, 1979).

8. See Bernard Weinberg, *French Realism: The Critical Reaction, 1830–1870* (New York: MLA, 1937), and Wellek, "The Concept of Realism."

9. See Everett Carter, "Taine in America," *Howells and the Age of Realism* (Philadelphia: Lippincott, 1954), 100.

10. Henry James, "William Dean Howells," *Harper's Weekly* 30 (19 June 1886), 394–95; reprinted in *Henry James: Literary Criticism*, Vol 1., ed. Leon Edel (New York: Library of America, 1984), 497–506.

11. Henry James, "William Dean Howells," *Henry James: Literary Criticism*, 502.

12. See Edwin H. Cady, *W. D. Howells as Critic* (London: Routledge & Kegan Paul, 1973) and the essays on literary criticism in Donald Pizer, *Realism and Naturalism in Nineteenth-Century American Literature* (Carbondale: Southern Illinois UP, 1966).

13. William Dean Howells, "Henry James, Jr.," *Century* 25 (November 1882): 25–29. Quoted from William Dean Howells, *Selected Literary Criticism, Vol. 1: 1859–1885*, ed. Ulrich Halfmann (Bloomington: Indiana UP, 1993), 322.

14. See William C. Frierson and Herbert Edwards, "Impact of French Naturalism on American Critical Opinion, 1877–1892," *PMLA* 63 (1948): 1007–16.

15. The phrase is Robert Falk's from "The Literary Criticism of the Genteel Decades," 149.

16. Hamilton Wright Mabie, "The Two Eternal Types of Fiction," *Forum* 19 (March 1895): 41–47.

17. Benjamin T. Spencer points out, in his "The New Realism and a National Literature," *PMLA* 56 (1941): 1116–32, that even in its own time many critics believed that local color was too parochial to achieve an expression of American life in general.

18. See also Donald A. Dike, "Notes on Local Color and Its Relation to Realism," *College English* 14 (1952): 81–88.

ONE

THE NOVEL AND ITS FUTURE

George Parsons Lathrop

George Parsons Lathrop (1851–98) was a busy late nine-teenth-century man of letters whose place in American literary history owes much to his early marriage, in 1871, to Rose Hawthorne, daughter of Nathaniel. Although he wrote prolifically in many forms and had as well an active career as a magazine and newspaper editor, he is perhaps best known for his important *A Study of Hawthorne* (1876) and as editor of Hawthorne's *Complete Works* (1883). Lathrop's "The Novel and Its Future" and its companion *Atlantic Monthly* essay "The Growth of the Novel" (June 1874) are among the first American efforts to discuss fiction within the assumptions of an aesthetic of realism.

Originating in the Greek romances of the fourth century, which were themselves the offspring of decline, the novel—this losel of literature and outcast of the wise—finds itself, after a long and adventurous career, at the head of all literary forms for present popularity and power. Called forth as a servant, to amuse some idle intellects, it has at length become the master, the instructor, the educator of vast modern audiences composed of thinking and progressive men. We must confess that, whatever our theoretic reverence for the drama, and whatever the triumphs it still achieves amongst us, the novel is still the more subtle, penetrative, and universal agent for the transmission of thought from poet to people.

Ours is essentially a period of prose. Versification, it is true, is a widespread accomplishment in these days, and there are instances enough of genius making it more than an accomplishment. But, on the whole, its frequency seems not so much to mark strengthening of its empire, as to emphasize the truth that things most in vogue are

Atlantic Monthly 34 (September 1874): 313–24.

most in danger of deterioration. As the quantity of verse increases, the merit has a tendency to subside to a common level. Instead of fountains of song bursting freely from the hill-sides, the nineteenth century maintains a large reservoir of liquid verse from which we may draw unlimitedly. The means of rhythmic expression are perhaps more varied and more perfect than at any previous epoch; but they assist lyrical demonstration, for the most part, — dramatic, seldom. It is the dramatic forms, however, which give the most manifold delight. Dramas are the cathedrals of poetry; the lyric verse is their adornment, rising in pinnacles. But we do not build cathedrals nor write great dramas. The novel, therefore, attracts to itself our chief energies. The novel is a portable drama, requiring no stage, no actors, no lights or scenery, no fixed time of enactment. Moreover, as we shall presently see, it embraces a wide range of subjects not fitted for the salient treatment of the playwright. It is, further, especially adapted to the various and complex inner life of the modern world. The very finest things of which the novel is now capable are rather calculated, in their delicate profundity, for private perusal than public recitation. There is a refined emanation from them which can be appreciated in silence and solitude only, or with but a chosen listener or two at hand to share the influence. But, if the vogue of verse be regarded as an intimation of impending decline, it will be asked why the multiplication of novels is not, in the same manner, to count for a sign of approaching decadence. That there is much danger of disaster to the novel is precisely what I should like to have most clearly understood; but there are reasons favoring its immediate and efficient advance which either cannot be supplied, or are not equally operative in the case of lyric poetry. In the first place it is an organism of a higher type than the lyric, being essentially and substantially dramatic; and in the second place the popular demand supplies it with an immense stimulus, while the lyric is sustained by smaller audiences and less frequent opportunities of devotion from its servants. The drama could alone compete successfully with the novel; but to do so it must undergo reforms more weighty than those which are needful to the perfection of the novel. Let us, however, before attempting to cast the horoscope of the latter form, consider the technical differences of drama and novel more closely, with a view to determining their respective advantages as artistic means.

A convenient starting-point for the discussion is to be found in Goethe's utterance on the subject. In the fifth book of Wilhelm Meister, he observes: "The difference between these sorts of fiction lies not merely in their outward form; not merely in the circumstance that the personages of the one are made to speak, while those of the other commonly have their history narrated for them. . . . But in the novel it is chiefly *sentiments* and *events* that are exhibited; in the drama it is *characters* and *deeds*. The novel must go slowly forward; and the sentiments of the hero must, by some means or other, restrain the tendency of the whole to conclude. The drama, on the other hand, must hasten, and the character of the hero must press forward to the end; it does not restrain, but is restrained. The novel-hero must be passive; at least he must not be active in a high degree; in the dramatic one we look for activity and deeds." But this definition is certainly inadequate. In reality, it applies to the novel as practiced by Goethe and Rousseau, rather than to the stature of the novel altered and strengthened by recent developments in its history. It is patent that characters and deeds are as requisite in the modern dramatically organized novel, as sentiments and events; and that they bear just the same relation to these as in the drama. We are far enough, also, from demanding that the novel shall "go slowly forward"—a mode of locomotion sustained in Wilhelm Meister with almost fatal indefatigableness. Compression and swiftness, on the contrary, are becoming marked characteristics of this species of composition. But it is important to observe Goethe's fundamental distinction,—that of the novel-hero's passivity; for he is still at liberty to retain this attitude whenever it may advantage him. And herein lies a special superiority of the novel over drama, in that it is thus fitted to exhibit the hero as the recipient of impressions only,—concentrating in him the phantasmagoric elaboration of all surrounding life through his individual senses and perceptions; while, at any moment, his position may be reversed, so that *his* views of things shall no longer predominate, a purely dramatic development being accorded to all alike. In this way a double order of effects lies open to the novelist. And it is from this source that the autobiographical novel derives a chief element of power; the suppression of internal history in every one but the first person leaving the characters of the rest to develop themselves in a wholly dramatic manner. The means to this end, in the drama, are the aside and the soliloquy. But people behind the footlights cannot find an escape for every significant emotion of a moment in asides; nor is facial expression always adequate to the occasion. Although of this latter resource it is only the intellectual effect which the novelist can convey, by those numerous brief, indescribable touches of intimation peculiar to his art; and although he surrenders the inexhaustible charm of actual impersonation, still his mode is the more natural. As for the soliloquy, that is a delicate instrument which must be used with the utmost care,—like the chemist's centigrade-weight, which he dares not lift with the fingers for fear of diminishing its accurate poise by the slight wear and moisture of manual contact.

> "And therefore; since I cannot prove a lover,
> To entertain these fair, well-spoken days,
> I am determined to prove a villain" —

I confess this jars upon me. This soliloquy of Richard's seems inferior to those of Hamlet and Wolsey, not only in poetical qualities but in its dramatic value. The same sense of inconvenience and unlikelihood attaches to the revery with which Iago closes the first act of Othello. Apparently, when the soliloquy must set forth in direct terms the speaker's motives to impending conduct, instead of dealing with wide-reaching speculations or emotions, it of necessity loses somewhat of its force. It would seem to be the sensitive organ in the constitution of a drama, in which the weaknesses of that order of composition manifest themselves most promptly. But even soliloquy becomes more probable and more acceptable when employed in the novel. For the narrator is an admitted entity from the start, and he enjoys the presumption of having either witnessed, or had faithfully described to him the circumstances of his story which he now gives in reproductive reminiscence. He does not require that we should believe in the instant presence of the persons and their personal responsibility for what they are saying, as the dramatist requires it. However the principles of dramatic development may be involved in his work, the whole affair is professedly drawn from something already past, is so represented; while in the drama we must relinquish, for the time being, even a subdominant consciousness that the scenes before us have been supplied by an already concluded episode of real life. But not only is the advantage greatly on the novelist's side, when the soliloquy is in question; he is also in great measure relieved from the necessity of using it at all, because licensed to come forward in his own person, when occasion strongly demands direct explanation or enlightenment—an interruption which, for the reasons already mentioned in support of soliloquy, cannot disturb us. The novelist's prerogative of description, too, though unconscionably abused in general, is in many situations, if properly respected by him, a palpable advantage. And in the matter of construction a gain is made over the dramatist's necessary restrictions in this particular, through the novelist's greater liberty of interrupting and rearranging the succession of incidents and events. With these technical advantages on its side, and being addressed to the reader at short range, so that its finest effects need not be lost or slurred over, if delicate and unobtrusive, the novel seems to offer a form in which subjects too little abounding in far-flashing externalities, to find successful embodiment in an acting play, may still be subjected to thoroughly dramatic processes.

Yet the prevalent opinions among too many novel-makers, as well as novel-consumers, in respect of what constitutes the dramatic, make it evident that this species of imaginative literature must clear itself of serious misconceptions, before it can proceed unimpeded in the direction of further improvement. An agitated notion seems generally to have gained ground—always reinforced, doubtless, by a benevolent forethought for those readers who choose their fiction from the book-stall mainly according to the broken and easy aspect of the pages—that the novel should be made above all things "conversational;" and to this mistake, serenity, and the contained and forcible utterance characterizing genuine mastery of the dramatic, are constantly sacrificed. But people have other ways of displaying their characters than by talking, and may be treated objectively by other means than those of conversation. Nor is the determined use of the present tense, by which writers occasionally (but too often) attempt to heighten the "graphic" effect of their scenes, at all essential, or even in any way an enhancement. We must take cognizance of a new modification of the dramatic, exemplified in some of the later achievements in the novel form. The stage necessarily appeals more broadly to the senses, and, in these days of excessive and corruptive mechanical contrivance, the sensuous agency has so far diminished the importance or infected the fineness of the subject-matter, as to charge the term, theatrical, with a certain implication of reproach. Those novels, therefore, which are most completely wrought out in the conversational manner, or in such fashion as to make a transposition to the stage an easy process, are not always the most dramatic, using the word at its best and highest. Dickens, Reade, Wilkie Collins, and Bulwer, have so written. And these possess in common a love of stimulating, melodramatic incident, unfolded in rapid and intricate succession. Collins, in particular is noted for his ingenious joiner-work, his elaborate and studied mechanism of incidents. The long "narratives" through which he conveys the same history, or different parts of it, by different persons, have, it is true, some faint flavor of the dramatic, being based on that unfailing surprise which arises from the partial and conflicting views taken by different people in regard to one and the same transaction. But all the true glory of dramatic abstemiousness is lost in his execution. His detail is excessive, and his accumulation of small items often redundant. The skill of selection which he exercises never rises above the plane of simple cleverness. He has arrived at a useful formula for methodic enumeration, of which he uniformly avails himself; displaying a surprising distrust of the reader's imaginative ability, or power of apprehending minor points, by a constant wordy explanation of the most trifling matters. A showy familiarity with the superficial aspects of human nature enables him to dazzle the reader, enough to conceal the fact that, for himself, he cares much more for his plot than for his persons. The latter are cut out to fit their places in the pieces; but their individuality in this way takes an artificial tone, and their narratives seem little more characteristic than affidavits in a police-trial—a kind of literature which we may suppose to have furnished Mr. Collins with a great part of his *motif*. In short, we possess in this noted sensationalist an inventor, not discoverer. He is a literary artisan, rather than an artist. Dickens and Reade, on the other hand, though theatrical in manner, possess real genius, which might have carried them higher, had they carefully pruned it and thrown its strength always to the upward. Dickens differs from Reade, in being far less studied: he is also more crude. Reade is apparently a careful student of the stage, while Dickens relied on the natural bent of his genius toward the theatrical. Collins, on the whole, is superior to Reade in the slow worrying and final decapitation of a mystery—a thing which the latter does not always and especially affect. But, on the other hand, Reade has a swift and sunny sympathy which Collins lacks; and his comparative openness in the matter of plot, leaves him free to develop incidents and characters together, by a series of stimulant surprises. His grand fund of spirits, and his quick sensibility to smiles or tears, are akin to attributes of the finest genius, and carry us on readily through all sorts of incongruities. But, once pausing or returning, to analyze the structure of his stuff, we find the conversation (at its liveliest) modeled on the rapid dialogues of brillant comedy. Mabel Vane, in Peg Woffington, exclaims to Triplet, "And you a poet!" "From an epitaph to an epic, madam," he answers. Her very next words, "A painter, too!" he meets with: "From a house front to an historical composition, ma'am." At other times, as in Love me Little, Love me Long, and later novels, we find Reade lost in the mire of multitudinous commonplace, apparently trying to reproduce life beyond all possibility of mistake, by letting loose upon us a flood of indiscriminate gabble. Thus he seems to waver between the farcically inclined talk of the stage, and a deadly literalism. In general, his pictures are not so much drawn from life itself, as they are spirited transcripts from stage-manners in the guise of real ones, and always strengthened by a considerable observation of real life, besides. But the novel has, by its history, assumed, and in this essay I have claimed, that it comes closer to real life than any antecedent form. By dropping into the stage-manner, however, the writer of a novel not only fails to draw nearer to life than before, but—what is still worse—separates himself from it by a double remove. As life has first been shown him under the gas-light of the theatre, so he kindles in his book a still fainter illumination, the reflection of a reflection. But, with all his brilliancy and energy, Reade disregards this, and plumes himself too openly upon his cleverness, obtruding the consciousness of his dexterity in the most ill-timed and annoying paragraphs of bold allusion to it. It cannot be denied that people relish this knowingness, as they do the equally omnipresent (though unspoken) knowingness of Dickens. Dickens's characters enter the arena with a jingling of the clown's cap and bells, as it were; and the audience sees at once that they are about to perform. There is a suggestion of the End Man's manner, in the way he has of opening a dialogue intended to be laughable. And (to return to our other simile) when the intervals of joking are over, we seem to hear the ring-master cracking his whip, as a signal for the serious and breathless business of riding bareback and jumping through paper hoops to begin again. This is a figure only partially true, yet with a truth worth heeding. The public likes this, I said: but it likes better things, as well. Yet there is an impartiality of omnivorousness, that it is not altogether desirable to sustain. We like to settle the respective merits of authors by the scale of avoirdupois. But, rather than magnitude, it is quality and radical tendency which we ought here to consider; for on these rests the future of fiction.

The more completely a novel remains a novel, the higher must it be rated, as being the more perfect representative of its class. Bulwer was both playwright and novelist, and he is conspicuous for the production of hybrids uniting the features of these two literary forms. His books are crowded with the stalest stage devices. One has but to look through the conversations in My Novel, Bulwer's most careful attempt at a reproduction of real life, to see how unshrinkingly he could dilute the pungent currents of nature with the flattest of liquids from the conventional theatrical tap. Much of the dialogue is given in the same form as if written for the stage. But in attempting, at the same time, to remain true to the aspect of common life, the author has been overcome by a disastrous inclination simply to *imitate* appearances; and the double desire to do this, and to be effective in the style of the stage, has resulted in something at once deplorably dull and intolerably conventional. Mere transcription of facts, aspects, and phases, actually observed by the writer, is—we find it necessary, notwithstanding its self-evidence, once more to announce—neither artistry, nor anything approaching it. On the other hand, conventionalisms, though they are sometimes very necessary, should never be relied on for more effect's sake, nor admitted at all unless they are genuine, thoughtful, brilliant, or forcible. Those which Bulwer introduces in My Novel and elsewhere are, it is true, pointed after a certain fashion: but they are whittled, rather than diamond-cut—sharp pegs, instead of sparkling gems crystallized by the invisible chemistry of genius. And yet these things would, no doubt, pass off well enough upon the stage. But the little green hedge of the foot-lights separates two territories of fiction in which the qualifications to success are, it would seem, by no means identical. Bulwer ignored this fact. Whether we skim the prattling shallows of Pelham, or turn the creaking leaves of Eugene Aram,—that heavy piece of melodramatic machinery,—or examine the dialogue of the Lady of Lyons, we shall hardly fail to meet everywhere the same prolix paucity, although less prolix, of course, in the plays, than in the novels. A knack of proportioning ingredients enabled Bulwer to give his works a pleasant taste to the public; but the critic, unfortunately knows too well that they were prepared according to recipe. Lord Lytton may be said to have maintained a flourishing "cheap store" or popular emporium of ready-made romance. His novels, like those of Anthony Trollope, though more pretentious and less neatly finished, bear the marks of the mold, still. The excessive activity of his invalid intellect never led him to a real originality. He searched for it on every side, imitating, in turn, Fielding, Sterne, Walter Scott, and Goethe; but had he possessed it, he would have learned this by simply looking within. Originality, it may observed here, has even more of sameness in it than of variety; for *this* lies in the subject-matter, and *that* is fundamental. Variety and versatility do not, of course, conflict with originality, any more than sameness is always the ensign of it. But it is the abiding peculiarities of a man's point of view (when these are developed, not derived) which make his writing original; and these continue to give it that character, so long as he abstains from conscious exertion to repeat and renew such peculiarities. From a stable and enduring quality of view, springs style, including not only phraseology, but the character of an author's observation, likewise. Thackeray, George Eliot, Hawthorne, Balzac, Turgenieff, possess distinct points of view, from which to contemplate the revolving world. Pausing at some standpoint of ideal perception, they let the variety of life pass under their eyes, and translate its meanings into the new language of their new genius. Hence comes it that large poetic genius is at once radical and conservative: it can look into the roots of things, but it also highly appreciates the value of calm, unchanging heights, upon which to build securely and live happily. Even when engaged in works of deracination and reform, you can see that, in spite of its intelligence, it loves and clings to what is old.

But Bulwer, and the other novelists of the theatrical group, almost wholly lack the distinction of style. Charles Reade is careless, and hardly more than a mannerist, even at his best. Wilkie Collins is lucid, without being concise; simple, not so much from severity, as because it is easy to be so, in the subjects and within the mental scope he allows himself; and devoid of any deep characteristics. Dickens, it may be urged, occupies an undeniably unique point of view. But his talent was even more accessory to his fame, than his genius. Talent is quick at catching a knack that will please the popular taste; but originally measures the sense of this taste, and guides more than it is guided by it. Shall we say that Dickens did not appreciate what was most genuine in himself; did not know in what proportion to combine with the more precious substance of his genius the common alloy of talent, to make it pass current, without debasing it? At all events, the deficiency in style exists. Who does not recall that droll and at the same time almost pitiable method of lengthening out sentences, to suit the increased suspense of a situation? To so many crowded and hurried emotions, we are allowed a corresponding number of clauses connected by colons, semicolons, and dashes,—like supplemental chairs at a hotel-table, to accommodate a rush of visitors. At other times, we accompany the author through long paragraphs of vague and confused description, at his own verbose leisure; and hardly do we find at any point the enhancement of a really beautiful, resonant, masterly verbal style, organically developed from the originality of his observation. Once let us recognize that this original observation is in great part superficial, taking the tint rather of a brilliant whimsicality than of a profound and vigorous insight, and we shall see why his style is poor and arid.

Balzac laid down the law, that the modern novelist must possess "*des opinions arrêtées*" that, in our phrase, he must have "views."[1] But nothing is more dangerous to the fiction-writer than views which are based upon prejudice. It is immaterial whether he supports himself with social tradition or commonsense, religious authority or unfettered theory: none of these will justify prejudice. These "views" should be the results of perfectly impartial observation of character, resembling somewhat the immovable, inclosing heavens of the old astronomy, which contained all the spheres and atmospheres. Yet they cannot be altogether, like this, changeless. It is simply profound and sympathetic penetration into character which is demanded. From positive views otherwise founded than upon patient and placid insight, spring the swarms of pamphleteering tales which are the bane of the fictionist's art in our time; and, in the domain of more genuine creation, they lead to the narrowness and limitations of Jane Austen, Miss Edgeworth, and Anthony Trollope. It is true, we should suffer irreparable loss if obliged to surrender Miss Austen and Miss Edgeworth. The world cannot afford to dispense with their pure and gentle feeling. What should we do, without the well-molded gelatinous "forms" of amiability, the excellent Potted Proprieties with which they have supplied us?—wholesome confections which it is to be hoped may regale many a generation yet to come. And yet, despite their charms, and that slow, sleepy spell which Trollope knows so well how to exercise, we cannot but think that writers treating human nature in this way are like placer miners, who, it is granted, may extract every grain of gold from their field of operations, but only by working in superficial deposits. And, when all is done, the gold-bearing stratum has been sacrificed, washed away in the process: only the barren bed-rock remains to aftercomers. These, truly, are the "novelists of manners," for they never get below the crust of society. A change in manners makes occasion for a new writer of the same stamp; and Anthony Trollope, in his generation, takes up the task of Jane Austen and Maria Edgeworth, in theirs. What is this remark of Dr. Johnson's, about Fielding giving us characters of manners, and Richardson characters of nature? It would be obviously unjust to Fielding, to place him with writers like Austen, Edgeworth, and Trollope, excellent as they are in their way.

Reade and Dickens, predominantly men of impulse, give no evidence in their works of having apprehended the importance of "arrested opinions." Dickens, indeed, went so far to follow our certain unsettled, impetuous feelings, which he mistook for convictions; and so became a propagator of prejudice (through doubtless effecting a great deal of transient good). Reade appreciating impartiality, and trying to avoid results of this kind, is content with treating mankind as an opportune and curious plaything for the amusement of himself and his reader. But in Victor Hugo we find an altogether singular writer, capable of genuine *opinions arrêtées*, and yet abounding in vagaries, and indulging an unlimited taste for the sensational-picturesque, which compel us to call him theatrical and a mannerist. Here is an author of undeniable genius, a great romantic dramatist, a delicate lyrist, exceptionally noble in his aims, and comprehending the value of an objective treatment of character; who at times delights us with simple and exquisite observation; yet who, for the most part, strays wholly from the ways of nature in his effects, and is wholly extravagant in style. As far as improbability is concerned, it may be said that objections to it, are too often and easily urged in a way to imply that such a thing were quite inadmissible. But if probability were in all cases an indispensable condition of poetic achievement, we should have to condemn much that is obviously above reproach. Nevertheless, it seems certain that the sentiment of probability should never be violated. If the artist should succeed with his illusion, there would be much to justify his use of the improbable. Still, it can scarcely be defended, if it does not also commend itself to the second thought; as it does in the case of Lady Macbeth, who has no children, but who nevertheless exclaims:

> "I have given suck; and know
> How tender 't is to love the babe that milks me."

The truth seems to be, that improbability is a potent means to effect; but when the effect obtained through it is momentary, rather than inherent in the situation's deepest truth, it becomes meretricious, and in degree as it is unessential. With such meretriciousness Victor Hugo seems fairly chargeable, in cases. The fire-cracker-like dialogues with which he emulates Dumas, and which so needlessly confuse us, at times, as to the succession of speakers; the multiplication of short paragraphs, that are in some danger of becoming no paragraphs at all—being often reduced to a single word; and his curious division of a novel into books and parts, with fresh titles and sub-titles as abundant as newspaper-headings, and chapters of every length, from a single paragraph upwards—all this is the issue of an undue desire to impress. Perhaps it should in some measure be excused, because of its service to the author, in carrying the average reader through much that would otherwise appear to him outrageously wearisome. For it is Hugo's plan to connect everything with infinity, on the shortest notice. To fly from the simplest fact into the far ether of abstract thought is his favorite exercise; and to render the reader capable of sharing in these aerial flights, he is obliged to wrap him in a magic cloak of invisibility, woven of sundry expansive and slightly windy phrases. He indites a chapter on a girl's hand, and reaches the weighty conclusion that "Déruchette smiling was simply Déruchette." In another place, describing the nature of a battle, he proudly convinces us, after a series of the most self-evident statements, that "he who leaves the field, is beaten." In fine, he wrestles with nothing, in these cases, as if it were a labor only to be ventured on by intellectual giants like himself; and he comes out of the fight with an immense appearance of victory. Under its guise of pompous emptiness, however, this method conceals capabilities of vigorous surprise and pathetic brevity. Very majestic, to my thinking, is that conclusion of Les Travailleurs de la Mer: "Nothing was now visible but the sea." But the defects of this method are more frequent than its beauties. Hugo's desire to air his enthusiasm and to expand in mystic revery furnishes another example of philosophy injuring art; in the same way that the inclination of George Eliot and Balzac toward philosophical parentheses and interspersed epigram fastens a clog on the dramatic movement of their stories. The novelist, it is true, may fulfill to some extent the functions of a chorus; but he should be very cautious in the fulfillment. Victor Hugo is guilty of "spouting." He tries to magnify, and often to distort, the proportions of all that comes in his way; but things sometimes refuse to be magnified, and leave him in rather a luckless plight. The elasticity and eccentricity of his form he seeks to defend by a mere hyperbole.

"This book," he says, in Cosette, "is a drama, the first person of which is the Infinite."

"Man is the second."

But it is difficult to reconcile ourselves on these easy terms with his reckless practice of "painting up" each and every separate picture in the series which compose a story, so that it may brave the glare of the combined exhibition. This whole question with which we are engaged, as to the grounds for discrimination between theatrical and dramatic novelist, culminates in Hugo's character as a writer of fiction. To get a fresh view of so important a figure, let us subject him to a contrast. Quitting the atmosphere of his lurid spectacles, let us enter the sad-colored every-day world in which rare Thackeray moves. Hugo and Thackeray both indulge in ample comment; but Thackeray's moralizing only partially impedes dramatic action, while Hugo's declamation is so interwoven with the story as to be almost beyond eluding, and is connected with a coarse and dazzling use of colors that reminds one of the scene-painter's trick. In Thackeray there is no hint of effect for effect's sake; but Victor Hugo's novels may be said almost to reek with it. An equally eloquent contrast is furnished by the romances of Hawthorne. "As the feeling with which we startle at a shooting star, compared with that of watching the sunrise at the preestablished moment," runs Coleridge's fine phrase, "such and so low is surprise as compared with expectation." Now, it is the determined preference of this lower pleasure that distinguishes novelists of the theatrical class. Observe, as opposed to this, that in The Scarlet Letter the identity of the unknown sharer in Hester's sin is clearly intimated in the opening scene, and the mind of the reader thus thrown forward, in an attitude of expectation, which the objective treatment pursued throughout the book is designed to assist. Such a master does not find any Jack-in-the-box surprise needful, to engage his audience. But Hawthorne stands in an atmosphere peculiar to himself. To distinguish him from Thackeray, by calling him an idealist, would entail misapprehension; for no novelist possessing genuine insight can fail to be in some sort an idealist. His personal impressions, and keen, unswerving perceptions must enter into the substance of his creation; idea will insensibly enter into every item of the representation. But thus much may be said, that Hawthorne's idealism is exceptionally free from all turbidness. It might be conceived of as a clear and stainless, rounded and buoyant sphere, and capable of bearing us serenely through the most solemn and awful spaces. So far is this idealism from being opposed to that of the acknowledged realistic writers, as people are often inclined to believe it, that we find Hawthorne's realism to be careful, detailed, perfectly true, and perfectly finished. But so suffused is it with fine spirituality, that it does not yet gain popular recognition. Some quality is perhaps wanting in his realism, which would make it more acceptable to the public; but Hawthorne, being engaged with the operation of spiritual laws, did not enter so industriously into descriptive realism as many others have done; although, with a true delight in appearances, he used those particular realistic means which were apt to his purpose with a complete mastery.

Let us consider the import of realism. It is, without doubt, an essential to the best dramatic novel-writing; though in the hands of different authors its manifestations must, of course, vary greatly. One reason for its value is, that it supplies the visual distinctness which is one great charm of the stage. But the necessity for it is more radical. As the painter will study anatomy, in order to a better structural idea of the human form, so the novelist will investigate the functions of all those complicated impulses, emotions, and impressions which we experience from hour to hour, from day to day, and by which our actions and characters are continually controlled, modified, or explained. With his investigation of psychological phenomena, or insight into the mysteries of spiritual being, he must unite the study of all that accompany these in the individual; as corporeality, with that curious net-work of appearances, habits, opinions, in which each human person is enveloped. Of all eminently realistic novelists, Turgénieff is, I imagine, the most vigorous, acute, and delicate. A little livelier play of fancy, he might, indeed, allow himself, without injury. That he is capable of it, certain rare touches seem to indicate. Speaking of a dandy, in Dimitri Roudine, he says: "He tried to give himself airs, as if he were not a human being, but his own statue, erected by national subscription." For freshness, airiness, and genial sarcasm, this equals the best flights of Dickens's fancy. Balzac, as well as Turgénieff, however, seems sometimes to fall below the level of completely artistic representation, simply from neglect of these more elastic motions of the mind. Balzac, in particular, is often too matter-of-fact, or too statistical in his statement of characters, situations, and appearances. It is important clearly to grasp the difference between realism and that which is merely literalism.

I. Realism sets itself at work to consider characters and events which are apparently the most ordinary and uninteresting, in order to extract from these their full value and true meaning. It would apprehend in all particulars the connection between the familiar and the extraordinary, and the seen and unseen of human nature. Beneath the deceptive cloak of outwardly uneventful days, it detects and endeavors to trace the outlines of the spirits that are hidden there; to measure the changes in their growth, to watch the symptoms of moral decay or regeneration, to fathom their histories of passionate or intellectual problems. In short, realism reveals. Where we thought nothing worthy of notice, it shows everything to be rife with significance. It will easily be seen, therefore, that realism calls upon imagination to exercise its highest function, which is the conception of things in their true relations. But a lucid and accurate statement of these relations, in so many words, does not meet the requirements of art. In certain portions of his work, Balzac seems to overlook this: he depends too much upon exact descriptions both of mental processes and physical appearances. He is too much the classifier. In his anxiety to be absolutely correct, he grafts upon his style whole technical vocabularies which confuse and discourage the reader. He often describes houses with a topographical minuteness that ends by effacing from our minds any picture the imagination had formed for itself, and leaving us without the ability to project a new one; and this, when his object is simply to give us a perfect physical impression. It is plan-drawing, rather than the painting of a picture; and this defect extends to his descriptions of persons. All description should be simple, pictorial, and devoid of technicalities. Otherwise, one kind of literalism is entailed upon us.

II. In this matter, Turgénieff completely surpasses Balzac. But there is a subtler truth which no pictorial description and no abstract exposition will suffice to convey; for the intimation of which, in fine, fancy alone is fitted. In apprehending this, Hawthorne is supreme. Dickens abounds in instances of fancy, grotesque, humorous, and pathetic; but he is not so uniformly true as Hawthorne. George Eliot, too, sometimes employs it gracefully. But George Eliot, Dickens, and Scott, all have, again, a somewhat excessive regard for the appearances of realness in and for itself, seen in their labored and frequently tiresome imitations of imperfect articulation. This, though undoubtedly a valuable auxiliary in some cases, is only occasionally essential to artistic representation. When carried too far, it makes the writer a copyist, an imitator,—merely a reporter of life. This sort of literalism is exemplified in still another way by the novels of Anthony Trollope, who accumulates irrelevancies with a persistence proving him to be for verisimilitude before all things. He will construct a long story out of atomic particles, making it as densely compact as a honey-comb—with the honey left out. He continually gives us, with the utmost gravity, the exact time to a minute, at which some one of his characters takes a train of cars, although this precision has no result in events. And an entire paragraph is consumed by the simple statement that two gentlemen went from the City to a London suburb, in a cab. First, he says that they went hence, and came hither; next, he repeats the declaration, adding that it was long since they had last done so; after which, he goes back and describes their meeting in the street—giving the precise insignificant words which they exchanged; and finally he crowns all with the triumphant announcement that they came home together (as he at first said)—this time explaining that they came by means of a cab. There is a certain fascination in all this: the natural man meets mediocrity half-way: but at bottom it is vicious. Trollope panders to an intellectual laziness which is, unfortunately, characteristic of novel-readers; and his books are pervaded by an unhealthy languor. His observation of character is timid and superficial, though abundantly clever; and his impartiality lapses into indifference, a dullness of sensibility. He has but one method of indicating a man's affection for a woman: that is, by making him put his arm around her waist. In Trollope, then, we see how thoroughly demoralizing literalism of this kind may become. It is impossible to prescribe any rules adequate to the various cases in which literalism may occur. But, in general terms, we may say that it is precipitated so soon as the aesthetic balance between idea and fact is, from whatever cause, at all unsettled. We have also seen that realism is assisted by fancy, and quick, pictorial language.

So much being supplied concerning the nature and requirements of realism, we are in a position to recognize the general community of aims in such masters as Hawthorne, George Eliot, Balzac, Thackeray, and Turgénieff. All these are leaders in the best dramatic novel-writing, and their example opposes itself, by its very nature, to the practices of Hugo, Dickens, Reade, and Bulwer. Among themselves, they of course differ in respect of quality and degree of realism, and as to their feeling for pure beauty. We have seen the positive character of Hawthorne's ideal tendency; that of the rest is more negative. Again, they vary in the degrees of pure dramatic effect achieved; and these particular differences are matters of vital consequence. Hawthorne, though thoroughly objective in his rendering, sustains throughout a resonant undertone of poetic revery; George Eliot and Balzac mingle analytical discourse and philosophic suggestion with the action—the latter, however, being by far the less diffuse, and having an easy grace in analysis which our great Englishwoman lacks. Thackeray, in his turn, takes the part of a grumbling and evil-predicting chorus; and Turgénieff claims little more than the right to introduce his persons, and tersely to explain the periods "supposed to have elapsed." There is fair room for choice among these several modifications of method. If Balzac and George Eliot make their books too much like treatises on human nature, anecdotically illustrated, it must still be said that their system is admirably adapted to bring men to a true appreciation of character; and there is small chance of mistaking the special truths which they wish to enforce in their "modern instances." So that what is lost to art, in their case, is possibly a gain to the direct instruction of the human race, in the problems of character and circumstance it constantly has to encounter. But that there is a loss to art, we cannot allow ourselves to forget. The highest dramatic skill would work upon us less directly: it would educate, instead of instructing us. By a gentle, if also searching satire, by a sunny insistence upon the joy of living (the joy of sadness, no less than that of gladness), and by the wise exercitation in us of noble emulation and noble pity, it would insensibly develop, and strengthen, and heal us. I think we are ready for something less medicinal than these magic potions—these bitter brews from sad experience, and deep, undeluded thought—with which the novelists, in these latter and greater days of their dynasty, have come to treat us.

In regard to form, it seems that Turgénieff's example is like to have the most general and far-reaching influence. His self-exclusion, however, is almost too rigid. This northern athlete demands a muscularity of apprehension in the reader nearly equal to that of his own style of presentation. It is sometimes too violent an exercise to read his books: they set every nerve quivering, hinting the agonies of a vivisection. Besides, he would seem to do himself injustice, in recounting such woeful histories as those he chooses, without allowing a single note of hope or of convincing joy to redeem their horror. He is too keenly responsive to outward beauty, to wish the destruction of our faith in some corresponding and essential beauty pervading and including all things. Yet, poet as he is, he finds the world all too unpoetical. To him, it is apparently not malleable in the fires of profound faith, but offers only fixed, enormous oppositions of loveliness and hideousness over which he will permit no veil of illusion to rest. There is truth in his picture; but it seems to deny beauty, and incites to despair. Does it not, then, verge upon error? In marked contrast to the great Russian, we find the Norwegian novelist and dramatist, Björnsen, who, while as strictly dramatic in the form and movement of his stores as Turgénieff, is an enthusiastic apostle of beauty, besides. It would be difficult to conceive of a more delicately inflected piece of dramatic recital, than his novelette called The Fisher Maiden. He has there given the history of an ingenuous, healthy, highly imaginative girl, whose glowing impulses involve her in a curious inconsistency and faithlessness with a pair of lovers, and bring temporary disgrace upon her mother. But at last her imagination makes an escape into art, and she becomes an actress. In the prejudiced community she lives in, she cannot do this without a struggle; and the climax of the tale is in her ultimate triumph, and her engagement at a theatre in the capital. We enter the theatre, to witness her performance; and the book closes with the rising of the curtain. How exquisite is this reticence, this reverence for his subject, that compels the poet to leave his revelation of that fresh maiden heart unspotted by any of the garish splendors or excitements with which novelists are wont so copiously to supply us! In general, they are only too willing to raise the curtain on all imaginable scenes, and to expose matters which should never be made the subject of spectacular interest (although admissible enough when handled with morally sensitive art). Fiction has too frequently indulged in what deserves no better name than downright debauchery. The advances it has made toward temperance, purity, health, and beauty are indeed surprising; but Björnsen, with his sweet and simple histories, has suggested the possibility of still greater refinement.

We already see the dawn of a new epoch. Christ's thought, however slow to manifest itself firmly in the details of our social, political, and religious organization, has assuredly taken root in the novel. Pity and charity, love, or admiration for the poor, the common, the unfortunate, and the unrecognized nobility of the world, are what it is continually endeavoring to arouse and propagate. Dickens's exaltation of the cruder or more ignorant classes was perhaps excessive; but there was much truth in his probably much-needed and opportune exaggeration. Thackeray stimulates inferences, by exposing false pretensions, and dethroning the unduly reverenced. The tragic element of frequency which George Eliot points out has, in fact, been already unconsciously accepted, and the moral value of the familiar seized by the artist. Our heroes and heroines are taken from the rank and file of the race, and represent people whom we daily encounter; indeed, we shall easily find our very selves depicted, if we look frankly for such depicture. There is no escaping the thoughtful and elevating influence of this. Nor need there be any implication of littleness or dullness in these aims. The great circle of the horizon may draw its ring around whatever spot shall be chosen as the groundwork of a fiction, and the exact zenith hang above the heads of its personages. Far from lessening the force of personality in fictitious characters, this choice of the frequent is most favorable to a true discrimination of qualities in character. When we have once become aware of the great number of points in which human beings are nearly identical; of the real coincidence of great people and little people, in minute traits no less than in fundamental characteristics; when, in fine, we perceive the incredible resemblances of men; then we shall best be able justly to estimate their equally astounding differences. The level of humanity is like that of the ocean; but each constitute particle rejoices in its own atomic being, and all have a chance to crest the highest waves, if wind and moon should conspire favorably. The instantaneous photograph is necessary to depict this ocean and its movements. But we must have more than any photograph can give us; with the accuracy of that, should be combined the aesthetic completeness of a picture and a poem in one,—and always of a picture and a poem.

NOTE

1. I translate so, because "opinions" to us, would hardly convey what I take to have been Balzac's meaning.

TWO

MODERN FICTION

Charles Dudley Warner

Charles Dudley Warner (1829–1900), a Massachusetts native and graduate of Hamilton College, spent his early career in newspaper work. While editor of the Hartford *Press* in the late 1860s, he helped found the Nook Farm literary community outside Hartford, which included Mark Twain and Harriet Beecher Stowe among its members. Although Warner collaborated with Twain on the satiric novel *The Gilded Age* (1873), by the late 1870s he was devoting himself principally to popular travel and essay writing and had become an influential spokesman for the literary and social position that was later to be called the Genteel Tradition. Among Warner's most widely read critical works are *Backlog Studies* (1873), *The Relation of Literature to Life* (1897), and *Fashions in Literature* (1902).

One of the worst characteristics of modern fiction is its so-called truth to nature. For fiction is an art, as painting is, as sculpture is, as acting is. A photograph of a natural object is not art; nor is the plaster cast of a man's face, nor is the bare setting on the stage of an actual occurrence. Art requires an idealization of nature. The amateur, though she may be a lady, who attempts to represent upon the stage the lady of the drawing-room, usually fails to convey to the spectators the impression of a lady. She lacks the art by which the trained actress, who may not be a lady, succeeds. The actual transfer to the stage of the drawing-room and its occupants, with the behavior common in well-bred society, would no doubt fail of the intended dramatic effect, and the spectators would declare the representation unnatural.

However our jargon of criticism may confound terms, we do not need to be reminded that art and nature are distinct; that art, though dependent on nature, is a

Atlantic Monthly 51 (April 1883): 464–74. Reprinted in *The Relation of Literature to Life* (New York: Harper, 1897). Text from the *Atlantic Monthly*.

separate creation; that art is selection and idealization, with a view to impressing the mind with human, or even higher than human, sentiments and ideas. We may not agree whether the perfect man and woman ever existed, but we do know that the highest representations of them in form—that in the old Greek sculptures—were the result of many living figures.

When we praise our recent fiction for its photographic fidelity to nature we condemn it, for we deny to it the art which would give it value. We forget that the creation of the novel should be, to a certain extent, a synthetic process, and impart to human actions that ideal quality which we demand in painting. Heine regards Cervantes as the originator of the modern novel. The older novels sprang from the poetry of the Middle Ages: their themes were knightly adventure, their personages were the nobility; the common people did not figure in them. These romances, which had degenerated into absurdities, Cervantes overthrew by Don Quixote. But in putting an end to the old romances he created a new school of fiction, called the modern novel, by introducing into his romance of pseudo-knighthood a faithful description of the lower classes, and intermingling the phases of popular life. But he had no one-sided tendency to portray the vulgar only; he brought together the higher and the lower in society, to serve as light and shade, and the aristocratic element was as prominent as the popular. This noble and chivalrous element disappears in the novels of the English who imitated Cervantes. "These English novelists since Richardson's reign," says Heine, "are prosaic natures; to the prudish spirit of their time even pithy descriptions of the life of the common people are repugnant, and we see on yonder side of the Channel those *bourgeoisie* novels arise, wherein the petty humdrum life of the middle classes is depicted." But Scott appeared, and effected a restoration of the balance in fiction. As Cervantes had introduced the democratic element into romances, so Scott replaced the aristocratic element, when it had disappeared, and only a prosaic, bourgeoisie fiction existed. He restored to romances the symmetry which we admire in Don Quixote. The characteristic feature of Scott's historical romances, in the opinion of the great German critic, is the harmony between the aristocratic and democratic elements.

This is true, but is it the last analysis of the subject? Is it a sufficient account of the genius of Cervantes and Scott that they combined in their romances a representation of the higher and lower classes? Is it not of more importance how they represented them? It is only a part of the achievement of Cervantes that he introduced the common people into fiction; it is his higher glory that he idealized this material; and it is Scott's distinction also that he elevated into artistic creations both nobility and commonalty. In short, the essential of fiction is not diversity of social life, but artistic treatment of whatever is depicted. The novel may deal wholly with another class, but it must idealize the nature it touches into art. The fault of the bourgeoisie novels, of which Heine complains, is not that they treated of one class only, and excluded a higher social range, but that they treated it without art and without ideality. In nature there is nothing vulgar to the poet, and in human life there is nothing uninteresting to the artist; but nature and human life, for the purposes of fiction, need a creative genius. The importation into the novel of the vulgar, sordid, and ignoble in life is always unbearable, unless genius first fuses the raw material in its alembic.

When, therefore, we say that one of the worst characteristics of modern fiction is its so-called truth to nature, we mean that it disregards the higher laws of art, and attempts to give us unidealized pictures of life. The failure is not that vulgar themes are treated, but that the treatment is vulgar; not that common life is treated, but that the treatment is common; not that care is taken with details, but that no selection is made, and everything is photographed regardless of its artistic value. I am sure that no one ever felt any repugnance on being introduced by Cervantes to the muleteers, contrabandistas, servants and serving-maids, and idle vagabonds of Spain, any more than to an acquaintance with the beggar-boys and street gamins on the canvases of Murillo. And I believe that the philosophic reason of the disgust of Heine and of every critic with the English bourgeoisie novels, describing the petty, humdrum life of the middle classes, was simply the want of art in the writers; the failure on their part to see that a literal transcript of nature is poor stuff in literature. We do not need to go back to Richardson's time for illustrations of that truth. Every week the English press—which is even a greater sinner in this respect than the American—turns out a score of novels which are mediocre, not from their subjects but from their utter lack of the artistic quality. It matters not whether they treat of middle-class life, of low, slum life, or of drawing-room life and lords and ladies; they are equally flat and dreary. Perhaps the most inane thing ever put forth in the name of literature is the so-called domestic novel, an indigestible, culinary sort of product, that might be named the doughnut of fiction. The usual apology for it is that it depicts family life with fidelity. Its characters are supposed to act and talk as people act and talk at home and in society. I trust this is a libel, but, for the sake of the argument, suppose they do. Was ever produced so insipid a result? They are called moral; in the higher sense they are immoral, for they tend to lower the moral tone and stamina of every reader. It needs genius to import into literature ordinary conversation, petty domestic details, and the commonplace and vulgar phases of life. A report of ordinary talk, which appears as dialogue in domestic novels, may be true to nature; if it is, it is not worth writing or worth reading. I cannot see that it serves any good purpose whatever. Fortunately, we have in our day illustrations of a different treatment of the vulgar. I do not know any more truly realistic pictures of certain aspects of New England life than are to be found in Judd's Margaret, wherein are depicted exceedingly pinched and ignoble social conditions. Yet the characters and the life are drawn with the artistic purity of Flaxman's illustrations of Homer. Another example is Thomas Hardy's Far from the Madding Crowd. Every character in it is of the lower class in England. But what an exquisite creation it is! You have to turn back to Shakespeare for any talk of peasants and clowns and shepherds to compare with the conversations in this novel, so racy are they of the soil, and yet so touched with the finest art, the enduring art. Here is not the realism of the photograph, but of the artist; that is to say, it is nature idealized.

When we criticise our recent fiction, it is obvious that we ought to remember that it only conforms to the tendencies of our social life, our prevailing ethics, and to the art conditions of our time. Literature is never in any age an isolated product. It is closely related to the development or retrogression of the time in all departments of life. The literary production of our day seems, and no doubt is, more various than that of any other, and it is not easy to fix upon its leading tendency. It is claimed for its fiction, however, that it is analytic and realistic, and that much of it has certain other qualities that make it a new school in art. These aspects of it I wish to consider in this paper.

It is scarcely possible to touch upon our recent fiction, any more than upon our recent poetry, without taking into account what is called the aesthetic movement,—a movement more prominent in England than elsewhere. A slight contemplation of this reveals its resemblance to the Romantic movement in Germany, of which the brothers Schlegel were apostles, in the latter part of the last century. The movements are alike in this: that they both sought inspiration in mediaevalism, in feudalism, in the symbols of a Christianity that ran to mysticism, in the quaint, strictly pre-Raphael art, which was supposed to be the result of a simple faith. In the one case, the artless and childlike remains of old German pictures and statuary were exhumed and set up as worthy of imitation; in the other, we have carried out in art, in costume, and in domestic life, so far as possible, what has been wittily and accurately described as "stained-glass attitudes." With all its peculiar vagaries, the English school is essentially a copy of the German, in its return to mediaevalism. The two movements have a further likeness, in that they are found accompanied by a highly symbolized religious revival. English aestheticism would probably disown any religious intention, although it has been accused of a refined interest in Pan and Venus; but in all its feudal sympathies it goes along with the religious art and vestment revival, the return to symbolic ceremonies, monastic vigils, and sisterhoods. Years ago, an acute writer in the Catholic World claimed Dante Rossetti as a Catholic writer, from the internal evidence of his poems. The German Romanticism, which was fostered by the Romish priesthood, ended, or its disciples ended, in the bosom of the Roman Catholic church. It will be interesting to note in what ritualistic harbor the aestheticism of our day will finally moor. That two similar revivals should come so near together in time makes us feel that the world moves onward, if it does move onward, in circular figures of very short radii. There seems to be only one thing certain in our Christian era, and that is a periodic return to classic models; the only stable standards of resort seem to be Greek art and literature.

The characteristics which are prominent, when we think of our recent fiction, are a wholly unidealized view of human society, which has got the name of realism; a delight in representing the worst phases of social life; an extreme analysis of persons and motives; the sacrifice of action to psychological study; the substitution of studies of character for anything like a story; a notion that it is not artistic, and that it is untrue to nature to bring any novel to a definite consummation, and especially to end it happily; and a despondent tone about society, politics, and the whole drift of modern life. Judged by our fiction, we are in an irredeemably bad way. There is little beauty, joy, or light-heartedness in living; the spontaneity and charm of life are analyzed out of existence; sweet girls, made to love and be loved, are extinct; melancholy Jaques never meets a Rosalind in the forest of Arden, and if he sees her in the drawing-room he poisons his pleasure with the thought that she is scheming and artificial; there are no happy marriages,—indeed, marriage itself is almost too inartistic to be permitted by our novelists, unless it can be supplemented by a divorce, and art is supposed to deny any happy consummation of true love. In short, modern society is going to the dogs, notwithstanding money is only three and a half percent. It is a gloomy business life, at the best. Two learned but despondent university professors met, not long ago, at an afternoon "coffee," and drew sympathetically together in a corner. "What a world this would be," said one, "without coffee!" "Yes," replied the other, stirring the fragrant cup in a dejected aspect,— "yes; but what a H. of a world it is with coffee!"

The analytic method in fiction is interesting, when used by a master of dissection, but it has this fatal defect in a novel,—it destroys illusion. We want to think that the characters in a story are real persons. We cannot do this if we see the author set them up as if they were marionettes, and take them to pieces every few pages, and show their interior structure, and the machinery by which they are moved. Not only is the illusion gone, but the movement of the story, if there is a story, is retarded, till the reader loses all enjoyment in impatience and weariness. You find yourself saying, perhaps, What a very clever fellow the author is! What an ingenious creation this character is! How brightly the author makes his people talk! This is high praise, but by no means the highest, and when we reflect we see how immediately inferior, in fiction, the analytic method is to the dramatic. In the dramatic method the characters appear, and show what they are by what they do and say; the reader studies their motives, and a part of his enjoyment is in analyzing them, and his vanity is flattered by the trust reposed in his perspicacity. We realize how unnecessary minute analysis of character and long descriptions are in reading a drama by Shakespeare, in which the characters are so vividly presented to us in action and speech, without the least interference of the author in description, that we regard them as persons with whom we might have real relations, and not as bundles of traits and qualities. True, the conditions of dramatic art and the art of the novel are different, in that the drama can dispense with delineations, for its characters are intended to be presented to the eye; but all the same, a good drama will explain itself without the aid of actors, and there is no doubt that it is the higher art in the novel, when once the characters are introduced, to treat them dramatically, and let them work out their own destiny according to their characters. It is a truism to say that when the reader perceives that the author can compel his characters to do what he pleases all interest in them as real persons is gone. In a novel of mere action and adventure, a lower order of fiction, where all the interest centres in the unraveling of a plot, of course this does not so much matter.

Not long ago, in Edinburgh, I amused myself in looking up some of the localities made famous in Scott's romances, which are as real in the mind as any historical places. Afterwards, I read the Heart of Midlothian. I was surprised to find that, as a work of art, it was inferior to my recollection of it. Its style is open to the charge of prolixity, and even of slovenliness in some parts; and it does not move on with increasing momentum and concentration to a climax, as many of Scott's novels do; the story drags alone in the disposition of one character after another. Yet, when I had finished the book and put it away, a singular thing happened. It suddenly came to me that in reading it I had not once thought of Scott as the maker; it had never occurred to me that he had *created* the people in whose fortunes I had been so intensely absorbed; and I never once had felt how clever the novelist was in the naturally dramatic dialogues of the characters. In short, it had not entered my mind to doubt the existence of Jeanie and Effie Deans, and their father, and Reuben Butler, and the others, who seem as real as historical persons in Scotch history. And when I came to think of it afterwards, reflecting upon the assumptions of the modern realistic school, I found that some scenes, notably the night attack on the old Tolbooth, were as real to me as if I had read them in a police report of a newspaper of the day. Was Scott, then, only a reporter? Far from it, as you would speedily see if he had thrown into the novel a police report of the occurrences at the Tolbooth, before art had shorn it of its irrelevances; magnified its effective and salient points; given events their proper perspective, and the whole picture due light and shade.

The sacrifice of action to some extent to psychological evolution in modern fiction may be an advance in the art as an intellectual entertainment, if the writer does not make that evolution his end, and does not forget that the indispensable thing in a novel is the story. The novel of mere adventure or mere plot, it need not be urged, is of a lower order than that in which the evolution of characters and their interaction make the story. The highest fiction is that which embodies both; that is, the story in which action is the result of mental and spiritual forces in play. And we protest against the notion that the novel of the future is to be, or should be, merely a study of, or an essay or a series of analytic essays on, certain phases of social life.

It is not true that civilization or cultivation has bred out of the world the liking for a story. In this the most highly educated Londoner and the Egyptian fellah meet on common human ground. The passion for a story has no more died out than curiosity, or than the passion of love. The truth is not that stories are not demanded, but that the born *raconteur* and story-teller is a rare person. The faculty of telling a story is a much rarer gift than the ability to analyze character, and even than that ability truly to draw character. It may be a higher or a lower power, but it is rarer. It is a natural gift, and it seems that no amount of culture can attain it, any more than learning can make a poet. Nor is the complaint well-founded that the stores have all been used, and the combinations of circumstances exhausted. It is no doubt our individual experience that we hear almost every day—and we hear nothing so eagerly—some new story, better or worse, but new in its exhibition of human character, and in the combination of events. And the strange, eventful histories of human life will no more be exhausted than the possible arrangements of mathematical numbers. We might as well say that there are no more good pictures to be painted as that there are no more good stories to be told.

Equally baseless is the assumption that it is inartistic and untrue to nature to bring a novel to a definite consummation, and especially to end it happily. Life, we are told, is full of incompletion, of broken destinies, of failures, of romances that begin but do not end, of ambitions and purposes frustrated, of love crossed, of unhappy issues, or a resultless play of influences. Well, but life is full, also, of endings, of the results in concrete action of character, of completed dramas. And we expect and give, in the stories we hear and tell in ordinary intercourse, some point, some outcome, an end of some sort. If you interest me in the preparations of two persons who are starting on a journey, and expend all your ingenuity in describing their outfit and their characters, and do not tell me where they went or what befell them afterwards, I do not call that a story. Nor am I any better satisfied when you describe two persons whom you know, whose characters are interesting, and who become involved in all manner of entanglements, and then stop your narration; and when I ask, say you have not the least idea whether they got out of their difficulties, or what became of them. In real life we do not call that a story where everything is left unconcluded and in the air. In point of fact, romances are daily beginning and daily ending, well or otherwise, under our observation.

Should they always end well in the novel? I am very far from saying that. Tragedy and the pathos of failure have their places in literature as well as in life. I only say that, artistically, a good ending is as proper as a bad ending. Yet the main object of the novel is to entertain, and the best entertainment is that which lifts the imagination and quickens the spirit; to lighten the burdens of life by taking us for a time out of our humdrum and perhaps sordid conditions, so that we can see familiar life somewhat idealized, and probably see it all the more truly from an artistic point of view. For the majority of the race, in its hard lines, fiction is an inestimable boon. Incidentally the novel may teach, encourage, refine, elevate. Even for these purposes, that novel is the best which shows us the best possibilities of our lives,—the novel which gives hope and cheer instead of discouragement and gloom. Familiarity with vice and sordidness in fiction is a low entertainment, and of doubtful moral value, and their introduction is unbearable if it is not done with the idealizing touch of the artist.

Do not misunderstand me to mean that common and low life are not fit subjects of fiction, or that vice is not to be lashed by the satirist, or that the evils of a social state are never to be exposed in the novel. For this, also, is an office of the novel, as it is of the drama, to hold the mirror up to nature, and to human nature as it exhibits itself. But when the mirror shows nothing but vice and social disorder, leaving out the saving qualities that keep society on the whole, and family life as a rule, as sweet and good as they are, the mirror is not held up to nature, but more likely reflects a morbid mind. Still it must be added that the study of unfortunate social conditions is a legitimate one for the author to make; and that we may be in no state to judge justly of his exposure while the punishment is being inflicted, or while the irritation is fresh. For, no doubt, the reader winces often because the novel reveals to himself certain possible baseness, selfishness, and meanness. Of this, however, I (speak for myself) may be sure: that the artist who so represents vulgar life that I am more in love with my kind, the satirist who so depicts vice and villainy that I am strengthened in my moral fibre, has vindicated his choice of material. On the contrary, those novelists are not justified whose forte it seems to be to so set forth goodness as to make it unattractive.

But we come back to the general proposition that the indispensable condition of the novel is that it shall entertain. And for this purpose the world is not ashamed to own that it wants, and always will want, a story,—a story that has an ending; and if not a good ending, then one that in noble tragedy lifts up our nature into a high plane of sacrifice and pathos. In proof of this we have only to refer to the masterpieces of fiction which the world cherishes and loves to recur to.

I confess that I am harassed with the incomplete romances, that leave me, when the book is closed, as one might be on a waste plain, at midnight, abandoned by his conductor, and without a lantern. I am tired of accompanying people for hours through disaster and perplexity and misunderstanding, only to see them lost in a thick mist at last. I am weary of going to funerals, which are not my funerals, however chatty and amusing the undertaker may be. I confess that I should like to see again the lovely heroine, the sweet woman, capable of a great passion and a great sacrifice; and I do not object if the novelist tries her to the verge of endurance, in agonies of mind and in perils, subjecting her to wasting sicknesses even, if he only brings her out at the end in a blissful compensation of her troubles, and endued with a new and sweeter charm. No doubt it is better for us all, and better art, that in the novel of society the destiny should be decided by character. What an artistic and righteous consummation it is when we meet the shrewd and wicked old Baroness Bernstein at Continental gaming-tables, and feel that there was no other logical end for the worldly and fascinating Beatrix of Henry Esmond! It is one of the great privileges of fiction to right the wrongs of life, to do justice to the deserving and the vicious. It is wholesome for us to contemplate this justice, even if we do not often see it in society. It is true that hypocrisy and vulgar self-seeking often succeed in life, occupy high places, and make their exit in the pageantry of honored obsequies. Yet always the man is conscious of the hollowness of his triumph, and the world takes a pretty accurate measure of it. It is the privilege of the novelist, without introducing into such a career what is called disaster, to satisfy our innate love of justice by letting us see the true nature of such prosperity. The unscrupulous man amasses wealth, lives in luxury and splendor, and dies in the odor of respectability. His poor and honest neighbor, whom he has wronged and defrauded, lives in misery, and dies in disappointment and penury. The novelist cannot reverse the facts without such a shock to our experience as shall destroy for us the artistic value of his fiction, and bring upon his work the deserved reproach of indiscriminately "rewarding the good and punishing the bad." But we have a right to ask that he shall reveal the real heart and character of this passing show of life; for not to do this, to content himself merely with exterior appearances, is for the majority of his readers to efface the lines between virtue and vice. And we ask this not for the sake of the moral lesson, but because not to do it is, to our deep consciousness, inartistic and untrue to our judgment of life as it goes on. Thackeray used to say that all his talent was in his eyes; meaning that he was only an observer and reporter of what he saw, and not a Providence to rectify human affairs. The great artist undervalued his genius. He reported what he saw as Raphael and Murillo reported what they saw. With his touch of genius he assigned to everything its true value, moving us to tenderness, to pity, to scorn, to righteous indignation, to sympathy with humanity. I find in him the highest art, and not that indifference to the great facts and deep currents and destinies of human life, that want of enthusiasm and sympathy, which has got the name of "art for art's sake." Literary fiction is a barren product, if it wants sympathy and love for men. "Art for art's sake" is a good and defensible phrase, if our definition of art includes the ideal, and not otherwise.

I do not know how it has come about that in so large a proportion of recent fiction it is held to be artistic to look almost altogether upon the shady and the seamy side of life, giving to this view the name of "realism;" to select the disagreeable, the vicious, the unwholesome; to give us for our companions, in our hours of leisure and relaxation, only the silly and the weak-minded woman, the fast and slangy girl, the *intrigante* and the "shady,"—to borrow the language of the society she seeks,—the hero of irresolution, the prig, the vulgar, and the vicious; to serve as only with the foibles of the fashionable, the low tone of the gay, the gilded riff-raff of our social state; to drag us forever along the dizzy, half-fractured precipice of the seventh commandment; to bring us into relations only with the sordid and the common; to force us to sup with unwholesome company on misery and sensuousness, in tales so utterly unpleasant that we are ready to welcome any disaster as a relief; and then—the latest and finest touch of modern art—to leave the whole weltering mass in a chaos, without conclusion and without possible issue.

And this is called a picture of real life! Heavens! Is it true that in England, where a great proportion of the fiction we describe and loathe is produced; is it true that in our New England society there is nothing but frivolity, sordidness, decay of purity and faith, ignoble ambition and ignoble living? Is there no charm in social life,—no self-sacrifice, devotion, courage to stem materialistic conditions, and live above them? Are there no noble women, sensible, beautiful, winning, with the grace that all the world loves, albeit with the feminine weaknesses that make all the world hope? Is there no manliness left? Are there no homes where the tempter does not live with the tempted in a mush of sentimental affinity? Or is it, in fact, more artistic to ignore all these, and paint only the feeble and the repulsive in our social state? The feeble, the sordid, and the repulsive in our social state, nobody denies, nor does anybody deny the exceeding cleverness with which our social disorders are reproduced in fiction by a few masters of their art; but is it not time that it should be considered good art to show something of the clean and bright side?

This is preëminently the age of the novel. The development of variety of fiction since the days of Scott and Cooper is prodigious. The prejudice against novel-reading is quite broken down, since fiction has taken all fields for its providence; everybody reads novels. Three quarters of the books taken from the circulating library are stories; they make up half the library of the Sunday-schools. If a writer has anything to say, or thinks he has, he knows that he can most certainly reach the ear of the public by the medium of a story. So we have novels for children; novels religious, scientific, historical, archaeological, psychological, pathological, total-abstinence; novels of travel, of adventure and exploration; novels domestic, and the perpetual spawn of books called novels of society. Not only is everything turned into a story, real or so called, but there must be a story in everything. The stump-speaker holds his audience by well-worn stories; the preacher wakes up his congregation by a graphic narrative; and the Sunday-school teacher leads his children into all goodness by the entertaining path of romance; we even had a President who governed the country nearly by anecdotes.

The result of this universal demand for fiction is necessarily an enormous supply, and as everybody writes, without reference to gifts, the product is mainly trash, and trash of a deleterious sort; for bad art in literature is bad morals. I am not sure but the so-called domestic, the diluted, the "goody," namby-pamby, un-robust stories, which are so largely read by school-girls, young ladies, and women, do more harm than the "knowing," audacious, wicked ones, also, it is reported, read by them, and written largely by their own sex. For minds enfeebled and relaxed by stories lacking even intellectual fibre are in a poor condition to meet the perils of life. This is not the place for discussing the stories written for the young and for the Sunday-school. It seems impossible to check the flow of them, now that so much capital is invested in this industry; but I think that healthy public sentiment is beginning to recognize the truth that the excessive reading of this class of literature by the young is weakening to the mind, besides being a serious hindrance to study and to attention to the literature that has substance.

In his account of the Romantic School in Germany, Heine says, "In the breast of a nation's authors there always lies the image of its future, and the critic who, with a knife of sufficient keenness, dissects a new poet can easily prophesy, as from the entrails of a sacrificial animal, what shape matters will assume in Germany." Now if all the poets and novelists of England and America to-day were cut up into little pieces (and we might sacrifice a few for the sake of the experiment), there is no inspecting augur who could divine therefrom our literary future. The diverse indications would puzzle the most acute dissector. Lost in the variety, the multiplicity of minute details, the refinements of analysis and introspection, he would miss any leading indications. For with all its variety, it seems to me that one characteristic of recent fiction is its narrowness,—narrowness of vision and of treatment. It deals with lives rather than with life. Lacking ideality, it fails of broad perception. We are accustomed to think that with the advent of the genuine novel of society, in the first part of this century, a great step forward was taken in fiction. And so there was. If the artist did not use a big canvas, he adopted a broad treatment. But the tendency now is to push analysis of individual peculiarities to an extreme, and to substitute a study of traits for a representation of human life.

It scarcely need be said that it is not multitude of figures on a literary canvas that secures breadth of treatment. The novel may be narrow, though it swarms with an hundred personages. It may be as wide as life, as high as imagination can lift itself; it may image to us a whole social state, though it puts in motion no more persons than we made the acquaintance of in one of the romances of Hawthorne. Consider for a moment how Thackeray produced his marvelous results. We follow with him, in one of his novels of society, the fortunes of a very few people. They are so vividly portrayed that we are convinced the author must have known them in that great world with which he was so familiar; we should not be surprised to meet any of them in the streets of London. When we visit the Charter House School, and see the old forms where the boys sat nearly a century ago, we have in our minds Colonel Newcome as really as we have Charles Lamb and Coleridge and De Quincey. We are absorbed, as we read, in the evolution of the characters of perhaps only half a dozen people; and yet all the world, all great, roaring, struggling London, is in the story, and Clive, and Philip, and Ethel, and Becky Sharpe, and Captain Costigan are a part of life. It is the flowery month of May; the scent of the hawthorn is in the air, and the tender flush of the new spring suffuses the Park, where the tide of fashion and pleasure and idleness surges up and down,—the sauntering throng, the splendid equipages, the endless cavalcade in Rotten Row, in which Clive descries afar off the white plume of his lady-love dancing on the waves of an unattainable society; the club windows are all occupied; Parliament is in session, with its nightly echoes of imperial politics; the thronged streets roar with life from morn till nearly morn again; the drawing-rooms hum and sparkle in the crush of a London season; as you walk the midnight pavement, through the swinging doors of the cider-cellars comes the burst of bacchanalian song. Here is the world of the press and of letters; here are institutions, an army, a navy, commerce, glimpses of great ships going to and fro on distant seas, of India, of Australia. This one book is an epitome of English life, almost of the empire itself. We are conscious of all this, so much breadth and atmosphere has the artist given his little history of half a dozen people in this struggling world.

But this background of a great city, of an empire, is not essential to the breadth of treatment upon which we insist in fiction, to broad characterization, to the play of imagination about common things which transfigures them into the immortal beauty of artistic creations. What a simple idyl in itself is Goethe's Hermann and Dorothea! It is the creation of a few master touches, using only common material. Yet it has in it the breadth of life itself, the depth and passion of all our human struggle in the world,—a little story with a vast horizon.

It is constantly said that the conditions in America are unfavorable to the higher fiction; that our society is unformed, without centre, without the definition of classes, which give the light and shade that Heine speaks of in Don Quixote; that it lacks types and customs that can be widely recognized and accepted as national and characteristic; that we have no past; that we want both romantic and historic background; that we are in a shifting, flowing, forming period which fiction cannot seize on; that we are in diversity and confusion that baffle artistic treatment; in short, that American life is too vast, varied, and crude for the purpose of the novelist.

These excuses might be accepted as fully accounting for our failure,—or shall we say our delay?—if it were not for two or three of our literary performances. It is true that no novel has been written, and we dare say no novel will be written that is, or will be, an epitome of the manifold diversities of American life, unless it be in the form of one of Walt Whitman's catalogues. But we are not without peculiar types; not without characters, not without incidents, stories, heroisms, inequalities; not without the charms of nature in infinite variety; and human nature is the same here that it is in Spain, France, and England. Out of these materials Cooper wrote romances, narratives stamped with the distinct characteristics of American life and scenery, that were and are eagerly read by all civilized peoples, and which secured the universal verdict which only breadth of treatment commands. Out of these materials, also, Hawthorne, child endowed with a creative imagination, wove those tragedies of inferior life, those novels of our provincial New England, which rank among the great masterpices of the novelist's art. The master artist can idealize even our crude material, and make it serve.

These exceptions to a rule do not go to prove the general assertion of a poverty of material for fiction here; the simple truth probably is that, for reasons incident to the development of a new region of the earth, creative genius has been turned in other directions than that of fictitious literature. Nor do I think that we need to take shelter behind the well-worn and convenient observations, the truth of which stands in much doubt, that literature is the final flower of a nation's civilization.

However, this is somewhat a digression. We are speaking of the tendency of recent fiction, very much the same everywhere that novels are written, which we have imperfectly sketched. It is probably of no more use to protest against it than it is to protest against the vulgar realism in pictorial art, which holds ugliness and beauty in equal esteem; or against aestheticism gone to seed in languid affectations; or against the enthusiasm of a social life which wreaks its religion on the color of a vestment, or sighs out its divine soul over an ancient pewter mug. Most of our fiction, in its extreme analysis, introspection and self-consciousness, in its devotion to details, in its disregard of the ideal, in its selection as well as in its treatment of nature, is simply of a piece with a good deal else that passes for genuine art. Much of it is admirable in workmanship, and exhibits a cleverness in details and a subtlety in the observation of traits which many great novels lack. But I should be sorry to think that the historian will judge our social life by it, and I doubt not that most of us are ready for a more ideal, that is to say a more artistic, view of our performances in this bright and pathetic world.

THREE

THE ART OF FICTION

Henry James

Although Henry James (1843–1916) had begun writing literary criticism during the 1860s, and was to produce a major body of work in this area during his lifetime, most of his writing about literature would today be called "practical"—that is, he eschewed the open discussion of general critical issues in favor of the detailed examination of specific writers and their work. "The Art of Fiction" is an exception, one which owes its existence to James's strong disagreement with Walter Besant's lecture "The Art of Fiction," which Besant delivered in April 1884. In addition, the cosmopolitan range of James's fictional interests—like Howells, he wrote often and fully about contemporary French, Russian, and English novelists—constituted in itself an indirect endorsement of the dominant realistic strain in late nineteenth-century European fiction. Among James's major works of criticism are *French Poets and Novelists* (1878), *Partial Portraits* (1888), and *Notes on Novelists* (1914).

I should not have affixed so comprehensive a title to these few remarks, necessarily wanting in any completeness upon a subject the full consideration of which would carry us far, did I not seem to discover a pretext for my temerity in the interesting pamphlet lately published under this name by Mr. Walter Besant. Mr. Besant's lecture at the Royal Institution—the original form of his pamphlet—appears to indicate that many persons are interested in the art of fiction, and are not indifferent to such remarks, as those who practise it may attempt to make about it. I am therefore anxious

Longman's 4 (September 1884): 502–21. Revised version in *Partial Portraits* (1888). Text is that of *Partial Portraits*, as reprinted in *The Art of Criticism: Henry James on the Theory and Practice of Fiction*, ed. William Veeder and Susan M. Griffin (Chicago: University of Chicago Press, 1986), pp. 165–83.

not to lose the benefit of this favourable association, and to edge in a few words under cover of the attention which Mr. Besant is sure to have excited. There is something very encouraging in his having put into form certain of his ideas on the mystery of story-telling.

It is proof of life and curiosity—curiosity on the part of the brotherhood of novelists as well as on the part of their readers. Only a short time ago it might have been supposed that the English novel was not what the French call *discutable*. It had no air of having a theory, a conviction, a consciousness of itself behind it—of being the expression of an artistic faith, the result of choice and comparison. I do not say it was necessarily the worse for that: it would take much more courage than I possess to intimate that the form of the novel as Dickens and Thackeray (for instance) saw it had any taint of incompleteness. It was, however, *naïf* (if I may help myself out with another French word); and evidently if it be destined to suffer in any way for having lost its *naïveté* it has now an idea of making sure of the corresponding advantages. During the period I have alluded to there was a comfortable, good-humoured feeling abroad that a novel is a novel, as a pudding is a pudding, and that our only business with it could be to swallow it. But within a year or two, for some reason or other, there have been signs of returning animation—the era of discussion would appear to have been to a certain extent opened. Art lives upon discussion, upon experiment, upon curiosity, upon variety of attempt, upon the exchange of views and the comparison of standpoints; and there is a presumption that those times when no one has anything particular to say about it, and has no reason to give for practice or preference, though they may be times of honour, are not times of development—are times, possibly even, a little of dulness. The successful application of any art is a delightful spectacle, but the theory too is interesting; and though there is a great deal of the latter without the former I suspect there has never been a genuine success that has not had a latent core of conviction. Discussion, suggestion, formulation, these things are fertilising when they are frank and sincere. Mr. Besant has set an excellent example in saying what he thinks, for his part, about the way in which fiction should be written, as well as about the way in which it should be published; for his view of the "art," carried on into an appendix, covers that too. Other labourers in the same field will doubtless take up the argument, they will give it the light of their experience, and the effect will surely be to make our interest in the novel a little more what it had for some time threatened to fail to be—a serious, active, inquiring interest, under protection of which this delightful study may, in moments of confidence, venture to say a little more what it thinks of itself.

It must take itself seriously for the public to take it so. The old superstition about fiction being "wicked" has doubtless died out in England; but the spirit of it lingers in a certain oblique regard directed toward any story which does not more or less admit that it is only a joke. Even the most jocular novel feels in some degree the weight of the proscription that was formerly directed against literary levity; the jocularity does not always succeed in passing for orthodoxy. It is still expected, though perhaps people are ashamed to say it, that a production which is after all only a "make-believe" (for what else is a "story"?) shall be in some degree apologetic—shall renounce the pretension of attempting really to represent life. This, of course, any sensible, wide-awake story declines to do, for it quickly perceives that the tolerance granted to it on such a condition is only an attempt to stifle it disguised in the form of generosity. The old evangelical hostility to the novel, which was as explicit as it was narrow, and which regarded it as little less favourable to our immortal part than a stage-play, was in reality far less insulting. The only reason for the existence of a novel is that it does attempt to represent life. When it relinquishes this attempt, the same attempt that we see on the canvas of the painter, it will have arrived at a very strange pass. It is not expected of the picture that it will make itself humble in order to be forgiven; and the analogy between the art of the painter and the art of the novelist is, so far as I am able to see, complete. Their inspiration is the same, their process (allowing for the different quality of the vehicle), is the same, their success is the same. They may learn from each other, they may explain and sustain each other. Their cause is the same, and the honour of one is the honour of another. The Mahometans think a picture an unholy thing, but it is a long time since any Christian did, and it is therefore the more odd that in the Christian mind the traces (dissimulated though they may be) of a suspicion of the sister art should linger to this day. The only effectual way to lay it to rest is to emphasize the analogy to which I just alluded—to insist on the fact that as the picture is reality, so the novel is history. That is the only general description (which does it justice) that we may give of the novel. But history also is allowed to represent life; it is not, any more than painting, expected to apologise. The subject-matter of fiction is stored up likewise in documents and records, and if it will not give itself away, as they say in California, it must speak with assurance, with the tone of the historian. Certain accomplished novelists have a habit of giving themselves away which must often bring tears to the eyes of people who take their fiction seriously. I was lately struck, in reading over many pages of Anthony Trollope, with this want of discretion in this particular. In a digression, a parenthesis or an aside, he concedes to the reader that he and this trusting friend are only "making believe." He admits that the events he narrates have not really happened, and that he can give his narrative any turn the reader may like best. Such a betrayal of a sacred office seems to me, I confess, a terrible crime; it is what I mean by the attitude of apology, and it shocks me every whit as much in Trollope as it would have shocked me in Gibbon or Macaulay. It implies that the novelist is less occupied in looking for the truth (the truth, of course I mean, that he assumes, the premises that we must grant him, whatever they may be), than the historian, and in doing so it deprives him at a stroke of all his standing-room. To represent and illustrate the past, the actions of men, is the task of either writer, and the only difference that I can see is, in proportion as he succeeds, to the honour of the novelist, consisting as it does in his having more difficulty in collecting his evidence, which is so far from being purely literary. It seems to me to give him a great character, the fact that he has at once so much in common with the philosopher and the painter; this double analogy is a magnificent heritage.

It is of all this evidently that Mr. Besant is full when he insists upon the fact that fiction is one of the *fine* arts, deserving in its turn of all the honours and emoluments that have hitherto been reserved for the successful profession of music, poetry, painting, architecture. It is impossible to insist too much on so important a truth, and the place that Mr. Besant demands for the work of the novelist may be represented, a trifle less abstractly, by saying that he demands not only that it shall be reputed artistic, but that it shall be reputed very artistic indeed. It is excellent that he should have struck this note, for his doing so indicates that there was need of it, that his proposition may be to many people a novelty. One rubs one's eyes at the thought; but the rest of Mr. Besant's essay confirms the revelation. I suspect in truth that it would be possible to confirm it still further, and that one would not be far wrong in saying that in addition to the people to whom it has never occurred that a novel ought to be artistic, there are a great many others who, if this principle were urged upon them, would be filled with an indefinable mistrust. They would find it difficult to explain their repugnance, but it would operate strongly to put them on their guard. "Art," in our Protestant communities, where so many things have got so strangely twisted about, is supposed in certain circles to have some vaguely injurious effect upon those who make it an important consideration, who let it weigh in the balance. It is assumed to be opposed in some mysterious manner to morality, to amusement, to instruction. When it is embodied in the work of the painter (the sculptor is another affair!) you know what it is: it stands there before you, in the honesty of pink and green and a gilt frame; you can see the worst of it at a glance, and you can be on your guard. But when it is introduced into literature it becomes more insidious—there is danger of its hurting you before you know it. Literature should be either instructive or amusing, and there is in many minds an impression that these artistic preoccupations, the search for form, contribute to neither end, interfere indeed with both. They are too frivolous to be edifying, and too serious to be diverting; and they are moreover priggish and paradoxical and superfluous, That, I think, represents the manner in which the latent thought of many people who read novels as an exercise in skipping would explain itself if it were to become articulate. They would argue, of course, that a novel ought to be "good," but they would interpret this term in a fashion of their own, which indeed would vary considerably from one critic to another. One would say that being good means representing virtuous and aspiring characters, placed in prominent positions; another would say that it depends on a "happy ending," on a distribution at the last of prizes, pensions, husbands, wives, babies, millions, appended paragraphs, and cheerful remarks. Another still would say that it means being full of incident and movement, so that we shall wish to jump ahead, to see who was the mysterious stranger, and if the stolen will was ever found, and shall not be distracted from this pleasure by any tiresome analysis or "description." But they would all agree that the "artistic" idea would spoil some of their fun. One would hold it accountable for all the description, another would see it revealed in the absence of sympathy. Its hostility to a happy ending would be evident, and it might even in some cases render any ending at all impossible. The "ending" of a novel is, for many persons, like that of a good dinner, a course of dessert and ices, and the artist in fiction is regarded as a sort of meddlesome doctor who forbids agreeable aftertastes. It is therefore true that this conception of Mr. Besant's of the novel as a superior form encounters not only a negative but a positive indifference. It matters little that as a work of art it should really be as little or as much of its essence to supply happy endings, sympathetic characters, and an objective tone, as if it were a work of mechanics; the association of ideas, however incongruous, might easily be too much for it if an eloquent voice were not sometimes raised to call attention to the fact that it is at once as free and as serious a branch of literature as any other.

Certainly this might sometimes be doubted in presence of the enormous number of works of fiction that appeal to the credulity of our generation, for it might easily seem that there could be no great character in a commodity so quickly and easily produced. It must be admitted that good novels are much compromised by bad ones, and that the field at large suffers discredit from overcrowding. I think, however, that this injury is only superficial, and that the superabundance of written fiction proves nothing against the principle itself. It has been vulgarised, like all other kinds of literature, like everything else to-day, and it has proved more than some kinds accessible to vulgarisation. But there is as much difference as there ever was between a good novel and a bad one: the bad is swept with all the daubed canvases and spoiled marble into some unvisited limbo, or infinite rubbish-yard beneath the back-windows of the world, and the good subsists and emits its light and stimulates our desire for perfection. As I shall take the liberty of making but a single criticism of Mr. Besant, whose tone is so full of the love of his art, I may as well have done with it at once. He seems to me to mistake in attempting to say so definitely beforehand what sort of an affair the good novel will be. To indicate the danger of such an error as that has been the purpose of these few pages; to suggest that certain traditions on the subject, applied *a priori*, have already had much to answer for, and that the good health of an art which undertakes so immediately to reproduce life must demand that it be perfectly free. It lives upon exercise, and the very meaning of exercise is freedom. The only obligation to which in advance we may hold a novel, without incurring the accusation of being arbitrary, is that it be interesting. That general responsibility rests upon it, but it is the only one I can think of. The ways in which it is at liberty to accomplish this result (of interesting us) strike me as innumerable, and such as can only suffer from being marked out or fenced in by prescription. They are as various as the temperament of man, and they are successful in proportion as they reveal a particular mind, different from others. A novel is in its broadest definition a personal, a direct impression of life: that, to begin with, constitutes its value, which is greater or less according to the intensity of the impression. But there will be no intensity at all, and therefore no value, unless there is freedom to feel and say. The tracing of a line to be followed, of a tone to be taken, of a form to be filled out, is a limitation of that freedom and a suppression of the very thing that we are most curious about. The form it seems to me, is to be appreciated after the fact: then the author's choice has been made, his standard has been indicated; then we can follow lines and directions and compare tones and resemblances. Then in a word we can enjoy one of the most charming of pleasures, we can estimate quality, we can apply the test of execution. The execution belongs to the author alone; it is what is most personal to him, and we measure him by that. The advantage, the luxury, as well as the torment and respon-

sibility of the novelist, is that there is no limit to what he may attempt as an execu-
tant—no limit to his possible experiments, efforts, discoveries, successes. Here it is
especially that he works, step by step, like his brother of the brush, of whom we may
always say that he has painted his picture in a manner best known to himself. His
manner is his secret, not necessarily a jealous one. He cannot disclose it as a general
thing if he would; he would be at a loss to teach it to others. I say this with a due
recollection of having insisted on the community of method of the artist who paints
a picture and the artist who writes a novel. The painter *is* able to teach the rudiments
of his practice, and it is possible, from the study of good work (granted the aptitude),
both to learn how to paint and to learn how to write. Yet it remains true, without
injury to the *rapprochement,* that the literary artist would be obliged to say to his
pupil much more than the other, "Ah, well, you must do it as you can!" It is a question of degree, a matter of delicacy. If there are exact sciences, there are also exact
arts, and the grammar of painting is so much more definite that it makes the difference.

I ought to add, however, that if Mr. Besant says at the beginning of his essay that
the "laws of fiction may be laid down and taught with as much precision and exactness as the laws of harmony, perspective, and proportion," he mitigates what might
appear to be an extravagance by applying his remark to "general" laws, and by expressing most of these rules in a manner with which it would certainly be unaccom-
modating to disagree. That the novelist must write from his experience, that his
"characters must be real and such as might be met with in actual life;" that "a young
lady brought up in a quiet country village should avoid descriptions of garrison life,"
and "a writer whose friends and personal experiences belong to the lower middle-
class should carefully avoid introducing his characters into society;" that one should
enter one's notes in a common-place book; that one's figures should be clear in outline; that making them clear by some trick of speech or of carriage is a bad method,
and "describing them at length" is a worse one; that English Fiction should have a
"conscious moral purpose;" that "it is almost impossible to estimate too highly the
value of careful workmanship—that is, of style;" that "the most important point of
all is the story," that "the story is everything": these are principles with most of
which it is surely impossible not to sympathise. That remark about the lower middle-
class writer and his knowing his place is perhaps rather chilling; but for the rest I
should find it difficult to dissent from any one of these recommendations. At the same
time, I should find it difficult positively to assent to them, with the exception, perhaps, of the injunction as to entering one's notes in a common-place book. They
scarcely seem to me to have the quality that Mr. Besant attributes to the rules of the
novelist—the "precision and exactness" of "the laws of harmony, perspective, and
proportion." They are suggestive, they are even inspiring, but they are not exact,
though they are doubtless as much so as the case admits of: which is a proof of that
liberty or interpretation for which I just contended. For the value of these different
injunctions—so beautiful and so vague—is wholly in the meaning one attaches to
them. The characters, the situation, which strike one as real will be those that touch
and interest one most, but the measure of reality is very difficult to fix. The reality of

Don Quixote or of Mr. Micawber is a very delicate shade; it is a reality so coloured by the author's vision that, vivid as it may be, one would hesitate to propose it as a model: one would expose one's self to some very embarrassing questions on the part of a pupil. It goes without saying that you will not write a good novel unless you possess the sense of reality; but it will be difficult to give you a recipe for calling that sense into being. Humanity is immense, and reality has a myriad forms; the most one can affirm is that some of the flowers of fiction have the odour of it, and others have not; as for telling you in advance how your nosegay should be composed, that is another affair. It is equally excellent and inconclusive to say that one must write from experience; to our supposititious aspirant such a declaration might savour of mockery. What kind of experience is intended, and where does it begin and end? Experience is never limited, and it is never complete; it is an immense sensibility, a kind of huge spiderweb of the finest silken threads suspended in the chamber of consciousness, and catching every airborne particle in its tissue. It is the very atmosphere of the mind; and when the mind is imaginative—much more when it happens to be that of a man of genius—it takes to itself the faintest hints of life, it converts the very pulses of the air into revelations. The young lady living in a village has only to be a damsel upon whom nothing is lost to make it quite unfair (as it seems to me) to declare to her that she shall have nothing to say about the military. Greater miracles have been seen than that, imagination assisting, she should speak the truth about some of these gentlemen. I remember an English novelist, a woman of genius, telling me that she was much commended for the impression she had managed to give in one of her tales of the nature and way of life of the French Protestant youth. She had been asked where she learned so much about this recondite being, she had been congratulated on her peculiar opportunities. These opportunities consisted in her having once, in Paris, as she ascended a staircase, passed an open door where, in the household of a *pasteur*, some of the young Protestants were seated at table round a finished meal. The glimpse made a picture; it lasted only a moment, but that moment was experience. She had got her direct personal impression, and she turned out her type. She knew what youth was, and what Protestantism; she also had the advantage of having seen what it was to be French, so that she converted these ideas into a concrete image and produced a reality. Above all, however, she was blessed with the faculty which when you give it an inch takes an ell, and which for the artist is a much greater source of strength than any accident of residence or of place in the social scale. The power to guess the unseen from the seen, to trace the implication of things, to judge the whole piece by the pattern, the condition of feeling life in general so completely that you are well on your way to knowing any particular corner of it—this cluster of gifts may almost be said to constitute experience, and they occur in country and in town, and in the most differing stages of education. If experience consists of impressions, it may be said that impressions *are* experience, just as (have we not seen it?) they are the very air we breathe. Therefore, if I should certainly say to a novice, "Write from experience and experience only," I should feel that this was rather a tantalising monition if I were not careful immediately to add, "Try to be one of the people on whom nothing is lost!"

I am far from intending by this to minimise the importance of exactness—of truth of detail. One can speak best from one's own taste, and I may therefore venture to say that the air of reality (solidity of specification) seems to me to be the supreme virtue of a novel—the merit on which all its other merits (including that conscious moral purpose of which Mr. Besant speaks) helplessly and submissively depend. If it be not there they are all as nothing, and if these be there, they owe their effect to the success with which the author has produced the illusion of life. The cultivation of this success, the study of this exquisite process, form, to my taste, the beginning and the end of the art of the novelist. They are his inspiration, his despair, his reward, his torment, his delight. It is here in very truth that he competes with life; it is here that he competes with his brother the painter in *his* attempt to render the look of things, the look that conveys their meaning, to catch the colour, the relief, the expression, the surface, the substance of the human spectacle. It is in regard to this that Mr. Besant is well inspired when he bids him take notes. He cannot possibly take too many, he cannot possibly take enough. All life solicits him, and to "render" the simplest surface, to produce the most momentary illusion, is a very complicated business. His case would be easier, and the rules would be more exact, if Mr. Besant had been able to tell him what notes to take. But this, I fear, he can never learn in any manual; it is the business of his life. He has to take a great many in order to select a few, he has to work them up as he can, and even the guides and philosophers who might have most to say to him must leave him alone when it comes to the application of percepts, as we leave the painter in communion with his palette. That his characters "must be clear in outline," as Mr. Besant says—he feels that down to his boots; but how he shall make them so is a secret between his good angel and himself. It would be absurdly simple if he could be taught that a great deal of "description" would make them so, or that on the contrary the absence of description and the cultivation of dialogue, or the absence of dialogue and the multiplication of "incident," would rescue him from his difficulties. Nothing, for instance, is more possible than that he be of a turn of mind for which this odd, literal opposition of description and dialogue, incident and description, has little meaning and light. People often talk of these things as if they had a kind of internecine distinctness, instead of melting into each other at every breath, and being intimately associated parts of one general effort of expression. I cannot imagine composition existing in a series of blocks, nor conceive, in any novel worth discussing at all, of a passage of description that is not in its intention narrative, a passage of dialogue that is not in its intention descriptive, a touch of truth of any sort that does not partake of the nature of incident, or an incident that derives its interest from any other source than the general and only source of the success of a work of art—that of being illustrative. A novel is a living thing, all one and continuous, like any other organism, and in proportion as it lives will it be found, I think, that in each of the parts there is something of each of the other parts. The critic who over the close texture of a finished work shall pretend to trace a geography of items will mark some frontiers as artificial, I fear, as any that have been known to history. There is an old-fashioned distinction between the novel of character and the novel of incident which must have cost many a smile to the intending fabulist who was keen about his work. It appears to me as little to the point as the equally celebrated distinction between the novel and the romance—to answer as little to any reality. There are bad novels and good novels, as there are bad pictures and good pictures; but that is the only distinction in which I see any meaning, and I can as little imagine speaking of a novel of character as I can imagine speaking of a picture of character. When one says picture one says of character, when one says novel one says of incident, and the terms may be transported at will. What is character but the determination of incident? What is incident but the illustration of character? What is either a picture or a novel that is *not* of character? What else do we seek in it and find in it? It is an incident for a woman to stand up with her hand resting on a table and look out at you in a certain way; or if it be not an incident I think it will be hard to say what it is. At the same time it is an expression of character. If you say you don't see it (character in *that—allons donc!*), this is exactly what the artist who has reasons of his own for thinking he *does* see it undertakes to show you. When a young man makes up his mind that he has not faith enough after all to enter the church as he intended, that is an incident, though you may not hurry to the end of the chapter to see whether perhaps he doesn't change once more. I do not say that these are extraordinary or startling incidents. I do not pretend to estimate the degree of interest proceeding from them, for this will depend upon the skill of the painter. It sounds almost puerile to say that some incidents are intrinsically much more important than others, and I need not take this precaution after having professed my sympathy for the major ones in remarking that the only classification of the novel that I can understand is into that which has life and that which has it not.

The novel and the romance, the novel of incident and that of character—these clumsy separations appear to me to have been made by critics and readers for their own convenience, and to help them out of their occasional queer predicaments, but to have little reality or interest for the producer, from whose point of view it is of course that we are attempting to consider the art of fiction. The case is the same with another shadowy category which Mr. Besant apparently is disposed to set up—that of the "modern English novel"; unless indeed it be that in this matter he has fallen into an accidental confusion of standpoints. It is not quite clear whether he intends the remarks in which he alludes to it to be didactic or historical. It is as difficult to suppose a person intending to write a modern English as to suppose him writing an ancient English novel: that is a label which begs the question. One writes the novel, one paints the picture, of one's language and of one's time, and calling it modern English will not, alas! make the difficult task any easier. No more, unfortunately, will calling this or that work of one's fellow-artist a romance—unless it be, of course, simply for the pleasantness of the thing, as for instance when Hawthorne gave this heading to his story of *Blithedale*. The French who have brought the theory of fiction to remarkable completeness, have but one name for the novel, and have not attempted smaller things in it, that I can see, for that. I can think of no obligation to which the "romancer" would not be held equally with the novelist; the standard of execution is equally high for each. Of course it is of execution that we are talking—that being the only point of a novel that is open to contention. This is perhaps too often lost sight of, only to produce interminable confusions and cross-purposes. We must grant the artist his subject, his idea, his *donnée*: Our criticism is applied only to what he makes of it. Naturally I do not mean that we are bound to like it or find it interesting: in case we do not our course is perfectly simple—to let it alone. We may believe that of a certain idea even the most sincere novelist can make nothing at all, and the event may perfectly justify our belief; but the failure will have been a failure to execute, and it is in the execution that the fatal weakness is recorded. If we pretend to respect the artist at all, we must allow him his freedom of choice, in the face, in particular cases, of innumerable presumptions that the choice will not fructify. Art derives a considerable part of its beneficial exercise from flying in the face of presumptions, and some of the most interesting experiments of which it is capable are hidden in the bosom of common things. Gustave Flaubert has written a story about the devotion of a servant-girl to a parrot, and the production, highly finished as it is, cannot on the whole be called a success. We are perfectly free to find it flat, but I think it might have been interesting; and I, for my part, am extremely glad he should have written it; it is a contribution to our knowledge of what can be done—or what cannot. Ivan Turgénieff has written a tale about a deaf and dumb serf and a lap-dog, and the thing is touching, loving, a little masterpiece. He struck the note of life where Gustave Flaubert missed it—he flew in the face of a presumption and achieved a victory.

Nothing, of course, will ever take the place of the good old fashion of "liking" a work of art or not liking it: the most improved criticism will not abolish that primitive, that ultimate test. I mention this to guard myself from the accusation of intimating that the idea, the subject, of a novel or a picture, does not matter. It matters, to my sense, in the highest degree, and if I might put up a prayer it would be that artists should select none but the richest. Some, as I have already hastened to admit, are much more remunerative than others, and it would be a world happily arranged in which persons intending to treat them should be exempt from confusions and mistakes. This fortunate condition will arrive only, I fear, on the same day that critics become purged from error. Meanwhile, I repeat, we do not judge the artist with fairness unless we say to him, "Oh, I grant you your starting-point, because if I did not I should seem to prescribe to you, and heaven forbid I should take that responsibility. If I pretend to tell you what you must not take, you will call upon me to tell you then what you must take; in which case I shall be prettily caught. Moreover, it isn't till I have accepted your data that I can begin to measure you. I have the standard, the pitch; I have no right to tamper with your flute and then criticise your music. Of course I may not care for your idea at all; I may think it silly, or stale, or unclean; in which case I wash my hands of you altogether. I may content myself with believing that you will not have succeeded in being interesting, but I shall, of course, not attempt to demonstrate it, and you will be as indifferent to me as I am to you. I needn't remind you that there are all sorts of tastes: who can know it better? Some people, for excellent reasons, don't like to read about carpenters; others, for reasons even better, don't like to read about courtesans. Many object to Americans. Others (I believe they are mainly editors and publishers) won't look at Italians. Some readers don't like quiet subjects; others don't like bustling ones. Some enjoy a complete illusion, others the consciousness of large concessions. They choose their novels accordingly, and if they don't care about your idea they won't, *a fortiori*, care about your treatment.

So that it comes back very quickly, as I have said, to the liking: in spite of M. Zola, who reasons less powerfully than he represents, and who will not reconcile himself to this absoluteness of taste, thinking that there are certain things that people ought to like, and that they can be made to like. I am quite at a loss to imagine anything (at any rate in this matter of fiction) that people *ought* to like or to dislike. Selection will be sure to take care of itself, for it has a constant motive behind it. That motive is simply experience. As people feel life, so they will feel the art that is most closely related to it. This closeness of relation is what we should never forget in talking of the effort of the novel. Many people speak of it as a factitious, artificial form, a product of ingenuity, the business of which is to alter and arrange the things that surround us, to translate them into conventional, traditional moulds. This, however, is a view of the matter which carries us but a very short way, condemns the art to an eternal repetition of a few familiar *clichés*, cuts short its development, and leads us straight up to a dead wall. Catching the very note and trick, the strange irregular rhythm of life, that is the attempt whose strenuous force keeps Fiction upon her feet. In proportion as in what she offers us we see life *without* rearrangement do we feel that we are touching the truth; in proportion as we see it *with* rearrangement do we feel that we are being put off with a substitute, a compromise and convention. It is not uncommon to hear an extraordinary assurance of remark in regard to this matter of rearranging, which is often spoken of as if it were the last word of art. Mr. Besant seems to me in danger of falling into the great error with his rather unguarded talk about "selection." Art is essentially selection, but it is a selection whose main care is to be typical, to be inclusive. For many people art means rose-coloured window-panes, and selection means picking a bouquet for Mrs. Grundy. They will tell you glibly that artistic considerations have nothing to do with the disagreeable, with the ugly; they will rattle off shallow commonplaces about the province of art and the limits of art till you are moved to some wonder in return as to the province and the limits of ignorance. It appears to me that no one can ever have made a seriously artistic attempt without becoming conscious of an immense increase—a kind of revelation—of freedom. One perceives in that case—by the light of a heavenly ray—that the province of art is all life, all feeling, all observation, all vision. As Mr. Besant so justly intimates, it is all experience. That is a sufficient answer to those who maintain that it must not touch the sad things of life, who stick into its divine unconscious bosom little prohibitory inscriptions on the end of sticks, such as we see in public gardens—"It is forbidden to walk on the grass; it is forbidden to touch the flowers; it is not allowed to introduce dogs or to remain after dark; it is requested to keep to the right." The young aspirant in the line of fiction whom we continue to imagine will do nothing without taste, for in that case his freedom would be of little use to him; but the first advantage of his taste will be to reveal to him the absurdity of the little sticks and tickets. If he have taste, I must add, of course he will have ingenuity, and my disrespectful reference to that quality just now was not meant to imply that it is useless in fiction. But it is only a secondary aid; the first is a capacity for receiving straight impressions.

Mr. Besant has some remarks on the question of "the story" which I shall not attempt to criticise, though they seem to me to contain a singular ambiguity, because I do not think I understand them. I cannot see what is meant by talking as if there were a part of a novel which is the story and part of it which for mystical reasons is not— unless indeed the distinction be made in a sense in which it is difficult to suppose that any one should attempt to convey anything. "The story," if it represents anything, represents the subject, the idea, the *donnée* of the novel; and there is surely no "school"—Mr. Besant speaks of a school—which urges that a novel should be all treatment and no subject. There must assuredly be something to treat; every school is intimately conscious of that. This sense of the story being the idea, the starting-point, of the novel, is the only one that I see in which it can be spoken of as something different from its organic whole; and since in proportion as the work is successful the idea permeates and penetrates it, informs and animates it, so that every word and every punctuation-point contribute directly to the expression, in that proportion do we lose our sense of the story being a blade which may be drawn more or less out of its sheath. The story and the novel, the idea and the form, are the needle and thread, and I never heard of a guild of tailors who recommended the use of the thread without the needle, or the needle without the thread. Mr. Besant is not the only critic who may be observed to have spoken as if there were certain things in life which constitute stories, and certain others which do not. I find the same odd implication in an entertaining article in the *Pall Mall Gazette*, devoted, as it happens, to Mr. Besant's lecture. "The story is the thing!" says this graceful writer, as if with a tone of opposition to some other idea. I should think it was, as every painter who, as the time for "sending in" his picture looms in the distance, finds himself still in quest of a subject—as every belated artist not fixed about his theme will heartily agree. There are some subjects which speak to us and others which do not, but he would be a clever man who should undertake to give a rule—an index expurgatorius—by which the story and the no-story should be known apart. It is impossible (to me at least) to imagine any such rule which shall not be altogether arbitrary. The writer in the *Pall Mall* opposes the delightful (as I suppose) novel of *Margot la Balafrée* to certain tales in which "Bostonian nymphs" appear to have "rejected English dukes for psychological reasons." I am not acquainted with the romance just designated, and can scarcely forgive the *Pall Mall* critic for not mentioning the name of the author, but the title appears to refer to a lady who may have received a scar in some heroic adventure. I am inconsolable at not being acquainted with this episode, but am utterly at a loss to see why it is a story when the rejection (or acceptance) of a duke is not, and why a reason, psychological or other, is not a subject when a cicatrix is. They are all particles of the multitudinous life with which the novel deals, and surely no dogma which pretends to make it lawful to touch the one and unlawful to touch the other will stand for a moment on its feet. It is the special picture that must stand or fall, according as it seems to possess truth or to lack it. Mr. Besant does not, to my sense, light up the subject by intimating that a story must, under penalty of not being a story, consist of "adventures." Why of adventures more than of green spectacles? He mentions a category of impossible things, and among them he places "fiction without adventure." Why without adventure, more than without matrimony, or celibacy, or parturition, or cholera, or hydropathy, or Jansenism? This seems to me to bring the novel back to the hapless little *rôle* of being an artificial, ingenious thing—bring it down from its large, free character of an immense and exquisite correspondence with life. And what *is* adventure, when it comes to that, and by what sign is the listening pupil to recognise it? It is an adventure—an immense one—for me to write this little article; and for a Bostonian nymph to reject an English duke is an adventure only less stirring, I should say, than for an English duke to be rejected by a Bostonian nymph. I see dramas within dramas in that, and innumerable points of view. A psychological reason is, to my imagination, an object adorably pictorial; to catch the tint of its complexion—I feel as if that idea might inspire one to Titianesque efforts. There are few things more exciting to me, in short, than a psychological reason, and yet, I protest, the novel seems to me the most magnificent form of art. I have just been reading, at the same time, the delightful story of *Treasure Island*, by Mr. Robert Louis Stevenson and, in a manner less consecutive, the last tale from M. Edmond de Goncourt, which is entitled *Chérie*. One of these works treats of murders, mysteries, island of dreadful renown, hairbreadth escapes, miraculous coincidences and buried doubloons. The other treats of a little French girl who lived in a fine house in Paris, and died of wounded sensibility because no one would marry her. I call *Treasure Island* delightful, because it appears to me to have succeeded wonderfully in what it attempts; and I venture to bestow no epithet upon *Chérie*, which strikes me as having failed deplorably in what it attempts—that is in tracing the development of the moral consciousness of a child. But one of these productions strikes me as exactly as much of a novel as the other, and as having a "story" quite as much. The moral consciousness of a child is as much a part of life as the islands of the Spanish Main, and the one sort of geography seems to me to have those "surprises" of which Mr. Besant speaks quite as much as the other. For myself (since it comes back in the last resort, as I say, to the preference of the individual), the picture of the child's experience has the advantage that I can at successive steps (an immense luxury, near to the "sensual pleasure" of which Mr. Besant's critic in the *Pall Mall* speaks) say Yes or No, as it may be, to what the artist puts before me. I have been a child in fact, but I have been on a quest for a buried treasure only in supposition, and it is a simple accident that with M. de Goncourt I should have for the most part to say No. With George Eliot, when she painted that country with a far other intelligence, I always said Yes.

The most interesting part of Mr. Besant's lecture is unfortunately the briefest passage—his very cursory allusion to the "conscious moral purpose" of the novel. Here again it is not very clear whether he be recording a fact or laying down a principle; it is a great pity that in the latter case he should not have developed his idea. This branch of the subject is of immense importance, and Mr. Besant's few words point to considerations of the widest reach, not to be lightly disposed of. He will have treated the art of fiction but superficially who is not prepared to go every inch of the way that these considerations will carry him. It is for this reason that at the beginning of these re-marks I was careful to notify the reader that my reflections on so large a theme have no pretension to be exhaustive. Like Mr. Besant, I have left the question of the mo-rality of the novel till the last, and at the last I find I have used up my space. It is a question surrounded with difficulties, as witness the very first that meets us, in the form of a definite question, on the threshold. Vagueness, in such a discussion, is fatal, and what is the meaning of your morality and your conscious moral purpose? Will you not define your terms and explain how (a novel being a picture) a picture can be either moral or immoral? You wish to paint a moral picture or carve a moral statue: will you not tell us how you would set about it? We are discussing the Art of Fiction; questions of art are questions (in the widest sense) of execution; questions of morality are quite another affair, and will you not let us see how it is that you find it so easy to mix them up? These things are so clear to Mr. Besant that he has deduced from them a law which he sees embodied in English Fiction, and which is "a truly admira-ble thing and a great cause for congratulation." It is a great cause for congratulation indeed when such thorny problems become as smooth as silk. I may add that in so far as Mr. Besant perceives that in point of fact English Fiction has addressed itself pre-ponderantly to these delicate questions he will appear to many people to have made a vain discovery. They will have been positively struck, on the contrary, with the moral timidity of the usual English novelist; with his (or with her) aversion to face the difficulties with which on every side the treatment of reality bristles. He is apt to be extremely shy (whereas the picture that Mr. Besant draws is a picture of boldness), and the sign of his work, for the most part, is a cautious silence on certain subjects. In the English novel (by which of course I mean the American as well), more than in any other, there is a traditional difference between that which people know and that which they agree to admit that they know, that which they see and that which they speak of, that which they feel to be a part of life and that which they allow to enter into literature. There is the great difference, in short, between what they talk of in conversation and what they talk of in print. The essence of moral energy is to survey the whole field, and I should directly reverse Mr. Besant's remark and say not that the English novel has a purpose, but that it has a diffidence. To what degree a purpose in a work of art is a source of corruption I shall not attempt to inquire; the one that seems to me least dangerous is the purpose of making a perfect work. As for our novel, I may say lastly on this score that as we find it in England to-day it strikes me as addressed in a large degree to "young people," and that this in itself constitutes a presumption that it will be rather shy. There are certain things which it is generally agreed not to discuss, not even to mention, before young people. That is very well, but the absence of discussion is not a symptom of the moral passion. The purpose of the English novel—"a truly admirable thing, and a great cause for congratulation"— strikes me therefore as rather negative.

There is one point at which the moral sense and the artistic sense lie very near to-gether; that is in the light of the very obvious truth that the deepest quality of a work of art will always be the quality of the mind of the producer. In proportion as that intelligence is fine will the novel, the picture, the statue partake of the substance of beauty and truth. To be constituted of such elements is, to my vision, to have purpose enough. No good novel will ever proceed from a superficial mind; that seems to me an axiom which, for the artist in fiction, will cover all needful moral ground: if the youthful aspirant take it to heart it will illuminate for him many of the mysteries of "purpose." There are many other useful things that might be said to him, but I have come to the end of my article, and can only touch them as I pass. The critic in the *Pall Mall Gazette*, whom I have already quoted, draws attention to the danger, in speaking of the art of fiction, of generalising. The danger that he has in mind is rather, I imagine, that of particularising, for there are some comprehensive remarks which, in addition to those embodied in Mr. Besant's suggestive lecture, might without fear of misleading him be addressed to the ingenuous student. I should remind him first of the magnificence of the form that is open to him, which offers to sight so few restrictions and such innumerable opportunities. The other arts, in comparison, appear confined and hampered; the various conditions under which they are exercised are so rigid and definite. But the only condition that I can think of attaching to the composition of the novel is, as I have already said, that it be sincere. This freedom is a splendid privilege, and the first lesson of the young novelist is to learn to be worthy of it. "Enjoy it as it deserves," I should say to him; "take possession of it, explore it to its utmost extent, publish it, rejoice in it. All life belongs to you, and do not listen either to those who would shut you up into corners of it and tell you that it is only here and there that art inhabits, or to those who would persuade you that this heavenly messenger wings her way outside of life altogether, breathing a superfine air, and turning away her head from the truth of things. There is no impression of life, no manner of seeing it and feeling it, to which the plan of the novelist may not offer a place; you have only to remember that talents so dissimilar as those of Alexandre Dumas and Jane Austen, Charles Dickens and Gustave Flaubert have worked in this field with equal glory. Do not think too much about optimism and pessimism; try and catch the colour of life itself. In France to-day we see a prodigious effort (that of Emile Zola, to whose solid and serious work no explorer of the capacity of the novel can allude without respect), we see an extraordinary effort vitiated by a spirit of pessimism on a narrow basis. M. Zola is magnificent, but he strikes an English reader as ignorant; he has an air of working in the dark; if he had as much light as energy, his results would be of the highest value. As for the aberrations of a shallow optimism, the ground (of English fiction especially) is strewn with their brittle particles as with broken glass. If you must indulge in conclusions, let them have the taste of a wide knowledge. Remember that your first duty is to be as complete as possible—to make as perfect a work. Be generous and delicate and pursue the prize."

FOUR

A TYPICAL NOVEL

Hamilton Wright Mabie

Hamilton Wright Mabie (1845–1916), though trained as a lawyer, devoted almost his entire career to a version of Christian apologetics in the form of essays and literary criticism. Indeed, much of his work appeared in the *Christian Union* and its successor, the *Outlook*. Though much respected in his day, by the 1920s he was frequently identified by H. L. Mencken and other radicals as the quintessential spokesman of the Genteel Tradition. Mabie was a prolific magazine writer whose volumes of collected essays appeared throughout his career. Among the most characteristic are *Short Studies in Literature* (1891) and *Essays in Literary Interpretation* (1892).

In "The Rise of Silas Lapham" Mr. Howells has given us his best and his most characteristic work; none of his earlier stories discloses so clearly the quality and resources of his gift or his conception of the novelist's art. As an expression of personal power and as a type of the dominant school of contemporary fiction in this country and in France, whence the special impulse of recent realism has come, this latest work of a very accomplished and conscientious writer deserves the most careful and dispassionate study. If Mr. Howells's work possessed no higher claim upon attention, its evident fidelity to a constantly advancing ideal of workmanship would command genuine respect and admiration; whatever else one misses in it, there is no lack of the earnestness which concentrates a man's full power on the thing in hand, nor of the sensitive literary conscience which permits no relaxation of strength on subordinate parts, but exacts in every detail the skill and care which are lavished on the most critical unfoldings of plot or disclosures of character. Mr. Howells evidently leaves nothing to the chance suggestion of an inspired moment, and takes nothing for granted; he verifies every insight by observation, fortifies every general statement by careful study of facts, and puts his whole force into every detail of his work. In spite

Andover Review 4 (November 1885): 417–29.

of its evident danger in any save the strongest hands, there is a tonic quality in this exacting conscientiousness which writers of a different school often lack, and the absence of which is betrayed by hasty, unbalanced, and incomplete workmanship. It is this quality which discovers itself more and more distinctly in Mr. Howells's novels in a constant development of native gifts, a stronger grasp of facts, and a more comprehensive dealing with the problems of character and social life to which he has given attention. In fact, this popular novelist is giving thoughtful readers of his books a kind of inspiration in the quiet but resolute progress of his gift and his art; a progress stimulated, no doubt, by success, but made possible and constant by fidelity to a high and disinterested ideal.

Nor has Mr. Howells spent his whole force on mere workmanship; he has made a no less strenuous endeavor to enlarge his knowledge of life, his grasp of its complicated problems, his insight into the forces and impulses which are the sources of action and character. If he has failed to touch the deepest issues, and to lay bare the more obscure and subtle movements of passion and purpose, it has been through no intellectual willfulness or lassitude; he has patiently and unweariedly followed such clews as he has been able to discover, and he has resolutely held himself open to the claims of new themes and the revelations of fresh contacts with life. The limitations of his work are also the limitations of his insight and his imagination, and this fact, fully understood in all its bearings, makes any effort to point out those limitations ungracious in appearance and distasteful in performance; if personal feeling were to control in such matters, one would content himself with an expression of hearty admiration for work so full of character, and of sincere gratitude for a delicate intellectual pleasure so varied and so sustained. The evidence of a deepened movement of thought is obvious to the most hasty backward glance from "The Rise of Silas Lapham" and "A Modern Instance" to "Their Wedding Journey" and "A Chance Acquaintance." In the early stories there is the lightness of touch, the diffused and delicate humor, which have never yet failed Mr. Howells; but there is little depth of sentiment, and almost no attempt to strike below the surface. These slight but very delightful tales discover the easy and graceful play of a force which deals with trifles as seriously as if it were handling the deepest and most significant problems of life. Seriousness is, indeed, the habitual mood of this novelist, and in his early stories it was the one prophetic element which they contained. There is a progressive evolution of power through "The Lady of the Aroostook," "The Undiscovered Country," "Dr. Breen's Practice," and "A Modern Instance"; each story in turn shows the novelist more intent upon his work, more resolute to hold his gift to its largest uses, more determined to see widely and deeply. His purpose grows steadily more serious, and his work gains correspondingly in substance and solidity. The problems of character which he sets before himself for solution become more complex and difficult, and, while there is nowhere a really decisive closing with life in a determined struggle to wring from it its secret, there is an evident purpose to grapple with realities and to keep in sympathy and touch with vital experience.

In "The Rise of Silas Lapham" Mr. Howells has made a study of social conditions and contrasts everywhere present in society in this country; not, perhaps, so sharply defined elsewhere as in Boston, but to be discovered with more or less definiteness of outline in all our older communities. His quick instinct has fastened upon a stage of social evolution with which everybody is familiar and in which everybody is interested. The aspect of social life presented in this story is well-nigh universal; it is real, it is vital, and it is not without deep significance; in dealing with it Mr. Howells has approached actual life more nearly, touched it more deeply, and expressed it more strongly than in any of his previous stories. The skill of his earliest work loses nothing in his latest; it is less evident because it is more unconscious and, therefore, more genuine and effective. There is the same humor, restrained and held in check by the major interests of the story, but touching here and there an idiosyncrasy, an inconsistency, a weakness, with all the old pungency and charm; a humor which is, in fact, the most real and the most distinctive of all Mr. Howells's gifts. There is, also, stronger grasp of situations, bolder portraiture of character, more rapid and dramatic movement of narrative. Still more important is the fact that in this novel life is presented with more of dramatic dignity and completeness than in any of Mr. Howells's other stories; there is a truer and nobler movement of human nature in it; and the characters are far less superficial, inconsequential, and unimportant than their predecessors; if not the highest types, they have a certain force and dignity which make us respect them, and make it worth while to write about them. Add to these characterizations of "The Rise of Silas Lapham" the statement that Mr. Howells has never shown more complete mastery of his art in dealing with his materials; that his style has never had more simplicity and directness, more solidity and substance, and it will be conceded that the sum total of excellence which even a reader who dissents from its underlying conception and method discovers in this story is by no means inconsiderable; is, indeed, such as to entitle it to very high praise, and to give added permanence and expansion to a literary reputation which, from the standpoint of popularity at least, stood in small need of these things.

And yet, when all this has been said, and said heartily, it must be added that "The Rise of Silas Lapham" is an unsatisfactory story; defective in power, in reality, and in the vitalizing atmosphere of imagination. No one is absorbed by it, nor moved by it; one takes it up with pleasure, reads it with interest, and lays it down without regret. It throws no spell over us; creates no illusion for us, leaves us indifferent spectators of an entertaining drama of social life. The novelist wrote it in a cool, deliberate mood, and it leaves the reader cold when he has finished it. The appearance and action of life are in it, but not the warmth; the frame, the organism, are admirable, but the divine inbreathing which would have given the body a soul has been withheld. Everything that art could do has been done, but the vital spark has not been transmitted. Mr. Howells never identifies himself with his characters; never becomes one with them in the vital fellowship and communion of the imagination; he constructs them with infinite patience and skill, but he never, for a moment, loses consciousness of his own individuality. He is cool and collected in all the emotional crises of his stories; indeed, it is often at such moments that one feels the presence of a diffused satire, as if the weakness of the men and women whom he is describing excited a little scorn in the critical mind of the novelist. The severest penalty of the persistent analytic mood is borne by the writer in the slight paralysis of feeling which comes upon him at the very moment when the pulse should beat a little faster of its own motion; in the subtle skepticism which pervades his work, unconsciously to himself, and like a slight frost takes the bloom off all fine emotions and actions. There are passages in Mr. Howells's stories in reading which one cannot repress a feeling of honest indignation at what is nothing more nor less than a refined parody of genuine feeling, sometimes of the most pathetic experience. Is Mr. Howells ashamed of life in its outcries of pain and regret? Does he shrink from these unpremeditated and unconventional revelations of character as vulgar, provincial, inartistic; or does he fail to comprehend them? Certainly the cool, skillful hand which lifts the curtain upon Silas Lapham's weakness and sorrows does not tremble for an instant with any contagious emotion; and whenever the reader begins to warm a little, a slight turn of satire, a cool phrase or two of analysis, a faint suggestion that the writer doubts whether it is worth while, clears the air again. Perhaps nothing more decisive on this point could be said of Mr. Howells's stories than that one can read them aloud without faltering at the most pathetic passages; the latent distrust of all strong feeling in them makes one a little shy of his own emotion.

This failure to close with the facts of life, to press one's heart against them as well as to pursue and penetrate them with one's thought; this lack of unforced and triumphant faith in the worth, the dignity, and the significance for art of human experience in its whole range; this failure of the imagination to bridge the chasm between the real and the fictitious reproduction of it, are simply fatal to all great and abiding work. Without faith, which is the very ground upon which the true artist stands; without love, which is both inspiration and revelation to him, a true art is impossible. Without faith there would never have come out of the world of the imagination such figures as Jeanie Deans, Colonel Newcome, Eugénie Grandet, Père Goriot, and Hester Prynne; without love—large, warm, generous sympathy with all that life is and means—the secret of these noble creations would never have been disclosed. Mr. Howells and Daudet practice alike the art of a refined realism, but what a distance separates the Nabob from Silas Lapham! Daudet is false to his theory and true to his art; life touches him deeply, fills him with reverence, and he can no more rid himself of the imagination than he can part the light from the flower upon which it falls. The Nabob might have suggested a similar treatment of Silas Lapham. How tenderly, how reverently, with what a sense of pathos, through what a mist of tears, Daudet uncovers to us the weakness and sorrows of Jansoulet! The Nabob is always touched by a soft light from the novelist's heart; poor Silas Lapham shivers in a perpetual east wind. Imagine the "Vicar of Wakefield" treated in the same spirit, and the fatal defect of Mr. Howells's attitude towards life is apparent at a glance.

The disposition to treat life lightly and skeptically, to doubt its capacity for real and lasting achievement, to stand apart from it and study it coolly and in detail with dispassionate and scientific impartiality, is at bottom decisive evidence of lack of power; that is, of the dramatic power which alone is able to reproduce life in noble dramatic forms. A refined realism strives to make up in patience what it lacks in genius; to make observation do the work of insight; to make analysis take the place of synthesis of character, and "a more analytic consideration of the appearance of things"—to quote Mr. James—the place of a resolute and masterly grasp of characters and situations. The method of the realism illustrated in "The Rise of Silas Lapham" is external, and, so far as any strong grasp of life is concerned, necessarily superficial. It is an endeavor to enter into the recesses of character, and learn its secret, not by insight, the method of the imagination, but by observation, the method of science; and it is an endeavor to reproduce that character under the forms of art, not by identification with it, and the genuine and almost unconscious evolution which follows, but by skillful adjustment of traits, emotions, passions, and activities which are the result of studies more or less conscientiously carried on. The patience and work involved in the making of some novels constructed on this method are beyond praise; but they must not make us blind to the fact that no method can take the place of original power, and that genius in some form—faith, sympathy, insight, imagination—is absolutely essential in all true art. The hesitation, the repression of emotion, the absence of color, are significant, not of a noble restraint of power, a wise husbanding of resources for the critical moment and situation, but of a lack of the spontaneity and overflow of a great force. Ruskin finely says that when we stand before a true work of art we feel ourselves in the presence, not of a great effort, but of a great force. In most of the novels of realism it is the effort which impresses us, and not the power. In Turgénieff and Björnson, masters of the art of realism, and yet always superior to it, the repression and restraint are charged with power; one feels behind them an intensity of thought and feeling that is at times absolutely painful. No such sensation overtakes one in reading "The Rise of Silas Lapham" or "The Bostonians;" there is no throb of life here; the pulse of feeling, if it beats at all, is imperceptible; and of the free and joyous play of that supreme force which we call genius there is absolutely not one gleam. If either novelist possessed it, no method, however rigidly practiced, could wholly confine it; it would flame like lightning, as in Björnson, or suffuse and penetrate all things with latent heat, as in Turgénieff, or touch all life with a soft, poetic radiance, as in Daudet.

Mr. Howells has said, in substance, that realism is the only literary movement of the day which has any vitality in it, and certainly no one represents this tendency on its finer side more perfectly than himself. Its virtues and its defects are very clearly brought out in his work: its clearness of sight, its fixed adherence to fact, its reliance upon honest work; and, on the other hand, its hardness, its lack of vitality, its paralysis of the finer feelings and higher aspirations, its fundamental defect on the side of the imagination. Realism is crowding the world of fiction with commonplace people; people whom one would positively avoid coming in contact with in real life; people without native sweetness or strength, without acquired culture or accomplishment, without that touch of the ideal which makes the commonplace significant and worthy of study. To the large, typical characters of the older novels has succeeded a generation of feeble, irresolute, unimportant men and women whose careers are of no moment to themselves, and wholly destitute of interest to us. The analysis of motives that were never worth an hour's serious study, the grave portraiture of frivolous, superficial, and often vulgar conceptions of life, the careful scrutiny of characters without force, beauty, aspiration, or any of the elements which touch and teach men, has become wearisome, and will sooner or later set in motion a powerful reaction. One cannot but regret such a comparative waste of delicate, and often genuine, art; it is as if Michael Angelo had given us the meaningless faces of the Roman fops of his time instead of the heads of Moses and Hercules.

It is certainly a mental or a moral disease which makes such trivial themes attractive to men of real talent. The "storm and stress" period returns at intervals, and, in spite of its extravagances of feeling, is respectable because of the real force and promise that are in it; one has a certain amount of patience with Werther, and with the hero of Schiller's "Robbers." But our modern misanthrope gropes feebly about for some clew to the mystery of his existence, and, not finding it ready to hand, snuffs out the flame of life in obedience, not to an honest conviction of the hopelessness of things, but because something goes wrong at the moment. Here is the modern hero skillfully displayed on a small canvas:—

"Vane walked up to Central Park, and returned to dress for dinner. Where was he to dine? The Club was the best place to meet people. His lodgings were dark, and he had some difficulty in finding a match; then he dropped one of his shirt-studs on the floor, and had to grope for it. Another one broke, and he threw open the drawer of his shaving-stand, impatiently, to find one to replace it. Lying in the drawer was an old revolver he had brought from Minnesota two years before. He took it out, placed the muzzle at his chest, and drew the trigger. As he fell to the floor, he turned over upon his side, holding up his hands before his eyes."

If such diseased and irresolute youths as Vane were the refuge of weak but ambitious writers groping for subjects with which to illustrate their own feebleness, there would be no significance in the fact; there is deep significance, however, in the fact that the man who wrote this story has genuine strength and skill. That such a character as Vane should attract such a writer, that Mr. James's stories should uniformly convey the impression, not of the tragic pathos of life, but of its general futility, that Mr. Howells should, for the most part, concern himself with men and women of very slender endowments and very superficial conceptions of life, are phenomena which lead us very directly to a conclusion somewhat similar to that reached by Mr. Stedman, after a survey of the present condition of poetry in this country, in his article on the "Twilight of the Poets" in a recent issue of the "Century Magazine." The work of the younger generation of American poets, in the judgment of this acute and accomplished critic, is full of the resources of a delicate art, and not without qualities of individual insight and imagination; but, as a whole, it lacks vigor, variety, grasp, and power. It is an interlude between the poetic activities of a generation now fast becoming silent and a generation not yet come to the moment of expression. Fiction has, however, a better outlook than poetry; there are already in the field novelists to whom life and art speak as of old with one voice, and who are illustrating under new forms those imperishable truths of character and destiny, the presence of which lifts the most obscure life into the realm of art, and the absence of which leaves life without a meaning, and devoid of all interest. It is very significant that realism either fails to grasp life firmly and present it powerfully, or else seizes upon its ignoble aspects; its vigor is mainly on the side of moral pathology.

The great name of Balzac is a word of power among the realists; and yet it is not easy to find in this master of fiction on a great scale either the principles or the method of the writers who profess to stand in direct line of succession from him. His realism was of that genuine order which underlies the noblest art of every age; it studies with most patient eye, and reproduces with most patient hand, the facts of life, in order that it may the more powerfully and the more faithfully discover the general law, the universal fact, which are the sole concern of art, behind them. The "more analytic consideration of the appearance of things" which one finds in Balzac is accompanied by a more powerful irradiation of the imagination. It is easy to understand Zola when he says "l'imagination de Balzac m'irrite;" it is just this imagination, this penetration of the real with the ideal, which makes the *Comédie Humaine* such a revelation of the age, such a marvelous reproduction of the complex life of the most complex epoch of history. The Naturalism of Zola, which is not psychological but physiological, which reduces life to its lowest factors, has little in common with the art of Balzac, which found all methods and facts inadequate for the complete illustration of the sublime, all-embracing fact of life. Naturalism is worthy of study, not only because of the great place it fills in contemporary literature, but because it is the logical result of realism, and, by exaggeration, makes the defects and limitations of realism more apparent.

The issue between the theoretical realism of the day and the older and eternal realism of fidelity to nature as the basis of all art is the more momentous because it is concealed in many cases by so much nice skill, and so much subtlety and refinement of talent. The divergence between the two is the nature of a great gulf fixed in the very constitution of things; it goes to the very bottom of our conceptions of life and art. To see nature with clear eyes, and to reproduce nature with deep and genuine fidelity, is the common aim of the old and the new realism; the radical character of the difference between them is made clear by the fact that the realists of the new school deny the existence in nature of the things which the older realists have held to be deepest and truest. The new realism is not dissent from a particular method; it is a fundamental skepticism of the essential reality of the old ends and subjects of art. It strikes at the very root of the universal art growth of the world: adherence to its fundamental precepts would have made Greek art an impossibility; would have cut the ground from under Aeschylus, Sophocles, and Euripides; would have prevented the new growth of art and literature in the Renaissance; would have paralyzed the old English drama, the classical French drama, and the late but splendid flowering of the German genius from Lessing to Heine. If the truth lies with modern realism, we must discard all those masters by whom the generations have lived and died, and seek out other teachers and shrines. Realism writes failure and barrenness across the culture of the world as the hand once wrote a similar judgment on the walls of an Assyrian palace. Fortunately, the parallel fails at the vital point; it requires a stronger faith than realism is able to furnish to identify the inspiration of the modern and the ancient interpreter, to discover in Zola the successor of Daniel.

The older art of the world is based on the conception that life is at bottom a revelation; that human growth under all conditions has a spiritual law back of it; that human relations of all kinds have spiritual types behind them; and that the discovery of these universal facts, and the clear, noble embodiment of them in various forms, is the office of genius and the end of art. The unique quality of the Greek race lay in its power to make these universal, permanent elements of life controlling. This is the secret of its marvelous and imperishable influence upon the minds of men. This was the work for which it was so lavishly endowed with genius. The art instinct among the Greeks was so universal and so controlling that all individual thought, feeling, and living seemed to be a kind of transparent medium for the revelation of elements and qualities which are common to the race. What was personal, isolated, unrelated to universal life has largely disappeared, and there remains a revelation, not of Greek character, but of human life of unequaled range and perfection. Every great Greek character is a type as truly as every Greek statue; and it is the typical quality which lifts the whole race into the realm of art. But modern realism knows nothing of any revelation in human life; of any spiritual facts of which its facts are significant; of any spiritual laws to which they conform in the unbroken order of the Universe. It does more than ignore these things; it denies them. Under the conditions which it imposes art can see nothing but the isolated physical fact before it; there are no mysterious forces in the soil under it; there is no infinite blue heaven over it. It forms no part of a universal order; it discovers no common law; it can never be a type of a great class. It is, in a word, practical atheism applied to art. It not only empties the world of the Ideal, but, as Zola frankly says, it denies "the good God;" it dismisses the old heaven of aspiration and possible fulfillment as an idle dream; it destroys the significance of life and the interpretative quality of art.

Such was not the conception of the great Balzac. With characteristic acuteness and clearness he puts the whole issue in a paragraph: "A writer who placed before his mind the duty of exact reproduction might become a painter of human types more or less faithful, successful, courageous, and patient; he might be the annalist of the dramas of private life, the archaeologist of the social fabric, the sponsor of trades and professions, the registrar of good and evil. And yet to merit the applause at which all artists should aim, ought he not also to study the reasons—or the reason—of the conditions of social life; ought he not to seize the hidden meaning of this vast accretion of beings, of passions, of events? Finally, having sought—I will not say found— this reason, this social mainspring, is he not bound to study natural law, and *discover why and when Society approached or swerved away from the eternal principles of truth and beauty?*" And he adds, to the same end, "History does not, like the novel, hold up the law of a higher ideal. History is, or should be, the world as it has been; the novel—to use a saying of Madame Necker, one of the remarkable minds of the last century—*should paint a possible better world.*" Readers of Balzac do not need to be told that his work, defective as it is on the side of moral insight, is still a commanding interpretation of life because it penetrates through individual fact to the universal fact, and through particular instances to the common law. It is only when one sees clearly this denial of the spiritual side of life, and sees it in all its results, that one understands why Naturalism inevitably portrays the repellant, and a refined realism the superficial, aspects of life. In this pregnant fact lies the secret of its rigidity, its coldness, its inevitable barrenness. A natural method, a true and vital conception, are always capable of further expansion. Is there anything beyond Zola? He has pressed his theory so far that even his hottest adherents see no step left for another to take. The energetic Naturalist—a man of great force and splendid working power—has left his followers not a single fig leaf to be plucked off the shameless nudity of the "bête humaine"—the human animal—in the delineation of which he rivals the skill of Barye. It is equally difficult to imagine any further progress along the lines of a refined realism; it has brought us face to face with the hard, isolated facts of life, and, having discarded the only faculty that can penetrate those facts to their depths and set them in the large order of the higher reason, there remains nothing more to be done by it. Materialism in art reaches its limits so soon that it never really gets into the field at all.

This denial of the imagination, this effort to discard it entirely and banish it into the region of moribund superstitions, is at bottom a confession of weakness. It is the refuge of writers who have inherited the skill, but not the impulse, of the great literary creators, and who are driven, unconsciously no doubt, to adopt a theory of art which makes the most of their strength and demands the least of their weakness. It is a new illustration of the old tendency to elevate individual limitations into universal laws, and to make the art bend to the man rather than the man to the art. We need not concern ourselves about the imagination, as if any man, or body of men, could discard it, or, for any long time, even obscure it; the imagination may safely be left to care for itself; what we need to concern ourselves about is the fact that we are on the wrong road, and that men of genius, unconsciously mistaking the way along which the sign-boards have all been carefully misplaced, may lose time and heart in the struggle to free themselves from misleading aims. We are in great danger of coming to accept as work of the first order that which has no claim to any such distinction, and adopt as the standards of the noblest literary art the very delightful but very inadequate creations of some of our contemporary writers. It is always wisest to face the truth; if the poets of the time lack the qualities which go to the making of great singers, let me acknowledge the fact and make the best of it; if our realistic novelists are more skillful than powerful, more adroit and entertaining than original and inspiring, let us admit this fact also. But, in the name and for the sake of art, let us decline to accept these charming story-tellers as the peers of the great masters, and above all, let us refuse to impose their individual limitations upon the great novelists of the future. "The Rise of Silas Lapham" and the novels of its class are additions to the literature of fiction for which we are grateful; but it is a great injustice to them and to their writers to insist upon placing them side by side with the great novels of the past.

What is needed now, in fiction as in poetry, is a revitalization of the imagination and a return to implicit and triumphant faith in it. The results of the scientific movement are misread by men of literary genius no less than by religious people; in the end, they will be found to serve the noblest uses of art no less than of religion. Their first effect is, indeed, to paralyze all superficial faiths and inspirations, by disturbing the order of facts upon which these rested, or from which they were derived; but, in the end, it will be found that the new order of the universe has under it a harmony of sublime conceptions such as no art has ever yet so much as dreamed of, and no religion ever yet grasped with clearness and certainty. Science not only leaves the imagination untouched, but adds indefinitely to the material with which it works. The more intelligent study of facts which it has made possible and inevitable purifies and enlarges in a corresponding degree the conceptions which underlie them, and will add in the end immeasurably to the scope and majesty of life. The hour is fast approaching for a new movement of the imagination; a new world awaits interpretation and reproduction in art at its hands. The first effects of the scientific tendency, evident in the uncertain note of contemporary poetry and the defective insight of realistic fiction, must not be mistaken for the final effects; it is this mistake which gives our poetry its elegiac note and our fiction its general confession of the futility of all things. Great works of art never come from hands afflicted with this kind of paralysis. The real outcome of the scientific spirit is something very different from the interpretation of realism; for its interpreters and prophets the time is fast approaching, and no blindness and faint-heartedness of this generation will delay their coming when the hour is ripe. They, too, will be realists as all the great artists have been; realists like Dante and Shakespeare; like Balzac and Thackeray; like the wise Goethe, who held resolutely to the fact because of the law behind it, who saw that the Real and the Ideal are one in the divine order of the universe, and whose clear glance into the appearance of things made him the more loyal to the Whole, the Good, and the True.

FIVE

SELECTIONS FROM THE "EDITOR'S STUDY"

William Dean Howells

William Dean Howells (1837–1920) not only published a great body of fiction over his long career but often combined his work as a novelist with sustained periods of productive association with a major magazine. Perhaps the most significant such conjunction occurred during the late 1880s and early 1890s. Already established along with James and Twain as one of the important novelists of the period, especially after the success of *The Rise of Silas Lapham* (1885), Howells agreed, in late 1885, to supply a monthly column on literary topics to *Harper's Monthly*. During the next six years, from January 1886 to early 1892—a period during which he was also producing some of his most significant fiction, including *A Hazard of New Fortunes* (1890)—Howells dealt with a wide variety of topics in his *Harper's* "Editor's Study" column but returned again and again to his preoccupation with the need for American fiction and criticism to adopt a realistic perspective. The column was widely discussed—newspapers often editorialized on its contents—as was Howells's collection of many of its more polemical portions in his *Criticism and Fiction* (1891). By the late 1880s Howells's name was a byword for realism in America. In addition to *Criticism and Fiction*, other major critical works by Howells are *My Literary Passions* (1895) and *Literature and Life* (1902). Howells's most significant criticism is collected in the three volumes of *Selected Literary Criticism* (1993) in the *Selected Edition of W. D. Howells*.

Each of the selections which follows appeared originally in *Harper's Monthly* and is collected in William Dean Howells, *Selected Literary Criticism. Vol. II: 1886–1897*, ed. Donald Pizer et al. (Bloomington: Indiana University Press, 1993). Specific bibliographical information is provided for each selection. The title of each selection is that which appears in *Selected Literary Criticism*; the columns were untitled in *Harper's Monthly*.

THE NEW "STUDY" AND THE USE
OF AMERICAN ENGLISH *

I.

There are few words so sympathetically compliant with a varied need as the word used to conceal the real character of this new department of the *New Monthly*. In almost every dwelling of any pretensions to taste there is nowadays a study, charmingly imagined by the architect and prettily equipped by the domestic powers, where the master of the house lounges away his leisure, scanty or abundant, and nobody apparently studies. From a very early time, or at least from the opening of the present genteel period when the whole race began to put on airs of intellectual refinement, the "study" has been known; and even in the *Book of Snobs* we read of Major Ponto's study, where "the library consisted mostly of boots," gardening tools, fishing-rods, whips, spurs, and pots of blacking; and such branches of literary inquiry were discussed as the fate of the calf or the sentence of the pig. This, to be sure, was the study of a country gentleman, and the study of an editor of such a magazine as ours is necessarily somewhat different, though its appointments are equally expressive, we hope, of cultivated pursuits. It is, in any case, not at all the kind of place which the reader, with his mind full of the Grub Street traditions of literature, would fancy—a narrow den at the top of the house, where the occupant, piled about with books and proofs and manuscripts, darkles in a cloud blown from his own cigar. The real editor, before whom contributors tremble, may be something like this in his habitat and environment; but the unreal editor, the airy, elusive abstraction who edits the Study, is quite another character, and is fittingly circumstanced. Heavy rugs silence the foot upon his floor; nothing but the costliest masterpieces gleam from his walls; the best of the old literatures, in a subtly chorded harmony of bindings, make music to the eye from his shelves, and the freshest of the new load his richly carved mahogany table. His vast windows of flawless plate look out upon the confluent waters of the Hudson and the Charles, with expanses, in the middle distance, of the Mississippi, the Great Lakes, and the Golden Gate, and in the background the misty line of the Thames, with reaches of the remoter Seine, and glints of the Tiber's yellow tide. The peaks of the Apennines, dreamily blending with those of the Sierras, form the vanishing-point of the delicious perspective; and we need not say that the edifice in which this study luxuriously lurks commands the very best view of the Washington Monument and the two-pair-front of the national Capitol. As a last secret we will own that the edifice is an American architect's adaptation of a design by the poet Ariosto, who for reasons of economy built himself a very small house in a back street of Ferrara,

---

*Harper's Monthly 72 (January 1886): 321, 324–25. Text from *Selected Literary Criticism*, pp. 3–6.

while he lavished his palaces on the readers of his poetry at no expense to himself; it was originally in the Spanish taste, but the architect has added some touches of the new Renaissance, and has done what he could to impart a colonial flavor to the whole.

In such keeping, the editor of the Study proposes to sit at a fine ease, and talk over with the reader—who will always be welcome here—such matters of literary interest as may come up from time to time, whether suggested by the new books of the day or other accidents of the literary life. The reader will, of course, not be allowed to interrupt the editor while he is talking; in return the editor will try to keep his temper, and to be as inconclusive as possible. If the reader disagrees with him upon any point, he will be allowed to write to him for publication, when, if the editor can not expose the reader's folly, he will be apt to suppress his letter. It is meant, in other terms, to make the Study a sort of free parliament, but for the presiding officer only; or, a symposium of one.

The editor comes to his place after a silence of some years in this sort, and has a very pretty store of prejudices to indulge and grudges to satisfy, which he will do with as great decency as possible. Their victims will at once know them for prejudices and grudges, and so no great harm will be done; it is impartiality that is to be feared in these matters, and a man who likes or dislikes can never be impartial—though perhaps a woman might. The editor will not deny that in addition to his prejudices and grudges he has some opinions, honest as opinions go, but cherished possibly because he has had no opportunity to exchange them with others. With a reader reduced to silence, the affair of their expression will be very simple; the reader will accept them or not as he likes, and having no chance to reply, will not be argued into them. While the editor's guest, he is invited to look at the same books and consider the same facts with him, and—tacitly, of course—may disable his judgment as much as he will. If he is not content with this, there will always be a vast body of literature not under discussion, and he may turn for relief to that.

*   *   *   *   *

IV.

We have the more patience because we hope that our inherited English may be constantly freshened and revived from the native sources which literary decentralization will help to keep open, and we will own that as we turned over those novels coming from Philadelphia, from New Mexico, from Boston, from Tennessee, from rural New England, from New York, every local flavor of diction gave us courage and pleasure. M. Alphonse Daudet, in a conversation which Mr. Boyesen has set down in a recently recorded interview with him, said, in speaking of Tourguéneff: "What a luxury it must be to have a great big untrodden barbaric language to wade into! We poor fellows who work in the language of an old civilization, we may sit and chisel our little verbal felicities, only to find in the end that it is a borrowed jewel we are polishing. The crown jewels of our French tongue have passed through the hands of so many generations of monarchs that it seems like presumption on the part of any late-born pretender to attempt to wear them."

This grief is, of course, a little whimsical. M. Daudet was expecting Mr. Boyesen to say, as he immediately said, that M. Daudet was himself a living refutation, and so forth, and so forth; yet it has a certain measure of reason in it, and the same regret has been more seriously expressed by the Italian poet Aleardi:

"Muse of an aged people, in the eve
Of fading civilization, I was born.
. . . . Oh, fortunate,
My sisters, who in the heroic dawn
Of races sung! To them did destiny give
The virgin fire and chaste ingenuousness
Of their land's speech; and, reverenced, their hands
Ran over potent strings."

It will never do to allow that we are at such a desperate pass in English, but something of this divine despair we may feel too in thinking of "the spacious times of great Elizabeth," when the poets were trying the stops of the young language, and thrilling with the surprises of their own music. We may comfort ourselves, however, unless we prefer a luxury of grief, by remembering that no language is ever old on the lips of those who speak it, no matter how decrepit it drops from the pen. We have only to leave our studies, editorial and other, and go into the shops and fields to find the "spacious times" again; and from the beginning Realism, before she had got a name or put on her capital letter, had divined this near-at-hand truth along with the rest. Mr. Lowell, the greatest and finest realist who ever wrought in verse, showed us that Elizabeth was still Queen where he heard Yankee farmers talk; and without asking that our novelists of the widely scattered centres shall each seek to write in his local dialect, we are glad, as we say, of every tint any of them gets from the parlance he hears; it is much better than the tint he will get from the parlance he reads. One need not invite slang into the company of its betters, though perhaps slang has been dropping its s and becoming language ever since the world began, and is certainly sometimes delightful and forcible beyond the reach of the dictionary. We would not have any one go about for new words, but if one of them came aptly, not to reject its help. For our novelists to try to write Americanly, from any motive, would be a dismal error, but being born Americans, we would have them use "Americanisms" whenever these serve their turn; and when their characters speak, we should like to hear them speak true American, with all the varying Tennesseean, Philadelphian, Bostonian, and New York accents. If we bother ourselves to write what the critics imagine to be "English," we shall be priggish and artificial, and still more so if we make our Americans talk "English." There is also this serious disadvantage about "English," that if we wrote the best "English" in the world, probably the English themselves would not know it, or, if they did, certainly would not own it. It has always been supposed by grammarians and purists that a language can be kept as they find it; but languages, while they live, are perpetually changing. God apparently meant them for the common people—whom Lincoln believed God liked because He had made so many of them; and the common people will use them freely as they use other gifts of God. On their lips our continental English will differ more and more from the insular English, and we believe that this is not deplorable, but desirable. Our tongue will always be intelligible enough to our cousins across seas to enable them to enjoy this department of the *New Monthly*, and we should not fear a diminished circulation of the Magazine among them if we became quite faithful in our written English to the spoken English of this continent.

BALZAC*

*   *   *   *   *

III.

It is droll to find Balzac, who suffered such bitter scorn and hate for his realism while he was alive, now become a fetich in his turn, to be shaken in the faces of those who will not blindly worship him. But it is no new thing in the history of literature: whatever is established is sacred with those who do not think. At the beginning of the century, when romance was making the same fight against effete classicism which realism is making to-day against effete romance, the Italian poet Monti declared that "the romantic was the cold grave of the Beautiful," just as the realistic is now supposed to be. The romance of that day and the realism of this are in certain degree the same. Romance then sought, as realism seeks now, to widen the bounds of sympathy, to level every barrier against aesthetic freedom, to escape from the paralysis of tradition. It exhausted itself in this impulse; and it remained for realism to assert that fidelity to experience and probability of motive are essential conditions of a great imaginative literature. It is not a new theory, but it has never before universally characterized literary endeavor. When realism becomes false to itself, when it heaps up facts merely, and maps life instead of picturing it, realism will perish too. Every true realist instinctively knows this, and it is perhaps the reason why he is careful of every fact, and feels himself bound to express or to indicate its meaning at the risk of over-moralizing. In life he finds nothing insignificant; all tells for destiny and character; nothing that God has made is contemptible. He cannot look upon human life and declare this thing or that thing unworthy of notice, any more than the scientist can declare a fact of the material world beneath the dignity of his inquiry. He feels in every nerve the equality of things and the unity of men; his soul is exalted, not by vain shows and shadows and ideals, but by realities, in which alone the truth lives. In criticism it is his business to break the images of false gods and misshapen heroes, to take away the poor silly toys that many grown people would still like to play with. He cannot keep terms with Jack the Giant-Killer or Puss in Boots, under any name or in any place, even when they reappear as the convict Vautrec, or the Marquis de Montrivaut, or the Sworn Thirteen Noblemen. He must say to himself that Balzac, when he imagined these monsters, was not Balzac, he was Dumas; he was not realistic, he was romantic.

---

*Harper's Monthly 72 (May 1886): 973. Text from *Selected Literary Criticism*, pp. 20–21.

*   *   *   *   *

DOSTOYEVSKY AND THE MORE
SMILING ASPECTS OF LIFE*

*   *   *   *   *

III.

M. Vogüé writes with perhaps too breathless a fervor, but his article is valuable for the light it casts upon the origins of Dostoïevsky's work, and its inspirations and motives. It was the natural expression of such a life and such conditions. But it is useful to observe that while *The Crime and the Punishment* may be read with the deepest sympathy and interest, and may enforce with unique power the lessons which it teaches, it is to be praised only in its place, and its message is to be received with allowances by readers exterior to the social and political circumstances in which it was conceived. It used to be one of the disadvantages of the practice of romance in America, which Hawthorne more or less whimsically lamented, that there were so few shadows and inequalities in our broad level of prosperity; and it is one of the reflections suggested by Dostoïevsky's book that whoever struck a note so profoundly tragic in American fiction would do a false and mistaken thing—as false and as mistaken in its way as dealing in American fiction with certain nudities which the Latin peoples seem to find edifying. Whatever their deserts, very few American novelists have been led out to be shot, or finally exiled to the rigors of a winter at Duluth; one might make Herr Most the hero of a labor-question romance with perfect impunity; and in a land where journeymen carpenters and plumbers strike for four dollars a day the sum of hunger and cold is certainly very small, and the wrong from class to class is almost inappreciable. We invite our novelists, therefore, to concern themselves with the more smiling aspects of life, which are the more American, and to seek the universal in the individual rather than the social interests. It is worth-while, even at the risk of being called commonplace, to be true to our well-to-do actualities; the very passions themselves seem to be softened and modified by conditions which cannot be said to wrong any one, to cramp endeavor, or to cross lawful desire. Sin and suffering and shame there must always be in the world, we suppose, but we believe that in this new world of ours it is mainly from one to another one, and oftener still from one to one's self. We have death in America, and a great deal of disagreeable and painful disease, which the multiplicity of our patent medicines does not seem to cure; but this is tragedy that comes in the very nature of things, and is not peculiarly American, as the large, cheerful average of health and success and happy life is. It will not do to boast, but it is well to be true to the facts, and to see that, apart from these purely mortal troubles, the race here enjoys conditions in which most of the ills that have darkened its annals may be averted by honest work and unselfish behavior. It is only

---

**Harper's Monthly* 73 (September 1886): 641–42. Text from *Selected Literary Criticism*, pp. 35–36.

now and then, when some dark shadow of our shameful past appears, that we can believe there ever was a tragic element in our prosperity. Even then, when we read such an artlessly impressive sketch as Mrs. Sarah Bradford writes of Harriet Tubman—once famous as the Moses of her people—the self-freed bondwoman who led three hundred of her brethren out of slavery, and with a price set upon her head, risked her life and liberty nineteen times in this cause; even then it affects us like a tale

> "Of old, unhappy, far-off things,
> And battles long ago,"

and nothing within the date of actual history. We cannot realize that most of the men and women now living were once commanded by the law of the land to turn and hunt such fugitives back into slavery, and to deliver such an outlaw as Harriet over to her owner; that those who abetted such outlaws were sometimes mulcted to the last dollar of their substance in fines. We can hardly imagine such things now for the purposes of fiction; all troubles that now hurt and threaten us are as crumpled rose leaves in our couch. But we may nevertheless read Dostoïevsky, and especially our novelists may read him, to advantage, for in spite of his terrible picture of a soul's agony he is hopeful and wholesome, and teaches in every page patience, merciful judgment, humble helpfulness, and that brotherly responsibility, that duty of man to man, from which not even the Americans are emancipated.

*   *   *   *   *

FALSE AND TRUTHFUL FICTION *

I.

It must have been a passage from Vernon Lee's *Baldwin*, claiming for the novel an indefinitely vast and subtle influence on modern character, which provoked the following suggestive letter from one of our readers:

"——, —— Co., Md., *Sept.* 18, 1886.
"Dear Sir,—With regard to article IV. in the Editor's Study in the September *Harper*, allow me to say that I have very grave doubts as to the whole list of magnificent things that you seem to think novels have done for the race, and can witness in myself many evil things which they have done for me. Whatever in my mental make-up is wild and visionary, whatever is untrue, whatever is injurious, I can trace to the perusal of some work of fiction. Worse than that, they beget such high-strung and supersensitive ideas of life that plain industry and plodding perseverance are despised, and matter-of-fact poverty, or every-day, commonplace distress, meets with no sympathy, if indeed noticed at all, by one who has wept over the impossibly accumulated sufferings of some gaudy hero or heroine.

Harper's Monthly 74 (April 1887): 824–26. Text from *Selected Literary Criticism*, pp. 43–47.

"Hoping you will pardon the liberty I have taken in addressing you, I remain,
"Most respectfully yours, —— ——."

We are not sure that we have the controversy with the writer which he seems to suppose, and we should perhaps freely grant the mischievous effects which he says novel-reading has wrought upon him, if we were not afraid that he had possibly reviewed his own experience with something of the inaccuracy we find in his report of our opinions. By his confession he is himself proof that Vernon Lee is right in saying, "The modern human being has been largely fashioned by those who have written about him, and most of all by the novelist," and there is nothing in what he urges to conflict with her claim that "the chief use of the novel" is "to make the shrewd and tolerant a little less shrewd and tolerant, and to make the generous and austere a little more skeptical and easy-going." If he will look more closely at these postulates, we think he will see that in the one she deals with the effect of the novel in the past, and in the other with its duty in the future. We still think that there "is sense if not final wisdom" in what she says, and we are quite willing to acknowledge something of each in our correspondent.

But novels are now so fully accepted by every one pretending to cultivated taste—and they really form the whole intellectual life of such immense numbers of people, without question of their influence, good or bad, upon the mind—that it is refreshing to have them frankly denounced, and to be invited to revise one's ideas and feelings in regard to them. A little honesty, or a great deal of honesty, in this quest will do the novel, as we hope yet to have it, and as we have already begun to have it, no harm; and for our own part we will confess that we believe fiction in the past to have been largely injurious, as we believe the stage play to be still almost wholly injurious, through its falsehood, its folly, its wantonness, and its aimlessness. It may be safely assumed that most of the novel-reading which people fancy is an intellectual pastime is the emptiest dissipation, hardly more related to thought or the wholesome exercise of the mental faculties than opium-eating; in either case the brain is drugged, and left weaker and crazier for the debauch. If this may be called the negative result of the fiction habit, the positive injury that most novels work is by no means so easily to be measured in the case of young men whose character they help so much to form or deform, and the women of all ages whom they keep so much in ignorance of the world they misrepresent. Grown men have little harm from them, but in the other cases, which are the vast majority, they hurt because they are not true—not because they are malevolent, but because they are idle lies about human nature and the social fabric, which it behooves us to know and to understand, that we may deal justly with ourselves and with one another. One need not go so far as our correspondent, and trace to the fiction habit "whatever is wild and visionary, whatever is untrue, whatever is injurious," in one's life; bad as the fiction habit is, it is probably not responsible for the whole sum of evil in its victims, and we believe that if the reader will use care in choosing from this fungus-growth with which the fields of literature teem every day, he may nourish himself as with the true mushroom, at no risk from the poisonous species.

The tests are very plain and simple, and they are perfectly infallible. If a novel flatters the passions, and exalts them above the principles, it is poisonous; it may not kill, but it will certainly injure; and this test will alone exclude an entire class of fiction, of which eminent examples will occur to all. Then the whole spawn of so-called unmoral romances, which imagine a world where the sins of sense are unvisited by the penalties following, swift or slow, but inexorably sure, in the real world, are deadly poison: these do kill. The novels that merely tickle our prejudices and lull our judgment, or that coddle our sensibilities, or pamper our gross appetite for the marvellous, are not so fatal, but they are innutritious, and clog the soul with unwholesome vapors of all kinds. No doubt they too help to weaken the mental fibre, and make their readers indifferent to "plodding perseverance and plain industry," and to "matter-of-fact poverty and commonplace distress."

Without taking them too seriously, it still must be owned that the "gaudy hero and heroine" are to blame for a great deal of harm in the world. That heroine long taught by example, if not precept, that Love, or the passion or fancy she mistook for it, was the chief interest of a life which is really concerned with a great many other things; that it was lasting in the way she knew it; that it was worthy of every sacrifice, and was altogether a finer thing than prudence, obedience, reason; that love alone was glorious and beautiful, and these were mean and ugly in comparison with it. More lately she has begun to idolize and illustrate Duty, and she is hardly less mischievous in this new role, opposing duty, as she did love, to prudence, obedience, and reason. The stock hero, whom, if we met him, we could not fail to see was a most deplorable person, has undoubtedly imposed himself upon the victims of the fiction habit as admirable. With him, too, love was and is the great affair, whether in its old romantic phase of chivalrous achievement or manifold suffering for love's sake, or its more recent development of the "virile," the bullying, and the brutal, or its still more recent agonies of self-sacrifice, as idle and useless as the moral experiences of the insane asylums. With his vain posturings and his ridiculous splendor he is really a painted barbarian, the prey of his passions and his delusions, full of obsolete ideals, and the motives and ethics of a savage, which the guilty author of his being does his best—or his worst—in spite of his own light and knowledge, to foist upon the reader as something generous and noble. We are not merely bringing this charge against that sort of fiction which is beneath literature and outside of it, "the shoreless lakes of ditch-water," whose miasms fill the air below the empyrean where the great ones sit; but we are accusing the work of some of the most famous, who have, in this instance or in that, sinned against the truth, which can alone exalt and purify men. We do not say that they have constantly done so, or even commonly done so; but that they have done so at all marks them as of the past, to be read with the due historical allowance for their epoch and their conditions. For we believe that, while inferior writers will and must continue to imitate them in their foibles and their errors, no one hereafter will be able to achieve greatness who is false to humanity, either in its facts or its duties. The light of civilization has already broken even upon the novel, and no conscientious man can now set about painting an image of life without perpetual question of the verity of his work, and without feeling bound to distinguish so clearly that no reader of his may be misled, between what is right, and what is wrong, what is noble and what is base, what is health and what is perdition, in the actions and the characters he portrays.

The fiction that aims merely to entertain—the fiction that is to serious fiction as the opéra bouffe, the ballet, and the pantomime are to the true drama—need not feel the burden of this obligation so deeply; but even such fiction will not be gay or trivial to any reader's hurt, and criticism will hold it to account if it passes from painting to teaching folly.

More and more not only the criticism which prints its opinions, but the infinitely vaster and powerfuler criticism which thinks and feels them merely, will make this demand. For our own part we confess that we do not care to judge any work of the imagination without first of all applying this test to it. We must ask ourselves before we ask anything else, Is it true?—true to the motives, the impulses, the principles that shape the life of actual men and women? This truth, which necessarily includes the highest morality and the highest artistry—this truth given, the book *cannot* be wicked and cannot be weak; and without it all graces of style and feats of invention and cunning of construction are so many superfluities of naughtiness. It is well for the truth to have all these, and shine in them, but for falsehood they are merely meretricious, the bedizenment of the wanton; they atone for nothing, they count for nothing. But in fact they come naturally of truth, and grace it without solicitation; they are added unto it. In the whole range of fiction we know of no *true* picture of life— that is, of human nature—which is not also a masterpiece of literature, full of divine and natural beauty. It may have no touch or tint of this special civilization or of that; it had *better* have this local color well ascertained; but the truth is deeper and finer than aspects, and if the book is true to what men and women know of one another's souls it will be true enough, and it will be great and beautiful. It is the conception of literature as something apart from life, superfinely aloof, which makes it really unimportant to the great mass of mankind, without a message or a meaning for them; and it is the notion that a novel may be false in its portrayal of causes and effects that makes literary art contemptible even to those whom it amuses, that forbids them to regard the novelist as a serious or right-minded person. If they do not in some moment of indignation cry out against all novels, as our correspondent does, they remain besotted in the fume of the delusions purveyed to them, with no higher feeling for the author than such maudlin affection as the *habitué* of an opium-joint perhaps knows for the attendant who fills his pipe with the drug.

II.

Or, as in the case of another correspondent of the Study, who writes that in his youth he "read a great many novels, but always regarded it as an amusement, like horse-racing and card-playing," for which he had no time when he entered upon the serious business of life, it renders them merely contemptuous. His view of the matter may be commended to the brotherhood and sisterhood of novelists as full of wholesome if bitter suggestion; and we urge them not to dismiss it with high literary scorn as that of some Boeotian dull to the beauty of art. Refuse it as we may, it is still the feeling of the vast majority of people for whom life is earnest, and who find only a distorted and misleading likeness of it in our books. We may fold ourselves in our scholars' gowns, and close the doors of our studies, and affect to despise this rude voice; but we cannot shut it out. It comes to us from wherever men are at work, from wherever they are truly living, and accuses us of unfaithfulness, of triviality, of mere stage-play; and none of us can escape conviction except he prove himself worthy of his time—a time in which the great masters have brought literature back to life, and filled its ebbing veins with the red tides of reality. We cannot all equal them; we need not copy them; but we can all go to the sources of their inspiration and their power; and to draw from these no one need go far—no one need really to go out of himself.

Fifty years ago, Carlyle, in whom the truth was always alive, but in whom it was then unperverted by suffering, by celebrity and despair, wrote in his study of Diderot:

> "Were it not reasonable to prophesy that this exceeding great multitude of novel-writers and such like must, in a new generation, gradually do one of two things; either retire into the nurseries, and work for children, minors, and semi-fatuous persons of both sexes, or else, what were far better, sweep their novel-fabric into the dust-cart, and betake themselves with such faculty as they have to understand and record what is true, of which surely there is, and will be forever, a whole infinitude unknown to us of infinite importance to us? Poetry, it will more and more come to be understood, is nothing but higher knowledge; and the only genuine Romance (for grown persons), Reality."

If after half a century fiction still mainly works for "children, minors, and semi-fatuous persons of both sexes," it is nevertheless one of the hopefulest signs of the world's progress that it has begun to work for "grown persons," and if not exactly in the way that Carlyle might have solely intended in urging its writers to compile memoirs instead of building the "novel-fabric," still it has in the highest and widest sense already made Reality its Romance. We cannot judge it, we do not even care for it, except as it has done this; and we cannot conceive of a literary self-respect in these days compatible with the old trade of make-believe, with the production of the kind of fiction which is too much honored by classification with card-playing and horse-racing.

* * * * *

STANDARDS AND TASTE IN FICTION*

* * * * *

III.

A more temperate critic than the one we have been quoting deplores in a New York journal the danger which attends the new fiction of the South from its prompt and

---

*Harper's Monthly 75 (September 1887): 639–40. Text from Selected Literary Criticism, pp. 62–64.

easy success. He calls himself a Southerner, and he thinks it would be well if there were a school of Southern criticism for the censure of Southern literature; but at the same time he is disposed to defend this literature against a charge which we agree with him cannot be against it alone. It has been called narrow, and he asks; "Is not the broadest of the new American fiction narrow, when compared, as it should be compared, with the authors of Russian fiction, French fiction, English fiction? Is there a living novelist of the North whose largest boundaries do not shrink to pitiful dimensions when put by the side of Tolstoi's or Balzac's, or Thackeray's?"

We do not know certainly whether a Southerner thinks narrowness a defect of Northern fiction or not, but upon the supposition that he does so, we remind him that both Thackeray and Balzac are dead, and that our recent novelists might as well, for all purposes of argument, be compared with Cervantes and Le Sage. Moreover, Balzac is rather a narrow writer in each of his books, and if we are to grant him breadth we must take him in the whole group which he required to work out his *comédie humaine*. Each one of Mr. Henry James's books is as broad as any one of Balzac's; and we believe his *Princess Casamassima* is of a scope and variety quite unknown to them. Thackeray, to be sure, wandered through vast spaces, but his greatest work was concerned with the very narrow world of English society; his pictures of life outside of society were in the vein of caricature. As for Tolstoi, he is the incomparable; and no novelist of any time or any tongue can fairly be compared with him, as no dramatist can fairly be compared with Shakespeare. Nevertheless, if something of this sort is absolutely required, we will instance Mr. J. W. De Forest, in his very inadequately named *Miss Ravenel's Conversion*, as presenting an image of American life during the late rebellion, both North and South, at home and in the field, which does not "shrink to pitiful dimensions" even when "put by the side of Tolstoi's" *War and Peace*; it is an admirable novel,—and spacious enough for the vast drama glimpsed in it. Mr. Cable's *Grandissimes* is large enough to reflect a civilization; and Mr. Bishop, in *The Golden Justice* and *The House of a Merchant Prince*, shows a feeling for amplitude in the whole design, as well as for close and careful work in the details.

The present English fiction is as narrow as our own; and if a Southerner had looked a little farther abroad he would have found that most modern fiction was narrow in a certain sense. In Italy he would have found the best men writing novels as brief and restricted in range as ours; in Spain the novels are intense and deep, and not spacious; the French school, with the exception of Zola, is narrow; the Norwegians are narrow; the Russians, except Tolstoi, are narrow, and the next greatest after him, Tourguénief, is the narrowest great novelist, as to mere dimensions, that ever lived, dealing nearly always with small groups, isolated and analyzed in the most American fashion. In fine, the charge of narrowness accuses the whole tendency of modern fiction as much as the American school. But we do not by any means allow that this superficial narrowness is a defect, while denying that it is a universal characteristic of our fiction; it is rather, for the present, a virtue. Indeed, we should call the present American work, North and South, thorough, rather than narrow. In one sense it is as broad as life, for each man is a microcosm, and the writer who is able to acquaint us intimately with half a dozen people, or the conditions of a neighborhood or a class, has done something which cannot in any bad sense be called narrow; his breadth is vertical instead of lateral, that is all; and this depth is more desirable than horizontal expansion in a civilization like ours, where the differences are not of classes, but of types, and not of types either so much as of characters. A new method was necessary in dealing with the new conditions, and the new method is world-wide, because the whole world is more or less Americanized. Tolstoi is exceptionally voluminous among modern writers, even Russian writers; and it might be said that the *forte* of Tolstoi himself is not in his breadth sidewise, but in his breadth upward and downward. *The Death of Ivan Illitch* leaves as vast an impression on the reader's soul as any episode of *War and Peace*, which indeed can only be recalled in episodes, and not as a whole. In fine, we think that our writers may be safely counselled to continue their work in the modern way, because it is the best way yet known. If they make it true, it will be large, no matter what its superficies are; and it would be the greatest mistake to try to make it big. A big book is necessarily a group of episodes more or less loosely connected by a thread of narrative, and there seems no reason why this thread must always be supplied. Each episode may be quite distinct, or it may be one of a connected group; the final effect will be from the truth of each episode, not from the size of the group.

*   *   *   *   *

THE GRASSHOPPER: THE SIMPLE, THE NATURAL, THE HONEST IN ART*

I.

The question of a final criterion for the appreciation of art, or of a "unity of taste," which Mr. J. Addington Symonds treated with so much reason, in the passage quoted from his last volumes in the Study for November, is one that perpetually recurs to those interested in any sort of aesthetic work. The reader will remember that Mr. Symonds held, in brief, that simplicity and naturalness and honesty were the lasting tests; moods and tastes and fashions change; people fancy now this and now that; but what is unpretentious and what is true is enduringly beautiful and good, and nothing else is so. This is not saying that fantastic and monstrous and artificial things do not please; everybody knows that they do please immensely for a time, and then, after the lapse of a much longer time, they have the charm of the *rococo*. Nothing is more curious than the fascination that fashion has. Fashion in women's dress, almost every fashion, is somehow delightful, else it would never have been the fashion; but if any one will look through a collection of old fashion plates, he must own that most fashions have been ugly. A few, which could be readily instanced, have been very pretty, and even beautiful, but it is doubtful if these have pleased the greatest number of

* *Harper's Monthly* 76 (December 1887): 153–55. Text from *Selected Literary Criticism*, pp. 71–75.

people. The ugly delights as well as the beautiful, and not merely because the ugly in fashion is associated with the young loveliness of the women who wear the ugly fashions, and wins a charm from them, not because the vast majority of mankind are tasteless, but for some cause that is not perhaps ascertainable. It is quite as likely to return in the fashions of our clothes, and houses and furniture, and poetry and fiction and painting, as the beautiful, and it may be from an instinctive or a reasoned sense of this that some of the extreme naturalists now refuse to make the old discrimination against it, or to regard the ugly as any less worthy of celebration in art than the beautiful; some of them, in fact, seem to regard it as rather more worthy, if anything. Possibly there is no absolutely ugly, no absolutely beautiful; or possibly the ugly contains always an element of the beautiful better adapted to the general appreciation than the more perfectly beautiful. This is a hazardous and somewhat discouraging conjecture, but we offer it for no more than it is worth; and we do not pin our faith to the saving of one whom we heard denying, the other day, that a thing of beauty was a joy forever. He contended that Keats's line should have read "Some things of beauty are sometimes joys forever," and that any assertion beyond this was hazardous.

II.

We should, indeed, prefer another line of Keats's, if we were to profess any formulated creed, and should feel much safer with his "Beauty is Truth, Truth Beauty," than even with our friend's reformation of the more quoted verse. It brings us back to the solid ground taken by Mr. Symonds, which is not essentially different from that taken in a book read last summer, at the season when the newspaper noticers of the magazines suppose their conductors to be sharing the luxurious disoccupation of the daily journalists. It was at that season when these children of inspiration invariably announce that the July *Century* or *Atlantic* or *Harper* betrays the enervating influences of the weather in the lax and flimsy character of its contents (the number having actually been made up in the eager air of early May, when the sleepless energies of the editor were irritated to their highest activity by the conviction that the winter was going to last forever); and at the same time there came to us a carefully marked paragraph assuring us, in the usual confident and unsparing terms, that we were mistaken in supposing that literature should be true to life—"it should be true to art." Out of the envious spirit which will be readily attributed to us we suppress the name of the newspaper; but there is no reason why we should withhold that of the book, which every reader of taste will suppose an intimacy with, as we should ourselves have done six months ago. It was the great Mr. Burke's *Essay on the Sublime and the Beautiful*—a singularly modern book, considering how long ago it was wrote (as the great Mr. Steele would have written the participle a little longer ago), and full of a certain well-mannered and agreeable instruction. In some things it is of that droll little eighteenth-century world, when philosophy had got the neat little universe into the hollow of its hand, and knew just what it was, and what it was for; but it is quite without arrogance; it is not even so confident as the newspaper which we are keeping back the name of. It will be seen that Mr. Burke differs radically with this other authority, which, however, he unwittingly owns to be of the sort called critical, and might almost be supposed to have had prophetically in mind.

"As for those called critics," he says, "they have generally sought the rule of the arts in the wrong place; they have sought among poems, pictures, engravings, statues, and buildings; *but art can never give the rules that make an art*. This is, I believe, the reason why artists in general, and poets principally, have been confined in so narrow a circle; they have been rather imitators of one another than of nature. Critics follow them, and therefore can do little as guides. I can judge but poorly of anything while I measure it by no other standard than itself. *The true standard of the arts is in every man's power; and an easy observation of the most common, sometimes of the meanest things, in nature, will give the truest lights*, where the greatest sagacity and industry that slights such observation must leave us in the dark, or, what is worse, amuse and mislead us by false lights."

III.

If this should happen to be true—and it certainly commends itself to our acceptance—it might portend an immediate danger to the vested interests of criticism, only that it was written a hundred years ago; and we shall probably have the "sagacity and industry that slights the observation of nature" long enough yet to allow most critics the time to learn some more useful trade than criticism as they pursue it. Nevertheless, we are in hopes that the communistic era in taste foreshadowed by Burke is approaching, and that it will occur within the lives of men now overawed by the foolish old superstition that literature and art are anything but the expression of life, and are to be judged by any other test than that of their fidelity to it. The time is coming, we trust, when each new author, each new artist, will be considered, not in his proportion to any other author or artist, but in his relation to the human nature, known to us all, which it is his privilege, his high duty, to interpret. "The true standard of the artist is in every man's power" already, as Burke says; Michelangelo's "light of the piazza," the glance of the common eye, is and always was the best light on a statue; Goethe's "boys and blackbirds" have in all ages been the real connoisseurs of berries; but hitherto the mass of common men have been afraid to apply their own simplicity, naturalness, and honesty to the appreciation of the beautiful. They have always cast about for the instruction of some one who professed to know better, and who browbeat wholesome common-sense into the self-distrust that ends in sophistication. They have fallen generally to the worst of this bad species, and have been "amused and misled" (how pretty that quaint old use of *amuse* is!) "by the false lights" of critical vanity and self-righteousness. They have been taught to compare what they see and what they read, not with the things that they have observed and known, but with the things that some other artist or writer has done. Especially if they have themselves the artistic impulse in any direction they are taught to form themselves, not upon life, but upon the masters who became masters only by forming themselves upon life. The seeds of death are planted in them, and they can produce only the still-born, the academic. They are not told to take their work into the public square and see if it seems true to the chance passer, but to test it by the work of the very men who refused and decried any other test of their own work. The young writer who attempts to report the phrase and carriage of everyday life, who tries to tell just how he has heard men talk and seen them look, is made to feel guilty of something low and unworthy by the stupid people who would like to have him show how Shakespeare's men talked and looked, or Scott's or Thackeray's, or Balzac's, or Hawthorne's, or Dickens's; he is instructed to idealize his personages, that is, to take the life-likeness out of them, and put the literary-likeness into them. He is approached in the spirit of the wretched pedantry into which learning, much or little, always decays when it withdraws itself and stands apart from experience in an attitude of imagined superiority, and which would say with the same confidence to the scientist: "I see that you are looking at a grasshopper there which you have found in the grass, and I suppose you intend to describe it. Now don't waste your time and sin against culture in *that* way. I've got a grasshopper here, which has been evolved at considerable pains and expense out of the grasshopper in general; in fact, it's a type. It's made up of wire and cardboard, very prettily painted in a conventional tint, and it's perfectly indestructible. It isn't very much like a real grasshopper, but it's a great deal nicer, and it's served to represent the notion of a grasshopper ever since man emerged from barbarism. You may say that it's artificial. Well, it *is* artificial; but then it's ideal too; and what you want to do is to cultivate the ideal. You'll find the books full of my kind of grasshopper, and scarcely a trace of yours in any of them. The thing that you are proposing to do is commonplace, but if you say that it isn't commonplace, for the very reason that it hasn't been done before, you'll have to admit that it's photographic."

IV.

As we said, we hope the time is coming when not only the artist, but the common, average man, who always "has the standard of the arts in his power," will have also the courage to apply it, and will reject the ideal grasshopper wherever he finds it, in science, in literature, in art, because it is not "simple, natural, and honest," because it is not like a real grasshopper. But we will own that we think the time is yet far off, and that the people who have been brought up on the ideal grasshopper, the heroic grasshopper, the impassioned grasshopper, the self-devoted, adventureful, good old romantic card-board grasshopper, must die out before the simple, honest, and natural grasshopper can have a fair field. We are in no haste to compass the end of these good people, whom we find in the mean time very amusing. It is delightful to meet one of them, either in print or out of it—some sweet elderly lady or excellent gentleman whose youth was pastured on the literature of thirty or forty years ago—and to witness the confidence with which they preach their favorite authors as all the law and the prophets. They have commonly read little or nothing since, or, if they have, they have judged it by a standard taken from these authors, and never dreamt of judging it by nature; they are destitute of the documents in the case of the later writers; they suppose that Balzac was the beginning of realism, and that Zola is its wicked end; they are quite ignorant, but they are ready to talk you down, if you differ from them, with an assumption of knowledge sufficient for any occasion. The horror, the resentment, with which they receive any question of their very peccable literary saints is to be matched only by the frenzy of the *Saturday Review* in defending the British aristocracy; you descend at once very far in the moral and social scale, and anything short of offensive personality is too good for you; it is expressed to you that you are one to be avoided, and put down even a little lower than you have naturally fallen.

These worthy persons are not to blame; it is part of their intellectual mission to represent the petrifaction of taste, and to preserve an image of a smaller and cruder and emptier world than we now live in, a world which was feeling its way toward the simple, the natural, the honest, but was a good deal "amused and misled" by lights now no longer mistakable for heavenly luminaries. They belong to a time, just passing away, when certain authors were considered authorities in certain kinds, when they must be accepted entire and not questioned in any particular. Now we are beginning to see and to say that no author is an authority except in those moments when he held his ear close to Nature's lips and caught her very accent. These moments are not continuous with any authors in the past, and they are rare with all. Therefore we are not afraid to say now that the greatest classics are sometimes not at all great, and that we can profit by them only when we hold them, like our meanest contemporaries, to a strict accounting, and verify their work by the standard of the arts which we all have in our power, the simple, the natural, and the honest.

PROPRIETY IN FICTION*

I.

One of the great newspapers the other day invited the prominent American authors to speak their minds upon a point in the theory and practice of fiction which had already vexed some of them. It was the question of how much or how little the American novel ought to deal with certain facts of life which are not usually talked of before young people, and especially young ladies. Of course the question was not decided, and we forget just how far the balance inclined in favor of a larger freedom in the matter. But it certainly inclined that way; one or two writers of the sex which is somehow supposed to have purity in its keeping (as if purity were a thing that did not practically concern the other sex, preoccupied with serious affairs) gave it a rather vigorous tilt to that side. In view of this fact it would not be the part of prudence to make an effort to dress the balance; and indeed we do not know that we were going to make any such effort. But there are some things to say, around and about the subject, which we should like to have some one else say, and which we may ourselves possibly be safe in suggesting.

II.

One of the first of these is the fact, generally lost sight of by those who censure the Anglo-Saxon novel for its prudishness, that it is really not such a prude after all; and that if it is sometimes apparently anxious to avoid those experiences of life not spo-

---

*Harper's Monthly 79 (June 1889): 151–54. Text from Selected Literary Criticism, pp. 118–23.

ken of before young people, this may be an appearance only. Sometimes a novel which has this shuffling air, this effect of truckling to propriety, might defend itself, if it could speak for itself, by saying that such experiences happened not to come within its scheme, and that, so far from maiming or mutilating itself in ignoring them, it was all the more faithfully representative of the tone of modern life in dealing with love that was chaste, and with passion so honest that it could be openly spoken of before the tenderest bud at dinner. It might say that the guilty intrigue, the betrayal, the extreme flirtation even, was the exceptional thing in life, and unless the scheme of the story necessarily involved it, that it would be bad art to lug it in, and as bad taste as to introduce such topics in a mixed company. It could say very justly that the novel in our civilization now always addresses a mixed company, and that the vast majority of the company are ladies, and that very many, if not most, of these ladies are young girls. If the novel were written for men and for married women alone, as in continental Europe, it might be altogether different. But the simple fact is that it is not written for them alone among us, and it is a question of writing, under cover of our universal acceptance, things for young girls to read which you would be put out-of-doors for saying to them, or of frankly giving notice of your intention, and so cutting yourself off from the pleasure—and it is a very high and sweet one—of appealing to these vivid, responsive intelligences, which are none the less brilliant and admirable because they are innocent.

III.

One day a novelist who liked, after the manner of other men, to repine at his hard fate, complained to his friend, a critic, that he was tired of the restriction he had put upon himself in this regard; for it is a mistake, as can be readily shown, to suppose that others impose it. "See how free those French fellows are!" he rebelled. "Shall we always be shut up to our tradition of decency?"

"Do you think it's much worse than being shut up to their tradition of indecency?" said his friend.

Then that novelist began to reflect, and he remembered how sick the invariable motive of the French novel made him. He perceived finally that, convention for convention, ours was not only more tolerable, but on the whole was truer to life, not only to its complexion, but also to its texture. No one will pretend that there is not vicious love beneath the surface of our society; if he did, the fetid explosions of the divorce trials would refute him; but if he pretended that it was in any just sense characteristic of our society, he could be still more easily refuted. Yet it exists, and it is unquestionably the material of tragedy, the stuff from which intense effects are wrought. The question, after owning this fact, is whether these intense effects are not rather cheap effects. We incline to think they are, and we will try to say why we think so, if we may do so without offence. The material itself, the mere mention of it, has an instant fascination; it arrests, it detains, till the last word is said, and while there is anything to be hinted. This is what makes a love intrigue of some sort all but essential to the popularity of any fiction. Without such an intrigue the intellectual equipment of the author must be of the highest, and then he will succeed only with the highest class of readers. But any author who will deal with a guilty love intrigue holds all readers in his hand, the highest with the lowest, as long as he hints the slightest hope of the smallest potential naughtiness. He need not at all be a great author; he may be a very shabby wretch, if he has but the courage of the trick of that sort of thing. The critics will call him "virile" and "passionate"; decent people will be ashamed to have been limed by him; but the low average will only ask another chance of flocking into his net. If he happens to be an able writer, his really fine and costly work will be unheeded, and the lure to the appetite will be chiefly remembered. There may be other qualities which make reputations for other men, but in his case they will count for nothing. He pays this penalty for his success in that kind; and every one pays some such penalty who deals with some such material. It attaches in like manner to the triumphs of the writers who now almost form a school among us, and who may be said to have established themselves in an easy popularity simply by the study of exotic shivers and fervors. They may find their account in the popularity, or they may not; there is no question of the popularity.

IV.

But we do not mean to imply that their case covers the whole ground. So far as it goes, though, it ought to stop the mouths of those who complain that fiction is enslaved to propriety among us. It appears that of a certain kind of impropriety it is free to give us all it will, and more. But this is not what serious men and women writing fiction mean when they rebel against the limitations of their art in our civilization. They have no desire to deal with nakedness, as painters and sculptors freely do in the worship of beauty; or with certain facts of life, as the stage does, in the service of sensation. But they ask why, when the conventions of the plastic and histrionic arts liberate their followers to the portrayal of almost any phase of the physical or of the emotional nature, an American novelist may not write a story on the lines of *Anna Karenina* or *Madame Bovary*. *Sappho* they put aside, and from Zola's work they avert their eyes. They do not condemn him or Daudet, necessarily, or accuse their motives; they leave them out of the question; they do not want to do that kind of thing. But they do sometimes wish to do another kind, to touch one of the most serious and sorrowful problems of life in the spirit of Tolstoi and Flaubert, and they ask why they may not. At one time, they remind us, the Anglo-Saxon novelist did deal with such problems—De Foe in his spirit, Richardson in his, Goldsmith in his. At what moment did our fiction lose this privilege? In what fatal hour did the Young Girl arise and seal the lips of Fiction, with a touch of her finger, to some of the most vital interests of life?

Whether we wished to oppose them in their aspiration for greater freedom, or whether we wished to encourage them, we should begin to answer them by saying that the Young Girl had never done anything of the kind. The manners of the novel have been improving with those of its readers; that is all. Gentlemen no longer swear or lie drunk under the table, or abduct young ladies and shut them up in lonely country houses, or so habitually set about the ruin of their neighbors' wives, as they once did. Generally, people now call a spade an agricultural implement; they have not grown decent without having also grown a little squeamish, but they have grown comparatively decent; there is no doubt about that. They require of a novelist whom they respect unquestionable proof of his seriousness, if he proposes to deal with certain phases of life; they require a sort of scientific decorum. He can no longer expect to be received on the ground of entertainment only; he assumes a higher function, something like that of a physician or a priest, and they expect him to be bound by laws as sacred as those of such professions; they hold him solemnly pledged not to betray them or abuse their confidence. If he will accept the conditions, they give him their confidence, and he may then treat to his greater honor, and not at all to his disadvantage, of such experiences, such relations of men and women as George Eliot treats in *Adam Bede*, in *Daniel Deronda*, in *Romola*, in almost all her books; such as Hawthorne treats in the *Scarlet Letter*; such as Dickens treats in *David Copperfield*; such as Thackeray treats in *Pendennis*, and glances at in every one of his fictions; such as Mrs. Gaskell treats in *Ruth Barton*; such as most of the masters of English fiction have at some time treated more or less openly. It is quite false or quite mistaken to suppose that our novels have left untouched their most important realities of life. They have only not made them their stock in trade; they have kept a true perspective in regard to them; they have relegated them in their pictures of life to the space and place they occupy in life itself, as we know it in England and America. They have kept a correct proportion, knowing perfectly well that unless the novel is to be a map, with everything scrupulously laid down in it, a faithful record of life in far the greater extent could be made to the exclusion of guilty love and all its circumstances and consequences.

We justify them in this view not only because we hate what is cheap and meretricious, and hold in peculiar loathing the cant of the critics who require "passion" as something in itself admirable and desirable in a novel, but because we prize fidelity in the historian of feeling and character. Most of these critics who demand "passion" would seem to have no conception of any passion but one. Yet there are several other passions: the passion of grief, the passion of avarice, the passion of pity, the passion of ambition, the passion of hate, the passion of envy, the passion of devotion, the passion of friendship; and all these have a greater part in the drama of life than the passion of love, and infinitely greater than the passion of guilty love. Wittingly or unwittingly, English fiction and American fiction have recognized this truth, not fully, not in the measure it merits, but in greater degree than most other fiction.

V.

Who can deny that it would be incomparably stronger, incomparably truer, if once it could tear off the habit which enslaves it to the celebration chiefly of a single passion, in one phase or another, and could frankly dedicate itself to the service of all the passions, all the interests, all the facts? Every novelist who has thought about his art knows that it would, and we think that upon reflection he must doubt whether his sphere would be greatly enlarged if he were allowed to treat freely the darker aspects of the favorite passion. But, as we have shown, the privilege, the right to do this is already perfectly recognized. This is proved again by the fact that serious criticism recognizes as master-works (we will not push the question of supremacy) the two great novels which above all others have moved the world by their study of guilty love. If by any chance, if by some prodigious miracle, any American should now arise to treat it on the level of *Anna Karenina* and *Madame Bovary*, he would be absolutely sure of success, and of fame and gratitude as great as those books have won for their authors.

But what editor of what American magazine would print such a story?

Certainly we do not think any one would; and here our novelist must again submit to conditions. If he wishes to publish such a story (supposing him to have once written it), he must publish it as a book. A book is something by itself, responsible for its character, which becomes quickly known, and it does not necessarily penetrate to every member of the household. The father or the mother may say to the child, "I would rather you wouldn't read that book"; if the child cannot be trusted, the book may be locked up. But with the magazine and its serial the affair is different. Between the editor of a reputable English or American magazine and the families which receive it there is a tacit agreement that he will print nothing which a father may not read to his daughter, or safely leave her to read herself. After all, it is a matter of business; and the insurgent novelist should consider the situation with coolness and common-sense. The editor did not create the situation; but it exists, and he could not even attempt to change it without many sorts of disaster. He respects it, therefore, with the good faith of an honest man. Even when he is himself a novelist, with ardor for his art and impatience of the limitations put upon it, he interposes his veto, as Thackeray did in the case of Trollope when Trollope approached the forbidden ground.

It does not avail to say that the daily papers teem with facts far fouler and deadlier than any which fiction could imagine. That is true, but it is true also that the sex which reads the most novels reads the fewest newspapers; and, besides, the reporter does not command the novelist's skill to fix impressions in a young girl's mind or to suggest conjecture. All this is very trite; it seems scarcely worth saying; and it appears pathetically useless to answer in the only possible way the complaint of the novelist that in the present state of the book trade it is almost impossible to get an audience for an American novel. That seems very likely, but, dear friend, your misfortune begins far back of the magazine editor. If you did not belong to a nation which would rather steal its reading than buy it, you would be protected by an international copyright law, and then you might defy the magazines and appeal to the public in a book with a fair hope of getting some return for your labor on it. But you *do* belong to a nation that would rather steal its reading than buy it, and so you must meet the conditions of the only literary form with which stolen literature cannot compete. The American magazine much more than holds its own against anything we can rob the English of. Perhaps it is a little despotic, a little arbitrary; but unquestionably its favor is essential to success, and its conditions are not such narrow ones. You cannot deal with Tolstoi's and Flaubert's subjects in the absolute artistic freedom of Tolstoi and Flaubert; since De Foe, that is unknown among us; but if you deal with them in the manner of George Eliot, of Thackeray, of Dickens, of society, you may deal with them even in the magazines. There is no other restriction upon you. All the horrors and miseries and tortures are open to you; your pages may drop blood; sometimes it may happen that the editor will even exact such strong material from you. But probably he will require nothing but the observance of the convention in question; and if you do not yourself prefer bloodshed he will leave you free to use all sweet and peaceable means of interesting his readers.

Believe us, it is no narrow field he throws open to you, with that little sign to keep off the grass up at one point only. Its vastness is still almost unexplored, and whole regions in it are unknown to the fictionist. Dig anywhere, and do but dig deep enough, and you strike riches; or, if you are of the mind to range, the gentler climes, the softer temperatures, the serener skies, are all free to you, and are so little visited that the chance of novelty is greater among them.

PALACIO VALDÉS, REALISM, AND EFFECTISM *

I.

How a better fashion can ever change for a worse; how the ugly can come to be preferred to the beautiful; in other words, how an art can decay, is a question which has often been approached, if not actually debated in this place. We do not know that we expect to debate it now; in the hurry of month after month, when the toe of September comes so near the heel of August, and March galls the kibe of February, the time never seems to arrive when the Study can really sweep and garnish itself, and quiet down to a season of serene inquiry upon such a point. At best it appears able only to cast some fitful gleams upon it, and then have its windows broken by all the little wanton boys of newspaper criticism, who like to throw stones at the light wherever they see it. The cost the Study is at in the mere matter of putty and glass, after one of their outbreaks, is such as would discourage a less virtuous apartment; but with the good conscience we have, and the faith we cherish that these *gamins* may yet grow up to be ashamed of themselves, we cheerfully pay the expense, and trim the lamp anew, and set it again where those who care may come to it. If they are not a great many, they are all the closer friends, perhaps, for being few; and it is in a kind of familiar intimacy that we turn to them with a question like that we have suggested. It has been coming up in our mind lately with regard to English fiction and its form, or rather its formlessness. How, for instance, could people who had once known the simple verity, the refined perfection of Miss Austen, enjoy anything less refined and less perfect?

With her example before them, why should not English novelists have gone on writing simply, honestly, artistically, ever after? One would think it must have been impossible for them to do otherwise, if one did not remember, say, the lamentable

Harper's Monthly 79 (November 1889): 962–67. Text from *Selected Literary Criticism*, pp. 126–34.

behavior of the people who support Mr. Jefferson, and their theatricality in the very presence of his beautiful naturalness. It is very difficult, that simplicity, and nothing is so hard as to be honest, as the reader, if he has ever happened to try it, must know. "The big bow-wow I can do myself, like any one going," said Scott, but he owned that the exquisite touch of Miss Austen was denied him; and it seems certainly to have been denied in greater or less measure to all her successors. But though reading and writing come by nature, as Dogberry justly said, a taste in them may be cultivated, or once cultivated, it may be preserved, and why was it not so among those poor islanders? One does not ask such things in order to be at the pains of answering them one's self, but with the hope that some one else will take the trouble to do so, and we propose to be rather a silent partner in the enterprise, which we shall leave mainly to Señor Armando Palacio Valdés.

II.

This delightful author will, however, only be able to answer our question indirectly from the essay on fiction with which he prefaces his last novel, and we shall have some little labor in fitting his saws to our instances. It is an essay which we wish every one intending to read, or even to write, a novel, might acquaint himself with; and we hope it will not be very long before we shall have it in English, together with the charming story of *The Sister of San Sulpizio*, which follows it. In the mean time we must go to the Spanish for some of the best and clearest things which have been said of the art of fiction in a time when nearly all who practice it have turned to talk about it.

Señor Valdés is a realist, but a realist according to his own conception of realism; and he has some words of just censure for the French naturalists, whom he finds unnecessarily, and suspects of being sometimes even mercenarily, nasty. He sees the wide difference that passes between this naturalism and the realism of the English and Spanish; and he goes somewhat further than we should go in condemning it. "The French naturalism represents only a moment, and an insignificant part of life. . . . It is characterized by sadness and narrowness. The prototype of this literature is the *Madame Bovary* of Flaubert. I am an admirer of this novelist, and especially of this novel; but often in thinking of it I have said, How dreary would literature be if it were no more than this! This is something antipathetic and gloomy and limited in it, as there is in modern French life;" but this seems to us exactly the best possible reason for its being. We believe with Señor Valdés that "no literature can live long without joy," not because of its mistaken aesthetics, however, but because no civilization can live long without joy. The expression of French life will change when French life changes; and French naturalism is better at its worst than French unnaturalism at its best. "No one," as Señor Valdés truly says, "can rise from the perusal of a naturalistic book . . . without a vivid desire to escape" from the wretched world depicted in it, "and a purpose, more or less vague, of helping to better the lot and morally elevate the abject beings who figure in it. Naturalistic art, then, is not immoral in itself, for then it would not merit the name of art; for though it is not the business of art to preach morality, still I think that, resting on a divine and spiritual principle, like the idea of the beautiful, it is perforce moral. I hold much more immoral other books which, under a glamour of something spiritual and beautiful and sublime, portray the vices in which we are allied to the beasts. Such, for example, are the works of Octave Feuillet, Arsène Houssaye, Georges Ohnet, and other contemporary novelists much in vogue among the higher classes of society."

III.

But what is this idea of the beautiful which art rests upon, and so becomes moral? "The man of our time," says Señor Valdés, "wishes to know everything and enjoy everything; he turns the objective of a powerful equatorial toward the heavenly spaces where gravitate the infinitude of the stars, just as he applies the microscope to the infinitude of the smallest insects; for their laws are identical. His experience, united with intuition, has convinced him that in nature there is neither great nor small; all is equal. All is equally grand, all is equally just, all is equally beautiful, because all is equally divine," as the Study has before now perhaps sufficiently insisted. But beauty, Señor Valdés explains, exits in the human spirit, and is the beautiful effect which it receives from the true meaning of things; it does not matter what the things are, and it is the function of the artist who feels this effect to impart it to others. We may add that there is no joy in art except this perception of the meaning of things and its communication; when you have felt it, and told it in a poem, a symphony, a novel, a statue, a picture, an edifice, you have fulfilled the purpose for which you were born an artist.

The reflection of exterior nature in the individual spirit, Señor Valdés believes to be the fundamental of art. "To say, then, that the artist must not copy but create is nonsense, because he can in no wise copy, and in no wise create. He who sets deliberately about modifying nature, shows that he has not felt her beauty, and therefore cannot make others feel it. The puerile desire which some artists without genius manifest to go about selecting in nature, *not what seems to them beautiful, but what they think will seem beautiful to others*, and rejecting what may displease them, ordinarily produces cold and insipid works. For, instead of exploring the illimitable fields of reality, they cling to the forms invented by other artists who have succeeded, *and they make statues of statues, poems of poems, novels of novels*. It is entirely false that the great romantic, symbolic, or classic poets modified nature; such as they have expressed her they felt her; and in this view they are as much realists as ourselves. In like manner if in the realistic tide that now bears us on there are some spirits who feel nature in another way, in the romantic way, or the classic way, they would not falsify her in expressing her so. Only those falsify her who, without feeling classic wise or romantic wise, set out being classic or romantic, wearisomely reproducing the models of former ages; and equally those who without sharing the sentiment of realism, which now prevails, force themselves to be realists merely to follow the fashion."

The pseudo-realists, in fact, are the worse offenders, to our thinking, for they sin against the living; whereas those who continue to celebrate the heroic adventures of Puss in Boots and the hair-breadth escapes of Tom Thumb, under various aliases, only cast disrespect upon the immortals, who have passed beyond these noises.

IV.

The ingenious English magazinist who has of late been retroactively fending the works of Tolstoi and Dostoyevsky from the last days of that saint of romance, George Sand, as too apt to inspire melancholy reflections in a lady of her life and literature, and who cannot rejoice enough that her dying hours were cheered by the writings of that reverend father in God, Alexander Dumas, *père*, would hardly be pleased, we suppose, with all the ideas of Señor Valdés concerning the novel, its nature, and its function, in modern life.

> "The principal cause," the Spaniard says, "of the decadence of contemporary literature is found, to my thinking, in the vice which has been very graphically called *effectism,* or the itch of awaking at all cost in the reader vivid and violent emotions, which shall do credit to the invention and originality of the writer. This vice has its roots in human nature itself, and more particularly in that of the artist; he has always something feminine in him, which tempts him to coquet with the reader, and display qualities that he thinks will astonish him, as women laugh for no reason, to show their teeth when they have them white and small and even, or lift their dresses to show their feet when there is no mud in the street. . . . What many writers nowadays wish, is to produce an effect, grand and immediate, to play the part of *geniuses.* For this they have learned that it is only necessary to write exaggerated works in any sort, since the vulgar do not ask that they shall be quietly made to think and feel, but that they shall be startled; and among the vulgar of course I include the great part of those who write literary criticism, and who constitute the worst vulgar, since they teach what they do not know. . . . There are many persons who suppose that the highest proof an artist can give of his fantasy is the invention of a complicated plot, spiced with perils, surprises, and suspenses; and that anything else is the sign of a poor and tepid imagination. And not only people who seem cultivated, but are not so, suppose this, but there are sensible persons, and even sagacious and intelligent critics, who sometimes allow themselves to be hoodwinked by the dramatic mystery and the surprising and fantastic scenes of a novel. They own it is all false; but they admire the imagination, what they call the 'power' of the author. Very well; all I have to say is that the 'power' to dazzle with strange incidents, to entertain with complicated plots and impossible characters, now belongs to some hundreds of writers in Europe; while there are not much above a dozen who know how to interest with the ordinary events of life, and with the portrayal of characters truly human. If the former is a talent, it must be owned that it is much commoner than the latter. . . . If we are to rate novelists according to their fecundity, or the riches of their invention, we must put Alexander Dumas above Cervantes,"

says Señor Valdés; but we must never forget that Dumas brought distraction if not peace to the death-bed of a woman who would probably have been unpleasantly agitated by those Russian authors who are apt to appeal to the imagination through the conscience.

"Cervantes," Señor Valdés goes on to say, "wrote a novel with the simplest plot, without belying much or little the natural and logical course of events. This novel, which was called *Don Quixote*, is perhaps the greatest work of human wit. Very well, the same Cervantes, mischievously influenced afterward by the ideas of the vulgar, who were then what they are now and always will be, attempted to please them by a work giving a lively proof of his inventive talent, and wrote the *Persiles and Sigismunda*, where the strange incidents, the vivid complications, the surprises, the pathetic scenes, succeed one another so rapidly and constantly that it really fatigues you. . . . But in spite of this flood of invention, imagine," says Señor Valdés, "the place that Cervantes would now occupy in the heaven of art, if he had never written *Don Quixote*," but only *Persiles and Sigismunda*!

From the point of view of modern English criticism, which likes to be melted, and horrified, and astonished, and blood-curdled, and goose-fleshed, no less than to be "chippered up" in fiction, Señor Valdés were indeed incorrigible. Not only does he despise the novel of complicated plot, and everywhere prefer *Don Quixote* to *Persiles and Sigismunda*, but he has a lively contempt for another class of novels much in favor with the gentilities of all countries. He calls their writers "novelists of the world," and he says that more than any others they have the rage of *effectism*. "They do not seek to produce effect by novelty and invention in plot. . . . they seek it in character. For this end they begin by deliberately falsifying human feelings, giving them a paradoxical appearance completely inadmissible. . . . Love that disguises itself as hate, incomparable energy under the cloak of weakness, virginal innocence under the aspect of malice and impudence, wit masquerading as folly, etc., etc. By this means they hope to make an effect of which they are incapable through the direct, frank, and conscientious study of character." He mentions Octave Feuillet as the greatest offender in this sort among the French, and Bulwer among the English; but Dickens is full of it (Boffin in *Our Mutual Friend* will suffice for all example), and the present loathsome artistic squalor of the English drama is witness of the result of *effectism* when allowed full play.

V.

But what, then, if he is not pleased with Dumas, who was sovereign for George Sand in sickness, and is good enough for the ingenious English magazinist in health, or with the *effectists* who delight genteel people at all the theatres, and in most of the romances, what, we ask, will satisfy this extremely difficult Spanish gentleman? He would pretend, very little. Give him simple, life-like character; that is all he wants. "For me, the only condition of character is that it be human, and that is enough. If I wished to know what was human, I should study humanity."

But, Señor Valdés! Do not you know that this small condition of yours implies in its fulfilment hardly less than the gift of the whole earth, with a little gold fence round it? You merely ask that the character portrayed in fiction be human; and you suggest that the novelist should study humanity if he would know whether his personages are human. This appears to us the cruelest irony, the most sarcastic affectation of humility. If you had asked that character in fiction be superhuman, or subterhuman, or preterhuman, or intrahuman, and had bidden the novelist go, not to humanity, but the humanities, for the proof of his excellence, it would have been all very easy. The books are full of those "creations," of every pattern, of all ages, of both sexes; and it is so much handier to get at books than to get at men; and when you have portrayed "passion" instead of feeling, and used "power" instead of commonsense, and shown yourself a "genius" instead of an artist, the applause is so prompt and the glory so cheap, that really anything else seems wickedly wasteful of one's time. One may not make one's reader enjoy or suffer nobly, but one may give him the kind of pleasure that arises from conjuring, or from a puppetshow, or a modern stage play, and leave him, if he is an old fool, in the sort of stupor that comes from hitting the pipe; or if he is a young fool, half crazed with the spectacle of qualities and impulses like his own in an apotheosis of achievement and fruition far beyond any earthly experience. If one is a very great master in that kind, one may survive to be the death-bed comfort of a woman who is supposed to have needed medicining of a narcotic kind from a past of inedifying experiences, and even to be the admiration of an ingenious English magazinist who thinks fiction ought to do the office of hyoscyamus or bromide of potassium.

But apparently Señor Valdés would not think this any great artistic result. Like Emerson, he believes that "the foolish man wonders at the unusual, but the wise man at the usual," that "the perception of the worth of the vulgar is fruitful in discoveries." Like Emerson, he "asks, not for the great, the remote, the romantic"; he embraces the common," he "sits at the feet of the familiar and the low." Or, in his own words,

> "Things that appear ugliest in reality to the spectator who is not an artist, are transformed into beauty and poetry when the spirit of the artist possesses itself of them. We all take part every day in a thousand domestic scenes, every day we see a thousand pictures in life, that do not make any impression upon us, or if they make any it is one of repugnance; but let the novelist come, and without betraying the truth, but painting them as they appear to his vision, he produces a most interesting work, whose perusal enchants us. That which in life left us indifferent, or repelled us, in art delights us. Why? Simply because the artist has made us see the idea that resides in it. Let not the novelists, then, endeavor to add anything to reality, to turn it and twist it, to restrict it. Since nature has endowed them with this precious gift of discovering ideas in things, their work will be beautiful if they paint these as they appear. But if the reality does not impress them, in vain will they strive to make their work impress others."

VI.

Which brings us again, after this long way about, to the divine Jane and her novels, and that troublesome question about them. She was great and they were beautiful because she and they were honest, and dealt with nature nearly a hundred years ago, as realism deals with it to-day. Realism is nothing more and nothing less than the truthful treatment of material, and Jane Austen was the first and the last of the English novelists to treat material with entire truthfulness. Because she did this, she remains the most artistic of the English novelists, and alone worthy to be matched with the great Scandinavian and Slavic and Latin artists. It is not a question of intellect, or not wholly that. The English have mind enough; but they have not taste enough; or rather their taste has been perverted by their false criticism, which is based upon personal preference, and not upon principle; which instructs a man to think that what he likes is good, instead of teaching him first to distinguish what is good before he likes it. The art of fiction, as Jane Austen knew it, declined from her through Scott, and Bulwer, and Dickens, and Charlotte Brontë, and Thackeray, and even George Eliot, because the mania of romanticism had seized upon all Europe, and these great writers could not escape the taint of their time; but it has shown few signs of recovery in England, because English criticism, in the presence of the Continental masterpieces, has continued provincial and special and personal, and has expressed a love and a hate which had to do with the quality of the artist rather than the character of his work. It was inevitable that in their time the English romanticists should treat, as Señor Valdés says, "the barbarous customs of the Middle Ages, softening and disfiguring them, as Walter Scott and his kind did"; that they should "devote themselves to falsifying nature, refining and subtilizing sentiment, and modifying psychology after their own fancy," like Bulwer and Dickens, as well as like Rousseau and Madame de Staël, not to mention Balzac, the worst of all that sort at his worst. This was the natural course of the disease; but it really seems as if it were their criticism that was to blame for the rest: not, indeed, for the performance of this writer or that, for criticism can never affect the actual doing of a thing; but for the esteem in which this writer or that is held through the perpetuation of false ideals. The only observer of English middle-class life since Jane Austen worthy to be named with her was not George Eliot, who was first ethical and then artistic, who transcended her in everything but the form and method most essential to art, and there fell hopelessly below her. It was Anthony Trollope who was most like her in simple honesty and instinctive truth, as unphilosophized as the light of common day; but he was so warped from a wholesome ideal as to wish at times to be like the caricaturist Thackeray, and to stand about in his scene, talking it over with his hands in his pockets, interrupting the action, and spoiling the illusion in which alone the truth of art resides. Mainly, his instinct was too much for his ideal, and with a low view of life in its civic relations and a thoroughly *bourgeois* soul, he yet produced works whose beauty is surpassed only by the effect of a more poetic writer in the novels of Thomas Hardy. Yet if a vote of English criticism even at this late day, when all continental Europe has the light of aesthetic truth, could be taken the majority against these artists would be overwhelmingly in favor of a writer who had so little artistic sensibility, that he never hesitated on any occasion great or small, to make a foray among his characters, and catch them up to show them to the reader and tell him how beautiful or ugly they were; and cry out over their amazing properties.

Doubtless the ideal of those poor islanders will be finally changed. If the truth could become a *fad* it would be accepted by all their "smart people," but truth is something rather too large for that; and we must await the gradual advance of civilization among them. Then they will see that their criticism has misled them; and that it is to this false guide they owe, not precisely the decline of fiction among them, but its continued debasement as an art.

SIX

REALISM AND ROMANCE

James Lane Allen

James Lane Allen (1849–1925) was born, raised, and educated in Kentucky. He was a schoolteacher for many years
while contributing regularly to magazines, but established
himself fully as a popular novelist in the 1890s with *A
Kentucky Cardinal* (1895) and *The Choir Invisible* (1897).
His literary criticism has never been collected. In addition
to noting Julian Hawthorne's remarks in the New York
World, Allen refers in the opening portion of his essay to
Henry James's "William Dean Howells," *Harper's Weekly*
30 (19 June 1886): 394–95 and Maurice Thompson's
"The Analysts Analyzed," *Critic* 9 (10 June 1886): 18–22.

Has any one remarked the fact that the critics have had of late a rather heated term?
If in a month's or two months' time I have happened upon a single notable piece of
perfectly amiable criticism, it has escaped my memory, and that, too, when the rarity
of the article would have made it peculiarly impressive. It would be difficult to say
just when the trouble began. Probably it was on the day that Mr. Howells took his
seat in "The Editor's Study." Such an event was of itself a signal for the commence-
ment of hostilities, as must readily have been foreseen by any one who understands
the sensitiveness and irritability of the literary temperament. The spectacle of a representative novelist and critical specialist taking his seat upon the throne of realism,
to wave the spectre of authority over a class of minds that profess to acknowledge
none, looked portentous of rebellion. Was it not subversive of the simplicity of freedom and general equality of democratic literary creeds and conditions? To change the
figure a little, it was evident that Mr. Howells would not sail through many of the
twelve monthly signs of the critical heavens before he encountered the zodiacal ram
mid-air or, may be, the goat. So, indeed, it happened; and from that day to this it has
been one prolonged case of lively and vigorous rebuttal. Even Mr. James, over the

New York *Evening Post*, 31 July 1886, p. 4; reprinted in *The Heritage of American Literature*, ed.
L. N. Richardson (Boston: Ginn, 1951), pp. 280–86. Text from the *Evening Post*.

quiet waters, suddenly grows rampant, and though well-nigh covered with the finest and whitest fleece of Parisian courtesy, still contrives to show a bulging forehead and curling horns; driving home at Mr. Howells with the blow that while he is devoted to the usual and the commonplace, life *does* sometimes exhibit the extraordinary and the wonderful in ways to make a man—or even a realistic ram—rub his eyes with incredulity. Then drawing back several paces, he pitches at him again with the forceful reminder that while his characters show great mutual toleration, there is really nothing much in them to tolerate but each other's manners! Think of one of the two great realists of the country telling the other that the only immoralities his books contain are little aberrations of thought and excesses of beer, and calling his strongest worst people ineffectual sinners! In the realism of this life, as we commonly know it, the sinners are only too effectual, as they are expected to find out in the world to come.

Well, Mr. Howells, sailing sturdily and serenely on as best he can (God speed him!) drops some words respecting Tolstoi and Russian criticism, applauding its enlightenment as contrasted with the crude, old-fashioned canons that still so largely dominate American methods and taste. Then Mr. Julian Hawthorne, looking out of the literary skylight of the *World* and seeing Mr. Howells passing overhead, hurls after him several columns of copy in minion type, designed to teach him and all of us, once and finally, just what this baneful thing realism is and what it isn't: more particularly that it is *not* art and never will be, and calling upon all professed realists and note-book representatives of the so-called scientific method, for decency's sake and consistency's sake, not to publish novels, but their note-books. Then somebody in Cincinnati ups and calls Mr. Hawthorne a born sneerer, having remembered against him all that he said years ago about the air, and the girls, and the home-life of a petty little country in Germany. Then Mr. Maurice Thompson, in Indianapolis, having impatiently waited until Mr. Howells reached his remote and rather lurid quarter of the heavens, all at once rushes round and round him like a headlong comet about a silvery sun— his orbit, it would seem, being determined about equally, though very strangely, by the forces of repulsion and attraction. Indeed, Mr. Thompson almost threatens to run into Mr. Howells and burn him up altogether. After letting him know that he has worse than no manners for criticising his betters and his contemporaries, who are just as good, he shows him that he is ridiculously wrong about this thing of realism, and winds up with blandly telling him that he is not, and never has been, a realist, but a romancer, and that nothing but romance has ever saved him!

Such is the angry condition of the times. Besides these larger bodies the atmosphere is full of nearly invisible small critical aerolites. But sooner or later, perhaps, these will all fall into Mr. Howells and increase his momentum and his mass.

All things considered, what a blessed thing it is to be away down here in Kentucky—unknown land—where no one ever quarrels (about books!), and where the spirit of criticism is supposed to rest as quietly as moonlight sleeping on a bank of moss. But at this safe distance and under cover of the general example of the times, what is even a Kentuckian to do but criticise somebody himself? This at any rate is his set and avowed intention. Of course one of the persons criticised will be Mr.

Howells. The man who cannot "criticise Howells" nowadays isn't respectable. He is a pariah—a pale shade—a nonentity. It is true that Mr. Howells has not yet attacked Kentucky; but sir, Kentucky sees in this fact no adequate reason for not attacking Mr. Howells. Sir, be it said to the pride of this State that she does not wait to be attacked. Mr. Howells may *intend* to attack her, which is the same thing. But before Mr. Howells must come a certain critic of *The Nation*, who recently had occasion to say that the South was now a favorite hunting-ground for the magazines. Whereupon he polished the nib of his pen with the following incisive observation: "Indeed, there is no country that will better bear exploration with respect to the picturesqueness of the land or the oddity of the inhabitants."

Thanks! Hereafter, when the editors of the great Northern magazines shall send to the South the query: "Have you anything in the way of available literary material?" and the reply comes back: "We are looking for picturesqueness and oddity," it will be for the entire South to rise up to a man and say: "Gentlemen, come down with your whole force; no country on the face of the globe can surpass us in these respects." If there is anything that should make the people of the South forget their millions of slaves and the civil war—forget all losses, trials, humiliations, and defeats—it ought to be the thought of the future which opens up before them in consequence of the fact that the editors of two or three magazines are coming down to explore them for picturesqueness and oddity. If there is anything that should double the circulation of those magazines in the North, and even carry them to those unclassified shreds and remnants of humanity which, in out-of-the-way fastnesses and islands of the earth, have hitherto by common consent of mankind been looked upon as above all other peoples picturesque and odd, it should be the announcement of the discovery that right here, in the southern part of the United States, are millions and millions of "inhabitants" who have never been excelled in the development of those delightful characteristics.

But I am not angry with this critic. He has not "hurt my feelin's." He meant well. He meant to be complimentary. He meant to recommend the South to further editorial consideration, and to suggest that picturesqueness and oddity were good things to begin with, which was all he knew. It probably never occurred to him that the South has always looked upon the "inhabitants" of the North as being "odd," without being picturesque. He never reflected that the coast-line from New York to New Orleans is not more crooked than the coast-line from New Orleans to New York. I have introduced him only for the purpose of saying that his point of view—in a somewhat modified form, it is true—is the most natural one in the world for a Northerner to entertain, and this mainly on account of Southern writers. It is a fact, curious and well worth noting, that the characteristic of Southern life most commonly and expressly emphasized is "oddity." We have had entire works on the oddities of Southern life and character. We have had short stories seemingly written to delineate this element, even to the manufacturing of the most impossible proper names. Garb, speech, conduct, incident, adventure, have all been made the materials of its exposition, or what is perhaps oftener true, of its outright and sheer imaginative embodiment. The abnormal nooks—the curious little byways of life have been and still are the places most keenly sought after and most gladly found. This pursuit of the minor and remote is in a measure the result of the premium that is set by the literary market upon the peculiar, the strange, the exceptional, the fresh—of the predominant demand for intense local color and extreme specialization of the field of work. Watch the imaginative prose contributions of Southern writers to the magazines. Almost invariably they are little byway studies—though excellent of their kind. Reflect for a moment upon the broad human characteristics of the larger work. Are not Cable's Creoles an odd and out-of-the-way set? Are not Miss Murfree's mountaineers an odd and out-of-the-way set? Is not "Uncle Remus" the oddest of Negroes? The whole vast, natural, typical life of the South—the whole vast system of facts and ideas which become the very earth of its historic development—the rich and profuse and splendid growth thereon of social forms and classes and conditions—the flowering forth and maturing of character types, the magnolias and jessamines of humanity, along with the cypresses and rank and noxious swamps—all these, with an atmosphere of passion and sentiment and Oriental sensuousness, do, indeed, as this critic of *The Nation* says, constitute a fresh field of exploration; but, in heaven's name! not for the sake of oddity.

That this great field is being entered here and there on the edges is perhaps a fact with the most interesting promise of any in the existing stage of our common literature. Miss Woolson has of late pressed its margin with a searching eye and resolute step. Mr. Cable made a stride into it when he wrote "Dr. Sevier" and came to Kentucky for his hero and his hero's father. I should like to say just here that those were true Kentucky types, but rare ones, and that John Richling's father was very rare for that time and well-nigh extinct now—an old Kentuckian with the mien of Napoleon at Marengo and with a dialect of provincial Johnsonese. Page has lately entered this same field from another quarter, but perhaps for excellent purposes of his own he chooses to portray the high, fine life of the South through the medium of the Negro character as its expositor and vital participant. This method imposes somewhat narrow limitations upon his exquisite art, which one could wish to see face to face with a larger canvas.

Is this literary movement in the South, which is beginning to embrace new names, broadly recognized as a fact of hopeful significance? Certainly it has not escaped observation abroad. Not long since I had a friend to spend the night with a literary Londoner, himself the author of a work on America. "What has come over you people in the southern part of the United States?" he exclaimed, "You are developing the most wonderful imaginative literature of the age. I have read 'In the Tennessee Mountains' time and again and tell everybody to read it that has not." Other writers were mentioned and recognized.

Here then we come upon Mr. Howells in "The Editor's Study." He has spoken encouragingly on this subject as follows: "Through such work as hers [Miss Murfree's] and Mr. Cable's the South is making itself heard in literature after a fashion likely to keep attention as well as to provoke it." Thanks again. But elsewhere he says, "These writers still permit themselves a certain romance of motive"; and of "The Prophet of the Great Smoky Mountain," "If the Prophet's substitution of himself for Micajah Green was voluntary, it was romantic, which is worse than uninteresting."

Now, why does Mr. Howells say "*still* permit"? Why "still"? Does it mean that Miss Murfree and Mr. Cable have been warned against this offence and continue to neglect the warning? Does it mean they are yet behind the times and may catch up by and by? Does it mean that their ideas of literary art and methods of work are in a state of development, and that, when the highest stage of this development is reached, they will lay the romantic motive aside? Or does it mean that those ideas and methods are of themselves wrong, whether developed or undeveloped, and should be abandoned for something better? And is the romantic motive worse than uninteresting?

Nothing is further from my wish than to come between Mr. Howells and Mr. Cable and Miss Murfree. The liberty has been taken of bringing them together in this connection, simply with the view of asking a question which this criticism gives point to and perhaps especial timeliness. That question is this: Is not the romantic motive as much at home in human nature as any other motive? There is just one reply to this question: "What do you mean by romantic?" Well, I should like to have the realist define that term. I should like him, in a manner diamond-clear and diamond-hard, with a pen dipped in the very spirit of precision and lucidity, to separate it from everything else and exhibit it in its sole and entire nature. Then we should understand each other. Then we should know exactly the grounds on which he pronounces it worse than uninteresting and condemns its presence in the novel. Until he does this, there is likely to be confusion of thought and wordy misunderstanding. The world in general will go on its old way and believe that the romantic motive *is* interesting; that romance is interesting; that romantic character, and incident, and adventure, and history, all are interesting, and such is the soul of man that they always will be interesting, until the great Note-Book is opened and we find ourselves—romance and all—analyzed on its pages by the master hand of the Great Realist.

It seems to me that there is but one definition of romantic that would justify the condemnation of it in the realistic novel; *i.e.*, not true of human nature, for if it *is* true of human nature, then least of all men is the realist, who must value the whole of human nature, competent to pronounce it uninteresting. But as soon as he gives this definition, will not half the world cry out and reject it? Will not half the world say, "The romantic *is* true of human nature—one of the deepest and truest things in it— we have the romantic tissue in our make-up; we have romantic temperaments, motives, and actions; we actually have known romantic people in this world, who were quite as real as any others"?

But, ah! this poor, sad business of criticism! At least *it* is nearly always realistic enough, as, for instance, when it charges Mr. Howells with being a time-server, and posing with self-admiration, and praising his own novels in the name of realism. That was an ungentle accusation; and if it is any comfort to him, he may feel sure that the cheek of every friend, whether romancer or realist, tingled with shame and indignation at the charge. And who has more friends than he?

SEVEN

CERTAIN TENDENCIES
IN CURRENT LITERATURE

Richard Watson Gilder

Richard Watson Gilder (1844–1909) was both a minor poet and a major force in American literary affairs. After serving in the Union army, he began a career in journalism that led to the editorship of the highly influential *Century* magazine, a post he held for almost forty years. In that role he was receptive to the work of the local colorists and of Henry James and Mark Twain (both *Adventures of Huckleberry Finn* and *The Bostonians* were serialized in the *Century* in 1885) and dismissive of any elements in submitted manuscripts that violated proprieties of middle-class taste, especially regarding the sexual. His essay on "Certain Tendencies in Current Literature" is one of his few efforts to express formally his critical beliefs.

I.

The somewhat desultory conflict which is now being waged in the literary field between "realism" and "idealism" is a most doubtful and subtle one; for there are few realists who have no ideality, and few idealists, few romanticists, who do not make use of the real. Shakspere was somewhat of a romanticist; somewhat of an idealist; and yet what realist of our day cuts deeper into the actual than he? In what realist of to-day can we find, for instance, a closer piece of observation than his where he speaks of the sleep that weighs down the eye-lids of the woman who nurses a child? And yet Shakspere gives this exquisite touch of reality lightly, as a simile. Cleopatra has placed the deadly aspick to her breast and is sinking into the oblivion of death:

> "Peace, peace!
> Dost thou not see my baby at my breast,
> That sucks the nurse asleep?"

New Princeton Review 4 (July 1887): 1–20.

Where, likewise, in all literature is there a more sublime and constant idealist, a more remorseless realist, than the great Tuscan poet-politician?

The fact is that all art is a selection. There is no *real* real in literature; and the world will have its own opinion of the taste and art of a writer who is swamped by the commonplace, or who betrays an engrossing love for the unlovely. Every writer must draw the line somewhere. To the unthinking it may appear that Zola saves himself that trouble; but he does not. We may suspect that there is always something more ghastly and abhorrent in real life than any realist of our time has yet cared fully to report, no matter how destitute of taste he may be, or rich in courage. Hateful is the false art that winces at every touch of unconventional and unrestrained vitality in nature and in society; and hateful, alike, the false art that delights in the disgusting. If a realist guide seizes upon you at the *gare* in Paris, drags you into one of their endless sewers and, after an all-day's journey, in slime and nausea, beneath that city of beauty, tells you that you have now, at last, seen Paris—he lies! For not less Paris is the unbelievable vista of the Champs Elyseés; not less Paris the Cathedral of Notre Dame; nor the palace of the Louvre, where the Venus of Milo keeps mankind forever aware of the ideal of human loveliness, and where Rembrandt, that ideal realist, shows us the unearthly face of the risen Christ.

But it is especially of fiction that we think when realism is spoken of; and it is evident that the definitely realistic school of our day and country is doing a great and needed work, both by example and precept. Let us not resent the zeal of some of its advocates, who at times assume that this school is the first and only enemy of the sentimental and the absurd. It is true that the walls of the unreal had begun to totter before a single blast was blown of their latter-day trumpets—for this is the age of science, of analysis, of remorseless, endless questioning. It is true that Benjamin Franklin, philosopher, drawing down with his kite the lightning of Jupiter, was the first American realist. But the message of the American literary realist of to-day, though not quite so novel as it appears to sound in his own ear, is timely and needed. It is the voice of conviction; the note of the genuine, of the exact; it is, perhaps, the fault of the situation that this voice is pitched at times in a tone more strenuous than alluring.

If it is asked what, precisely, is understood by this new gospel of realism, and if I hesitate to attempt a full and categorical reply, it is because I do not care to undertake a definition which I am sure can be much better elaborated by others. There are sceptics who would say that the present realism in fiction is in France a discovery of the unclean, and in America a discovery of the unimportant. But this would be a petulant and shallow answer. The serious explanation of the sympathizer might be that modern realism is everywhere, at home and abroad, a discovery of life.

To use so epoch-making a name as Rousseau; to quote examples of realism or of realistic imagination from writers before or after the author of *The Confessions*; to say that any one of these was at times a realist; that Balzac was especially a realist, and may be considered the founder of this school in fiction, unless the date be moved on to Flaubert's day; though a method and a tendency might thus be indicated, still such examples would not thoroughly illustrate the present realistic movement. This movement could be more clearly explained by an examination of contemporaneous continental novels, chiefly of those belonging to the reigning school of Paris, and distinguished at this moment by the work of men as different from each other as Zola, Daudet, and "Pierre Loti;" even more powerfully explained by the books of Tolstoi, a writer whose extraordinary artistic career is now passing into a religious and political propagandism no less extraordinary; explained more satisfactorily still by the stories of the late Russo-Parisian, Turgeneff, the most delicately proportioned, the most artistic, flower of the school. In America the movement could be illustrated by reference to writers with whom all are familiar, and whom it is unnecessary to name.

But in lieu of exact definition and copious illustration, the realistic method may be indicated in a general way by negative description. Strictly realistic fiction is averse to caricature; it may, perhaps complain that even Balzac has a touch too much of this, and it looks upon that masterly and astonishingly real writer as somewhat unduly given to the romantic. Modern realistic fiction does not take kindly to the conventional hero and heroine, nor to elaborate plots, nor to melodramatic situations, and "romantic" disguises. Its method would scarcely include such a line as that in *The Lady of the Lake*, which has brought to their feet, with startled delight, more readers than any other single line in the English language:

"And Snowdoun's knight is Scotland's king!"

Realism is, in fact, something in the air which even those who do not think of it by name must necessarily feel. Its influence in America, as elsewhere, is not confined to those writers who proclaim themselves of the faith; it is the Time-Spirit. Even our broader humorists feel the influence; as well as the writers of fairy tales, vagaries, and romances. Even in the minds of many who think themselves free from its influence it remains as a test of everything they write or read. Though some of its apostles say "Romance not at all!", the Time-Spirit will permit you to romance, if you manifest a certain deference, even though unconsciously, for the real. The Time-Spirit does not, thank heaven! object to the inimitable invention of Stockton, nor to the stern and breathless fantasy of Stevenson; because each of these so different purveyors of impossibilities still keeps a firm hold upon the world we live in.

Realism is a state of mind, and it is the state of mind of the nineteenth century. It affects the poet, fictionist, humorist, journalist, essayist, historian; the religionist; the philosopher; the natural scientist; the social scientist; the musician, the dramatist, the actor, the painter, the sculptor.

How intimately the various branches of intellectual activity are affected by the realistic spirit, it would be an interesting task to inquire, but a task beyond the range of this writing. An essay might well be devoted to the philosophic field alone. In the religious field, the realistic influence might be pointed out in an important work just issued from the American press. Theodore Munger, a divine of the keenest spiritual insight, calls his very latest book *The Appeal to Life*, and as realism may be called the discovery of life, so this book, or rather the method it elucidates, may be called the discovery of God in human life. Says its author:

"If we can interpret the human heart as it feels and hopes and strives in the natural relations of life; if we can measure the play of the human mind in the family, in society, and in the nation, we shall find both the field of the Gospel and its vindication. The thing to be done at present . . . is to set forth the identity of the faith with the action of man's nature in the natural relations of life."

The social scientist feels this influence, and forbids you to put your hand in your pocket and give a real dime to a romantic beggar.

The musician, from the time of Beethoven's "Pastoral Symphony" to that of Wagner and the modern so-called "programme-music," has felt increasingly the realistic influence.

The actor feels it; and the finest comedian of America exemplifies on the stage, to the never-ending delight of his fellow-countrymen, the absolutely satisfying union of nature and the imagination, of the real and the ideal. Contrast his exquisite, unfailing, and always elevating art with that of another comedian; a man of most desirable and commendable originality, dealing freshly and strongly, as author and actor, with seldom-seized phases of our modern life, but capable of illustrating, unconsciously, in his own person, one of those current tendencies which make the judicious grieve. I have seen this doting-piece of the realists devote a large part of an evening to the absolutely natural depiction of the effects of the juice of the American tobacco-plant, when applied internally to the system of a (naturalized) American citizen. The actor feels it; and the greatest tragedian of our age, greatest both by popular applause and critical assent, shows in his art that idealization of the real and realization of the ideal—that fusing of both in the white heat of passion—which marks the highest intensity of imaginative art.

The painter feels it, and two among the most salient art movements of our time, disassociated and strangely dissimilar—in many respects directly opposed each to the other—are yet each distinctly in the line of modern realism: the pre-Raphaelite movement in England, and the Impressionist movement in France. The painter feels it, I say, and the peasant of Normandy who spent his life on the edge of the forest of Fontainebleau painted this unescapable realism of the nineteenth century into that picture of the ideal "Sower," which stands in many minds as the most typical, the most thrilling, the most lofty work of modern art.

The sculptor feels it; and in a work like St. Gaudens's Lincoln, (yet in the studio,) gives us a realistic and yet ideal portrait of a statesman of our own day; a man of intense individuality; gaunt; long-drawn-out; clothed, not in the typical toga, but in the homely and typical broadcloth; a statue which startles with its impression of the man—not of the man's external traits alone, but also of that humorous, shrewd, far-seeing, just, tender, melancholy spirit which ruled an empire by the force of imagination and the power of a great heart.

I have cited these examples of imaginative art in other fields than literature, to show that realism is all about us; that when properly understood and intelligently practised it is something to be rejoiced in and not to be deplored; that, in fact, this age demands reality with greater insistence than any preceding age; but still demands it not as a solitary and morbid function, but as a part only of the make-up of the consecrated artist.

The more reality the better! But let it be reality all the way through; reality of the spirit as well as of the flesh; not a grovelling reality; not a reality microscopic, or photographic, or self-conscious, or superficial; not a reality that sees ugliness but is blind to beauty; not a reality which sees the little yet neither sees nor feels the great; not a reality which ignores those social phenomena, those actual experiences of the heart, those natural passions and delights which have created in man "the romantic spirit"; those experiences of the soul which have created in him "the religious spirit," and which are facts of existence certainly no less important than any other.

Some of us remember how captivated we were many years ago, when stereoscopic views were first introduced as a parlor toy, and little twin photographs of in-door groups, colored just like life, were used, like music at the play, to make endurable the "waits" of the social drama. You lifted the machine from the white marble centre-table, looked through the eye-pieces, and could see these people, standing up and sitting down, posing quite naturally. You could actually look under the table. You could see all around the separate figures. It was most curious; most "real." Yet how soon every one tired of this bogus reality. It is like this with some, by no means all, of the work of our modern American realists. It is curious; it is a sort of discovery. You can see under the table and all around the little man with a blue coat and striped trousers; but it is not art, and it will not last.

Yet a great deal of the American realism of to-day *will* last for its own worth, for its revelation of ourselves to ourselves, and as a hint for the work of future days. What is it but realism, as understood by various minds, as interpreted by many and various artistic temperaments, in all sorts of surroundings, and among "all sorts and conditions of men," that is at this moment vitalizing American literature and attracting to it the attention of the world? We do not want less realism, but more of it; and better, fuller, than we now have! In some of our current realistic work a true method, used awkwardly by men freshly and deeply enamoured therewith, becomes obvious and ineffectual. The result is a straining after novelty; the elevation of the insignificant; in a word, a lack of proportion, a lack of art. But when these very men fully master their method they will preach more acceptably their artistic faith; the faith of their great European masters, living and dead. Above all they will feel that the realization in fiction of the petty, the disagreeable, and the loathsome can only be tolerated where there is a background either of genuine and living humor, or of the most powerful human passion.

II.

Along with the growth of the realistic comes a cry from some of our authors for a greater freedom of subject and expression: a freedom which, they declare, is denied to them by that class of the public for which they are compelled to write. They complain that American men are too busy to be novel-readers; at least, that there are not enough men-readers to constitute a paying audience—a statement which, by the way, it would be hard to prove. They declare that they are in mortal terror of the young girl of the period, who is at once the source of their income and the arbiter of their destiny. Professor Boyesen has put the confession and complaint of some of our

American novelists into frank and unmistakable language, in an article published in the *Forum*. He writes with a sore heart; and if some part of the impetuous confession fails to do justice to the best in himself, and belittles his own beautiful, and, surely not altogether insincere work, let us not misunderstand a cry of distress like that; let us, on the contrary, give earnest heed to what he has to say.

"I confess," says the author of *Gunnar,* "The Story of an Outcast," and *Truls, the Nameless*— "I confess I have never written a book without helplessly deploring the fact that young ladies were to be the arbiters of its fate; that young persons whose opinions on any other subject, involving the need of thought or experience, we should probably hold in light esteem, constitute collectively an Areopagus from whose judgments, in matters relating to fiction, there is no appeal. To be a purveyor of amusement (especially if one suspects that he has the stuff in him for something better) is not at all amusing. To be obliged to repress that which is best in him and offer that which is of no consequence is the plight to which many a novelist, in this paradise of women, is reduced. Nothing less is demanded of him by that inexorable force called public taste, as embodied in the editors of the paying magazines, behind whom sits, arrayed in stern and bewildering loveliness, his final judge, the young American girl. She is the Iron Madonna who strangles in her fond embrace the American novelist."[1]

Professor Boyesen mentions certain modern American novels which he regards as exceptions to the rule, such as Mr. Howells's *A Modern Instance* and *The Rise of Silas Lapham*. And he refers to De Forest's *Honest John Vane* and Eggleston's *Roxy*, as exceptions which prove the rule that the capable novelist of to-day avoids politics. He thinks the novelist has a greater freedom, and therefore does greater work, in all the countries of continental Europe. He implies that England is in the same condition as America, but he does not go into detail with regard to that country, though, since the publication of Mr. Boyesen's *Forum* article, Mr. Rider Haggard has sent up a similar note of distress in regard to the present supposed limitations of the English novelist.

Let us assume that Professor Boyesen is right, and that the young woman of America is as he depicts her, a terror to manly genius and the devastator of American literature. But, then, are there no compensations? The kind of freedom that Professor Boyesen individually yearns for might, in his own literature, be a boon and not a burden to the community. But if we go without freedom, do we not also go without filth? "No," you say, "we import a plenty of that." Yes, a great plenty, but is it not a bit staler and less offensive after its translation to our shores? Is there, or is there not, a greater delicacy and decency of speech in America than on the European continent? There are many who believe that America has the purest society in the world. Is not this purity worth paying for with a little prudery? To what a fathomless pit of shame has so-called "liberty" brought a large part of the literature of France! Even were the restrictions of the American novelist as great as Professor Boyesen believes them to be, I can see another side of the shield. But I do not think it is as bad as he thinks it is. As for the young American girl of the period, I have not as poor an opinion of her as have some of her critics. She has, I take it, a good deal of penetration, of sympathy, of enthusiasm; her intelligent interest and curiosity cover a wide and widening field; and in the matter now at issue she probably occasions more alarm than she suffers.

The impartial observer will agree to this, that while, according to Professor Boyesen, the American novelist has been making his living out of the young American girl, he has never yet quite done her justice in fiction. Perhaps we can now understand the reason why; for it seems that he may have at the same time exaggerated her dominance, and underrated her common-sense.

But, without badinage, is it not true that, as a general thing, our authors have expressed themselves frankly, faithfully, and naturally; and not least acceptably when most faithfully? Professor Boyesen, as noted above, gives a brief list of exceptions to what he holds to be the rule. The full list of virile works of fiction, published in American magazines during the last fifteen or twenty years, would be a long one, and would represent with insight and accuracy the various phases of life in the new world. But the American author has, besides, the privilege—and an extending privilege it is—to print, as in France, in the newspapers; and book publication, also, is nearly always possible in some quarter. I certainly do not believe that works of real art, of real power, can be prevented from reaching the public in America. Some periodical, some publisher, will send them forth, and the author will reap a generous reward.

Every one, nevertheless, who is sincerely interested in the development of American literature, should welcome the discussion which Professor Boyesen's protest has occasioned. I cannot but believe that he has exaggerated the difficulties of the situation, but he has called attention to a vital question, and one that deserves to be honestly and fully discussed. He, however, has overlooked the fact that one of the very magazines to which he refers was before him in sounding a note of warning. As much as two years ago it acknowledged, in fact, some of the very limitations to which he now calls attention, doing this for the purpose of helping to spread abroad a more genuine literary hospitality, and to assist in procuring for all writers a greater liberty of theme and opinion.

"There are some," says the editorial to which we refer, "who deprecate the very existence of the popular magazines upon which our American writers are so largely dependent—especially dependent in the deplorable absence of international copyright laws, which would not only give them revenue from abroad, but protect them at home from the base competition of stolen literary wares. There are some, we say, who fear that our literature may lose in frankness and in force from the supposed necessity of trimming too consciously to the taste of an audience which has many sensitive and hypercritical elements. There is some truth in this. It cannot be denied that much of the world's most valuable literature, sacred and secular, could never reach the public through the pages of the 'family magazine.' There is, moreover, a certain unwritten guarantee which every periodical evolves from its own history and habit. It behooves all concerned to see to it that the limitations of the popular periodical do not have a narrowing or flattening effect upon current literature; do not put our best writers into a sort of literary bondage; do not repress originality and individuality either of style or of opinion. It may be said on this point that while the world will always have its share of the long-eared race, fortunately the number of the over-anxious and the hypersensitive seems to be growing yearly less considerable; and the idea is rapidly passing away that editors are bound to the infinite task of themselves entertaining every shade of opinion and belief expressed by the various writers for the periodical with which they are connected. Readers afford help to editors by being tolerant, open-minded, and sympathetic with 'many moods of many minds,' as editors themselves must be."[2]

III.

The more closely, then, we study the foreign and native influences at work upon American literature, and the more keenly we appreciate the aesthetic tendencies of the present age, the more must we be convinced that our American literature is destined to show, even to a greater degree than it does at present, a specifically realistic tendency. And at the same time our authors are sure to assert, more and more, the liberty of discussion; the right to a freer report and criticism of the whole range of modern life and modern thought.

If this be so, how increasingly great the responsibility our current literature is assuming. Will the reaction against the unreal carry, especially our novelists, to excess? We must expect this here and there. Will an overdone realism have the effect of the juice of "the little western flower" on Titania's eyelids, and will the muse of fiction "be enamour'd of an ass"? We are sometimes called to witness that phenomenon already. In fact, so imminent is the harm from the overzeal of the proselytizer, and from the reckless performance of the unintelligent or conscienceless disciple, that no serious worker in even the most advanced group of the realistic propaganda should take unkindly either the questioning challenge of unbelievers, or the sympathetic warning of those who think they descry dangers in the path.

"Reality, reality, reality?" cries the novelist, appealing for freedom. Let him have his reality, but not until he proves that he has mastered that watchword of subtler power, "Imagination, imagination, imagination!" Nor let him think that he is prepared to undertake a more pressing and intimate mission to humanity till he assures himself of a decent and artistic taste, a clean heart, and a pure purpose. No one can read the pronouncements of the American realists without feeling that they have a mission. But suppose one thinks he discovers evil tendencies along with the good in this movement, shall he be silent lest he be misunderstood? Heaven forbid! Let us each be true to his own nature and conscience.

IV.

Now, in the strictly realistic movement in this country, along with the wholesome, there are certain other tendencies which some of us who read cannot do otherwise than deplore and condemn. These tendencies are partly aesthetic, partly moral.

We deplore the fact that while preaching industry and accuracy to the literary neophyte, and in striving to get false and conventional notions of art and life out of his head, these men mislead alike the would-be artist and his public by views of the artistic faculty as false in one direction as are those they would supplant in the other; for though it is well to play the part of the severe uncle to the heir of genius, it is a cruelty both to the individual and to the reading-world to encourage great expectations in ambitious mediocrity.

We deplore, moreover, a tendency to underrate that unnameable and not to be analyzed quality in a painting, in a book, which constitutes the essential difference between one so-called work of art and another. We deplore the tendency to ignore or depreciate what is most subtle, evanescent, indescribable, and valuable in art,

"The light that never was on sea or land."

We who read deplore, on the one hand, a loss of the old love of beauty—of beauty "for its own sake"—and on the other an apparent lack of interest in the deeper ranges of man's spiritual nature.

We deplore and condemn also a tendency toward what seems to us an un-ideal standard, not of literature only, but also of life. I speak of this tendency with diffidence, for I know that the tone to which I allude is taken conscientiously, and is the result of close and long study and experience. The evident desire is to substitute sensible and accurate views of life for high-flown and misleading views; the idea also seems to be that it is better to set the moral aim not too high, for then there is more likelihood of hitting the mark, and less chance of disastrous discouragement. But what if, in stamping out sentimentality, true sentiment now and then suffers outrageously? And as for aim, why not let it be high? Why not the highest?

"The aim, if reached or not, makes great the life."

Let not those be censured who would bid the archer point his arrow at the moon rather than at the street-lamp, thinking there were better chance to bring down a star.

The pronounced realist may say that a sane archer does not shoot either at moons, stars, or street-lamps. Well, then, let us put it in a less poetic way, and declare that in our experience the more a man of business, or any citizen, aesthetic or otherwise, cherishes ideal aims—aims tinctured with imagination, even, it may be, with romance and mysticism—the more apt he is to act justly and live honorably and usefully among his fellow-men.

V.

The pronounced realist is a useful fellow-creature, but so also is the pronounced idealist—stouten his work though you well may with a tincture of modern reality. For let us confess—knowing that if the narrow realist frown (or, more likely, smile) at the confession, not so will that wiser realist, the Spirit of our Time—let us confess there are some of us who thirst now and again for deep draughts of old-time heroism, romance, faery; some of us who cannot live without the clear, pure atmosphere of the over-world; who, in all our wanderings, must, with Dante, keep our eyes upon "the most sweet stars"; who need all the Bibles and Divine Comedies, all the Lears, Midsummer-Night's Dreams, Miltons, Wordsworths, Emersons, Brownings; all the loftiest musicians and painters; all the supernal imaginings, most devoted affections, most sacred associations, and inspired communions of which our souls are capable; who need all these to make life "less forlorn"; to bring

"that blessed mood,
In which the burthen of the mystery,
In which the heavy and the weary weight
Of all this unintelligible world,
Is lightened";

who need, it may be, all these and more to keep us out of the penitentiary or the mad-house.

So sordid is life that sometimes it seems as if the current of moral progress had come to a stand-still, or was even actually turning back. At times the tendencies toward the base, the un-ideal, affright us with their nearness and force. But recall the voyage down the St. Lawrence. For miles there is no smallest craft in sight. How smooth the waters! How swiftly we glide, now in the middle of the mighty stream, now darting strangely near the woody banks! The wheels of the steamer have suddenly stopped; but watch the shore; the boat is driving on, not of its own force, but the slave of the rushing current. A breathless moment, and the vessel plunges across the topmost wave of the rapids, and shoots onward—downward. But see; the ocean-like billows in front, on either side, curve backward instead of on, and the giant river seems to be returning upward to its source. But it is not; it is pouring forever toward the ocean—its goal.

So, in the current of life, the superficial waves sometimes break backward; but may it not mean that the waters are hurrying faster to the ocean of everlasting truth and right? Notwithstanding all that is sordid, petty, unclean, and menacing in politics, in the press, in society strictly so-called, in the greater social world—no matter what may threaten the literature of our age or country, let us be sure that the deepest and strongest tendencies are wholesome and true.

Broadly speaking, the great artist, in every art and in every age, unites the functions of the realist with those of the idealist; but it is the ideal side of art and of life that makes the other worth while, and raises mankind ever higher above the beasts. It is the ideal side of our nature that stands in greatest need of culture: and surely none the less in a realistic age like this. Let us not be ashamed to listen to the voices that come to us from the heights.

He the great World-Musician at whose stroke
The stars of morning into music broke;
He from whose Being Infinite are caught
All harmonies of light, and sound, and thought;
Once in each age, to keep the world in tune,
He strikes a note sublime; nor late, nor soon,
A god-like soul—music and passion's birth—
Vibrates across the discord of the earth
And sets the world aright.
    O, these are they
Who on men's hearts with mightiest power can play—

The master-poets of humanity,
Send down from heaven to lift men to the sky.

NOTES

1. *The Forum*, February, 1887.
2. *The Century*, May, 1885.

EIGHT

THE NEW BATTLE
OF THE BOOKS

George Pellew

George Pellew (1859–92) was born in England but educated at Harvard, where he was a student of Howells's
friend Thomas Sergeant Perry. While practicing law in
Boston and New York, he contributed frequently to magazines and newspapers in support of social reform and
Howellsian realism until his early death.

For a long time a wordy war has raged in the magazines and the newspapers between
so-called realists and romanticists. In "Harper's Monthly" Mr. Howells has for years
been asserting the importance of novels that keep close to the facts of life; and the
critics and criticasters have daily attacked his teaching and practice as materialistic
and debasing, as disregarding "the depth, variety, and beauty of life." Mr. George
Saintsbury has recently enunciated as "the first rule of literature, . . . that what is presented shall be presented not merely as it is, but transformed, or, if I may say so, dis-
realized." "As a merely mimetic process," says Mr. J. A. Symonds, "art is so conspicuously a failure, that the artist must resign the attempt to do again what nature
does, . . . and all his realistic skill must finally subserve the expression of the thought
and emotion which himself contains." Even Mr. Andrew Lang and Mr. Edgar Fawcett have been drawn into the fray, and at length certain rules have been formulated
by a deft and charming writer, Mr. R. L. Stevenson. The young author, he asserts,
must first select a motive either of character or passion, and then make everything in
the novel subservient to that motive; he should remember always that a novel is "not
a transcript of life;" he must not suffer "his style to play below the level of the argument," and must "pitch the key of conversation, not with any thought of how men
talk in parlors, but with a single eye to the degree of passion he may be called on to
express;" finally, he is not even to "care particularly if he miss the pungent material
of the day's manners, the reproduction of the atmosphere and the environment."

Forum 5 (July 1888): 564–73.

One critic violently denounces Rider Haggard's "She," and another, with equal vehemence, derides Howells's "April Hopes." The ground is strewn with dead and dying reputations. Is it not time, perhaps, to call a parley, and to consider terms of peace? In all this confusion there must be some principles to guide us, some truths generally admitted that may serve as a basis for compromise. Let us for a moment try to discuss this matter calmly, with what impartiality and lucidity we may. The controversy has become mainly one of words, a question of "right naming;" let us try to ascertain the facts that these words but half reveal.

No one, doubtless, ever tried to paint a picture or to tell a story untrue to fact in every particular; certainly, no one ever succeeded in such an attempt. Even an angel in a church window has some resemblance to a human being, and the action of even the most romantic hero is not inspired by the weakest motive. At the outset, then, one may say that every work of fiction ever written has been, to some extent at least, realistic. The question becomes at once a question of the degree of realism that is permissible. In a matter of such delicacy it would seem that every man must be a law to himself, for where can any authoritative rules be found? A novelist may copy the practice of previous novelists, but whence comes their authority? or he may copy nature, carefully retaining the color of his own spectacles and the effect of his own prejudices; but why should his personal defects of judgment or vision be of enduring interest? or he may copy nature with an endeavor to be as impartial and unprejudiced and clear-sighted as his character and education permit, and if he does so what Daniel is there who can say that he does wrong?

In the old romances of chivalry "all reference to real life or real geography," to quote the words of Ticknor, "was apparently thought inappropriate, and the heroes, who were invariably princes in disguise, always expressed themselves with that noble elegance supposed to be characteristic of the speech of princes." In "Palmerin of Great Britain" the Green Sword Knight had a lively contest with the dragon Endriago, and, "before its soul departed, the devil flew from its mouth and went through the air with a clap of thunder." The typical hero, as in the later romance of "Cassandre," whatever else he might be, was never commonplace; always "his face was marvelously handsome; and through a beauty which had nothing effeminate one might observe something so martial, so sparkling, and so majestic, as might in all hearts make an impression of love, fear, and respect, at once. His stature exceeded that of the tallest man, but the proportion of it was wonderfully exact, and all the motions of his body had a grace and liberty that was nothing common."

In Greene's "Arcadia," even a poor gentlewoman living with shepherds could not change her dress without quoting Latin: "Aulica vita splendida miseria; . . . then, Lamedon, will I disguise myself, . . . for being poorly attired, I shall be meanly minded, and measure myself by my present estate, not by former fortunes." The Amadis romances were still more extravagant, and are to the modern reader still more unreadable. Did a generation more imaginative than ours delight in such romances simply because they were unreal, because the heroes talked like gods and loved like madmen? In those days the "Amadis" must have seemed far more lifelike than the only other fiction to be had, stories from classical mythology and jest-books of anecdotes ancient as the Sanscrit. Knight-errantry, moreover, was more real and lasted longer than we can well believe. In the time of Ferdinand and Isabella several distinguished noblemen journeyed into foreign countries, "in order to try the fortune of arms with any cavalier that might be pleased to adventure it with them," and it was well on in the sixteenth century when Ulrich von Hutten, "the last of the knights-errant," sallied forth from his study to attack "three abbots on the highway in the Palatinate," and later fought, single-handed, five of the retinue of the French ambassador at Viterbo. It could not, indeed, have been the unreality of the romances that charmed their readers, since they are known to have been regarded as literally true.

Even in the romances most remote from actual life there are occasional natural touches. Many a valiant knight must have sympathized with Amadis at the tournament when, "his arms in pieces and without a sword, . . . he looked toward Oriana's window, and seeing her back toward him, knew why she had turned away," and got fresh courage; for Oriana could not bear to see his danger, and yet would comfort him with the sight of her long hair.

It may well, then, have been the truth rather than the untruth, the realism rather than the exaggeration, in the romances of chivalry that made them interesting to the dames and damsels left at home in the old castles of Castile; and it was certainly because of the unreality of the prolific brood of Amadis that they vanished forever at the first prick of Don Quixote's lance. Cervantes had, indeed, as he confessed, "no other desire than to render abhorred of men the false and absurd stories of the books of chivalry;" and ridicule he found, as it ever is, a rapid solvent of everything save truth.

The long survival of unreal characters and of literary traditions that have lost their meaning is often surprising, but still more significant is the inevitable certainty with which real life reappears, though in the most conventional of disguises, in every romance of more than a day's popularity. In the "Astrée" the masques of nymphs and shepherds but half concealed the faces of ladies and nobles that every one recognized. In "Cassandre" the author professed to avoid "all improbable actions and extravagant adventures," and to supplement rather than to contradict the historians. The romances *de longue haleine* that Mlle. de Scudéry adroitly constructed from the ruins of the pastorals and the books of chivalry merely transplanted contemporary life to the banks of the Tiber or the Euphrates in the days of Tarquin or Darius. The hero of "Le Grand Cyrus" is Condé, whose victories, and even military strategy, are described with minute exactitude; and in the fifteen volumes of "Clélie" the conversations between the ladies whose fates are ruled by the stars of Brutus and Amilcar obviously but repeat the long discussions that beguiled the afternoons at the Hôtel de Rambouillet and at Mlle. de Scudéry's own *salon* on her famous *Samedis*.

Richardson brought the romances down to earth from cloudland, and ridiculed their "high ideas of first impressions, of eternal constancy, of love raised to a pitch of idolatry." Sir Charles Grandison, with all his perfections, was more human than Amadis, and has survived him. Fielding, in his turn, ridiculed Richardson, and Fielding is not yet dethroned, though some of his most highly finished conversations were condemned by a young lady of the time for reasons since regarded as conclusive. "It is such sort of stuff," said she, "as passes every day between me and my own maid." Was not Squire Western's brutal coarseness intensely realistic, and is not Squire Western one of the best-remembered characters in "Tom Jones"? Even Horace Walpole professed to make the servants at Otranto talk as servants talked at Strawberry Hill, and justified himself for such an innovation by the example of Shakespeare. The fear and terror, at least, of Mrs. Radcliffe's heroines are natural enough, and it was their naturalness, rather than their absurdity, that shook the nerves of hysterical young-ladydom. Jane Austen's little world still continues its tranquil existence of mild flirtation and petty sinning in many a green corner of memory, simply because she had keen eyes, a truthful heart, and, to Miss Mitford's fancy, "an entire want of taste which could produce so pert, so worldly a heroine" as Elizabeth Bennett. At the tragic horrors of "The Mysteries of Udolpho" Jane Austen laughed. Against the still more unnatural inventions of "The Castle of Otranto" Dr. Johnson raised the formidable club of his logic. Said he, "A story is a picture either of an individual or of human nature in general. If it be false, it is a picture of nothing." The eccentric characters in "Evelina" were criticised sharply by Macaulay. "They are rare," said he, "in real life, and ought to be sparingly introduced into works which profess to be pictures of real life." Time has justified these judgments, for to-day, while one reads Horace Walpole, and two or three read Fanny Burney, Jane Austen is the delight of a thousand.

In "The Old English Baron" Miss Reeve tried to modernize the Gothic tale, and in this country Charles Brockden Brown set himself to replace by ventriloquism and semi-scientific marvels what he called "the puerile superstitions, exploded manners, Gothic castles, and chimeras, the material usually used" by the novelist. No tale could be more ludicrously sentimental than "The Genuine Distresses of Damon and Celia," yet its author knew the best way to appeal to the heart. "Will not a plain, unvarnished tale—the genuine history of two children of affliction—excite all the generous pity of the public, to whom these unhappy sufferers plead for compassion and redress?" The appeal of "Damon and Celia" falls upon deaf ears in this generation because we disbelieve in its sincerity, not because our hearts are grown hard.

"Romanticism" we now speak of as the opposite or reverse of "realism." Romantic writers, so called, of our day, seem to think that the impossible, the preposterous, or the non-existent is more interesting than the actual; that the incidents of life as they know them to occur must be distorted or over-emphasized to become significant or impressive. Is it possible that of all literary movements romanticism alone should have originated in an intentional exaggeration or falsification of facts? History shows us nothing so improbable. Alike in their methods and their aims the first romanticists were realists. "Let us strike at theories, *artes poeticoe*, and systems," wrote Victor Hugo in his preface to "Cromwell." "The poet has to study only nature, truth, and his inspiration, which also is truth and nature." The "three unities" were destroyed; the pseudo-Greeks and pseudo-Romans were driven from the stage, in the name of truth and nature. To free the modern novel from the restrictions of a conventional plot, and from all unnatural and pseudo-human characters, is but to strike a second blow in the same eternal cause. To an age that had fought and won the battle of will against the conventions of a dozen centuries, force of will and persistence in endeavor seemed all-powerful and all-important, transcending and uncontrolled by material circumstance. In comparison with the pallid passions of the order-loving heroes of the family novel, the most eccentric sentimentality, the most impetuous weeping, the wildest frenzy, seemed more human. The survivors of the Revolution could be impressed only by the utmost development of emotion and passion. What matters the shape of the crucible, if the rising bubbles attest the gold in the quicksilver? Why question the probability of the situation, if it discloses the intensity of love, the fervor of self-sacrifice, the awfulness of unrelenting vengeance? The romanticists sacrificed one truth to save another truth; they disregarded society to magnify the individual; they painted with a big brush; they sifted life through a coarse sieve, and all that escaped them they thought insignificant. It was the truths they discerned and stated that gave them the victory, not their blindness to other truths; the reality of their heroes' passions, not the unnaturalness of their plots. From nature they took the passions, and only the plots from invention, and the plots were chosen so as to exhibit the passions best. Pseudo-romanticists of our day go to school only to their invention, and to the works of these great masters, whose extravagances they imitate, but not their truth.

The more famous novelists of late years have done otherwise. Slowly they have deserted the extraordinary and remote, and have found in denizens of city slums and country villages, passion and pain, hatred and jealousy, pity and love as poignant and pathetic as in any Greek corsair or Heaven-gifted musician. "I have purposely dwelt," said Dickens, "on the romantic side of familiar things." But still the plots were unusual and the characters eccentric, since the emotions had to be extreme, until Thackeray introduced the world to Arthur Pendennis, "with all his faults and shortcomings, who does not claim to be a hero, but only a man and a brother;" and until George Eliot bespoke our sympathy for Amos Barton, "a man whose virtues were not heroic, and who had no undetected crime within his breast; who had not the slightest mystery hanging over him, but was palpably and unmistakably commonplace." "We have many weaknesses, said Thackeray again, "but we are not ruffians of crime. No more was my friend Lovel."

In the beginning of the century the influence of heredity and the dependence of the individual character upon the social environment were not understood. An honest return, therefore, to the point of view of the early romanticists is now impossible, and such novels as they wrote cannot be written now without affectation. Human sympathy has broadened, society has become more democratic; a scientific study of history has shown the interdependence of all men, the comparative unimportance of exceptional men, and the all-importance of those commonplace individuals who form the mass of a people, who stamp the character of a nation's government, its art, and its religion, who alone make possible the achievements of its great men.

"But ah!" cry the sentimental critics, "where are the blue roses? They were so sweet, the roses of the Brenta. Imagination has departed, and the light that never was on sea or land." Their lament is baseless. The "blue roses" remain in the realistic novel as in life, where alone they ever were, in the hopes of the boy or the maiden, in the innocent heart, in the dreaming soul. But to say the roses in the hedge are blue for all to see, and the heroine perfectly beautiful for all to love, that is to be false to life and to one's self. "Is all that a good novelist needs, then," ask the critics, "keen observation? Instead of an imaginative artist is he to become a mere mechanical photographer or statistician?" No, is the answer. Observation without imagination can discern only the motions, not the emotions, of other men; can see men but "as trees walking." With due respect to M. de Maupassant, who has recently made so brave a plea for freedom in fiction, a purely objective novel, if such a thing were possible, would be a most incomplete and unintelligible representation of human life. The simplest action, if unexplained in terms of thought and feeling, may be a comedy or a tragedy, most trivial or pregnant with tremendous purpose; but which, no one can tell except the actor or the author. The sudden blush of a girl may indicate a torn dress or a broken heart. The accurate novelist must express the thoughts and feelings of his characters, if they are to be men and not puppets; and only by experience, sympathy, and vivid imagination can one tell what is passing in any head except one's own. To do so with general correctness is the greatest and the rarest achievement of the disciplined imagination; but incorrectness often attracts the attention and impresses the mind more than correctness; the flawless workmanship of perfect skill seems easy, while inferior and inaccurate work is miscalled great.

What, indeed, is imagination, except the more or less unconscious putting together in the mind of images and fragmentary recollections originally given by experience. The result may correspond to something that actually exists, or it may not; it may be a horse or a griffin, and of the two a griffin can be drawn by a child in the nursery, and his griffin can hardly be proved inferior to any other griffin. If, however, imagination deals only with recollections of experiences, the only possible test of its use or misuse is the correspondence of its productions with experience.

In the old romances there were no plots, in the modern sense of the word; the notion of a plot was derived rather from the eighteenth century theory of the requirements of the stage. Let us not carp at those who still write dramas in prose and call them novels; but let us remember that, if the characters are true to life, the absence of a plot does not lessen the demand on the imagination of the reader. "Ah, now I am glad!" said Verena in "The Bostonians," when she reached the street with Ransom, her betrothed lover, from the hall where her lecture had been so rudely interrupted. "But though she was glad, Ransom presently discerned that beneath her hood she was in tears." To the imaginative reader this is as good an ending as though the marriage bells were pealing and in his ears the sweet words were ringing, "and they lived happily ever after;" so far as Verena and Ransom resemble human beings, a discerning mind may follow their footsteps through many nights and days with perfect confidence, since their after history is implicit in their characters.

The aims, then, of romanticists and realists, when intelligently understood and pursued, are identical; but the words "romanticism" and "realism," as commonly used, indicate slightly different points of view. The romanticist thinks the realist is like an ignorant man who tries to give an idea of a complicated machine by a photograph of it, taken indifferently from any side; and that he himself is like a mechanical draughtsman who detects first the plane that reveals most of the mainsprings and peculiarities of the machine, and then draws that one plane in its simplest outlines. The realist in his turn would say that he tries to give both the drawing and the photograph, but that the romanticist, without studying the thing at all, evolves from his inner consciousness a rough design of how such a noble machine ought to look.

"What matter whether you call it pantheism or pottheism, if the thing be true?" asked Carlyle. What matter whether a work is called romantic or realistic, if the thing be true? It makes no matter. What does matter is, that any restrictions whatever should be imposed upon the writer who thinks he has something to say and tries to say it, who thinks he has observed something and tries to describe it. The vigorous men who founded schools always held themselves bound by no conventions; those who insist on following blindly in some master's path deprive themselves of the advantage of any special skill of theirs or opportunity, and adopt by choice the master's errors, while it is only by accident if they possess a single one of the qualities that made his merits possible. "We are bid to study the ancients," said wiser Goethe, "yet what does that avail us, if it does not teach us to study the real world and reproduce that? for that was the source of the power of the ancients."

To reproduce the real world in its entirety is impossible, or even to reproduce precisely its smallest particle, but the attempt to do so need not therefore be discouraged. It is enough that novelists may approximate to a perfect representation of life indefinitely. In other arts perfection is not supposed to be common, but it is not on that account deemed an undesirable ideal. Many men, working with the utmost of their personal intelligence, expressing in words that to them seem fittest the thoughts and the scenes that to them are nearest and most familiar, may each in his measure reproduce something of true that has eluded the vision and the grasp of all other men. To shackle such liberty of choice may lose for humanity something irretrievable, something of incalculable worth.

NINE

SELECTIONS FROM *THE ETHICS OF LITERARY ART*

Maurice Thompson

Although Maurice Thompson (1844–1901) was born in Indiana, he was raised in Georgia and served in the Confederate army during the Civil War. Returning to Indiana after the war, he practiced law while writing poetry and historical romances. In 1889 he became editor of the *Independent* magazine and made it a major vehicle for the expression of conservative social and literary beliefs. His historical romance *Alice of Old Vincennes* (1900) was a popular success.

Joseph Addison undertook to define critical taste in literature, and called it "that faculty of the soul which discerns the beauties of an author with pleasure, and the imperfections with dislike." But what is the distinguishing mark between "beauties" and "imperfections"? If ethics is the "art of conduct," it steps in to suggest moral responsibility. Sir Philip Sidney, that flower of manhood, declared that the end of all earthly learning must be "virtuous action"; and that the chief function of art seemed to be the engendering of good impulses, — "it moveth one to do that which it doth teach." Certainly this moving power is our test of genius. But too often genius sets its face the wrong way, and then, if we are moved by it, our impulse is toward evil. An attack upon our sensibility is more dangerous than one upon our mere intellectuality; the secret sources of action, no matter what materialists may guess, lie deeper than the brain. We may not find the seat of moral pleasure in any particular nerve-cell, dissect no matter how carefully. Men of easy leisure can perhaps afford to enjoy theories as a sort of luxuries, as the gourmand enjoys his *pâté de foie gras*; but in active, militant life most of us must crush facts together, and knead them rapidly into available forms of aliment for body and soul. And it is a rule of Nature that what is good for the body is good for the soul. Health in the broadest sense is the state of happi-

---

The Ethics of Literary Art (Hartford: Hartford Seminary Press, 1893), pp. 7–37.

ness. Ethics, therefore, has perfect health in view; a sound pure body and a sound pure mind with which to pursue the conduct of life. What is good for the soul is good for the body.

I assume that human ethics is the perfection of selfishness—but the selfishness of the perfect man who can see that the good of all mankind is his good, and that the only way to do self the highest service is to serve the race. To accept individual happiness, a variable commodity measured by dispositions as different as persons, and make it the criterion, would be to embrace anarchy. The wholesome notion of right must be human, not personal.

If ethics broadly stated is the art of conduct, in our present discussion we shall find it to be the conduct of art. And if human happiness, in the highest sense, is the end of ethics, no one will doubt that the ethical end of art is the same. To please the most perfectly organized and most nobly refined human taste would be the aim of true art, as it is the ethical desire to have all mankind fitted to enjoy true art. In this view the ethical and the aesthetical lines coincide throughout.

Many persons nurse a remarkable fear of didactic art; but these are not clear thinkers. All art is didactic, positively or negatively, and wields an influence by attraction or repulsion. Perhaps it would be better to say that every form of art creation attracts us toward or away from that equilibrium of good which is the perfection of human conduct.

I note that certain critics, who in one way or another are apologists for immoral literature, seem fond of the phrase, "artistic conscience." As if the artist must have a conscience different from that of any other good man! He is a coward who in any exigency makes his own case a special one. The moral responsibility of the artist offers no secret and private avenues of confession and avoidance, and if it does, a true man ought to be too proud to use them. In literature, as in every other sphere of human conduct, we must have vast charity for the man, but no charity for the man's evil. Proper critical appreciation of Shelley's poetry, for example, does not involve any such reckless eulogy of Shelley's character as has been the recent vogue in America and England. Charity covers faults, but it never lies about them or excuses them. Ethics draws no distinction between the wife-murderer who cleans stables or keeps a dive, and the wife-murderer who writes a "Prometheus Unbound," or an "Ode to a Skylark." The right of the aristocrat is not available as a shield against the operation of moral responsibility. The glamour of genius cannot blind the eyes of God.

It has ever been the function of evil to progress by means of fascination, and this fascination is loosely and mistakenly regarded as pleasure or happiness. The thrill of the unholy is mistaken for the calm and lofty ecstasy of pure joy. Ethics does not recognize the legitimacy of evil delights, come from what source they may. The making of a poem which appeals to base sympathies, no matter how perfect the art, is as vile an act as though it were vulgarly done in prose. Our conception of the notion of art takes its color from the surroundings we give to it. If we deny it an ethical environment, we make the artist a being specially privileged to do evil for art's sake. Such a conception robs the creative act of every connection with the sources of true conscience, and sets artistic results apart as excrescences on the substance of life. If the poet, for example, is an agent with power to affect the currents of human conduct, what law of nature exempts him from the common obligation to affect them in a way to do the greatest good to the greatest number? A ribald song may appeal to a vast audience; it may have a haunting melody; but is it justified?

It is in one of the plays of Aristophanes, "The Birds," that a nightingale sings and, as one of the listeners remarks, "makes the wilderness sweet with tender breath of music." Here is a conception of pure and wholesome art in the wilderness of life; it breathes a civilizing sweet round about. The Greeks called the Muses "the lamps of the earth," as if to make them guides to lead out of darkness; and this is the key-note of Greek art, the fine note of open illumination. Matthew Arnold denied to the Greeks that magic of genius which he found in the Celts; but what magic is more sure or more potent than this light direct, this surprise of sound and joyous conception? Mind, I do not here speak of subject-matter, nor of treatment, but of the conception of the function of art—namely, to lead by the cord of delight.

Suddenly the question, Whither is the young mind led by unbridled "art for art's sake"? I freely grant full sway to the phrase, "a clean mind can cleanly contemplate evil"; but can a clean mind be delectated with what is unclean? Surely we may discern the distinction here suggested. Youth is the period of happiness and desire, and to youth art makes its most moving appeal. Take the novel, the most popular form of art, and you note that it is the young who read and are swayed by powerful fiction. The tremendous fascination of evil gives to an immoral novel an impetus in the grooves of commerce. Young people, even the purest of them, are curious to know what lies between the lids of a scarlet book. A high ethical conception cannot license art to generate such curiosity and then feed it.

But certain artists say that their business is not to furnish food for babes. Very well. Is the adult liberated to delectate himself with evil? By what ethical law can the distinction be recognized? If art is a factor in the conduct of life, our conception of it must be that it symbolizes an act of the collective human body and expresses an aspiration. In every area of human action, except, as it would seem, the field of fine art, we are required to avoid evil aspirations and to shun the company of vice and filth. Even the crudest observation and the most rudimentary experience of life convince us that we must grow like what we contemplate, and that intellectual associations give color to the soul. There are no more intimate and subtle intellectual associations than those effected through literature. The man or woman we meet in a book walks into our sanctuary of character and writes maxims on its walls. If we are libertines in art, what are we in the finest tissues of character? The conduct of the imagination is the chemistry of life. Physiological study leads more and more toward the conclusion that thought-habit largely influences what we may call nervous alimentation, and nothing is more certainly known than that character-quality depends upon the health of the nerve centers. It is therefore of ethical importance to study the connection between the development of art and the evolution of character.

One theory is that civilization shapes art to suit its changes. The other theory views art as a factor in developing civilization. A sound thinker who has read history and observed life will blend the two theories into a reciprocal one; but the ethical importance of art will be found in its influence in shaping conduct. Without this influence it is a mere efflorescence of life. To my mind genius loses its salient value when it takes the attitude of accident and poses as a mere *lusus naturae*, like a gall-nut on an oak leaf, or a wart on your hand. I like to regard it as a healthy fruit tree, bearing wholesome and invigorating fruit; a perfect soul working consciously and with conscience to delight and refine all other souls.

And yet my conception of art does not recognize obvious didactics, or accept the limitations of any arbitrary system of morals. The key to art is taste, and taste is the finest secret of conduct. Behind taste lies moral bias, from which the initial impulse of every art movement springs; for it is moral bias that controls every conception of the form and the function of art. This bias gets into the air of an age; it is miasm or ozone; it is a coefficient operating with conscience or inspiring irresponsible revolt. Now, the deepest reach of art is to engender a right bias, so that good taste shall become hereditary. Says De Quincey, "the writer is not summoned to convince, but to persuade"; and Joubert adds, "it is not enough that a work be good; it must be done by a good author." At the present moment of history we seem to be hesitating whether or not, after all, literature shall be regarded as a mere mode of commercial motion. "The first value of a book," said a publisher, "is its salability." This is a conception which destroys every imaginable basis of conscience in literary life, unless we can make good books salable; for the publisher holds command.

Both church and state have tried to educate taste by means of legal censorship. The practice has been as futile as the principle is despicable. Indeed, the circulation of a bad book is always urged to the maximum by legal prohibition. Human perversity is an element in every problem of reform. A man told me that he never thirsted for whisky save when in a prohibition state. To reform conduct we must educate life. If a man is suffering from blood-poisoning, we do not cure him by local treatment; we try to cleanse his whole system. Ethics must regard the collective body as one patient whose disease is constitutional. The quack doctor panders to a maudlin weakness of chronic invalids. So in art a certain school of quacks, like Ibsen and Tolstoi, fatten upon the liberality of hysterical souls.

Speaking of false critics, sturdy and right-minded John Dryden said: "All that is dull, insipid, languishing, and without sinews in a poem they call an imitation of nature." In our day the so-called realists answer to Dryden's description. They boast of holding up a mirror to nature; but they take care to give preference always to ignoble nature. They never hold up their mirror to heroic nature. Have you observed how, as a man becomes a realist, he grows fond of being narrow and of playing with small specialties? Have you thought out the secret force which controls the movements of this so-called realism, and always keeps its votaries sneering at heroic life, while they revel in another sort of life, which fitly to characterize here would be improper? I can tell you what that force is. It is unbelief in ideal standards of human aspiration, and it is impatient scorn of that higher mode of thought which has given the world all the greatest creations of imaginative genius. It is a long cry from Homer and Aeschylus and Shakespeare and Scott to Zola and Ibsen and Tolstoi and Flaubert; but it is exactly measured by the space between a voice which utters the highest note of its time and civilization, and one that utters the lowest. I say that these modern realists utter the cry of our civilization's lowest and most belated element; and they call it the cry of modern science. But science has nothing to do with it. Science never disports itself in the baleful light of mere coarseness; nor does it choose dry or commonplace investigations simply because they are dry and commonplace. In its true sphere science aims to lift us above mysteries. The same may be said of all the great masters of art; they lift us above the mire of degrading things. True, we find coarseness amounting to what is foul in all the ancient classics, and even in Chaucer and Shakespeare; but we cannot take shelter behind these to cast forth upon the world our own surplus of filth. The custom of critics is in charity to refer the obscenities of old writers to the moral taste of the time. Shall we credit our own civilization with an appetency for the *Kreützer Sonata, Leaves of Grass*, and *Madame Bovary*? Have we moved no farther than this during these centuries of Christianity?

I know absolutely nothing about theology, which is doubtless to be counted in reckoning what I come to, and I frankly say that I could not, to save me, tell the difference between one creed and another; but I have it clearly in mind that Christianity is responsible for our civilization, and is the datum-line to which we must refer in all our measurements. Our enlightenment may be imaginary, the gleam of a myth, but it comes from the Star of Bethlehem.

Every reader is aware that there exists a certain strained relation between art and moral responsibility. The first impulse of a solicitous parent is toward forbidding novels and dramatic literature to his children. The college and the pulpit wrestle with a giant doubt in the matter of approving the current conception of art. We all feel that the contemporary artistic influence is subtly opposed to the ethical verities. We find that in fiction and poetry we are hobnobbing with persons with whom we could not in real life bear a moment's interview. It is not so much the scenes and characters chosen; we might regard these, as in real life, with a deep regret; but the conception of art and its function represented by such a choice of subject and treatment suggests a vicious trend of life.

Matthew Arnold's theory of "sweetness and light" may be a trifle flabby when put to the average test of practical experience; yet to irradiate light and to instill sweetness can never be amiss; this indeed seems to me the only excuse for art. Culture must, however, have its root nourished in a stronger soil than that of mere amiability. Art should stand for more than an expression of good-natured commentary on current life, or of ill-natured caricature of humanity's frailties. "What is realism?" inquired a young woman the other day. Her friend answered, "It's writing what we are too clean to speak, and reading about what we would blush to look at. It is going in books where to go in actual life would disgrace us." Prudery does not appeal to a sound soul, and our strictures on art ought not to be different from our strictures on life. Our associations in art should not be lower than our associations in life. Indeed, to me the main service of imaginative activities is in giving higher experiences than ordinary life can afford. In life we aim at the higher life; in art, why not at the higher life? The most abject prudery is that which makes us ashamed to insist upon cleanness and soundness; the vilest dishonesty suggests that we account for literary villainy on the score of compulsion by "artistic conscience." Evil is the great foe of true happiness; but art must give canvas-room for this dark figure with all its scowls and all its fascinating smiles; it has a mighty value when set over against goodness to the effect that the conception holds fast to the right. But let us not pass the limit of freedom into the domain of license. In life we face the ills and evils of our state; we must do the same in art, and in both life and art there must be moral responsibility. If in writing a book, we must not steal the thought-work of a fellow, surely in the same pages we must avoid breaking the other nine commandments. Still I have known a man who complained loud and long of the immorality of a publisher who had failed to make accurate copyright reports of sales in the matter of a vilely impure novel. This is the special pleading which in another form demands that the artist clothe himself before painting a naked picture.

Plato's dreams and Aristotle's facts may come at last into coincidence, and yet Plato's conception is the only safe ground of art. An imagination which never goes above "scientific dissections" may state conditions; but a flash of empyrean fire cuts through conditions and illuminates the remote high area of the unconditional. Plato's attitude was supremely artistic; Aristotle's posture was realistic. The utilitarian, who measures life by material units, is a peripatetic; the true artist is platonic, and wherever we find him indicating an ethical conception, it is a universal one. The old Dorian notion was the elemental one, that morality was not of the individual but of the people, and this is the poet's notion in all ages.

But how is ethical leaven to work in literary art? We cannot brook legal censorship, and, if we could, the remedy would be worse than the disease. Freedom must be next to absolute in letters. The one feasible scheme of ethical reform is education. And here arises the abrupt question, By what particular channel of education can literary taste be most readily purified? It is safe to assume that a wholesome conception of art is the first stage of reform needed, and I suggest that sound criticism would be a potent factor in the work; but I speak of criticism in its most liberal sense, certainly not in the sense which would make the critic a mere friendly purveyor of appreciation, a sycophant self-trained to lick boots. The zealous fault-hunter, to be sure, is not a critic; no more is the fault-dodger. I like to read Sainte-Beuve; but I lay at his door and Wordsworth's much of the insignificance of literary art at this moment. The conception of art in the body of Wordsworth's poetry and the notion of criticism in Sainte-Beuve's essays have easily formed the whey of commonplace and the curd of "appreciation."

It is the habit of certain editors, I am told, to have their book reviews written by persons who will be sure to praise each work. This is but another expression of that irresponsibility behind which literary folk delight to huddle. The same weakness affects the whole modern theory of criticism. What avails teaching if in the same school every theory, no matter how debauching, has its expert apologist? If criticism is nothing more than sympathetic exposition by a special pleader, it amounts simply to the critic's saying: "I can make this artist's purpose and meaning plainer and more enjoyable than he could himself."

Criticism is the measuring of conduct—the conduct of life, the conduct of art.

Viewed broadly, it is the fine residuum of sound morals left over after the solution of ethical problems. One man is not a critic; it is the intelligent majority. Say what we may, the average mind is the triumphant criterion; by it life wins or loses in all that concerns the body of humanity. What does not concern humanity as a body ought not to concern any man. We are the Adam and Eve of to-day; it is mankind that must make the long run, not the individual. If we suffer from the old Adam's fall, what countless millions must writhe far down the future because we, the new Adam, ate a more deadly fruit! Verily, the day is ours and the light of it.

It will be felt that I am suggesting immanent criticism, the floating, general, vital impression out of which the elusive but powerful influence of art is so largely drawn. What makes a book popular? No number of favorable reviews can do it—no amount of advertising or puffing. The secret lies in touching the nerve of average taste. Every proposition submitted to mankind is at last solved by this average immanent criticism. Artists may rebel; but the democracy of human economy always prevails, and that picture, that poem, that story which appeals to and satisfies a common and steadfast human longing is the lasting and influential one. Ethics, then, as it regards art, must respect the average, and the ethical aim must be to lift the line of mean human aspiration. To have no privileged class and to admit no special pleading in favor of genius by which strict moral responsibility may be avoided in art, are prerequisites of critical honesty. The average mind may be easily convinced of the justice of this democratic rule, and to this end should education tend. The higher we urge the mean level of immanent human criticism, the higher will rise the surface of human conduct. The conduct of art has no special exemption.

The chief office of art is to teach through fascination, not openly and dictatorially, but almost unawares. Its appeal is the charm of beauty, the lure of symmetry, the perfume of truth; or it is the imperious fascination of evil clothed in a counterfeit divinity. This is the old demarcation between good and evil. I repeat that neither genius nor art can successfully slink out of responsibility through a special side gate. To prevent this cowardice the old Greeks invented dialectics and discussed life vigorously in their schools. We may say that they were heathens; but what would they say of us with our Christian theories and our pagan practices? Nakedness, physical and spiritual, in art was a sincere reflect of Greek religion, Greek civilization. It was unconsciously projected. Not so with us; when we go naked it is done self-consciously, with the full understanding that nakedness is not decent. We do it in sheer defiance of immanent criticism.

Is there a man or a woman in the world who believes that any person ever read a novel or a poem for the stark purpose of moral reform? Do you ever read a novel expecting thereby to wash away some stain from your character. Be honest and answer that in every quest pleasure is your goal. From the notion of heaven down to the wish for a tin whistle your aim is pleasure. You imagine you would enjoy heaven; you feel sure that a tin whistle would delight you. If you buy *Anna Karénina* or *Madame Bovary*, it is for delectation and not for personal purification. Speaking of cant, what cant is worse than that of the artist who entertains you at the table of vice with the avowed purpose of sweetening your life?

It is that wonderful Joubert again who says, "Naturally, the soul repeats to itself all that is beautiful or all that seems so." The writer writes what he likes, the reader reads what is to his taste. Ah, taste! there is the foundation. Can you for a moment credit any man's statement that he reads for delectation and yet against his taste? Perhaps I am a Philistine; at all events I do not hesitate here flatly to charge insincerity. Who could possibly be more hopelessly insincere than the avowedly pure woman who tells you that she has fortified her virtue by reading Ibsen's picture of Hedda Gabler? Woman, you have taken Ibsen's arm and have gone with him into vile company and have been delighted with the novelty of it. The smack of hell is sweet to your lips, as it was to those of new-made Eve. It would be strictly true for such a woman to say, "Yes I read these novels of impure passion, and there is a strain in my taste which enjoys these pictures of temptation and of evil pleasures. Secretly I like a peep into debauchery; but then I hold on to my own rectitude." The word "rectitude" as here used means formal rectitude of life's exterior; the intrinsic muscles have responded to a coarse and beastly impulse.

In producing works of art having evil for their source of fascination, and in reading such works, we are tainting the most secret veins of immanent criticism. Civilization inevitably responds to these influences working at the farthest tips of its tenderest roots. Vitiate imagination and you destroy character. No pure woman ever wrote a fiction of illicit love; if she began pure, she ended soiled. Her soul followed her pen. Druggists and physicians have told me that a person who takes to opium-eating will lie, steal, or barter body and soul for a morsel of dried poppy-juice. Never in my life have I known a man or a woman given over to the pleasure of writing or of reading novels based on illicit love who did not habitually lie to avoid the application of personal responsibility.

To the perfectly unbiased observer nothing is clearer than that forbidden fruit is always in demand, and will be as long as human perversity fortifies human animalism. If the author of *Tess of the D'Urbervilles* would say the truth, he would flatly confess that he wrote that brilliantly fascinating, filthy novel, not to make poor young girls cling to virtue, not to prevent rich young men from being villains at heart; but to make a fiction that would appeal to human perversity and delectate human animalism. He reckoned safely; the book sold almost as fast as whisky. It was named by the author "the story of a pure woman." This woman, after being easily led to shame once prior to marriage, fell again during wedlock, and then committed murder and was executed. This is no extreme case; I cite it as typical. Nearly all of the critics were loud in praise of this novel—thousands of good people read it. And to justify themselves both critics and readers claimed for it a high moral influence. What I see wrong in this is that it claims for fiction a power and an exemption not possible to real life. How can association with immoral and debauching people and conditions in our reading differ from our association with them in life? If art is chiefly for delectation, is it not a species of debauchery to indulge in art which takes its fascination from forbidden sources? As I have said, human perversity demands the forbidden. A publisher told me that for a novel to gain the reputation of being written in the highest strain of art and yet on a subject not considered clean was a sure guaranty of success;

"and yet," said he, "popular sentiment is strong against such books." Here is the fascination of the unclean—the very fascination which it is the duty of all to avoid and which it is the highest mission of Christian civilization to extinguish. And yet Christian artists demand the right to make commerce of this same evil fascination, and in this demand they are upheld by Christian critics.

In a word, I conclude this part of my argument by propounding a question, Has the immanent meaning of Christian civilization yet showed itself in art? Or, negatively, Is not fine art, and especially literary fine art, still essentially heathen? Is not the most direct and vigorous appeal of current poetry and fiction made to the ancient, elemental, conscienceless substance of humanity? One of two things is certainly true,—the artist is specially exempt from moral responsibility, or he is just as responsible as any other person.

To me it appears that the commercial value of literary filth is really behind every argument in favor of the moral force assumed by authors and critics to be inherent in the dramatic presentation of illicit love. We must admit that novels and poems on this subject are immensely fascinating and that in a cold commercial view they are good property. In the same view whisky and gambling rooms are excellent investments. Gilded dives pay large dividends in the lawful currency. St. Peter's Church has fewer visitors than Monte Carlo. What do you make of this? Is it the true conception of art that the artist may live in honor by the same appeal which enriches the faro-dealer, the saloon-keeper, and the princess of a bagnio? Is the money earned by writing and selling *Tess of the D'Urbervilles* one whit cleaner than that earned by any other play upon the human weakness for unclean things?

It is not clear why a feeling should prevail that, to be robust, art must show a great deal of vulgarity. The best athlete carries but little flesh, and I find that the muscles and sound nerves go farther than fat. Grossness, indeed, is as far removed from true virility as one pole from the other. Mere audacity in handling things not considered by the spirit of our civilization touchable cannot win the badge of Homer or of Horace. Homer sang strictly within the spirit of his age and voiced its characteristic aspiration. Horace did no violence to the civilization that inspired him. Full, close, sympathetic touch with Christianity (not with dry dogma, creed, ritual, or sect, or denomination), close touch with Christianity, I say, can give the only true conception of the new art of our just dawning era.

You will observe that I do not hesitate to speak of Christianity as distinct from church, priesthood, theology, and formal religion,—as a mode of progress, a great mood of civilization, broadening, deepening, warming day by day. It is moving toward the republic in everything; not backward toward the republic of the heathen, but forward to the republic of the Christian. Wherefore the conception of art, to be adequate, must apprehend this future while availing itself of the past. The point where the old orb and the new blend the rays of warning and of prophecy is the true focus of inspiration. We must know where we are. There is no return. The Greek with his jocund heathen song is dead; gone is the heathen grace of Virgil; gone the goatherd genius from the fells of Sicily; gone Anacreon, the ruddy bibber, and gone the strange cry:

῎Ω παῖ παρθένιον βλέπων

Not much less remote echoes the Dantesque strain, half Christian, half heathen. It is time for the key-note of our era to sound; it is time for genius to speak in the true, in the highest terms of our civilization.

"Well," says some practical soul, "when, where, and to what purpose?" I answer: When we make for genius the true Christian atmosphere; in that atmosphere will he thrive; not in the dust of dogma; not in the twilight of cathedrals; not yet in the cramped sanctuary of tradition. He shall inhale the rich air, which is buoyant with the significance of our era, and his purpose shall be the good of the brotherhood of man.

TEN

REALISM IN LITERATURE AND ART

Clarence Darrow

Clarence Darrow (1857–1938), born and raised in Ohio but Chicago-based for most of his career, was perhaps the most famous lawyer in America between the 1890s and the 1930s. A staunch liberal Democrat with socialist leanings as well as a free thinker, he defended, among others, the Haymarket anarchists, Eugene Debs, Big Bill Hayward, and John Scopes. Darrow published widely on legal, social, and literary issues and also wrote several novels. The *Arena* magazine, in which "Realism in Literature and Art" appeared, was, under the editorship of B. O. Flower, one of the principal outlets for radical ideas during the late 1880s and early 1890s.

Man is nature's last and most perfect work; but however high his development or great his achievements, he is yet a child of the earth and the forces that have formed all the life that exists thereon. He cannot separate himself from the environment in which he grew, and a thousand ties of nature bind him back to the long-forgotten past, and prove his kinship to all the lower forms of life that have sprung from that great common mother, earth.

As there is a universal law of being which controls all forms of life, from the aimless movement of the mollusk in the sea to the most perfect conduct of the best developed man, so all the varied activities of human life, from the movements of the savage digging roots to the work of the greatest artist with his brush, are controlled by universal laws, and are good or bad, perfect or imperfect, as they conform to the highest conditions nature has imposed.

The early savage dwelt in caves and cliffs, and spent his life in seeking food and

Arena 9 (December 1893): 98–113. Reprinted in *A Persian Pearl and Other Essays* (East Aurora, NY: Roycroft Shops, 1893), pp. 113–42. Text from the *Arena*.

providing some rude shelter from the cold. He looked at the earth, the sun, the sea, the sky, the mountain peak, the forest, and the plain, at the vegetable and animal life around, and all he saw and heard formed an impression on his brain, and aided in his growth.

Like a child he marvelled at the storm and flood; he stood in awe as he looked upon disease and death; and to explain the things he could not understand, he peopled earth and air and sea with gods and demons and a thousand weird creations of his brain.

All these mysterious creatures were made in the image of the natural objects that came within his view. The gods were men grown large, and endowed with marvellous powers, while tree and bird and beast were used alike as models for a being greater far than any nature ever formed.

It was an angry god that made the rivers overrun their banks and leave destruction in their path. An offended god it was who hurled his thunderbolts upon a wicked world or sent disease and famine to the sinning children of the earth; and to coax these rulers to be merciful to man, the weak and trembling people of the ancient world turned their thoughts to sacrifice and prayer.

The first clouded thoughts of these rude men were transcribed on monument and stone, or carved in wood, or painted with the colors borrowed from the sun and earth and sky; in short, the first rude art was born to sing the praise, and tell the fame, and paint the greatness of the gods. But all of this was natural for the time and place; and the graven images, the chiselled hieroglyphics, and all this rude beginning of literature and art were formed upon what men saw and heard and felt, enlarged and magnified to fit the stature of the gods.

As the world grew older, art was used to celebrate the greatness and achievements of kings and rulers as well as gods, and their tombs were ornamented with such decorations as these early ages could create; but yet all literature and art was only for the gods and the rulers of the world. Then, even more than now, wealth and power brought intellect to do their will, and all its force was spent to sing the praises of the rulers of the earth and air.

The basis of all this art of pen and brush was the reality of the world; but this was so magnified and distorted for the base use of kings and priests, that realism in the true sense could not exist.

It would not do to paint a picture of a king resembling a man of flesh and blood, and of course a god must be far greater than a king. It would not do to write a tale in which kings and princes, lords and ladies, should act like men and women—else what difference between the ruler and the ruled? The marvellous powers which romance and myth had given to gods and angels were transferred to those of royal blood. The wonderful achievements of these knights and princes could be equalled only by the gods; and the poor dependents of the world, who lived for the glory of the great, were fed with legends and with tales that sang the praises of the great.

Literature, sculpture and painting, music and architecture, indeed, all forms of art, were the exclusive property of the great and strong; and the artist, then, like most of those today, was retained to serve the great and maintain the status of the weak.

No one dreamed that there was any beauty in a common human life or any romance in a fact. The greatest of the earth had not yet learned to know that every life is a mystery and every death a tragedy; that the spark of the infinite, which alone transforms clay to life, animates alike the breast of the peasant and the soul of the prince. The world had not learned that the ant hill was as great as Mont Blanc and the blade of grass as mysterious as the oak. It is only now that the world is growing so delicate and refined that it can see the beauty of a fact; that it is developing a taste so rare as to distinguish between the false and true; that it can be moved by the gentle breeze as well as by the winter's gale; that it can see a greater beauty in a statement true to life than in the inflated tales which children read.

Most of the literature and art the world has known has been untrue. The pictures of the past have been painted from the distorted minds of visionists and the pliant brains of tools. They have represented impossible gods and unthinkable saints, angels and cherubs and demons—everything but men and women. Saints may be all right in their place, but a saint with a halo around his head was born of myth and not of art. Angels may be well enough, but all rational men prefer an angel with arms to an angel with wings. When these artists were not busy painting saints and Madonnas, they were spending their time painting kings and royal knaves, and the pictures of the rulers were as unlike the men and women whom they were said to represent as the servile spirit of the painter was unlike the true artist of to-day. Of course an artist would not paint the poor. They had no clothes that would adorn a work of art, and no money nor favors that could pay him for his toil. An ancient artist could no more afford to serve the poor than a modern lawyer to defend the weak.

After literature had so far advanced as to concern other beings than gods and kings, the authors of these ancient days endowed their characters with marvellous powers; knights with giant strength and magic swords; princes with wondrous palaces and heaps of gold; travellers who met marvellous beasts and slew them in extraordinary ways; giants with forms like mountains and strength like oxen, and who could vanquish all but little dwarfs. Railroads were not invented in those early days, but travel was facilitated by the use of seven-league boots. Balloons and telescopes were not yet known, but this did not keep favored heroes from peering at the stars or looking down from on high upon the earth. They had but to plant a magic bean before they went to bed at night, and in the morning it had grown so tall that it reached up to the sky; and the hero, although not skilled in climbing, needed simply to grasp the stalk and say, "Hitchety, hatchety, up I go. Hitchety, hatchety, up I go," and by this means soon vanished in the clouds.

Tales of this sort used once to delight the world, and the readers half believed them true. We give them to children now, and even the least of these view them with a half contempt.

The modern man who still reads Walter Scott does not enjoy these ancient myths. He relishes a lie, but it must not be too big; it must be so small that, although he knows in his inmost soul that it is not true, he can yet half make himself believe it is not false. Most of us have cherished a pleasant waking dream, and fondly clung to the sweet delusion while we really knew it was not life. The modern literary stomach is becoming so healthy that it wants a story at least half true; should the falsehood be too strong, it acts as an emetic instead of food.

These old fairy tales have lost their power to charm, as the tales of the gods and kings went down before. They have lost their charm; for as we read them now, they awake no answering chord born of the experiences that make up what we know of human life.

When the beauty of realism shall be truly known, we shall read the book, or look upon the work of art, and, in the light of all we know of life, shall ask our beings whether the image that the author or the painter creates for us is like the one that is born of the consciousness which moves our souls, and the experiences that life has made us know.

Realism worships at the shrine of nature. It does not say that there may not be a sphere in which beings higher than man can live, or that some time an eye may not rest upon a fairer sunset than was ever born behind the clouds and sea; but it knows that through countless ages nature has slowly fitted the brain and eye of man to the earth on which we live and the objects that we see, and the perfect earthly eye must harmonize with the perfect earthly scene. To say that realism is coarse and vulgar, is to declare against nature and her works, and to assert that the man she made may dream of things higher and grander than nature could unfold.

The eye of the great sculptor reveals to him the lines that make the most perfect human form, and he chisels out the marble block until it resembles this image so perfectly that it almost seems to live. Nature, through ages of experiment and development, has made this almost faultless form. It is perfect because every part is best fitted for the separate work it has to do. The artist knows that he could not improve a single organ if he would, for all the rest of nature must be adjusted to the change. He has the skill to reproduce this perfect shape in lasting stone, and the human brain could not conceive a form more beautiful and fair. Here is a perfect image of the highest work that countless centuries of nature's toil has made; and yet some would seek to beautify and sanctify this work by dressing it in the garb that shifting fashion and changing fancy make for men.

It was only the vulgar superstition of the past that ever suggested that the reproduction of human forms in stone was an unholy work. Through long, dark centuries religion taught that the human form was vile and bad, and that the soul of man was imprisoned in a charnel house, unfit for human sight. They wounded, bruised, and maimed their house of clay; they covered it with skins that under no circumstances could be removed, and many ancient saints lived and died without ever having looked upon the bodies nature gave to them. The images of saints and martyrs, which in the name of religion were scattered through Europe, were covered with paint and clothes, and were nearly as hideous as the monks who placed them there.

When the condition of Europe and its religious thought is clearly understood, it is not difficult to imagine the reception that greeted the first dawn of modern realistic art. Sculpture and painting deified the material. It told of beauty in the human form which thousands of years of religious fanaticism had taught was bad and vile.

If the flesh was beautiful, what of the monks and priests who had hidden it from sight; who had kept it covered night and day through all their foolish lives; who maimed and bruised, cut and lacerated it for the glory of the spirit which they believed was chained within? The church had taught that the death of the flesh was the birth of the soul, and they therefore believed that the artist's resurrection of the flesh was the death of the soul.

This old religious prejudice, born of a misty, superstitious past, has slowly faded from the minds of men, but we find its traces even yet; the origin of the feeling against realistic art has well-nigh been forgot, but much of the feeling still remains. No one now would pretend to say that all the body was unholy or unfit for sight, and yet years of custom and inherited belief have made us think that a part is good and the rest is bad; that nature, in her work of building up the human form, has made one part sacred and another vile. It is easy to mistake custom for nature, and inherited prejudice for morality.

There is not a single portion of the human body which some people have not believed holy, and not a single portion which some have not believed vile. It was not shame that made clothing, but clothing that made shame. If we should eradicate from our beliefs all that inheritance and environment have given, it would be hard for us to guess how much would still remain. Custom has made almost all things good and nearly all things bad, according to the whim of time and place. To find solid ground we must turn to nature, and ask her what it is that conduces to the highest happiness and the longest life. The realistic artist cannot accept the popular belief, whatever that may be, as to just where the dead line on the human body should be drawn that separates the sacred and profane.

There are realists who look at all the beauty and loveliness of the world, and all its maladjustments, too, and who do not seek to answer the old, old question, whether back of this is any all-controlling and designing power. They do not answer, for they cannot know; but they strive to touch the subtle chord which makes their individual lives vibrate in harmony with the great heart of that nature which they love, and they cannot think but what all parts of life are good, and that, while men may differ, nature must know best.

Other realists there are who believe they see in nature the work of a divine Maker, who created man in His own image as the last and highest triumph of His skill; that not the minutest portion of the universe exists except because He wished it thus. To the realist who accepts this all-controlling power, any imputation against a portion of his Master's work must reach back to the author who designed it all.

We need not say that the human body might not be better than it is. We only need to know that it is the best that man can have, and that its wondrous mechanism has been constructed with infinitely more than human skill; that every portion is adapted for its work, and through the harmony of every part the highest good is reached, and that all is beautiful, for it makes the perfect being best adapted to the earth. Those who denounce realistic art deny that knowledge is power, and that wisdom only can make harmony; but they insist, instead, that there are some things vital to life and happiness that we should not know, or that, if we must know these things, we at all events should pretend that we did not.

One day the world will learn to know that all things are good or bad according to the service they perform. A great brain which is used by its owner for his selfish ends, regardless of all the purposes that are sacrificed to attain the goal, is as base and bad as the mind can well conceive; while a great brain dedicated to the right and just, and freely given to the service of the world, is high and grand. One day it ought to learn that the power to create immortality, through infinite succeeding links of human life, is the finest and most terrible that nature ever gave to man; and to ignore this power or call it bad, to fail to realize the great responsibility of this tremendous fact, is to cry out against the power that gave us life, and commit the greatest human sin, for it may be one that never dies.

The true artist does not find all beauty in the human face or form. These are a part of a mighty whole. He looks upon the sunset, painting all the clouds with rosy hue, and his highest wish is to create another scene like this. He never dreams that he could paint a sunset fairer than the one that lights the fading world. A fairer sunset would be something else. He sees beauty in the quiet lake, the grassy field, and running brooks. He sees majesty in the cataract and mountain peak. He knows that he can paint no streams and mountain peaks more perfect that the ones that nature made.

The growth of letters has been like that of art, from the marvellous and mythical to the natural and true. The tales and legends of the ancient past were not of common men and common scenes. These could not impress the undeveloped intellects of long ago. A man of letters could not deify a serf or tell the simple story of the poor. He must write to maintain the status of the world, and please the prince who gave him food. So he told of kings and queens, of knights and ladies, of strife and conquest, and the coloring he used was human blood.

The world has grown accustomed to those ancient tales—to scenes of blood and war, and novels that would thrill the soul and cause the hair to stand on end. It has read them so long that the true seems commonplace and not fit to fill the pages of a book. But all the time we forget the fact that the story could not charm unless we half believed it true. The men and women in the tale we learn to love and hate; we take an interest in their lives; we hope they may succeed or fail; we must not be told at every page that the people of the book are men of straw, that no such beings ever lived upon the earth. We could take no interest in men and women who were myths conjured up to play their parts, remind us in every word they spoke that, regardless of the happiness or anguish the author made them feel, they were but puppets, and could know neither joy nor pain. It may be that the realistic story is commonplace, but so is life, and the realistic tale is true. Among the countless millions of the earth it is only here and there, and now and then, that some soul is born from out the mighty depths that does not soon return to the great sea, and leave no ripple on the waves.

In the play of life each actor seems important to himself; the world he knows revolves around him as the central figure of the scene; his friends rejoice in all the fortune he attains, and weep with him in all his griefs. To him the world is bounded by the faces that he knows and the scenes in which he lives; he forgets the great surging world outside, and cannot think how small a space he fills in that infinity which bounds his life. He dies; a few sorrowing friends mourn him for a day, and the world does not know he ever lived or ever died. In the ordinary life almost all events are commonplace, but a few important days are thinly sprinkled in among all of those that intervene between the cradle and the grave. We eat and drink, we work and sleep, and here and there a great joy or sorrow creeps in upon our lives, and leaves a day that stands out in the monotony of all the rest, like the pyramids upon the level plains. But there are very, very few, and are important only to ourselves; and for the rest, we walk with steady pace along the short and narrow path of life, and rely upon the common things alone to occupy our minds and hide from view the marble stone that here and there we cannot fail to see, as it gleams upon us through the overhanging trees just where the road leaves off.

The highest mountain range, when compared with all the earth, is no larger than a hair upon an ordinary globe; and the greatest life bears about the same resemblance to the humanity of which it is a part.

The old novel, which we used to read and to which the world so fondly clings, had no idea of relation or perspective. It had a hero and a heroine, and sometimes more than one. The revolutions of the planets were less important than their love. War, shipwreck, and conflagration all conspired to produce the climax of the scene, and the whole world stood still until their hearts and hands were joined. Wide oceans, burning deserts, Arctic seas, impassable jungles, irate fathers, and even designing mothers were helpless against the decree that fate had made; and when all the barriers were passed, and love had triumphed over impossibilities, the tale was done. Through the rest of life nothing of interest could transpire. Sometimes in the progress of the story, if the complications were too great, a thunderbolt or an earthquake was introduced to destroy the villain and help out the match. Earthquakes sometimes happen, and the realistic novelists might write a tale of a scene like this; but then the love affair would be an incident of the earthquake, and not the earthquake an incident of the love affair.

In real life the affections have played an important part, and sometimes great things have been done in the name of love; but most of the affairs of the human heart have been as natural as the other events of life.

The true love story is generally a simple thing. On a sloping hill, beside a country road, lives a farmer, in the house his father owned before. He has a daughter, who skims the milk, and makes the beds, and goes to singing school at night. There are other members of the household, but our tale is no concern of theirs. In the meadow, back of the house, a woodchuck has dug his hole, and reared a family in its humble home. Across the valley, only a mile away, another farmer lives. He has a son who ploughs the fields, and does the chores, and goes to singing school at night. He cannot sing, but he attends the school as regularly as if he could. Of course he does not let the girl go home alone! and in the spring, when singing school is out, he visits her on Sunday evening without excuse. If the girl had not lived so near, the farmer's son would have fancied another girl about the same age who also went to singing school. Back of the second farmer's house is another woodchuck hole and woodchuck home.

After a year or two of courtship, the boy and girl are married, as their parents were before, and they choose a pretty spot beside the road, and build another house between the two, and settle down to common life—and so the world moves on. And a woodchuck on one farm makes the acquaintance of a woodchuck on the other, and they choose a quiet place beside a stump, in no one's way, where they think they have a right to be, and dig another hole and make another home. For after all, men and animals are much alike, and nature loves them both and loves them all, and sends them forth to drive the loneliness from off the earth, and then takes them back into her loving breast to sleep.

It may be that there are few great incidents in the realistic tale; but each event appeals to life, and cannot fail to wake our memories and make us live the past again. The great authors of the natural school, Tolstoi, Daudet, Howells, Ibsen, Kielland, Flaubert, Zola, Hardy, and the rest, have made us think and live. Their words have burnished up our thoughts and revealed a thousand pictures that hung upon the walls of memory, covered with the dust of years and hidden from our sight. Sometimes, of course, we cry with pain at the picture that is thrown before our view; but life consists of emotions, and we cannot truly live unless the depths are stirred.

These great masters, it is true, may sometimes shock the over-sensitive with the stories they tell of life; but if the tale is true, why hide it from our sight? Nothing is more common than the protest against the wicked books of the realistic school, filled with delineations of passion and of sin; but he who denies passion ignores all the life that exists upon the earth, and cries out against the mother that gave him birth; and he who ignores this truth passes with contempt the greatest fact that nature has impressed upon the world.

Those who condemn as sensual the tales of Tolstoi and Daudet still defend the love stories of which our literature is full—those weak and silly tales that make women fit only to be the playthings of the world, and deny to them a single thought of right except to serve their master, man. These objectors do not contend that stories dealing with the feelings and affections shall not be told—they approve these, but they simply insist that they shall be false, instead of true.

The old novel filled the mind of the school girl with a thousand thoughts that had no place in life—with ten thousand pictures she could never see. It taught that some time she would meet a prince in disguise, to whom she should freely give her hand and heart. So she went out upon the road to find this prince; and the more disguised he was, the more certain did she feel that he was the prince for whom she sought.

The realist paints the passions and affections as they are. Both man and woman can see their beauty and their terror, their true position and the relation that they bear to all of life. He would not beguile the girl into the belief that her identity should be destroyed and merged for the sake of this feeling; which not once in ten thousand times could realize the promises that the novel made, but would leave her as an individual to make the most she could and all she could of life, with all the chance for hope and conquest which men have taken for themselves. Neither would the realist cry out blindly against these deep passions that have moved men and women in the past, and which must continue fierce and strong so long as life exists. He is taught by the scientist that the fiercest heat may be transformed to light, and is shown by life that from the strongest passions are sometimes born the sweetest and the purest human souls.

In these days of creeds and theories, of preachers in the pulpit and out, we are told that all novels should have a moral and be written to serve some end. So we have novels on religion, war, marriage, divorce, socialism, theosophy, woman's rights, and other topics without end. It is not enough that the preachers and lecturers shall tell us how to think and act; the novelist must try his hand at preaching, too. He starts out with a theory, and every scene and incident must be bent to make it plain that the author believes certain things. The doings of the men and women in the book are secondary to the views the author holds. The theories may be very true, but the poor characters who must adjust their lives to these ideal states are sadly warped and twisted out of shape.

The realist would teach a lesson, too, but he would not violate a single fact for all the theories in the world, for a theory could not be true if it did violence to life. He paints his picture so true and perfect that all men who look upon it know that it is a likeness of the world that they have seen; they know that these are men and women and little children whom they meet upon the streets, and they see the conditions of their lives, and the moral of the picture sinks deeply into their minds.

There are so-called scientists who make a theory, and then gather facts to prove their theory true; the real scientist patiently and carefully gathers facts, and then forms a theory to explain and harmonize these facts.

All life bears a moral, and the true artist must teach a lesson with his every fact. Some contend that the moral teacher must not tell the truth; the realist holds that there can be no moral teaching like the truth.

The world has grown tired of preachers and sermons; to-day it asks for facts. It has grown tired of fairies and angels, and asks for flesh and blood. It looks on life as it exists to-day—both its beauty and its horror, its joy and its sorrow. It wishes to see all; not only the prince and the millionnaire, but the laborer and the beggar, the master and the slave. We see the beautiful and the ugly, and know what the world is and what it ought to be, and the true picture which the author saw and painted stirs the heart to holier feelings and to grander thoughts.

It is from the realities of life that the highest idealities are born. The philosopher may reason with uttering logic and show us where the world is wrong; the economist may tell us of the progress and poverty that go hand in hand. But these are theories, and the abstract cannot suffer pain.

Dickens went out into the streets of the great city, and found poor little Jo sweeping the crossing with his broom. All around were the luxury and elegance which the rich have appropriated to themselves—great mansions, fine carriages, beautiful dresses,—but in all the great city of houses and homes poor little Jo could find no place to lay his head. His home was in the street; and every time he halted for a moment in the throng, the policeman touched him with his club and bade him to "move on." At last, ragged, wretched, nearly dead with "moving on," he sank down upon the cold stone steps of a magnificent building erected for "The Propagation of the

Gospel in Foreign Parts." As we think of wretched, ragged Jo in the midst of all this luxury and wealth, we see the tens of thousands of other waifs in the great cities of the world, and we condemn the so-called civilization of the earth that builds the mansions of the rich and great upon the rags and miseries of the poor.

The true realist cannot worship at the shrine of power nor prostitute his gifts for gold. With an artist's eye he sees the world exactly as it is, and he tells the story faithfully to life. He feels for every heart that beats, else he could not paint them as he does. It takes the soul to warm a statue into life and make living flesh and coursing blood, and each true picture that he paints or draws makes the world a better place in which to live.

Read Daudet and Flaubert and Maupassant, and you can see living images that think and move and feel. It needs no analysis of character to tell us what they think. You see them move, and you know the motives that inspired the act. You can hear the murmuring of the waterfall, no louder than it ought to be; and as you look upon the foliage of the trees, you fancy that the leaves are almost stirred by a gentle southern breeze.

You can see and feel the social life, and the gulf that separates the rich and poor. If you would know the differences that divide French country life, look but a moment at the part which Flaubert paints, and you can see the gay faces and rich costumes of the dancers in the hall, and the stolid countenances and uncouth garbs of the peasants who look through the windows, from their world outside, at this fairy scene within.

The artists of the realistic school have a sense so fine that they cannot help catching the inspiration that is filling all the world's best minds with the hope of greater justice and more equal social life. With the vision of the seer they feel the coming dawn, when true equality shall reign upon the earth—the time when democracy shall no more be confined to constitutions and to laws, but will be a part of human life.

The greatest artists of the world today are telling facts and painting scenes that cause humanity to stop and think, and ask why one shall be a master and another a serf—why a portion of the world should toil and spin, should wear away their strength and lives, that the rest may live in idleness and ease.

The old-time artists thought they served humanity by painting saints and Madonnas and angels from the myths they conjured in their brains. They painted war with long lines of soldiers dressed in new uniforms, and looking plump and gay, and a battle scene was always drawn from the side of the victorious camp, with the ensign proudly planting his bright colors on the rampart of the foe. One or two were dying, but always in their comrades' arms and listening to shouts of victory that filled the air, and thinking of the righteous cause for which they fought and died. In the last moments they dreamed of pleasant burial-yards at home, and of a grave kept green by loving, grateful friends, and a smile of joy lit up their fading faces, so sweet that it seemed a hardship not to die in war. They painted peace as a white-winged dove settling down upon a cold and "farewell" earth. Between the two it was plain which choice a boy would make, and thus art served the state and king.

But Verestchagin painted war so true to life that as we look upon the scene we long for peace. He painted war as war has ever been and will ever be—a horrible and ghastly scene, where men, drunk with blind frenzy,—which rulers say is patriotic pride,—and made mad by drums and fifes and smoke and shot and shell and flowing blood, seek to maim and wound and kill, because a ruler gives the word. He paints a battle-field a field of life and death, a field of carnage and of blood. And who are these who fight like fiends and devils driven to despair? And what cause is this that makes these men forget that they are men, and vie with beasts to show their cruel thirst for blood? They shout of home and native land; but they have no homes, and the owners of their native land exist upon their toil and blood. The nobles and princes, for whom this fight is waged, are sitting far away upon a hill, beyond the reach of shot and shell; and from this spot they watch their slaves pour out their blood to satisfy their rulers' pride and lust of power. And what is the enemy they fight? Men, like themselves, who blindly go to death at another king's command; slaves who have no land, who freely give their toil or blood—whichever one their rulers may demand. These fighting soldiers have no cause for strife, but their rulers live by kindling in their hearts a love of native land—a love which makes them hate their brother laborers of other lands, and dumbly march to death, to satisfy a king's caprice.

But let us look once more, after the battle has been fought. Here we see the wreck and ruin of the strife. The field is silent now, given to the dead, the beast of prey, and night. A young soldier lies upon the ground. The snow is falling fast around his form. The lonely mountain peaks rise up on every side. The wreck of war is all about. His uniform is soiled and stained. A spot of red is seen upon his breast. It is not the color that his country wove upon his coat to catch his eye and bait him to his death; it is hard and jagged and cold; it is his life's blood that leaked out through a hole that followed the point of a sabre to his heart. His form is stiff and cold, for he is dead. The cruel wound and the icy air have done their work. The government which took his life taught this poor boy to love his native land. As a child he dreamed of scenes of glory and of power, and the great, wide world just waiting to fall captive to his magic strength. He dreamed of war and strife, and of victory and fame. If he should die, kind hands would smooth his brow, and loving friends would keep his grave and memory green, because he died in war. But no human eye was there at last, as the mist of night and the mist of death shut out the lonely mountains from his sight. The snow is all around, and the air above is gray with falling flakes. These would soon hide him from the world; and when the summer time should come again, no one could tell his bleaching bones from all the rest. The only life upon the scene is the buzzard, slowing circling in the air above his head, waiting to make sure that death has come. The bird looks down upon the boy, upon the eyes which first looked out upon the great, wide world, and which his mother fondly kissed. Upon these eyes the buzzard will begin his meal.

Not all the world is beautiful, and not all of life is good. The true artist has no right to choose only the lovely spots, and make us think that this is life. He must bring the world before our eyes, and make us read and think. As he loves the true and noble, he must show the false and bad. As he yearns for true equality, he must paint the master and the slave. He must tell the truth; must tell it all; must tell it o'er and o'er again, till the deafest ear will listen and the dullest mind will think. He must not swerve to please the world by painting only pleasant sights and telling only lovely tales. He must paint and write and work and think until the world shall learn so much, and grow so good, that the true will be all beautiful, and all the real be ideal.

ELEVEN

THE PROGRESSIVE REALISM OF AMERICAN FICTION

H. H. Boyesen

Hjalmar Hjorth Boyesen (1848–95) immigrated from his native Norway to America in 1869. After several years of newspaper work, he became a professor of Germanic languages, first at Cornell and then for the remainder of his life at Columbia. He published actively in various fields, including literary criticism, Scandivanian studies, and novels with strong social themes, of which *The Mammon of Unrighteousness* (1891) and *The Golden Calf* (1892) were the most well received. He was frequently identified during the late 1880s and early 1890s as a strong supporter of Howellsian realism.

In a letter to his friend Zelter (Vol. IV., p. 343), Goethe, in his disgust at the extravagances of the Romantic School, quotes a verse, which he has just written, prophetic of the future of American literature. Although it makes no claim to poetic merit, the sentiment which it expresses is sufficiently remarkable to deserve translation:

America, thy happy lot
Above old Europe's I exalt;
Thou hast no castle ruin hoar
No giant columns of basalt.
Thy soul is not troubled
In living light of day
By useless traditions,
Vain strife and affray.

Literary and Social Silhouettes (New York: Harper's, 1894), pp. 58–78.

Grasp but the present that is thine,
And when thy children take to writing,
May kindly Fate preserve their tales
From robbers, knights, and ghosts affrighting.

I fancy Goethe must have been aware when he wrote this verse (June 21, 1827) that the Americans had already taken to writing, and that their famous novelist, James Fenimore Cooper, was treading this very path from which he hoped that kindly Fate would preserve him. Knights and ruined castles he was, to be sure, by the necessities of the case, forced to eschew; but I doubt not that he regarded it as a dire deprivation. Robbers, red and white, are his stock characters, and, if I remember rightly, he also dealt in ghosts. Edgar Allan Poe revelled in horrors, and our other pioneer novelist, Charles Brockden Brown, of Philadelphia, had all the qualities which would have recommended him to Goethe's particular detestation, being slipshod in style and exhibiting a sovereign disregard of reality. His works abound in psychological curiosities and superingenious mysteries, exulting, like those of his romantic compeers, in all the calamities from which in the Prayer Book we ask God to deliver us.

From the romanticism of Brown and Poe to that of Hawthorne, who chronologically follows the latter as the next notable dispenser of American fiction, we take a long stride forward. Brown's productions belonged to the family of Mrs. Radcliffe and Godwin, and owned only the airiest allegiance to American soil and climate. Hawthorne, on the other hand, was so distinctly a product of New England blood and environment, that he would have been absolutely inconceivable in any other setting. As he disclaims, however, the title of novelist, preferring that of romancer, it would be unfair to measure him by any standard of mere fidelity to fact.

He says, in the preface to *The House of the Seven Gables*:

"When a writer calls his work a Romance, it need hardly be observed that he wishes to claim a certain latitude, both as to its fashion and material, which he would not have felt entitled to assume had he professed to be writing a novel."

This very romance, however, has, with all its fanciful psychology, so unmistakable a New England flavor as almost to make the disclaimer of the preface superfluous. Though the human conscience, with its mysterious heritage of sin and woe, was his theme, the spiritual climate in which his strange blossoms unfolded their hectic beauty was that of the New World; and with their singular delicacy of form and texture they could never have grown anywhere else. The disadvantages under which he labored as a romancer in a world ostensibly devoid of romance, are strongly, almost amusingly, insisted upon in his preface to *The Marble Faun*:

"No author without a trial can conceive of the difficulty of writing a romance about a country where there is no shadow, no antiquity, no mystery, no picturesque and gloomy wrong nor anything but a commonplace prosperity, in broad and simple daylight, as is happily the case with my dear native land. Romance and poetry, ivy, lichens, and wall-flowers need ruin to make them grow."

That he was by no means lacking in the sense of the reality is shown by the exquisite delicacy with which he reproduces the atmospheric tone and color of any locality which forms the setting of his more important scenes; and if further testimony is needed, his note-books will furnish it in abundance.

Mrs. Harriet Beecher Stowe, whose popularity reached further than that of any of her predecessors, had no intellectual affinity to Hawthorne; but her kinship with her greater contemporary, Charles Dickens, is unmistakable. Eva, in *Uncle Tom's Cabin*, belongs to the same lachrymose family as Little Nell, and they both die (one might almost say) with the same emotional extravagance. The inimitable drollery and genial satire of Dickens are absent in Mrs. Stowe; but the tearful sentimentalism which exhibits itself in a kind of hysterical pathos they both have in common. The notion I had formed of the negroes from my first perusal of *Uncle Tom's Cabin* was that they were a kind of archangels in black, hounded, tortured, and abused by the fiendish whites on account of their moral superiority. It took me some time and cost me not a little money to correct this impression after my arrival in the United States. Though in all Mrs. Stowe's romances the tendency is perceptible, she has, as she grew older, abandoned much of her early extravagance, which was defensible enough in the cause of reform, and has steered closer and closer to the shores of reality. In *Oldtown Folks*, and particularly in the Sam Lawson sketches, she betrays a power of minute observation and an appreciation of local color which might almost entitle her to the name of a realist.

Another conspicuous representative of the school of Dickens is Bret Harte, who, however, in *Gabriel Conroy*, plays at ducks and drakes with probability in a way that would have given even Dickens a qualm.

It is the first chapter of *Bleak House* which contains the famous description of a London fog, worked up, as it appears to me, to a strained, tensely quivering pitch, when a single more wrench at the screw would snap the string. Where Dickens has fog everywhere, Bret Harte substitutes "snow everywhere," as the season demands, and proceeds to describe it, not with the same words, but in the same key as Dickens, with the same dithyrambic vehemence. The rhetorical cadence of the two passages is so strikingly similar that I cannot forbear to quote. Here is Dickens:

"Fog everywhere. Fog up the river, where it flows among green aits and meadows; fog down the river, where it rolls defiled among the tiers of shipping, and the waterside pollutions of a great and dirty city. Fog on the Essex Marshes, fog on the Kentish Heights. Fog creeping into the cabooses of collier brigs; fog lying out on the yards, and hovering in the rigging of great ships; fog drooping on the gunwales of barges and small boats," etc., etc.

Gabriel Conroy opens as follows:

"Snow everywhere as far as the eye could reach—fifty miles looking southward from the highest peak—filling ravines and gulches, and dropping from the walls of canons in white, shroud-like drifts, fashioning the dividing line into the likeness of a monstrous grave, hiding the bases of giant pines, completely covering young trees and larches, rimming with porcelain the bowl-like edges of still, cold lakes, undulating in motionless white billows to the edge of the distant horizon. Snow everywhere over the California Sierras on the 15th of March, 1884, and still falling."

The travelling earthquake and all the stage machinery of romantic melodrama, which Mr. Harte brings into action in *Gabriel Conroy* point, however, not to Dickens, but rather to Eugene Sue's *Wandering Jew*. The ancestry of his noble villains, the magnanimous gamblers with seraphic tenor voices, the chivalrous murderers, the generous strumpets, may be traced to that high-priest of romanticism, Victor Hugo, who delighted in the same sort of violent antitheses, defying probability and straining our credulity beyond endurance. The general attitude towards life, however lawless, exhibited in his early California tales, his disposition to find virtue in the vicious, to exalt the lowly at the expense, perhaps, of those who regard themselves as their superiors, shows the direct influence of the author of *Bleak House* and *The Christmas Carols*.

But Harte is, to my mind, the last American novelist of any eminence who can be classed as a romanticist. All our contemporary authors, with a few notable exceptions, such as Marion Crawford and Amélie Rives Chanler, deal frankly and honestly with American life, as they know it and see it; and though there are varying degrees in their power to grasp and vividly present what they see, I cannot think of one who does not aim to chronicle the particular phases of American life with which he is most intimately acquainted. While Mr. W. D. Howells (who in point of rank is *facile princeps*) preached his entertaining gospel of realism in the "Editor's Study" of *Harper's Monthly*, the critics (who as a rule are far behind the time) railed at him and professed to regard his postulate, that the novelist had to be true to the logic of life, as a piece of amusing eccentricity. He was, in their opinion, merely trying to justify his own practice. But in spite of all ridicule this proposition has, outside of England, come to be pretty generally accepted; and though the witty and genial Andrew Lang and that brilliant antediluvian, Robert Louis Stevenson, may be terribly shocked at his disrespect for Walter Scott, Mr. Howells has a valuable ally in what is called the spirit of the age, and he is bound in the end to prevail. For, as P. G. Hamerton happily puts it:

"The important service it [literature] renders to mankind is the *perpetual registering of the experiences of the race*. . . . Without a literature to record it, the experiences of dead generations could never be fully available for the living one."

Whether the majority of our contemporary novelists would subscribe to this view of their calling I do not know; but, whether they would or not, their practice sustains it. If we have an American Haggard or an American Stevenson among us, where is he? and what rank does he hold within the guild of letters? I am aware that Mr. Julian Hawthorne some years ago, entered into partnership with Inspector Byrnes and wrote some grewsome detective stories in the style of Gaboriau; and I have also seen recent tales of his in the *New York Ledger* which in blood-curdling horror rivalled *The Strange Case of Dr. Jekyl and Mr. Hyde*. But I cannot be persuaded to believe that either he or any one else regards them as serious contributions to literature. I do not question that Mr. Hawthorne is by conviction, as by inheritance, a romanticist; but there is a wide distance between the romanticism of *Bressant*, and *Beatrix Randolph* and that of *A Tragic Mystery* and *Section 558, or the Fatal Letter*.

If besides the versatile Amélie Rives we have another adherent of the defunct school among us, it is probably Mr. Harry Harland (Sydney Luska), whose first books, *As it is Written* and *Mrs. Peixada*, certainly dealt with abnormal and exceptional phases of life, and sometimes made heavy drafts upon our credulity. But if we are to judge from Mr. Harland's later works, he is rapidly shedding his romantic plumage and assuming his permanent colors among the serious chroniclers of contemporary life and manners. At all events, one will have to look very far for a more delightful bit of realism than *The Land of Love* (a study of life in the Latin Quarter in Paris); and as regards *Grandison Mather*, depicting the struggles of a young man of letters and his wife in New York, it is only less charming, but not less realistic. I have been told by those who are anxious to acquit a novelist of the charge of fidelity (they usually say "sordid fidelity") to the humdrum prose of life that Mr. Edgar Fawcett is a romancer. In order to convince myself on this point, and correct previous impressions which might prove to be erroneous, I recently re-read three or four of Mr. Fawcett's books; and I must confess that if he is to be judged by his best, I am not for a moment in doubt as to where he properly belongs. In his admirable novel, *An Ambitious Woman*, he has given a picture of New York life which in delicate veracity and vividness is as yet unsurpassed. Mr. Fawcett knows his New York (both its upper and its nether side) as does no other American novelist, unless it be Mr. H. C. Bunner; and if it were not for the breathless haste he displays in his prolific productivity he could scarcely fail to be recognized as the brilliant and faithful chronicler of metropolitan manner that he undoubtedly is. Take such a book as *The Evil That Men Do*, which no one can read without being impressed with the enormous amount of accurate local knowledge which it implies. I take it to be no mean achievement to have painted in such striking colors the physiognomy of lower New York—the Bowery, Great Jones Street, and all the labyrinthine tangle of malodorous streets and lanes, inhabited by the tribes of Israel, the swarthy Italian, the wily Chinaman, and all the other alien hordes from all the corners of the earth. The man who can do this, and whose impulse leads him to explore with so minute an interest that *terra incognita* of polite fiction, is, whatever his friends may say to the contrary, a realist. Let them judge him by *Rutherford* and *Salarion*. I shall still persist in judging him by *An Ambitious Woman* and *The Evil That Men Do*.

To Mr. Howells, more than to any one else are we indebted for the ultimate triumph of realism in American fiction. For that realism has triumphed or is triumphing no one will seriously deny who has kept track of American literature during the last quarter of a century. I do not mean by realism, of course, merely the practice of that extreme wing of the school which believes only that to be true which is disagreeable, and conscientiously omits all cheerful phenomena. Nor do I confine my definition to that minute insistence upon wearisome detail which, ignoring the relation of artistic values, fancies that a mere agglomeration of incontestable facts constitutes a truthful picture. Broadly speaking, a realist is a writer who adheres strictly to the logic of reality, as he sees it; who, aiming to portray the manners of his time, deals by preference with the normal rather than the exceptional phases of life, and, to use Henry James's felicitous phrase, arouses not the pleasure of surprise, but that of recognition. I would, therefore, include in my pantheon of realists George Eliot, Thackeray, Anthony Trollope, and Thomas Hardy; while I exclude Dickens, Wilkie Collins, Stevenson, and Haggard. I am aware that I am not in full agreement with Mr. Howells in this classification. In his recent book, *Criticism and Fiction*, he is disposed to draw the lines rather more narrowly. He puts not only Walter Scott and Dickens, but the genial biographer of Pendennis and Becky Sharp, into the outer darkness. It is, therefore, conceivable that he might also disagree with my classification of American authors, and label not only Marion Crawford and Amélie Rives, but G. W. Cable, Harold Frederic, and the late admirable Miss Woolson, with the opprobrious epithet "romantic." My space does not permit me to defend them here, but only to remark that they all have chronicled certain phases of American life with a brilliancy, delicacy, and truthfulness which no one will question. I admit that both Frederic and Miss Woolson have a lingering romantic strain which displays itself in fondness for murders; but their treatment of these sensational incidents is as realistic as that of Inspector Byrnes (in his official, not in his literary capacity). Murder in *Anne* is somehow divested of its sensational character by this insistence upon verisimilitude, which compels our credulity to keep pace with the author's invention.

Mr. Frederic has in *Seth's Brother's Wife* made the same concession to romanticism in a novel which, to those who know rural New York, is charged from beginning to end with an authenticity which enforces belief. This book, as well as *The Lawton Girl* (the scene of which is also a rural town in Central New York), has a closeness of texture and convincing quality hinting at ample stores of experience.

And this brings me to the main point of my argument. Nothing could testify with more force to the fact that we have outgrown romanticism than this almost unanimous desire, on the part of our authors, to chronicle the widely divergent phases of our American civilization. There are scarcely a dozen conspicuous States now which have not their own local novelist. Howells, T. B. Aldrich, Miss Jewett, and Miss Wilkins have described with the pictorial minuteness and delicacy of a Meissonier the life of New England in village, city, and country. New York follows not far behind with Julien Gordon, the vivid chronicler of our fashionable life, Frederic, Fawcett, W. H. Bishop (the author of *The Home of a Merchant Prince*), H. C. Bunner, Miss Woolson, and a dozen of minor lights. Creole Louisiana has found a most faithful and delightfully artistic biographer in G. W. Cable. Virginia boasts Thomas Nelson Page, Constance Cary Harrison, and I might add Amélie Rives Chanler, if it were not for the fact that her stories must just as well be located in the moon.

Georgia's biographer, than whom I know few with a vivider touch and a more masterly grasp of character, is Richard Malcolm Johnston, the author of the delightful *Dukesborough Tales*. Tennessee has suddenly raised her head among her sister States as an aspirant for literary glory since Miss Murfree (Charles Egbert Craddock) published her beautiful collection of tales, *In the Tennessee Mountains*. Through these and *The Despot of Broomsedge Cove*, *In the Clouds*, and *Where the Battle was Fought*, we have acquired a realizing sense of the distinctness of physiognomy which the neighbor of Kentucky presents to the world. What was hitherto a mere geographical conception, made up of some rather arbitrary lines on the map, has, through Miss Murfree's art, become an individuality, with a living countenance. For so great a service she surely deserves a monument. Of the throng of brilliant writers who have raised California to the pinnacle of a world-wide (though not quite enviable) renown, I have already mentioned Bret Harte; and Mark Twain, whose *Life on the Mississippi* and *Roughing It*, in spite of their occasional grotesqueness, are important documents of social history, has furnished the comic counterpart to Bret Harte's heroics. There are fully a dozen more who have followed in their wake; and only their number prevents me from mentioning them.

Pennsylvania and the Middle States have, so far, lagged behind in the literary movement, and are still awaiting their authentic biographers. If Edward Eggleston had not abandoned Indiana, after his promising debut with his *Hoosier Schoolmaster, Roxy*, etc., he might have claimed the same identification with her name as Cable and R. M. Johnston with their respective States. But in his latest novel, *The Faith Doctor*, he has moved to New York, and left James Whitcomb Riley in full possession. For Riley is a Hoosier to the backbone; and though he is primarily a poet, he possesses, in prose as in verse, the vitalizing touch of genius, which stamps everything that he produces with a vivid individuality. Illinois,[1] as far as I know, has as yet no novelist who is peculiarly her own; and Ohio, Kansas, and all the stripling States that stretch away to the Pacific have perhaps failed to display as yet a sufficiently distinct type to have need of a biographer. For all that, a "prairie State" furnished the scene of that remarkable novel, *The Story of a Country Town*, by E. W. Howe; and Hamlin Garland (the most vigorous realist in America) has caught the very soul of that youthful virgin, Dakota, and held up to her a mirror of most uncompromising veracity.

The "Philadelphia flavor," which I am told is something very fine and very distinct, has hitherto scorned to put itself on record in literature; but recently Mr. Thomas Janvier captured it, as it were, on the wing, and wafted it into the nostrils of an expectant and appreciative world. Mr. Janvier possesses the distinction of being, up to date, the only American novelist who can boast such an achievement; though I seem to remember that a thin ghost of Philadelphia pervaded a short story which appeared in the *Century*, many years ago, by Miss Sprague, the author of *An Earnest Trifler*. I am also aware that the late Bayard Taylor was a Pennsylvanian, and that he wrote several novels (*Hannah Thurston, The Story of Kennett*, etc.), descriptive of the life of his native State; but he forsook his career as a novelist at too early a date to accomplish the task which once must have attracted him, and for which he had a most admirable equipment. His ballads "Jane Reed" and "The Old Pennsylvania Farmer" show what an exquisitely sympathetic biographer the Quaker lost in him.

It is because the American novel has chosen to abandon "the spirit of romance," which never was indigenous on this continent, and devoted itself to the serious task of studying and chronicling our own social conditions, that it is to-day commanding the attention of the civilized world. It is because Realism has ousted or is ousting Romanticism from all its strongholds that we have a literature worthy of serious consideration, and growing every year more virile, independent, and significant.

NOTE

1. Since the above was written a promising Illinois novelist, of realistic tendencies, has appeared in the person of Henry B. Fuller of Chicago, the author of *The Cliff Dwellers*.

TWELVE

PRODUCTIVE CONDITIONS OF AMERICAN LITERATURE

Hamlin Garland

Hamlin Garland (1860–1940) burst upon the literary scene in the early 1890s as a radical voice from the Midwest preaching the doctrines of local sovereignty in literary expression, Henry George's single tax in economic policy, and the People's Party (or Populism) in political matters. Soon after reaching Boston in 1884 by way of Iowa, Wisconsin, and South Dakota, Garland became a major defender of Howells's fiction and critical beliefs. During these years of intense productivity and social and literary activism, from approximately the mid-1880s to the mid-1890s, Garland wrote in a variety of forms, including drama, poetry, fiction, and polemic essays on literary and social issues. His most noteworthy work of this period includes the collection of short stories *Main-Travelled Roads* (1891), the essay collection *Crumbling Idols* (1894), and the novel *Rose of Dutcher's Coolly* (1895). Garland's essay "Productive Conditions of American Literature" conveniently summarizes the salient ideas of *Crumbling Idols*.

American literature must be faithful to American conditions. Granting the variations in the personal comment of each artist, the output must be in its general character creative, not imitative. It should rise out of our conditions as naturally as the corn grows. It must be distinctly and unmistakably American. This is a fundamental characteristic of the American realist (or veritist)—there are others which separate him more or less widely from the romanticist and idealist. I use the word "veritist" be-

Forum 17 (August 1894): 690–98.

cause "realism" has been indiscriminately applied to everything from a tract on Christian Science down to a tank drama. I ask indulgence for the word; there is no other which expresses my meaning in dealing with the new literary method.

The meaning of the word "realism" varies with the outlook of every person who uses it. Mr. Howells calls it "the truthful treatment of material." Véron states it to be the realistic imitation of actual things. Verestchagin advises the young artist to bring every event into harmony with the time, place, and light selected. Valdés advises the artist to treat of the thing he loves and it will no longer be prosaic or dull. My own conception is that realism (or veritism) is the truthful statement of an individual impression corrected by reference to the fact.

The difference between the veritist and the romanticist is expressed, first, by choice of subject. The veritist chooses for his subject not the impossible, not even the possible, but always the probable. He does not seek the exceptional, the sensational; he *naturally* finds the probable more interesting than the impossible. Certainly he does not choose it because it pays better, for it does not. The larger portion of the public is composed of grown-up children, and tales of blood and intrigue please them much better than stories of the probable and the wholesome. Mr. Rider Haggard's books sell better than Miss Wilkins's. Thus the poor veritist is too often a martyr to his care for probabilities.

He sees Mr. Marion Crawford and Mr. Conan Doyle winning loud applause and much money by easy-going tales of love and war, the while his unexciting stories of normal human life find only an occasional reader. This is in the nature of things. The new art, the modern statement, must make its way against the traditional. It is like making a new road in the forest. To rouse passion is an easy trick; to produce intellectual emotion is an art. Even to read an original novel requires brains. The veritist chooses a modern theme necessarily. His love of life and his distaste for imitation prevent him from "novelizing" history in the manner of the school of historical novelists, and keeps him from the worn-out themes of the Middle Ages. He feels entirely willing that other men should write "The Iron Mask" and "The Glittering Glaive." To him such work is a waste of time.

The veritist chooses a native story, a near-by theme, and he deals with probable characters. They live,—his men and women; you can find them at home if you call. Having chosen probable characters he does not put them through impossible paces. He does not distort their lives. He respects the characters of his story as if they were personages in life. He cannot shove them about, nor marry them, nor kill them. What they do, they do by their own will or through nature's arrangement. Their very names come by some singular attraction. The veritist cannot name his characters arbitrarily. He cannot call them "Maud St. Ayr" or "Hubert De Montford." They are sometimes named "Maud Jones" or "Percy B. Wilson,"—the corrective influence of fact is shown in the surname. There is more of the whole question in this matter of names than one would think.

The veritist loves his characters not because they do, but because they are; not because they are heroes and heroines, but because they are men and women. The veritist has wearied of gods and heroes; he wants men. He has wearied of maidens who are willowy of form and star-eyed. He has wearied of the constant appeal to the sensual which the tricky novelist knows is organic in every man and woman. He therefore takes an interest in plain women of character. He tells of middle-aged people. He seeks not mere beauty, but beauty and significance. This led Octave Thanet to write of "Whitsun Harp," and Joseph Kirkland of "Zury." They did this, not out of theory, but because they found more to interest, more to depict, in such lives.

A mere love-story has become the most hackneyed theme in the world. Miss Wilkins writes mainly of old people and themes of filial or fraternal love. James Whitcomb Riley put the same themes in verse. In choosing these, they undoubtedly sacrifice a certain kind of success. The easiest way to succeed in a monetary way is by the delineation of the erotic in the life of youth. Nothing is easier than the excitation of men and women by tales of love and war. It lacks distinction, however, and the veritist finds himself naturally averse to running in such well-worn ruts. He prefers to treat of other affections and interests—as, for example, where Henry James writes the story of a boy-pupil, or Herman Chaplin studies of "Eli."

The veritist sees the individual rather than the type. If the individual chances to be a widely recognized type, well and good—but the individual comes first. Nothing is permitted to overshadow character. The question is not so much, What did they do? as, What did they think? With a background which he loves, and characters which he knows, the veritist begins to write, not in another's way, but in his own way, corrected by reference to life. To allow the fantastic, or the improbable, or the impossible to come in, would destroy the unity of his story. It would be untrue, and would be unjust to his characters, for the action springs from them, and is controlled by them or by social forces around them. The introduction of a sensual or bloody incident into "Silas Lapham" would be monstrous—impossible.

The veritist has wearied of the expected also. He does not contrive to have things come out all right in the end to satisfy some sentimentalist who wants "him" to always marry "her." He cannot provide such endings in opposition to the logic of all that has gone before. If the drift of the action is in a certain direction, it can be changed only by the will of the character or by the working of characters upon social environment.

Neither does he enjoy the fortuitous. The chance thing, the curious coincidence, has small value to the veritist. To him the sunny, the regular, the normal is miraculous. He studies stars, not comets. The spy who is condemned to death is *not* a son of the general, nor a nephew,—not even a son of an old classmate; he is a stranger. This lessens the agony, but raises the novelist's art. In the drama the hero does not rush in at the last moment and bid the villain "stand back." The son and husband who goes off to the war, and whom everybody supposes to be dead, continues to be dead, notwithstanding the need of him at home. The old curmudgeon who holds the mortgage has not the slightest desire to possess the widow—he wants the interest. In this novel the hero does not hear of the heroine's danger; the will stays lost, and the wife marries again, and her step-children get on peaceably with her.

All this because the veritist does not constantly ask himself: "Will this create an effect?" or "Could this happen?"—but asks himself, "*Would* this happen?" He does not say it never happens that the spy looks like the general's classmate, or that the will turns up; he merely knows that it is not probable. In short, life goes on in this novel as under the sun and in the open air. The central figures do not necessarily marry or die at the end of the book—they walk on over the hill. I am quite willing to grant that this is distressing to certain minds, but the writers of such stories are not writing to please or to distress romantically inclined readers, but to satisfy their own ideas of art. That is to say, the veritist forms his novel upon life, not upon some other man's book; not even upon his own caprice, but upon his personal impression of the fact.

It is not true to say that there is no imagination involved. Imagination is generally taken to mean the creation of weird, unnatural, impossible, or pathologic situations. The people who use the word thus are mistaken in their psychology. These are merely the more hackneyed forms of the imagination. Imagination is not a thing possessed only by an occasional morbid writer of sensational fiction. It is a faculty possessed by the bridge-builder, the inventor, the business man, often in far higher degree. To imagine vice and crime and salacious incidents is not to my mind a very high exercise of the imagination. The imagination involved in the writing of truthful novels is just as certainly creative as that used in the "Lone Horseman" or in "Dr. Jekyll and Mr. Hyde." It is a little saner and more wholesome; that is all. That it is not photography or flat reporting can be proved by this fact: the critic cannot distinguish between the entirely fictitious characters of the veritistic novel and the characters drawn from life. The critic is challenged to point out in "A Modern Instance" the characters "photographed" from life.

We are now to consider the objection so often raised that the veritist is a gloomy and depressing writer. The romanticist, notwithstanding his themes of blood and lust and tears, is supposed to be a wholesome and inspiring creature. He can slay men in war, and imprison maidens in donjon keeps, and hound poor peasants to death, and yet be called a joyous and lovely teacher of the splendor and glory of life. Miss Repplier is fond of celebrating such books. Mr. Haggard, Mr. Doyle, Mr. Weyman, and Mr. Crawford act upon this theory. Because the romancer puts his scene afar off and clothes his assassin in scarlet-and-green doublet and in gold-inlaid steel, it is all beautiful and moral and inspiring for our sons and daughters to read! He may reflect for the thousandth time the heartless cruelty and injustice of the Middle Ages; he may perpetuate sordid and lustful views of life; he may celebrate the ideals of feudalism, and repeat age-worn slanders against women,—and yet be considered excellent food for American youth! But the man who stands for individuality and freedom; who puts woman on an equality with man, making her a human being; who stands for a pure man as well as a pure woman; who stands for an altruistic and free state where involuntary poverty does not exist; who teaches the danger and degradation of lust and greed, and who inculcates a love for all who live, teaching justice and equal rights,—this novelist is depressing in his effect upon his readers!

The absurdity involved in this needs no exegesis. It will appear in the mere statement. As a matter of fact the "romance" dulls thought. It is a lie that lulls the conscience to sleep. The novel or drama of life stings, arouses, fires with exultant and awakened humanitarian religion. To one the reader goes to dream, to sensuously enjoy; from the other, the reader rises with broader sympathy, with more complete knowledge, better fitted to think and act in the interest of truth and freedom.

In advocating veritism I am not to be understood as apologizing for the so-called French realists. In fact they are not realists from my point of view. They seem to me to be sex-mad. I do not believe they are true to the men and women who make up the great body of citizens in France. I believe the average man or woman in France is sane and wholesome. I know this is true in America. They may be rough and sordid, and grim with a life of toil, but as a rule Americans are not sex-maniacs. No nation can endure and transact business whose citizens are as depraved as those set forth by Zola or his feeble imitators here in America. Even were his books true of the French, it would not justify a vile imitation of them on this side of the ocean. To imitate a grace is weakness; to imitate a vice is criminal. Veritism shuts out those novelists who think that only crime is real and only vice interesting. It does not include dramas which deal with diseased persons. Zola is a great writer, a terrible satirist: he is not what I mean by "veritist."

It will be seen that the work of the veritist is most difficult. He sets himself a most arduous task. His art consists in making others feel his individual and distinctive comment on the life around him. He cannot allow mere incident to cover up lack of characterization. He cannot fly to rape and arson to keep up the interest of his readers. He relies upon the power and variety and dignity of truth. He has faith in the physiology rather than in the pathology in human life. It requires more insight and more creative intelligence to write twenty successful novels—as Mr. Howells has done—without a single crime or unnatural vice in any of them, than to write a score of romances made up of murder, adultery, suicide, manslaughter, and all the other indispensable elements of the present-day romance. To write "A New England Nun," or "The Grandissimes," or "The Cliff-Dwellers," requires something better than mechanics and situations. To write "Shore Acres" requires a conscience, a human sympathy, and the power to individualize. To write the ordinary melodrama requires only scissors and the carpenter's hammer.

There is one characteristic which I believe marks the difference between the veritist and all romancers or idealists. The veritist loves actual life; the romancers shrink from it as if from cold water. The veritist loves realities, is moved and exalted by them. He fights greed and depravity face to face. He discerns nobility among his street companions. He laughs with them, not at them. He feels the waves of life beat upon him, and is moved and nerved as if by the dash of ocean spray. He loves the sun and air. He sees the drama of street and market-place. He finds significance and beauty in the things near at hand. He feels no need of "escaping from life."

The romanticist is the opposite of all this, however. As he approaches the idealist, he places great stress on the beautiful. The castle is more interesting than the railway station. He loves subdued lights and retired places. His characters move in a mist of sentiment. He does not enjoy close contact with life. The smell of workmen disgusts him. Business men, and keen, sensible women, alarm him or annoy him. He withdraws into a world of dead people who will keep their distance and nod when he pulls the string. He charters a vessel and goes round the world in search of a motive.

When he uses the near-at-hand he distorts and exaggerates it and lights it up with red fire. He lacks repose. He troubles himself much about effect. He organizes ordeals and puts his characters through triumphantly in the face of enormous odds. His story comes out right, finishes, "rounds up," not because it would do so in life, but because it does not do so in life. He treats of people who are not his neighbors, because he does not like common people in real life and of course could not like them better in books. (In this he is essentially aristocratic and lacking in sympathy and insight, from the veritist's point of view.) The brave youth always succeeds; the pure girl secures the approbation of heaven; the immoral are miraculously changed by the power of some good woman. The drunkard keeps his pledge; the villain dies endowing an orphan asylum—all contrary to life as a matter of common observation. This does not disturb the idealist romancer. "It is not true to life," cries the veritist. "No, but it *ought* to be," calmly replies the idealist.

I am not crying out against this. On the contrary I hope it will continue, at least so long as it is a sincere expression of a certain outlook on life. When it is mere effectism I desire to see it fail and die. These qualifications and descriptions do not all apply to any one writer, but only in part. The romancer is really of all shades and grades. At one extreme he deals in melodrama, at his simplest he approaches the veritist. Often the veritist lapses into the romanticist or idealist momentarily.

It all comes down to a matter of temperament. Certain minds find greater value in realities than others. One mind loves and values the near-at-hand; another finds only the blue distance enchanting. I have no war with any sincere artist, but I despise imitation and effectism. No great art ever rose or ever can rise that is based upon imitation or that sacrifices truth for effect. The romanticist as well as every other artist should ask himself whether he is working to please some cult—some reader. To write in imitation of Zola is as fatal to real utterance as to write in imitation of Scott. Veritism imagines in the image of life. Idealism imagines in the image of some ideal, which is generally of the past. It is not always conventional, not always of the past, but it is apt to be so in form if not in spirit. To create in the image of life is the only road to never-ending art. That means progress, and forever progress. To create in the image of models is to take a road which leads in a circle that never rises but always descends. To create in the image of an ideal, ignoring the earth, is like painting the clouds without landscape.

To recapitulate a little: In the Novel, veritism demands simplicity, genuineness, wholesomeness, perfect truth to the conditions of American life, and unity of effect. It demands significance as well as beauty, and a bold, unshrinking contact with life, but it gives the latitude of personal impression of the fact. It has produced such diverse novelists as Mr. Howells, Mr. James, Miss Wilkins, Miss French ("Octave Thanet"), Mr. Harold Frederic, the late Mr. Joseph Kirkland, Miss Murfree, Mr. Cable, and many more. It is true that some of these writers have their romantic moments; it is true that some of them decline to be classed as veritists. Such things do not disturb the critic. Seeing that their work is based upon truth to certain localities and conditions, and allowing for all extravagances, they certainly represent those localities and conditions with sufficient faithfulness to be classed as veritists.

In Poetry it leads to freedom of form—that is, to a closer approach to the passionate speech of modern men. It leads to disuse of conventional words and phrases and hackneyed themes. It modifies the classic and fixed forms. Whitman stood for one phase of it, Sidney Lanier for another, James Whitcomb Riley for still another. Whitman was a powerful iconoclast and teacher of freedom. Lanier enlarged and modified the ancient forms which Whitman threw away. Riley is striving after the actual emotional utterances of the people. These poets only prophesy change; they do not complete a cycle; let that be stated again.

In Sculpture, veritism demands freedom from the abstract. It demands a return to the same source from which all true art has sprung—study of actual life. It will lead to the delineation of the habits, amusements, characters of modern life. Whatever the sculptor loves and desires to embody in stone or bronze—that thing is suitable. In this way will original work be done and imitation die out. No great sculpture will come till it comes out of spontaneous effort. The sculptor who chisels a nude figure with the right leg advanced and calls it "Charity," and another similar figure with the left foot advanced and calls it "Faith," is not American, and his work is not art. Better "The Checker-Players" of John Rogers, for that is measurably true—has humor and life in it. The work of a man like Edward Kemys, once a hunter and trapper, now a great sculptor of wild animals, shows the real development. Lanceray's groups in bronze show the marvellous inclusiveness of the word "sculptor," once we are free from conventional adherence to the nude and to the ideal.

In the Drama, veritism demands the abolition of formal plot, of set villains, of asides and soliloquies. It advances the study of human life. It widens the dramatic vocabulary. It relates action on the stage to action in life. It leads to the use of the probable and the wholesome, as in the novel. It discards the abnormal, the exceptional, the diseased, the criminal, in order to deal with the affairs of normal human life, making the drama co-extensive with the novel in the scope of its possible themes. In this connection the dramas of Mr. Herne and Mr. Thomas have significance. Mr. Herne has discarded the soliloquy, the aside, the fixed complication, and the villainous villain. Mr. Thomas, Mr. Matthews, Mr. Fitch, and Mr. Barnard are attempting simple scenes of American life. "Shore Acres" and "In Mizzoura" announce an American drama. They will encourage still more faithful and sympathetic studies of American life.

Finally veritism, as I see it, does not enslave, it sets free. It does not even say, "Idealize life—seek out the beautiful." It places the artist alone before life and says: "You are alone with the fact and your literary conscience. Your product is your own—or should be. It should be your individual comment upon life. Be yourself. Do not cringe or prostrate yourself; above all, do not imitate. As a creative mind, the great masters of the past have nothing for you. There is nothing for you to do but ignore them, as they ignored the masters who came before their time. All that Shakespeare or Goethe knew of humanity, you may know; not through them, not at second or third hand, but through a study of present life—by contact with men and women and with physical nature."

Every creative artist in the past, small or great, created in the image of life as he knew it and loved it. Shakespeare wrote great plays by studying life, not by studying Shakespeare. Were he living to-day he would be writing novels and dramas of living men and women, not imitations of the dramas of feudalism. The only justification for an American writer, painter, or sculptor is that he add something to the literature or other art of the world. To imitate, to shirk, to write for mere gain or to satisfy vanity, will not add a lasting word to any art. The American artist must grow out of American conditions and reflect them without deprecatory shrug or spoken apology. He may not always keep himself on the highest level, but it should be his constant care to be faithful to the fact in the light of his literary conscience. In this way he will at least escape imitation, and he may speak a new work about the soul or catch a new light breaking amid the reeds of the river bank.

THIRTEEN

THE NEW STORY-TELLERS AND THE DOOM OF REALISM

William Roscoe Thayer

William Roscoe Thayer (1859–1923) was closely associated with Boston and Harvard for his entire life. Born in
Boston, he was educated at Harvard and served the university in various capacities for the remainder of his career,
principally as editor of the *Harvard Graduates' Magazine*
from 1892 to 1915. A major historian of Italian life as well
as a biographer of American political figures, Thayer was
president of the American Historical Association during
1918–19.

Eight years ago, in writing on "Realism in Literature," I called attention to the then
recently printed essays of M. Emile de Vogüé. That excellent critic, who has since
been admitted to the French Academy, had in the essays referred to pointed out indications that realistic fiction—at least in France—was fast nearing the high-water
mark, and he confidently expected that the turn in the tide would be followed by
fiction of a purer, different sort. Only eight years have elapsed, yet no one can doubt
that, so far as Realism is concerned, M. de Vogüé was a far-seeing observer. M. Zola,
the arch-priest of the obscene rites of French Realism, has ceased to have any formative influence on French novelists; he has ceased to be called "maître," or to be imitated by disciples; his own books are still widely read, for obvious reasons, among
which his talent as an advertiser is not the least; but they beget no warfare among
critics and their power as literary epoch-makers has vanished. Even the stories of Guy
de Maupassant, the Realist who presented his delicately-wrought immoralities to you
with silver tongs, instead of Zola's coal-shovel, we were told the other day by another

Forum 18 (December 1894): 470–80.

watcher of French literature, have lost their vogue: and yet Maupassant is but two years dead.

I refer first to France because France is still the initiator of novelties, whether in politics, literature, or millinery; and when she does not originate she is usually the first to give world-currency to what other have initiated. But the symptoms observed in France have been widespread, and the change they betoken is working most healthily in England and America. We violate no confidences in declaring that Realism in fiction is passing away. Eight years ago the "Realists"—who ought rather to be called the "Epidermists"—had the cry; to-day you have only to look at the publishers' announcements, or at the volumes in everybody's hand, to see what fiction is popular. Caine, Doyle, Zangwill, Weyman, Crockett, Du Maurier,—not Realists but Romanticists, not analysts but story-tellers,—are writing the novels which the multitude are sitting up late to read. And Stevenson and Crawford, whose reputation dates from the very heyday of Realism, have certainly not lost popularity during the past decade, while—worse and worse!—two separate popular editions of Scott, and new translations of Dumas *père*, have just come out, in spite of the assertions of the Epidermists that not even schoolboys could now be coaxed to read Sir Walter. Above all, Rudyard Kipling, who was so recently characterized by Mr. Howells as merely a young man with his hat cocked over one eye, holds the entire English-speaking world in fee as no other story-teller since Dickens has held it.

Now this change deserves attention, even from those of us who read very little current fiction, but who realize how important a symptom is the popular demand for it. To follow the statistics of the circulation of novels may lead to conclusions not less significant than do the statistics of the annual consumption of malt and fermented liquors. If you found, for instance, that the nation had in the course of ten years given up whiskey and taken to beer, you might be able to demonstrate the close relation between strong drink and crime; and so we may be sure that the change in taste which has led the public back to romantic fiction has for its basis something deeper than caprice. It is too soon to say how deep the meaning really is, or what may come of it, but it is not too soon to look back over the losing fight of Realism and to specify some of its traits.

In the first place, the tide turned much earlier than most of us expected. Ten years ago few of us dared hope that the exposure of Zola's plausible fallacy would so soon be generally agreed to. He had been captivated by the eminent physiologist, Claude Bernard, who found medicine an art and left it a science, and reasoning from analogy, he had concluded that fiction might be subjected to a similar evolution. Observation and experiment, these were the two methods by which the "experimental novelist," subsequently miscalled "Realist," should produce his work. We all know with what vigor and plausibility Zola set forth this doctrine, which had all the more attractiveness in that it seemed to tally with the scientific spirit of the age. Everything was tinctured with science; the very word "scientific" had become a shibboleth: we had "scientific" clothespins, "scientific" liverpads,—why not "scientific" novels?

And in due time "scientific" novels came,—"Nana," "L'Assommoir," and the rest; but I suspect that Zola's literary philosophy would have achieved notoriety much more slowly had he not chosen topics either brutally obscene or horrible, which at once excited the jaded Parisian palate. And as the author of these works proclaimed that he was personally as impartial towards virtue and vice as a chemist is towards acids and alkalies, and that he did not make it his business to correct nature, but simply to photograph her, his aim being scientific truth, many persons read his abominations who could not have been induced to do so but for the seductive catchword "scientific." Many others read, and still read, Zola, regardless of any literary theory to gratify their pornographic appetite; for it required no keenness to perceive that decency, modesty, sanctity,—conceptions which after many painful centuries, the more civilized minority of the human race has begun to venerate,—could not protect themselves against the brazen presumptions of Realism. Zola and his fellows, at home and abroad, tore the veil away with an affectation of scientific impartiality even more repulsive than the downright prurience of the avowed worshippers of lubricity. Strenuously have they protested that their goddess is the naked Truth, but we may well ask, as we look at the product of their school, whether it has not been the nakedness rather than the divinity of Truth which has attracted them.

When realism had thus assumed the proportion of a literary movement, the historians of literature went back to discover M. Zola's precursors. They traced, with what accuracy I know not, the roots of Realism down through Flaubert and Balzac to Stendhal. The disciples of the new school had no scruple in asserting that it was not only the school of the present and future, but that it would utterly supersede previous literature; its novels were to all previous novels as modern invention to old-fashioned handiwork. It would soon make even school-girls ashamed to admit that they enjoyed romances. Poetry, of course, could no more exist in its presence than frost before a blow-pipe. "There shall never be any more plots," was one of the edicts of the new law-givers. Not since the memorable conflict of the Romanticists and the Classicists had so pretentious a movement been seen; a movement, moreover, which affected, or tended to affect, not merely the writing of novels and all imaginative literature, but also our established views of morals.

I fear that we must confess that this Realistic movement has been, on the whole, less memorable than we should have predicted of a revolution which boldly took upon itself the task of creating a new heaven and a new earth. It has certainly been less spectacular, amusing, and attractive than the Romantic movement which culminated sixty-five years ago. Victor Hugo led that, as Zola has led this. Hugo was very human, and abounded in qualities which drew enthusiastic disciples round him. We cannot think of Zola as a man whom anybody can love; we think of him as a coldly calculating doctrinaire, a chemist who has invented a process for making top-dressing cheap and has the shrewdness to sell it at an enormous profit. In France, the quarrel has been rather *banal*, not enlivened by any such scenes as those which signalized the triumph of Hugo's supporters at the production of "Hernani."

In America, however, the warfare has not failed to amuse us, thanks to the wit of Mr. Howells. Yet even his wit has lacked the picturesqueness of Théophile Gautier's famous flaming waistcoat, which glows upon us from the records of the warfare of Romanticism. At the outset, however, Mr. Howells gave promise of being both picturesque and lively. We all remember how, after his first naïf declaration that the art of fiction as practised by Mr. Henry James and himself is a finer art than that of Dickens, Thackeray, and George Eliot, a burst of genial laughter swept over the continent and re-echoed even in England. Mr. Howells did not directly name himself, of course, but the implication was not to be escaped. The public laughed because it thought it had caught a man-of-the-world—one, moreover, who had been publishing books for a quarter of a century—in a perfectly indiscreet bit of egotism. The fact is, however, that Mr. Howells told the plain truth,—the art of fiction as practised by him and Mr. James is a finer art than that of Dickens or Thackeray, just as the art of the cameoist is "finer" than that of the sculptor.

Mr. Howells, being thoroughly in earnest, probably did not mind the laughter. At any rate no convert from one religion to another could be more zealous than he was during five or six years. He bore witness to his faith by example not less than by precept; and as he had the good fortune to be able to use as mouthpiece a magazine with a very large circulation, he spread the gospel of Realism in a brief time before multitudes who are usually slow to feel the direction of literary currents. Whatever opinion readers might have had of the novel by Mr. Howells in the earlier part of the magazine, they were sure to be informed in a crisp, satirical essay farther on that only fools and old fogies tolerated fiction produced by other than Realistic methods.

A propagandist as witty, resourceful, and assured as he, has not for so many years together and from so conspicuous a pulpit preached any literary gospel, good or bad, in America; and there were many of us who, while we read very little of his novels, never missed one of his monthly essays. They were significant, if only as symptoms; and then, perhaps the doctrine they uttered might be true. At any rate, it was very wholesome, if somewhat bewildering, at the start, to have our venerable idols challenged, and to receive from the lips of an evangelist the message which was to revolutionize literature, casting out its false gods, dethroning its arrogant sovereigns, levelling its exclusive aristocracies, and establishing a Simon-pure democracy which should be run forever on scientific principles. It took fortitude, until custom made us callous, to watch Mr. Howells, like another Tarquin, go up and down the poppy-field of literature, lopping off head after head which had brought delight to millions. The Greeks, of course, were smitten very early: they are always the first to excite the righteous rage of all sorts of reformers, and have been demolished so many times! Artistic principles—symmetry, grace, condensation, beauty—went next: Realism, we perceived, knew not beauty, and despised literary neatness as your true son of the soil is supposed to despise those who indulge in soap and water. Poetry, too, had its death-warrant signed. Even Shakespeare was not spared. At his martyrdom, we knew that genius too must go, and soon the dictum came that "there is no such thing as genius," that what the unscientific foreworld called by that name is only a strong congenital predisposition *plus* indefatigable perseverance.

Incidentally we learned the tenets of Realism, and month by month we were introduced to Spanish and Russian masters of the new creed. A little later than some of us, but earlier than the masses, Mr. Howells discovered Tolstoi, and then we knew why the Greeks and art and Shakespeare had been previously swept away. For the great

Russian, though he be in many aspects a master, has certainly no inkling of the Greek conception of art, no spark of Shakespeare's dramatic intensity. The Greek made his effects by selection, Tolstoi makes his by cumulation; the Greek's motto was, "Nothing superfluous"; Tolstoi's is, "Put in everything, and then add a little more." If you think of Russia as a vast flat prairie land, in which even a tree or hillock is an important feature, you may be reminded of Tolstoi; if you remember Greece, with its infinite variety of chiselled mountains and valleys, its individual headlands, its islands and lovely bays, with a luminous sky above and beautiful color on all below, you have, in contrast with him, the Greek. No Greek could so have sinned against his instinct for symmetry as to write "War and Peace," a story, or congeries of stories, stretching through twenty-five hundred pages—the equivalent in space of fifty "Antigones" and of seven or eight Iliads. The Iliad is getting well on in years, and yet, if there existed a company for insuring the lives of literary works, some of us think that the Iliad would prove a better risk than "War and Peace": for one good reason, it is only one eighth as bulky as the Russian masterpiece; and bulk is an element which will count more and more in the longevity of books.

I pause at Tolstoi, because Mr. Howells assured us that his works not only form the culminating glory of Realism, but practically render obsolete all other works not produced by that system. So we accepted the reign of Czar Lyoff, although for a while, after the immolation of Shakespeare and the great companions of our youth, the world seemed empty, lonesome. It was as if the sun had been stolen, and the thief had hung-up a locomotive headlight in its stead. But, on closer examination of Tolstoi, we were surprised to find that he wrote almost always with a strong moral purpose; and this, we had been so often assured, was one of the foul practices of the old school of novelists which Realism would abolish. For, to the genuine Realist, virtue and vice are what acids and alkalies are to the chemist: therefore, he cannot prefer, cannot have, an ethical purpose.

Reading Mr. Howells's preachments month by month, while we could but admire his versatility in iconoclasm, and his unquestioning zeal,—he swallowed Tolstoi's "Kreutzer Sonata" and Zola's "La Terre," and smacked his lips, bidding us all do likewise,—we saw that we had to do with a very clever disciple and not at all with a master. As certainly as Mr. Howells is a more graceful and clever writer than M. Zola, so certainly is M. Zola profounder and more philosophical than Mr. Howells. The Frenchman had, indeed, thought out and formulated his system, and his essays in "Le roman expérimental" remain the chief document of the theory of Realism. Them, the serious student of literary and spiritual movements may consult, but Mr. Howells's critical writings take on more and more the aspect of being merely the register of the vagaries of a mind alert rather than cultured, and of a generous spirit which cannot resist becoming the champion of crude causes. Not impossibly, therefore, these writings of his will be valued less and less as orthodox Realistic tracts, and more and more as data for studying the psychological development of an interesting personality.

Nevertheless, Mr. Howells had the satisfaction, for the time being, of making Realism the chief topic of discussion, and of encouraging the belief in innumerable crude minds that you have only to report word for word the morning gossip of idle women on a summer hotel piazza, or the rusticities in wit and grammar of the patrons of the corner grocery, in order to produce a work beside which Shakespeare's pages look faded. Perhaps no higher compliment can be paid to Mr. Howells than to state that those who undertake to write about Realism in America will inevitably find themselves dealing with it as though it were his private property, instead of with the doctrines and assertions of a system. And yet for a dozen years a horde of Realists, great and small, have been filling the magazines with their products and turning out an average of two novels a day.

And now Realism—a movement which, but for the deep matters it involves, we might call a fad—is on the wane. It has been the logical outcome of our age, whose characteristic is analysis. Our modern science, abandoning the search for the Absolute, has been scrutinizing every atom, to weigh and name it, and to discover its relations with its neighbors. "Relativity" has been the watchword. Science literally knows neither great nor small: it examines the microbe and Sirius with equal interest; it draws no distinction between beauty and ugliness—having no preference for the toadstool or the rose, the sculpin or the trout: it is impartial; it seeks only to know. By observation and experiment, by advancing from the known to the unknown, science has begun to make the first accurate inventory of the substance, laws, and properties of the world of matter. Its achievements have already been stupendous. Its methods have dominated all the other works in our time; it was inevitable that they should encroach on the sphere of art and of literature.

Arguing from analogy, the Realist persuaded himself that the only means for attaining perfect accuracy in fiction must be experiment and observation, which had brought such rich returns to Science. He disdained anything except an exact reproduction of real life—hence his name, Realist. To him, as to the man of science, there should be, he declared, neither beauty nor ugliness, great nor small, goodness nor evil; he was impartial; he eliminated the personal equation; he would make his mind as unprejudiced as a photographic plate. To Pyrrhonism so thoroughgoing, considerations of interest and charm appealed no more than did considerations of morals or of beauty. The Realist frankly announced that the precise record of the humblest mind was just as important as one of Shakespeare's mind would be. So we have been regaled by our English and American Realists with interminable inspection and introspection of commonplace intellects; and if we have yawned, we have been told that we were still poisoned with Romanticism, and still had a childish desire to read about persons with high titles, moving in the upper circles. Realism, we were assured, was the application of democratic principles to fiction. When, on the other hand, the foreign Realists dealt chiefly in moral filth, we were children for our squeamishness, and informed that, since depravity exists, the Realist is in duty bound to make impartial studies of it.

I need not point out that such doctrines reduce literature, art, and morals to anarchy. The "scientific method," applied in this way, is not the method for portraying human nature. Only the human can understand, and consequently interpret, the human: how, therefore, shall a man who boasts that he has *dehumanized* himself so that his mind is as impartial as a photographic plate, enabling him to look on his fellow-beings without preferring the good to the bad, the beautiful to the ugly,—how shall he be qualified to speak for the race which does discriminate, does prefer, does feel? The camera sees only the outside; the Realist sees no more, and so it would be more appropriate to call him "Epidermist," one who investigates only the surface, the cuticle of life,—usually with a preference for very dirty skin.

And, in truth, he deceives himself as to the extent of his scientific impartiality. He, too, has to select; he cannot set down every trivial thought, cannot measure every freckle. His work is fiction—a consideration which he had forgotten. But since he is forced to select, he cannot escape being judged by the same canons as all other artists. Do they not all aim at representing life? Is *Silas Lapham*, produced by Epidermist methods, more real than *Shylock* or *Hamlet*? Will he be thought so three hundred years hence, or will he seem odd and antiquated, a mere fashion, like the cut of old garments? Only the human can understand and interpret the human; and our Epidermists also will, in time, perceive that not by relying on the phonograph and kodak can they come to know the heart of man. They have mistaken the dead actual for reality, the show of the moment for the essence, the letter for the spirit.

By the imagination have all the highest creations of art and literature been produced, and the general truths of science and morals been discovered: for the imagination is that supreme faculty in man which beholds reality; it is the faculty, furthermore, which synthetizes, which vivifies, which constructs. The Epidermist, whose forte is analysis, discarding the imagination, has hoped by accumulating masses of details to produce as sure an effect of reality, as genius produces by using a few essentials. Yet, merely in the matter of illusion, this is an inferior method: if Mr. Kipling, for instance, can in a paragraph illude his readers to the extent he desires, whereas it takes Mr. Howells or Mr. James ten pages to produce an illusion, the chances are ten to one against Epidermism as a means of literary expression.

That heaping up of minute details which is proper in scientific investigation has influenced immensely all our intellectual processes for the past fifty years. There was a time when theology was the absorbing interest, and even non-theological works of that time, the fiction and poetry, are inevitably saturated with theology. We can detect it plainly and can pronounce it just so far a detriment to the novel or poem in which we find it. So science has permeated our time, encroaching upon, and inevitably vitiating, departments over which it has no jurisdiction. The multitude has been willing to accept the products of Epidermism, because its own imagination has been dulled, and it has come to suppose that observation and experiment were the only methods by which truth can be discovered. Hence the tanks of *real* water and the *real* burglars and the *real* fire-engines in our recent plays, and hence the predominance of Realism in fiction.

But the knell of the Epidermists has sounded. The novels that are everywhere in demand are the novels with a story. Individually, they may be good or bad—it matters not: the significant fact is that the public taste has turned, and that that instinct which is as old as the children of Adam and Eve, the instinct for a story, has reasserted itself.

Realism, therefore, has been a phase, indicating the decadence of fiction, and not, as the Epidermists themselves believed, its regeneration. It represents the period during which fiction has been enslaved by scientific methods, a period when the imagination has lain dormant, and other—lower—faculties have essayed to do her work. The novels produced by Realism will not, I suppose, occupy the attention of the world sixty years from now to the same extent that the products of Romanticism still occupy our attention. Certainly, the polemics of Realism have produced nothing so striking as Hugo's and Manzoni's and Heine's essays on Romanticism; nothing that has the lasting quality of Wordsworth's prefaces, or of Coleridge's criticism on Wordsworth. I hazard the prediction that our children, if they ever turn the pages of the masterpieces of Realism, will wonder how we could once have read them: and that, not because they will find in those pages much that is nasty (under the plea of "science"), and much that is morbid, and more that is petty, but because the prevailing note is dulness. Against dulness, the gods themselves have no refuge save flight.

Eight years ago all this was less evident than it is now. We could not say with assurance eight years ago that the movement had reached its logical culmination. To-day we can say this. Doubtless its votaries will not abandon it suddenly; but when they find the story-tellers getting all the readers, they will know their doom. Epidermism has already found its true habitat in the sensational daily press: there, the kodak and the phonograph and the eavesdropper have untrammelled play; and moreover, the persons portrayed are really alive—which gives them an advantage against which the make-believe real people of Mr. Howells cannot in the long run compete; for if *realness* be the final test, the really real heroes of the newspapers must excel the make-believe real characters of Epidermist fiction. What chance has *Silas Lapham* with the barber or bootblacks described, with illustrations, any day in the New York "Scavenger"? Another product of Epidermism, the dialect story, will soon, we may hope, be banished from the magazines to the transactions of the dialect societies, which have been providentially springing up. Of the shameless products—the obscenities and filth—we can at least predict that the time for foisting them, and all other matters not pertinent to fiction, upon us, under the plea of scientific impartiality, has passed; though doubtless from time to time some angel of the pit, some new Zola, will come to stir the surface of the cesspools of society.

Realism, or Epidermism, passes; but at least the example of sincerity which many of its devotees have given will not be lost. And now, as the atmosphere is clearing, the dear and venerable masters greet us in their majesty undiminished. Shakespeare—whose laurel has been prematurely claimed so many times by ardent partisans for the brows of ephemeral idols—Shakespeare and Dante, and the spokesmen of antiquity, confer serenely together. Near them, in another group, are Scott and Hawthorne and Thackeray, unconscious that they were so recently ostracized from Olympus. Could their words reach us, assuredly they would confirm the message written through all their books: "The lamp of Art differs from the lamp of Science; confound not their uses. Think not by machine or tool, which is material, to discover the secret of the heart of man, who is spiritual. The Real includes the Ideal; but the Real without the Ideal is as the body without life, a thing for anatomists to dissect. Only the human can understand and interpret the human."

FOURTEEN

THREE ESSAYS ON NATURALISM

Frank Norris

Although Frank Norris (1870–1902) was born in Chicago and did not move to San Francisco until 1884, he is known principally as a California author. Four years at the University of California (1890–94) were followed by a year at Harvard and several years as a jack-of-all-trades writer for the San Francisco weekly *The Wave*. Norris had come deeply under the influence of Zola while still at Berkeley, and his early novels *McTeague* (1899) and *Vandover and the Brute* (posthumously published in 1914) are often Zolaesque in material and method while expressing as well Norris's distinctive vision of experience. After a series of popular novels written to establish himself professionally, Norris returned to major fiction with the two completed volumes of his Trilogy of the Wheat, *The Octopus* (1901) and *The Pit* (1903). Norris wrote much journalistic literary criticism throughout his brief career, sometimes to keep the pot boiling but frequently as well to express his beliefs about such topics related to his fiction as the nature of naturalism, the character of western fiction, and the role of the writer in a democratic society. A selection of Norris's criticism appeared after his death in the volume *The Responsibilities of the Novelist* (1903).

"Zola as a Romantic Writer," San Francisco *Wave*, 27 June 1896, p. 3; "Frank Norris' Weekly Letter," Chicago *American*, 3 August 1901, p. 5; "A Plea for Romantic Fiction," Boston *Evening Transcript*, 18 December 1901, p. 14. "A Plea for Romantic Fiction" reprinted in *The Responsibilities of the Novelist* (1903). All three essays reprinted in *The Literary Criticism of Frank Norris*, ed. Donald Pizer (Austin: University of Texas Press, 1964), pp. 71–78. Text from *The Literary Criticism of Frank Norris*.

ZOLA AS A ROMANTIC WRITER

It is curious to notice how persistently M. Zola is misunderstood. How strangely he is misinterpreted even by those who conscientiously admire the novels of the "man of the iron pen." For most people Naturalism has a vague meaning. It is a sort of inner circle of realism—a kind of diametric opposite of romanticism, a theory of fiction wherein things are represented "as they really are," inexorably, with the truthfulness of a camera. This idea can be shown to be far from right, that Naturalism, as understood by Zola, is but a form of romanticism after all.

Observe the methods employed by the novelists who profess and call themselves "realists"—Mr. Howells, for instance. Howells's characters live across the street from us, they are "on our block." We know all about them, about their affairs, and the story of their lives. One can go even further. We ourselves are Mr. Howells's characters, so long as we are well behaved and ordinary and bourgeois, so long as we are not adventurous or not rich or not unconventional. If we are otherwise, if things commence to happen to us, if we kill a man or two, or get mixed up in a tragic affair, or do something on a large scale, such as the amassing of enormous wealth or power or fame, Mr. Howells cuts our acquaintance at once. He will none of us if we are out of the usual.

This is the real Realism. It is the smaller details of every-day life, things that are likely to happen between lunch and supper, small passions, restricted emotions, dramas of the reception-room, tragedies of an afternoon call, crises involving cups of tea. Every one will admit there is no romance here. The novel is interesting—which is after all the main point—but it is the commonplace tale of commonplace people made into a novel of far more than commonplace charm. Mr. Howells is not uninteresting; he is simply not romantic. But that Zola should be quoted as a realist, and as a realist of realists, is a strange perversion.

Reflect a moment upon his choice of subject and character and episode. The Rougon-Macquart live in a world of their own; they are not of our lives any more than are the Don Juans, the Jean Valjeans, the Gil Blases, the Marmions, or the Ivanhoes. We, the bourgeois, the commonplace, the ordinary, have no part nor lot in the *Rougon-Macquart*, in *Lourdes, or in Rome*; it is not our world, not because our social position is different, but because we are *ordinary*. To be noted of M. Zola we must leave the rank and the file, either run to the forefront of the marching world, or fall by the roadway; we must separate ourselves; we must become individual, unique. The naturalist takes no note of common people, common in so far as their interests, their lives, and the things that occur in them are common, are ordinary. Terrible things must happen to the characters of the naturalistic tale. They must be twisted from the ordinary, wrenched out from the quiet, uneventful round of every-day life, and flung into the throes of a vast and terrible drama that works itself out in unleased passions, in blood, and in sudden death. The world of M. Zola is a world of big things; the enormous, the formidable, the terrible, is what counts; no teacup tragedies here. Here Nana holds her monstrous orgies, and dies horribly, her face distorted to a frightful mask; Etienne Lantier, carried away by the strike of coal miners of *Le Voreux*, (the strike that is almost war), is involved in the vast and fearful catastrophe that comes as a climax of the great drama; Claude Lantier, disappointed, disillusioned, acknow-ledging the futility of his art after a life of effort, hangs himself to his huge easel; Jacques Lantier, haunted by an hereditary insanity, all his natural desires hideously distorted, cuts the throat of the girl he loves, and is ground to pieces under the wheels of his own locomotive; Jean Macquart, soldier and tiller of the fields, is drawn into the war of 1870, passes through the terrible scenes of Sedan and the Siege of Paris only to bayonet to death his truest friend and sworn brother-at-arms in the streets of the burning capital.

Everything is extraordinary, imaginative, grotesque even, with a vague note of ter-ror quivering throughout like the vibration of an ominous and low-pitched diapason. It is all romantic, at times unmistakably so, as in *Le Rêve* or *Rome*, closely resembling the work of the greatest of all modern romanticists, Hugo. We have the same huge dramas, the same enormous scenic effects, the same love of the extraordinary, the vast, the monstrous, and the tragic.

Naturalism is a form of romanticism, not an inner circle of realism. Where is the realism in the *Rougon-Macquart*? Are such things likely to happen between lunch and supper? That Zola's work is not purely romantic as was Hugo's, lies chiefly in the choice of Milieu. These great, terrible dramas no longer happen among the personnel of a feudal and Renaissance nobility, those who are in the fore-front of the marching world, but among the lower—almost the lowest—classes; those who have been thrust or wrenched from the ranks, who are falling by the roadway. This is not romanti-cism—this drama of the people, working itself out in blood and ordure. It is not re-alism. It is a school by itself, unique, somber, powerful beyond words. It is natural-ism.

FRANK NORRIS' WEEKLY LETTER

It is not more than a week ago since the present writer, in going through the daily batch of volunteer manuscripts submitted to a certain firm of New York publishers, came across a letter pinned to the typewritten draft of a novel. The letter was, in a way, a note and commentary upon the novel, and its writer declared with some vehe-mence, and more than once, that the events in the novel were true—were taken from real life—actually occurred, etc., etc. The inference was plain as paint. The author believed his story to be better by just so much, because the things in it were taken from actual life, were based on fact—must, therefore, be true to life. Now, here is the point. Is an event that is taken from actual life, true to life? Let us consider now. Sup-pose one had overlooked this author's letter, and had written to him to say that one of the faults of his story lay in the fact that it was not true to life. What a chance! How that author would have countered! How he would have forever demolished the critic, or the reader, with the one phrase, "But, sir, it actually happened." Therefore, it must be true.

Well, I say no. Let us talk about this Truth in Fiction, and with a certain provincial magistrate ask—in the name of American literature—"What is Truth?" A thing has actually happened; that is the proposition. Given to prove that it is not necessarily true when told as fiction—not necessarily true even when told with the most scrupulous adherence to fact, even when narrated with the meticulous science of the phonograph or pictured with the incontestable precision of the photograph.

Perhaps we will get a good grip of the problem at the outset if we make a difference, a wide difference, between Accuracy and Truth. A story can be accurate and yet lamentably—even wickedly—untrue. As, for instance, let us suppose that you have never seen a sheep, and that it devolves upon me to give you an idea of the animal—describe it, in fact. I go out into the fields and select a sheep. In size, build, habits, weight, wool-producing qualities and the like it is precisely like other sheep—but it is black. To you, then I bring this sheep, I call your attention to the characteristics. I falsify nothing, conceal nothing. I present the creature fairly in every detail, in ever particular. I am, in a word, accurate. But what is the result? To your notion all sheep are black, which is an untruth.

So that Accuracy is not necessarily Truth, and the novelist who relies upon the accurate presentation of a crisis in life, hoping by this means to create the impression of Truth, is leaning upon a broken reed.

For further—Life itself is not necessarily True—not necessarily True to life. I admit that this is much easier to assert than to prove, and the sound of it is that of a flippant paradox. Let us try an illustration or two. How many times—how almost invariably, especially with us stoical Anglo-Saxons—do men or women confronted suddenly with great tragedy or great joy fail to "rise to the occasion." How seldom is it that their actions or words at the moment are adequate, are interpretive of their emotions, give an expression of themselves. Mr. Davis tells of a condemned murderer who received the news of his pardon with the words:

"That's good. That's good."

Death-bed scenes are notoriously tame; heroic rescuers are most frequently silent at their work; the soldier receiving a mortal wound, when not struck unconscious, shouts "Gee!" and sits down suddenly with straddled legs. Wellington, at Waterloo, never cried "Up guards and at 'em!" Louis Napoleon's tame eagle refused to fly at the fortress of Ham; and Newton, when his little dog, by overturning a lamp, had irreparably destroyed fifty years of work, could only exclaim, "Ah, Flo, Flo, thou little knowest the ruin thou hast wrought!" Suppose Newton had acted and spoken in proportion to the poignancy of his grief, what a noble, heroic strain of tragedy would have been given to the world. But if we all gave true expression to our feelings under stress there would be no need nor place for fiction.

And here comes the dividing line. Here stands the crux. Is it too much to say that fiction can be truer than Life itself? I take it that we can say this and yet be well within conservatism. For fiction must not be judged by standards of real life, but both life and fiction referred to a third standard. The expression "true to life" is false, is inadequate, for life itself is not always true.

To what, then, should the truth of a novel be referred—to what standard? By what touchstone may we recognize the true metal?

Difficult question. Standards vary for different works of fiction. We must not refer Tolstoy to the same standard as Victor Hugo—the one a realist, the other a romanticist. We can conceive of no standard which would be large enough to include both, unless it would be one so vague, so broad, so formless as to be without value. Take the grand scene in *Hernani*. How would Tolstoy have done it? He would have brought it home as close to the reader as possible. Hugo has elevated it as far as he could in the opposite direction. Tolstoy would have confined himself to probabilities only. Hugo is confined by nothing save the limitations of his own imagination. The realist would have been accurate—only in this case he would not have chosen a black sheep. The romanticist aims at the broad truth of the thing—puts into his people's mouths the words they would have spoken if only they could have given expression to his thoughts.

Then the conclusion. Is it permissible to say that Accuracy is realism and Truth romanticism? I am not so sure, but I feel that we come close to a solution here. The divisions seem natural and intended. It is not difficult to be accurate, but it is monstrously difficult to be True; at best the romanticists can only aim at it, while on the other hand, mere accuracy as an easily obtainable result is for that reason less worthy.

Does Truth after all "lie in the middle"? And what school, then, is midway between the Realists and Romanticists, taking the best from each? Is it not the school of Naturalism, which strives hard for accuracy and truth? The nigger is out of the fence at last, but must it not be admitted that the author of *La Débâcle* (not the author of *La Terre* and *Fécondité*) is up to the present stage of literary development the most adequate, the most satisfactory, the most just of them all?

A PLEA FOR ROMANTIC FICTION

Let us at the start make a distinction. Observe that one speaks of Romanticism and not of sentimentalism. One claims that the latter is as distinct from the former as is that other form of art which is called Realism. Romance has been often put upon and overburdened by being forced to bear the onus of abuse that by right should fall to sentiment; but the two should be kept very distinct, for a very high and illustrious place will be claimed for Romance, while sentiment will be handed down the scullery stairs.

Many people today are composing mere sentimentalism, and calling it and causing it to be called Romance, so with those who are too busy to think much upon these subjects, but who none the less love honest literature, Romance too has fallen into disrepute. Consider now the cut-and-thrust stories. They are all labelled Romances, and it is very easy to get the impression that Romance must be an affair of cloaks and daggers, or moonlight and golden hair. But this is not so at all. The true Romance is a more serious business than this. It is not merely a conjurer's trick box, full of flimsy quackeries, tinsel and clap traps, meant only to amuse, and relying upon deception to do even that. Is it not something better than this? Can we not see in it an instrument, keen, finely tempered, flawless—an instrument with which we may go straight through the clothes and tissues and wrappings of flesh down deep into the red, living heart of things?

Is all this too subtle, too merely speculative and intrinsic, too *précieuse* and nice and "literary"? Devoutly one hopes the contrary. So much is made of so-called Romanticism in present day fiction, that the subject seems worthy of discussion, and a protest against the misuse of a really noble and honest formula of literature appears to be timely—misuse, that is, in the sense of limited use. Let us suppose for the moment that a Romance can be made out of the cut-and-thrust business. Good Heavens, are there no other things that are romantic, even in this—falsely, falsely called—humdrum world of today? Why should it be that so soon as the novelist addresses himself—seriously—to the consideration of contemporary life he must abandon Romance and take up that harsh, loveless, colorless, blunt tool called Realism?

Now, let us understand at once what is meant by Romance and what by Realism. Romance—I take it—is the kind of fiction that takes cognizance of variations from the type of normal life. Realism is the kind of fiction that confines itself to the type of normal life. According to this definition, then, Romance may even treat of the sordid, the unlovely—as for instance, the novels of M. Zola. (Zola has been dubbed a Realist, but he is, on the contrary, the very head of the Romanticists.) Also, Realism, used as it sometimes is as a term of reproach, need not be in the remotest sense or degree offensive, but on the other hand respectable as a church and proper as a deacon—as, for instance, the novels of Mr. Howells.

The reason why one claims so much for Romance, and quarrels so pointedly with Realism, is that Realism stultifies itself. It notes only the surface of things. For it Beauty is not even skin-deep, but only a geometrical plane, without dimensions of depth, a mere outside. Realism is very excellent so far as it goes, but it goes no farther than the Realist himself can actually see, or actually hear. Realism is minute, it is the drama of a broken teacup, the tragedy of a walk down the block, the excitement of an afternoon call, the adventure of an invitation to dinner. It is the visit to my neighbor's house, a formal visit, from which I may draw no conclusions. I see my neighbor and his friends—very, oh, such very! probable people—and that is all. Realism bows upon the doormat and goes away and says to me, as we link arms on the sidewalk: "That is life." And I say it is not. It is not, as you would very well see if you took Romance with you to call upon your neighbor.

Lately you have been taking Romance a weary journey across the water—ages and the flood of years—and haling her into the fubsy, musty, worm-eaten, moth-riddled, rust-corroded "Grandes Salles" of the Middle Ages and the Renaissance, and she has found the drama of a bygone age for you there. But would you take her across the street to your neighbor's front parlor (with the bisque fisher boy on the mantel and the photograph of Niagara Falls on glass hanging in the front window); would you introduce her there? Not you. Would you take a walk with her on Fifth avenue, or

Beacon street, or Michigan avenue? No indeed. Would you choose her for a companion of a morning spent in Wall Street, or an afternoon in the Waldorf-Astoria? You just guess you would not.

She would be out of place, you say, inappropriate. She might be awkward in my neighbor's front parlor, and knock over the little bisque fisher boy. Well, she might. If she did, you might find underneath the base of the statuette, hidden away, tucked away—what? God knows. But something which would be a complete revelation of my neighbor's secretest life.

So you think Romance would stop in the front parlor and discuss medicated flannels and mineral waters with the ladies? Not for more than five minutes. She would be off upstairs with you, prying, peeping, peering into the closets of the bedroom, into the nursery, into the sitting-room; yes, and into that little iron box screwed to the lower shelf of the closet in the library; and into those compartments and pigeonholes of the *secrétaire* in the study. She would find a heartache (may-be) between the pillows of the mistress's bed, and a memory carefully secreted in the master's deedbox. She would come upon a great hope amid the books and papers of the study table of the young man's room, and—perhaps—who knows—an affair, or, great heavens, an intrigue, in the scented ribbons and gloves and hairpins of the young lady's bureau. And she would pick here a little and there a little, making up a bag of hopes and fears, and a package of joys and sorrows—great ones, mind you—and then come down to the front door, and stepping out into the street, hand you the bags and package, and say to you—"That is Life!"

Romance does very well in the castles of the Middle Ages and the Renaissance chateaux, and she has the entrée there and is very well received. That is all well and good. But let us protest against limiting her to such places and such times. You will find her, I grant you, in the chatelaine's chamber and the dungeon of the man-at-arms; but, if you choose to look for her, you will find her equally at home in the brownstone house on the corner and in the office building downtown. And this very day, in this very hour, she is sitting among the rags and wretchedness, the dirt and despair of the tenements of the East Side of New York.

"What?" I hear you say, "look for Romance—the lady of the silken robes and golden crown, our beautiful, chaste maiden of soft voice and gentle eyes—look for her among the vicious ruffians, male and female, of Allen street and Mulberry Bend?" I tell you she is there, and to your shame be it said you will not know her in those surroundings. You, the aristocrats, who demand the fine linen and the purple in your fiction; you, the sensitive, the delicate, who will associate with your Romance only so long as she wears a silken gown. You will not follow her to the slums, for you believe that Romance should only amuse and entertain you, singing you sweet songs and touching the harp of silver strings with rosy-tipped fingers. If haply she should call to you from the squalor of a dive, or the awful degradation of a disorderly house, crying: "Look! listen! This, too, is life. These, too, are my children, look at them, know them and, knowing, help!" Should she call thus, you would stop your ears; you would avert your eyes, and you would answer, "Come from there, Romance. Your place is not there!" And you would make of her a harlequin, a tumbler, a sword dancer, when, as a matter of fact, she should be by right divine a teacher sent from God.

She will not always wear the robe of silk, the gold crown, the jeweled shoon, will not always sweep the silver harp. An iron note is hers if so she choose, and coarse garments, and stained hands; and, meeting her thus, it is for you to know her as she passes—know her for the same young queen of the blue mantle and lilies. She can teach you, if you will be humble to learn. Teach you by showing. God help you, if at last you take from Romance her mission of teaching, if you do not believe that she has a purpose, a nobler purpose and a mightier than mere amusement, mere entertainment. Let Realism do the entertaining with its meticulous presentation of teacups, rag carpets, wall paper and haircloth sofas, stopping with these, going no deeper than it sees, choosing the ordinary, the untroubled, the commonplace.

But to Romance belongs the wide world for range, and the unplumbed depths of the human heart, and the mystery of sex, and the problems of life, and the black, unsearched penetralia of the soul of man. You, the indolent, must not always be amused. What matter the silken clothes, what matter the prince's houses? Romance, too, is a teacher, and if—throwing aside the purple—she wears the camel's hair and feeds upon the locusts, it is to cry aloud unto the people, "Prepare ye the way of the Lord; make straight his path."

FIFTEEN

THE RESPONSIBILITIES OF THE NOVELIST

Frank Norris

It is not here a question of the "unarrived," the "unpublished"; these are the care-free irresponsibles whose hours are halcyon and whose endeavors have all the lure, all the recklessness of adventure. They are not recognized; they have made no standards for themselves, and if they play the *saltimbanque* and the charlatan nobody cares and nobody (except themselves) is affected.

But the writers in question are the successful ones who have made a public and to whom some ten, twenty or a hundred thousand people are pleased to listen. You may believe if you choose that the novelist of all workers is independent, that he can write what he pleases, and that certainly, certainly he should never "write down to his readers," that he should never consult them at all.

On the contrary, I believe it can be proved that the successful novelist should be more than all others limited in the nature and character of his work; more than all others he should be careful of what he says; more than all others he should defer to his audience; more than all others—more even than the minister and the editor—he should "feel his public" and watch his every word, testing carefully his every utterance, weighing with the most relentless precision his every statement; in a word, possess a sense of his responsibilities.

For the novel is the great expression of modern life. Each form of art has had its turn at reflecting and expressing its contemporaneous thought. Time was when the world looked to the architects of the castles and great cathedrals to truly reflect and embody its ideals. And the architects—serious, earnest men—produced such "expressions of contemporaneous thought" as the castle of Coucy and the church of Notre Dame. Then with other times came other customs, and the painters had their day. The men of the Renaissance trusted Angelo and da Vinci and Velásquez to speak for them, and trusted not in vain. Next came the age of the drama. Shakespeare and Marlowe found the value of x for the life and the times in which they lived. Later on contemporary life had been so modified that neither painting, architecture, nor

Critic 16 (December 1902): 537–40. Reprinted in *The Responsibilities of the Novelist* (1903). Reprinted in *The Literary Criticism of Frank Norris*, ed. Donald Pizer (Austin: University of Texas Press, 1964), pp. 94–98. Text from *The Literary Criticism of Frank Norris*.

drama was the best vehicle of expression, the day of the longer poems arrived, and Pope and Dryden spoke for their fellows.

Thus the sequence. Each age speaks with its own peculiar organ, and has left the Word for us moderns to read and understand. The castle of Coucy and the church of Notre Dame are the spoken words of the Middle Ages. The Renaissance speaks—and intelligibly—to us through the sibyls of the Sistine chapel and the "Mona Lisa." *Macbeth* and *Tamburlaine* résumé the whole spirit of the Elizabethan age, while the "Rape of the Lock" is a wireless message to us straight from the period of the Restoration.

To-day is the day of the novel. In no other way and by no other vehicle is contemporaneous life so adequately expressed; and the critics of the twenty-second century, reviewing our times, striving to reconstruct our civilization, will look not to the painters, not to the architects nor dramatists, but to the novelists to find our idiosyncrasy.

I think this is true. I think if the matter could in any way be statisticized, the figures would bear out the assumption. There is no doubt the novel will in time "go out" of popular favor as irrevocably as the long poem has gone, and for the reason that it is no longer the right mode of expression.

It is interesting to speculate upon what will take its place. Certainly the coming civilization will revert to no former means of expressing its thought or its ideals. Possibly music will be the interpreter of the life of the twenty-first and twenty-second centuries. Possibly one may see a hint of this in the characterization of Wagner's operas as the "Music of the Future."

This, however, is parenthetical and beside the mark. Remains the fact that to-day is the day of the novel. By this one does not mean that the novel is merely popular. If the novel was not something more than a simple diversion, a means of whiling away a dull evening, a long railway journey, it would not, believe me, remain in favor another day.

If the novel then is popular it is popular with a reason, a vital inherent reason; that is to say, it is essential. Essential—to resume once more the proposition—because it expresses modern life better than architecture, better than painting, better than poetry, better than music. It is as necessary to the civilization of the twentieth century as the violin is necessary to Kubelik, as the piano is necessary to Paderewski, as the plane is necessary to the carpenter, the sledge to the blacksmith, the chisel to the mason. It is an instrument, a tool, a weapon, a vehicle. It is that thing which, in the hand of man, makes him civilized and no longer savage, because it gives him a power of durable, permanent expression. So much for the novel—the instrument.

Because it is so all-powerful to-day, the people turn to him who wields this instrument with every degree of confidence. They expect—and rightly—that results shall be commensurate with means. The unknown archer who grasps the bow of Ulysses may be expected by the multitude to send his shaft far and true. If he is not true nor strong he has no business with the bow. The people give heed to him only because he bears a great weapon. He himself knows before he shoots whether or no he is worthy.

It is all very well to jeer at the People and at the People's misunderstanding of the arts, but the fact is indisputable that no art that is not in the end understood by the People can live or ever did live a single generation. In the larger view, in the last analysis, the People pronounce the final judgment. The People, despised of the artist, hooted, caricatured, and vilified, are after all, and in the main, the real seekers after Truth. Who is it after all, whose interest is liveliest in any given work of art? It is not now a question of *aesthetic* interest; that is the artist's, the amateur's, the *cognoscente's*. It is a question of *vital* interest. Say what you will, Maggie Tulliver—for instance—is far more a living being for Mrs. Jones across the street than she is for your sensitive, fastidious, keenly critical artist, litterateur, or critic. The People—Mrs. Jones and her neighbours—take the life history of these fictitious characters, these novels, to heart with a seriousness that the aesthetic cult have no conception of. The cult consider them almost solely from their artistic sides. The People take them into their innermost lives. Nor do the People discriminate. Omnivorous readers as they are to-day, they make little distinction between Maggie Tulliver and the heroine of the last "popular novel." They do not stop to separate true from false, they do not care.

How necessary it becomes, then, for those who, by the simple act of writing, can invade the heart's heart of thousands, whose novels are received with such measureless earnestness—how necessary it becomes for those who wield such power to use it rightfully. Is it not expedient to act fairly? Is it not in Heaven's name essential that the People hear, not a lie, but Truth? If the novel were not one of the most important factors of modern life, if it were not the completest expression of our civilization, if its influence were not greater than all the pulpits, than all the newspapers between the oceans, it would not be so important that its message should be true.

But the novelist to-day is the one who reaches the greatest audience. Right or wrong the People turn to him the moment he speaks, and what he says they believe.

For the million, Life is a contracted affair, is bounded by the walls of the narrow channel of affairs in which their feet are set. They have no horizon. They look to-day as they never have looked before, as they never will look again, to the writer of fiction to give them an idea of Life beyond their limits, and they believe him as they never have believed before and never will again.

This being so, is it not difficult to understand how certain of these successful writers of fiction—these favored ones into whose hands the gods have placed the great bow of Ulysses—can look so frivolously upon their craft? It is not necessary to specify. One speaks of those whose public is measured by "one hundred and fifty thousand copies sold." We know them, and because the gods have blessed us with wits beyond our deserving we know their work is false. But what of the "hundred and fifty thousand" who are not discerning and who receive this falseness as Truth, who believe this topsy-turvy picture of Life beyond their horizons is real and vital and sane?

There is no gauge to measure the extent of this malignant influence. Public opinion is made no one can say how, by infinitesimal accretions, by a multitude of minutest elements. Lying novels, surely, surely in this day and age of indiscriminate reading contribute to this more than all other influences of present-day activity.

The Pulpit, the Press and the Novel—these indisputably are the great moulders of Public opinion and Public morals to-day. But the Pulpit speaks but once a week; the Press is read with lightning haste and the morning news is wastepaper by noon. But the novel goes into the home to stay. It is read word for word, is talked about, discussed; its influence penetrates every chink and corner of the family.

Yet novelists are not found wanting who write for money. I do not think this is an unfounded accusation. I do not think it asking too much of credulity. This would not matter if they wrote the Truth. But these gentlemen who are "in literature for their own pocket every time" have discovered that for the moment the People have confounded the Wrong with the Right, and prefer that which is a lie, to that which is true. "Very well then," say these gentlemen. "If they want a lie they shall have it"; and they give the People a lie in return for royalties.

The surprising thing about this is that you and I and all the rest of us do not consider this as disreputable, do not yet realize that the novelist has responsibilities. We condemn an editor who sells his editorial columns, and we revile the Pulpit attainted of venality. But the venal novelist,—he whose influence is greater than either the Press or Pulpit,—*him* we greet with a wink and the tongue in the cheek.

This should not be so. Somewhere the protest should be raised, and those of us who see the practice of this fraud should bring home to ourselves the realization that the selling of one hundred and fifty thousand books is a serious business. The People have a right to the Truth as they have a right to life, liberty, and the pursuit of happiness. It is *not* right that they be exploited and deceived with false views of life, false characters, false sentiment, false morality, false history, false philosophy, false emotions, false heroism, false notions of self-sacrifice, false views of religion, of duty, of conduct, and of manners.

The man who can address an audience of one hundred and fifty thousand people who—unenlightened—*believe what he says* has a heavy duty to perform, and tremendous responsibilities to shoulder; and he should address himself to his task not with the flippancy of the catch-penny juggler at the county fair, but with earnestness, with soberness, with a sense of his limitations, and with all the abiding sincerity that by the favor and mercy of the gods may be his.

SIXTEEN

TRUE ART SPEAKS PLAINLY

Theodore Dreiser

Theodore Dreiser (1871–1945) was born in Terre Haute, Indiana, and raised in various Indiana towns until his move to Chicago in his mid-teens. After some years as a newspaper reporter in Chicago, St. Louis, and Pittsburgh, he established himself during the late 1890s as a magazine editor and free-lance writer in New York. His first novel, *Sister Carrie* (1900), which deals evocatively with working and lower middle class life in Chicago and New York, was praised by some for its honesty and power but was chastised as well for its uncouth material and ungainly style. Dreiser went on to attempt a second novel, *Jennie Gerhardt,* but at the time he wrote "True Art Speaks Plainly" for a Philadelphia magazine he was deeply depressed both by the reception of *Sister Carrie*, which he believed had been suppressed by its publisher, and by the state of his personal affairs. Dreiser was to write frequently on literary matters for the remainder of his long career, but almost entirely on specific writers and their work or on the relation of fiction to various social and philosophical issues.

The sum and substance of literary as well as social morality may be expressed in three words—tell the truth. It matters not how the tongues of the critics may wag, or the voices of a partially developed and highly conventionalized society may complain, the business of the author, as well as of other workers upon this earth, is to say what he knows to be true, and, having said as much, to abide the result with patience.

Booklovers Magazine 1 (February 1903): 129. Reprinted in *Theodore Dreiser: A Selection of Uncollected Prose*, ed. Donald Pizer (Detroit: Wayne State University Press, 1977), pp. 155–56. Text from *Theodore Dreiser: A Selection of Uncollected Prose*.

Truth is what is; and the seeing of what is, the realization of truth. To express what we see honestly and without subterfuge: this is morality as well as art.

What the so-called judges of the truth or morality are really inveighing against most of the time is not the discussion of mere sexual lewdness, for no work with that as a basis could possibly succeed, but the disturbing and destroying of their own little theories concerning life, which in some cases may be nothing more than a quiet acceptance of things as they are without any regard to the well-being of the future. Life for them is made up of a variety of interesting but immutable forms and any attempt either to picture any of the wretched results of modern social conditions or to assail the critical defenders of the same is naturally looked upon with contempt or aversion.

It is true that the rallying cry of the critics against so-called immoral literature is that the mental virtue of the reader must be preserved; but this has become a house of refuge to which every form of social injustice hurries for protection. The influence of intellectual ignorance and physical and moral greed upon personal virtue produces the chief tragedies of the age, and yet the objection to the discussion of the sex question is so great as to almost prevent the handling of the theme entirely.

Immoral! Immoral! Under this cloak hide the vices of wealth as well as the vast unspoken blackness of poverty and ignorance; and between them must walk the little novelist, choosing neither truth nor beauty, but some half-conceived phase of life that bears no honest relationship to either the whole of nature or to man.

The impossibility of any such theory of literature having weight with the true artist must be apparent to every clear reasoning mind. Life is not made up of any one phase or condition of being, nor can man's interest possibly be so confined.

The extent of all reality is the realm of the author's pen, and a true picture of life, honestly and reverentially set down, is both moral and artistic whether it offends the conventions or not.

THE EARLY MODERN
PERIOD, 1915–1950

INTRODUCTION

For much of the first half of the twentieth century, the academic study of literature in English was confined principally to the work of British authors. American literature did of course receive some attention. *The Cambridge History of American Literature* (1917–21), an enterprise prompted in part by America's emergence as a world power, was a significant effort, and standard literary histories and biographies of major early figures were common.[1] Scholarly attention to late nineteenth-century American literature, however, was handicapped by doubts related to both its recent vintage and its quality. As in the 1880s and 1890s, therefore, the critical discussion of American realism and naturalism was conducted as a public debate centering on the implications of these forms of expression for contemporary American life. Although some writers participating in the debate were members of the academy—Stuart P. Sherman, V. L. Parrington, and Lionel Trilling, for example—the criticism of this period differed little from that of the earlier in its vehemence and partisanship.

The early twentieth-century phase of the debate did differ significantly, however, in its focus on literary naturalism and above all on Theodore Dreiser, a naturalist whose career spanned the late nineteenth and early twentieth centuries and whose fiction evoked strong reactions. On the contrary, Howellsian realism, except for Howells's later socialist phase, was a dead issue insofar as it was related to twentieth-century interests. Few contemporary novelists could be identified as writing in the spirit of Howells, and Howells's literary ideals were often distorted for polemical purposes into an unthinking endorsement of Victorian prudery and blind optimism.[2] Naturalism, on the other hand, not only continued as a living presence—initially with Dreiser and then, in the 1930s, in the fiction of a number of other major figures—but appeared to address the intellectual and social preoccupations of the period. Although these resembled the issues that had occupied nineteenth-century critics, they were reformulated to reflect specific twentieth-century intellectual concerns and social conditions.

During the late teens and early 1920s, the debate over naturalism swirled around its ethical character. Did it constitute, as Randolph Bourne and H. L. Mencken claimed, a true portrait of man, a portrait stripped of illusions and lies? Or was it, as Stuart P. Sherman, Paul Elmer More, and the New Humanist critics declared, a foreign incursion capable of undermining the moral fabric of American life? In the late 1920s and throughout the 1930s, V. L. Parrington, Alfred Kazin, and a host of critics deeply affected by a potent mix of dire economic conditions and Marxist idealism adapted the social implications of Howellsian realism and Dreiserian naturalism into a model of social engagement for the American writer. And, finally, during the 1940s and 1950s, many of the leading critics of the age, including Philip Rahv,[3] Malcolm Cowley, and Lionel Trilling, reexamined naturalism from the perspective of the relationship between its intellectual limitations and those of a now discredited communist ideology. For much of the early twentieth century, therefore, the critical debate over naturalism, and especially Dreiserian naturalism, served as a means for the discussion of such deeply evocative social and intellectual issues as the relationship between the traditional ethical character of American life and its new ethnic culture, the centrality of economic reality in the lives of most Americans, and the danger of authoritarian ideologies.

Stuart P. Sherman's 1915 "The Naturalism of Mr. Dreiser" marks the onset of Dreiser's preeminent role in discussions of American naturalism. Dreiser had reentered the fictional arena with *Jennie Gerhardt* in 1911 followed by his controversial novels *The Financier* in 1912 and *The "Genius"* in 1915. He had also been taken up by a group of young critics, led by H. L. Mencken and Randolph Bourne, who were eager to proclaim him as a new voice in opposition to the puritan ethos still dominating American public taste. Sherman's essay, as well as the heavy attack on Dreiser by the New Humanists in the 1920s, thus arose out of a need by conservative-minded critics to counter the claim that Dreiser's naturalism constituted the emergence of a truer and more meaningful American fiction.

Sherman's three-pronged attack both harks back to the arguments used against realism and naturalism in the 1880s and 1890s and looks forward to their continued exploitation as late as the 1950s. Dreiser's fiction, Sherman claims, is amoral in its concept of human nature, is unrepresentative of American experience, and is artistically inept. Life to Dreiser, Sherman states in a series of highly quotable aphorisms, is a jungle in which irrational man functions largely as a creature of his appetites. Taking advantage of the anti-German sentiment already abroad in 1915, Sherman attributes this "new note" in American literature to the " 'ethnic' element of our mixed population" (189). Dreiser's rejection of eternal moral truths is thus "curiously outside American society" (193). And of course the intellectual clumsiness associated with an inadequate ethical philosophy and a foreign origin helps explain Dreiser's fictional limitations.

The long shelf life of Sherman's reading of Dreiser's naturalism is exemplied initially by its adoption by the New Humanists.[4] Led by Irving Babbitt and Paul Elmer More, this largely academic group of critics sought to counter the new writing of the 1920s by a call for literature to express traditional ethical values and the need for individual moral discipline. As More noted in his *The Demon of the Absolute* in 1928, the cult of science and the concomitant primacy of the natural had resulted in a lessening of the role of ethical norms in life and literature. In a diction and tone suggestive of the 1880s, More remarks of Dreiser's *An American Tragedy*, "If only [Dreiser] knew the finer aspects of life as he knows its shabby underside; if only his imagination had been trained in the larger tradition of literature instead of getting its bent from the police court and the dregs of science. . . . "[5]

The vitality of Sherman's polemic is also indicated by the need felt by Randolph Bourne, in his 1917 "The Art of Theodore Dreiser," and by H. L. Mencken, in his "The Dreiser Bugaboo" of the same year, to respond directly to it. Their arguments would also reappear in many later efforts to explain and defend American naturalism as an art form that draws its significance from its close relationship to the conditions of American life. If Dreiser dramatizes American experience with a raw immediacy that places him outside the conventional platitudes governing the interpretation of American life, it is because, Bourne claims, he speaks to our new condition of "conglomerate Americanism" (200), that is, to our social reality as a nation of recent immigrants. He does not shape his fiction around the ethical certainties of the past but rather seeks to "to make something artistic out of the chaotic materials that lie around us in American life. . . . He expresses an America that is in process of forming" (200). Bourne and Mencken link their belief that Dreiser's fiction is a kind of unmediated response to the actualities of experience to his power as a tragic writer. Dreiser's commitment to what Sherman had labeled "a theory of animal behavior" (196) is refined by Bourne and Mencken into Dreiser's rendering of the complex mix of beauty and tragedy inherent in man's sexual nature. Dreiser's crime as an artist, Mencken comments, is that his novels fail to endorse

> the rubber-stamp formulae of American fiction . . . ; instead of reducing the inexplicable to the obvious, they lifted the obvious to the inexplicable; one could find in them no orderly chain of causes and effects, of rewards and punishments; they represented life as a phenomemon at once terrible and unintelligible, like a stroke of lightning.[6]

In short, Mencken concludes, echoing one of the defenses of realism employed by an earlier generation, Sherman was offended not by "Dreiser's shortcomings as an artist, but Dreiser's shortcomings as a Christian and an American."[7]

Mencken's and Bourne's essays in support of Dreiser indicate the larger cultural dimensions of the early twentieth-century debate over naturalism. At stake was less the value of a specific kind of fiction than the conflicting claims of older and newer ways of conceiving of America. Could the traditional belief in a moral universe, as exemplified in the shared values of a homogeneous culture, prevail? Or did twentieth-century America reveal, as a consequence of its new and diverse cultural makeup, the conflicts, chaos, and mystery at the heart of all life?

By the late 1920s, however, as is suggested by V. L. Parrington's preparation during this period of his *Main Currents in American Thought*, American critics were shifting the focus of their engagement with American writing from the ethical to the economic and political. The stock market crash of 1929 and the depression of the 1930s of course intensified the progress of this change. As far as the critical examination of late nineteenth-century American literature is concerned, this new emphasis is especially apparent in a reconceptualization of Howellsian realism and Dreiserian naturalism.

Parrington's monumental intellectual history was to serve as the key interpretation of the American experience for an entire generation of American critics. Its hold is suggested by Lionel Trilling's effort, some twenty years after its appearance, to deflate its role as the preeminent history of American literature and thought.[8] In his account of Howells, Parrington, like most 1930s critics who were to follow his lead, concentrated on the post-Haymarket Riot Howells of the late 1880s and 1890s, the Howells whose social conscience has been awakened by the excesses of American capitalism and by his new-found socialist beliefs. H. L. Mencken's timid and complacent Victorian is replaced in Parrington's account by a generous-spirited observer of the destructive economic system of his time who is nevertheless tragically prevented by the literary conventions of his moment from translating Marxist ideology into a full-scale indictment of his society.

Parrington's polarization of late nineteenth-century America into a powerless reflowering of Jeffersonian idealism and an overwhelming and destructive capitalism was echoed throughout the 1930s and early 1940s, most notably in Granville Hicks's influential *The Great Tradition* of 1933 and Alfred Kazin's widely read *On Native Grounds* of 1942. Parrington's equally pervasive interpretation of late nineteenth-century naturalism also rests on the evocative image of the beleaguered individual rendered impotent by an unjust but all-powerful economic and social system. He begins his account of naturalism by detailing its scientism, objectivity, and amorality, and concludes with a precise definition that was to be endlessly repeated in literary histories and classrooms. "Naturalism is pessimistic realism, with a philosophy that sets man in a mechanical world and conceives of him as victimized by that world" (212). To Parrington, the significance of this concept, no matter how flawed its translation into fiction by American naturalists, is that it correctly renders late nineteenth-century social and psychological reality. The average man of the period, whatever the rhetoric of freedom in which he lived, was imprisoned in a world of machine industrialism, untrammeled great wealth, and huge anonymous cities. Naturalism as an ideology of pessimistic determinism is the appropriate response, Parrington and most 1930s critics agreed, to these conditions.[9] Whatever the naturalist writer's pose of objectivity, his truthful depiction of these conditions was a cry of pain and anger at the perversion of Jeffersonian ideals that they represented. In all, despite his role in helping to perpetuate a formulaic definition of the movement, Parrington's account of late nineteenth-century naturalism opened up two rich veins for later, more fully realized exploration. He stressed the native social as well as foreign literary roots of the movement, and he highlighted the role of naturalism in not only reflecting but protesting against the oppression of the individual by his society.

Whatever the efforts of Parrington, Kazin, and various left-wing critics of the 1920s and 1930s to formulate a positive role for late nineteenth-century naturalism as a critique of American capitalism, the reputation of the movement declined sharply from the late 1930s to the early 1950s. Many American intellectuals reacted to the Stalinist purges and Soviet-Nazi pact of the late thirties by repudiating their earlier identification with Communist Party ideals and goals, a change in the political climate that was paralleled by a shift in the politics of literary reputation. Put oversimply, such major critics as Malcolm Cowley and Lionel Trilling shaped an argument that began with the premise that many leading American novelists of the 1920s and 1930s, led by Dreiser and including James T. Farrell, John Dos Passos, and John Steinbeck, were both naturalist in fictional method and left-wing or communist in political leaning. Since the political inclinations of these novelists revealed their basic shallowness of perception and intellect, their naturalism was equally tainted. Inevitable conclusion as far as naturalism as a whole was concerned: It was a morally and intellectually bankrupt literature wherever it was found, including the late nineteenth century. In brief, in order to cleanse American writing of the contamination of its flirtation with communism during the 1930s, it was necessary to establish the limitations of mind and spirit of a literary movement closely associated with an acceptance of this now rejected ideology. And as is not uncommon in the history of conversion from one faith to another, the vehemence of the attack on naturalism by this group of critics is in part explained by their own endorsement, earlier in their careers, of far-left positions.[10]

The essays by Cowley and Trilling, though differing in what each critic singles out as the salient weakness of naturalism, are similar in their common device of reductivism. If naturalism as a world-wide movement has its principal model and spokesman in Zola, Cowley (and also Oscar Cargill in his influential study of 1940, *Intellectual America*), discovers its American version to be completely derivative. If naturalism often stresses the overpowering role of the social conditions in which we live, Trilling finds that it eliminates entirely consciousness as a subject and theme and is thus incapable of achieving either a tragic effect or a full rendering of the complexity of experience. And if naturalism depicts the role of the instinctive in man's nature, Cowley announces that it is totally committed to representing the "beast within" (226). Both critics either explicitly or implicitly accept the convention that naturalists write within a formula of pessimistic determinism and that they are therefore indeed formulaic, mechanical, superficial, and ultimately mindless in their fiction.

Cowley's essay was frequently cited in later discussions of American naturalism, but it is Trilling's "Reality in America" that has received the greatest attention and is perhaps the most commonly known general discussion of the movement.[11] Trilling nowhere mentions naturalism and he alludes to communism only at the close in brief references to F. O. Matthiessen's praise of Dreiser's *The Bulwark* (Matthiessen was an open party supporter) and to Robert Elias's defense of Dreiser's late gesture of joining the party. Rather, Trilling dissects Parrington's critical beliefs and Dreiser's ideas and fiction to express his contempt for their shared simplicity of mind. Both figures, Trilling holds—in a charge that harks back to nineteenth-century attacks on realism—are guilty of a naturalistic metaphysics in which only the material and physical are real. Parrington believed that reality is "fixed and given" (240) and Dreiser displayed a "vulgar materialism" (249) in every aspect of his thought and writing. "In the American metaphysic," as defined by these writers and their "liberal intellectual" (read far-left) supporters, "reality is always material reality, hard, resistant, unformed, impenetrable, and unpleasant. And that mind is alone felt to be trustworthy which most resembles this reality by most nearly reproducing the sensations it affords" (245).

Trilling's conflation of a suspect literary movement and an even more deeply suspect political belief into an implicit indictment of the socially engaged novelist and critic was to have a long life given the widespread suspicion of this role that accompanied the anti-communist sentiment of the Cold War decades. But James T. Farrell's essay of the same year, "Some Observations on Naturalism, So Called, in Fiction," contains a different approach to the movement, one which was to flourish in later academic criticism. Himself an apostate of the far left but also a novelist often identified as a naturalist, Farrell's principal effort is to free interpretations of naturalism from reductive and formulaic approaches. The American naturalist, according to Farrell, owes little to Zola other than an acceptance of his belief in observable causes. He is not seeking to demonstrate a philosophy of pessimistic determinism but is rather attempting to represent the impact of external event on belief and action. The naturalistic novel is thus capable of a tragic effect, though within a reformulated conception of the nature of the tragic in modern life, and it also differs widely in its expression among American novelists. Farrell thus posits a naturalistic tradition in America that exhibits certain shared qualities but that is above all varied and complex in its depiction of American life. Although not all later critics of American naturalism were to accept Farrell's interpretation of the movement, his effort to divorce its discussion from the worn paths created by the critical wars of the early twentieth century was increasingly to be the model for serious accounts of naturalism in American fiction.

NOTES

1. See Kermit Vanderbilt, *American Literature and the Academy: The Roots, Growth, and Maturity of a Profession* (Philadelphia: U of Pennsylvania P, 1986).

2. See H. L. Mencken, "The Dean," *Prejudices, First Series* (1919) and "Puritanism as a Literary Force," *A Book of Prefaces* (1917); and Sinclair Lewis, "The American Fear of Literature" (The Nobel Prize Address), in *The Man from Main Street: A Sinclair Lewis Reader*, ed. Harry E. Maule and Melville H. Cane (New York: Random House, 1953), 4–17.

3. See Rahv's "On the Decline of Naturalism," *Partisan Review* 9 (Nov.–Dec. 1942): 483–93. Reprinted in his *Image and Idea: Fourteen Essays on Literary Themes* (1949).

4. See J. David Hoeveler, Jr., *The New Humanism: A Critique of Modern America, 1900–1940* (Charlottesville: UP of Virginia, 1977).

5. Paul Elmer More, *The Demon of the Absolute* (Princeton: Princeton UP, 1928), 68.

6. H. L. Mencken, "The Dreiser Bugaboo," *Seven Arts* (Aug. 1917); rpt. in *Critical Essays on Theodore Dreiser*, ed. Donald Pizer (Boston: G. K. Hall, 1981), 25.

7. Mencken, "The Dreiser Bugaboo," 22.

8. See Trilling's "Reality in America" below (239–50).

9. See, for example, Alfred Kazin, "American Naturalism: Reflections from Another Era," in *The American Writer and the European Tradition*, ed. Margaret Denny and William H. Gilman (Minneapolis: U of Minnesota P, 1950), 121–31.

10. See Alan M. Wald, *The New York Intellectuals: The Rise and Decline of the Anti-Stalinist Left from the 1930s to the 1980s* (Chapel Hill: U of North Carolina P, 1987).

11. See William M. Chace, *Lionel Trilling: Criticism and Politics* (Stanford: Stanford UP, 1980).

SEVENTEEN

THE NATURALISM OF
MR. DREISER

Stuart P. Sherman

Stuart P. Sherman (1881–1926) was educated at Williams College and Harvard, where he was a student of Irving Babbitt, who was later to become a leader of the conservative New Humanist movement, and where he was awarded a Ph.D. in 1906. Sherman taught for most of his career at the University of Illinois. He was a frequent contributor to the *Nation*, which, under the editorship of Paul Elmer More, undertook to counter the modernist literary positions advanced by H. L. Mencken in the *Smart Set*. Sherman collected his essays in a number of volumes, of which *On Contemporary Literature* (1917) represents him at the most conservative stage of his thinking.

The layman who listens reverently to the reviewers discussing the new novels and to the novelists discussing themselves can hardly escape persuasion that a great change has rather recently taken place in the spirit of the age, in the literature which reflects it, and in the criticism which judges it. The nature of the supposed revolution may be briefly summarized.

The elder generation was in love with illusions, and looked at truth through a glass darkly and timorously. The artist, tongue-tied by authority and trammelled by aesthetic and moral conventions, selected, suppressed, and rearranged the data of experience and observation. The critic, "morally subsidized," regularly professed his disdain for a work of art in which no light glimmered above "the good and the beautiful."

The present age is fearless and is freeing itself from illusions. Now, for the first time in history, men are facing unabashed the facts of life. "Death or life," we cry, "give

Nation 101 (2 December 1915): 648–50. Reprinted as "The Barbarous Naturalism of Theodore Dreiser," *On Contemporary Literature* (1917). Text from the *Nation*.

us only reality!" Now, for the first time in the history of English literature, fiction is become a flawless mirror held up to the living world. Rejecting nothing, altering nothing, it presents to us—let us take our terms from the bright lexicon of the reviewer—a "transcript," a "cross-section," a "slice," a "photographic" or "cinematographic" reproduction of life. The critic who keeps pace with the movement no longer asks whether the artist has created beauty or glorified goodness, but merely whether he has told the truth.

Mr. Dreiser, in his latest novel, describes a canvas by a painter of this austere modern school: "Raw reds, raw greens, dirty gray paving stones—such faces! Why, this thing fairly shouted its facts. It seemed to say: 'I'm dirty, I am commonplace, I am grim, I am shabby, but I am life.' And there was no apologizing for anything in it, no glossing anything over. Bang! Smash! Crack! came the facts one after another, with a bitter, brutal insistence on their so-ness." If you do not like what is in the picture, you are to be crushed by the retort that perhaps you do not like what is in life. Perhaps you have not the courage to confront reality. Perhaps you had better read the chromatic fairy-tales with the children. Men of sterner stuff exclaim, like the critic in this novel, "Thank God for a realist!"

Mr. Dreiser is a novelist of the new school, for whom we have been invited off and on these fourteen years to thank God—a form of speech, by the way, which crept into the language before the dawn of modern realism. He has performed with words what his hero performed with paint. He has presented the facts of life "one after another with a bitter, brutal insistence on their so-ness," which marks him as a "man of the hour," a "portent"—the successor of Mr. Howells and Mr. James. In the case of a realist, biographical details are always relevant. Mr. Dreiser was born of German-American parents in Terre Haute, Indiana, in 1871. He was educated in the Indiana public schools and at the State University. He was engaged in newspaper work in Chicago, St. Louis, New York and elsewhere, from 1892 to 1910. He has laid reality bare for us in five novels published as follows: "Sister Carrie," 1901; "Jennie Gerhardt," 1911; "The Financier," 1912; "The Titan," 1914; and "The Genius," 1915. These five works constitute a singularly homogeneous mass of fiction. I do not find any moral value in them, nor any memorable beauty—of their truth I shall speak later; but I am greatly impressed by them as serious representatives of a new note in American literature, coming from that "ethnic" element of our mixed population which, as we are assured by competent authorities, is to redeem us from Puritanism and insure our artistic salvation. They abundantly illustrate, furthermore, the methods and intentions of our recent courageous, veracious realism. Before we thank God for it, let us consider a little more closely what is offered us.

I

The first step towards the definition of Mr. Dreiser's special contribution is to blow away the dust with which the exponents of the new realism seek to becloud the perceptions of our "reverent layman." In their main pretensions, there are large elements of conscious and unconscious sham.

It should clear the air to say that courage in facing and veracity in reporting the facts of life are no more characteristic of Theodore Dreiser than of John Bunyan. These moral traits are not the peculiar marks of the new school; they are marks common to every great movement of literature within the memory of man. Each literary generation detaching itself from its predecessor—whether it has called its own movement Classical or Romantic or what not—has revolted in the interest of what it took to be a more adequate representation of reality. No one who is not drunken with the egotism of the hour, no one who has penetrated with sober senses into the spirit of any historical period anterior to his own, will fall into the indecency of declaring his own age preëminent in the desire to see and to tell the truth. The real distinction between one generation and another is in the thing which each takes for its master truth—in the thing which each recognizes as the essential reality for it. The difference between Bunyan and Dreiser is in the order of facts which each reports.

It seems necessary also to declare at periodic intervals that there is no such thing as a "cross-section" or "slice" or "photograph" of life in art—least of all in the realistic novel. The use of these catchwords is but a clever hypnotizing pass of the artist, employed to win the assent of the reader to the reality of the show, and, in some cases, to evade moral responsibility for any questionable features of the exhibition. A realistic novel no more than any other kind of a novel can escape being a composition, involving preconception, imagination, and divination. Yet, hearing one of our new realists expound his doctrine, you might suppose that writing a novel was a process analogous to photographing wild animals in their habitat by trap and flashlight. He, if you will believe him, does not invite his subjects, nor group them, nor compose their features, nor furnish their setting. He but exposes the sensitized plate of his mind. The pomp of life goes by, and springs the trap. The picture, of course, does not teach nor preach nor moralize. It simply represents. The only serious objection to this figurative explanation of the artistic process is the utter dissimilarity between the blank impartial photographic plate, commemorating everything that confronts it, and the crowded inveterately selective human mind, which, like a magnet, snatches the facts of life that are subject to its influence out of their casual order and redisposes them in a pattern of its own.

In the case of any specified novelist, the facts chosen and the pattern assumed by them are determined by his central theory or "philosophy of life"; and this is precisely criticism's justification for inquiring into the adequacy of any novelist's general ideas. In vain, the new realist throws up his hands with protestations of innocence, and cries: "Search me. I carry no concealed weapons. I run life into no preconceived mould. I have no philosophy. My business is only to observe, like a man of science, and to record what I have seen." He cannot observe without a theory, nor record his observations without betraying it to any critical eye.

As it happens, the man of science who most profoundly influenced the development of the new realistic novel—Charles Darwin—more candid than the writers of "scientific" fiction—frankly declared that he could not observe without a theory. When he had tentatively formulated a general law, and had begun definitely to look for evidence of its operation, then first the substantiating facts leaped abundantly into his vision. His "Origin of Species" has the unity of a work of art, because the recorded observations support a thesis. The French novelists who in the last century developed the novel of contemporary life learned as much, perhaps, from Darwin's art as from his science. Balzac emphasized the relation between man and his social *milieu*; the Goncourts emphasized the importance of extensive collection of "human documents"; Zola emphasized the value of scientific hypotheses. He deliberately adopted the materialistic philosophy of the period as his guide in observation and as his unifying principle in composition. His theory of the causes of social phenomena, which was derived largely from medical treatises, operated like a powerful magnet among the chaotic facts of life, rejecting some, selecting others, and redisposing them in the pattern of the *roman naturaliste*. Judicious French critics said: "My dear man," or words to that effect, "your representations of life are inadequate. This which you are offering us with so earnest an air is not reality. It is your own private nightmare." When they had exposed his theory, they had condemned his art.

Let us, then, dismiss Mr. Dreiser's untenable claims to superior courage and veracity of intention, the photographic transcript, and the unbiased service of truth; and let us seek for his definition in his general theory of life, in the order of facts which he records, and in the pattern of his representations.

II

The impressive unity of effect produced by Mr. Dreiser's five novels is due to the fact that they are all illustrations of a crude and naively simple naturalistic philosophy, such as we find in the mouths of exponents of the new *Real-Politik*. Each book, with its bewildering masses of detail, is a ferocious argument in behalf of a few brutal generalizations. To the eye cleared of illusions it appears that the ordered life which we call civilization does not really exist except on paper. In reality our so-called society is a jungle in which the struggle for existence continues, and must continue, on terms substantially unaltered by legal, moral, or social conventions. The central truth about man is that he is an animal amenable to no law but the law of his own temperament, doing as he desires, subject only to the limitations of his power. The male of the species is characterized by cupidity, pugnacity, and a simian inclination for the other sex. The female is a soft, vain, pleasure-seeking creature, devoted to personal adornment, and quite helplessly susceptible to the flattery of the male. In the struggles which arise in the jungle through the conflicting appetites of its denizens, the victory goes to the animal most physically fit and mentally ruthless, unless the weaklings, resisting absorption, combine against him and crush him by sheer force of numbers.

The idea that civilization is a sham Mr. Dreiser sometimes sets forth explicitly, and sometimes he conveys it by the process known among journalists as "coloring the news." When Sister Carrie yields to the seductive drummer, Drouet, Mr. Dreiser judicially weighs the advantages and disadvantages attendant on the condition of being a well-kept mistress. When the institution of marriage is brushed aside by the heroine of "The Financier," he comments "editorially" as follows: "Before Christianity was man, and after it will also be. A metaphysical idealism will always tell him that it is better to preserve a cleanly balance, and the storms of circumstance will teach him a noble stoicism. Beyond this there is nothing which can reasonably be imposed upon the conscience of man." A little later in the same book he says: "Is there no law outside of the subtle will and the power to achieve? If not, it is surely high time that we knew it—one and all. We might then agree to do as we do; but there would be no silly illusion as to divine regulation." His own answer to the question, his own valuation of regulation, both divine and human, may be found in the innumerable contemptuous epithets which fall from his pen whenever he has occasion to mention any power set up against the urge of instinct and the indefinite expansion of desire. Righteousness is always "legal"; conventions are always "current"; routine is always "dull"; respectability is always "unctuous"; an institution for transforming schoolgirls into young ladies is presided over by "owl-like conventionalists"; families in which parents are faithful to each other lead an "apple-pie order of existence"; a man who yields to his impulses yet condemns himself for yielding is a "rag-bag moralistic ass." Jennie Gerhardt, by a facile surrender of her chastity, shows that "*she could not be readily corrupted by the world's selfish lessons* on how to preserve oneself from the evil to come." Surely, this is "coloring the news."

By similar devices Mr. Dreiser drives home the great truth that man is essentially an animal, impelled by temperament, instinct, physics, chemistry—anything you please that is irrational and uncontrollable. Sometimes he writes an "editorial" paragraph in which the laws of human life are explained by reference to the behavior of certain protozoa or by reference to a squid and a lobster fighting in an aquarium. His heroes and heroines have "cat-like eyes," "feline grace," "sinuous strides," eyes and jaws which vary "from those of the tiger, lynx, and bear to those of the fox, the tolerant mastiff, and the surly bulldog." One hero and his mistress are said to "have run together temperamentally like two leopards." The lady in question, admiring the large rapacity of her mate, exclaims playfully: "Oh, you big tiger! You great, big lion! Boo!" Courtship as presented in these novels is after the manner of beasts in the jungle. Mr. Dreiser's leonine men but circle once or twice about their prey, and spring, and pounce; and the struggle is over. A pure-minded serving-maid, who is suddenly held up in the hall by a "hairy, axiomatic" guest and "masterfully" kissed upon the lips, may for an instant be "horrified, stunned, *like a bird in the grasp of a cat*." But we are always assured that "through it all something tremendously vital and insistent" will be speaking to her, and that in the end she will not resist the urge of the *élan vital*. I recall no one of all the dozens of obliging women in these books who makes any effective resistance when summoned to capitulate. "The *psychology of the human animal*, when confronted by these tangles, these ripping tides of the heart," says the author of "The Titan," "has little to do with so-called reason or logic." No; as he informs us elsewhere with endless iteration, it is a question of chemistry. It is the "chemistry of her being" which rouses to blazing the ordinarily dormant forces of Eugene Witla's sympathies in "The Genius." If Stephanie Platow is disloyal to her married lover in "The Titan," "let no one quarrel" with her. Reason: "She was an unstable chemical compound."

Such is the Dreiserian philosophy.

III

By thus eliminating distinctively human motives and making animal instincts the supreme factors in human life, Mr. Dreiser reduces the problem of the novelist to the lowest possible terms. I find myself unable to go with those who admire the powerful reality of his art while deploring the puerility of his philosophy. His philosophy quite excludes him from the field in which a great realist must work. He has deliberately rejected the novelist's supreme task—understanding and presenting the development of character; he has chosen only to illustrate the unrestricted flow of temperament. He has evaded the enterprise of representing human conduct; he has confined himself to a representation of animal behavior. He demands for the demonstration of his theory a moral vacuum from which the obligations of parenthood, marriage, chivalry, and citizenship have been quite withdrawn or locked in a twilight sleep. At each critical moment in his narrative, where a realist like George Eliot or Thackeray or Trollope or Meredith would be asking how a given individual would feel, think, and act under the manifold combined stresses of organized society, Mr. Dreiser sinks supinely back upon the law of the jungle or mutters his mystical gibberish about an alteration of the chemical formula.

The possibility of making the unvarying victoriousness of jungle-motive plausible depends directly upon the suppression of the evidence of other motives. In this work of suppression Mr. Dreiser simplifies American life almost beyond recognition. Whether it is because he comes from Indiana, or whether it is because he steadily envisages the human animal, I cannot say; I can only note that he never speaks of his men and women as "educated" or "brought up." Whatever their social status, they are invariably "raised." Raising human stock in America evidently includes feeding and clothing it, but does not include the inculcation of even the most elementary moral ideas. Hence Mr. Dreiser's field seems curiously outside American society. Yet he repeatedly informs us that his persons are typical of the American middle class, and three of the leading figures, to judge from their names—Carrie Meeber, Jennie Gerhardt, and Eugene Witla—are of our most highly "cultured" race. Frank Cowperwood, the hero of two novels, is a hawk of finance and a rake almost from the cradle; but of the powers which presided over his cradle we know nothing save that his father was a competent official in a Philadelphia bank. What, if anything, Carrie Meeber's typical American parents taught her about the conduct of life is suppressed, for we meet the girl in a train to Chicago, on which she falls to the first drummer who accosts her. Eugene Witla emerges in his teens from the bosom of a typical middle-class American family—with a knowledge of the game called "post office," takes the train for Chicago, and without hesitation enters upon his long career of seduction. Jennie Gerhardt, of course, succumbs to the first man who puts his arm around her; but, in certain respects, her case is exceptional.

In the novel "Jennie Gerhardt" Mr. Dreiser ventures a disastrous experiment at making the jungle-motive plausible without suppressing the evidence of other motives. He provides the girl with pious Lutheran parents, of fallen fortune, but alleged to be of sterling character, who "raise" her with the utmost strictness. He even admits that the family were churchgoers, and he outlines the doctrine preached by Pastor

Wundt: right conduct in marriage and absolute innocence before that state, essentials of Christian living; no salvation for a daughter who failed to keep her chastity unstained or for the parents who permitted her to fall; Hell yawning for all such; God angry with sinners every day. "Gerhardt and his wife, and also Jennie," says Mr. Dreiser, "accepted the doctrines of their church without reserve." Twenty pages later Jennie is represented as yielding her virtue in pure gratitude to a man of fifty, Senator Brander, who has let her do his laundry and in other ways has been kind to her and to her family. The Senator suddenly dies; Jennie expects to become a mother; Father Gerhardt is broken-hearted, and the family moves from Columbus to Cleveland. This first episode is not incredibly presented as a momentary triumph of emotional impulse over training—as an "accident." The incredible appears when Mr. Dreiser insists that an accident of this sort to a girl brought up *under the conditions stated* is not necessarily followed by any sense of sin or shame or regret. Upon this simple pious Lutheran he imposes his own naturalistic philosophy, and, in analyzing her psychology before the birth of her illegitimate child, pretends that she looks forward to the event "without a murmur," with "serene, unfaltering courage," "the marvel of life holding her in trance," with "joy and satisfaction," seeing in her state "the immense possibilities of racial fulfilment." This juggling is probably expected to prepare us for her instantaneous assent, perhaps a year later, when a healthy, magnetic manufacturer, who has seen her perhaps a dozen times, claps his paw upon her and says, "You belong to me," and in a perfectly cold-blooded interview proposes the terms on which he will set her up in New York as his mistress. Jennie, who is a fond mother and a dutiful daughter, goes to her pious Lutheran mother and talks the whole matter over with her quite candidly. The mother hesitates—not on Jennie's account, gentle reader, but because she will be obliged to deceive old Gerhardt; "the difficulty of telling this lie was very great for Mrs. Gerhardt"! But she acquiesces at last. "I'll help you out with it," she concludes—"with a little sigh." The unreality of the whole transaction shrieks.

Mr. Dreiser's stubborn insistence upon the jungle-motive results in a dreary monotony in the form and substance of his novels. Interested only in the description of animal behavior, he constructs his plot in such way as to exhibit the persistence of two or three elementary instincts through every kind of situation. He finds, for example, a subject in the career of an American captain of industry, thinly disguised under the name of Frank Cowperwood. He has just two things to tell us about Cowperwood: that he has a rapacious appetite for money, and that he has a rapacious appetite for women. In "The Financier" he "documents" those two truths about Cowperwood in seventy-four chapters in each one of which he shows us how his hero made money or how he captivated women in Philadelphia. Not satisfied with the demonstration, he returns to the same theses in "The Titan," and shows us in sixty-two chapters how the same hero made money and captivated women in Chicago and New York. He promises us a third volume, in which we shall no doubt learn in a work of sixty or seventy chapters—a sort of huge club-sandwich composed of slices of business alternating with erotic episodes—how Frank Cowperwood made money and captivated women in London. Meanwhile Mr. Dreiser has turned aside from his great "trilogy of desire" to give us "The Genius," in which the hero, Witla, alleged to be a great realistic painter, exhibits in 101 chapters, similarly "sandwiched" together, an appetite for women and money indistinguishable from that of Cowperwood. Read one of these novels, and you have read them all. What the hero is in the first chapter, he remains in the hundred-and-first or the hundred-and-thirty-sixth. He acquires naught from his experience but sensations. In the sum of his experiences there is nothing of the impressive mass and coherence of activities bound together by principles and integrated in character, for all his days have been but as isolated beads loosely strung on the thread of his desire. And so after the production of the hundredth document in the case of Frank Cowperwood, one is ready to cry with fatigue: "Hold! Enough! We believe you. Yes, it is very clear that Frank Cowperwood had a rapacious appetite for women and for money."

If at this point you stop and inquire why Mr. Dreiser goes to such great lengths to establish so little, you find yourself once more confronting the jungle-motive. Mr. Dreiser, with a problem similar to De Foe's in "The Apparition of Mrs. Veal," has availed himself of De Foe's method for creating the illusion of reality. The essence of the problem and of the method for both these authors is the certification of the unreal by the irrelevant. If you wish to make acceptable to your reader the incredible notion that Mrs. Veal's ghost appeared to Mrs. Bargrave, divert his incredulity from the precise point at issue by telling him all sorts of detailed credible things about the poverty of Mrs. Veal's early life, the sobriety of her brother, her father's neglect, and the bad temper of Mrs. Bargrave's husband. If you wish to make acceptable to your reader the incredible notion that Aileen Butler's first breach of the seventh article in the decalogue was "a happy event," taking place "much as a marriage might have," divert his incredulity by describing with the technical accuracy of a fashion magazine not merely the gown that she wore on the night of Cowperwood's reception, but also with equal detail the half-dozen other gowns that she thought she might wear, but did not. If you have been for three years editor-in-chief of the Butterick Publications, you can probably perform this feat with unimpeachable verisimilitude; and having acquired credit for expert knowledge in matters of dress and millinery, you can now and then emit unchallenged a bit of philosophy such as "Life cannot be put in any one mould, and the attempt may as well be abandoned at once. . . . Besides, whether we will or no, theory or no theory, the large basic facts of chemistry and physics remain." None the less, if you expect to gain credence for the notion that your hero can have any woman in Chicago or New York that he puts his paw upon, you had probably better lead up to it by a detailed account of the street-railway system in those cities. It will necessitate the loading of your pages with a tremendous baggage of irrelevant detail. It will not sound much like art. It will sound more like one of Lincoln Steffens's special articles. But it will produce an overwhelming impression of reality, which the reader will carry with him into the next chapter where you are laying bare the "chemistry" of the human animal.

IV

It would make for clearness in our discussions of contemporary fiction if we withheld the title of "realist" from a writer like Mr. Dreiser, and called him, as Zola called himself, a "naturalist." While asserting that all great art in every period intends a representation of reality, I have tried to indicate the basis for a working distinction between the realistic novel and the naturalistic novel of the present day. Both are representations of the life of man in contemporary or nearly contemporary society, and both are presumably composed of materials within the experience and observation of the author. But a realistic novel is a representation based upon a theory of human conduct. If the theory of human conduct is adequate, the representation constitutes an addition to literature and to social history. A naturalistic novel is a representation based upon a theory of animal behavior. Since a theory of animal behavior can never be an adequate basis for a representation of the life of man in contemporary society, such a representation is an artistic blunder. When half the world attempts to assert such a theory, the other half rises in battle. And so one turns with relief from Mr. Dreiser's novels to the morning papers.

EIGHTEEN

THE ART OF THEODORE DREISER

Randolph Bourne

Randolph Bourne (1886–1918) suffered throughout his life from major physical handicaps but nevertheless played a significant role in American intellectual life during his brief career as a spokesman for radical literary and social positions. While still a Columbia undergraduate (1909–13), his contributions to journals on the new American society arising out of an immigrant culture and changing sexual mores drew much attention. It is not surprising that he became one of the most outspoken defenders of Theodore Dreiser during the period when Dreiser's work was under heavy attack both for its sexual themes and its "foreign" character. The best of Bourne's essays were collected after his death by Van Wyck Brooks in *The History of a Literary Radical and Other Essays*.

Theodore Dreiser has had the good fortune to evoke a peculiar quality of pugnacious interest among the younger American *intelligentsia* such as has been the lot of almost nobody else writing to-day unless it be Miss Amy Lowell. We do not usually take literature seriously enough to quarrel over it. Or else we take it so seriously that we urbanely avoid squabbles. Certainly there are none of the vendettas that rage in a culture like that of France. But Mr. Dreiser seems to have made himself, particularly since the suppression of "The 'Genius,' " a veritable issue. Interesting and surprising are the reactions to him. Edgar Lee Masters makes him a "soul-enrapt demi-urge, walking the earth, stalking life"; Harris Merton Lyon saw in him a "seer of inscrutable mien"; Arthur Davison Ficke sees him as master of a passing throng of figures, "labored with immortal illusion, the terrible and beautiful, cruel and wonder-laden

Dial 62 (14 June 1917): 507–9. Reprinted in *The History of a Literary Radical and Other Essays* (1920). Text from the *Dial*.

illusion of life"; Mr. Powys makes him an epic philosopher of the "lifetide"; H. L. Mencken puts him ahead of Conrad, with "an agnosticism that has almost passed beyond curiosity." On the other hand, an unhappy critic in the "Nation" last year gave Mr. Dreiser his place for all time in a neat antithesis between the realism that was based on a theory of human conduct and the naturalism that reduced life to a mere animal behavior. For Dreiser this last special hell was reserved, and the jungle-like and simian activities of his characters rather exhaustively outlined. At the time this antithesis looked silly. With the appearance of Mr. Dreiser's latest book, "A Hoosier Holiday," it becomes nonsensical. For that wise and delightful book reveals him as a very human critic of very common human life, romantically sensual and poetically realistic, with an artist's vision and a thick, warm feeling for American life.

This book gives the clue to Mr. Dreiser, to his insatiable curiosity about people, about their sexual inclinations, about their dreams, about the homely qualities that make them American. His memories give a picture of the floundering young American that is so typical as to be almost epic. No one has ever pictured this lower middle-class American life so winningly, because no one has had the necessary literary skill with the lack of self-consciousness. Mr. Dreiser is often sentimental, but it is a sentimentality that captivates you with its candor. You are seeing this vacuous, wistful, spiritually rootless, middle-Western life through the eyes of a naïve but very wise boy. Mr. Dreiser seems queer only because he has carried along his youthful attitude in unbroken continuity. He is fascinated with sex because youth is usually obsessed with sex. He puzzles about the universe because youth usually puzzles. He thrills to crudity and violence because sensitive youth usually recoils from the savagery of the industrial world. Imagine incorrigible, sensuous youth endowed with the brooding skepticism of the philosopher who feels the vanity of life, and you have the paradox of Mr. Dreiser. For these two attitudes in him support rather than oppose each other. His spiritual evolution was out of a pious, ascetic atmosphere into intellectual and personal freedom. He seems to have found himself without losing himself. Of how many American writers can this be said? And for this much shall be forgiven him,— his slovenliness of style, his lack of nuances, his apathy to the finer shades of beauty, his weakness for the mystical and the vague. Mr. Dreiser suggests the oversensitive temperament that protects itself by an admiration for crudity and cruelty. His latest book reveals the boyhood shyness and timidity of this Don Juan of novelists. Mr. Dreiser is complicated, but he is complicated in a very understandable American way, the product of the uncouth forces of small-town life and the vast disorganization of the wider American world. As he reveals himself, it is a revelation of a certain broad level of the American soul.

Mr. Dreiser seems uncommon only because he is more naïve than most of us. It is not so much that he swarms his pages with sexful figures as that he rescues sex for the scheme of personal life. He feels a holy mission to slay the American literary superstition that men and women are not sensual beings. But he does not brush this fact in the sniggering way of the popular magazines. He takes it very seriously, so much so that some of his novels become caricatures of desire. It is, however, a misfortune that it has been Brieux and Freud and not native Theodore Dreiser who soaked the sexual imagination of the younger American *intelligentsia*. It would have been far healthier to have absorbed Mr. Dreiser's literary treatment of sex than to have gone hysterical over its pathology. Sex has little significance unless it is treated in personally artistic, novelistic terms. The American tradition had tabooed the treatment of those infinite gradations and complexities of love that fill the literary imagination of a sensitive people. When curiosity got too strong and reticence was repealed in America, we had no means of articulating ourselves except in a deplorable pseudo-scientific jargon that has no more to do with the relevance of sex than the chemical composition of orange paint has to do with the artist's vision. Dreiser has done a real service to the American imagination in despising the underworld and going gravely to the business of picturing sex as it is lived in the personal relations of bungling, wistful, or masterful men and women. He seemed strange and rowdy only because he made sex human, and American tradition had never made it human. It had only made it either sacred or vulgar, and when these categories no longer worked, we fell under the dubious and perverting magic of the psychoanalysts.

In spite of his looseness of literary gait and heaviness of style Dreiser seems a sincere groper after beauty. It is natural enough that this should so largely be the beauty of sex. For where would a sensitive boy, brought up in Indiana and in the big American cities, get beauty expressed for him except in women? What does mid-Western America offer to the starving except its personal beauty? A few landscapes, an occasional picture in a museum, a book of verse perhaps! Would not all the rest be one long, flaunting offense of ugliness and depression? "The 'Genius,' " instead of being that mass of pornographic horror which the Vice Societies repute it to be, is the story of a groping artist whose love of beauty runs obsessingly upon the charm of girlhood. Through different social planes, through business and manual labor and the feverish world of artist, he pursues this lure. Dreiser is refreshing in his air of the moral democrat, who sees life impassively, neither praising nor blaming, at the same time that he realizes how much more terrible and beautiful and incalculable life is than any of us are willing to admit. It may be all *apologia*, but it comes with the grave air of a mind that wants us to understand just how it all happened. "Sister Carrie" will always retain the fresh charm of a spontaneous working-out of mediocre, and yet elemental and significant, lives. A good novelist catches hold of the thread of human desire. Dreiser does this, and that is why his admirers forgive him so many faults.

If you like to speculate about personal and literary qualities that are specifically American, Dreiser should be as interesting as any one now writing in America. This becomes clearer as he writes more about his youth. His hopelessly unorientated, half-educated, boyhood is so typical of the uncritical and careless society in which wistful American talent has had to grope. He had to be spiritually a self-made man, work out a philosophy of life, discover his own sincerity. Talent in America outside of the ruling class flowers very late, because it takes so long to find its bearings. It has had almost to create its own soil, before it could put in its roots and grow. It is born shivering into an inhospitable and irrelevant group. It has to find its own kind of people and piece together its links of comprehension. It is a gruelling and tedious task, but those who come through it contribute, like Vachel Lindsay, creative work that is both novel and indigenous. The process can be more easily traced in Dreiser than in almost any-body else. "A Hoosier Holiday" not only traces the personal process, but it gives the social background. The common life, as seen throughout the countryside, is touched off quizzically, and yet sympathetically, with an artist's vision. Dreiser sees the American masses in their commonness and at their pleasure as brisk, rather vacuous people, a little pathetic in their innocence of the possibilities of life and their optimistic trust-fulness. He sees them ruled by great barons of industry, and yet unconscious of their serfdom. He seems to love this countryside, and he makes you love it.

Dreiser loves, too, the ugly violent bursts of American industry,—the flaming steel-mills and gaunt lakesides. "The Titan" and "The Financier" are unattractive novels, but the are human documents of the brawn of a passing American era. Those steno-graphic conversations, webs of financial intrigue, bare bones of enterprise, insult our artistic sense. There is too much raw beef, and yet it all has the taste and smell of the primitive business-jungle it deals with. These crude and greedy captains of finance with their wars and their amours had to be given some kind of literary embodiment, and Dreiser has hammered a sort of raw epic out of their lives.

It is not only his feeling for these themes of crude power and sex and the American common life that make Dreiser interesting. His emphases are those of a new America which is latently expressive and which must develop its art before we shall really have become articulate. For Dreiser is a true hyphenate, a product of that conglomerate Americanism that springs from other roots than the English tradition. Do we realize how rare it is to find a talent that is thoroughly American and wholly un-English? Culturally we have somehow suppressed the hyphenate. Only recently has he forced his way through the unofficial literary censorship. The *vers-librists* teem with him, but Dreiser is almost the first to achieve a largeness of utterance. His outlook, it is true, flouts the American canons of optimism and redemption, but these were never anything but conventions. There stirs in Dreiser's book a new American quality. It is not at all German. It is an authentic attempt to make something artistic out of the chaotic materials that lie around us in American life. Dreiser interests because we can watch him grope and feel his clumsiness. He has the artist's vision without the sure-ness of the artist's technique. That is one of the tragedies of America. But his faults are those of his material and of uncouth bulk, and not of shoddiness. He expresses an America that is in process of forming. The interest he evokes is part of the eager interest we feel in that growth.

NINETEEN

WILLIAM DEAN HOWELLS AND THE REALISM OF THE COMMONPLACE

V. L. Parrington

Vernon Louis Parrington (1871–1929) was Illinois born and Kansas bred. He received a B.A. from Harvard and taught in Kansas and Oklahoma before moving to the University of Washington in 1908, where he remained until his death. Parrington is known almost entirely for his monumental three-volume *Main Currents in American Thought* (1927–30), the third volume of which was published in incomplete form in 1930 after his death. A full generation of American literary and intellectual historians, until the domination of the field by the New Criticism in the 1950s, was deeply influenced by Parrington's reading of America's past in terms of his Jeffersonian and economic determinism beliefs.

*   *   *   *   *

From such nostalgia [that of Henry James], that left a note of wistfulness in his pages, William Dean Howells was saved by his frank and undivided loyalties. Intellectually and emotionally he was native to the American soil, and however widely he might range he remained always a conscious American. He had no wish to Europeanize his mind; he felt no secret hankerings for the ways of Mayfair or the culture of the Quartier Saint Germain. The homely American reality satisfied the needs of his art, and he accepted it with the finality of Walt Whitman. If he failed to depict it in all its sprawl-

The Beginnings of Critical Realism in America: An Interpretation of American Literature from the Beginnings to 1920 (Vol. 3 of *Main Currents in American Thought*) (New York: Harcourt Brace, 1930), pp. 241–58. Copyright 1930 by Harcourt Brace & Company and renewed 1958 by V. L. Parrington Jr. Reprinted by permission of the publisher.

ing veracity, if much of its crude robustness never got into his pages, the lack was due to no self-imposed alienation, but to the temperament of the artist and the refined discretions of his environment.

The current school of realism is inclined to deal harshly with Howells. His quiet reticences, his obtrusive morality, his genial optimism, his dislike of looking ugly facts in the face, are too old-fashioned today to please the professional purveyors of our current disgusts. They find his writings as tedious as the gossip of old ladies. To their coarser palates his respectable commonplace is as flavorless as biscuit and tea. Yet it must not be forgotten that for years he was reckoned new-fashioned. Whatever may be one's final judgment on his work it is certain that for twenty years he was a prophet of realism to his generation, the leader of a movement to turn American literature from the path of romanticism and bring it face to face with the real and actual. It was not his fault that the ways of one generation are not those of another, and it is well to remember that if his realism seems wanting to a generation bred up on Theodore Dreiser, it seemed a debasement of the fine art of literature to a generation bred up on Thomas Bailey Aldrich. Realism like dress changes its modes.

The Howells we know best was not a simple child of the frontier, like Mark Twain, whom all could laugh with and love because the sallies of his wit awakened a native response. He did not remain completely native to the older folk-ways. He was rather a composite of the ideals reckoned excellent by the postwar generation—an American Victorian, kindly, urbane, tolerant, democratic, accepting America as a land that God's smile rests on, and convinced that here, wedded to a generous democracy, culture must eventually produce offspring finer than the world has hitherto known. Bred up in the mystical Swedenborgian faith, he shrank from all fleshliness and loved purity with the devotion of a Galahad. A child of the Ohio frontier, he retained to the last the western feeling of democratic equality. An adopted son of Brahmin Cambridge, he immersed himself in culture—Italian, English, Yankee—and served the ideal of excellence with a lifelong devotion; a reverent pilgrim to the shrine of truth, he followed such paths as his generation knew to lay his art at the high altar. In all these things—in his ample culture, his kindly democracy, his high standards of workmanship—as well as in the instinctive reverences of a clean and sweet nature, he was an embodiment of the best in American life, a child of Jacksonian democracy who made use of his freedoms to serve the excellent cause of culture.

But he was much more than that, and if the critics who are wont to damn his Victorian squeamishness would penetrate to the inner core of Howells they would discover an intellectual, alert and sensitive to changing currents of thought, seeing with his own eyes, pursuing his own ends, who wrought out for himself a culture that was individual and native. If he was not, like Henry Adams, plagued with an itch of curiosity, he traveled widely in the realm of the mind. Culture meant to him open-mindedness, familiarity with diverse schools of thought, a willingness to venture upon the unorthodox and to defend the unpopular. He was never a child of the Gilded Age. He was unsoiled by its vulgarity, unconcerned with its sordid ambitions. Neither at heart was he a child of Brahmin culture. He loved Lowell and Norton and Godkin and Aldrich, and he wanted to be approved by them; but he ranged far more widely than they, into places they thought indiscreet. The mature Howells came to stand apart from Brahminism, dissatisfied with a literary Toryism, convinced that a sterile genteel tradition could not suffice the needs of American literature. His very drift toward realism was a negation of the Brahmin influence. On the whole it was unfortunate that he lived so long in the Cambridge atmosphere. The New England influence may not have been a factor in shaping his too leisurely technique, but certainly it postponed the day of his intellectual release. If he had removed to New York a decade earlier, before his literary method hardened into rigidity, his technique might have changed with his more radical intellectual outlook and become the vehicle of a more adequate realism than he ever achieved.

But the significant thing is that the mind of Howells refused to imprison itself in Brahmin orthodoxies, but set forth on perilous expeditions while Lowell and Norton were discreetly evading the intellectual heresies raging outside their libraries. While Henry James was moving towards aristocratic Mayfair, Howells was journeying towards the proletarian East Side. The scientific revolution seems early to have washed in upon him, undermining the theological cosmos of his youth and turning him into a liberal freethinker. His scientific views very likely came to him secondhand, through the medium of literature; but with his wide reading in Continental fields—Spanish, French, German, Scandinavian—he could not fail to become saturated with the evolutionary view then permeating all current letters. In this he was only following with John Fiske and Henry Holt and Henry Adams the path of a new orthodoxy; nevertheless in applying the scientific spirit to fiction and espousing an objective realism, he quite definitely broke with Brahmin tradition. And when, under the guise of fiction, he turned to social questions, and wove into the placid texture of his work the vexing problem of social justice, he ventured on perilous ground where his Brahmin friends would not follow. To espouse the teachings of Herbert Spencer was one thing, to espouse the teachings of Karl Marx was quite another.

Howells came late to an interest in sociology, held back by the strong literary and aesthetic cast of his mind. But in the eighties, when he had reached middle life, he was no longer able to ignore or evade the economic maladjustments of the Gilded Age. The social unrest that was coming to bloody issue in strikes and lockouts gave him acute concern, and slowly under pressure of a sensitive social conscience there began a quiet intellectual revolution that was to transform the detached observer of the American scene into a Marxian socialist. A democrat, a lover of his kind, a just soul endowed with a tender conscience, an idealist who dreamed of a brotherhood of free men who should create in America a civilization adequate to human needs, what else could he do? He loved peace but war was all about him. And so in the mid-afternoon of life he turned to the work of spreading the gospel of social democracy in the America of the Gilded Age. He had no private or personal causes to serve. He had not, like Godkin and Dana, given hostages to fortune in the shape of a newspaper or magazine; he had no call to be partisan to his own interests. He was free to plead the cause of justice in his own way and at his own time. It is easy for the later radical to sneer at him as a parlor socialist who talked well but carefully refrained from disturbing the capitalistic machine from which he drew his income; but that is to ignore the courage of the artist in confronting a hostile world. He stood stoutly for the rights of workingmen that the passions of the times swept rudely away. When the Haymarket Riot in Chicago brought its shameful hysteria, and all respectable America was crying for blood, Howells was one of the few intellectuals who spoke for justice, one of the few who held aloof from the mob spirit, thereby bringing on his head a wave of criticism. It was a brave thing in 1886 to speak for the "Chicago anarchists."

But it was not till his removal to New York, where he found himself at the center of the great revolution, that he set about seriously studying the way of plutocracy. For the student of Cambridge society it involved a mental upheaval. The urbanity of his literary-manner conceals for most readers the intensity of emotion that underlies his quiet style; yet it is clear enough that having examined the ways of private capitalism and considered its works, he rejected it. Thenceforth to the end of his life he hated the thing and quietly preached against it. His affections went back fondly to the earlier agricultural order that had shaped his youth, and in the character of Dryfoos, in *A Hazard of New Fortunes*, he suggests the moral degeneration that he believed followed in the train of the substitution of a speculative capitalist economy for the wholesomer agrarian economy. But though, remembering his frontier youth, he might prefer the older ways, he was realist enough to understand that capitalism was the order of his generation, and he turned eagerly to explore the new proletarian philosophies that came out of Germany. Howells was the first distinguished American man of letters to espouse Marxian socialism. For a cultivated American in the Gilded Age to sympathize with proletarian theory and to proclaim himself a socialist, was enough to excite amazement in his fellows. In the eighties American social thought was still naïve and provincial. Old-world theories were as alien as old-world institutions, and in spite of the wide interest aroused by *Looking Backward* the intelligent American in 1890 knew as little about Marxianism as he knows today about Bolshevism.

The doubts and hesitations that troubled Howells during these years of changing outlook, are skillfully dramatized in *A Hazard of New Fortunes*. The story of the removal of the Marshes from New England to New York, told with more than usual leisureliness, is the story of the transition from the peacefulness of his earlier literary life to the anxieties of his later thought. Slowly into a story of the familiar Howells commonplace comes the note of social dissension. Antagonistic social philosophies meet and clash, and the movement draws inevitably to the great climax of the strike that brings tragedy into the scene. Of the mood that grew upon him as he wrote he afterwards said:

> It became, to my thinking, the most vital of my fictions; through my quickened interest in the life about me, at a moment of great psychological import. We had passed through a period of strong emotioning in the direction of humaner economics, . . . the rich seemed not so much to despise the poor, and the poor did not so hopelessly repine. That shedding of blood which is for the remission of sins had been symbolized by the bombs and scaffolds of Chicago, and the hearts of

those who felt this bound up with our rights, the slavery implicated in our liberty, were thrilling with griefs and hopes hitherto strange to the average American breast. Opportunely for me there was a great street-car strike in New York, and the story began to find its way to issues nobler and larger than those of the love-affairs common to fiction.[1]

The years of unrest marked by the great agrarian revolt were years of great intellectual activity for Howells, during which his thought ripened and mellowed. His own liberal spirit drew to him the liberal spirits of the younger generation, and he became the counselor and friend of many of the young rebels of the day. His sympathy went out to all who were concerned at the injustice of the world. He questioned the right of none to uphold his creed, nor sought to impose his own beliefs upon others. As he watched the great struggle of the times his heart was always on the side of the weak and exploited. Very likely he knew little about the economics of money and finance, over which rival partisans were quarreling savagely, but he understood the human side of the farmers' problem and it was always the balance in the human ledger that weighed with him.

He was a friend of Hamlin Garland and rejoiced when *Main-Travelled Roads* was given to the world, writing for it an introduction warmly and tenderly sympathetic. As an artist he grew concerned lest under the stimulus of B. O. Flower the zeal of the propagandist should submerge the art of the story-teller; but he had no quarrel with the "causes" that were fermenting in the mind of the young Populist, and would not lessen one whit the ardor of his social faith. Throughout the passionate campaign of 1896, that brought most of his friends to a blind and scurrilous partisanship of the gold standard, his heart kept his mind just and his sympathy for the unrequited producers served as counterbalance to the shrill vituperation of his friend Godkin. He had thought too long and too honestly to be moved by the *claque* of the press.

It was in the black days of the panic of '93 that he seems to have brooded most thoughtfully over the ways of capitalistic America, and in the following year he published *The Traveller from Altruria*, the first of his two Utopian romances in which he subjected the system of capitalism to critical analysis. It is a clever book that quite disarms the reader. Howells delivers no broadside attack on the capitalistic system, and he suggests its mean and selfish exploitation with such genial urbanity, such sly satire, as to arouse no sleeping lions. The concern in his heart is belied by the twinkle in his eye. He hints that the Altrurian critic is only the figment of a dream, and he smilingly suggests the sources of the Altrurian commonwealth in the long line of Utopian dreamers from Plato and Sir Thomas More to Bellamy and William Morris. But the urbanity is only a mask. Protected by it Howells delivers many a shrewd thrust at the ways of capitalism. American democracy does not show to advantage under his analysis. The Altrurian comes upon the canker of social injustice in every chink and cranny of life—a canker that is slowly destroying democratic America; and Howells takes a sly pleasure in contrasting our democratic professions with our plutocratic practice. There is a delightful irony in his attack on the professional classes—

the professor, the minister, the writer—for their quick defense of the exploiting classes. What may we expect of the science of economics, he suggests, when our academic economists are only apologists for the existing order?

The Traveller from Altruria is a shrewd analysis of American life set against a Marxian background, and in forecasting the future Howells follows the Marxian law of concentration. The Age of Accumulation, with its gigantic monopolies gathered in ever fewer hands, prepared the way for a new order when industrialism, grown over-big, falls into the control of the state as naturally as the harvest is gathered into the granary. There was no need of a class war. When the times were ripe political means sufficed, for the democracy retained the effective weapon of the vote. Thirteen years later Howells completed his Utopian venture with *Through the Eye of the Needle*, in which he sketches in fuller detail the order of life in Altruria. It was not till men learned that cooperation is a better social cement than competition, altruism than egoism, that the new order was possible; and in this later work he depicts the kindly, rational society that emerged when men left off fighting each other and turned to working together instead. On every page the influence of William Morris is revealed—not only in the rejection of an urban society founded on the machine and a return to a decentralized anarchistic order, but in the emphasis on the psychology of work and the satisfactions that spring from free creative labor. *Through the Eye of the Needle* is curiously reminiscent of *News from Nowhere* and suggests how sympathetically Howells followed English social thought in its reaction against industrialism.

It was while he was thus engaged that he put into compact form his speculations on the theory of realism. For more than a decade he had been the most distinguished advocate of realism in America, and for longer still his successive novels had revealed to a critical world what substance and form he believed the realistic novel should possess. The immediate sources of his theory are obscure, though it is clear enough that the work of Jane Austen was a creative influence. From the school of French and Russian naturalism, then at the height of its vigor, he drew back in repulsion, and it was not till after his technique was matured that Tolstoi became an influence in his intellectual life. It is reasonable to assume that his realism was a native growth, the result of temperament unfolding through quiet years of reading in the English classics. A quizzical observer with the gift of humor is not likely to run into romanticism, and a youthful passion for Pope and Heine is not the best preparation for it. His intense dislike of the romantic, that led him to an inadequate and partial conception of it, seems to have sprung from certain instinctive feelings and convictions that strengthened with the years; a deep and sincere love of truth, a native sympathy with the simple homely phases of life, a quiet loyalty to American fact, and a sharp distrust of the aristocratic spirit. Endowed with such feelings he came to ascribe his own partisanships to literary methods; the romantic became for him the aristocratic, and the realistic became the democratic. As an American he was content to take the common stuff of life, as he found it in America, and depict it in unpretentious sincerity. Plain American life was not only worthy of literature, he was convinced, but the only material worthy of American literature. The path to the universal runs as directly through the commonplace American parlor as through the hall of the medieval baron or the drawing-room of Mayfair.

In *Criticism and Fiction* (1894), Howells ascribes the rise of modern realism to the twin sources of science and democracy. From science it derives its passion for truth, for "realism," he asserts, "is nothing more and nothing less than the truthful treatment of material." "We must ask ourselves before we ask anything else, Is it true?—true to the motives, the impulses, the principles, that shape the life of actual men and women." The question, what is essential truth, that has been the apple of discord amongst the realists, Howells answers in democratic fashion by appealing to the average. The "foolish man," he says, "wonders at the unusual, but the wise man at the usual." The realist, therefore, will deal objectively with the usual and common rather than with the unusual or strange, and in so doing he draws closer to the common heart of humanity, and learns the respect for simple human nature that is the source and wellspring of democracy. In delineating truthfully the prosaic lives of common people realism reveals the essential dignity and worth of all life. The romantic, on the other hand, is aristocratic. "It seeks to withdraw itself, to stand aloof; to be distinguished and not to be identified." "The pride of caste has become the pride of taste," and romance is the last refuse of the aristocratic spirit that, defeated elsewhere, has taken refuge in culture. Not aloofness, but comradeship, is the need of the world; not distinction, but identity. Realism is the child of democracy because the realist is one who "feels in every nerve the equality of things and the unity of men," and the great artist is one with a talent "robust enough to front the everyday world and catch the charm of its work-worn, care-worn, brave, kindly face."

To this characteristic conception that realism is democratic Howells adds certain other dicta that to his own generation seemed as true as to ours they seem doubtful: that art must serve morality, that it must teach rather than amuse, and that truthfulness to American life requires a note of cheerfulness. Art cannot flout the "eternal amenities," Howells asserted, for "morality penetrates all things, it is the soul of all things." Nor can it stand aloof, disdaining the office of teacher, for unless it "tends to make the world better and kinder" it is empty and futile; and it can do this only "from and through the truth." But the truth that will uplift society does not dwell in the kennel and pigsty; it will not be come upon by exploring the animal in man, or in wrapping the shroud of pessimism about life. In America at least, realism must concern itself with the "large cheerful average of health and success and happy life," for after all "the more smiling aspects of life" are "the more American." From such postulates Howells developed his familiar technique, which in minimizing plot, rejecting the unusual and strange and heroic, reduced his stories to the drab level that bores so many of his readers, and evokes the criticism that in elaboration of the commonplace he evades the deeper and more tragic realities that reach to the heart of life.

The criticism is just. More than any other thing this concern for the usual weakens Howells's work and renders it trivial. He does not probe the depths of emotional experience. Neither the life of the spirit nor the passions of the flesh is the stuff from which he weaves his stories. The lack—and allowing for all his solid excellence it remains grave—sprang in part from his own timid nature that recoiled from the gross and the unpleasant, and in part from the environment in which he perfected his technique. For years he lived in an atmosphere of complacent convention, a society dominated by women, culture, and conscience. Cambridge and Boston in the seventies and eighties were still in the Age of Innocence greatly concerned with erecting defenses against the intrusion of the unpleasant, reverencing the genteel in life and letters, soberly moral and making much of the eternal verities. In such a world of refined manners and narrow outlook what should the realist do but report faithfully of what he saw and heard? And so Howells, perforce, became a specialist in women's nerves, an analyst of the tenuous New England conscience, a master of Boston small-talk. It was such materials that shaped his leisurely technique until it falls about his theme with the amplitude of crinoline.

Through these chronicles of the Age of Innocence runs a persistent note of the neurotic. There are more scruples to a page of Howells than in any other writer except Henry James—for the most part filmy cobwebs invisible to the coarser vision of a later generation. The action percolates through the sand of small-talk, welling up from the tiniest springs and stopped by the smallest obstruction. Like Franklin's two-headed snake his characters are in danger of dying from thirst because of much argument over the right path to water. It is hard to weave a substantial fabric from such gossamer threads, and when in *The Rise of Silas Lapham* endless pages are devoted to the ethical subtleties of a woman's accepting the hand of a man who the family had believed was in love with his sister, or when in *April Hopes* the fantastic scruples of a neurotic girl are elaborated with a refinement of art worthy of a Fra Angelico Madonna, the stuff is too filmy to wear well. Commonplace men and neurotic women are poor materials from which to fashion an adequate realism, and with the passing of the Age of Innocence the scruples of Howells went out of fashion.

The fault, in part at least, must be traced to the artist's deep reverence for New England. From his youth he had cherished an exalted notion of the sufficiency of New England culture, and had accepted its parochialisms as ultimate standards. To a bookish lad, inclined to be too consciously literary, such loyalty to a declining school could only accentuate his native aloofness from life. His four years at Venice had been given over to an ardent pursuit of culture, as culture was understood by Lowell and Norton. It was the natural impulse of a sensitive mind, conscious of its limitations, reveling for the first time in the wealth that had been denied his frontier boyhood. His poetic *Venetian Days* was an infallible passport to Boston favor, and when after his return he was taken up by the *Atlantic* group he carried with him to Boston an unconscious inferiority complex that did his genius an evil turn. It was natural for the self-taught western youth to be reverent in presence of the great of earth; but it is not well for the artist to be humble in the presence of his masters. Unless he is something of a rebel, given to questioning the dogmas of the schools, he will never ripen into creative originality.

An inferiority complex is a common mark of the frontier mind that finds itself diffident in presence of the old and established, and Howells suffered from it greatly. For years his keen eyes lacked their usual shrewdness in judging Boston ways, and to the end of his life he overestimated the greatness of the men to whom his youthful loyalty had gone out. Not only did he accept Lowell and Holmes and Longfellow at the Boston rating, but he regarded the lesser group of cultivated Boston gentlemen with partial eyes. It would have been far better for his art if like Hamlin Garland he had never been received within the charmed circle; if he had had to make his way alone. To justify his acceptance Howells felt that he must prove himself as completely Bostonian as the best, and in consequence he sloughed off his western heritage, perverted his genius, and shaped his realism to the slender materials discovered in Back Bay drawing-rooms. The genteel tradition was in the way of strangling his realism.

Subjected to such refinements his realism in the end became little more than technique—a meticulous transcription of New England conventions, the casual action submerging itself in an endless stream of talk. No doubt Howells was true to what he saw; certainly no one has ever fixed more exactly the thin substance of the Age of Innocence. Nevertheless the fidelity of his observation, the refinement of his prose style, and the subtlety of his humor that plays lambently about the edges of his words, do not compensate for the slightness of his materials. The record he has left is not that of a great soul brooding over the meaning of life, puzzled, uncertain, yet tender toward the victims that fate has seized and crushed. He was restrained by too many inhibitions to deal frankly with natural human passions. He felt deeply and tenderly, but he was too diffident to let himself go. It is likely that Howells never realized the inadequacy of his temperament and the futility of his method to any serious realism. Even in his acutest study *A Hazard of New Fortunes*, which comes upon brutal economic reality, the story is entangled in a mass of minute detail and never quite breaks through. The indecisions, the repetitions, the whimsical descriptions, the drifting talk, are all true to life, but they are not essential or vital truth. The real issue toward which the story moves—the problem of social justice and the contrasting systems of wage-slavery, bond-slavery, and social democracy—is obscured in a welter of asides and never quite reaches the front of the stage. He is more effective in such works as *Indian Summer*, when he deals with characters on vacation who play whimsically with love, and in *April Hopes*, when he dwells fondly on the infinitely eloquent trivialities of young love-making. In such studies the minute fidelity to word and gesture, the humorous playing with invisible scruple, is a pleasant substitute for solider material.

Howells had real gifts, of which he made the most. Refinement, humor, sympathy—fidelity to external manner and rare skill in catching the changing expression of life—a passion for truth and a jealous regard for his art: he had all these qualities, yet they were not enough to make him a great realist. He belonged to the Age of Innocence and with its passing his works have been laid away. He has had no followers to keep his method alive. If one may hazard an explanation of the lot that has befallen him, it would be this. Howells the artist mistook his calling. He was not by temperament a novelist. He lacked the sense of drama, a grasp of the rough fabric of life, the power to deal imaginatively with the great and tragic realities. His genius was rather that of a whimsical essayist, a humorous observer of the illogical ways of men. He was an eighteenth-century spirit—a subtler Goldsmith—set down in another age and an uncongenial world. In his later years he must have come to realize this, for more and more he turned to the essay form. There his quiet humor and shrewd observation fitted his sinuous prose style to a nicety. In such sketchy autobiography as *My Literary Passions*, and more whimsically in such genial travel essays as *Certain Delightful English Towns*, his refined art arrived at its most perfect expression. Not an original genius like Mark Twain, far from a turbulent soul like Herman Melville, Howells was the reporter of his generation—the greatest literary figure of a drab negative age when the older literary impulse was slackening, and the new was slowly displacing it. He marks the transition between the earlier idealism and the later naturalism. A humane and lovable soul, he was the embodiment of all that was kindly and generous in an America that was not wholly given over to the ways of the Gilded Age—an America that loved beauty and served culture even amidst the turmoil of revolution.

NOTE

1. Quoted in "The Social Consciousness of William Dean Howells," *New Republic*, Vol. 26, p. 193.

TWENTY

NATURALISM IN AMERICAN FICTION

V. L. Parrington

Naturalism originated in France. Term first used by Zola. Chief example—Flaubert's *Mme. Bovary*. Contrast between Zola and Flaubert reveals two diverse tendencies of the movement—a sociological study of background, with a multitude of characters dwarfed by the *milieu*; and psychological study of individual character.

Naturalism a child of nineteenth-century thought—offspring of Darwin, Marx, Comte, Taine. The scientific movement created a scientific attitude of mind and emphasized the law of causation. From this emerged two fruitful ideas: (1) biological determinism, (2) economic determinism. So Zola and Flaubert. Influence of Claude Bernard—"We take men from the hands of the physiologist solely . . . to solve scientifically the question of how men behave in society."

The criteria of naturalism are:

1. Objectivity. Seek the truth in the spirit of the scientist. "We naturalists, we men of science," Zola says, accepting Bernard's position, "we must admit of nothing occult; men are but phenomena and the conditions of phenomena."

2. Frankness. A rejection of Victorian reticence. The total man and woman must be studied—the deeper instincts, the endless impulses. The three strongest instincts are fear, hunger, sex. In the life of the ordinary person, the third is most critical, hence the naturalist makes much of it.

3. An amoral attitude toward material. The naturalist is not a judge, he holds no brief for any ethical standards. He records what happens. He "must possess a knowledge of the mechanisms inherent in man, show the machinery of his intellectual and sensory manifestations, under the influence of heredity and environment, such as physiology shall give them to us, and then finally, to exhibit man living in social conditions, produced by himself, which he modifies daily and in the heart of which he is undergoing constant transformation." (Zola.) This is difficult to accept. Puritanism.

4. A philosophy of determinism. This is the vital principle of naturalism, setting it

The Beginnings of Critical Realism in America: An Interpretation of American Literature from the Beginnings to 1920 (Vol. 3 of *Main Currents in American Thought*) (New York: Harcourt Brace, 1930), pp. 323–34. Copyright 1930 by Harcourt Brace & Company and renewed 1958 by V. L. Parrington Jr. Reprinted by permission of the publisher. (A publisher's note accompanying this material explained that it consisted of notes prepared by Parrington for a lecture at the University of California.)

off from realism. The scientist has turned philosopher. It is the residuum of much pondering over life and its meaning, and may result from:

    a. Sociological emphasis—study of heredity and environment.

    b. A broader mechanistic philosophy—Flaubert, Dreiser.

    c. Fatalism: a world of malignant chance—Hardy.

    5. A bias toward pessimism in selecting details. A reaction from the romantic conception of a purposive will.

Romance springs from the longings of a baffled and thwarted will, creating a world as we should like it wherein to find refuge. But the naturalist will tolerate no such refuge. He will envisage the truth, and the truth that he sees is that the individual is impotent in the face of things. Hence it is as the victim, the individual defeated by the world, and made a sardonic jest of, that the naturalist chooses to portray man. Always that conception creeps in. It is seen and felt throughout the texture of the story—a fate lurking in the background and visible to the reader—and at some dramatic moment the conviction comes home to the victim and is crystallized in bitter words wrenched from his baffled will. The business of the story is to lead him up to this crystallization.

There are two main forms—(1) Life is a trap. (2) Life is mean. So Strindberg's Countess Julie: "Everything is wreckage, that drifts over the water until it sinks, sinks." So Ray Pearson in Sherwood Anderson's *Winesburg, Ohio*: "Tricked, by Gad, tricked by life and made a fool of." So D. H. Lawrence: "We are prostituted, oh, prostituted by life." To Ma Westcott "Life is duty. It is a lie." This pressure may come from without—*milieu*—or from within—imperious desires—but the outcome is usually hopeless sorrow—sometimes stolid resignation, sometimes fierce protest, but with no other end than annihilation. An exception is Maugham's *Of Human Bondage*.

    6. A bias in selection of characters. The naturalist commonly chooses one of three types:

    a. Characters of marked physique and small intellectual activity—persons of strong animal drives. They range all the way from morons like Norris's McTeague, Zola's Nana, and Dreiser's Jennie Gerhardt to natures like Hardy's Tess, and Sallie in *Of Human Bondage*.

    b. Characters of excited, neurotic temperament, at the mercy of moods, driven by forces that they do not stop to analyze. Such are Strindberg's Countess Julie, Sue, Emma Bovary, and the hero in *Of Human Bondage*. Sometimes this is aggravated by some physical defect, like a club-foot.

    c. An occasional use of a strong character whose will is broken. Thus Hardy's Jude and the doctor in Strindberg's *By the Open Sea*. But such are comparatively infrequent.

Naturalism is pessimistic realism, with a philosophy that sets man in a mechanical world and conceives of him as victimized by that world. *Certain unconscious exaggerations of naturalism.* Since men are victimized either by outer forces—the *milieu*—or by inner drives—impulses and instincts—the naturalist from much brooding is subject to certain temptations:

1. From concern over a devastating *milieu* he may end in desiring to change that *milieu* to the end that men may achieve happiness. Hence he tends to lose his objectivity and scientific detachment, and becomes a partisan to a cause. Such as the fate of Zola. The philosopher of naturalism, in practice he abandoned his principles and became a reformer, attacking the church, the capitalistic order, etc. His *J'accuse* letter is characteristic of this. *Nana*, almost alone, preserves the naturalistic attitude. This was the failure of the first group of American naturalists—Frank Norris, Robert Herrick, Jack London.

2. From much study of inner drives of low-grade characters the naturalist is in danger of creating grotesques. Behavioristic psychology may prove to be a further temptation, in creating a "sex complex." So Masters's *Spoon River Anthology*, Sherwood Anderson, D. H. Lawrence, Frank Norris. Most common in the later American naturalists. So Brander Matthews.

3. From much emphasis on animal impulses the naturalist may turn man into an animal. Men are more than sex-driven creatures—the city is more than the slums. There are sewers, but why not accept the sewer without messing over its contents as they flow to disintegration? This is the commonest objection to naturalism. So Meredith: "The naturalist sees the hog in nature, and takes nature for the hog." It is certainly an overcorrection—a reaction against the complacent optimism of romanticism—against too much shutting of the eyes to slums and filth and sewers. To a mechanist like Dreiser, who traces life and conduct back to chemistry, or to the behaviorist, who traces it to ducts and glands, it is rational. The charge may be true of Zola, of De Maupassant, of Anderson, of Lawrence, but it is not true of Hardy, of Maugham.

Naturalism and the Conception of Tragedy. Naturalistic books are almost inevitably tragedies, but the philosophy of naturalism that underlies them has played havoc with the Aristotelian conception of tragedy. As Ludwig Lewisohn says, it has "rendered the traditional principle of tragedy wholly archaic." According to the Aristotelian tradition, tragedy results when an essentially noble character of heroic proportions transgresses an immutable moral law by a self-originating will and suffers the punishment dealt by poetic justice. So Macbeth, Othello, Lear, Hamlet. But this assumes two thing: (1) an eternally changeless moral law; (2) the existence of a purposive will. Both of these the naturalist refuses to accept. Compare Hardy.

> It became clear that the self-originating element in human action is small. The individual acts in harmony with his character, which is largely the result of complex and uncontrollable causes. It became even clearer that among the totality of moral values an absolute validity can be assigned to a few only. Hence the basic conception of tragic guilt was undermined from within and from without. The transgression of an immutable moral law by a self-originating will was seen to be an essentially meaningless conception, since neither eternally changeless moral law nor an un-caused volition is to be found in the universe that we perceive.[1]

The tragedy of naturalism lies in the disintegration and the pity or irony with which we contemplate man and his fate in the world.

Naturalism and the Traditional American Temper. The two most characteristic qualities of the American temper are Puritanism and optimism—the belief in the supremacy of the moral law, and the conviction that this is a good world that man shapes to his will. This is to be believed historically: the former is traditionally English, the latter a product of new-world economics—a decentralized society. Pessimistic determinism results inevitably from the sense of social pressure on the individual. Social complexity entails a feeling of coercive regimentation by forces too strong to contend against. These forces are both internal and external: environment or the social machine; heredity or the physical machine. The most complete dwarfing of the individual will and significance takes place in the most crowded societies, producing a corresponding philosophy and psychology. So the fatalism of the Orient and the dream of Nirvana. The first widespread philosophy of determinism among English people was spread by Calvinism. Predestination was an alien thought, the last expression of a world depressed by Roman regimentation and degeneration. Augustine preached that men are evil, and men are doomed. This old-world dogma was brought to America, where regimentation was impossible. A free economics created a free-will philosophy and psychology. The will to succeed. This flowered in Emerson. Philosophical optimism. The world is good, man is good: let him stand upon his instincts and there abide and the whole world will come round to him. "Trust thyself." Since Emerson's time a new world has been emerging. The old shadow is falling across the American mind. Determinism is in the air.

Complexity and American Determinism. Complexity springs from:

1. Machine industrialism. The bigness of the economic machine dwarfs the individual and creates a sense of impotency.

2. The great city reduces the individual to a unit. By machine methods of transportation and quantity output individual differences are worn away. We dress, live, think, work, play, alike. The *Saturday Evening Post* is fast regimenting the American mind. Standardization.

3. Centralization of wealth is creating a caste regimentation.

4. A mechanistic psychology. Behaviorism: stimulus and response; ducts and glands. The individual conceived as a mechanism, driven by instincts and habits.

America today is the greatest, most complex machine the world has ever known. Individualism is giving way to regimentation, caste, standardization. Optimism is gone; pessimism is on the horizon. The psychology of naturalism is being prepared.

Three American writers began an experiment in naturalism in the middle nineties—Stephen Crane, Frank Norris, and Harold Frederic. The early death of all three stopped the movement, which was speedily overwhelmed by the romantic deluge and the muckraking zeal. Crane was tubercular and died at twenty-nine; Norris was cut down in the early thirties; Harold Frederic removed to England, where he died.

NOTE

1. Ludwig Lewisohn, *Modern Drama*, New York, 1915, p. 3.

TWENTY-ONE

THE OPENING STRUGGLE
FOR REALISM

Alfred Kazin

Alfred Kazin (1915–) was born in Brooklyn, received a
B.A. from City College of New York in 1935, and an M.A.
from Columbia in 1938. While still an undergraduate, he
contributed reviews to major New York journals, and
throughout his early career he played a significant role in
the vibrant group of anti-Stalinist leftists centered around
the *Partisan Review*. Kazin's first book, *On Native
Grounds* (1942), was greeted as a major achievement, both
for its remarkable range and vigorous style and for its interpretation of the progress of American literature and culture since the 1890s as dependent on the writer's full and
honest depiction of America's social ills. Most of Kazin's
later work, except for his autobiographical volumes, has
been in the essay form, with *The Inmost Leaf* (1955) and
Contemporaries (1962) among the most notable. Kazin
has taught at a number of universities, including the State
University of New York at Stony Brook.

As an idea, as a token of change, as something peculiarly French and unwholesome,
but portentously significant, the theory of realism had by 1890 almost gained a certain respectability in America. Even Zola—perhaps because he was Zola—who had,
after the American publication of *L'Assommoir* in 1879, been accused of pander-
ing to the wicked, had by 1888 gained a certain tolerance for *La Terre*. In 1882, the
Critic, a fashionable literary journal of the day, had declared Zola a literary outlaw,
and insane. In 1892 it pronounced: "It was a brilliant idea to introduce the scientific

On Native Grounds: An Interpretation of Modern American Prose Literature (New York:
Harcourt Brace, 1942), pp. 12–24. Copyright 1942 and renewed 1970 by Alfred Kazin. Reprinted by
permission of Harcourt Brace & Company.

spirit of the age into the novel, and Zola set to work upon it with his immense energy and his unshakable resolution. One by one the evils of his time have been taken up by this prodigious representative of Latin realism and laid before the world in all their enormity." By 1900, largely because of his stand in the Dreyfus case, Zola was beginning to be openly accepted almost everywhere and acclaimed a prophet. Yet Howells was not acclaimed much of anything for his stand in the Haymarket affair, and American realists had still to struggle to make themselves heard. By a curious irony, indeed, this had even become more difficult, for as realism in America came of age and passed into naturalism, its very foundations in thought and experience were overrun by the tide of Graustark fiction, the decorative trivialities of the fin de siècle, and the growing complacency of the American middle class in the epoch of imperialism. Where the opponents of realism had once barked at it as immoral, they now patronized it and called it dull. So Howells was told over and again in fashionable literary papers that while he was the noblest of men and his motives indubitably of the loftiest, his novels were a bore. So Eugene Field, who at his Punchinello best liked to josh Garland and other solemn young realists with plotting the destruction of a social order founded on the full dinner-pail and the G.O.P., wrote excessively whimsical papers in his newspaper column, *Sharps and Flats*, on the dreariness of realism.[1] Traditional romanticism, which from the eighties on had flourished in prosperity and yielded dolefully to realism in periods of crisis and panic, was to attain unparalleled confidence in the expansive years after the Spanish-American War; and it was particularly humiliating to compete with Richard Harding Davis and the Gibson girl after twenty years of struggle and devotion.

Yet it was entirely characteristic of the quality and the history of American realism that it should be opposed by the senile and the complacent, by academic reactionaries who feared what they did not understand, and by cynical businessmen of letters like F. Marion Crawford who had made a good thing of superplush fiction. For realism in America, which struggled so arduously to make itself heard and understood, had no true battleground, as it had no intellectual history, few models, virtually no theory, and no unity. In France realism and Zolaism had been contested by Ferdinand Brunetière and Anatole France on esthetic as well as moral grounds; it had possessed a school, a program, a collective energy, the excitement that grew out of the modern novelist's sense, as Henry James described it, of his "sacred office"—of being in the direct line of the sages and chroniclers of history. In Scandinavia and Russia the epoch of realism had evoked national energies and ideals, had burst upon a Europe groping its way through the collapse of the old faiths to announce the dignity of art and the recovery of truth. So Zola had written in the general notes to the Rougon-Macquart cycle that he based it "upon a truth of the age: the upheaval of ambitions and appetites." So naturalism, denounced for its crudity and its "atheism," had been founded, whatever its pretentiousness and savagery, upon the logic of science. "I believe above all in a constant march toward truth," Zola had cried. "It is only from the knowledge of virtue that a better social state can be born. . . . My study then is simply a piece of analysis of the world as it is. I only state facts." So the European romantic poet—Shelley, Leopardi, Pushkin—bestriding the world in radiant indignation, became the ubiquitous naturalist reporter, notebook in hand, glorying in the fetid metropolitan air, the mortuary, the sewer, the slum, the prison hospital, convinced that the truth does make men free.

What if naturalism did surrender to the materialism it aimed to expose, and was bogged down too often in the worship of Fact? It had at least shed the rhetoric of romanticism with romantic energy. Henry James saw the matter with almost classic penetration when he wrote in an essay on contemporary fiction that "M. Zola is magnificent, but he strikes an English reader as ignorant; he has an air of working in the dark. If he had as much light as energy, his results would be of the highest value." Yet James knew that the conception of realism of which Zola was at best only an extravagant and even a self-imposed symbol, had in it the seeds of a moving greatness. To the novelist of the future he wrote:

> Enjoy [the novelist's freedom] as it deserves; take possession of it, explore it to its utmost extent, publish it, rejoice in it. All life belongs to you, and do not listen either to those who would shut you up into corners of it and tell you that it is only here and there that art inhabits, or to those who would persuade you that this heavenly messenger wings her way outside of life altogether, breathing a superfine air, and turning away her head from the truth of things. There is no impression of life, no manner of seeing it and feeling it, to which the plan of the novelist may not offer a place.

At the moment, however, this was too exalted for an American realism which was still laboring in the nineties to establish elementary principles of candor and seriousness. For how was one to foster those principles when the movement depended upon the business cycle like any industry and was, indeed, principally the by-product of an economic revolution? Everything that is significant in the history of American realism stems from the fact, confirmable over fifty years of subsequent literary experience, that while in Europe realism and naturalism grew out of the positivism of Continental thought and the conviction that one literary movement had subsided and another was needed, realism in America grew out of the bewilderment, and thrived on the simple grimness, of a generation suddenly brought face to face with the pervasive materialism of industrial capitalism.[2] Realism in Europe found its philosophy in mechanism, its cosmogony in the Newtonian conception of the universe, its authority in Comte, Darwin, and Taine, its artistic quintessence in artists like Flaubert and Ibsen, who by their own careers signified the irrepressible movement of the literary mind from romanticism to scientific "objectivity" in literature. Realism in America, whatever it owed to contemporary skepticism and the influence of Darwinism, poured sullenly out of agrarian bitterness, the class hatreds of the eighties and nineties, the bleakness of small-town life, the mockery of the nouveaux riches, and the bitterness in the great new proletarian cities. Its primitivism as a literary movement was such that some of the most vigorous pioneer realists—Ed Howe, Harold Frederic, Hamlin Garland—were engaged in precisely the same labor of elementary truth-telling about farm life that had impelled George Crabbe a hundred years before to rebel against Goldsmith's sentimental bucolic elegies. Its leaders were the unhappy sons of prairie families, shriveled New England bluestockings acidly recording the narrowness and meanness of small-town life, romantic academicians like Hjalmar Boyesen, Chicago journalists who enjoyed riddling *le bourgeois*. Realism came to America from everywhere and nowhere ("no one invented it," said Howells, "it came"), and it had no center, no unifying principle, no philosophy, no joy in its coming, no climate of experiment. There was something dim, groping, unrealized in American realism even when it found its master in Dreiser, and long before Dreiser (himself so perfect a symbol of the crudity and emotional depths of American realism) it foundered on a dozen religious and moral taboos. Like so many of the innovations and literary revolutions that were to compose the subsequent history of modern American literature, that pioneer realism utterly lacked a coherent and dynamic orientation. Thus Howells, despite his cultivation, remained something of a provincial to the very end, and as late as 1883 could write to John Hay that Zola's *Nana* was a bad book because "its bad art in one respect arose from the bad French morality." A decade later he was to justify the "purity" of the American novel on the ground that it satisfied the aspirations of the feminine reading audience of America, while in Europe the novel was written principally for "men and married women." So, too, the career of so aggressive a naturalist as Frank Norris was to prove that an American novelist had to grope over Stevenson in order to reach Zola, and that the violence of Wild West stories was the only available introduction to the violence of naturalism—the violence of the modern mind. Indeed, Norris's mind was to suggest that romanticism had not yet even begun to express itself fully in America when it slipped into naturalism.

Yet it is to these primitive realists—to a Joseph and Caroline Kirkland, a Rebecca Harding Davis, an Ed Howe, a Hamlin Garland, a Henry Fuller, as it is to Howells, that contemporary literature in America owes the paramount interests that have dominated it for fifty years, and the freedoms it takes for granted. It is to these lone protestants of their time, who did not always know that they were writing "realism," to Jeffersonian hearts plagued by a strangely cold and despotic America, to writers some of whom lacked every capacity for literature save a compelling passion to tell the truth, that the emancipated and metropolitan literature of contemporary America owes its very inception. It was these early realists, with their baffled careers and their significant interest in "local color," cultivating their own gardens, who encouraged in America that elementary nationalism, that sense of belonging to a particular time and a native way of life, which is the indispensable condition of spiritual maturity and a healthy literature.

It was this insight and this need that Hamlin Garland proclaimed in his naturalist's manifesto, *Crumbling Idols*, when he wrote proudly that the history of literature in America is the history of the slow development of a distinctive utterance. He appealed, at the pitch of Wordsworth's appeal in the Preface to the *Lyrical Ballads*, for that independence of outlook and democratic freedom of mind which signified nothing less than loyalty and affection to native resources. Of what value was the social and political militancy of the West, Garland cried, if it yielded timidly to copy-book maxims and a copy-book art? At a time when colonial antiquarianism and snobbery dominated the respectable imagination, Garland exulted in the candor and bitterness of those young Western writers who, whatever their crudities (not that Garland was particularly aware of those crudities), were devoting themselves to an American, a regional, a democratic art. Garland's regionalism, as it happens, drew him to an exaggerated regional jingoism, but he could claim with perfect justice that the whole school of local color (launched before the Civil War) was an attempt to explore the different resources of the national character.

At the very moment that these pioneer realists marshaled their hopes for a literature appropriate to the new age, however, they were forced into a faltering struggle with the forces of that new age. Out of the first embattled years of the new industrial epoch there developed the abiding quality of an American literature which has ever since been significantly alien to a domineering capitalism and half-nostalgic for a preindustrial society. The cleavage between the artist and capitalist society that runs all through the history of modern Western literature found its first expression in America in people who were themselves, as citizens, stricken by industrial capitalism and frightened by it; citizens who did not so much rebel against the new order as shrink from it. American thought had as traditional a hatred of commercialism and the "cash nexus" as any culture in the world, and had memorialized it imperishably in an Emerson, a Thoreau, a John Humphrey Noyes, in the impulse that had founded a Brook Farm, a Fruitlands, an Ephrata. But the new America that was cradled in the Civil War, baptized by the Bessemer process and married too early in life to the Republican party, the new America that came in rudely through Gettysburg and the Wilderness, stamping across a hundred thousand corpses, blaring its tariffs, sniggering its corruption, crying "Nothing is lost but honor"—that America was so strange, shocking, and new that its impact on the first postbellum generations still reverberates in the American mind. What wonder, then, that the first realists of the period, so many of whom were farmers and small villagers, were almost devastated by it? The only dissent they knew was rhetorical, "Jeffersonian," bound to a preindustrial and precorporate way of life. What was there in Emerson (who now seemed to speak from another world), in any previous tradition of dissent on American soil,[3] by which to oppose or even to understand the Crédit Mobilier and railroad strikes, Pinkertons and Anarchists, trusts and Mark Hanna, or the unforgettable dictum of George F. Baer, the railway official: "The rights of the laboring man will be protected and cared for, not by labor agitation, but by the Christian men to whom God in His infinite wisdom has given control of the property interests of the country"? These pioneer realists, pioneer moderns, in truth, were as unprepared for the onslaught of a capitalist order and its corresponding ethic as European writers implemented by the tireless criticisms of a Marx, a Ruskin, an Arnold, a Tolstoy, a William Morris, were prepared; and they foundered. In their foundering is half the story of their time and of our own.

It is this alienation from the new postbellum order, with its confusions rather than its hatreds, its perplexity rather than its penetration, that marks the beginning of the modern spirit in America. To the historian, as to the revolutionary, the domination of the nineteenth century by the bourgeois mind records a process, a phase of development. To the student who knows that the literary imagination of America has more

often been embedded in the Zeitgeist than reflective of it, the anxieties and bewilderment of the distraught folk literature that grew out of the eighties are profoundly
significant and moving. The evocation of a new order in literature is to contemporary
observers often an unconscious process, but the sense of its presence in the literature
of America after 1880 is almost intolerably intense. The conception of the Civil War
as "the second American revolution" has already become platitudinous, but the living
significance of the contest between Southern plantation owners and Northern manu-
facturers—between "feudalism" and "capitalism"—was not lost to the postwar
mind. John Jay Chapman put it best when he said that the whole history of America
after the Civil War was the story of a railroad passing through a town, and then
dominating it. So forty years later Sherwood Anderson was to describe in *Poor White*
a little town in Ohio whose habitants suddenly knew, one hushed poignant afternoon, "when the stumps had been cleared, the Indians driven away," that they were
waiting for the new order to overtake them.[4]

When Frederick Jackson Turner told the eighteen-nineties that the era of expansion
was over, the frontier forever closed, he told something less than the whole truth; but
The Significance of the Frontier in American History, whatever its value as a contemporary analysis, had a more direct influence as a contribution to the climate of opinion. Whether writers read Turner or not, the implications of his thesis soon became
popular enough, and the image of a closed frontier, of a corporation economy, of a
city proletariat oppressed and rebellious, darkened the mind. Even Howells—whose
seemingly complacent pronouncement that "the smiling aspects of life are the more
American" earned him the contempt of two generations of modernists—added in
the same context, however, that while "the sum of hunger and cold is comparatively
small in a land where journeymen carpenters and plumbers strike for four dollars a
day and the wrong from class to class has been almost inappreciable, all this is changing for the worse." In the first of his Utopias, *A Traveler from Altruria*, he had one
character describe the transformation of American life between 1850 and 1890:

> If [in 1850] a man got out of work, he turned his hand to something else; a man
> failed in business, he started again from some other direction; as a last resort, in
> both cases, he went West, pre-empted a quarter section of public land, and grew
> up with the country. Now the country is grown up; the public land is gone; busi-
> ness is full on all sides, and the hand that turned itself to something else has lost
> its cunning. The struggle for life has changed from a free fight to an encounter of
> disciplined forces, and the free fighters that are left get ground to pieces between
> organized labor and organized capital.

Henry Adams, who invested his life with the dignity of tragedy because, as the legend had it, he had missed the dignity of office, saw the matter now fiercely, now petu-
lantly; but he saw it to its depths when he wrote in an early letter to his brother
Brooks: "Our so-called civilization has shown its movement, even at the centre, arrested. It has failed to concentrate further. Its next effort may succeed, but it is more
likely to be one of disintegration, with Russia for the eccentric on one side and America on the other." Writing in the *Education* of the new reign of power, of the engi-

neer-statesmen of this new era who were "trustees for the public," he had pointed out that these men were controlled by others, and said:

> The work of internal government has become the task of controlling these men, who are socially as remote as heathen gods, alone worth knowing, but never known, and who could tell nothing of political value if one skinned them alive. Most of them have nothing to tell, but are forces as dumb as their dynamos, absorbed in the development or economy of power. They are trustees for the public, and whenever society assumes the property, it must confer on them that title; but the power will remain as before, whoever manages it, and will then control society without appeal, as it controls its stokers and pit-men. Modern politics is, at bottom, a struggle not of men but of forces. The men become every year more and more creatures of force, massed about central power-houses. The conflict is no longer between the men, but between the motors that drive the men, and the men tend to succumb to their own motive forces.

As the little men lost their confidence, admiration for the *novi homines* of the "heroic age of business enterprise" began to wane. Trust-busting, which was to exhaust so much of the middle-class ardor of the Progressive period, came only *after* the acceptance of capitalism; but it was just at that crucial period when Mark Hanna became one of the great villains of contemporary folklore and Opper's caricatures of barrel-shaped magnates were being scanned with relish, that big business made its boldest bid for power, invaded Washington as a political force, and displayed that ostentatious "reign of gilt" and contempt for society that were to obsess social novelists before the muckraking novel appeared.[5] For at least a decade before the Bryan-McKinley campaign crystallized the social antagonisms of the postbellum era, writers not particularly more sensitive than the great body of the middle class knew that the businessman had become the legendary archetype, even the hero, of the new order. By 1880 there were already a hundred millionaires in the United States (Emerson died only two years later), and the upstarts who built their imitation châteaux pretentiously also built them solidly, as if to signify that they had come to stay.

The age of the individualist was at its height; never before had the commercial mind displayed so much power or so much confidence in its culture, its profits, and its future. Never in the history of business, Miriam Beard has observed, "had such reaches of the earth come into the possession of men of affairs; always, in previous times, the soil had to be taken by the sword, and the merchant, less martial or less interested in the furrow, had not wrested great dominions from feudal chivalry. . . . For the first time, and in America, businessmen acquired territories of regal extent, without lifting a battleaxe." One man owned a million acres alone in the Texas Panhandle; another, Joseph Leiter, offered to buy the Great Wall of China. The father of William Randolph Hearst, as if to anticipate the exploitation of literary wares that was to make his son's reputation, hired Ambrose Bierce to defame Collis Huntington in a skirmish of the many California railroad wars. In 1896 a stranger asked Mark Hanna if he was not related to Herman Melville, the last the middle name of Hanna's brother. Uncle Mark scratched. "What the hell kind of job does Melville want?" So wild was the extravagance of the new American plutocracy, so mad its pace of acquisition, that even European financiers were shocked by the intensity of its lust. Orgiastic in their greed, the "titans of industry" had become rich so explosively that while they could buy the world's fine art, they themselves could boast no cultivation. In a world of businessmen like Cecil Rhodes, Gustav Stressmann, Walter Rathenau, their only intellectual distinction was James Ford Rhodes's "businesslike" *History of the United States* in seven volumes. They could hardly remember with pleasure the verdict passed by another businessman who also wrote history, Charles Francis Adams. The brother of Brooks and Henry Adams wrote in a famous passage of his *Autobiography*:

> As I approach the end I am more than a little puzzled to account for the instances I have seen of business success—money getting. It comes from a rather low instinct. Certainly, so far as my observation goes, it is rarely met with in combination with the finer or more interesting traits of character. I have known, and known tolerably well, a good many "successful" men—"big" financially—men famous during the last half-century; and a less interesting crowd I do not care to encounter. Not one that I have ever known would I care to meet again, either in this world or the next; nor is one of them associated in my mind with the idea of humor, thought or refinement. A set of mere money-getters and traders, they were essentially unattractive and uninteresting.

Yet what if the businessman in America had produced nothing of "culture"? In politics he had attained a classic glory when he fostered a Warwick in Mark Hanna; in the arts, a Morgan raiding the Old World of its bibelots, its holograph Bunyan and Milton, its Italian masters. What need had the business mind to apologize for itself? The new commercialism was to become the theme, even the obsession, of a hundred histories, plays, novels, satires; to be analyzed and excoriated and praised with a ferocious interest that was itself the highest flattery. What need had the businessman to scribble or philosophize when he dominated the imagination of his time and the frantic materialism that was his principle of existence had become the haunting central figure in contemporary life?[6]

NOTES

1. Typical of these was an imaginary dialogue between Garland and Tolstoy in a Russian railway train:

> " 'From bad humanity goes to worse. Its condition becomes harder and harder all the time. This barren country about us will eventually be cultivated, these trees felled, these mountains quarried, these plains plowed and irrigated.'
> 'And all involves more labour, more suffering, more sorrow!'
> 'That will be the harvest of realism,' continued the 'younger genius.' 'There will be more sweat, more sore feet, more lame backs, more callous hands, more evil smells, a greater destitution of socks, and a vaster plentitude of patched pants than the philosophy of veritism even dreams of in these days.'

'And we shall not be here to enjoy these miseries and the telling of them! It is this thought that makes our lot even more wretched!' " — C. H. Dennis, *Eugene Field's Creative Years*, Doubleday, Page and Company, 1924, p. 135.

2. Which is not to say that American realism did not find its characteristic motivations and forms in many sections and for many reasons. *As a doctrine*, realism in America has a suggestive history, but one only passingly relevant to the purposes of this essay. It may, for example, be ascribed to, or linked with, the doctrinal Yankee homeliness of Emerson; the example of Whitman; the appearance of the daguerreo-type; the school of nineteenth-century "open-air" painters, notably Thomas Eakins and W. S. Mount. (There is a very rich and illuminating discussion of this aspect in F. O. Matthiessen's monumental study, *American Renaissance*.) It is an interesting commentary on the history of realism in America to remember that one of our earliest realists, Caroline Stansbury Kirkland (d. 1864), began to write her trenchant little sketches of frontier life in opposition to Chateaubriand's *Atala*, which she had taken with her as a bride to her frontier home. Edward Eggleston, who published *The Hoosier Schoolmaster* in 1871, found his spur in a copy of Taine's *Art in the Netherlands*, which showed him "that the artist of originality will work courageously with the materials he finds in his own environment." The history of realism in America after the Civil War is a history of grievances, and the most important thing about it is its cardinal and poignant simplicity — how much audacity it took merely to say: "Write of what you know! Write of your very own!"

3. Forty years after he had read *Walden*, Howells once confessed that he had never looked at the book afterward. In somewhat the same spirit Charles Eliot Norton wrote, in a letter of 1870: "No best man with us has done more to influence the nation than Emerson, — but the country has in a sense outgrown him. He was the friend and helper of its youth; but for the difficulties and struggles of its manhood we need the wisdom of the reflective and rational understanding, not that of the intuitions. Emerson . . . belongs to the pure and innocent age of the Presidency of Monroe or John Quincy Adams, — to the time when Plancus was Consul, — to the day of Cacciaguida." Howells did, of course, add in the same passage in *Literary Friends and Acquaintance* a famous tribute to Thoreau's prophetic criticism of the "unworthiness" of modern civilization — the civilization of industrial slavery. Yet it is significant, as Henry Seidel Canby notes in his *Thoreau*, that it was the nascent British Labor party that used *Walden*; no American social group ever did. American writers admired Emerson and Thoreau; Europeans and Asiastics — Tolstoy and Gandhi are the most famous examples — profited by them.

4. As early as the eighties, indeed, the concept of superhuman centralization, of vast interlocking combines, so haunted the contemporary imagination that it provoked a remarkably copious Utopian literature which has no parallel in other periods or literatures. *Looking Backward* stimulated hundreds of "Nationalist" clubs to spread its gospel, sold hundreds of thousands of copies a week in the late eighties, and even provoked Morris to write *News from Nowhere* — he had pronounced *Looking Backward* "a horrible cockney dream." The significance of these Utopian novels (even Howells wrote two, and the literary-minded Populist, Ignatius Donnelly, one) lies not only in the startling immediacy of their response to a transformed civilization or the avidity with which the middle class devoured them, but in the simplicity with which Bellamy and his many imitators accepted the industrial era as the herald of a beneficent Socialist totalitarianism. Though they proved themselves as vulgar on occasion as any manufacturer worshiping his machine, and antedated the American advertising mystics of the latest gadget, they were — like all their generation — children playing with fire. Like the late Utopian novelist Bradford Peck, who entitled his thriller *The World a Department Store*, they took the most inane or sinister implications of a profit economy on trust, and asked only to be allowed

the destruction of "institutions." So Bellamy, whose state was built like a corporation, unconsciously anticipated the conscripted labor armies of the GPU and the Nazi Labor Front in his suggestion that labor could be organized into an industrial army.

5. "You Americans believe yourselves to be excepted from the operation of general laws. You care not for experience. I have lived seventy-five years, and all that time in the midst of corruption. I am corrupt myself, only I do have courage to proclaim it, and you others have it not. Rome, Paris, Vienna, Petersburg, London, all are corrupt, only Washington is pure! Well, I declare to you that in all my experience I have found no society which has had elements of corruption like the United States. The children in the street are corrupt, and know how to cheat me. The cities are all corrupt, and also the towns and the counties and the States' legislatures and the judges. Everywhere men betray trusts both public and private, steal money, run away with public funds. Only in the Senate men take no money." —Baron Jacobi in Henry Adams's *Democracy*.

6. "As energetic young Frenchmen in Froissart's day turned to war, as energetic young Americans of 1800 turned to pioneering, so the young Americans of Rockefeller's day turned to business. They looked to it for distinction, power, and the joys of self-expression." —Allan Nevins, *John D. Rockefeller: The Heroic Age of Business Enterprise*.

TWENTY-TWO

"NOT MEN"

A Natural History of American Naturalism

Malcolm Cowley

Malcolm Cowley (1898–1989) had a lengthy and influential career as an American man of letters. Harvard educated, Cowley served in the American ambulance corps during World War I and then returned to Europe as an expatriate poet during the early 1920s. During the 1930s, he became one of the country's leading Marxist critics in his role as literary editor of the *New Republic*. For the remainder of his extraordinarily long career, Cowley's lengthy essays and introductions could make or break a literary reputation. Many of his most significant essays are collected in *A Many-Windowed House: Collected Essays on American Writers and American Writing* (1970).

There have been too many unfruitful arguments over Naturalism in American fiction. Now that the movement has flourished for half a century, we can forget to attack or defend it, and instead can look back in an objective or Naturalistic spirit at the work of the many authors it inspired. We can note that their line extends from Norris and the early Dreiser through Farrell and Steinbeck. We can describe their principles, note how these were modified in practice, and finally try to reach some judgment of their literary remains.

Naturalism has been defined in two words as pessimistic determinism, and the definition is true so far as it goes. The Naturalistic writers were all determinists in that

The Kenyon Review 9 (Summer 1947): 414–35. Reprinted in revised and expanded form as "Naturalism in American Literature" in *Evolutionary Thought in America*, ed. Stow Persons (1950) and as "A Natural History of American Naturalism" in *A Many-Windowed House: Collected Essays on American Writers and American Writing*, ed. Henry Dan Piper (1970). Text from *The Kenyon Review*. Copyright 1947 by Kenyon College. Reprinted by permission of *Kenyon Review*.

they believed in the omnipotence of abstract forces. They were pessimists so far as they believed that men and women were absolutely incapable of shaping their own destinies. They regarded the individual as "a pawn on a chessboard"; the phrase recurs time and again in their novels. They felt that he could not achieve happiness by any conscious decision and that he received no earthly or heavenly reward for acting morally; man was, in Dreiser's words, "the victim of forces over which he had no control." Frank Norris was sometimes more extreme in his magnification of forces and minification of persons. "Men were nothings, mere animalculae, mere ephemerides that fluttered and fell and were forgotten between dawn and dusk," he says in the next-to-last chapter of *The Octopus*. "Men were naught, life was naught; FORCE only existed—FORCE that brought men into the world, FORCE that crowded them out of it to make way for the succeeding generation, FORCE that made the wheat grow, FORCE that garnered it from the soil to give place to the succeeding crop."

But Norris, like several other Naturalists, was able to combine this romantic pessimism about individuals with romantic optimism about the future of mankind. "The individual suffers, but the race goes on," he says at the very end of the novel. "Annixter dies, but in a far distant corner of the world a thousand lives are saved. The larger view always and through all shams, all wickednesses, discovers the Truth that will, in the end, prevail, and all things, surely, inevitably, resistlessly work together for good." This was, in its magniloquent way, a form of the belief in universal progress announced by Herbert Spencer, but it was also mingled with native or Emersonian idealism, and it helped to make Naturalism more palatable to Norris' first American readers.

Zola had also declared his belief in human perfectibility, in what he called "a constant march toward truth"; and it was from Zola rather than Spencer or any native source that Norris had borrowed most of his doctrines. Zola described himself as "a positivist, an evolutionist, a materialist." In his working notes, which Norris of course had never seen, but which one might say that he divined from the published text of the novels, Zola had indicated some of his aims as a writer. He would march through the world observing human behavior as if he were observing the forms of animal life. "Study men as simple elements and note the reactions," he said. And again, "What matters most to me is to be purely naturalistic, purely physiological. Instead of having principles (royalism, Catholicism) I shall have laws (heredity, atavism)." And yet again, "Balzac says that he wishes to paint men, women and things. I count men and women as the same, while admitting their natural differences, and *subject men and women to things*." In that last phrase, which Zola underlined, he expressed the central Naturalistic doctrine: that men and women are part of nature and subject to the same indifferent laws.

A favorite theme in Naturalistic fiction is that of the beast within. As the result of some crisis—usually a fight, a shipwreck or an expedition into the Arctic—the veneer of civilization drops or is stripped away and we are faced with "the primal instinct of the brute struggling for its life and for the life of its young." The phrase is Norris', but it might have been written by any of the early Naturalists. When evolution is treated in their novels, it almost always takes the opposite form of devolution or degeneration. Instead of moving from the simple to the complex, as Herbert Spencer tells us that everything does in this world, the Naturalists keep moving from the complex to the simple, by a continual process of reduction. They speak of the nation as "the tribe," and a moment later the tribe becomes a pack. Civilized man becomes a barbarian or a savage, the savage becomes a brute, and the brute is reduced to its chemical elements. "Study men as simple elements," Zola had said; and many years later Dreiser followed his advice by presenting love as a form of electromagnetism and success in life as a question of chemical compounds; thus, he said of his brother Paul that he was "one of those great Falstaffian souls who, for lack of a little iron or sodium or carbon dioxide in his chemical compost, was not able to bestride the world like a Colossus."

There was a tendency in all the early Naturalistic writers to identify social laws with biological or physical laws. For Jack London, the driving force behind human events was always biology—"I mean," says his autobiographical hero, Martin Eden, "the real interpretative biology, from the ground up, from the laboratory and the test tube and the vitalized inorganic right on up to the widest aesthetic and social generalizations." London believed that such biological principles as natural selection and the survival of the fittest were also the laws of human society. Thomas Hardy often spoke as if men's destinies were shaped by the physical sciences. He liked to say that his characters were doomed by the stars in their courses; but actually they were doomed in a more interesting fashion by human conflicts or by the still Puritan conventions of middle-class England. Norris fell into the same confusion between the physical and the social world when he pictured the wheat as "a huge Niagara . . . flowing from West to East." In his novels wheat was not a grain improved by men from various wild grasses and grown by men to meet human needs; it was an abstract and elemental force like gravity. "I corner the wheat!" says Jadwin, the hero of *The Pit*. "Great heavens, it is the wheat that has cornered me."

Just as the wheat is described as having grown itself, so, in the first volume of Norris' trilogy, the Pacific and Southwestern Railroad has built itself, as if without human intervention. Even Shelgrim, the great-souled president of the railroad, is merely the agent of a superhuman power. At the end of *The Octopus* he gives a lecture to Presley, the poet in the novel who often speaks for Norris himself. It is a lecture that overwhelms the poet and leaves him feeling that it rang "with the clear reverberation of truth." "You are dealing with forces," Shelgrim says, "when you speak of Wheat and the Railroads, not with men. There is the Wheat, the supply. It must be carried to the People. There is the demand. The Wheat is one force, the Railroad, another, and there is the law that governs them—supply and demand. Men have little to do with the whole business." If the two forces came into conflict—if the employees of the railroad massacred the wheat ranchers and robbed them of their land—then Presley should "blame conditions, not men."

The effect of Naturalism as a doctrine is to subtract from literature the whole notion of human responsibility. "Not men" is its constant echo. If Naturalistic stories had tragic endings, these were not to be explained by human wills in conflict with each other or with fate; they were the blind result of conditions, forces, physical laws or nature herself. "There was no malevolence in Nature," Presley reflects after meeting the railroad president. "Colossal indifference only, a vast trend toward appointed goals. Nature was, then, a gigantic engine, a vast, cyclopean power, huge, terrible, a leviathan with a heart of steel, knowing no compunction, no forgiveness, no tolerance; crushing out the human atom standing in its way, with nirvanic calm." Stephen Crane had already expressed the same attitude toward nature in a sharper image and in cleaner prose. When the four shipwrecked men in *The Open Boat* are drifting close to the beach but are unable to land because of the breakers, they stare at a windmill that is like "a giant standing with its back to the plight of the ants. It represented in a degree, to the correspondent, the serenity of nature amid the struggles of the individual—nature in the wind, and nature in the visions of men. She did not seem cruel to him, then, nor beneficent, nor treacherous, nor wise. But she was indifferent, flatly indifferent."

2.

All these beliefs of the first American Naturalists might have been deduced from their original faith in Darwinian evolution and in its application to human affairs. But they had other characteristics that were more closely connected with social conditions in their own time.

The last decade of the 19th Century, when they started their literary careers, was an age of contrasts and sudden changes when America, to quote from Dreiser's memoirs, "was just entering upon the most lurid phase of that vast, splendid, most lawless and most savage period in which the great financiers were plotting and conniving at the enslavement of the people and belaboring each other." During this battle of the Titans, ordinary citizens found it difficult to plan their futures and even began to suspect that they were, in a favorite Naturalistic phrase, "the playthings of forces beyond human control." The American faith that was preached in the pulpits and daily reasserted on editorial pages had lost its connection with American life. It was not only an intolerable limitation on American writing, as all the rebel authors had learned; it also had to be disregarded by anyone who hoped to rise in the business world and by anyone who, having failed to rise, wanted to understand the reasons for his failure.

In its simplest terms, the American faith was that things were getting better year by year, that the individual could solve his problems by moving, usually westward, and that virtue was rewarded with wealth, the greatest virtue with the greatest wealth. Those were the doctrines of the editorial page; but reporters who worked for the same newspaper looked around them and decided that wealth was more often the fruit of selfishness and fraud, whereas the admirable persons in their world—the kind, the philosophic, the honest and the open-eyed—were usually failures by business standards. Most of the early Naturalistic writers, including Stephen Crane, Harold Frederic, David Graham Phillips and Dreiser, were professional newspaper men; while the others, except the poets, either worked for short periods as reporters or wrote series of newspaper articles. All were affected by the moral atmosphere of the city room; and the fact is important, since the newspaper men of the 1890's and 1900's were a special class or type. "Never," says Dreiser, speaking of his colleagues

on the Pittsburgh *Dispatch*, "had I encountered more intelligent or helpful or com-
panionable albeit more cynical men than I met here"; and the observation leads to
general remarks about the reporters he had known:

> One can always talk to a newspaper man, I think, with the full confidence that
> one is talking to a man who is at least free of moralistic mush. Nearly everything
> in connection with those trashy romances of justice, truth, mercy, patriotism,
> public profession of all sorts, is already and forever gone if they have been in the
> business for any length of time. The religionist is seen by them for what he is: a
> swallower of romance or a masquerader looking to profit and preferment. Of the
> politician, they know or believe but one thing: that he is out for himself.

Essentially the attitude forced upon newspaper men as they interviewed politicians,
evangelists and convicted criminals was the same as the attitude they derived or
might have derived from popular books on evolution. Reading and experience led to
the same convictions: that Christianity was a sham, that moral professions were false,
that there was nothing real in the world but force and, for themselves, no respectable
role to play except that of detached observers gathering the facts and printing as
many of them as their publishers would permit. They drank by conviction, talked
with prostitutes, played enormous practical jokes and dreamed about writing stark,
honest, cynical books. "Most of these young men," Dreiser says, "looked upon life as
a fierce, grim struggle in which no quarter was given or taken, and in which all men
laid traps, lied, squandered, erred through illusion: a conclusion with which I now
most heartily agree." His novels one after another would be based on what he had
learned in his newspaper days.

In writing their novels, most of the Naturalists pictured themselves as expressing a
judgment of life that was scientific, dispassionate and, to borrow one of their own
phrases, completely unmoral; but a better word for their attitude would be "rebellious." Try as they would, they could not remain merely observers. They had to revolt
against the moral standards of their time; and the revolt involved them more or less
unconsciously in the effort to impose new standards that would be closer to what
they regarded as natural laws. Their books are full of little essays or sermons addressed to the reader; in fact they suggest a Naturalistic system of ethics complete
with its vices and virtues.

Among the vices, those most often mentioned are hypocrisy, intolerance, conven-
tionality and unwillingness to acknowledge the truth. Among the virtues, perhaps
the first is strength, which is presented as both a physiological and a moral quality; it
implies the courage to be strong in spite of social restraints. A second virtue is naturalness, that is, the quality of acting in accordance with one's nature and physical
instincts. A third virtue is complete candor about the world and oneself; a fourth is
pity for others; and a fifth is tolerance, especially of moral rebellion and economic
failure. Most of the characters presented sympathetically in Naturalistic novels are
either the victors over moral codes which they defy (like Cowperwood in *The Financier* and Susan Lenox in the novel by David Graham Phillips about her fall and rise)
or else victims in the economic struggle, paupers and drunkards with infinitely more

wisdom than the respectable citizens who avoid them. A great deal of Naturalistic writing, including the early poems of Edwin Arlington Robinson, is a hymn to loneliness and failure as the destiny, in America, of most superior men.

There are other qualities of American Naturalism that are derived not so much from historical conditions as from the example of the two novelists whom the younger writers regarded as leaders or precursors. Norris first and Dreiser after him fixed the patterns that the others would follow.

Both men were romantic by taste and temperament. Although Norris was a disciple of Zola's, his other favorite authors belonged in one way or another to the romantic school; they included Froissart, Scott, Dickens, Hugo, Kipling and Stevenson. Zola was no stranger in that company, Norris said; on one occasion he called him "the very head of the Romanticists." "Terrible things must happen," he wrote, "to the characters of the Naturalistic tale. They must be twisted from the ordinary, wrenched from the quiet, uneventful round of everyday life and flung into the throes of a vast and terrible drama that works itself out in unleased passions, in blood and sudden death. . . . Everything is extraordinary, imaginative, grotesque even, with a vague note of terror quivering throughout like the vibration of an ominous and low-pitched diapason." Norris himself wished to practise Naturalism as a form of romance, instead of taking up what he described as "the harsh, loveless, colorless, blunt tool called Realism." Dreiser in his autobiographical writings often refers to his own romantic temper. "For all my modest repute as a realist," he says, "I seem, to my self-analysing eyes, somewhat more of a romanticist." He speaks of himself in his youth as "a creature of slow and uncertain response to anything practical, having an eye single to color, romance, beauty. I was but a half-baked poet, romancer, dreamer." The other American Naturalists were also romancers and dreamers in their fashion, groping among facts for the extraordinary and even the grotesque. They believed that men were subject to natural forces, but they felt those forces were best displayed when they led to unlimited wealth, utter squalor, collective orgies, blood and sudden death.

Among the romantic qualities they tried to achieve was "bigness" in its double reference to size and intensity. They wanted to display "big"—that is, intense—emotions against a physically large background. Bigness was the virtue that Norris most admired in Zola's novels. "The world of M. Zola," he said, "is a world of big things; the enormous, the formidable, the terrible, is what counts; no teacup tragedies here." In his own novels Norris looked for big themes; after his trilogy on the wheat, he planned to write a still bigger trilogy on the three days' battle of Gettysburg, with one novel devoted to the events of each day. The whole notion of writing trilogies instead of separate novels came to be connected with the Naturalistic movement, although it was also adopted by the historical romancers. Before Norris there had been only one planned trilogy in serious American fiction: *The Littlepage Manuscripts*, written by James Fenimore Cooper a few years before his death; it traces the story of a New York State landowning family through a hundred years and three generations. After Norris there were dozens of trilogies, with a few tetralogies and pentalogies: to mention some of the better known, there were Dreiser's trilogy on the career of a financier, T. S. Stribling's trilogy on the rise of a poor-white family, Dos Passos' trilogy on the U.S.A. from 1900 to 1930, Farrell's trilogy on Studs Lonigan, and O'Neill's trilogy of plays, *Mourning Becomes Electra*.

Later O'Neill set to work on a trilogy of trilogies, a drama to be complete in nine full-length plays. Farrell wrote a pentalogy about the boyhood of Danny O'Neill and then attacked another theme that would require several volumes, the young manhood of Bernard Clare. Trilogies expanded into whole cycles of novels somehow related in theme. Thus, after the success of *The Jungle*, which dealt with the meat-packing industry in Chicago, Upton Sinclair wrote novels on other cities (Denver, Boston) and other industries (oil, coal, whiskey, automobiles); finally he settled on a character, Lanny Budd, whose adventures were as endless as those of Tarzan. Sinclair Lewis dealt one after another with various trades and professions: real estate, medicine, divinity, social service, hotel management and the stage; there was no limit to the subjects he could treat, so long as his reader's patience was equal to his own.

With their eyes continually on vast projects, the American Naturalists were careless about the details of their work and indifferent to the materials they were using; often their trilogies resembled great steel-structural buildings faced with cinder blocks and covered with cracked stucco ornaments. Sometimes the buildings remained unfinished. Norris set this pattern, too, when he died before he could start his third novel on the wheat. Dreiser worked for years on *The Stoic*, which was to be the sequel to *The Financier* and *The Titan*; but he was never satisfied with the various endings he tried and the book had to be completed by others after his death. Lewis never wrote his novel on labor unions, although he spent months or years gathering material for it and spoke of it as his most ambitious work. In their effort to achieve bigness at any cost, the Naturalists were likely to undertake projects that went beyond their physical or imaginative powers, or in which they discovered too late that they weren't really interested.

Meanwhile they worked ahead in a delirium of production, like factories trying to set new records. To understand their achievements in speed and bulk, one has to compare their output with that of an average novelist. There is of course no average novelist, but there are scores of men and women who earn their living by writing novels, and many of them try to publish one book each year. If they spend four months planning and gathering material for the book, another four months writing the first draft (at the rate of about a thousand words a day) and the last four months in revision, they are at least not unusual. Very few of the Naturalists would have been satisfied with that modest rate of production. Harold Frederic wrote as much as 4,000 words a day and often sent his manuscripts to the printer without corrections. At least he paused between novels to carry on his work as a foreign correspondent; but Jack London, who wrote only 1,000 words a day, tried to meet that quota six days a week and fifty-two weeks a year; he allowed himself no extra time for planning or revision. He wrote fifty books in seventeen years and didn't pretend that all of them were his best writing. "I have no unfinished stories," he told an interviewer five years before his death. "Invariably I complete every one I start. If it's good, I sign it and send it out. If it isn't good, I sign it and send it out." David Graham Phillips finished his first novel in 1901 and published sixteen others before his death in 1911, in addition to the articles he wrote for muckraking magazines. He left behind him the manuscripts of six novels (including the two-volume *Susan Lenox*) that were published posthumously. Upton Sinclair set a record in the early days when he was writing half-dime novels for boys. He kept three secretaries busy; two of them would be transcribing notes while the third was taking dictation. By that method he once wrote 18,000 words in a day. He gained a fluency that helped him later when he was writing serious books, but he also acquired a contempt for style that made them painful to read, except in their French translations. Almost all the Naturalists read better in translation; that is one of the reasons for their international popularity as compared with the smaller audience that some of them found at home.

3.

The Naturalistic writers of all countries preferred an objective or scientific approach to their material. As early as 1864 the brothers Goncourt had written in their journal, "The novel of today is made with documents narrated or selected from nature, just as history is based on written documents." A few years later Zola defined the novel as a scientific experiment; its purpose, he said in rather involved language, was to demonstrate the behavior of given characters in a given situation. Still later Norris advanced the doctrine "that no one could be a writer until he could regard life and people, and the world in general, from the objective point of view—until he could remain detached, outside, maintain the unswerving attitude of the observer." The Naturalists as a group not only based their plots on current scientific theories, but tried to copy scientific methods in planning their novels. They were writers who believed, or claimed to believe, that they could deliberately choose a subject for their work instead of being chosen by a subject; that they could go about collecting characters as a biologist collected specimens; and that their fictional account of such characters could be as accurate and true to the facts as the report of an experiment in the laboratory.

It was largely this faith in objectivity that led them to write about penniless people in the slums, whom they regarded as "outside" or alien subjects for observation. Some of them began with a feeling of contempt for the masses. Norris during his college years used to speak of "the canaille" and often wished for the day when all radicals could be "drowned on one raft." Later this pure contempt developed into a contemptuous interest, and he began to spend his afternoons on Polk Street, in San Francisco, observing with a detached eye the actions of what he now called "the people." The minds of the people, he thought, were simpler than those of persons in his own world; essentially these human beings were animals, "the creatures of habit, the playthings of forces," and therefore they were ideal subjects for a Naturalistic novel. Some of the other Naturalists revealed the same rather godlike attitude towards workingmen. Nevertheless they wrote about them, a bold step at a time when most novels dealt only with ladies, gentlemen and faithful retainers; and often their contemptuous interest was gradually transformed into sympathy.

Their objective point of view towards their material was sometimes a pretense that deceived themselves before it deceived others. From the outside world they chose the subjects that mirrored their own conflicts and obsessions. Stephen Crane said that his aim in writing *Maggie* was "to show that environment is a tremendous thing and often shapes lives regardlessly. If I could prove that theory," he continued, "I would make room in Heaven for all sorts of souls (notably an occasional street girl) who are not confidently expected to be there by many excellent people." On the subjective level, however, the novel revealed an obsessive notion about the blamelessness of prostitutes that affected his career from beginning to end; it caused a series of scandals, involved him in a feud with the vice squad in Manhattan and finally led him to marry the madam of a bawdy house in Jacksonville. Norris' first novel, *Vandover and the Brute*, is an apparently objective study of degeneration, but it also mirrors the struggles of the author with his intensely Puritan conscience; Vandover is Norris himself. He had drifted into some mild dissipations and pictured them as leading to failure and insanity.

Dreiser in *Sister Carrie* was telling a story based on the adventures of one of his sisters; that explains why Carrie Meeber is "Sister" Carrie even though her relatives disappear after the first few pages. "My mind was a blank except for the name," Dreiser said when explaining how he came to write the novel. "I had no idea who or what she was to be. I have often thought that there was something mystic about it, as if I were being used, like a medium." In a sense he was being used by his memories, which had become subconscious. There was nothing mystic to Upton Sinclair about his fierce emotion in writing *The Jungle*; he knew from the beginning that he was expressing a personal emotion. "I wrote with tears and anguish," he says in his memoirs, "pouring into the pages all that pain which life had meant to me. Externally the story had to do with a family of stockyard workers but internally it was the story of my own family. . . . Our little boy was down with pneumonia that winter, and nearly died, and the grief of that went into the book." Indeed, there is grief and fury and bewilderment in all the most impressive Naturalistic novels. They are at their best, not when they are scientific or objective, in accordance with their own theories, but when they are least Naturalistic, most personal and lyrical.

If we follow William James and divide writers into the two categories of the tough and the tender-minded, then most of the Naturalists are tender-minded. They write shocking books because they have been shocked. The sense of moral fitness is strong in them; they believe in their hearts that nature *should* be kind, that virtue *should* be rewarded on earth, that men *should* control their own destinies. More than other writers, they are wounded by ugliness and injustice, but they will not close their eyes to either; indeed, they often give the impression of seeking out ugliness and injustice in order to be wounded again and again. They have hardly a trace of the cynicism that is often charged against them. It is the quietly realistic or classical writers who are likely to be cynics, in the sense of holding a low opinion of life and human beings; that low estimate is so deeply ingrained in their thought that they never bother to insist on it—for why should they try to make converts in such a hopeless world? The Naturalists are always trying to convert others and themselves, and sometimes they build up new illusions simply to enjoy the pain of stripping them away. It is their feeling of fascinated revulsion towards their subject matter that makes some of the Naturalists hard to read; they seem to be flogging themselves and their audience like a band of Penitentes.

4.

So far I have been trying to present the positive characteristics of a movement in American letters, but Naturalism can also be defined in terms of what it is not. Thus, to begin a list of negations, it is not journalism in the bad sense, merely sensational or entertaining or written merely to sell. It has to be honest by definition, and honesty in literature is a hard quality to achieve, one that requires more courage and concentration than journalists can profitably devote to writing a novel. Even when an author holds all the Naturalistic doctrines, his books have to reach a certain level of observation and intensity before they deserve to be called Naturalistic. Jack London held the doctrines and wrote fifty books, but only three or four of them reached the required level. David Graham Phillips reached it only once, with *Susan Lenox*, if he reached it then.

Literary Naturalism is not the sort of doctrine that can be officially sponsored and taught in the public schools. It depends for too many of its effects on shocking the sensibilities of its readers and smashing their illusions. It always becomes a threat to the self-esteem of the propertied classes. *Babbitt*, for example, is Naturalistic in its hostile treatment of American business men. When Sinclair Lewis defended Babbittry in a later novel, *The Prodigal Parents*, his work had ceased to be Naturalistic.

For a third negative statement, Naturalism is not what we have learned to call literature "in depth." It is concerned with observed behavior and with explanations of that behavior in terms of heredity or environment. It presents the exterior world, often on a broad scale and in striking visual images; but unlike the work of Henry James or Sherwood Anderson or William Faulkner—to mention only three writers in other traditions—it does not try to explore the world within. Faulkner's method is sometimes described as "subjective Naturalism," but the phrase is self-contradictory, almost as if one spoke of "subjective biology."

Naturalism does not deal primarily with individuals in themselves, but rather with social groups or settings or movements, or with individuals like Babbitt and Studs Lonigan who are regarded as being typical of a group. The Naturalistic writer tries not to identify himself with any of his characters, though he doesn't always succeed; in general his aim is to present them almost as if they were laboratory specimens. They are seldom depicted as being capable of moral decisions. This fact makes it easy to distinguish between the early Naturalists and some of their contemporaries like Robert Herrick and Edith Wharton who also tried to write about optimistic illusions. Herrick and Wharton, however, dealt with individuals who possessed a degree of moral freedom; and often the plots of their novels hinge on a conscious decision by one of the characters. Hemingway, to mention a later author often confused with the Naturalists, writes stories that reveal some moral quality, usually stoicism or the courage of a frightened man.

Many Naturalistic works are valuable historical documents, but the authors in

general have little sense of history. They present each situation as if it had no historical antecedents, and their characters might be men and women created yesterday
morning, so few signs do they show of having roots in the past. "Science," for Naturalistic writers, usually means laboratory science, and not the study of human institutions or patterns of thought that persist through generations.

With a few exceptions they have no faith in reform, whether it be the reform of an
individual by his own decision or the reform of society by reasoned courses of action.
The changes they depict are the result of laws and forces and tendencies beyond
human control. That is the great difference between the Naturalists and the proletarian or Marxist novelists of the 1930's. The proletarian writers—who were seldom
proletarians in private life—believed that men acting together could make a new
world. But they borrowed the objective and exterior technique of the Naturalists,
which was unsuited to their essentially religious purpose. In the beginning of each
book they portrayed a group of factory workers as the slaves of economic conditions,
"the creatures of habit, the playthings of forces"; then later they portrayed the conversion of one or more workers to Communism. But conversion is a psychological,
not a biological, phenomenon, and it could not be explained purely in terms of conditions or forces. When the conversion took place, there was a shift from the outer
to the inner world, and the novel broke in two.

It was not at all extraordinary for Naturalism to change into religious Marxism in
the middle of a novel, since it has always shown a tendency to dissolve into something
else. On the record literary Naturalism does not seem to be a doctrine or attitude to
which men are likely to cling through their whole lives. It is always being transformed
into satire, symbolism, lyrical autobiography, utopian socialism, Communism, Catholicism, mysticism, Freudian psychology, hack journalism or the mere assembling
of facts. So far there is not in American literature a single instance in which a writer
has remained a Naturalist from beginning to end of a long career; even Dreiser before
his death became a strange mixture of Communist and mystic. There are, however, a
great many works that are predominantly Naturalistic; and the time has come to list
them in order to give the basis for my generalities.

I should say that those works, in fiction, were *Maggie* and *George's Mother*, by
Stephen Crane, with many of his short stories. *The Damnation of Theron Ware*, by
Harold Frederic; *Vandover*, *McTeague* and *The Octopus* (but not *The Pit*), by Frank
Norris; *The Call of the Wild*, which is a sort of Naturalistic Aesop's fable, besides *The
Sea Wolf* and *Martin Eden*, by Jack London; *The Jungle*, by Upton Sinclair, as far as
the page where Jurgis is converted to socialism; *Susan Lenox*, by David Graham Phil-
lips; all of Dreiser's novels except *The Bulwark*, which has a religious ending written
at the close of his life; all the serious novels of Sinclair Lewis between *Main Street*
(1920) and *Dodsworth* (1929), but none he wrote aftwards; Dos Passos' *Manhattan
Transfer* and *U.S.A.*; James T. Farrell's work in general, but especially *Studs Lonigan*;
Richard Wright's *Native Son*; and most of John Steinbeck's novels, including *In Dubious Battle* and all but the hortatory passages in *The Grapes of Wrath*. But the Naturalistic movement, though strongest in fiction, has extended into many other fields.
In poetry there is Robinson's early verse (*The Children of the Night*) and there is

Edgar Lee Masters' *Spoon River Anthology*. In the drama there are the early plays of Eugene O'Neill, from *Beyond the Horizon* to *Desire Under the Elms*. Among essays there are H. L. Mencken's *Prejudices* and Joseph Wood Krutch's *The Modern Temper*, which is the most coherent statement of the Naturalistic position. There are other Naturalists in all fields, especially fiction, and other Naturalistic books by several of the authors I have mentioned; but these are the works by which the school is likely to be remembered and judged.

5.

And what shall we say in judgment?—since judge we must, after this long essay in definition. Is Naturalism true or false in its premises and good or bad in its effect on American literature? Its results have been good, I think, in so far as it has forced its adherents to stand in opposition to American orthodoxy. Honest writing in this country has almost always been the work of an opposition, chiefly because the leveling and unifying elements in our culture have been so strong that a man who accepts orthodox judgments is in danger of losing his literary personality. Catullus and Villon might be able to write their poems here; with their irregular lives they wouldn't run the risk of being corrupted by the standards of right-thinking people. But Virgil, the friend of Augustus, the official writer who shaped the myth of the Roman state, would be a dubious figure as an American poet. He would be tempted to soften his values in order to become a prophet for the masses. The American myth of universal cheap luxuries, pearly bathrooms, patented automatic, silent, odorless kitchens and service with a smile would hardly provide him with the basis for an epic poem.

The Naturalists, standing in opposition, have been writers of independent and strongly marked personalities. They have fought for the right to speak their minds and have won a measure of freedom for themselves and others. Yet it has to be charged against them that their opposition often takes the form of cheapening what they write about; of always looking for the lowdown or the payoff, that is, for the meanest explanation of everything they describe. I have mentioned a tendency in literary Naturalism—as distinguished from philosophical Naturalism, which is not my subject—always to explain the complex in terms of the simple, society in terms of self, man in terms of his animal inheritance and the organic in terms of the inorganic. The result is that something is omitted at each stage in the process of reduction. To say that man is a beast of prey or a collection of chemical compounds omits most of man's special nature; it is a metaphor, not a scientific statement.

This scientific weakness of Naturalism involves a still greater literary weakness, for it leads to a conception of man that makes it impossible for Naturalistic authors to write in the tragic spirit. They can write about crimes, suicides, disasters, the terrifying and the grotesque; but even the most powerful of their novels and plays are case histories rather than tragedies in the classical sense. Tragedy is an affirmation of man's importance; it is "the imitation of noble actions," in Aristotle's phrase; and the Naturalists are unable to believe in human nobility. With their emphasis on "conditions not men," they have to present victims instead of heroes. "We write no tragedies today," said Joseph Wood Krutch in his early book, *The Modern Temper*, which might better have been called "The Naturalistic Temper." "If the plays and novels of today deal with littler people and less mighty emotions, it is not because we have become interested in commonplace souls and their unglamorous adventures but because we have come, willy-nilly, to see the soul of man as commonplace and its emotions as mean." But Krutch was speaking only for those who shared the Naturalistic point of view. There are other doctrines held by modern writers that make it possible to endow their characters with human dignity. Tragic novels and plays have been written in these years by Christians, Communists, Humanists and even by Existentialists, all of whom believe in different fashions and degrees that men can shape their own fates.

For the Naturalists, however, men are "human insects" whose brief lives are completely determined by society or nature. The individual is crushed in a moment if he resists; and his struggle, instead of being tragic, is merely pitiful or ironic, as if we had seen a mountain stir itself to overwhelm a fly. Irony is a literary effect used time and again by all the Naturalistic writers. For Stephen Crane it is the central effect on which almost all his plots depend: thus, in *The Red Badge of Courage*, the boy makes himself a hero by running away. In "A Mystery of Heroism," a soldier risks his life to bring a bucket of water to his comrades, and the water is spilled. In "The Monster," a Negro stableman is so badly burned in rescuing a child that he becomes a faceless horror; that is his reward for valor; and the child's father, a physician, loses his practice as a reward for sheltering the stableman. In Dreiser's novels the irony depends on an unspoken contrast between conventional morality and the situations he describes: thus, Carrie Meeber loses her virtue and succeeds in her career; Jennie Gerhardt is a kept woman with higher principles than any respectable wife. In Sinclair Lewis the irony is reduced to an obsessive and irritating trick of style; if he wants to say that a speech was dull and stupid, he has to call it "the culminating glory of the dinner" and then, to make sure that we catch the point, explain that it was delivered by Mrs. Adelaide Tarr Gimmitch, "known throughout the country as 'the Unkies' Girl.' " The reader, seeing the name of Gimmitch, is supposed to smile a superior smile. There is something superior and ultimately tiresome in the attitude of many Naturalists towards the events they describe. Irony—like pity, its companion—is a spectator's emotion, and it sets a space between ourselves and the characters in the novel. They suffer, but their cries reach us faintly, like those of dying strangers we cannot hope to save.

There is nothing in the fundamental principles of Naturalism that requires a novel to be written in hasty or hackneyed prose. Flaubert, the most careful stylist of his age, was a predecessor and guide of the French Naturalists. Among the Naturalistic writers of all countries who wrote with a feeling for language were the brothers Goncourt, Ibsen, Hardy and Stephen Crane. But it was Norris, not Crane, who set the standards for Naturalistic fiction in the United States, and Norris had no respect for style. "What pleased me most in your review of *McTeague*," he said in a letter to Isaac Marcosson, "was 'disdaining all pretensions to style.' It is precisely what I try most to avoid. I detest 'fine writing' 'rhetoric,' 'elegant English'—tommyrot. Who cares for fine style. Tell your yarn and let your style go to the devil. We don't want literature, we want life." Yet the truth was that Norris' novels were full of fine writing and lace-curtain English. "Untouched, unassailable, undefiled," he said of the wheat, "that mighty world force, that nourisher of nations, wrapped in Nirvanic calm, indifferent to the human swarm, gigantic, resistless, moved onward in its appointed grooves." He never learned to present his ideas in their own clothes or none at all; it was easier to dress them in borrowed plush; easier to make all his calms Nirvanic and all his grooves appointed.

Yet Norris wrote better prose than most of his successors among the American Naturalists. With a few exceptions like Dos Passos (who seems a little ashamed of writing vividly) and Steinbeck (who likes to glitter in short sentences), they have all used language as a blunt instrument; they write as if they were swinging shillelaghs. O'Neill is a great dramatist, but he has never had an ear for speech of living persons. Lewis used to have an ear, but now listens only to himself. He insists on being arch and ironical about his characters until we want to snarl at him, "Quit patronizing those people! Maybe they'd have something to say if you'd only let them talk." Farrell writes well when he is excited or angry, but most of the time he keeps his readers trudging through vacant lots in a South Chicago smog. Dreiser is the worst writer of all, but in some ways the least objectionable; there is something native to himself in his misuse of the language, so that we come to cherish it as a sign of authenticity, like the tool marks on Shaker furniture. Most of the others simply reach for the nearest and oldest and easiest phrase.

But although the Naturalists as a group are men of defective hearing, they almost all have keen eyes for new material. Their interest in themes that others regarded as too unpleasant or ill-bred for literary treatment has immensely broadened the scope of American fiction. Moreover, they have had enough vitality and courage to be exhilarated by the American life of their own times. From the beginning they have exulted in the wealth and ugliness of American cities, the splendor of the mansions and the squalor of the tenements. They compared Pittsburgh to Paris and wrote about New York as if they were describing imperial Rome. Frank Norris thought that his own San Francisco was the ideal city for story-tellers; "Things happen in San Francisco," he said. Dreiser remarked of Chicago, "It is given to some cities, as to some lands, to suggest romance, and to me Chicago did that hourly. . . . Florence in its best days must have been something like this to young Florentines, or Venice to the young Venetians." The Naturalists for all their faults were embarked on a bolder venture than those other writers whose imaginations can absorb nothing but legends already treated in other books, prepared and predigested food. They tried to seize the life around them, and at their best they transformed it into new archetypes of human experience. We look for Studs Lonigan in the Chicago streets as our grandfathers looked for Leatherstocking in the forest. Just as Cooper had shaped the legend of the frontier and Mark Twain the legend of the Mississippi, so the Naturalists have been shaping the harsher legends of an urban and industrial age.

TWENTY-THREE

REALITY IN AMERICA

Lionel Trilling

Lionel Trilling (1905–75), perhaps America's most influential literary critic from the early 1950s until his death, was born in New York and educated at Columbia, receiving his Ph.D. in 1938. Trilling also taught at Columbia for most of his career. Like many of his generation, Trilling's early Marxist idealism shifted during the mid-1930s to a suspicion of leftest values and methods. By the 1950s he was often expressing conservative cultural and political beliefs while still maintaining a fully engaged interest in modern thought and literature. After early book-length studies of Matthew Arnold and E. M. Forster, almost all of Trilling's later work was in the essay form. His most noteworthy essay collections are *The Liberal Imagination: Essays in Literature and Society* (1950), *The Opposing Self: Nine Essays in Criticism* (1955), and *Beyond Culture: Essays on Literature and Learning* (1966).

i.

It is possible to say of V. L. Parrington that with his *Main Currents in American Thought* he has had an influence on our conception of American culture which is not equaled by that of any other writer of the last two decades. His ideas are now the accepted ones wherever the college course in American literature is given by a teacher who conceives himself to be opposed to the genteel and the academic and in alliance with the vigorous and the actual. And whenever the liberal historian of America finds occasion to take account of the national literature, as nowadays he feels it proper to do, it is Parrington who is his standard and guide. Parrington's ideas are the more

Part i, *Partisan Review* 7 (January-February 1940): 24–40; Part ii, *Nation* 162 (20 April 1946): 466–72. Reprinted, with major revisions, in *The Liberal Imagination* (New York: Scribner's, 1950), pp. 3–21. Text from *The Liberal Imagination*. Permission to reprint granted by the Estate of Lionel Trilling, Diana Trilling, Executor.

firmly established because they do not have to be imposed—the teacher or the critic who presents them is likely to find that his task is merely to make articulate for his audience what it has always believed, for Parrington formulated in a classic way the suppositions about our culture which are held by the American middle class so far as that class is at all liberal in its social thought and so far as it begins to understand that literature has anything to do with society.

Parrington was not a great mind; he was not a precise thinker or, except when measured by the low eminences that were about him, an impressive one. Separate Parrington from his informing idea of the economic and social determination of thought and what is left is a simple intelligence, notable for its generosity and enthusiasm but certainly not for its accuracy or originality. Take him even with his idea and he is, once its direction is established, rather too predictable to be continuously interesting; and, indeed, what we dignify with the name of economic and social determinism amounts in his use of it to not much more than the demonstration that most writers incline to stick to their own social class. But his best virtue was real and important—he had what we like to think of as the saving salt of the American mind, the lively sense of the practical, workaday world, of the welter of ordinary undistinguished things and people, of the tangible, quirky, unrefined elements of life. He knew what so many literary historians do not know, that emotions and ideas are the sparks that fly when the mind meets difficulties.

Yet he had after all but a limited sense of what constitutes a difficulty. Whenever he was confronted with a work of art that was complex, personal and not literal, that was not, as it were, a public document, Parrington was at a loss. Difficulties that were complicated by personality or that were expressed in the language of successful art did not seem quite real to him and he was inclined to treat them as aberrations, which is one way of saying what everybody admits, that the weakest part of Parrington's talent was his aesthetic judgment. His admirers and disciples like to imply that his errors of aesthetic judgment are merely lapses of taste, but this is not so. Despite such mistakes as his notorious praise of Cabell, to whom in a remarkable passage he compares Melville, Parrington's taste was by no means bad. His errors are the errors of understanding which arise from his assumptions about the nature of reality.

Parrington does not often deal with abstract philosophical ideas, but whenever he approaches a work of art we are made aware of the metaphysics on which his aesthetics is based. There exists, he believes, a thing called *reality*; it is one and immutable, it is wholly external, it is irreducible. Men's minds may waver, but reality is always reliable, always the same, always easily to be known. And the artist's relation to reality he conceives as a simple one. Reality being fixed and given, the artist has but to let it pass through him, he is the lens in the first diagram of an elementary book on optics: Fig 1, Reality; Fig. 2, Artist; Fig. 1′, Work of Art. Figs. 1 and 1′ are normally in virtual correspondence with each other. Sometimes the artist spoils this ideal relation by "turning away from" reality. This results in certain fantastic works, unreal and ultimately useless. It does not occur to Parrington that there is any other relation possible between the artist and reality than this passage of reality through the transparent artist; he meets evidence of imagination and creativeness with a settled hostility the expression of which suggests that he regards them as the natural enemies of democracy.

In this view of things, reality, although it is always reliable, is always rather sober-sided, even grim. Parrington, a genial and enthusiastic man, can understand how the generosity of man's hopes and desires may leap beyond reality; he admires will in the degree that he suspects mind. To an excess of desire and energy which blinds a man to the limitations of reality he can indeed be very tender. This is one of the many meanings he gives to *romance* or *romanticism*, and in spite of himself it appeals to something in his own nature. The praise of Cabell is Parrington's response not only to Cabell's elegance—for Parrington loved elegance—but also to Cabell's insistence on the part which a beneficent self-deception may and even should play in the disappointing fact-bound life of man, particularly in the private and erotic part of his life.[1]

The second volume of *Main Currents* is called *The Romantic Revolution in America* and it is natural to expect that the word romantic should appear in it frequently. So it does, more frequently than one can count, and seldom with the same meaning, seldom with the sense that the word, although scandalously vague as it has been used by the literary historians, is still full of complicated but not wholly pointless ideas, that it involves many contrary but definable things; all too often Parrington uses the word romantic with the word romance close at hand, meaning *a* romance, in the sense that *Graustark* or *Treasure Island* is a romance, as though it signified chiefly a gay disregard of the limitations of everyday fact. Romance is refusing to heed the counsels of experience (p. iii); it is ebullience (p. iv); it is utopianism (p. iv); it is individualism (p. vi); it is self-deception (p. 59)—"romantic faith . . . in the beneficent processes of trade and industry" (as held, we inevitably ask, by the romantic Adam Smith?); it is the love of the picturesque (p. 49); it is the dislike of innovation (p. 50) but also the love of change (p. iv); it is the sentimental (p. 192); it is patriotism, and then it is cheap (p. 235). It may be used to denote what is not classical, but chiefly it means that which ignores reality (pp. ix, 136, 143, 147, and *passim*); it is not critical (pp. 225, 235), although in speaking of Cooper and Melville, Parrington admits that criticism can sometimes spring from romanticism.

Whenever a man with whose ideas he disagrees wins from Parrington a reluctant measure of respect, the word romantic is likely to appear. He does not admire Henry Clay, yet something in Clay is not to be despised—his romanticism, although Clay's romanticism is made equivalent with his inability to "come to grips with reality." Romanticism is thus, in most of its significations, the venial sin of *Main Currents*; like carnal passion in the *Inferno*, it evokes not blame but tender sorrow. But it can also be the great and saving virtue which Parrington recognizes. It is ascribed to the transcendental reformers he so much admires; it is said to mark two of his most cherished heroes, Jefferson and Emerson: "they were both romantics and their idealism was only a different expression of a common spirit." Parrington held, we may say, at least two different views of romanticism which suggest two different views of reality. Sometimes he speaks of reality in an honorific way, meaning the substantial stuff of life, the ineluctable facts with which the mind must cope, but sometimes he speaks of it pejoratively and means the world of established social forms; and he speaks of realism in two ways: sometimes as the power of dealing intelligently with fact, sometimes as a cold and conservative resistance to idealism.

Just as for Parrington there is a saving grace and a venial sin, there is also a deadly sin, and this is turning away from reality, not in the excess of generous feeling, but in what he believes to be a deficiency of feeling, as with Hawthorne, or out of what amounts to sinful pride, as with Henry James. He tells us that there was too much realism in Hawthorne to allow him to give his faith to the transcendental reformers: "he was too much of a realist to change fashions in creeds"; "he remained cold to the revolutionary criticism that was eager to pull down the old temples to make room for nobler." It is this cold realism, keeping Hawthorne apart from his enthusiastic contemporaries, that alienates Parrington's sympathy—"Eager souls, mystics and revolutionaries, may propose to refashion the world in accordance with their dreams; but evil remains, and so long as it lurks in the secret places of the heart, utopia is only the shadow of a dream. And so while the Concord thinkers were proclaiming man to be the indubitable child of God, Hawthorne was critically examining the question of evil as it appeared in the light of his own experience. It was the central fascinating problem of his intellectual life, and in pursuit of a solution he probed curiously into the hidden, furtive recesses of the soul." Parrington's disapproval of the enterprise is unmistakable.

Now we might wonder whether Hawthorne's questioning of the naïve and often eccentric faiths of the transcendental reformers was not, on the face of it, a public service. But Parrington implies that it contributes nothing to democracy, and even that it stands in the way of the realization of democracy. If democracy depends wholly on a fighting faith, I suppose he is right. Yet society is after all something that exists at the moment as well as in the future, and if one man wants to probe curiously into the hidden furtive recesses of the contemporary soul, a broad democracy and especially one devoted to reality should allow him to do so without despising him. If what Hawthorne did was certainly nothing to build a party on, we ought perhaps to forgive him when we remember that he was only one man and that the future of mankind did not depend upon him alone. But this very fact serves only to irritate Parrington; he is put out by Hawthorne's loneliness and believes that part of Hawthorne's insufficiency as a writer comes from his failure to get around and meet people. Hawthorne could not, he tells us, establish contact with the "Yankee reality," and was scarcely aware of the "substantial world of Puritan reality that Samuel Sewall knew."

To turn from reality might mean to turn to romance, but Parrington tells us that Hawthorne was romantic "only in a narrow and very special sense." He was not interested in the world of, as it were, practical romance, in the Salem of the clipper ships; from this he turned away to create "a romance of ethics." This is not an illuminating phrase but it is a catching one, and it might be taken to mean that Hawthorne was in the tradition of, say, Shakespeare; but we quickly learn that, no, Hawthorne had entered a barren field, for although he himself lived in the present and had all the future to mold, he preferred to find many of his subjects in the past. We learn too that his romance of ethics is not admirable because it requires the hard, fine pressing of ideas, and we are told that "a romantic uninterested in adventure and afraid of sex is likely to become somewhat graveled for matter." In short, Hawthorne's mind was a thin one, and Parrington puts in evidence his use of allegory and symbol and the very severity and precision of his art to prove that he suffered from a sadly limited intellect, for so much fancy and so much art could scarcely be needed unless the writer were trying to exploit to the utmost the few poor ideas that he had.

Hawthorne, then, was "forever dealing with shadows, and he knew that he was dealing with shadows." Perhaps so, but shadows are also part of reality and one would not want a world without shadows, it would not even be a "real" world. But we must get beyond Parrington's metaphor. The fact is that Hawthorne was dealing beautifully with realities, with substantial things. The man who could raise those brilliant and serious doubts about the nature and possibility of moral perfection, the man who could keep himself aloof from the "Yankee reality" and who could dissent from the orthodoxies of dissent and tell us so much about the nature of moral zeal, is of course dealing exactly with reality.

Parrington's characteristic weakness as a historian is suggested by his title, for the culture of a nation is not truly figured in the image of the current. A culture is not a flow, nor even a confluence; the form of its existence is struggle, or at least debate—it is nothing if not a dialectic. And in any culture there are likely to be certain artists who contain a large part of the dialectic within themselves, their meaning and power lying in their contradictions; they contain within themselves, it may be said, the very essence of the culture, and the sign of this is that they do not submit to serve the ends of any one ideological group or tendency. It is a significant circumstance of American culture, and one which is susceptible of explanation, that an unusually large proportion of its notable writers of the nineteenth century were such repositories of the dialectic of their times—they contained both the yes and the no of their culture, and by that token they were prophetic of the future. Parrington said that he had not set up shop as a literary critic; but if a literary critic is simply a reader who has the ability to understand literature and to convey to others what he understands, it is not exactly a matter of free choice whether or not a cultural historian shall be a literary critic, nor is it open to him to let his virtuous political and social opinions do duty for percipience. To throw out Poe because he cannot be conveniently fitted into a theory of American culture, to speak of him as a biological sport and as a mind apart from the main current, to find his gloom to be merely personal and eccentric, "only the atrabilious wretchedness of a dipsomaniac," as Hawthorne's was "no more than the skeptical questioning of life by a nature that knew no fierce storms," to judge Melville's response to American life to be less noble than that of Bryant or of Greeley, to speak of Henry James as an escapist, as an artist similar to Whistler, a man characteristically afraid of stress—this is not merely to be mistaken in aesthetic judgment; rather it is to examine without attention and from the point of view of a limited and essentially arrogant conception of reality the documents which are in some respects the most suggestive testimony to what America was and is, and of course to get no answer from them.

Parrington lies twenty years behind us, and in the intervening time there has developed a body of opinion which is aware of his inadequacies and of the inadequacies of his coadjutors and disciples, who make up what might be called the literary academicism of liberalism. Yet Parrington still stands at the center of American thought about American culture because, as I say, he expresses the chronic American belief that there exists an opposition between reality and mind and that one must enlist oneself in the party of reality.

ii.

This belief in the incompatibility of mind and reality is exemplified by the doctrinaire indulgence which liberal intellectuals have always displayed toward Theodore Dreiser, an indulgence which becomes the worthier of remark when it is contrasted with the liberal severity toward Henry James. Dreiser and James: with that juxtaposition we are immediately at the dark and bloody crossroads where literature and politics meet. One does not go there gladly, but nowadays it is not exactly a matter of free choice whether one does or does not go. As for the particular juxtaposition itself, it is inevitable and it has at the present moment far more significance than the juxtaposition which once used to be made between James and Whitman. It is not hard to contrive factitious oppositions between James and Whitman, but the real difference between them is the difference between the moral mind, with its awareness of tragedy, irony, and multitudinous distinctions, and the transcendental mind, with its passionate sense of the oneness of multiplicity. James and Whitman are unlike not in quality but in kind, and in their very opposition they serve to complement each other. But the difference between James and Dreiser is not of kind, for both men addressed themselves to virtually the same social and moral fact. The difference here is one of quality, and perhaps nothing is more typical of American liberalism than the way it has responded to the respective qualities of the two men.

Few critics, I suppose, no matter what their political disposition, have ever been wholly blind to James's great gifts, or even to the grandiose moral intention of these gifts. And few critics have ever been wholly blind to Dreiser's great faults. But by liberal critics James is traditionally put to the ultimate question: of what use, of what actual political use, are his gifts and their intention? Granted that James was devoted to an extraordinary moral perceptiveness, granted too that moral perceptiveness has something to do with politics and the social life, of what possible practical value in our world of impending disaster can James's work be? And James's style, his characters, his subjects, and even his own social origin and the manner of his personal life are adduced to show that his work cannot endure the question. To James no quarter is given by American criticism in its political and liberal aspect. But in the same degree that liberal criticism is moved by political considerations to treat James with severity, it treats Dreiser with the most sympathetic indulgence. Dreiser's literary faults, it gives us to understand, are essentially social and political virtues. It was Parrington who established the formula for the liberal criticism of Dreiser by calling him a "peasant": when Dreiser thinks stupidly, it is because he has the slow stubbornness of a peasant; when he writes badly it is because he is impatient of the sterile literary gentility of the bourgeoisie. It is as if wit, and flexibility of mind, and perception, and knowledge were to be equated with aristocracy and political reaction, while dullness and stupidity must naturally suggest a virtuous democracy, as in the old plays.

The liberal judgment of Dreiser and James goes back of politics, goes back to the cultural assumptions that make politics. We are still haunted by a kind of political fear of the intellect which Tocqueville observed in us more than a century ago. American intellectuals, when they are being consciously American or political, are remarkably quick to suggest that an art which is marked by perception and knowledge, although all very well in its way, can never get us through gross dangers and difficulties. And their misgivings become the more intense when intellect works in art as it ideally should, when its processes are vivacious and interesting and brilliant. It is then that we like to confront it with the gross dangers and difficulties and to challenge it to save us at once from disaster. When intellect in art is awkward or dull we do not put it to the test of ultimate or immediate practicality. No liberal critic asks the question of Dreiser whether *his* moral preoccupations are going to be useful in confronting the disasters that threaten us. And it is a judgment on the proper nature of mind, rather than any actual political meaning that might be drawn from the works of the two men, which accounts for the unequal justice they have received from the progressive critics. If it could be conclusively demonstrated—by, say, documents in James's handwriting—that James explicitly intended his books to be understood as pleas for cooperatives, labor unions, better housing, and more equitable taxation, the American critic in his liberal and progressive character would still be worried by James because his work shows so many of the electric qualities of mind. And if something like the opposite were proved of Dreiser, it would be brushed aside—as his doctrinaire anti-Semitism has in fact been brushed aside—because his books have the awkwardness, the chaos, the heaviness which we associate with "reality." In the American metaphysic, reality is always material reality, hard, resistant, unformed, impenetrable, and unpleasant. And that mind is alone felt to be trustworthy which most resembles this reality by most nearly reproducing the sensations it affords.

In *The Rise of American Civilization*, Professor Beard uses a significant phrase when, in the course of an ironic account of James's career, he implies that we have the clue to the irrelevance of that career when we know that James was "a whole generation removed from the odors of the shop." Of a piece with this, and in itself even more significant, is the comment which Granville Hicks makes in *The Great Tradition* when he deals with James's stories about artists and remarks that such artists as James portrays, so concerned for their art and their integrity in art, do not really exist: "After all, who has ever known such artists? Where are the Hugh Verekers, the Mark Ambients, the Neil Paradays, the Overts, Limberts, Dencombes, Delavoys?" This question, as Mr. Hicks admits, had occurred to James himself, but what answer had James given to it? "If the life about us for the last thirty years refused warrant for these examples," he said in the preface to volume xii of the New York Edition, "then so much the worse for that life. . . . There are decencies that in the name of the general self-respect we must take for granted, there's a rudimentary intellectual honor to which we must, in the interest of civilization at least pretend." And to this Mr. Hicks, shocked beyond argument, makes this reply, which would be astonishing had we not heard it before: "But this is the purest romanticism, this writing about what ought to be rather than what is!"

The "odors of the shop" are real, and to those who breathe them they guarantee a sense of vitality from which James is debarred. The idea of intellectual honor is not real, and to that chimera James was devoted. He betrayed the reality of what is in the interests of what ought to be. Dare we trust him? The question, we remember, is asked by men who themselves have elaborate transactions with what ought to be. Professor Beard spoke in the name of a growing, developing, and improving America. Mr. Hicks, when he wrote *The Great Tradition*, was in general sympathy with a nominally radical movement. But James's own transaction with what ought to be is suspect because it is carried on through what I have called the electrical qualities of mind, through a complex and rapid imagination and with a kind of authoritative immediacy. Mr. Hicks knows that Dreiser is "clumsy" and "stupid" and "bewildered" and "crude in his statement of materialistic monism"; he knows that Dreiser in his personal life—which is in point because James's personal life is always supposed to be so much in point—was not quite emancipated from "his boyhood longing for crass material success," showing "again and again a desire for the ostentatious luxury of the successful business man." But Dreiser is to be accepted and forgiven because his faults are the sad, lovable, honorable faults of reality itself, or of America itself—huge, inchoate, struggling toward expression, caught between the dream of raw power and the dream of morality.

"The liability in what Santayana called the genteel tradition was due to its being the product of mind apart from experience. Dreiser gave us the stuff of our common experience, not as it was hoped to be by any idealizing theorist, but as it actually was in its crudity." The author of this statement certainly cannot be accused of any lack of feeling for mind as Henry James represents it; nor can Mr. Matthiessen be thought of as a follower of Parrington—indeed, in the preface to *American Renaissance* he has framed one of the sharpest and most cogent criticisms of Parrington's method. Yet Mr. Matthiessen, writing in the *New York Times Book Review* about Dreiser's posthumous novel, *The Bulwark*, accepts the liberal cliché which opposes crude experience to mind and establishes Dreiser's value by implying that the mind which Dreiser's crude experience is presumed to confront and refute is the mind of gentility.

This implied amalgamation of mind with gentility is the rationale of the long indulgence of Dreiser, which is extended even to the style of his prose. Everyone is aware that Dreiser's prose style is full of roughness and ungainliness, and the critics who admire Dreiser tell us it does not matter. Of course it does not matter. No reader with a right sense of style would suppose that it does matter, and he might even find it a virtue. But it has been taken for granted that the ungainliness of Dreiser's style is the only possible objection to be made to it, and that whoever finds in it any fault at all wants a prettified genteel style (and is objecting to the ungainliness of reality itself). For instance, Edwin Berry Burgum, in a leaflet on Dreiser put out by the Book Find Club, tells us that Dreiser was one of those who used—or, as Mr. Burgum says, utilized—"the diction of the Middle West, pretty much as it was spoken, rich in colloquialism and frank in the simplicity and directness of the pioneer tradition," and that this diction took the place of "the literary English, formal and bookish, of New England provincialism that was closer to the aristocratic spirit of the mother country than to the tang of everyday life in the new West." This is mere fantasy. Hawthorne, Thoreau, and Emerson were for the most part remarkably colloquial—they wrote, that is, much as they spoke; their prose was specifically American in quality, and, except for occasional lapses, quite direct and simple. It is Dreiser who lacks the sense of colloquial diction—that of the Middle West or any other. If we are to talk of bookishness, it is Dreiser who is bookish; he is precisely literary in the bad sense; he is full of flowers of rhetoric and shines with paste gems; at hundreds of points his diction is not only genteel but fancy. It is he who speaks of "a scene more distingué than this," or of a woman "artistic in form and feature," or of a man who, although "strong, reserved, aggressive, with an air of wealth and experience, was *soi-disant* and not particularly eager to stay at home." Colloquialism held no real charm for him and his natural tendency is always toward the "fine:"

> ... Moralists come and go; religionists fulminate and declare the pronouncements of God as to this; but Aphrodite still reigns. Embowered in the festal depths of the spring, set above her altars of porphyry, chalcedony, ivory and gold, see her smile the smile that is at once the texture and essence of delight, the glory and despair of the world! Dream on, oh Buddha, asleep on your lotus leaf, of an undisturbed Nirvana! Sweat, oh Jesus, your last agonizing drops over an unregenerate world! In the forests of Pan still ring the cries of the worshippers of Aphrodite! From her altars the incense of adoration ever rises! And see, the new red grapes dripping where votive hands new-press them!

Charles Jackson, the novelist, telling us in the same leaflet that Dreiser's style does not matter, remarks on how much still comes to us when we have lost by translation the stylistic brilliance of Thomas Mann or the Russians or Balzac. He is in part right. And he is right too when he says that a certain kind of conscious, supervised artistry is not appropriate to the novel of large dimensions. Yet the fact is that the great novelists have usually written very good prose, and what comes through even a bad translation is exactly the power of mind that made the well-hung sentence of the original text. In literature style is so little the mere clothing of thought—need it be insisted on at this late date?—that we may say that from the earth of the novelist's prose spring his characters, his ideas, and even his story itself.[2]

To the extent that Dreiser's style is defensible, his thought is also defensible. That is, when he thinks like a novelist, he is worth following—when by means of his rough and ungainly but no doubt cumulatively effective style he creates rough, ungainly, but effective characters and events. But when he thinks like, as we say, a philosopher, he is likely to be not only foolish but vulgar. He thinks as the modern crowd thinks when it decides to think: religion and morality are nonsense, "religionists" and moralists are fakes, tradition is a fraud, what is man but matter and impulses, mysterious "chemisms," what value has life anyway? "What, cooking, eating, coition, job holding, growing, aging, losing, winning, in so changeful and passing a scene as this, important? Bunk! It is some form of titillating illusion with about as much import to the superior forces that bring it all about as the functions and gyrations of a fly. No more. And maybe less." Thus Dreiser at sixty. And yet there is for him always the vulgarly saving suspicion that maybe, when all is said and done, there is Something Behind It All. It is much to the point of his intellectual vulgarity that Dreiser's anti-Semitism was not merely a social prejudice but an idea, a way of dealing with difficulties.

No one, I suppose, has ever represented Dreiser as a masterly intellect. It is even commonplace to say that his ideas are inconsistent or inadequate. But once that admission has been made, his ideas are hustled out of sight while his "reality" and great brooding pity are spoken of. (His pity is to be questioned: pity is to be judged by kind, not amount, and Dreiser's pity—*Jennie Gerhardt* provides the only exception—is either destructive of its object or it is self-pity.) Why has no liberal critic ever brought Dreiser's ideas to the bar of political practicality, asking what use is to be made of Dreiser's dim, awkward speculation, of his self-justification, of his lust for "beauty" and "sex" and "living" and "life itself," and of the showy nihilism which always seems to him so grand a gesture in the direction of profundity? We live, understandably enough, with the sense of urgency; our clock, like Baudelaire's, has had the hands removed and bears the legend, "It is later than you think." But with us it is always a little too late for mind, yet never too late for honest stupidity; always a little too late for understanding, never too late for righteous, bewildered wrath; always too late for thought, never too late for naive moralizing. We seem to like to condemn our finest but not our worst qualities by pitting them against the exigency of time.

But sometimes time is not quite so exigent as to justify all our own exigency, and in the case of Dreiser time has allowed his deficiencies to reach their logical, and fatal, conclusion. In *The Bulwark* Dreiser's characteristic ideas come full circle, and the simple, didactic life history of Solon Barnes, a Quaker business man, affirms a simple Christian faith, and a kind of practical mysticism, and the virtues of self-abnegation and self-restraint, and the belief in and submission to the hidden purposes of higher powers, those "superior forces that bring it all about"—once, in Dreiser's opinion, so brutally indifferent, now somehow benign. This is not the first occasion on which Dreiser has shown a tenderness toward religion and a responsiveness to mysticism. *Jennie Gerhardt* and the figure of the Reverend Duncan McMillan in *An American Tragedy* are forecasts of the avowals of *The Bulwark*, and Dreiser's lively interest in power of any sort led him to take account of the power implicit in the cruder forms of mystical performance. Yet these rifts in his nearly monolithic materialism cannot quite prepare us for the blank pietism of *The Bulwark*, not after we have remembered how salient in Dreiser's work has been the long surly rage against the "religionists" and the "moralists," the men who have presumed to believe that life can be given any law at all and who have dared to suppose that will or mind or faith can shape the savage and beautiful entity that Dreiser liked to call "life itself." Now for Dreiser the law may indeed be given, and it is wholly simple—the safe conduct of the personal life requires only that we follow the Inner Light according to the regimen of the Society of Friends, or according to some other godly rule. And now the smiling Aphrodite set above her altars of porphyry, chalcedony, ivory, and gold is quite forgotten, and we are told that the sad joy of cosmic acceptance goes hand in hand with sexual abstinence.

Dreiser's mood of "acceptance" in the last years of his life is not, as a personal experience, to be submitted to the tests of intellectual validity. It consists of a sensation of cosmic understanding, of an overarching sense of unity with the world in its apparent evil as well as in its obvious good. It is no more to be quarreled with, or reasoned with, than love itself—indeed, it is a kind of love, not so much of the world as of oneself in the world. Perhaps it is either the cessation of desire or the perfect balance of desires. It is what used often to be meant by "peace," and up through the nineteenth century a good many people understood its meaning. If it was Dreiser's own emotion at the end of his life, who would not be happy that he had achieved it? I am not even sure that our civilization would not be the better for more of us knowing and desiring this emotion of grave felicity. Yet granting the personal validity of the emotion, Dreiser's exposition of it fails, and is, moreover, offensive. Mr. Matthiessen has warned us of the attack that will be made on the doctrine of *The Bulwark* by "those who believe that any renewal of Christianity marks a new 'failure of nerve.' " But Dreiser's religious avowal is not a failure of nerve—it is a failure of mind and heart. We have only to set his book beside any work in which mind and heart are made to serve religion to know this at once. Ivan Karamazov's giving back his ticket of admission to the "harmony" of the universe suggests that *The Bulwark* is not morally adequate, for we dare not, as its hero does, blandly "accept" the suffering of others; and the Book of Job tells us that it does not include enough in its exploration of the problem of evil, and is not stern enough. I have said that Dreiser's religious affirmation was offensive; the offense lies in the vulgar ease of its formulation, as well as in the comfortable untroubled way in which Dreiser moved from nihilism to pietism.[3]

The Bulwark is the fruit of Dreiser's old age, but if we speak of it as a failure of thought and feeling, we cannot suppose that with age Dreiser weakened in mind and heart. The weakness was always there. And in a sense it is not Dreiser who failed but a whole way of dealing with ideas, a way in which we have all been in some degree involved. Our liberal, progressive culture tolerated Dreiser's vulgar materialism with its huge negation, its simple cry of "Bunk!," feeling that perhaps it was not quite intellectually adequate but certainly very *strong*, certainly very *real*. And now, almost as a natural consequence, it has been given, and is not unwilling to take, Dreiser's pietistic religion in all its inadequacy.

Dreiser, of course, was firmer than the intellectual culture that accepted him. He *meant* his ideas, at least so far as a man can mean ideas who is incapable of following them to their consequences. But we, when it came to his ideas, talked about his great brooding pity and shrugged the ideas off. We are still doing it. Robert Elias, the biographer of Dreiser, tells us that "it is part of the logic of [Dreiser's] life that he should have completed *The Bulwark* at the same time that he joined the Communists." Just what kind of logic this is we learn from Mr. Elias's further statement. "When he supported left-wing movements and finally, last year, joined the Communist Party, he did so not because he had examined the details of the party line and found them satisfactory, but because he agreed with a general program that represented a means for establishing his cherished goal of greater equality among men." Whether or not Dreiser was following the logic of his own life, he was certainly following the logic of the liberal criticism that accepted him so undiscriminatingly as one of the great, significant expressions of its spirit. This is the liberal criticism, in the direct line of Parrington, which establishes the social responsibility of the writer and then goes on to say that, apart from his duty of resembling reality as much as possible, he is not really responsible for anything, not even for his ideas. The scope of reality being what it is, ideas are held to be mere "details," and, what is more, to be details which, if attended to, have the effect of diminishing reality. But ideals are different from ideas; in the liberal criticism which descends from Parrington ideals consort happily with reality and they urge us to deal impatiently with ideas—a "cherished goal" forbids that we stop to consider how we reach it, or if we may not destroy it in trying to reach it the wrong way.

NOTES

1. See, for example, how Parrington accounts for the "idealizing mind"—Melville's—by the discrepancy between "a wife in her morning kimono" and "the Helen of his dreams." Vol. II, p. 259.

2. The latest defense of Dreiser's style, that in the chapter on Dreiser in the *Literary History of the United States*, is worth noting: "Forgetful of the integrity and power of Dreiser's whole work, many critics have been distracted into a condemnation of his style. He was, like Twain and Whitman, an organic artist; he wrote what he knew—what he was. His many colloquialisms were part of the coinage of his time, and his sentimental and romantic passages were written in the language of the educational system and the popular literature of his formative years. In his style, as in his material, he was a child of his time, of his class. Self-educated, a type or model of the artist of plebeian origin in America, his language, like his subject matter, is not marked by internal inconsistencies." No doubt Dreiser was an organic artist in the sense that he wrote what he knew and what he was, but so, I suppose, is every artist; the question for criticism comes down to what he knew and what he was. That he was a child of his time and class is also true, but this can be said of everyone without exception; the question for criticism is how he transcended the imposed limitations of his time and class. As for the defense made on the ground of his particular class, it can only be said that liberal thought has come to a strange pass when it assumes that a plebeian origin is accountable for a writer's faults through all his intellectual life.

3. This ease and comfortableness seem to mark contemporary religious conversions. Religion nowadays has the appearance of what the ideal modern house has been called, "a machine for living," and seemingly one makes up one's mind to acquire and use it not with spiritual struggle but only with a growing sense of its practicability and convenience. Compare *The Seven Storey Mountain*, which Monsignor Sheen calls "a twentieth-century form of the *Confessions of St. Augustine*," with the old, the as it were original, *Confessions of St. Augustine*.

TWENTY-FOUR

SOME OBSERVATIONS ON NATURALISM, SO CALLED, IN FICTION

James T. Farrell

James T. Farrell (1904–79) was born and raised in south Chicago and was graduated from the University of Chicago in 1929. A prolific novelist who published forty-one works of fiction during his lifetime, he is identified above all with his early *Studs Lonigan Trilogy* (1932–35), a painfully honest depiction of the limitations of Chicago Irish-American life that has often been cited as evidence of the persistence of American naturalism in the 1930s. Farrell moved to New York in 1932, where he became a stalwart member of the anti-Stalinist left. His *A Note on Literary Criticism* (1936) was hotly debated because of its rejection of the absolutes of party-line literary values. Farrell's "Some Observations on Naturalism, So Called, in Fiction," derives in part from his lifelong admiration for Dreiser's fiction, an admiration cemented by his friendship with Dreiser during the early 1940s.

I

Emile Zola is usually characterized as the father of modern naturalism. And quite frequently Zola's "The Experimental Novel" is cited by critics as the gospel of literary naturalism. More than one critic has judged any number of books to be defective, and even dangerous, on the assumption that these books are illustrations of what Zola wrote in this particular essay in the year 1878.

Antioch Review 10 (Summer 1950): 247–64. Reprinted in *Reflections at Fifty and Other Essays* (New York: Vanguard, 1954), 142–55. Text from *Reflections at Fifty*. Reprinted by permission of Cleo Paturis, Executor of the Estate of James T. Farrell.

Now, what did Zola really say in "The Experimental Novel"? He relied heavily on the writing of a French physiologist, Claude Bernard.[1] In a time when it was argued that medicine was not a science but an art, Bernard claimed that it could become a science. Zola applied this and many other concepts of Bernard almost literally to the field of the novel. He equated art and science without making any clear distinction between them. Zola did not look upon the questions he raised in terms of the difference between problems in the laboratory and those in the writer's study.

What was paramount with Zola was determinism. Paraphrasing Bernard, he declared: "There is an absolute determinism in the existing conditions of natural phenomena, for the living and for inanimate bodies."

Zola conceived of determinism as "determining the conditions necessary for the manifestation of phenomena." Noting that Claude Bernard had found that there were fixed laws governing the human body, he wrote that it could be proclaimed without fear of error that the hour would come when the laws of thought and of passion would be formulated in a like manner. And he asserted that in terms of this determinism, the naturalistic novelist was a scientist who was analyzing man in both his individual and his social relations. Thus, he declared: " . . . We [novelists] operate on the characters, the passions, on the human and social data, in the same way that the chemist and the physicist operate on living beings. Determinism dominates everything."

A longer quotation will give a fuller sense of Zola's view:

Man is not alone: he lives in society, in a social condition: and consequently, for us novelists, the social condition increasingly modifies the phenomenon. Indeed our great study is just there, a reciprocal effect of society upon the individual and the individual on society. . . . We are not able yet to prove that the social condition is . . . physical and chemical. . . . We can act upon the social condition, in acting upon the phenomena of which we have made ourselves masters of men. And this is what constitutes the experimental novel: to possess a knowledge of the mechanism of the phenomena inherent in man, to show the masking of the intellectual and sensory manifestations under the influence of heredity and environment, such as physiology shall give them to us, then finally to exhibit man living in a social condition produced by himself, which modifies daily, and in the heart of which he himself experiences a continual transformation. Thus, then, we lean on physiology: we take man from the hand of the physiologist solely in order to continue the solution of the problem, and to solve scientifically how men behave when they are in society.

Affirming these views, Zola looked forward to the day when the experimental novelist, the naturalist, would bring forth decisive results of a scientific character. He emphasized the word *experimental*, declaring that the novelist would show by experiments the ways that passion acts under certain given conditions, that these experiments would serve as a means of going from the known to the unknown, and that the experimental novelist would thus act as a scientist who went from the known to the unknown insofar as man was concerned. As such, he was to be contrasted with the "idealistic novelist" who deliberately remained in the unknown, and who clung to all sorts of religious and philosophical prejudices "under the extraordinary pretense that the unknown is nobler and more beautiful than the known."

In answer to the charge that the work of experimental novelists needed justification because it dealt with the ugly, Zola quoted Bernard as follows:

"You will never reach fully fruitful and luminous generalizations on the phenomena of life until you have experimented yourself and stirred up in hospital, the amphitheater, the laboratory, the fetid or palpitating source of life. If it were necessary for me to give a comparison which would explain my sentiments on the science of life, I should say that it is a superb salon, flooded with light, which you can only reach by passing through a long and nauseating kitchen."

Zola saw the experimental method as a means whereby scientific authority would be substituted for personal authority. With this, he also asserted that naturalism is not a school: " . . . it is nothing but a vast movement, a march forward in which everyone is a workman according to his genius. All theories are admitted and the theory which carries the most weight is the one which explains the most."

Zola was opposed to the supernatural. He believed that science had already demonstrated that the supernatural was not real or true. He saw in science the source of intellectual leadership in the nineteenth century, and he insisted that the novelist have a place in this scientific movement. Opposing scientists who would not give writers such a place, he declared:

I have remarked that a great many of the most intelligent savants, jealous of the scientific authority which they enjoy, would very willingly confine literature to the ideal. They themselves seem to feel the need of taking a little recreation in the world of lies after the fatigue of their exact labor, and they are fond of amusing themselves with the most daring hypotheses, and with fictions which they know perfectly well to be false and ridiculous.

To Zola, romanticism and the ideal were lies—unreal and untrue and undemonstrable. Rather than trade in these "lies," as he styled them, the novelist should have equal place with the scientist, and should work as he does. Zola here established a conception of truth as the ideal, and he held that the artist must adhere to it. He believed that the feeling of the artist must "always be subject to the higher law of truth and nature." And he added that " . . . each time that a truth is established by the savants," the writers should immediately abandon their hypotheses to adopt this truth; otherwise they will remain deliberately in error without benefiting anyone. And in terms of these attitudes he also proclaimed the death of "metaphysical man" and the advent of the "physiological man."

In a lecture "From Poe to Valéry," delivered at the Library of Congress, T. S. Eliot made an excellent observation which can be applied to Zola's theory of the experimental novel. Speaking of the theory which Valéry held as a poet, Eliot said:

Here I should like to point out the difference between a theory of poetry propounded by a student of aesthetics, and the same theory as held by a poet. It is one thing when it is simply an account of how the poet writes without knowing it, and another thing when the poet himself writes consciously according to that theory. In affecting writing, the theory becomes a different thing from what it was merely as an explanation of how the poet writes.

Zola wrote consciously in terms of his theory. But if we wish to understand what has happened and what is still happening in literature, we must not test Zola, and a whole series of novels which have been written since Zola's time, by making a literal-minded effort to correlate and to judge specific works in terms of this theory. We must not forget that, up to the present time, no one has succeeded in creating a perfect theory of aesthetics.

Zola's attempt to embody scientific methods, procedures, and conclusions in the novel should be seen as an effort to incorporate in literature something of the developing mental climate of his own time. Today it is rather easy to make detailed criticisms of his theory, to formulate a clearer statement of scientific method, and to displace the copy theory of knowledge implied in his ideas with a better theory of epistemology.

The late V. L. Parrington, in *The Beginnings of Critical Realism in America* (Volume III of his *Main Currents in American Thought*), discussed the influence of science in American thought during the latter part of the nineteenth century. He observed:

> To speak exactly, it is not so much science that has taken possession of the mind, as certain postulates of science, certain philosophies presumably derived from science, and justified by science, which we have felt bound to incorporate in our thinking as a hundred years before the conclusions of the Enlightenment had been incorporated.

Parrington's observations can be applied to Zola. The novelist did set down a series of postulates, "presumably derived from science," which permitted him to widen the boundaries of that which was admissible in modern literature. He contributed to enlarging the area of human conduct which can be described by a novelist: he also changed and expanded the kind of theme which could be embodied in novels. He contributed to greater liberty of expression for the artist. His postulates, drawn from science, also gave him greater confidence, provided him with hypotheses which would help him look anew at the material of life, of characters and events. He risked hypotheses concerning heredity which, he recognized, were not completely established by science in his own time but which seemed plausible and for which there appeared to be some scientific evidence. Was he scientific or unscientific?

The American philosopher George Herbert Mead, in *The Philosophy of the Act*, made a pertinent distinction between scientific knowledge and information about science. Mead saw science as an evolving system of knowledge. In this evolving system, he contended that what remained of scientific endeavor were the facts discovered.

And his theories indicated that, while he was a relativist, he more or less held that a fact had the character of factualness and was valid within its proper frame of reference. But Mead pointed out that in this system of science the generalizations or conclusions change. We know this to be so. Mead further asserted that scientific knowledge was really gained only when you performed the experiments yourself, when you actually experienced the gaining of the knowledge, the finding out of the facts. Merely to read about this finding of the fact, as Mead properly noted, only gives us information. Zola, then, when he wrote about science, and when he stated his conclusions and hypotheses, was speaking largely in terms of information, the scientific information of his time. When he went out and gathered facts, and was proceeding with the scientific spirit and method, he was gaining knowledge. He was, then, trying to write with respect for the spirit of truth. This is part of what remains important in his legacy.

Zola's theory of naturalism is not so important today for its scientific as for its historical relevance. His theory should not be regarded simply as pessimistic determinism applied to literature. Nor has he been responsible for a school of novelists who have written books which only describe man as a "trapped animal," or, as the critics of naturalism have declared, as a rat in a cage. It should be obvious to us, in the present, that scientific advances, both theoretical and practical, have changed not only our mental universe but our way of life. Zola sensed that this was happening in his own day and attempted to deal with such a change as it might affect literature.

II

Just what has the problem of free will versus determinism to do with literature? Discussions of this problem are now usually of a piece with those concerning heredity versus environment, in which both elements appear to be solid forces in absolute conflict to one another. When we deal with such broad and all-inclusive categories it is more than well for us to recall an observation by Whitehead, who warned against committing the "fallacy of misplaced concretion." It is important here to observe that usually those who pose this question pose it in terms of a flat either/or. Is man free or is he not free? Does man have free will, or is he completely determined?[2] To me, this is an unanswerable question.

What has this to do with a novel? How will the assumption that man has free will make someone a better writer? In what way does one or another answer to the question of free will versus determinism relate to the work of fiction? When a critic of naturalism logically demonstrates the existence of free will he is merely proving what he wants to prove. But you cannot prove that anything exists in the world with pure logic. If the question is put as an empirical one, then all that these literary critics can do is to build up a case on the basis of information. Their arguments have no more necessary scientific ground than do the assertions about heredity which Zola held and applied in his novels. As literary people, we are either reducing literature to a question of logic, or we are trying to resolve literary questions by talking in terms of sciences which we do not work in. The empirical answer to this question would demand scientific work in specialized fields, such as physiology and biology, as well as psychiatry. In addition, deterministic hypotheses, whether we call them true or false, have had a value in science. Those who dispute over literary naturalism in terms of free will versus determinism are generally opposing the scientific spirit. Zola's attitude was scientific, even though limited. That of many of his latter-day critics is antiscientific.

Zola denied that art was an expression of personal views. He insisted that scientific authority must be established in place of the personal authority of the artist. I think he was mistaken. Today we are inclined to be much less optimistic than Zola was. We are aware that we can know less than we would like to pretend to, and that the unknown is far vaster than many imagined it to be in the nineteenth century. We cannot proclaim, as Zola did, that the artist must abandon theories when science has disproved them. Proof is a much more complicated process than he thought it would be. Some scientific warrant can even be given, at least tentatively, to substantiate the possible validity of types of art which Zola might have described as unrealistic, idealistic, metaphysical, or romantic—as lies.

We can translate Zola's theories so that, with many qualifications, they can have one significant value at the present time. Zola insisted that the experimental novelist must apply methods of observation and analysis. He attempted to do this. Serious writers at the present time make a similar attempt. In some instances a writer will start with a metaphysical orientation. Or he may start with attitudes or postulates which have some ground in scientific discovery. Marcel Proust, for instance, organized his books in terms of metaphysical conceptions which had some correspondence with Bergson's theories of time and continuity. Was or was not Proust a realist? Was or was not Proust a naturalist? Whether we answer these questions yes or no, we will still face the question of what Proust means to us when we read him. Do we get any fresh insight? Do we feel anything? Do we learn anything? Are we excited? What happens to our emotions? When you read a book, the handling of your own emotions, the resolution of your own feelings is much more important than any kind of judgment you make about whether the book is good or bad, especially if that judgment is made in terms of questions which are pseudophilosophical and pseudoscientific.

III

Words such as *realism* and *naturalism* have been applied to many writers. Various definitions of these words have been given. One is that of Oscar Cargill, who, in *Intellectual America: Ideas on the March*, says that naturalistic writers have in common a theory of pessimistic determinism. Others, in attempting to establish a common meaning for naturalism, have come forth with definitions which are mutually exclusive. Some hold that naturalism is optimistic.[3] Others believe it pessimistic, and will say that if a book has a hopeful ending it can't be naturalistic. I do not know all of the definitions of naturalism but I have come across enough to know they are many. I am reminded of the state of psychology fifty or sixty years ago, when a so-called instinct psychology was dominant. Apparently there was a competition among academic psychologists at that time for finding new phrases for new instincts, real or alleged. The same kind of competition must be going on among those who are attempting to get a definition of naturalism. If you accept someone else's definition, you are not original.

I have been called a naturalist and I have never denied it. However, my own conception of naturalism is not that which is usually attributed to me. By naturalism I mean that whatever happens in this world must ultimately be explainable in terms of events in this world. I assume or believe that all events are explainable in terms of natural origins rather than of extranatural or supernatural origins. Although this assumption underlies what I have written, I do not write novels to prove or disprove this assumption. I write novels to try to reveal what life seems to me to be like. I write novels as part of an attempt to explore the nature of experience.

IV

Another way of looking at these questions is in terms of necessity and of tragedy. Some contemporary criticism bases itself on the Aristotelian concept of tragedy. At its most banal level, this is not analysis at all, but often merely a kind of self-evident criticism to the effect that such and such a modern writer is not as great as Goethe or Euripides. When such criticism goes beyond the self-evident, certain points based upon Aristotle's conception of tragedy are applied.

Aristotle held that in order for a character to be a tragic figure that character must be superior. Of tragedy he said: "A tragedy . . . is the imitation of an action that is serious, and also, as having magnitude, complete in itself." And he added: "Tragedy is essentially an imitation not of persons, but of action and of life, of happiness and misery." The function of the poet was to describe not the thing that had happened, but "a kind of thing that might happen," i.e., what is possible is deemed "probable or necessary." When a play is truly tragic, it induces pity and terror in the audience: "pity is occasioned by undeserved misfortune, and fear [terror] by that of one like ourselves."

The tragic deeds of characters in the Aristotelian conception were necessary either to be done or not to be done, and the action could be undertaken either knowingly or unknowingly. This exhausted all of the possibilities. But for the character to be tragic he had to be "better than the ordinary man."

The two points to be stressed are the conception of the hero as a superior person, and the conception of Fate in the Greek drama. The Greek conception of Fate or Nemesis involves the actions of a god who controlled human destinies. The tragic hero, superior to the ordinary man, a male rather than a female or a slave, met his fate and suffered; therein lies the essence of his tragedy. It well may be that writers today are far inferior to the Greek dramatists. However, this inferiority cannot be cured by adopting the attitudes of the Greeks to Fate or Nemesis, or the conception of a tragic character as a superior person. In modern life few people can be superior in the Greek sense. And the ordinary person today does not possess the freedom in circumstances necessary to a tragedy after the manner of Greek drama.

Quite frequently, tragedy in our society has a representational and a social character. Involved in modern tragic characters are such factors as powerlessness because of one's economic position; lack of experience because of social and economic position, or because of accidents at birth which are the result of the type of parents one has; suffering of consequences of an economic and political character which are far beyond a person's individual control. All of this is obvious, and yet the obvious is overlooked when a literal conception of tragedy based upon Aristotle's theory and the example of Greek drama is rigidly held. Today we assume, with some warrant, that social forces, social factors, social pressures and tendencies play a role similar to that played by the gods, by Fate and Nemesis, in ancient Greece. And this is not reducible to mere difference in postulates. It involves social and technological changes, and also what Whitehead styled "a mental climate."

We live in a different society and we live in a different mental climate from that of Aristotle. Man does not, today, believe himself to be the center of the world, as he once did. He does not now look upon his life as a drama of salvation in the way and to the extent that he did in the Middle Ages. Even the character and the nature of knowledge is different. This is to be seen in the scientific superseding of the Aristotelian world. Substantially, it is revealed in a conception of the world in terms of relationships rather than of essence. All of these changes have been and will continue to be registered in literature. We must take these developments into account when we concern ourselves with the reasons naturalism, so called, has developed. It has been an attempt to meet and to reveal and to explore the nature of experience in the modern world.

V

Many writers, strikingly different from one another, have been called naturalists; thus the brothers Goncourt, Flaubert, Zola in France, and in America Frank Norris, Stephen Crane, Theodore Dreiser, John Dos Passos. Those linked together as naturalists in terms of a definition like that of Professor Cargill are too often taken as representatives of a school. General similarities are stressed while significant differences are neglected. Within the framework of the naturalistic tradition there is an extraordinary variety of theme, subject matter, attitude, ideas expressed or implied, types of character. *Madame Bovary* by Flaubert, *Germinal* by Zola, *The Red Badge of Courage* by Stephen Crane, *Sister Carrie* by Dreiser, *U.S.A.* by Dos Passos, could be cited as naturalistic novels. But what insight do we gain by linking them together in terms of a watered-down generalization?

These and other books, linked together in this tradition, are all part of the effort by writers of the nineteenth and twentieth centuries to come to terms with experience. They have been written in the spirit of truth. If they are part of a tradition, that tradition has had more force and more impact, and has been able to nourish and give more energy to successive generations than any other tradition. This is especially so in America. The majority of critics of this tradition have been exponents of another, the genteel tradition in America. Speaking of the latter, Parrington aptly observed that its essence was to be found in "a refined aestheticism, that professed to discover the highest virtue in shutting one's eyes to disagreeable fact and the highest law in the law of convention." So-called American realistic writers have grown up in a different

American world from that of nineteenth-century New England. They have lived different kinds of lives. They have different origins.

But they are attacked in the name of nineteenth-century writers. In the light of this, I should like to quote from a long review, "The Deflowering of New England," by the critic Stanley Edgar Hyman in *The Hudson Review* (Winter, 1950). Mr. Hyman who shares at least some of the attitudes to which I have alluded, criticizes a number of biographies of Hawthorne, Henry James, Thoreau, Emerson, and Henry Adams and Melville—all of whom I admire as writers. He writes:

> . . . there is the embarrassing and confusing question of the private domestic lives of these writers, that is, not to put too fine a point on it, sex. On a scale of healthy and normal domestic life, Thoreau, priggish, terrified of women, dependent on his mother, and frigidly ascetic, would be at the bottom, followed closely by the spinsterish James; and Hawthorne and Adams, both of them fortunate in story-book marriages (until the death of Marian Adams) would be somewhere at the top. And yet, dare we say that the latter lives were fuller, or rounder, or even happier? Wouldn't a scale of tough-mindedness, of living in ecological balance with the world and dying with a minimum of whining be just as apt to run the other way? If Emerson's first marriage was passionate, short-lived, and tragic, and his second cold, long-lived, fecund, contented, which one helped his work? What is the condition of health for the artist, is there any, and how would we know it if we saw it?

And then at the end of the review: " . . . we are all simmering: who will be the new Emerson, or even the exhumer of the old Emerson, to bring us to a boil?"

In this quotation, as in the writings of many critics of the so-called naturalistic tradition, I see an insecurity, a lack of sureness, a timidity, although it is often marked by an authoritative use of the hallowed names of the past and by an association with these hallowed names. I see a tendency to cling to stereotypes of what literature and the artist should be, to cling to these in times when literature is slowly being remade and changed in a world that is both changing and dangerous.

It is a curious fact that it is the writers of the so-called naturalistic tradition who constantly have had to bear the brunt of the struggle for freedom of literary expression. It is the writers of this tradition who constantly have been haled into court, who have had to defend their work at law, who have had to face the application of the police power. It is the writers of this tradition whose books have been excluded from libraries, from colleges, from bookstores, even excluded from being transported across the boundaries of democratic countries. The consequences of the best work in this tradition have been an increase in feeling and a desire for more freedom, more frankness, more understanding in the world.

The consequences of the obscurantist criticism of this tradition have been more or less in the direction of censorship, or narrowness, or tightness of feeling and thought. Today, much of this criticism seems strangely arrogant. It is today's advocates of the new gentility who are looking for something in the past which will steam them up to the boiling point.

I have always maintained that all artistic tendencies should have free play for expression, and that there should be a kind of free competition between them so that each may have its chance to attract those who may gain from it. I have always believed that there should be richness and variety and art in literature, in philosophy, and in thought. In speaking of naturalism, I do not want to establish it in any authoritative way over any other tendency. All I would state is that realism and naturalism have been in the forefront in the last century in shaping contemporary literature. These have encouraged a spirit of truth and free inquiry. The problems over which psychologists, sociologists, and many others today show great concern are the very problems that agitated, concerned, and provoked many of the realistic writers and stimulated the creation of their books, some of which became lasting works in world literature.

"It is only those," writes Alfred Kazin, in *On Native Grounds*, "who have no culture and no belief in culture who resent differences among men and the exploration of the human imagination." The naturalistic tradition, so called, has been one means of this exploration.

NOTES

1. I have not read the work of Claude Bernard, but Zola quotes him so copiously in this, as well as in other essays, that one gets a fairly clear idea of the outlines of Bernard's thought.

2. It is my personal opinion that a number of the literary critics of "naturalism" who base their criticisms on free will do so on grounds of temperament. This is understandable. However, a man's temperamental bent cannot be accepted as a justification for the distortion of facts, the false attribution of views to others, and, worse, downright slander. I am not a monistic determinist. I do not, however, look on free will as an inherent attribute of man; rather, I believe that free will is an achievement of men, gained individually and collectively, through knowledge and the acquisition of control, both over nature and over self. Let me suggest here, to the interested reader, William James's essay, "The Dilemma of Determinism" in *The Will to Believe*. I do not agree with it wholly, but consider it, unlike many discussions of this question, illuminating and instructive.

3. In passing, let me say that despite his determinism, despite the character of many of his novels, Zola was fundamentally an optimist: Zola was a man who proudly declared: "The truth is on the march." The man who boldly assumes that the truth is on the march cannot be such a die-hard pessimist.

PART TWO

Modern Academic
Criticism, 1951–1995

INTRODUCTION

The prevalence of academic studies of late nineteenth-century American realism and naturalism since the early 1950s is related to the general phenomenon in American intellectual life of the decline of the man of letters and the burgeoning of academic scholarship.[1] Instead of a widely known literary figure (William Dean Howells or Edmund Wilson, for example) addressing an engaged middle-class audience, the critic of American literature in the post-World War II period was more apt to be a professional scholar teaching at a large research university and writing principally for other scholars. The academic literary historian, however, whatever his degree of commitment to the scholarly ideals of archival research and critical objectivity, was often as much influenced in his interpretation of late nineteenth-century fiction by the intellectual and cultural issues of his own time as earlier critics had been by the major concerns of their moment. Although pursued in a less polemical mode and in a narrower forum, the questions addressed by post-World War II literary historians— whether the fiction of late nineteenth-century realism and naturalism truthfully depicted American life and whether it did so in successful art forms—were similar to those of earlier critics and were still areas of controversy. Now, however, the debate was, broadly speaking, between two generations of literary historians, with the questions answered affirmatively in varying ways and to varying degrees through the 1970s and less positively since the early 1980s.

One of the initial efforts of post-World War II scholars of late nineteenth-century fiction was to confirm the validity of the field as an area of inquiry within the accepted criteria of literary research of the time—that is, to find that it contained a distinctive and coherent body of values and beliefs about society and literature within a specific time frame. As Robert Falk summarized in his 1953 essay on "The Rise of Realism," "American literary realism was a genuine cultural movement in itself with fairly definite chronological limits and recognizeable aesthetic principles and techniques."[2]

263

Naturalism, as Falk makes clear by omitting it from his essay and as Charles C. Walcutt sought to demonstrate in his *American Literary Naturalism* of 1956, was a similarly conceptualized but different movement that followed hard on realism. And both phases, as Everett Carter's "Taine in America" (1954) and Walcutt's "New Ideas in the Novel" (1956) reveal, are defined principally by their dominant ideas, ideas which are traced from their European origins through their adoption and modification by major American writers. The application of scholarly method to the interpretation of literary history, in other words, produced above all a belief in periodization as the principal means of writing literary history, with changes in ideas constituting the basic focus of critical analysis. Indeed, the period concept was to continue as the central premise in the study of American realism and naturalism through the major literary histories in the 1960s by Warner Berthoff and Jay Martin[3] to the more specialized period studies of the 1960s and 1970s by Robert Falk, Donald Pizer, Harold H. Kolb, Edwin H. Cady, and others. It was only with the shift in the late 1970s to an emphasis on literature as a cultural phenomenon inseparable from underlying economic and social conditions and thus less tied to conscious belief that the period ideal lost some of its hold.

The postwar reading of late nineteenth-century realism and naturalism as phases of American expression having both internal coherence and a significant relationship to American life and values arose from a number of impulses and contained various threads. Most of all, it was closely related to the state of mind that sought to portray American literature as a vigorous expression of American ideals and values, including the American tradition of dissent, a state of mind which had its origins in America's postwar status as a superpower whose role among nations was to exemplify and promote the acceptance of democratic ideals. Despite the reservations held by many intellectuals about the legitimacy of America's pursuit of its aims by means of an absolutist anti-Communist policy abroad and McCarthyite methods at home, it was difficult for historians of American literature to write outside of the felt belief that our power as a nation lay not only in our material strength but in our values as expressed in our literature.

One of the clearest examples of the effect of this postwar climate of belief on the interpretation of late nineteenth-century literature was the widespread celebration of Howells as an exponent of democratic values. From Everett Carter's seminal *Howells and the Age of Realism* (1954) through such major efforts as Harold H. Kolb's *The Illusion of Life: American Realism as a Literary Form* (1965), William J. McMurray's *The Literary Realism of William Dean Howells* (1967), and Edwin H. Cady's *The Light of Common Day: Realism in American Fiction* (1971), and reaching as far forward as Alfred Habegger's *Gender, Fantasy and Realism in American Fiction* (1982), Howellsian realism was found to affirm our basic values as a nation. With some variations, these interpretations stressed Howells's faith in what Harold Kolb summarized as the "pragmatic, relativistic, democratic, and experimental" (311) in human affairs. Howells (and to a considerable degree Mark Twain as well) was expressing through his fiction and criticism the practical wisdom of a nation of problem solvers who rejected dogmatism and absolutism in any form and who therefore accepted the social and moral implications of a shared vision of experience—that is, that a normative interpretation of life arising out of our engagement with daily experience could provide the basis for a free and strong nation. Howellsian realism, Edwin Cady claims, appeals to "some of the sanest and most useful processes of the human mind" (334) and thus can provide the foundation for a common and binding national faith.

A complementary process of legitimization was also occurring in the interpretation of late nineteenth-century naturalism during the postwar years, with Charles C. Walcutt's *American Literary Naturalism, A Divided Stream* (1956) and Richard Chase's *The American Novel and Its Tradition* (1957) two significant examples. Walcutt rejects the widely accepted premise that naturalism is largely a foreign import with little relationship to American beliefs and experience. Rather, naturalism plays a vital role in dramatizing the great schism of belief in nineteenth-century American thought between systems of value and faith stressing the spiritual and intuitive and those affirming the material and objective. The anomalous mix in an American naturalist novel of reform and deterministic strains of belief, for example, reveals its participation in this "divided stream." Thus American naturalism as a whole, from its origins to its twentieth-century manifestations, embodies and expresses one of the great philosophical issues of modern life.

Walcutt, while seeking to validate American naturalism as a significant fiction closely related to basic issues in American life, held that the American naturalist novelist was unable to find a fictional form to express his often irreconcilable themes. Richard Chase, however, discovered coherence in the shape of the naturalist novel by establishing continuity between its conventions of form and those of the romance tradition in American fiction. Adopting Lionel Trilling's notion that American literature was essentially dialectic in nature—that it expressed a constantly changing dialogue about the nature of the American experience rather than, as Parrington believed, a main current—Chase proceeded to the idea that the romance, because its devices of melodrama, sensationalism, and single-dimensional characterization made it amenable to the symbolic expression of ideas, was the chief vehicle for the American writer's engagement in the ideological arguments of his time. Naturalism, and specifically the work of Frank Norris, perhaps the most naturalist of the American naturalists, was an extension of this ideological and symbolic use of romance conventions into the intellectual and social conflicts of the late nineteenth century. Like Walcutt, therefore, but with an emphasis on fictional form rather than history of ideas, Chase sites late nineteenth-century naturalism firmly within an American tradition of expression.

Present throughout much of this effort to raise the stature of late nineteenth-century realism and naturalism by relating the movements firmly to American belief was the complementary attempt to assert the artistic strength of major realistic and naturalistic novels. Here the assumptions and methods of the New Criticism, which had begun to leave its mark on American academic criticism in the late 1930s but which did not significantly influence the reading of fiction until the 1950s, played a primary role.[4] The application of New Critical methodology to late nineteenth-century novels is seemingly anomalous, since the conservative ideology underlying the New Criticism would appear to be incompatible with the reform impulse present in much of this fiction. Nevertheless, an entire generation of critics now sought to explicate the major works of late nineteenth-century realism and naturalism—initally the fiction of James, Twain, and Crane, but later that of Howells, Norris, and Dreiser as well—by means of New Critical tools of formalistic analysis. In Harold Kolb's and Edwin Cady's studies of realism, for example, as well as in such an explicitly formalistic analysis as Janet H. McKay's *Narrative and Discourse in American Realistic Fiction* (1982), the novels of Howells, James, and Twain are examined for their organic unity, symbolic structure, dramatic narrative modes, and other evidence of their author's sophisticated manipulation of fictional devices. Much of the same effort was occurring in the interpretation of the formal characteristics of naturalism, as Frederick Hoffman's "From Document to Symbol" (1960)[5] and Donald Pizer's *Realism and Naturalism in Nineteenth-Century American Literature* (1966) make clear. Reversing both the long-standing belief that the naturalist novel consists of a crude massing of documentary detail and Walcutt's more recent assumption that its form mirrors its thematic incoherence, Hoffman, Pizer, and the many close readers of Crane's fiction during the 1960s sought to uncover the ways in which naturalist themes and methods were not incompatible with complex and successful fictional constructs.

Beginning in the late 1970s, however, and reaching full expression by the early 1980s, these various efforts to view late nineteenth-century realism and naturalism in positive terms have frequently been challenged. This change appears to be related to the widespread disillusionment with American political and social institutions by American intellectuals that accompanied and followed the upheavals of the Viet Nam and Watergate era of the late 1960s and early 1970s. The university students of that period had by the 1980s become the new generation of literary scholars. They often brought to the study of earlier phases of American life a political sensibility alive to the possibility that those in power seek to maintain their power by disguising motives, manipulating truth, and exploiting fear. This mind set, with its powerful undercurrent of suspicion of received values and beliefs, received confirmation and an explicit critical methodology and vocabulary from both a new wave of Marxist literary theory and a linguistically based form of literary analysis know as deconstruction. The first posits a model of literary production in which it is almost impossible for a writer's work—whatever his ostensible beliefs—not to express the dominant cultural ethos of his moment, and more specifically for western industrial societies, the consumerism and commodification values of capitalism.[6] The second deploys the demonstration by modern philosophers of the instability of meaning inherent in language to reject the Aristolelian claim that fiction can mirror life. A novel is therefore its own meaning, and the function of the critic is to reveal the almost infinite possibilities of meaning within a work, many of which run counter to ostensible meaning. These two critical movements, though seemingly unrelated in that one has its roots in social concerns, the other in a theory of language, nevertheless join in a number of recent critics to constitute a large-scale reorientation of emphasis in the study of late nineteenth-century American realism and naturalism. The movements are not what they are usually held to be—forms of productive engagement with and critques of late nineteenth-century American life—but are rather unconscious endorsements of the very values they seemingly oppose.

Several common threads are apparent in this reorientation in the study of late nineteenth-century American writing that has occurred during the last two decades. One is the frequent conflation in many studies—as in *American Realism: New Essays* (1982), edited by Eric J. Sundquist, *The Social Construction of American Realism* (1988) by Amy Kaplan, and *The Problem of American Realism* (1993) by Michael Davitt Bell—of realism and naturalism into a single movement called realism. This change reflects the effort by these and other recent critics to shift the discussion of late nineteenth-century American literary history from its conventional structure of two generations of writers, each with distinctive themes and forms, to that of a single cultural era in which all writers are subject to the same economic and social conditions and pressures of a post-Civil War industrialized America. Thus, the obvious differences between a Howells and Dreiser novel, for example, are less significant than (and even obscure) the participation of both works in the similar class and gender assumptions of the period between the Civil War and World War I. A second common thread is the marginalization or denigration of Howells's criticism and fiction. Gone is the role that Howells played, in the eyes of the previous generation of critics, as the icon of American democratic idealism. Now, as in Eric Sundquist's "The Country of the Blue" (1982), Howells's work is often viewed as uncharacteristic of his moment because of his attempt to find a common ground of belief during a period when the brutal realities of American life occasioned among almost all other writers far more extreme responses.

The most significant common element in recent criticism of late nineteenth-century realism and naturalism has been the practice of "cultural poetics" or "cultural logistics"[7]—a form of analysis of the relationship between literature and its social and ideological context that stresses the writer's unconscious absorption and thus indirect but nevertheless significant expression of the dominant cultural values of his day whatever his more conscious stance toward these values. This kind of criticism takes various directions related to the specific social phenomena the critic chooses to stress. So Sundquist emphasizes in his "The Country of the Blue" the engulfment of the late nineteenth-century writer in the psychic anxieties caused by a machine culture and market economy, and June Howard, in her *Form and History in American Literary Naturalism* (1985), concentrates on middle-class fears occasioned by mass immigration and a brutalized work force. Walter Benn Michaels, in his much-discussed *The Gold Standard and the Logic of Naturalism* (1987), is concerned primarily with problems of knowledge and issues of social power present in a consumer-based economy; Mark Seltzer, in *Bodies and Machines* (1992), deals with the various ways in which the biological and mechanical interact within the beliefs and expression of the age; and Michael Davitt Bell, in *The Problem of American Realism* (1993), examines the role of gender politics in the fiction and literary polemics of the day.[8] The tone of these studies varies from Sundquist's sympathetic portrayal of the beleaguered late nineteenth-century writer taking refuge in the "country of the blue" of his imagination to Michaels's and Bell's air of superiority and even contempt in their accounts of the ways in which such seeming critics of their society as Howells, Dreiser, and Norris were in fact complicit in maintaining the status quo by their expression of the underlying middle-class assumptions of their time. As was true of a good deal of socially based literary history and criticism of the 1930s, this recent stress on the novel as a kind of unmediated conduit for the expression of the dominant beliefs of its historical moment contains two major hazards. It can reduce what Henry James most admired in the genre of the novel, its capacity to represent the full range of human experience, to the single interest of its expression of cultural ideology. And it can misread specific works as it ahistorically applies what are assumed to be universal ideological constructs to the distinctive ideologies present in the works of a distinctive historical moment.[9]

Although Amy Kaplan's *The Social Construction of American Realism* (1988), Kenneth W. Warren's *Black and White Strangers* (1993), and Elizabeth Ammons's "Expanding the Canon of American Realism" (1995) display various degrees of participation in this recent strain of criticism, they suggest new directions as well. To Kaplan, the inseparability of the writer and his cultural moment can take the form of a productive engagement rather than of a complete capitulation. Realism to her is not a mode of escape or surrender but "a strategy for imagining and managing the threats of social change" (411) by constructing narratives that seek to mediate and thus "control" the violent upheavals in belief and value of their time. Kaplan seeks to reinstate the writer as a conscious participant in the social crises of his moment. This effort is also apparent, though in different form, in the essays by Warren and Ammons. Both critics still subscribe to the belief that a middle-class culture imprisons its artists within its assumptions. Thus Warren describes James's unconscious reflection of black stereotypes in his fiction, and Ammons notes the exclusion of women and racial and ethnic minorities from the canon of realism by several generations of white male critics. But they also examine those who speak from outside the dominant culture—W. E. B. Du Bois's vigorous critique of the white culture of his times, and the "new" voices in what Ammons calls the "realisms" (442) of late nineteenth-century American writing—and who thereby paradoxically express the full richness of that culture.

Criticism of late nineteenth-century realism and naturalism since World War II has thus come considerable distance from the widespread attempt by post-war critics to demonstrate the common commitment of writers of the period to depicting the ways in which American society had fallen away from the ideals of a democratic faith. Both assumptions underlying this earlier body of criticism—that writers can stand apart from their culture and criticize it and that a culture is best represented by writers from its dominant strains—have been frequently and strongly challenged. What appears to remain as a residue from a recognition of the strengths and weaknesses of these earlier critical beliefs and of those that have replaced them is an acceptance of the premises that criticism of the period should concern itself with the complex ways in which a novel and a novelist interact with a social moment and that the field of inquiry for this concern is much richer and wider than has been realized.

NOTES

1. See Daniel Aaron, "The Man of Letters in American Culture," *American Notes: Selected Essays* (Boston: Northeastern UP, 1994), 179–98.

2. Robert Falk, "The Rise of Realism, 1871–1891," *Transitions in American Literary History*, ed. H. H. Clark (Durham: Duke UP, 1953), 383.

3. Warner Berthoff, *The Ferment of Realism: American Literature, 1884–1919* (New York: Free Press, 1965) and Jay Martin, *Harvests of Change: American Literature, 1865–1914* (Englewood Cliffs, NJ: Prentice-Hall, 1967).

4. See Vincent B. Leitch, *American Literary Criticism from the Thirties to the Eighties* (New York: Columbia UP, 1988).

5. Hoffman's essay, though published in 1976, was originally delivered as a conference paper in 1960.

6. Two major sources of ideas and of critical practice in this area are Fredric Jameson, *The Political Unconscious: Narrative as a Socially Symbolic Act* (Ithaca: Cornell UP, 1981) and, more specifically for nineteenth-century fiction, Leo Bersani, *A Future for Astyanax: Character and Desire in Literature* (Boston: Little, Brown, 1976).

7. The first phrase occurs in the University of California Press series "The New Historicism: Studies in Cultural Poetics," the second in Mark Seltzer's *Bodies and Machines* (New York: Routledge, 1992), 4.

8. For a variation on the theme of the text as social palimpsest, one in which the writer himself is commodified within his profession of authorship, see Daniel Borus, *Writing Realism: Howells, James, and Norris in the Mass Market* (Chapel Hill: U of North Carolina P, 1989).

9. Omitted from this account are two recent studies that use traditional history-of-ideas and formalistic analysis in an attempt to reestablish the centrality of philosophical determinism in late nineteenth-century American naturalism: John J. Conder, *Naturalism in American Fiction: The Classic Phase* (Lexington: UP of Kentucky, 1984) and Lee Clark Mitchell, *Determined Fictions: American Literary Naturalism* (New York: Columbia UP, 1989).

TWENTY-FIVE

TAINE IN AMERICA

Everett Carter

Everett Carter (1919–) was educated at the University of
California, Los Angeles (B.A., 1939; Ph.D., 1947) and was
for many years a member of the faculty and administration
of the University of California, Davis. In addition to *Howells and the Age of Realism* (1954), Carter has published
*The American Idea: The Literary Response to American
Optimism* (1977).

"Try to understand yourself. . . . "

In France, a generation earlier, a philosopher had come forth who had made the techniques and attitudes of the new science the basis of a system of thought. August
Comte had proclaimed that the scientific attitude towards society and its problems
was the right one. Just as it had alone proven of use in unlocking the mysteries of the
physical universe, so it would alone be of use in solving the questions of the moral
universe. Comte aimed at taking human social thought out of the two childlike and
adolescent stages of development—the theological, in which all phenomena are ascribed to supernatural causes, and the metaphysical, in which preformulated, *a priori*
principles are considered the causes of events. The new stage, said Comte, the positive
stage, is one in which the supernatural is ignored and the metaphysical is discarded,
and observation, analysis, and classification take their place.

Hippolyte Taine took positivism and made it into a literary credo, and it was
Taine's positivistic theory of the source and function of literary expression that became the basis of conscious American realism.

Taine was almost unknown in America before 1870. There had been a review of
his work in 1861 when M. H. Harisse had summarized the latest developments in
French criticism for the *North American Review*. But the attitude of this early notice

"Taine and American Realism," *Revue de Littérature Comparée* 26 (1952): 357–64. Reprinted in
revised form in *Howells and the Age of Realism* (Philadelphia: Lippincott, 1954), pp. 94–102. Text
from *Howells and the Age of Realism*, by Everett Carter. Copyright 1950, 1952, 1954 by Everett
Carter. Reprinted by permission of HarperCollins Publishers, Inc.

was that here is a young and brilliant Frenchman with a rather difficult philosophy of aesthetics and criticism in which we are interested but with which we cannot wholly agree. Then Edward Eggleston read Taine's *Philosophy of Art in the Netherlands*, and wrote a brief review of it for the *Independent* in 1870. A few months later, he was encouraged to write a story for *Hearth and Home*. The story extended through three issues; and while he was writing it, Eggleston remembered the philosophy of art formulated by Taine—that to be a great artist, one must express one's own times, and the attitudes of one's own people; that the greatness of the art of the Netherlands was its willingness to use common materials and familiar subjects. Eggleston came to his brother, George Cary Eggleston, and announced that he was going to "write a three-number story, founded upon your experiences at Riker's Ridge." Then, George recorded, the incipient novelist went on to "set forth his theory of art—that the artist, whether with pen or brush, who would do his best work, must choose his subjects from the life that he knows." And to justify his choice of theme, Eggleston "cited the Dutch painters" as well as referring to "Lowell's success with the Biglow papers."[1]

Out of this fortuitous combination, out of Taine, Lowell, and the desire of the *Hearth and Home* for a story from Eggleston, came *The Hoosier Schoolmaster*, an early landmark in the development of realism in America. Despite its open mawkish sentimentalism, the novel was rich with regional dialect, and remorseless in its truthful portrayal of the hard-shelled farmers of Indiana. And in 1874, Eggleston added to his picture of the Midwest in *The Circuit Rider*. In the preface to this book, he expressed with clarity and precision the aim of realism in literature, and it was an expression which clearly shows the influence of the Frenchman who pointed out that an artist must deal with his contemporaries. Eggleston asked the reader who might be offended by his treatment of the rougher side of religion to remember "the solemn obligations of a novelist to tell the truth." He insisted that the title of "novelist" could only be given to him who tries with whole soul "to produce the higher form of history, by writing truly of men as they are, and dispassionately of those forms of life that come within his scope."

Howells had hailed *The Hoosier Schoolmaster* as a contribution to the development of a native school of realism. But this review had been one of a group which Howells wrote from 1867 to 1872 which had shown a catholicity of taste confounding to any attempt to draw consistent attitudes from them. They had praised historical romances and imaginative fantasies by Edward Everett Hale, and Dion Boucicault, as well as the realism of De Forest and Eggleston. But in 1872 Howells, too, read and reviewed a work of Taine's—his *History of English Literature*.

Taine's transformation of Comte's philosophy of social positivism into the conception of literature as a product of the *"race, milieu, et moment"* of each author is well known. What has not been so well remembered was Taine's penetrating formulation of the justification for, even the necessity of, a literature which plays its part in the positivist program. Literature, Taine said in essence, must be the principal method by which society and men are observed, analyzed, and classified. Fiction should be the scientific laboratory of society—the laboratory in which the complex components of our social system are mixed with each other, so that the race may watch the experiment, see the result, and be better able to make decisions affecting its life.

The romantics, said Taine, had been afflicted by the malady of the age—the bewilderment that came from the "reign of democracy which excited our ambitions without satisfying them" and the "philosophy which kindled our curiosity without satisfying it." The romantics had agreed that "there is a monstrous disproportion between the different parts of our social structure," and had seen that "human destiny is vitiated by this disagreement." But the answers of these "unfortunates" had been to "let deep and strong sensations reign upon you . . . cultivate your garden, re-enter the flock . . . take holy water, abandon your mind to dogmas."

These answers, said Taine, proved ineffectual, and his generation saw the true reply, the "deeper answer . . . in which issue all the labor and experience of the age, and which may perhaps be the subject matter of future literature: 'Try to understand yourself, and things in general.' " Yes, said this observer from France, his generation, too, was afflicted with the malady of the age, and all it could hope to do, in hopes of an eventual cure, was to strive to arrive at the truth; it must study man; he is not "an abortion or a monster, but he is in his place and completes a chain. . . . He is like everything else, a product, and as such it is right he should be what he is." The task of literature is to seek the truth about him, in all his relations. In this employment of science, and in its counterpart in letters—realistic fiction—"there is a new art, a new morality, a new polity, a new religion."[2]

Howells reviewed Taine's *History of English Literature*, in the February, 1872, issue of the *Atlantic*. His notice was concerned with the one-sidedness of Taine's approach to literature. He called his method of showing the influence of environment upon art "admirably brilliant and effective," but he warned the reader against a too inflexible application of this theory. Howells pointed out that the personality of each great writer must be considered along with the general circumstances of his time and people.[3]

Then, a year later, Howells became thoroughly saturated with Taine's theory of realistic literature as the laboratory of mankind. For in April, 1873, A. G. Sedgwick, normally the political reporter for the *Atlantic*, stepped out of his conventional role and wrote a review of George Eliot's *Middlemarch* which applied the philosophy of Taine to contemporary literature in English. Sedgwick was trying to discover why Eliot's detailed analysis of human action made her so great a figure in contemporary literature. He found the answer in Taine. He started his review with a long quotation from the *History of English Literature*, and these are the words which Howells, if he had not already read them, must have read and reread in manuscript, proof, and final form in the office of the magazine he was editing. For he was an uncommonly scrupulous reader of the material that went into the *Atlantic*. Besides his reading of manuscripts before their acceptance, he went over the proofs of each article "making what changes" he chose to make, and "verifying every quotation, every date, every geographical and biographical name, every foreign word to the last accent, every technical and scientific term." The article was then sent back to the author, and after author's changes, was read by Howells again.[4]

What he read and reread in Sedgwick's article was a summary of Taine's justification for literature in an age of science. Sedgwick quoted the French critic on the failure of the romantic writers from 1800 to 1830 to give any answers to the great problems facing the nineteenth century, and then continued the long quotation, which is worth reproducing in full, for it seems to have struck exactly the note which writers in America, seeking the reasons for their instinctive yearning towards the actualities of their provincial environments, found so sympathetic. Of the great romantic writers, of Byron and Shelley and Keats, and their sensitivity to the monstrous disproportions which they felt to be the fact of their society, Taine asked the following questions, and Sedgwick reproduced these questions, and Taine's answers to them in their entirety:

"What advice have they given us for its remedy? They were great: were they wise? 'Let deep and strong sensations reign upon you; if your machine breaks, so much the worse. . . . Cultivate your garden, busy yourself in a little circle; re-enter the flock, be a beast of burden. . . . Turn believer again, take holy water . . . aspire to power, honor, wealth.' Such are the various replies of artists and citizens, Christians and men of the world. . . . There is another and deeper answer, which Goethe was the first to give, which we begin to conceive, in which issue all the labor and experience of the age, and which may perhaps be the subject matter of future literature. 'Try to understand yourself and things in general.' A strange reply, seeming barely new, whose scope we shall only hereafter discover. For a long time yet, men will feel their sympathies thrill at the . . . sobs of their great poets. For a long time they will rage against a destiny which opens to their aspirations the career of limitless space, to shatter them, within two steps of their goal, against a wretched post which they had not seen. For a long time they will bear, like fetters, the necessities which they must embrace as laws. Our generation, like the preceding, has been tainted by the malady of the age, and will never more than half be quit of it. We shall arrive at the truth, not at calm. All we can heal at present is our intellect; we have no hold upon our sentiments. But we have a right to conceive for others the hopes which we no longer entertain for ourselves, and to prepare for our descendants the happiness which we shall never enjoy."

But, Sedgwick wrote, we are not anywhere near those fortunate times which Taine foresaw in the future. "For the present, we," like the romantics, "live in a period of intellectual and moral tumult." Modern life is "too complicated, too revoluntionary, too full of sudden surprises and absurdities, too sad, too merry, too horribly real, too shamefully false. . . . Our business is *not creation, but criticism*." Eliot's maxim, and our motto is, only slightly to alter Taine's words: "Know thyself and things in general."[5]

Before Sedgwick's article appeared, Howells had seemed in doubt about the purpose which he felt literature should have. In his February, 1873, review of Turgenev, he had declared: "It is hard to reconcile the sense of . . . artistic impartiality with one's sense of the deep moral earnestness of the author's books."[6] But in 1874, nine months after Sedgwick's forceful recapitulation of Taine, Howells seemed able to reconcile art and morality, and the reconciliation was based upon the positivistic philosophy of the French critic. In that year, Howells wrote that autobiography is "the most precious contribution to men's knowledge of each other," and that inventive writing reaches its greatest ethical heights when it enables men to know each other better by giving the reader the "facts in man's consciousness or experience."[7]

In the same year, Howells ran a searching article on *The Growth of the Novel* by G. P. Lathrop, in which Lathrop took up the question of fictional morality in an age of science, and gave it Taine's answer. Lathrop scoffed at the attempts of Richardson and the sentimentalists to "impose a mechanical morality upon us," and then went on to underscore the positivist's contention that morality in the novel can only consist in telling us the truth about our actions, so that we may have clear understanding of what we are like. "It is only through clear perceptions into the true quality of our common nature," wrote Lathrop, "that the *foundations* of morality are deepened and secured."[8] And in 1885, Howells, through one of his most sympathetically portrayed characters, pointed out the immorality of sentimental literature, when viewed from the standpoint of positivist ethics. The Reverend Mr. Sewell turns to the Coreys' dinner guests in *The Rise of Silas Lapham* and tells them flatly that "those novels with the old-fashioned heroes and heroines in them . . . are ruinous." He goes on to explain his startling statement by saying: "The novelists might be the greatest possible help to us if they painted life as it is, and human feelings in their true proportion and relation, but for the most part they have been and are altogether noxious."

The following year Howells began writing the series of monthly essays in *Harper's* called "The Editor's Study," and for six years he made these articles the medium through which he tried to convince the public of the merits of positivism as a basis for morality in literature. To enable humanity to know itself better—this is the burden of literature, he repeated again and again through the pages of the magazine. It was in one of these essays that he echoed Sedgwick's paraphrase of Taine, and said that he could not thank the writer of false fiction who "teaches us not to know, but to unknow our kind."[9] This direct echo of Taine's justification for fiction in a scientific age Howells repeated in many ways. Fiction, he said, in commenting upon Mary Chase Wyman's "powerful sketches" is a place where "men and women . . . wish to meet other men and women in literature . . . to hear them speak out the heart of human passion in the language of life."[10] Someone wrote to him and complained about false and injurious notions that could be traced back to the reading of novels. Howells agreed with his correspondent, but claimed that the term "novel" could not be rightly given to works which falsify life. Before we can call it a novel, especially before we can call it a good novel, he said, "We must ask ourselves . . . is it true?— true to the motives, the impulses, the principles that shape the life of actual men and women?" And then he specifically gave the positivist's justification for this kind of truthfulness: "If the book is true to what men and women know of one another's souls it will be true enough, and it will be great and beautiful."[11]

The reason for this equivalence of truth and beauty, Howells believed, lay in the function of literature as the laboratory of man's behavior, where a reader may watch an experiment in social relationships, and can find out what will happen, given certain personalities reacting to each other under certain conditions. Just as an experiment would be false and injurious if it were "rigged," so a novel would be misleading and harmful if the people, or the circumstances, were contrived and arranged without regard to the truth of men's motives and passions, and the facts of their physical surroundings. Like the scientist, the novelist, Howells felt, "contributes his share to a thorough knowledge of groups of the human race under conditions which are full of inspiring novelty and interest."[12]

In this feeling, of course, he was elaborating and adapting to American conditions the basic ideas of Hippolyte Taine. And he continued to the end to feel that any philosophy of art must be based upon what men know of the laws of natural science. At the beginning of the twentieth century, as we shall see, Howells realized that his own view of truth as that which might be perceived by the senses and objectively analyzed and classified was being replaced by more subtle and complex considerations. He was not able to grasp the new conceptions, but was entirely willing to admit their truth. In an "Easy Chair" essay in 1903, he conducted an imaginary conversation in which he brought out the parallel between the inductive method of science and the realistic method of fiction. The inductive method, he showed, was the objective assembling of facts from which the scientist could draw generalizations; the technique of the realistic novelist was the objective assembling of facts of human nature under conditions of "novelty and interest" which would enable the reader to make valid and usable generalizations about human nature. But a philosopher who is present points out that induction is being gradually replaced by a newer method—that of "boldly supposing a case . . . and then looking for occurrences to verify it." The new scientific way is "first the inference and then the fact." The favorite literature of the new reading public, it is then suggested, is "quite in the spirit of the new science. . . . Its bold events, its prodigious characters, its incredible motives, were they not quite of the nature of the fearless conjecture which imagined long and short electric waves, and then spread a mesh of wire to intercept them and seize their message?"[13] All this is said, of course, in a tone of almost disbelieving good humor, the product of a state of mind which can intellectually grasp the possibilities of truth in the statement, but cannot constitutionally be convinced of it. But nevertheless, the possibility is stated, and stated convincingly, and shows the essential liberality of the man who is perfectly willing to change his basic creed of fiction to meet changed conditions of man's perception of truth. His own life and his own art were dominated by the positivistic concern with the objective observation, analysis, and classification of human life.

NOTES

1. George Cary Eggleston, *The First of the Hoosiers* (Philadelphia, 1903), 297.
2. Hippolyte Taine, *History of English Literature* (Philadelphia, 1908), IV, 66 ff.
3. [William Dean Howells,] "*History of English Literature*, by H. Taine," *Atlantic*, XXIX, 241 (February, 1872).
4. Willian Dean Howells, *Literary Friends and Acquaintances* (New York, 1900), 138–39.
5. [A. G. Sedgwick,] "*Middlemarch*, by George Eliot," *Atlantic*, XXXI, 492 (April, 1873).

6. [William Dean Howells,] "*Liza*, by Ivan Turgenieff," *Atlantic*, XXXI 239 (February, 1873).

7. [William Dean Howells,] "*Threading My Way*, by Robert Dale Owen," *Atlantic*, XXXIII, 232 (February, 1874).

8. G. P. Lathrop, "Growth of the Novel," *Atlantic*, XXXIII, 695 (June, 1874).

9. *Criticism and Fiction* (New York, 1891), 112.

10. "Editor's Study," *Harper's*, LXXIV, 483 (April, 1887).

11. *Ibid.*, 826 (April, 1887).

12. *Ibid.*, 641 (September, 1887).

13. "Editor's Easy Chair," *Harper's*, CVII, 806 (October, 1903).

TWENTY-SIX

NEW IDEAS IN THE NOVEL

Charles C. Walcutt

Charles C. Walcutt (1908–89) received his Ph.D. from the University of Michigan in 1937 and spent the bulk of his career at Queens College of New York and the Graduate Center of the City University of New York. Walcutt's *American Literary Naturalism, A Divided Stream* (1956) was the most influential academic study of American naturalism for over thirty years. Walcutt is also the author of *Man's Changing Mask: Modes and Methods of Characterization in Fiction* (1966).

Something extraordinary happened to the American novel about 1890, when what is called the Naturalistic Movement began to gather momentum. It was a wonder, a scandal, and a major force. Its effects appear everywhere today, both in fiction and in popular attitudes, for it reflects at once our faith in science and our doubts about the modern "scientific" world. And perhaps because the effects of science have been so disturbing and ambiguous, the true character of naturalism has not been determined. In one form it appears a shaggy, apelike monster; in another it appears a godlike giant. Shocking, bestial, scientific, messianic—no sooner does its outline seem to grow clear than, like Proteus, it slips through the fingers and reappears in another shape. The critics reflect its elusiveness. Whereas one authority describes it as an extreme form of romanticism, another counters that it is the rigorous application of scientific method to the novel. When others say it is desperate, pessimistic determinism, they are answered by those who insist that it is an optimistic affirmation of man's freedom and progress.

These authorities are not all mistaken. On the contrary, they are all correct. But each has reached his conclusion by looking at different aspects of naturalism, at different times between 1890 and about 1940, and having committed himself to a confining definition he has found it difficult to consider other areas and aspects of the

American Literary Naturalism, A Divided Stream (Minneapolis: University of Minnesota Press, 1956), pp. 3–39. Reprinted by permission of the University of Minnesota Press.

subject. The Beast, which cannot be named until it is caught, is indeed of a Protean slipperiness. But if it may not be caught and held in a single form, it may be observed in enough of its forms so that we can finally mark the varieties and the limits of its changes. Only in this way can naturalism be explained and defined. Seeing it in perspective involves a considerable step backward through the centuries; but it can be taken quickly.

THE EMERGENCE OF NATURALISM

All literature is founded on some concept of the nature of man. When a major new literary trend appears it either assumes or defines some new concept of man and therefore of his place in the world. Such a new image takes its shape against the background from which it has emerged and against which it has in some way reacted. Naturalism has its roots in the Renaissance, its backgrounds in the Middle Ages. The medieval idea of man (which lived on, indeed, through the nineteenth century) was of a fallen creature in a dualistic universe. This dual universe was divided into heaven and earth, God and Satan, eternal and temporal, and, in man, soul and body. Its values pointed always toward the eternal, toward salvation and God—away from the temporal, the worldly, and the natural; for nature was under God's curse. Man too, by his own Fall, was under God's curse. Having both body and soul, he was torn in the eternal battle between good and evil. Man's physical nature—his desires and instincts—was, by and large, the Devil's playground; it had contributed to the original Fall and it continued to corrupt his will and his reason. Nonhuman nature was not only under God's curse; it was also unpredictable because of the workings upon it of fiends and the occasional miraculous intervention of God or a saint.

Reliable truth came from God to man through particular miraculous revelations and through the permanent miraculous authority of the Scriptures, which were interpreted and systematized by the Church. The Church was ordained by God; its head, the Pope, was divinely inspired. Emphasis on authority prevailed: in matters of dogma the Church Fathers of the fourth and fifth centuries were consulted; religious practices and personal morality were rigidly prescribed by the wisdom of the past, for neither man's impulses nor his reason could be trusted; the sovereign, divinely appointed, was not subject to popular mandate; and for the final word on nature men turned not to experiment but to books—to the antique wisdom of Aristotle, Pliny, or Isadore of Seville. Authority dominated then, as reason and observation do today. Science, called "natural philosophy," was not an end in itself; it was "the handmaid of theology," pursued for the glory of God.

The subordination of nature and its dualistic separation from spiritual matters began to vanish during the Renaissance, as a new concept of the nature of man took shape. The change began with astronomy, the science furthest from man and society, but it got to man very rapidly, in a series of great intellectual strides that may be reviewed briefly by reference to the thinkers who made them.

Late in the seventeenth century, Sir Isaac Newton formulated mechanical laws that explained the movements of the planets in our solar system. He calculated their masses, velocities, and gravitational attractions; suggested that the energy and matter in the universe were constant and indestructible; and speculated that the universe was composed of billions of minute particles in ceaseless motion. The work of many astronomers and philosophers—Copernicus, Kepler, Galileo, Descartes—had already pointed this way, but Newton's system seemed mathematically perfect and irrefutable (even Einstein has only modified it). It dignified nature and implied that its laws were not subject to God's miraculous intervention. This system did not consider the problems of form and growth, because according to it all forms were reducible to the same particles and hence the varying forms themselves were not within the scope of mechanical science. In other words, it dealt with phenomena in terms of ultimate constituents, and so it had no tools for the consideration of complex forms like life. The problems of mind and will were not considered, although God and the soul were not denied. But even though not carried to its logical conclusions, the system itself was essentially materialistic and supplied both the method and the direction for later thought. Applied to the individual, the Newtonian system would produce determinism; it would subject man to natural law.

Oddly enough, the outlines of a popular philosophy called deism, which anticipated the social and moral consequences of Newton's theories, were set forth some twenty years before the publication of his *Principia Mathematica* (1687). The deists appealed to man's nature as evidence against the orthodox belief that he was fallen. They said that man was innately and instinctively good; they doubted creeds and authority; and during the following century they put increasing emphasis on the worship of nature as God's only revelation. In this latter respect, a popular theology was drawing on science; yet its actual import—and certainly its literary expression—appeared in the belief that the essence of God, nature, and man was to be found in the noble principle of reason. By the end of the eighteenth century, deism's corollary, the philosophy of naturalism (so called because it joined man and God through nature's law of reason), was widely influential; but because science had not yet adequately implemented it with biological data, it was not rigorously applied to man, the works of "necessitarians" like Bentham and Godwin exercising the fascination of rhetorical novelty rather than basically altering the popular belief in the existence of the soul and in man's freedom to sin and be eternally punished therefor. It was in the nineteenth century that scientific method, deistic faith, and biological discoveries began seriously to converge upon man and to suggest not only that his nature was good but also that his natural self was his ultimate self. This trend was soon to be tremendously accelerated by the positivism of Auguste Comte and the Darwinian theory of evolution.

Positivism was presented as an empirical, naturalistic method of finding truth. It stresses accuracy and objectivity and affirms that the only significant reality is the content of experience. The function of science is to observe facts and formulate laws which explain those facts. But positivism was much more than a method. It was a torch to burn the dark rubbish of the past and to light the way into the future. Living in the period following the French Revolution, Comte was impelled by a desire to establish society and its institutions on a more solid foundation. To that end he sought a new faith that would use the intellectual advantages of the age to unite men in a common purpose. In his *Cours de Philosophie Positive* (1830) he devised his famous law of the three stages of thought as it progresses toward maturity. They are the theological, the metaphysical, and the scientific, to which he applied the very prejudiced terms *fictitious* (i.e., mythical), *abstract*, and *positive*, respectively, the last being the triumphant stage at which mankind will for the first time in history enjoy a reliable basis for progress. In this final stage science is descriptive rather than—as philosophy had attempted to be—explanatory. Comte rejects the pursuit of first causes and absolute truths; he wants "effective" causes from which useful laws may be deduced, and he firmly asserts that all phenomena are subject to physical laws. Here is a sweeping rejection of the authority and supernaturalism of the past.

Comte went on to classify the sciences in the order of their complexity, dependency, and perfectibility. He arrived at the conclusion that sociology was the last in each of these categories: it was the most complex; it required the preexistence of the other sciences; and it would be the last to attain the perfection of positive method. Sociology thus became the unifying discipline of human thought and its purpose the perfect organization of human society. A religion of progress was offered to replace the darkness of antique superstition.

Darwin's *Origin of Species* (1859) was a culmination in the field of biology of the naturalistic temper of the period, presenting a hypothesis toward which many streams of thought and investigation had been converging. A hundred years earlier Montesquieu (*Esprit des Lois*, 1748) had proclaimed the influence of environment in all human affairs. Malthus had written (*Essay on the Principle of Population*, 1798) on the over-fecundity of nature. Wallace, unknown to Darwin, worked in the same area toward the same conclusions. Darwin employed the positive method to show how natural selection operated to produce new species. His theory challenged the prevailing belief of biologists in the immutability of species; it challenged the teleological concepts of "purpose" and "design" in the universe, for it attributed the physical changes of evolution to millions of accidents, innumerable false starts, and the pitiless waste of individuals and even of whole species. Studying man in the perspective of his biological development, it inevitably emphasized his animal nature. To the horror of the pious, it appeared to destroy the foundations of religion and (consequently) of morality. Scientists and the scientifically minded, on the contrary, did not consider it immoral to know the truth; and though some of them said that truth could not damage religion, others were eager to jettison unwieldly dogma and sail with clear fact into the hopeful future.

The works of Comte and Darwin—who are only illustrious figures in a great movement—brought the promise of Newton's mathematics home to man and society. They did not abolish dualism and dispose of the supernatural once and for all, but they made it possible to believe that man could be completely accounted for by physical, psychological, and social facts. When this program won a limited assent, naturalistic fiction could be conceived and attempted.

Herbert Spencer converted Darwin's biological hypothesis into a cosmic generalization. With Comte, he considered that sociology was the end of science; and, like Ernst Haeckel after him, he was deeply impressed by the theory of the conservation of energy, a theory that was implicit in the Newtonian system but was not actually expounded until the nineteenth century. From 1860 to 1902 he labored over the volumes of his famous *Synthetic Philosophy* which attempted to assemble all the special sciences into a whole whose unifying principle was evolution. Just as the sidereal universe had evolved from a gaseous nebula, he maintained, so complex species developed from simple cells and the human will out of elementary sensations and reflexes. From this broad conviction it was only a step to moral and social implications of great significance. For example: Pleasure and good are identified with adaptability. Evolution moves society toward the good life. Ethics are improved as society evolves. Perfection is the final outcome of change. Human nature improves with its improving environment. Evolution toward more complex forms is nature's ultimate law.

The early effect of these beliefs was to affirm the idea of progress and provide a powerful impetus to scientific investigation, although the Darwinian hypothesis could have been—and later was—interpreted as defining a condition of endless and hopeless flux, in which improvement and decay alternated with no discernible purpose. But Spencer affirmed that once society had evolved to perfection it could maintain itself in that state indefinitely.

These naturalistic patterns exclude and indeed frequently assail the supernatural. About the human will, which is by definition "uncaused" and therefore not a material phenomenon, they are not so consistent. Spencer recognized the individual will as an element in natural processes, but he deplored as unnatural the social or collective will. He believed that the "natural" working of economic process included the individual wills and motives of intelligently selfish men—so that social evolution was guided by this trustworthy ingredient. Political and economic *laissez faire* brought about the survival of the socially fittest and thus contributed to evolution's majestic movement toward perfection. But Spencer placed so much importance on the "struggle for existence" and the "survival of the fittest" (this was his phrase, not Darwin's) that he could not look with approval on any organized exercise of the social will that might in any way protect the unfit. He condemned as "unnatural" everything from labor unions to pure food and drug laws. Contrariwise, Marx, on the left wing, interpreting this same "struggle for existence" in terms of class warfare, found the bourgeoisie, which produced for profit, guilty of interfering with the working man's "natural" instinct to produce well and abundantly. So the liquidation of the capitalists was to aid the survival of the more productive and therefore more "fit" workers.

Both Spencer and Marx invoked natural law, which they asserted would inevitably produce certain results; both stressed the power of the human will; and both with similar illogic became morally indignant at those who would presume to interfere with the "inevitable" natural processes. If this mixture, on both sides, of fervid exhortation with concepts of majestic inevitableness evokes a smile today, it also serves to remind us that naturalistic theory was never able to free itself from human passion. All the critical problems ultimately derive from this conflict.

THE DIVIDED STREAM

The zeal of these researchers and theorists shows that the restoration of nature to importance does not, even when carried to the conclusion that all truth is to be found in her provinces, satisfy man's doubts or answer his emotional needs. Naturalistic philosophers since the Renaissance have been motivated by wonder and passion and fear. Just as deism leaped to worship reason long before it could prove that the cosmos was reasonable, so the assault on orthodox dualism sprang from need for a faith that could be united with fact—for a binding principle, an explanation that would unite the scientific and the spiritual domains. The answer came as transcendentalism, a philosophy which in its popular American form converted the formalized and somewhat arid faith of the deists into a dynamic and emotional creed. Deism sustained the wonderful reasonableness of the Founding Fathers; transcendentalism became the spirit of American expansion, the statement of the American Dream of individual opportunity, freedom, and greatness. Transcendentalism rises through the belief that knowledge brings liberty, to its apotheosis of making man equivalent to God.

The essence of transcendentalism is to be found in Emerson's repeated statement that Nature is a symbol of Spirit. This means that what is ideal or absolute as spirit is translated into physical laws and perfectly embodied (incarnated) as nature. It is a monistic philosophy which attempts to draw together the nature-spirit poles of orthodox dualism until they are touching, until, indeed, they are one. The relationship of spirit and nature in this monism can be simply represented as identical to the relation which relativity physicists have discovered between energy and matter: they are two forms of the same one. What seems ultimately to be an electric charge expresses itself as all the forms of the physical universe; taking a metaphysical step, one can infer that all the forms of the universe are latent or *ideal* in that charge. Give energy a moral quality, and you have Spirit. When a modern physicist like Sir James Jeans says that reality seems ultimately to correspond to a thought in a logical mind, he is expressing a version of transcendentalism. If, as Emerson says, "Every natural fact is a symbol of a spiritual fact [i.e., an idea]," it follows that the physical is a form of the divine. "The axioms of physics translate the laws of ethics," and nothing in the world fails to have spiritual significance.

In Emerson's system, man's mind is an aspect of spirit, his body a fact of nature. Thus through the mind, by what the transcendentalists called reason or intuition, man can directly experience truth—or call it the Absolute—because he is that Absolute. He can also approach truth through science, because every natural fact is a symbol of a spiritual fact and when penetrated by the mind will give up its ultimate or spiritual meanings. The mind's contemplation of itself and the study of nature are equally spiritual quests. The system stresses responsibility but not authority: every man is as great as he makes himself; truth is his if he will seek it; no church or power is its special custodian.

Henry Thoreau's successful quest for peace through intuition was achieved by a devoted examination of nature: "God himself culminates in the present moment, and will never be more divine in the lapse of all the ages," he says in *Walden*, and he continues that "we are enabled to apprehend at all what is sublime and noble only by the perpetual instilling and drenching of [ourselves by] the reality that surrounds us." Whitman's early delight in the phenomenal world conveys the same idea of unity:

> You have waited, you always wait, you dumb, beautiful
> ministers [i.e., phenomena]
> We receive you with free sense at last, and are insatiate
> henceforward . . .
>
> "Crossing Brooklyn Ferry," 1856

Emerson left the ministry because he could not be bound by a doctrine of special or limited access to the divine:

> The word unto the prophet spoken . . .
> Still floats upon the morning wind,
> Still whispers to the willing mind.
>
> "The Problem," 1839

The transcendental ideal of freedom through knowledge expresses America's belief in science and in physical progress as an image of spiritual progress. It unites the practical world and the spiritual world, in a spiritual quest for perfection through mastery of nature. Reason and instinct, fact and faith, join in the image of a perfectible present, a physical world whose conquest would be not only a symbol but also an embodiment of spiritual conquest.

This idea, which is the American Dream, stands somewhere between medieval otherworldliness and the skepticism of the twentieth century. In the Middle Ages revelation was the source of spiritual truth. Natural truth was both unimportant and unreliable. Today we are very skeptical of any ultimate design in nature, for we are apt to believe that the human species is about to prove the absence of design by destroying itself—leaving the world to the next species, as the dinosaurs left it to us. Between these extremes, in the nineteenth century man believed in a divine plan that was to be found in nature. Nature was the physical expression of divine reason, and in its laws revealed the forms and purposes of God. The scientific penetration of nature became a spiritual quest, therefore, into absolute Being. The philosophical basis of this quest is *monistic*: spirit and nature, soul and body, are various expressions of one unified reality. There can be no basic separation of them, as there was in the medieval view of the cosmos.

This monism was the dream that glowed behind naturalism in American thought. But the monist sea (a favorite nineteenth-century symbol of unity) did not stay one. Just as the language of analysis divided it with the words spirit and nature, showing how difficult it is to think a monism, so time and experience divided it into streams of optimism and pessimism, freedom and determinism, will and fate, social reformism and mechanistic despair. When the Nature which was assumed to be a symbol and version of God and of man's spirit grew under scientific analysis into a force which first controlled man's will and presently made it seem an illusion, then it became alien and terrifying; and man's nature too revealed, upon further exploration, depths that were repellent rather than godlike.

The American Dream was a theory, an abstraction, that never completely dispelled old taboos or eliminated the traditional distrust of emotion and impulse. The struggle against authority, which brought in the Renaissance, liberated reason first and emotion a slow second. Indeed, reason had a long head start. Even in the Middle Ages it was the delight of all thoughtful people, though "officially" distrusted. The Puritans likewise were indefatigable rationalists and disputants, always happy to match wits with the benighted. But man's emotions had been distrusted for so many centuries that they could not easily win free from the taint of sin. It was popular during the eighteenth century to say that man's impulses were humane and beautiful; but in America the Puritan tradition kept the flesh a disgrace. Our leading transcendentalist thinkers—Emerson, Thoreau, Alcott—were proper and inhibited to an extreme. Emerson recognized a disciple in Whitman but urged him to suppress physical details in *Leaves of Grass*. When naturalistic writings ignored sexual taboos, they offended other people than Emerson and impelled them back toward the old dualist position that the flesh was, indeed, vile. Monist theory that the instincts were divine could not remove old attitudes. It became easy to denounce frankness as sensationalism, as morbid, as a rejection of American optimism.

Freedom from the taboos of conservative taste and propriety could be a means to a host of desirable ends—ends of truth, freedom, and candor. But when such freedom turned into sensationalism, which seemed to be an end in itself, the reaction toward propriety and conservatism was understandable. The reaction, furthermore, isolated the sensationalism from the more acceptable theoretical expressions of the American Dream. Nor was this entirely a conservative reaction; it is possible for the most liberal reader to find the naturalists' exploration of the dark alleys of human experience obsessive. Sensationalism as a means, pursued thus obsessively, becomes an end. This metamorphosis of means into ends occurs in other areas. It is interesting to turn back to the treatises of Adam Smith or John Stuart Mill and see how completely they subordinated economic activity and democratic process to the ideal of personal freedom and enrichment which they held always before them as the true reward of productive efficiency or progress in democracy. Today, by a metamorphosis that helps to explain this other debasement of idealism into sensationalism, productive efficiency has become an end in itself. The old goal of personal fulfillment deteriorates as the economic means have become ends. In the same way, we have seen scientists abdicate social responsibility, even while they have been rediscovering transcendental unity through relativity physics. The escape from taboo, like the expansion of economic process, can become obsessive and defeat its own ideal ends.

Recent "science fiction" reveals exactly the same processes. Writers like Ray Bradbury, A. A. Van Vogt, Henry Kutter, and a host of others (Orwell's *1984* is in the same class) have been exploring the social and human prospects of a future in which first the machine and then the techniques of mass manipulation have taken charge of man. Society depends upon technological powers to the point where individual freedom cannot be tolerated. The little man must be oriented and organized to the machine. As he becomes more dependent upon it and as its complexities multiply, society itself becomes part of a mechanism.

These dire prophesies of brain-wash and total propaganda come from writers who are devoted to the ideal of human freedom. Their exploration of the ways in which the human spirit may be suppressed has some of the obsessive quality of Swift's fascination with what he found repulsive in man. But their exploration of this horror has had the effect of domesticating it. Being described again and again, often with great imagination, it acquires the fascination of the abomination. It comes to constitute, through repetition and imaginative identification, the only possible future. Youthful readers of science fiction abound who do not suspect the moral implications of these tales and who regard the coming of brain-wash and thought-police as among the inevitable corollaries of space travel.

And thus it would be possible, if not just, to accuse these writers of promoting the very horror they set out to expose. They might be denounced by social "idealists" — whom they in turn would accuse of being the very ostriches who by their willful blindness to what is happening today make the horror of the future probable. This was the situation, early in this century, of the naturalists and their various indignant critics. Both sides believed in Man. Both were moral in intention. Yet each saw the other as the enemy of the Dream. If it is true that science fiction conditions us to expect the Total State, it may be true that naturalistic fiction was an influence in the movement toward pessimism, materialism, and despair. However confidently and happily it was undertaken, the demonstration that social forces operate to control human lives communicated grim pictures of physical deprivation, thwarted hopes, and human frustration. The conviction grew that man could not control the giant forces about him.

There are many other manifestations of the divided stream of transcendentalism. The transcendentalist union of reason and instinct has since deteriorated, on the one hand, into the popular notion that the educated don't have horse sense, that instinct is killed by cultivation, that "nature" is good but knowledge and reason are bad. On the other hand, when human and physical nature becomes unpleasant or unmanageable, it requires only the smallest step to separate good from evil by denouncing the refractory as essentially bad and falling back on authority for standards by which to exhort or chastise rebellious nature. We have still not adjusted the cultural lag that made emotion and instinct suspect. The idea of a whole which embraces nature, spirit, and the sum of human qualities, in perfect harmony, has been easier to define than to maintain.

Still another example of this divided stream has to do with scientific theory on the highest level—the level for which mathematics is the only accurate language—where the emotions of some of the world's leading physicists have become characteristically involved. The aim of Max Planck's quantum theory is, so far as a layman can trust the language, to determine the smallest possible unit of matter or energy. And it seems that the apparent continuous flow or continuity of matter and energy can be reduced, ultimately, to a succession of separate "jumps" by separate "particles." This smallest quantity Planck labeled a *quantum*. It further appears that these particles are known only by the jumps they take—and that the jumps are so quick that it is impossible to determine the position of a particle at any instant during the almost infinitely short time of its jump. Two conclusions have emerged from these investigations: first, that "matter" and "energy" are separate names for things that cannot be separated, since the "particle" and its "jump" are known only in terms of each other, and the particle in effect does not exist except when it is jumping, although its place at any point within the jump cannot be determined; second, that in measurements there is a final irreducible minimum of error which is due to the fact that the tiny "jump" of the "particle" is so quick that it is impossible for human measurement to determine where the particle is at any moment of its jump. (Our language, say the physicists, breaks down here, in this use of "jump" and "particles," but it is the best we can do.) Planck's great contribution was to formulate a theory (called the Indeterminancy Principle) and an equation which would account for this irreducible minimum of error.

It would occasion no surprise if laymen misinterpreted Planck's findings. According to the physicists it is impossible really to understand the quantum theory in any language but mathematics. But what are we to think when certain very eminent physicists seize upon Planck's concept of this irreducible area of ignorance and build upon it whole volumes devoted to reintroducing an element of "freedom" or "will" or "uncaused effects" into the realms of material causation? This is what Arthur Eddington in *The Nature of the Physical Universe* (1928) and James Jeans in *The Universe Around Us* (1929) have done. These volumes were received enthusiastically by those who found in them an attack on the chain of physical causation with which science had for more than a generation been fettering the human spirit.

The reader need not accept the word of a layman on this matter, for Max Planck himself published a volume (*Where is Science Going?* 1932) in which he sought to combat these writings of Eddington and Jeans by reaffirming that man's inability to measure certain phenomena did not prove that they were "uncaused" and hence evidence of "freedom." In a colloquium appended to this volume, Albert Einstein explained that Eddington and Jeans were moved by the British literary tradition, a tradition that is rich indeed in its affirmation of the human spirit, to write volumes that went counter to what they as scientists must have known about the proper application of Planck's theory.

These literary physicists are in effect transcendentalists: they want to fuse mind or spirit with matter and thus to give nature a moral drive. But their use of Planck's equation to justify a reaffirmation of freedom shows that they do not really see the cosmos as one, for they reveal themselves as trying to widen a crack in the wall of physical law through which they can let freedom wiggle in—rather than seeing the whole range of physical law as an expression of spirit and therefore a *projection* of man's freedom throughout nature. Their hearts are not satisfied by their new monism, and they seek to temper the rigidity of their own laws. Their minds flow in the divided stream.

The elements of these contradictions, which I have illustrated at such length, are contained in every piece of naturalistic writing. There is always the tension between hope and despair, between rebellion and apathy, between defying nature and submitting to it, between celebrating man's impulses and trying to educate them, between embracing the universe and regarding its dark abysses with terror. The dynamics of transcendentalism demanded evolution, in order to give life to the system. Emerson frequently refers to the "aspiration" in nature: "Striving to be man, the worm Mounts through all the spires of form." Spencer used his evolutionary philosophy to justify predatory capitalism and the elimination of the "unfit" in sweatshops or mine explosions. Another version of cosmic process saw man as an accident in a movement toward eventual lifeless rest (entropy, it was called) when all cosmic energy would be absorbed and everything would be dead and uniform. This prospect justified ruthless self-expression, the brutal "superman" who smashed his way over natural and human obstacles. Yet Nietzsche's superman, Jack London's Wolf Larsen, and, a couple of generations down the scale, Mickey Spillane's Mike Hammer are all moral idealists.

These varieties of social and ethical confusion never entirely thrust from the writer's mind the orthodox Christian dualism that provides the framework within which naturalism reveals its intention and its meaning. The belief in free will and ethical responsibility, in a universe of rewards and punishments, in a world dominated by purpose and meaning, hovers like a ghost over almost every variety of naturalism in fiction. The naturalistic novelist was inspired by a zeal which he did not precisely relate to his avowed determinism and which therefore frequently turned him back toward dualism. He fell back, that is, on the tradition of Christian orthodoxy from which he had derived, unconscious of any inconsistency, the moral sanction for his belief in social justice and human rights.

From this point we can extend some of the historical perspectives of our problem: The Middle Ages saw revelation and authority solidly established over reason and nature, for reason was fallen and nature was under God's curse. But within the premises set by authority, reason was phenomenally active, and there was certainly more respect for *logical consistency* in those times than there is today. Today we are so used to assuming an absolute union of logical consistency with *exact observation* that we must be reminded that such a connection is not inevitable, that, in fact, it required five or six centuries for exact observation to overtake logical consistency. Medieval logicians could define their premises and argue from them as well as most modern scientists—perhaps better—but if there was an issue between observation and authority they automatically relied on the latter. Perhaps the cardinal fact of modern times is not that people observe more carefully, but that they rate observation first. Somewhere between the Middle Ages and the high Renaissance the premise that observation was more reliable than authority took hold. This process of taking hold extended painfully over at least a couple of centuries, for it took the idea that long to become established. But never completely established, for it is deeply seated in human psychology that one always tends to see what he expects to see—what his previous experience has conditioned him to look for. As far back as the thirteenth century a monk named Roger Bacon wrote a book on optics in which he explained the form and position of the rainbow with a perfect union of objective observation and logical consistency. As recently as the eighteenth century vaccination for smallpox was assailed with absolute horror by the medical profession; and less than a hundred years ago, clear proof that the infection of puerpural fever could be carried from one mother to another on the hands of a doctor was passionately rejected.

Nevertheless, at some point the premise was accepted and firsthand observation became as important as logical consistency. As this premise gained strength slowly and unevenly over the years, now in one area of knowledge, now in another, depending upon the religious, the social, the economic, or merely the emotional convictions that were challenged by such observation, nature—the thing that yielded truth to observation—rose in status, enjoying attention, respect, reverence, and fear in proportions that reflected the fluctuations of attraction and repulsion for instinct, which we have already considered.

During the seventeenth century astronomy made prodigious strides, and John Locke laid the foundations of mechanistic psychology. In the eighteenth century nature was sentimentalized under a myth that human nature was the pattern and model of divine reason:

The proper study of mankind is man.

Ecstasy over this idea produced more complacent speculation about "nature" than observation of it. In the early nineteenth century, the romantic fusion of nature and reason, whether in Wordsworth's "presence Whose dwelling is the light of setting suns, And the round ocean and the living air," or in Thoreau's enraptured contemplation, achieved the emotional force of religion. Then, later in the century, the worship of reason-nature gathered momentum as an assault on convention, on moral and social values, hitherto unquestioned, that rested on the dualist religious authority of the past. It swept on into an affirmation of progress through knowledge of hard scientific fact; and then the facts grew dark, inscrutable, overpowering, and man cowered under the threat of forces he could not control.

SOME CRITERIA OF LITERARY NATURALISM

Literary naturalism moves among three patterns of ideas: the religion of reason-nature, revealed in an enraptured contemplation of Process; the attack on the dualist (therefore unscientific) values of the past; the recognition and slowly growing fear of natural forces that man might study but apparently could not control.

Out of the never-resolved tension between the ideal of perfect unity and the brutal facts of experience come the themes, motifs, forms, and styles through which naturalism found literary expression. These are all part of the picture of naturalism, although some are there more or less by chance. To list them briefly is to suggest the rather disorderly composition of this picture.

The major themes and motifs are *determinism, survival, violence,* and *taboo.* The theme of determinism, which is of course basic, carries the idea that natural law and socioeconomic influences are more powerful than the human will. The theme of survival grows out of the application of determinism to biological competition; the notion that survival is the supreme motive in animal life provides a point of view from which all emotion, motivation, and conflict may be approached; it fastens man to his physical roots. The theme of violence grows with the transfer of emphasis from tradition (ultimately supernatural tradition) to survival. Animal survival is a matter of violence, of force against force; and with this theme there emerge various motifs having to do with the expression of force and violence and with the exploration of man's capacities for such violence. "The lower nature of man," in short, is revealed, explored, emphasized. It is also defiantly and triumphantly brandished; it may indeed be worshiped! A generation later this theme will be found to have modulated into the discovery of psychic recesses—the acknowledgement of new kinds and qualities of emotional experience. The last link in this chain, dangling from survival and violence, comes as an assault on taboo; a host of topics that had been considered improper—sex, disease, bodily functions, obscenity, depravity—were found to be in the province of physical survival. In that province, where the naturalists focused their attention, they could not be ignored. Nobody wanted to ignore them.

The forms which the naturalistic novel assumes are *clinical, panoramic, slice-of-life, stream of consciousness*, and *chronicle of despair*. When the idea of the free, responsible human will, making ethical choices that control its fate, is set aside in favor of such concepts as determinism and survival, a new notion of social process has appeared. It is dramatized (or enacted) in these new kinds of novels. Biological determinism can be set forth in a clinical study of disease or deterioration, in which the course of the malady or mania is traced step by step as it destroys the individual. When these forces operate in or through the whole body of society, a panoramic novel appears. Zola's *Germinal*, which "studies" a coal mining community and shows the miners helplessly squeezed to the edge of starvation by laissez-faire capitalism, is the classic of this form and the archetype of the proletarian novel. The minute and faithful reproduction of some bit of reality, without selection, organization, or judgment, every smallest detail presented with "scientific" fidelity, is the formless form of a slice-of-life novel. The same approach, but to the content of the mind (all the data of experience) rather than to external reality, gives a stream of consciousness novel, in which every smallest detail of thought is presented without selection, organization, or judgment. And finally there is the chronicle of despair, in which a whole life is depicted as the weary protagonist trudges across the dreary wastes of the modern world and finds, usually, an early death. *Studs Lonigan* in 1930 or Motley's *Knock on Any Door* in 1950 have almost exactly the same form.

The reader who has followed through the second part of this chapter will by now be uncomfortable in his recognition that these five forms do not—any of them—allow for both parts of the divided stream or for the tensions which I have said were inseparable from naturalism. The point is that naturalism involved a continual *search* for form. These are the forms it would have attained if its materialistic premises had been wholly and consistently followed. The fact that such premises were not—and probably could not have been—consistently maintained accounts for the complexity and fascination of literary naturalism as a problem. The question will be explored in the last section of this chapter.

Naturalistic styles cannot be defined in any exclusive sense. They can be listed, perhaps, as *documentary*, *satiric*, *impressionistic*, and *sensational*; but these are not very accurate terms for describing styles, and they are certainly not exclusive. The ideal of a fact-freighted, uncolored, objective, "scientific" style can be stated, but it is not easy to find an example of it in the novel. Frequently the most superficially objective or restrained style is the most highly charged with bitterness or indignation—as in the minute and faithful reproductions of stupid conversations by, say, James T. Farrell, or the vitriolic attacks on the middle class by contemporaries of de Maupassant in France. At the other extreme, the style of Zola, the fountainhead of naturalism, is recognized as highly romantic by all the critics, as is the style of his closest follower in America, Frank Norris, who went to considerable pains in one of his essays to explain that naturalism was romantic rather than realistic. In a "naturalistic" novel, where the subject matter is sensational, the style is likely to be restrained and objective; where the subject matter is commonplace, the style is likely to be turbulent or "romantic."

For these reasons, there cannot be a "naturalistic style." When applied to a literary movement, the term *naturalism* indicates the philosophical orientation outlined in the previous sections of this chapter. The term *romantic*, in this connection, indicates an attitude or quality—an exuberance or intensity of approach, a sense of vitality or richness, a feeling that the demands of the human spirit cannot be met by the commonplace or typical occasions of life. This romantic quality is frequently achieved by naturalistic subject matter presented (because it is sensational) in a style that is restrained and objective; here the effect would be called romantic, whereas the style would be called realistic. Where the subject matter is typically romantic, as for example in Melville's *Typee*, the romantic effect is rendered through a realistic style. Realism in style is, as everyone knows, relative: the "realistic" Dickens style has been turned by the passage of years into what might today be called romantic. Even in our time, what was the poignant, intense realism of Hemingway in 1927 has come to be considered romantic and even (God save the mark!) sentimental. When novels like Zola's *Germinal* and Norris's *McTeague* are considered naturalistic in philosophy, romantic in effect, and (though not consistently) realistic in style, it becomes very apparent that the three terms are not mutually exclusive; no one of them can characterize a novel to the exclusion of the other two. I use the term *naturalism* to indicate a philosophical orientation; *romanticism* to indicate extremes or intensities of effect; *realism* to indicate the apparent fidelity, through style, to details of objects, manners, or speech.

FROM SCIENTIFIC THEORY TO AESTHETIC FACT

The word *naturalistic*, then, labels a philosophy fairly adequately, but by the time we have passed through the varieties of social and ethical application that have been drawn from it and listed the forms, styles, and motifs that it has evoked, we dare speak of the "*naturalistic*" novel only with the reservations implied by quotation marks. The significant form of a novel cannot be deduced from the fact that its writer is a philosophical naturalist, for naturalism does not account for spirit, imagination, and personality. A work that was perfectly controlled by the theory of materialistic determinism would not be a novel but a report. It is not surprising, therefore, that critics have run aground or afoul of each other when they have tried to characterize the naturalistic novel with sweeping generalizations. Current theories about the nature of naturalism disagree in general and in detail. They disagree so fundamentally that they give diametrically contrary statements about the matter. The focus of discord seems to be the question of whether the naturalistic novel is "optimistic" or "pessimistic." Some critics insist that the essence of naturalism is "pessimistic determinism," expressing resignation or even despair at the spectacle of man's impotence in a mechanistic universe; others claim that the naturalistic novel is informed with a bright, cheerful, and vigorous affirmation of progress—of man's ability through science to control his environment and achieve Utopia.[1]

The hostility of such points of view might lead one to expect that their proponents were writing about entirely different groups of books, but they are not. It is true that one writer excludes Dreiser from the naturalistic movement, whereas another finds its epitome in his work; but on the whole these antipodal camps are dealing with the same works. The cause of the discord lies in the relation between science and literature: specifically, in the idea that scientific attitudes produce equivalent aesthetic effects. One group starts with the assumption that science is essentially optimistic and concludes that the naturalistic novel must therefore express an optimistic social purpose. Another group starts at the opposite end with the assumption that most novels of the naturalistic movement reveal a "pessimistic determinism" and concludes that the materialism of science must therefore be a philosophy of gloom and despair and that no novel written from its tenets can express any social purpose. A third set of critics, realizing that naturalistic novels embody "pessimistic determinism" and that scientists are generally idealists, innovators, and believers in progress, conclude that in the critical woodpile there is indeed a nigger, whom they cannot find.

The key to this puzzle (for it can be solved) lies in a distinction between what the socially minded man thinks and what the work of art is. The scientist who wants to improve the lot of man through knowledge and manipulation of the material world faces two obstacles: lethargy and unbelief. Some people think mankind is doing well enough. Others do not think that anything can be accomplished with "human nature" by scientific methods. The scientist-reformer therefore has to establish the validity of two assumptions: that the state of man needs to be improved, and that human conditions are determined by the operation of material causes which can be traced, recorded, understood, and, finally, controlled. The pieces of the puzzle fall into place when we understand that the best possible way to illustrate and validate these two assumptions is to write a "naturalistic" tragedy in which a human being is crushed and destroyed by the operation of forces which he has no power to resist or even understand. The more helpless the individual and the more clearly the links in an inexorable chain of causation are defined, the more effectively documented are the two assumptions which underlie the scientists' program of reform, for the destruction of an individual demonstrates the power of heredity and environment over human destinies. And if the victim's lot is sordid, the need for reform is "proved." The more helpless the character, the stronger the proof of determinism; and once such a thesis is established the scientist hopes and believes that men will set about trying to control the forces which now control men.

Thus can the scientists' "optimistic" purpose be served by a "pessimistic" novel; and thus we see how the deduction that both must be either optimistic or pessimistic is untrue. In the works of Zola we frequently see pictures of degeneration and depravity flourished with the enthusiasm of a side-show barker describing a two-headed lady. The zeal is such that one imagines the author rubbing his hands in delight over his monsters. The most casual reading of *L'Assommoir* will identify this fusion of opposites—of sordid degeneracy and soaring enthusiasm—which troubles only the logical and abstracting critic.

The optimism of the scientist is undeniable; I shall not discuss here the formidable probability that it is not justified by his philosophy of naturalism. Nor do I mean to maintain that naturalistic novelists like Zola and Frank Norris grasped the distinction between a social policy, which proposes action, and a work of art, which is essentially self-contained. There is, on the contrary, a sharp discrepancy between what Zola announced in *Le Roman Expérimental* and what he performed in his novels; it corresponds to the discrepancy between Theodore Dreiser's socialism and the inexorable fatality that controls *An American Tragedy*. Returning for a moment to our optimism-pessimism dilemma, we should not be surprised to find the critic who proceeds from social theory to literary practice affirming that *An American Tragedy* is authentic naturalism because Dreiser suggests that "radical social reforms are imperative";[2] whereas another might deduce, if he proceeded from the novel to the social theory, that the philosophy of naturalism is grimly pessimistic because the protagonist of the novel is utterly helpless to control his fate. But I should say that the novel is an almost ideal example of naturalism because within its framework Dreiser makes no proposals. He shows how, given certain hereditary and environmental conditions, what did happen had to happen; and he communicates this conviction because he is able to present so detailed an account of events that Clyde Griffiths is shown as powerless to choose at the very climax of the action and is never held morally responsible for his "crime."

Within its aesthetic frame the novel is completely deterministic and might be called pessimistic (though I should prefer merely to call it faithful to fact); it is for this reason that it can be considered an unusually consistent (and powerful) expression of the naturalistic philosophy. No novel, of course, can actually render the total context of an event. But it can create the *illusion* of doing so; and this is the fundamental aim, as well as the criterion, of this type of naturalistic novel. The writer's opinions about social justice cannot and will not interfere with the form of the work.

Observing the operation of determinism in *An American Tragedy*, the reader may well be led to conclude that something should be done to change the conditions that produce such tragedies. But this happens to the reader, not in the novel; and I believe it can be shown that it happens after and apart from the aesthetic experience of the novel, although of course it is an effect of the book and undoubtedly the author's intention. The force of this social conclusion depends, paradoxically, on the very inexorable fatality of the action. The ultimate social implications of the action are doubtless with the reader as he reads, too, since no man can stay constantly within the framework or be constantly and exclusively controlled by the assumptions of the work he is reading; indeed his awareness of social conditioning and of the effect of social and financial ambition on Clyde Griffiths is an important element in his awareness that the work of art which he contemplates is unique and self-contained. The conditions as given are absolute for Clyde, although for America they can be improved. Reading a naturalistic tragedy in which the hero appears to have no freedom, one can know that one is performing an act of freedom in reading the book, and can sense that the author is by no means contained by the determinism which controls his novel, for he appeals to the reader's freedom and idealism as he shows that his hero is trapped. Thus the heightening of the reader's social consciousness (and any impulse to social action which he may subsequently experience) comes precisely because the movement of *An American Tragedy* is so perfectly "fatalistic," presenting in its massive and lumbering fashion a superb integration of structure and underlying philosophy. Observing this, the reader enjoys an access of wisdom that would not come if he were being systematically exhorted to action.

But *can* anything but despair emerge from such a spectacle? And by what right do we call a naturalistic novel tragic, when its premises strip the protagonist of will and ethical responsibility? The answer lies, surely, in the fact that will is not really absent from the naturalistic novel. It is, rather, taken away from the protagonist and the other characters and transferred to the reader and to society at large. The reader acknowledges his own will and responsibility even as he pities the helpless protagonist. But the protagonist is not an automaton: his fall is a tragic spectacle because the reader participates in it and feels that only by a failure of his will and the will of society could it have taken place. What appears as an error of choice or a weakness of character in the plays of Aeschylus and Shakespeare is thus transferred to society in the naturalistic tragedy; society has destroyed the hero and thus has destroyed a part of its immortal self—and pity and guilt result. It is guilt instead of terror, because the social forces which crush a hero are finally subject to man's will and do not have the fatal power and mystery of cosmic forces. This curious wrenching of the novel's enclosing frame, which permits the "guilty" reader to enter the action, explains, in part, why so much criticism of naturalism has dealt with the problem of social intent. It also shows that the Aristotelian definition of tragedy is so fundamentally true that even a writer who believes he denies its premises nevertheless contrives to fulfill its conditions. If we can admit that *An American Tragedy* is tragic in this quasi-Aristotelian sense, we can take a further step and conclude that it is irrelevant to ask whether it is optimistic or pessimistic. The question is whether it is true. And whatever its ultimate social intent, naturalistic fiction does not exhort the reader to action. If some of Zola's best novels are still read it is because of their logical, integrated, relentless movement toward disaster—not that *L'Assommoir* will discourage drunkenness, or *Germinal* usher in the Revolution, or *Nana* apprise us of the evils of sexual license in a decadent society.

When we grant that a novelist may promote his ideas on social reform by writing a novel in which he seeks to embody a thorough-going materialistic determinism, we evoke two formidable objections. First, carried through to perfection, such a work would be a report, uncolored by ideas of human personality or recognition of the freedom of the human spirit. Such a work does not exist as a novel, and one would be fairly safe in affirming that it could not exist and be a novel. Second, the conflict between confidence in progress through human-effort and a belief in scientific determinism is not reconciled by my showing that "tragic" novels can document social optimism. The conflict remains. It is the chief problem that any "naturalistic" novel presents to a thoughtful reader; and we shall watch its Protean changes in the novels discussed in this volume. Like the critical controversy over optimism and pessimism, it is evidence of the divided stream—of a profound uncertainty as to whether science liberates the human spirit or destroys it. Novels, novelists, and critics consistently reflect this modern tension between science as god and science as devil, between progress and despair, between the hope of the future and the values of the past, between the two faces of human and physical nature.

A final observation on these contradictions: Naturalistic fiction which purports to receive its sanction from the scientific method and deterministic philosophy usually reveals, to the dispassionate observer, affiliations with several aspects of the aesthetic of ugliness, and these are apt to play a larger part in the novel's form than may appear to us if we keep our attention too closely on such concepts as science and reform. Art is anthropocentric. It is created by men whose dominant concern is to domesticate the physical universe to the uses of man's spirit. This aim is accomplished—or approached—by the artist's attempts to impose patterns of human thought upon the endless and eternal complexity of the physical universe. No matter how ardently he appears to be denying the worth or importance of man, the autonomy of the will, the permanence of life, the value of man's spirit, or the power of his knowledge, he is always in some fashion affirming these very things, for art is exercise and proof of them. The naturalistic novelist while he portrays with loathing and bitterness the folly and degradation of man is also affirming his hope and his faith, for his unspoken strictures imply an equally unspoken ideal which stimulates and justifies his pejorative attitude toward the world about him. The act of criticism, furthermore, is an exercise of creative intelligence which in itself denies what it may be saying about the futility of life and the folly of man.

This denial is a term in the dialectic of art; it is as much a part of the total effect of the work of art as its stated or implied scientific hypothesis. Hence all "naturalistic" novels exist in a tension between determinism and its antithesis. The reader is aware of the opposition between what the artist says about man's fate and what his saying it affirms about man's hope. Both of these polar terms are a part of the "meaning" of a naturalistic novel.

NOTES

1. A quasi-political grouping of left-center-right will orient us among the major critical approaches to naturalism that are current. The right wing is conservative and "pessimistic"; the left stresses social progress; the center tries to reconcile the extremes.

The right wing is represented by Harry Hartwick, *The Foreground of American Fiction* (New York, 1934); he maintains that the determinism of the naturalists was so pessimistic that they conceived of nature as a vast, horrible, indifferent mechanism, a "contrivance of wheels within wheels; man is a piece of fate caught in the machinery of Nature . . . Man's only duty is to discharge his energies and die, at the same time expressing his individuality as best he can." (Pp. 17–18.) Naturalism, he says, destroyed religious faith and inspired literature reflecting the conviction that might is right, that "men should court the simple atavistic behavior of children and savages, who have not yet been corrupted by ideas." (Pp. 18–19.) Here we see the simplest false correlation between the treatment of sordid or brutal characters in a novel and the author's own moral position. Actually it reveals a great interest in ideas on the part of the author when he attempts to dramatize the "struggle for existence" in a novel of violence. Jack London, for example, is a novelist of ideas, intensely *interested* in the "atavistic behavior of children and savages" and frontiersmen; but he does not advocate mindless violence. An equally extreme right-wing position appears in Oscar Cargill, *Intellectual America* (New York, 1941). Mr. Cargill concludes that naturalism is pessimistic determinism (a phrase he uses repeatedly), according to which failure and degeneracy are the natural ends of man, who is helpless to better his condition; no naturalistic work, he says, can show any hope for man or any ideas about social reform. If it has an affirmative note, it is not naturalistic. His entire structure of theory rests on the single point that determinism eliminates human freedom.

The extreme left-wing position appears in George W. Meyer's "The Original Social Purpose of the Naturalistic Novel," *Sewanee Review*, October 1942. Mr. Meyer argues from Zola's statement in *Le Roman Expérimental* that science will find the truth that will set men free; if this is Zola's belief, then no genuine naturalistic novel can evince any pessimistic determinism. Mr. Meyer goes a step further to accept Zola's distinction between fatalism and determinism: Zola said the latter was optimistic, because it could be used by the scientist as the instrument for controlling nature, and therefore Mr. Meyer concludes that a deterministic novel must be optimistic and progressive. Mr. Meyer shows that Mr. Cargill is in error when he labels the philosophy of naturalism "pessimistic," but he too is in error when he insists that the naturalistic novel must be "optimistic." Mr. Meyer's error is not serious, because in its larger social context even a depressing novel like *An American Tragedy* communicates, as I have said, the conviction that social ills can be cured by the will of man—and there is buoyant enthusiasm apparent everywhere in Zola's gloomiest works. But in theory, at least, it is not possible to distinguish between that for which God is responsible and that for which "man is at least partly responsible." (P. 6.) To separate fatalism from determinism is to deny the "monism of the cosmos" which is the foundation rock of naturalistic theory. In *theory*, Zola recognizes neither God nor the human will—only law. And law is neither optimistic nor pessimistic.

2. Meyer, op. cit., p. 7.

TWENTY-SEVEN

NORRIS HISTORICALLY VIEWED

Richard Chase

Richard Chase (1914–62) received his Ph.D. from Columbia in 1946 and became a member of the Columbia faculty
in 1949. Chase quickly established a major reputation
with a series of studies on nineteenth-century American figures, notably *Herman Melville: A Critical Study* (1949)
and *Emily Dickinson* (1951). But it was his *The American
Novel and Its Tradition* (1957), with its vigorously pursued
thesis that the distinctive character of American fiction lay
in its relationship to the romance, that was his most influential work. For over a generation it was impossible to discuss the general nature of the American novel without reference to Chase's romance thesis.

What we usually have, then, in the novels of Norris (and this would apply to Zola as
well) is the chronicle of the degeneration of characters under the pressure of heredity
and environment, the tone of the story varying from straight novelistic realism to
melodrama, epic, and grotesque comedy. Norris makes of his naturalism, even though
it may seem to be merely a ruthless realism, a means of restoring to the novel some of
the dramatic actions, mysteries, colorful events, and extreme situations, along with
the mythic and symbolic motives, that used to be brought into the novel under other
auspices. He does not, in other words, abandon the romance or romance-novel; he
merely recreates it and reconstitutes it on new grounds.

Different as he was in temperament and background from the older American romancers, and limited though his genius was, Norris continued in certain respects the
tradition of Brockden Brown, Hawthorne, and Melville, a process that was inherent

in his attempt to adapt the practice of Zola to American conditions. Historians have often observed how easily in many people's minds Calvinism modified itself during the nineteenth century into the philosophical determinism that stood behind the naturalistic movement in fiction. The "dark necessity" that rules Hawthorne's Chillingworth and Melville's Ahab differs from that which rules Norris's McTeague, because Hawthorne and Melville understand fate as being an inner or psychic predisposition. The ruin of the hero, or hero-villain as he often is, comes about as a result of the clash between his will and the adamant circumstances he finds himself in. Naturalistic doctrine, on the other hand, assumes that fate is something imposed on the individual from the outside. The protagonist of a naturalistic novel is therefore at the mercy of circumstances rather than of himself, indeed he often seems to *have* no self. Psychologically he is a simplified character compared even with the already simplified characters in the older romances, although by way of compensation his life is more richly endowed with concrete detail than is theirs. Nevertheless the sense of the dark necessity that controls human actions is vividly caught by both the naturalists and the older romancers. And despite the shifting of the spotlight from the inner mind to the outer world, it is often caught by the same procedures. Norris, for example, shares with the older writers a melodramatic extravagance, a tendency towards a stiff and abstract conventionalism of plot, a tendency toward the tone if not the actual method of allegory, and an interest in symbols (cf. the gold symbolism in *McTeague*).

To be sure, much had happened to the American novelist since the time of Cooper, Hawthorne, and Melville. What had happened can be suggested by the words realism and anti-intellectualism. The realism which was introduced into the older romance-novels only sporadically became after the Civil War the primary prerequisite of the serious novel, whether as practiced by James, Howells, Mark Twain, Stephen Crane, or Norris. With the advent of these writers an era began which has not yet been superseded, and perhaps never will be—an era in which all the imaginative dimensions of the novel begin on the operational base of realism. Historically involved with this realism, although not logically necessitated by it, is the anti- or non-intellectualism shown by most of the important modern novelists except those who belong to the school of James and Howells. The older writers, from Brown and Cooper to Melville, thought of themselves, not perhaps as "intellectuals" in any of the modern senses of this term, but at least as writers a part of whose task it was to have a commerce with the life of ideas and with certain traditional values. Norris is a classic case of the modern lowbrow novelist, something of an intellectual himself to be sure, and yet a lowbrow because of his native temperament and conviction—but also because, let us not fail to add, lowbrowism is one of the most successful literary poses in modern America.

Compared with Cooper and Melville, nurtured as they were on a fairly complex Anglo-American culture, Frank Norris is a semibarbarian out of the new West. And yet nothing so confirms one's belief in the existence of an American tradition of the romance-novel as the fact that Norris's background and upbringing furnish him with an imagination which is so similar to that derived from quite different sources by the older writers. Take, for example, two of the leading imaginative ideas of Melville; first, the golden age with its simple life of innocence and genial emotions, which he generically calls "Typee"; and, second, his idea of Evil, the "great power of black-ness" which, as we have noted in an earlier chapter, he finds in Hawthorne's tales and which he thinks "derives its force from its appeals to that Calvinistic sense of Innate Depravity and Original Sin, from whose visitations, in some shape or other, no deeply thinking mind is always and wholly free." To a considerable extent Melville con-sciously derives these two leading ideas from literary and intellectual tradition, how-ever native they may have been to the demands of his temperament.

One finds new versions of Melville's ideas in the novels of Frank Norris. But they have been derived not so much from reflection and reading as from Norris's instinc-tive imaginative sympathy with the doctrines of American Populism, the movement of agrarian protest and revolt which was in its heyday when Norris was forming his ideas in the 1880's and 1890's. The importance of Populist doctrine in understanding the art of Frank Norris is suggested by his own remark, cited above, that romance derives from the "People."

It was not really the plain facts and concrete injustices behind the Populist protest that appealed to Norris. Rather, it was what Richard Hofstadter calls (in *The Age of Reform*) "the folklore of Populism." For our purpose, this folklore may be under-stood as having two origins. First, there is what Mr. Hofstadter calls the "agrarian myth" that ever since the time of Jefferson has haunted the mind, not of the vast com-mercialized middle class or perhaps after the earliest times the farmers either, but of reformers and intellectuals. This "myth" involves the idea of a pastoral golden age— a time of plain living, independence, self-sufficiency and closeness to the soil—an idea which has been celebrated in various ways by innumerable American writers. Second, there is the mythology of Calvinism which especially in the rural West and South has always infused Protestantism, even the non-Calvinist sects, with its particu-lar kind of Manichaean demonology.

If, as we have been saying in this book, American fiction has traditionally enhanced realism with nostalgic idyl and with melodrama, it is evidently akin in its imagination to "the folklore of Populism," which has always done the same. This is pointed up sharply when we perceive how close a writer like Norris actually is to Populism—not, it must be re-emphasized, to its genuinely liberal or its genuinely realistic reformist program but to its vaunting, mythic ideology (an ideology often reactionary in its political implication). In Norris's *McTeague* and *The Octopus* one finds this ideology more or less exactly represented; one finds what Mr. Hofstadter calls "the idea of a golden age. . . . the dualistic version of social struggles; the conspiracy theory of his-tory; and the doctrine of the primacy of money."

McTeague is not literally an agrarian hero; yet he does come out of a simple rural America, and he is corrupted and defeated by the customs and laws of the evil city. The fact that nature is thoroughly Darwinized in Norris's imagination and that McTeague, though appealing in his masculine simplicity, is not far above the brute, does not quite conceal the underlying myth of Adam and the fall from Eden that makes McTeague a sort of brutalized Billy Budd. The dualistic version of social struggles is apparent in *McTeague*, though not nearly so strongly dramatized as it is in *The Octopus*. In both books the social question is conceived as a clear-cut, black-and-white war between the grasping capitalist and the plain American. And although Norris does not campaign for silver, he accepts the idea of the primacy of money. Gold is shown, especially in *McTeague*, to be as fertile a source of evil and misery as the devil himself and its sinister powers are melodramatized with an exaggerated symbolism. In *The Octopus* we find a full use of the conspiracy theory of history—the theory that all would be well with American life if only it were not for the machinations of the money power—the bankers, the railroad magnates, and their panoply of venal journalists and lawyers, suborned marshals, and hired assassins.

The main difference between the folklore of Populism and the imagination of Frank Norris is that naturalist doctrine has given him an underlying pessimism about nature itself and man's place in it. Norris appears to accept what Mr. Hofstadter calls "the concept of natural harmonies," a utopian faith in the natural order and in the virtue of man's living in harmony with it; but this view of things always has to contend in Norris's mind with a radically pessimistic view. As with most American naturalistic novelists, the pessimism wins out in the end, but in doing so it seems to take over from the idyl of nature some of its poetic, utopian quality, so that what we have is not hardheaded Darwinism but romantic nihilism, the final implication of which is that death itself is utopia.

Norris's romance-novels succeeded in reclaiming for American fiction an imaginative profundity that the age of Howells was leaving out—a fact which Norris's crudity and passages of bad writing cannot conceal. *McTeague* introduced to the novel a new animal vitality and a new subject matter drawn from lower-class life. From a moral and intellectual point of view, *The Octopus* has to be called a sort of subnovel. Yet no sympathetic reader can forget its enormous panoramic power. The book has, as D. H. Lawrence says, a brooding primitive tone, an astonishing sense of a world instinct with sinister forces, that remind one of Cooper's *The Prairie*.

In view of their imaginative achievement one does not worry too much, in reading Norris's books, about their sentence-to-sentence faults of syntax and language, although like Dreiser, Norris was unable to tell whether the English he himself wrote was good or bad. *McTeague* and *The Octopus* prove again that it is possible to master certain fundamental aspects of the art of prose fiction despite the imperfection of the language in which the feat is achieved. One does not destroy either Norris or Dreiser by pointing out their bad grammar and their false rhetoric. On the other hand neither can you write a very great novel unless you are master of your language, as Hawthorne, Melville, Mark Twain, James, and Faulkner are masters. And then again you may be the perfect master of your language without being a great master of the art of the novel; Hemingway is an example.

Many later writers, the two greatest being Dreiser and Faulkner, have shown that naturalism remains a usable technique. Dreiser performed the considerable service of adapting the colorful poetry of Norris to the more exacting tasks imposed upon the social novelist—very much as James assimilated Hawthorne's imagination of romance into his novels. Faulkner, a more universal genius than Dreiser and less specifically deriving from Norris, allies the naturalistic procedures with certain of the classic motives of fiction. But it is in Norris that we see the glories and perils of naturalism in their sheerest form.

TWENTY-EIGHT

MARK TWAIN AND THE EARLIER REALISM

Robert Falk

Robert Falk (1914–96) received his Ph.D. from the University of Wisconsin in 1941 and in 1951 joined the faculty of the University of California, Los Angeles, where he remained until his retirement. In addition to his book-length study of American realism in *The Victorian Mode in American Fiction* (1965), Falk contributed a series of major essays on various aspects of the movement to the volumes *Transitions in American Literary History*, ed. Harry H. Clark (1954); *The Development of American Literary Criticism*, ed. Floyd Stovall (1955); and *The Gilded Age: A Reappraisal*, ed. H. Wayne Morgan (1963).

V. L. Parrington, in the first comprehensive discussion of Victorian realism in America, used the language of evolution to describe the period after the Civil War as arising out of "the ashes of romantic faith." He dismissed the work of Howells and Henry James as genteel and ineffectual, out of harmony with the steady march of the realistic emphasis. Now, however, his basic assumption of an evolutionary "rise" of literary aspirations from "gaudy romantic altars" and decadent social patterns to new and vitally "real" ones has ceased to carry the conviction it once had. It is no longer possible to accept his premise of an upward-curving spiral toward "reality," or to share his condescension toward nineteenth-century America. The decades here designated as "Victorian Realism" constituted more than a "transitional" phase of literary history. Both in its social and its literary manifestations the period deserves to be considered not as a side current in the stream of letters, but as an independent unit of cultural history. It had a development of its own marked by distinct chronological and historical limits—from the end of the war to the outbreak, about 1885,

The Victorian Mode in American Fiction, 1865–1885 (East Lansing: Michigan State University Press, 1965), pp. 159–66. Reprinted by permission of Michigan State University Press.

of a new form of turbulence and social strife—and it accomplished a life cycle of its own. It coincided with the formative and maturing years of three of America's leading novelists. During that period the novel was a potent social force and an accurate barometer of taste and manners. Literature was both an art and a social record, but it was not yet an instrument of reform. As a cultural unit, the period is one of great interest to the student of the American mind. And in its purely literary manifestations—the critical issues raised, the flourishing "monthlies" read and supported, the excited discussions of "art" and "reality," the lively exchanges of letters among its major writers—the age of Victorian realism had all the signs of a "movement."

The heated critical battles in the journals marked the literary phase of the larger struggle of intellectual conflict and swift social change. Great issues hovered in the background. The ideals of the Enlightenment and the political experiment of 1776 seemed to hang in the balance. As a moment of intellectual history, the twenty years between 1865 and 1885 were the stage-setting for a drama of survival in which the promise of democratic idealism and the threat of a deterministic and mechanistic philosophy seemed in fatal opposition. A reorientation of American thought took place in which social Darwinism and the Victorian orthodoxy represented the polar extremities. Between these two extremes thoughtful Americans sought some new basis and a new stabilization of opposing pressures.

The rapid movement after the war of social and economic forces toward an industrial economy, the aggregation of capital, and the consequent rise of the leaders of finance found philosophic sanction both in the traditional American faith in the individual and in the evolutionary argument of natural selection. This powerful swing of the pendulum toward integration, however, created the momentum for a reverse movement—labor and agrarian protest, group psychology, and a class-conscious society. Collectivism gradually drew support in opposition to rugged individualism and business enterprise. The intellectual expression of this conflict was a gradual reorientation of the prewar attitudes of individualism and equalitarianism. Psychological and analytical study of the springs of conduct supplanted the older exaltation of individual worth; similarly, economic and sociological disciplines, based upon science, took the place of the earlier philosophic abolitionism with its ethical concept of human rights. Both the new psychology and the new sociology contained seeds of determinism. Regional oppositions grew more complex. The rapid expansion westward into the unsettled frontier established a third section with its own claim to recognition to complicate the existing tensions between North and South. New rights of man needed to be integrated with the old—the rights of women, the rights of sections, the rights of labor. Increasingly diversified religious and racial types sought a place alongside the predominantly Anglo-Protestant strain. The impact of such forces upon the earlier idealistic-individualistic heritage produced a climate of intellectual and social disparity.

Against this background of controversy intellectuals and literary-minded men and women envisioned some sort of synthesis of opposing points of view. Sensitive to both the old and the new, they sought a temporary equilibrium of conflicting forces. It is this quest, as it took shape in the two decades following the truce of 1865, that one must regard as the essence of the problem of realism in fiction and criticism. For the most part, it was a conservative quest. American critics, for instance, did not turn at once to espouse a critical realism of protest against political corruption and economic graft. Instead, they grounded their hopes upon a return to the earlier democratic faith that the individual consciousness contained the will and strength to bring about necessary reforms in society. In short, the Victorian orthodoxy was conservative in temper, Christian in spirit, and humanitarian in outlook. It turned away from militant and outward means to reform, and, sustained by the strong infusion of mid-century idealism, it looked to the natural endowments of the democratic man to bring about the American dream. It is inaccurate to regard this effort as a genteel escape or a priestly withdrawal into the academy and drawing room. More sympathetically seen, it was a belief that the frictions of society might be assuaged by a literature which, without sacrificing the authenticity of the newer analytical methods and contemporary themes, could still maintain inherited standards of ethical and aesthetic idealism. During the twenty years we have been considering, the literary pendulum swung back and forth between the ideals of "romance" and those of "realism," and the values which emerged from this controversy may be discovered in the antithetical and reinforcing counterpoint between the two.

There were various literary "realisms." In one meaning, the word was associated with the novel as opposed to the "romance." In another, it signified realism of the commonplace and "poor real life" which Howells found so precious. The realism of contemporary life found expression in the work of De Forest, Howells, and James. Anti-romanticism was still another form of realism, and Henry James became the master of transposed melodrama. Victorian realism, when broadly defined, contained something of all these attitudes and points of view. There remains to be accounted for in the literary climate of the Seventies and Eighties another form of realism—the realism of native humor and local color. The frontier thesis as applied to literary history, puts this tradition in a conspicuous place in the growth of a realistic literature. Its roots lie far back in the nineteenth century, but in the early work of Mark Twain it became something more than dialect humor and newspaper eccentricity. It achieved the status of a genuine American style.

Although Mark Twain's best books have achieved the rank of greatness in American and world literature, it is difficult to define his precise relationship to the pattern of realism as we have attempted to portray it. In his own way Mark Twain was both a realist and a Victorian, yet his literary method and his highly original personality place him somehow outside of the tradition of Victorian literary realism. His best books depicted an earlier, rural America. His angle of vision was reminiscent, nostalgic, retrospective. His genius was unique and his method autobiographical. He was uninterested in aesthetic ideas or the art of fiction. Analysis and psychological character delineation were not in his repertoire. He did not carry over, as did James and Howells, a strong heritage of transcendental idealism. Criticism, metaphysics, philosophy, and social criticism were outside the circle of his interests which he once described as "history, biography, travels, curious facts, strange happenings, and science."[1] He once told Howells that he could not stand George Eliot, Hawthorne "and all those people." He detested Jane Austen and preferred to be damned to John Bun-yan's heaven than be forced to read *The Bostonians*. Scott and Cooper were not liter-ary models to be followed, but convenient targets for burlesque. In contemporary fiction he read only the novels of Howells for enjoyment, more out of his strong friendship and attachment than from any special interest in realistic fiction. His own books he wrote, he once said, with one eye on the lecture platform and the other on sales.[2]

Still, Mark Twain's contribution to a realistic literary attitude was important and lasting. In the 1870's it took the form of burlesquing the excesses of what he felt was an outworn romanticism. Building upon the dialect and tall-tale tradition of western humor, he wrote in *Innocents Abroad* and *Roughing It* books which were implicitly and explicitly broadsides against the serious tradition of letters. He poked fun at Ben-jamin Franklin's moral earnestness, parodied Scott and Coleridge, rebuked the noble savage, and slashed away at European culture and American tourists who became cathedral-hounds and culture-seekers. Together with his predecessors and contempo-raries in this humor tradition, he attacked by means of colloquialism, slang, parody, buffoonery, and plain ridicule all forms of "goody-goody-ism," "flim-flam charlatan-ism," and "sappy inanities." By deflating the polite tradition of the East and the cul-ture of Europe, he contributed to an amorphous but effective campaign of deflation and demonstrated in riotous terms the *un*importance of being earnest. Along with John Phoenix, Artemus Ward, G. W. Harris, Bill Nye, John Hay, and others, Mark Twain sought to expose artifice, sentiment, and pretentiousness and thus helped clear the ground for others to articulate a more positive program for realism.

But in more constructive ways Mark Twain contributed to the literary climate of realism during the Seventies and Eighties. His humor was in itself a protest against what he once called "a sad false delicacy" which had emasculated literature and feminized culture. If his humor more often ran to travesty, burlesque, or ribaldry, he could also employ satire as a weapon of the realist, and he once drew a distinction between travesty, which left the reader a "joked and defrauded victim," and satire which had as its aim the advancement of knowledge or wisdom. In his special prov-ince of western life, Mark Twain sought for veracious coloring and authentic tones. He was offended, for instance, when Bret Harte referred in one of his early stories to "twilight" along the Pacific slope, remarking that there was no such phenomenon. Commenting upon a painting by Bierstadt, he pronounced the peaks and valleys cor-rect, but objected that the "atmosphere" in the picture was "imported." Nothing like it, he noted, "was ever seen in California." Making a comment on E. W. Howe's *The Story of a Country Town*, he said it was "vivid and true. I know for I have seen and lived it all." He distrusted the meretricious wherever he found it. Summing up his literary creed late in life, he felt that he had experienced much that had equipped him for the building of novels. "I surely have the equipment," he said, "and a wide culture and all of it real, none of it artificial, for I don't know anything about books."

The association of realism with local color and especially with the western story was Twain's one positive contribution to theoretical criticism of the novel. Looking at his own career in retrospect he concluded that it was only through years of "unconscious absorption" that a writer can report the soul of a nation—its very life and speech and thought. But even this is too broad a scope for a single novelist. He must not try to generalize a nation.

No, he lays before you the ways and speech and life of a few people grouped in a certain place—his own place—and that is one book. In time he and his brethren will report to you the life and the people of the whole nation.[3]

Every section and racial type can provide subject matter for the writer and not until "a thousand able novels have been written," can you have "the soul of the people, the life of the people, the speech of the people; and not anywhere else can these be had."[4] Thus Mark Twain defined the place and function of local color. In his cooperative approach to the American novel he was characteristically western. He agreed with a fellow westerner, Eggleston, who said in 1892 discussing the regional movement and its achievement in Americanizing our literature:

The taking up of life in this regional way has made our literature really national by the only process possible. . . . 'The great American novel' for which prophetic critics yearned so fondly twenty years ago, is appearing in sections.[5]

Hamlin Garland likewise found localism to be the key to the realistic trend and saw the work of Cable, Joel Chandler Harris, Eggleston, Jewett, Wilkins, and Harte as "varying phases of the same movement which is to give us at last a really vital and original literature."[6] The local color movement seemed to Garland a signal for "the advance of the democratization of literature."[7]

In a different perspective, however, Mark Twain's relation to realism in the 1880's paralleled that of Howells and brought him closer to the pattern of Victorian realism as we have indicated it. Like Howells, he reached his artistic peak in the early and middle Eighties when *Life on the Mississippi* and *Huckleberry Finn* were published. In 1883 he wrote to Howells that he was piling up manuscript rapidly for the new book: "I'm booming these days—got health and spirits to waste—got an overplus."[8] The humor of *Innocents Abroad* and *Roughing It* was the rollicking gayety and coarse laughter of the romantic West. Although the satire of *The Gilded Age* was sharp at times it was without rancor; but in the Nineties his humor had turned to bitterness and misanthropic scorn in *The Mysterious Stranger* and *What is Man?* Somewhere between *Tom Sawyer* (1876) and *A Connecticut Yankee* (1889) Clemens achieved a period of adjustment and equilibrium among the variable and quixotic elements of his literary personality. It was not the middle zone of romance and realism which Howells sought, nor the "ideal real" of Henry James, but rather the coming to terms in middle life with the psychic conflict between his youthful enthusiasm and the cynicism of age. Passages of reminiscence in *Life on the Mississippi* contained this note of ripeness. But in *Huckleberry Finn* the mood was sustained throughout in a stronger handling of plot structure, social history, symbolism and skillful characterization. The nice adjustment of point of view, for instance, between the realist Huck and the romantic Tom show the two sides of Twain's nature in happy combination. This greater depth and harmony of mood indicates his work at its best. *Life on the Mississippi* and *Huckleberry Finn* are fundamentally great regional portraits. In them the romancer and the poet, the humorist and the cynic, the realist and the satirist, and the rich narrator of the American past were all suffused by the imaginative strength of his style. It was in the early Eighties that he found the most successful expression for his theories of localism, his keen ear for dialect, his nostalgia, and his autobiographical understanding of people and scenes along the Mississippi. In these ways he made significant contributions to the development of literary realism.

Much importance has been attached to the incident by which *Huckleberry Finn* was banned as an indecent book by the Concord Library Association. The *Springfield Republican* called it "trashy and vicious," its moral level low, and Clemens's sense of propriety unreliable, as in the notorious speech at the *Atlantic* dinner.[9] But the few authentic voices of criticism which were heard in review of the book recognized at once its superior artistry. T. S. Perry in the *Century* praised the humor, descriptive power, and characterization. He called Huck "its immortal hero," and a young scapegrace whose "undying fertility of invention, his courage, his manliness in every trial, are an incarnation of the better side of the ruffianism that is one result of the independence of Americans." He likewise admired its "autobiographical form" which gave the book a unity of narration superior to the more fragmentary *Tom Sawyer*. In the Grangerford-Shepherdson feud, Perry saw the method of Twain at its best. Here was "objectivity" and truth, one of the marks of realism in its mature form. The account is told as it appears to "a semi-civilized boy of fourteen, without the slightest condemnation or surprise."

> That is the way a story is best told, by telling it, and letting it go to the reader unaccompanied by signposts or directions how he shall understand it and profit by it. Life teaches its lessons by implication, not by didactic preaching; and literature is at its best when it is an imitation of life and not an excuse for instruction.[10]

Brander Matthews, one of the so-called "genteel" critics, likewise recognized that *Huckleberry Finn* was more than the work of a funny man. In an article entitled "Mark Twain's Best Story" he wrote: "that Mark Twain is a literary artist of a very high order all who have considered his later writings critically cannot but confess." Matthews acknowledged the "marvelous" skill of characterization and, like Perry, complimented him upon his objectivity and refusal to moralize. He thought the scene between Colonel Sherburn and the mob "one of the most vigorous bits of writing Mark Twain has done." On the subject of the portrayal of Huck, Matthews anticipated and refuted the expected genteel criticism of the novel: "Old maids of either sex will wholly fail to understand him, or to like him, or to see his significance and his value." Huck and Jim were both true to life, he thought, and concluded:

> That Mr. Clemens draws from life, and yet lifts his work from the domain of the photograph to the region of art, is evident to anyone who will give his writing the attention it deserves.[11]

There is, indeed, ample evidence that the vituperation and abuse of Mark Twain's vulgarity and buffoonery which greeted many of his books is hardly a fair representation of the criticism which the "Age of Decorum" rendered him. Setting aside comments by European critics such as those of Andrew Lang and Kipling, who ranked him with Cervantes, one recalls Howells's high opinion of his work and Joel Chandler Harris's defense of the wholesomeness of *Huckleberry Finn*.[12] J. G. Huneker followed Perry and Matthews in the serious view of his work. He wrote in 1899:

> Mr. Clemens is one of the most original writers America has produced and more of an artist than is generally believed. Being a humorous soul the public was slow to recognize his power in other fields. I pin my faith to 'Huckleberry Finn.' For me it is the great American novel, even if it is written for boys.[13]

Mark Twain was in many respects typical of the age whose name he coined. He was typical of its puzzling contradictions and disharmonies. He shared with Colonel Sellers dreams of great wealth. Money was his theme, but unlike Horatio Alger his endings were often bitter and disillusioning. He was defensive about art, Europe, age, tradition, culture, and bookishness. Yet he was one of the most widely travelled of his contemporaries. Full of ribaldry and profanity, he was a sensitive writer and one of the most "exquisite" of men. Travel made him the more conscious of his own limitations and threw him back upon the main affirmation of his life—a democratic faith in the value and dignity of the individual. His realism was a special blend, born of experience and frontier skepticism, schooled by such hard disciplines as the printing office of a newspaper or the pilot house of a Mississippi steamboat. But in his best books of the middle 1880's he found a successful harmony in his strain of idealism and his love of authentic reporting and local color. In his own way he portrayed a passing America with accuracy and with skill. If it was not the contemporary world of the eastern seaboard or the international set, it was a significant phase of the American experience which has remained in myth and imagination and belonged as much to the period as did the more serious fiction of James and Howells and De Forest.

After 1885 it became increasingly difficult for writers and thoughtful Americans to maintain a moderate attitude toward social problems. A change began to manifest itself in many areas of the national life which marked the decline of the earlier form of realism and transformed the ideas and tastes which we have called "Victorian." The intensification of conflicts between labor and capital, the alarming increase in strikes, the emotional response to the Haymarket "anarchists," and the tendency once more to take sides in social disputes brought about a period during the late 1880's and early 1890's which can be called "The Years of Protest." Utopian and socialistic solutions like Edward Bellamy's *Looking Backward* caught the popular fancy and liberals like Lawrence Gronlund, Richard T. Ely, and Jacob Riis proposed remedies and pointed out the seriousness of the disparities between "haves" and "havenots." In fiction the change in Howells's novels was symptomatic of the socio-economic trend of the late Eighties. In his vigorous championing of liberal causes, he became the guide and inspiration for a group of younger writers whose interests had been formed by the Populist movement and the mood of protest. But the moderate realism of Howells's best books of the mid-Eighties was not equalled in his reform novels. The plots moved more slowly, interrupted by long sermonic passages, and the characters became symbols of class distinctions. Only *A Hazard of New Fortunes* among his books of this period achieved something of the balance between a social thesis and a psychological study of character. More and more he allowed his sympathy for social betterment to color his reading of human nature.

By 1890 Henry James had lost touch with the American scene as a subject for fiction and turned to London theater for new worlds to conquer. Mark Twain, beset by personal trials and financial reverses, had grown embittered by "the damned human race" and, despite desperate efforts to recover the mood of *Huckleberry Finn*, he was not able to achieve anything like its harmony of tone and style. The critical battles in the journals between the adherents of "realism" and those of "romance" continued, but the debates grew shrill and acrimonious and produced little of the blending that had marked the earlier period. A younger generation of novelists and critics began to explore different areas of the national experience in an atmosphere which could less and less be termed "Victorian." The essential tone and quality of the earlier realism had changed and the literary world had begun to search for another and greatly altered concept of reality.

NOTES

1. A. B. Paine, *Mark Twain; A Biography* (New York, 1912), I, p. 512.

2. *Mark Twain's Letters*, ed. A. B. Paine (New York, 1917), I, p. 145.

3. "What Paul Bourget Thinks of Us," *Literary Essays* (New York, 1899), pp. 146–47.

4. *Ibid.*, p. 147.

5. Preface, Library Edition (1892) *The Hoosier Schoolmaster* (New York, 1899), pp. 6–7. See for a discussion of the relation of the American novel to regionalism and nationalism B. T. Spencer, "The New Realism and a National Literature," *Publications of the Modern Language Association*, LVI (Dec., 1941), pp. 1129–31.

6. *New England Magazine*, II, n.s. (1890), p. 243.

7. *Literary News*, IX (1888), pp. 236–37.

8. *Mark Twain's Letters*, I, p. 434.

9. See *Critic*, VI (March 28, 1885), p. 155. For a discussion of the reception of *Huckleberry Finn* cf. A. L. Vogelback, "The Publication and Reception of *Huckleberry Finn* in America," *American Literature*, XI (Nov., 1939), pp. 260–72.

10. *Century Magazine*, XXX (May, 1885), pp. 171–72.

11. *Americanisms and Briticisms* (New York, 1892), pp. 153–61.

12. *Critic*, VII (Nov. 28, 1885), p. 253.

13. *Musical Courier*, XXXVIII (June 28, 1899), p. 23.

TWENTY-NINE

AMERICAN REALISM DEFINED

Harold H. Kolb Jr.

Harold H. Kolb Jr. (1933–) received his Ph.D. from Indiana University in 1968. He has taught at the University of Virginia since 1967. In addition to *The Illusion of Life: American Realism as a Literary Form* (1969), he is the author of *A Field Guide to the Study of American Literature* (1976).

"Realism," according to the *Guide to the Study of the United States of America*, "is a semantic house of many mansions."[1] Having considered previous discussions of realism, we are now in a position to suggest a structural definition for that particular mansion which houses nineteenth-century American realism—a definition that is partially a synthesis of previous work and partially new. Identifying characteristics of the realistic writing which culminated in the mid-1880's can be found in four areas: philosophy, subject matter, morality, and style. These areas are, of course, finally inseparable, but considering each one individually gives us a convenient method for confronting the full dimensions of American realism.

The philosophy of American realism is not a philosophy in a specialized, technical sense, but rather a loosely organized and often generalized set of convictions and attitudes—an after-dinner brandy-and-cigars philosophy, rather than an epistemologically sound academic system. It is best introduced by first considering the beliefs of an earlier generation of writers, beliefs which the realists oppose and reject. In "The Poetic Principle," Poe maintains that art must reflect man's immortal search for higher beauty: "Inspired by an ecstatic prescience of the glories beyond the grave, we struggle by multiform combinations among the things and thoughts of Time to attain a portion of that Loveliness whose very elements perhaps appertain to eternity

The Illusion of Life: American Realism as a Literary Form (Charlottesville: University Press of Virginia, 1969), pp. 36–58. Reprinted by permission of the University Press of Virginia.

alone."[2] Wordsworth states that the function of art is to "exhilarate the spirit," to reflect

That most noble attribute of man . . .
That wish for something loftier, more adorned,
Than is the common aspect, daily garb,
Of human life.[3]

Many romantic writers compose variations on a theme by Emerson—that succinct statement in *Nature* which is fundamental to romantic thought on both sides of the Atlantic: "Every natural fact is a symbol of some spiritual fact."[4] Carlyle, for example, finds that "all visible things are emblems; what thou seest is not there on its own account; strictly taken, is not there at all: Matter exists only spiritually, and to represent some Idea, and *body* it forth."[5] The implications of this romantic philosophy for literature were flatly summarized by Longfellow in *Kavanagh*, in 1849: "Literature is rather an image of the spiritual world than of the physical, is it not?"[6]

Separated by a generation from the romantics and by the greater gulf of Lyell's *Principles of Geology* (1830–33), Strauss' *Leben Jesu* (1835–36, translated by George Eliot in 1846), Darwin's *Origin of Species* (1859), Mill's *Utilitarianism* (1861), and Marx' *Das Kapital* (vol. I, 1867, translated 1886), the American realists answer Longfellow's question with a resounding no. They reject not only Poe's ideas but his entire vocabulary of "supernal Beauty," "immortal instinct," "crystal springs," "sublime angels," and "elevated souls." They deny Carlyle's definition of mankind— "light-sparkles floating in the aether of Deity!"[7] The philosophy of American realism, to borrow Carlyle's term, is "descendental," or, more accurately, nontranscendental. The realists cannot accept supernaturalism, Platonic idealism, and the worlds of spirit. They do not necessarily deny the validity of such worlds; they simply ignore them as unknowable in ordinary human terms and thus irrelevant to ordinary human experience. The American realists agreed with John Stuart Mill's formulation of the utilitarian position in his *Coleridge*:

We see no ground for believing that anything can be the object of our knowledge except our experience, and what can be inferred from our experience by the analogies of experience itself; nor that there is any idea, feeling or power in the human mind, which, in order to account for it, requires that its origin should be referred to any other source. . . . There is no knowledge *a priori*; no truths cognizable by the mind's inward light, and grounded on intuitive evidence.[8]

This unidealized view of human experience has an artistic corollary. The realists believe that the purpose of art, as always, is to instruct and to please—*aut prodesse aut delectare*. But the instruction and the pleasure lie in giving shape to life's meaning by seeing into human experience, rather than seeing through it to spirit, ideal, or godhead. It is not, as Hamilton Wright Mabie claimed, "practical atheism applied to art,"[9] but rather practical agnosticism applied to art. Mabie's nineteenth-century theological bias is clear, but there has been a more recent misunderstanding of the realists' position. The philosophical aspect of realism, according to George Becker, held that "life had no meaning, no telic motion, and that man was a creature barely escaped from the level of animal behavior and driven by forces over which he had no control and in which he could discern no purpose."[10] The basic problem here is the common confusion of realism and naturalism. The two movements are related, but they must be kept separate since they have very different attitudes toward human experience and society. In the mid-1880's the realists denied idealism without embracing pessimism; they rejected the affirmations of Longfellow and Tennyson without accepting the environmental web of Frank Norris and Thomas Hardy. In their best work the realists were pragmatic, relativistic, democratic, and experimental. They were not committed to dogmatic theories or fixed formulas, insisting only that fiction be true to life, that it be interesting, that it be honest, that it be the result of a direct impression of life. In 1885, the house of fiction had "not one window, but a million."[11]

The subject matter of the American realists in the 1880's provides another basis for definition, for all writers are defined to some extent by what they write about. The realistic subject matter is derived directly from the realistic philosophy. Subjects are drawn from "our experience, and what can be inferred from our experience by the analogies of experience itself."[12] The realists write about the common, the average, the unextreme, the representative, the probable. They concern themselves with ordinary human lives seen in the context of normal social relationships. They concentrate on what people are rather than what they ought to be, on men rather than Man. Much of the fiction written in the mid-1880's is topical; the Boston reform movement, feminism, the problem of the new American businessman, the European underground revolutionary movement. Most of the fiction deals with recognizable geographic locations—Boston's Beacon Street; Hannibal, Missouri; Cairo, Illinois; London's Buckingham Palace Road; the Ponte Vecchio in Florence.

Arguing from the "Editor's Study" in *Harper's*, Howells noted the difficulty of breaking the new literary ground of realistic subject matter and the resistance that it invariably caused. He went on to quote selected sections from Emerson's "The American Scholar" and "The Poet," excerpts which constitute an accurate definition of the subject matter of American realism:

> I ask not for the great, the remote, the romantic. . . . I embrace the common; I sit at the feet of the familiar and the low. . . . Man is surprised to find that things near are not less beautiful and wondrous than things remote. . . . The perception of the worth of the vulgar is fruitful in discoveries. . . . The foolish man wonders at the unusual, but the wise man at the usual. . . . To-day always looks mean to the thoughtless; but to-day is a king in disguise. . . . Banks and tariffs, the newspaper and caucus, Methodism and Unitarianism, are flat and dull to dull people, but rest on the same foundations of wonder as the town of Troy and the temple of Delphos.[13]

Howells' quotations from Emerson were extracted with some care, as the many ellipses indicate. Emerson does embrace the common, the familiar, and the low, but he also sees these as emblems of the spiritual, as links to a higher world. Howells, of course, breaks the links and denies the emblems. What he carefully did not quote in these essays tells as much about realism, by contrast, as what he did: "Nature is a symbol"; "The near explains the far"; "The Universe is the externalization of the soul"; "Each believes himself inspired by the Divine Soul which also inspires all men"; "I think nothing is of any value in books excepting the transcendental and extraordinary"; "This is the reward; that the ideal shall be real to thee, and the impressions of the actual world shall fall like summer rain, copious, but not troublesome to thy invulnerable essence."[14]

The Emersonian vocabulary—Divine Soul, transcendental, Universe, invulnerable essence—well represents those aspects which the realists discard as subject matter. Their rejection of the transcendental thus eliminates the wild fantasies of the supernatural, the grotesque and the arabesque, the foreign and the strange, angels and devils, heroes and villains. It denies the "everlasting itch for things remote," which motivates Ishmael in the first chapter of *Moby Dick:* "I love to sail forbidden seas, and land on barbarous coasts." Instead of barbarous coasts and great leviathans of the deep, flaming letters in the sky, or miraculous voices in the night, we have a makeshift Mississippi raft, the problems of a paint manufacturer, a meeting of disheveled reformers in Boston's South End. In 1885 the proper study of mankind was man.

The realists' concern with common experience, contemporary issues, and Baedeker topography should not lead us into the trap of discussing realism in terms of photographic portrayal, statistical norms, a one-to-one correspondence with reality, or a slice of life.[15] A slice of life, like a pound of flesh, is a messy affair. Fiction in the mid-1880's is still fictitious, and James, Howells, and Mark Twain do not choose their topics from raw and unrefined experience. The realists' representation of the common experience is ultimately achieved through imaginative realization rather than reportorial or statistical method. James' short tale, "The Real Thing," treats precisely this point. The artist of the story finds that truly genteel Major and Mrs. Monarch are unsatisfactory as models for illustrations of ladies and gentlemen. The drawings of Mrs. Monarch make her seem seven feet tall; the Major is useful only for brawny giants. The real thing, for the puzzled artist, keeps coming out larger than life, and he discovers "an innate preference for the represented subject over the real one: the defect of the real one was so apt to be a lack of representation."[16]

Another qualification concerning the realists' subject matter needs to be made. The common life and the ordinary characters on which the realists presumably depend are, upon close inspection, not so common and ordinary after all. Runaway slaves, millionaires, revolutionary suicides, and princesses (even democratic ones) are somewhat exceptional. And no important character in the fiction of Henry James can be lightly accused of being ordinary. Even Huck Finn is chosen as much for his unique social position as for his common humanity. "His liberties were totally unrestricted," said Mark Twain of Huck's prototype, Tom Blankenship of Hannibal. "He was the only really independent person—boy or man—in the community."[17] It is Huck's unique freedom which makes possible both the narrative structure of the book and its criticism of contemporary life, for his freedom gives him a distance from the community which makes critical perception possible (at least for the reader, through the point of view of the naïve narrator). Floating down the Mississippi on a raft has been seen as the great American experience. How many Americans have ever done it? The realists concern themselves with characters and events which are imaginatively representative of the common experience, even though the characters and events themselves may be somewhat out of the ordinary, outside the range of the statistical norm.

This point helps to explain the inappropriateness of Gordon Haight's witty rejoinder to Howells' praise of realistic subject matter in the "Editor's Study." In the most interesting American fiction, according to Howells,

nothing happens; that is, nobody murders or debauches anybody else; there is no arson or pillage of any sort; there is not a ghost, or a ravening beast, or a hairbreadth escape, or a shipwreck, or a monster of self-sacrifice, or a lady five thousand years old in the whole course of the story.[18]

Professor Haight comments:

Despite [Howells'] insistence that realism "prefers to avoid all manner of strange coincidences and dire catastrophes," his books abound in them. Three plots turn on train wrecks, three on fires; two characters are removed by brain fever, a number by sudden sickness; two commit suicide with poison; one hero is shot, another knocked down by a horsecar, and two others killed by locomotives.[19]

Realistic subject matter does have room for the exceptional, if it is the humanly exceptional (not the superhumanly or subhumanly exceptional, as in romantic and naturalistic writing). And it should be noted that Professor Haight's list is not quite analogous to Howells'. Fires, sicknesses, and train wrecks do happen, and with somewhat greater frequency than ladies five thousand years old. On Boston's Beacon Street in 1885, horsecars were more likely to be encountered than ghosts.

The subject matter of the realists is chosen from a middle ground. They reject the romance of the gutter as well as the romance of the ideal, a point not always clearly recognized. Charles Dudley Warner, writing in 1883, stated that "it is held to be artistic to look almost altogether upon the shady and the seamy side of life, giving to this view the name of 'realism'; to select the disagreeable, the vicious, the unwholesome." Warner concluded his catalogue of realistic subject matter with an exclamation that must have swayed the lambrequins in nineteenth-century parlors; "And this is called a picture of real life! Heavens!"[20] This common opinion concerning realism can be seen in the eleventh edition of the *Encyclopaedia Britannica*, which defined the realist as one who "describes ugly things and brings out details of an unsavoury sort,"[21] a definition epigrammatized by the acid pen of the devil's lexicographer, Ambrose Bierce: "Realism, n. The art of depicting nature as it is seen by toads."[22] George Becker, tracing realism well into the twentieth century, speaks of the subject matter of the "lower social levels," a view supported by Willard Thorp (realistic characters include "servants, laborers, privates in the army, immigrants, derelicts, the lonely ones, prostitutes, inhabitants of the urban slums and the worn-out farms") and James

Colvert ("like the realists, Crane chose certain characteristic subjects and themes—slum life, war, prostitution, and alcoholism").[23]

Once again, however, we must separate realism from naturalism. The subject matter in the novels of the mid-1880's represents a *via media* between the castles of the romancers and the slums of the naturalists. The characters are essentially middle class, and the concerns of the novels are, for the most part, middle-class concerns. The realists open new areas of subject matter for fiction, but they do not open all areas. Overt sexuality, for example, was simply not possible in public American literature in the 1880's just as the bikini bathing suit was not possible on public American beaches in the nineteenth century. Even Mark Twain, who relished ribald tales and regretted that he had to modify for public printing the extravagant and gorgeous language of Jim Gillis of Jackass Gulch, spoke of fiction which poured from "Zola's sewer."[24] Howells' portraits of middle-class women and working girls—Marcia Hubbard, Zerrilla Millon Dewey, Statira Dudley, Amanda Grier—seem tame enough today, but they caused a momentous stir in their time. "How dare you speak out your beliefs as you do?" asked a letter to Howells, a letter not from Anthony Comstock or Agnes Repplier, but from the bold and masculine John William De Forest, a former combat commander of Company I of the Twelfth Connecticut Volunteers:

> You spare neither manhood nor womanhood, and especially not the latter, though it furnishes four-fifths of *our* novel-reading public. . . . Indeed I wonder in my admiration of your heroism, if you quite know what you are about. You are exposing to view the base metal and coarse clay of which nearly the whole American people is fabricated; and meantime this slag and half-baked mud is so conceited of itself, and so shop-girlishly touchy in its conceit![25]

Howells, of course, did not deal with sexuality or the lowest social levels, but he and the other realists helped to make these subjects possible for later writers. The realistic movement away from idealism, sentimentality, and romance is evolutionary: Statira Dudley and Zerrilla Dewey are a step toward Crane's Maggie and Dreiser's Carrie. The overtones of Lesbianism in *The Bostonians* are muted but unmistakable.[26] Howells and James, while not dealing directly with sex, do shatter the idealistic (yet hypocritical) nineteenth-century feminine pedestal and open up the entire question of the status of women and their relations with men. Romantic novelist Amelia Barr criticized the realists for depicting girls who were not "nice," girls who were frank, highhanded, freethinking, and contemptuous of authority, girls who rode bicycles, played tennis, and rowed boats—"altogether in accord with an epoch that travels . . . sixty miles an hour."[27] Charles Dudley Warner also condemned the realists for their portraits of "the silly and weak-minded woman, the fast and slangy girl, the *intrigante* and the 'shady.' "[28] It must have distressed Warner to find that the issue of the *Atlantic* which carried his condemnation had, as its leading piece, James' three-act dramatic version of *Daisy Miller*.

This context of nineteenth-century thought and the realists' dynamic innovations have been ignored by the shortsighted critics who condemn Howells and James (and Mark Twain, to a lesser extent) for the restricted range of their subject matter. It is the realists' extension of the subject matter previously available to fiction that has opened the door to modern literature (a door which, in recent decades, has been taken off its hinges). Such critics as Van Wyck Brooks, H. L. Mencken, Sinclair Lewis, V. L. Parrington, Granville Hicks, Maxwell Geismar, and Leslie Fiedler are suffering from the historical fallacy of judging the past by the present—a process which tends effectively to obscure both past and present.[29]

"Humor," said Mark Twain, "must not professedly teach and it must not professedly preach, but it must do both if it would live forever."[30] Howells and James would agree, and would expand the statement from humor to all fiction, for the ethical content of realistic novels is so essential that it demands a place as an integral part of the definition of realism. The morality of realism has not always been recognized. Nineteenth-century critics attacked *The Rise of Silas Lapham* as "a book whose moral tone was so unpleasantly, so hopelessly bad."[31] The Concord Library Committee stumbled into fame by calling *Adventures of Huckleberry Finn* "rough, coarse, and inelegant . . . the veriest trash" and banning the book from the library's refined, elegant, and grammatical shelves. The Library Committee was not, as is sometimes thought, simply another isolated manifestation of Massachusetts contrariness. The committee's opinion was apparently a majority one, and was seconded by such diverse publications as the *Arkansaw Traveler* ("Mark Twain's latest book . . . is vulgar and coarse") and the Springfield *Republican* (The "moral level [of Twain's books] is low, and their perusal can not be anything less than harmful").[32]

Other critics questioned the moral vision of the realists, but on different grounds. Charles F. Richardson accused realistic writing of being amoral, rather than immoral: "For the purpose of the present study it may be sufficient to say that it [realism] stands without, not within; gives no evidence of personal sympathy; seldom indulges in reflections upon the narrative it offers; leaves the reader to draw his own conclusions concerning right, wrong, progress, and remedy."[33] Richardson's charge of amorality has been repeated by some twentieth-century critics, who are often more concerned with aesthetics than with ethics. The realist's illusion of "objectivity" has led some readers to suppose that the realist "served no interest and adhered to no philosophy of social action." Or, if the realist is unable to maintain his uncommitted "objectivity," he arrives at "the delicate point at which realism ends and overt social criticism begins."[34] The charge of amorality has also been made against Henry James, on somewhat different grounds. James, it is often said, sacrifices morality on the all-consuming altar of his Art. He has substituted "psychological for ethical measurements of good and evil,"[35] although it is by no means clear what the difference is.

In spite of these criticisms, perceptive readers have long been aware of the fundamental moral orientation of American realism. Joel Chandler Harris immediately recognized that "there is not in our fictive literature a more wholesome book than 'Huckleberry Finn.' . . . We are taught [by it] the lesson of honesty, justice, and mercy."[36] Unlike many contemporary critics, Harris realized that the ethical force of *Huckleberry Finn* and the other realistic novels was not based upon external spiritual forces but upon the confrontation of human beings in a humanly created social environment. The realists' morality is intrinsic, integral, relativistic; it arises from the characters and the narrative action, rather than being superimposed upon them. Significant fiction has always been ethical, and the realists come to rather conventional conclusions about the qualities men must have in dealing with each other—honesty, justice, mercy, love. What is new in 1885 is that these qualities are no longer sought in an external, transcendental system of values. Realistic protagonists are forced to work out their own codes of behavior, appropriate to their individual circumstances.

Howells, James, and Mark Twain do not professedly teach or preach. They do not step to the front of the stage and tell the reader how to interpret their puppets. On the other hand, the realists do not ignore interpretation. Since the moral arises from the fabric of the fictional experience, interpretation is built into the narrative. The reader makes the interpretation for himself, but if he is a careful reader he makes the interpretation that the author desires. The reader's freedom to choose, like the realist's "objectivity," is largely an illusion.

Alfred Kazin has remarked that Howells' morality, like Tolstoy's, meant "the relation of man to his society."[37] The observation is valid for all the realists, and the fiction of the mid-1880's explores the relations between man and society in a variety of ways. *Adventures of Huckleberry Finn* contains a double pattern: the condemnation of religious, political, and social opinions which are held by fools and exploited by knaves and the affirmation of brotherhood through the relation of Huck and Jim. Huck faces a dilemma common in realistic fiction. When he finds that Jim has been sold back into slavery by the King, Huck is forced to decide between a fixed code of public morality and an inner ethical impulse—a conflict which he resolves at the climax of *Huckleberry Finn*:

> I was a trembling, because I'd got to decide, forever, betwixt two things, and I knowed it. I studied a minute, sort of holding my breath, and then says to myself: "All right, then, I'll *go* to hell."[38]

Huck chooses hell and humanity; his sound heart triumphs over the conscience which has been deformed by a morally corrupt society.[39]

Huck's sound heart can be heard beating in another of Mark Twain's works published in 1885, "The Private History of a Campaign That Failed," which tells of Sam Clemens' two-week fling at soldiering in the summer of 1861. Like most of Twain's autobiographical writings, the "Campaign" has only a casual acquaintance with historical accuracy; but whether fact or fiction, the central episode of the piece, and Twain's treatment of it, is revealing. The holiday spirit of the boys in Twain's company is broken when, dazed with fear, they shoot an unarmed stranger who happens by their camp at night. The death preys on young Clemens:

> I could not get rid of it. I could not drive it away, the taking of that unoffending life seemed such a wanton thing. And it seemed an epitome of war; that all war must be just that—the killing of strangers against whom you feel no personal ani-

mosity; strangers whom, in other circumstances, you would help if you found them in trouble, and who would help you if you needed it.[40]

This taste of war added a new activity to Twain's growing list of publicly sanctioned insanities and immoralities and ended his brief experience as a Confederate irregular. He soon lit out for the Territory with his brother Orion.

Like Huck Finn, Silas Lapham struggles with a difficult and lonely moral decision for which he has no precedent, and, like Huck, he wins a moral victory. Lapham's final rise is an ethical one, climaxed when he refuses to sell his western milling property, which he knows to be of little value, to English buyers. This decision is made difficult by Lapham's cascading series of financial disasters and more difficult by the apparent dishonesty of the Englishmen, who represent "rich and charitable" investors who will not feel the loss of the money which could save Lapham. A further loophole is provided by Colonel Lapham's ex-partner Rogers, who offers to serve as a middleman in the purchase and thus relieve Lapham of any legal responsibility. He is tempted and confused, but Lapham resists the offer until it is no longer feasible. Morally strengthened by this victory of hesitation, he is then easily able to refuse to sell the paint works in Vermont to a New York agent who is unaware of the declining market value of Lapham's mineral paint. Silas Lapham's fall from business, from wealth, and from Beacon Street is complete. He retires to his Vermont farm, and taking his poverty with better grace than his success, closes his story with a laconic but sincere testimony to morality: "I don't know as I should always say it paid; but if I done it, and the thing was to do over again, right in the same way, I guess I should have to do it."[41]

Howells' two other novels in the period also demonstrate ethical concerns. In *Indian Summer* Theodore Colville achieves an amiable moral victory over his illusions of youth and is conventionally rewarded with the hand of Mrs. Bowen, a widow who, like Colville, is enjoying the agreeable weather in the afternoon of life. But underneath the placid surface and the pleasant ironies of *Indian Summer* is a tough-minded attack on conventional romantic notions and heroic self-sacrifice, favorite Howellsian targets. Colville's dishonest dream of himself lies shattered along the banks of the Arno, just as that corrupt steamboat, the *Walter Scott*, is wrecked along the Mississippi in *Huckleberry Finn*.

In *The Minister's Charge; or, The Apprenticeship of Lemuel Barker* Howells develops another moral theme which he uses for the rest of his career—complicity.[42] The Reverend David Sewell discovers that he is responsible for Lemuel Barker, a Willoughby Pastures boy who is accidentally introduced to the complexities of Boston life by Sewell. Barker himself learns that he is responsible for Statira Dudley, a working girl whom he gradually transcends in his social rise. All of the proper Bostonians learn that they cannot insulate themselves from the swindlers on the Common, the line-up at the city police station, and the indigent tramps at the Wayfarers' Lodge. And the reader is enlightened by a series of discussions on complicity which culminate in Howells' recapitulation of Sewell's sermon:

No one for good or for evil, for sorrow or joy, for sickness or health, stood apart from his fellows, but each was bound to the highest and the lowest by ties that centered in the hand of God. No man, he said, sinned or suffered to himself alone; his error and his pain darkened and afflicted men who never heard of his name. If a community was corrupt, if an age was immoral, it was not because of the vicious, but the virtuous who fancied themselves indifferent spectators.[43]

Howells' three novels in the mid-1880's not only show a concern for ethics, they also demonstrate a pattern of moral development, a pattern which accurately reflects Howells' continually deepening thought. *Indian Summer*, written first, contains the lesson that we must live honestly with ourselves. *Silas Lapham* extends the point, for Lapham discovers that honesty to self demands honesty to others. And the reader of *The Minister's Charge* learns the fundamental Christian doctrine that honesty is not enough, that we must involve ourselves with mankind. The Reverend Mr. Sewell comes to realize, somewhat to his surprise, that even a Boston minister is a piece of the continent, a part of the main.

In the closing pages of *Silas Lapham*, Mr. Sewell (one of several peripatetic characters who appear in different Howells novels) observes that "we can trace the operation of evil in the physical world . . . but I'm more and more puzzled about it in the moral world. There its course is often so very obscure. . . . " Henry James would thoroughly agree, for, characteristically, the morality of his novels is less obvious than that of Howells, but no less central to his artistic purpose. *The Bostonians* is a novel without a hero, and emphatically a novel without a heroine. There is no moral mouthpiece, no center of reference, for Basil Ransom is no more "right" than the Bostonians to whom he is a foil. The moral, as usual for James, must be drawn by inference, by implication—ultimately, by character. With the exception of Verena Tarrant, the malleable prize, all of the characters, whether reformers or reactionaries, Northerners or Southerners, are motivated by selfishness. The main conflict, that of Basil and Olive over Verena, is one of will rather than of love, and each wants her for his own satisfaction. Selah Tarrant, like Hollingsworth, his spiritual ancestor in Hawthorne's *Blithedale Romance*, is a "moralist without moral sense,"[44] who rents his daughter to Olive on a yearly basis. The reform movement itself, with its sacrifices and its martyrdoms, is seen as an exercise in ego. The entire group is transfixed on the shrill point of Olive's despairing concern for herself: "I shall see nothing but shame and ruin!" The novel's coda is provided, ironically, by self-seeking Mrs. Tarrant: "It's the most horrible, wicked, immoral selfishness I ever heard in my life!"[45]

In *The Princess Casamassima* the reformers are changed to revolutionaries, and shame and ruin of a different sort stalk the novel's anguished protagonist, Hyacinth Robinson. Intellectually and emotionally torn, Hyacinth cannot carry out his mysterious assignment. His revolutionary convictions are not strong enough to overcome his morality, and unable to assassinate the duke, Hyacinth shoots himself instead, through the heart.

In spite of the variety of these six works, their underlying moral orientation is clear. In addition, they have many ethical points in common. Both *Indian Summer* and *The Bostonians* show that self-sacrifice is often self-aggrandizement. Complicity is the official lesson of *The Minister's Charge*, but it applies as well to *Huckleberry Finn*. James' portraits of selfishness are reverse images of the Howellsian doctrine of complicity, for the preoccupation with self precludes involvement with others. Howells, James, and Mark Twain agree that we fully become human beings only when we escape the prison of the ego. This affirmation of basic human values should exculpate the realists from charges of immorality and amorality, although such moral themes are not new, by any means. Huck's raft was preceded by a good many vessels, the *Pequod* among them, for the lesson of the monkey-rope is as applicable to Huck and Jim as it is to Ishmael and Queequeg, even though Twain, characteristically, refuses to editorialize or overtly symbolize the relationship. What the realists contribute in their discussion of human values is the emphasis on the complexity of moral choice and the necessity of individual decision in a human context, unassisted by external spiritual forces. And these values are dramatized rather than sermonized in the novels of the mid-1880's (with the minor exception of the sermons of the Reverend Mr. Sewell, which are, after all, occupationally justified), for the realist refuses to "stand about in his scene, talking it over with his hands in his pockets, interrupting the action, and spoiling the illusion."[46]

The relation of moral content to dramatization, theme to technique, leads us to the fourth significant category which can be used to define American realism in the 1880's—style. Realistic style is the vehicle which carries realistic philosophy, subject matter, and morality. It is the link between the theory and its artistic application, between the idea and the narrative, which converts concepts into patterns of words, paragraphs, and chapters.

There is a curious irony concerning discussions of realistic style. In the wake of the New Criticism, scholars are virtually unanimous in their statements of the significance of the realists' technique. There is an impressive chorus of critical comment which sings the importance of style in realism. Ian Watt differentiates between "realism of assessment" and "realism of presentation" and states that "the novel's realism does not reside in the kind of life it presents, but in the way it presents it."[47] Marcus Cunliffe notes that "with Mark Twain, *content*—like Western life—had a mongrel incongruity; but *form* began the lineage that has led to Hemingway."[48] Gordon Haight claims that "realism is determined less by choice of material than by intention and method of treatment."[49] Similar views are held by Wallace Stegner ("realism of *method*"), H. Wayne Morgan ("By realism, I mean simply a literary technique"), Lars Ahnebrink ("a manner and method of composition"), L. W. Smith ("Realism is willing to remain a literary method"), James D. Hart ("Realistic technique continues to be dominant"), and George Becker ("The perennial phase . . . is what may be called realism of method").

Having sung these brief introductory anthems, the voices stop. For many critics, the mere statement that style is an important part of realism is enough, and they fail to discuss what that style is and how it operates. Others go further, and discuss objective presentation, realistic details, and the vernacular, but they do not take full advantage of realistic technique as a useful handle for definition.[50] The following chapters will consider in detail the main aspects of nineteenth-century American realistic style—its antiomniscient point of view, its complexity and ambiguity, its concern with character, and its tendency to be imagistic rather than symbolic. Such emphasis on technique is, in many respects, the best introduction to realistic fiction, for the realists strongly believed in (and skillfully practiced) the concept of organic form, the appropriateness of technique to subject. Thus style can be a useful key in unlocking the novels and in analyzing the similarities and differences between realism and other kinds of writing.

Recent decades have too often seen the exploitation of the stylistic approach and its degeneration into metaphor mongering and syntax torture, but such excesses do not negate the method. A consideration of technique, like every critical approach, is justified only if it leads to a deeper understanding of the work at hand. For the fiction of the mid-1880's, stylistic analysis is useful both in the consideration of individual works and in defining the movement as a whole, since style is ultimately the means of embodying the realistic sensibility in literary works of art. From this point on, then, our purpose, as Milton observed over three centuries ago, will be "not to make verbal curiosities the end, that were a toylsom vanity, but to be an interpreter & relater of the best and sagest things."[51]

NOTES

1. Washington: Library of Congress, 1960, p. 64.

2. *The Complete Poems and Stories of Edgar Allan Poe*, ed. A. H. Quinn and E. H. O'Neill (New York: Alfred A. Knopf, 1951), II, 1026. In an adjacent passage Poe considers, and rejects the realistic sensibility: "He who shall simply sing, with however glowing enthusiasm, or with however vivid a truth of description, of the sights, and sounds, and odors, and colors, and sentiments, which greet *him* in common with all mankind—he, I say, has yet failed to prove his divine title."

3. *The Prelude* (1850 ed.), ed. Ernest De Selincourt (London: Oxford University Press, 1926), pp. 141, 167 (bk. V., lines 108, 573, 575–77).

4. *Selections from Ralph Waldo Emerson*, ed. Stephen E. Whicher (Boston: Houghton Mifflin Co., 1957), p. 32.

5. *Sartor Resartus, The Works of Thomas Carlyle* (London: Chapman & Hall, 1896), I, 57 (bk. I, ch. 11).

6. *Henry Wadsworth Longfellow: Prose Works* (Boston: Houghton, Mifflin & Co., 1904), II, 426. There is not space here to enter the controversy concerning the definition of romanticism—that is another war. But if the views of Peckham, Lovejoy, Wellek, Abrams, *et al.* are taken together, a central point does emerge. By almost every definition, romanticism involves a belief in a higher, transcendent, spiritual reality, which can inspire and transform men's lives. The realists cannot accept such superlunar reality, and in this respect, perhaps more than others, it is appropriate to speak of an opposition between romanticism and realism.

7. *Sartor Resartus*, p. 43 (bk. I, ch. 8). Scotty Briggs well expressed the realists' reaction to Carlyle's definition in his reply to the elegant statements of an Eastern clergyman: "You ruther hold over me, pard. I reckon I can't call that hand. Ante and pass the buck" (*Roughing It, The Writings of Mark Twain* [New York: Harper & Bros., 1929], IV, 45).

8. *On Bentham and Coleridge*, introd. F. R. Leavis (New York: Harper & Bros., 1962), pp. 114, 109.

9. "A Typical Novel," *Andover Review*, IV (November 1885), 426. The *Andover Review* was subtitled *A Religious and Theological Monthly* and was edited by the faculty of the Andover Theological Seminary. Mabie was an editor for the *Christian Union*.

10. "Realism: An Essay in Definition," *Modern Language Quarterly*, X (June 1949), 192.

11. Henry James, Preface to *The Portrait of a Lady*, in *The Art of the Novel: Critical Prefaces*, ed. R. P. Blackmur (New York: Charles Scribner's Sons, 1934), p. 46. This preface and "The Art of Fiction" (1884) contain James' statements concerning the "direct impression of life." The latter is the best statement of the realists' belief in variety, freedom, and experimentation in fiction.

12. *On Bentham and Coleridge*, p. 114.

13. LXXV (October 1887), 803.

14. *Selections from Emerson*, pp. 78, 80, 227, 236, 240.

15. Cf. C. D. Warner's "Modern Fiction," *Atlantic Monthly*, LI (April 1883) 464 ("photographic fidelity to nature"); William F. Thrall and Addison Hibbard's *A Handbook to Literature*, rev. and enl. by C. Hugh Holman (New York: Odyssey Press, 1960), p. 398 ("a one-to-one correspondence between the representation and the subject"); and Becker's "Realism: An Essay in Definition," p. 187 (the realist "keeps his eye on a statistical norm").

16. *The Complete Tales of Henry James*, ed. Leon Edel (Philadelphia: J. B. Lippincott Co., 1962–64), VIII, 237.

17. *The Autobiography of Mark Twain*, ed. Charles Neider (New York: Harper & Row, 1959), p. 73.

18. *Harper's Monthly*, LXXXI (October 1890), 804.

19. "Realism Defined: William Dean Howells," *Literary History of the United States: History*, ed. R. E. Spiller et al., 3d ed., rev. (New York: Macmillan Co., 1963) p. 894. Cf. Oscar W. Firkins, *William Dean Howells* (New York: Russell & Russell, 1963; orig. pub. 1924), pp. 230–232.

20. "Modern Fiction," p. 471. It is difficult to reconcile this essay with Warner's collaboration with Mark Twain on *The Gilded Age*.

21. XXII, 941.

22. *The Devil's Dictionary* (New York: Hill & Wang, 1957, p. 152. Orig. pub., in part, as *The Cynic's Word Book* in 1906.

23. Becker, "Realism: An Essay in Definition," p. 191; Thorp, Introduction to *Great Short Works of American Realism* (New York: Harper & Row, 1968), p. xiv; Colvert, Introduction to *Great Short Works of Stephen Crane* (New York: Harper & Row, 1968), p. vii.

24. *Mark Twain: Life as I Find It*, ed. Charles Neider (Garden City, N.Y.: Hanover House, 1961), p. 214. Private printing was another matter; witness *1601*.

25. James F. Light, *John William De Forest* (New York: Twayne Publishers, 1965), p. 166. De Forest himself had difficulty in finding publishers for his candid fiction.

26. James once complained that "we grope in darkness—that airless gloom of false delicacy in which the light of life quite goes out" ("The Novel of Dialect; W. D. Howells," *Literature* [9 July 1898]; quoted in *Henry James: The American Essays*, ed. Leon Edel [New York: Vintage Books, 1956], p. 252).

27. "The Modern Novel," *North American Review*, CLIX (November 1894), 598. Mrs. Barr sighed for those good old-fashioned girls "who thought their parents infallible and who were reverent Church-women—the girls who were so shrinkingly modest, and yet so brave in great emergencies—the girls who were so fully accomplished and so beautiful, and who yet had

no higher ambition than to be the dearly loved wife of a noble-hearted man and the good house-mother of happy children."

28. LI (April 1883), 471.

29. These opinions are by no means limited to the more outspoken (if not outrageous) critics. Professor Samuel Chew, for example, is convinced that James' restricted subject matter has doomed his literary reputation: "With the disappearance of his 'world' the books . . . are likely to become, save in the estimation of a small and diminishing band of devotees, mere documents in the history of a phase of European sensibility almost as remote from today's actualities as is the *Carte du Tendre*" (in *A Literary History of England*, ed. A. C. Baugh [New York: Appleton-Century-Crofts, 1948], p. 1551). That small band of devotees seems to consist of avid book buyers, for there are currently one hundred thirty-four volumes and collections of James' works in print, according to Bowker's *Books in Print* (1967). The charges of avoiding experience which have been leveled against James blatantly ignore *The Bostonians* and *The Princess Casamassima*. Moreover, they ignore James' entire commitment to experience, summarized by his prefatory highlighting of the essence of *The Ambassadors*: "Live all you can; it's a mistake not to." And it is James who has drawn the classic portrait of the man who refused experience—John Marcher in "The Beast in the Jungle." The fact that James uses a Hemingway metaphor of hairy-chested experience—the final, fatal spring of the hideous beast—to capture Marcher's realization of his tragedy of nothingness, well expresses the depth of James' irony and his art.

30. *Autobiography*, ed. Neider, p. 298. Characteristically, Mark Twain goes on to deflate his own rhetoric: "By forever, I mean thirty years."

31. "Novel-Writing as a Science," *Catholic World*, LXII (November 1885), 279.

32. Arthur L. Vogelback, "The Publication and Reception of *Huckleberry Finn* in America," *American Literature*, XI (November 1939), 269–271.

33. *American Literature: 1607–1885* (New York: G. P. Putnam's Sons, 1888), II, 431–32. The leader of the realistic school was Henry James, according to Richardson. Mark Twain is almost totally ignored in the two-volume study, and if Richardson read *Huckleberry Finn*, he didn't admit it.

34. Becker, "Realism: An Essay in Definition," p. 188.

35. Robert E. Spiller, *The Cycle of American Literature* (New York: New American Library, 1957), p. 135.

36. *Critic*, VII (28 November 1885), 253. Quoted by Vogelback, "Publication of *Huckleberry Finn*," p. 271.

37. *On Native Grounds* (Garden City, N.Y.: Doubleday & Co., 1956), p. viii.

38. *Adventures of Huckleberry Finn* (New York: Charles L. Webster & Co., 1885), p. 272.

39. Twain once referred to *Huckleberry Finn* as "a book of mine where a sound heart & a deformed conscience come into collision & conscience suffers defeat" (Notebook no. 28a [I], TS, p. 35 [1895], Mark Twain Papers, University of California Library, Berkeley); quoted in *Adventures of Huckleberry Finn*, ed. Henry Nash Smith (Boston: Houghton Mifflin Co., 1958), p. xvi. Huck's decision is totally serious, but it suggests an idea that runs through much of Mark Twain's lighter work: Heaven for climate; hell for society.

40. *Century Magazine*, XXXI (December 1885), p. 203. In 1909 Thomas Hardy expressed the same thought in "The Man He Killed," a poem based upon a remarkably similar dramatic situation:

"Yes; quaint and curious war is!
    You shoot a fellow down

You'd treat if met where any bar is,
    Or help to half-a-crown."

(Reprinted with permission of The Macmillan Company from *Collected Poems* by Thomas Hardy, p. 269. Copyright 1925 by The Macmillan Company.)

41. *The Rise of Silas Lapham, Century Magazine*, XXX (August 1885), 526.

42. The word "complicity" has an almost exclusively negative meaning in the twentieth century, probably because of its use in legal terminology and its guilt-by-association relationship to "accomplice." *Webster's New World Dictionary* gives "partnership in wrongdoing." Howells, of course, with an eye to the Latin root ("weave together"), means partnership in mankind.

43. *The Minister's Charge, Century Magazine*, XXXIII (December 1886), 191. Privately, out of his pulpit, Sewell puts his doctrine more simply: "Everybody seems to be tangled up with everybody else" (p. 191).

44. *Century Magazine*, XXIX (April 1885), 907.

45. *Ibid.*, XXXI (January 1886), 341; XXXI (February 1886), 597.

46. "Editor's Study," *Harper's Monthly*, LXXIX (November 1889), 967.

47. *The Rise of the Novel* (Berkeley, Calif.: University of California Press, 1962), pp. 290–91.

48. *The Literature of the United States* (Baltimore: Penguin Books, 1954), p. 169.

49. "Realism Defined: William Dean Howells," *Literary History of the U.S.: History*, p. 894.

50. There is as little critical agreement about the meaning of the word "style" (and such terms as form, technique, structure, and texture) as there is concerning realism. For the purposes of this discussion and the chapters to follow, style is synonymous with form and technique. It is used in the broad sense defined by Mark Schorer in his discussion of technique: "Modern criticism has shown us that to speak of content as such is not to speak of art at all, but of experience; and that it is only when we speak of the *achieved* content, the form, the work of art as a work of art, that we speak as critics. The difference between content, or experience, and achieved content, or art, is technique. When we speak of technique, then, we speak of nearly everything. For technique is the means by which the writer's experience, which is his subject matter, compels him to attend to it; technique is the only means he has of discovering, exploring, developing his subject, of conveying its meaning, and finally, of evaluating it. . . . In this sense, everything is technique which is not the lump of experience itself" ("Technique as Discovery," *Hudson Review*, I [Spring 1948], 67, 69). Cf. M. H. Abrams: "Style . . . is how a speaker or writer says whatever he says" (*A Glossary of Literary Terms* [New York: Holt, Rinehart & Winston, 1957], p. 91).

51. *The Reason of Church-Government Urg'd against Prelaty* (1641), *The Works of John Milton* (New York: Columbia University Press, 1931), III, pt. 1, 236.

THIRTY

"REALISM"

Toward a Definition

Edwin H. Cady

Edwin H. Cady (1917–) received his Ph.D. from the University of Wisconsin in 1943 and has held teaching positions at Syracuse University (1946–59), Indiana University (1959–73), and Duke University (1973–1987), where he was Mellon Professor in the Humanities. A major interpreter of late nineteenth century American literature and culture, Cady's publications include *The Gentleman in America: A Literary Study in American Culture* (1949), a two-volume biography of William Dean Howells (1956, 1958), *Stephen Crane* (1962), and a collection of essays, *The Light of Common Day: Realism in American Fiction* (1971).

The face of the water, in time, became a wonderful book—a book that was a dead language to the uneducated passenger, but which told its mind to me without reserve, delivering its most cherished secrets as clearly as if it uttered them with a voice. . . . There never was so wonderful a book written by man; never one whose interest was so absorbing, so unflagging, so sparklingly renewed with every re-perusal. . . . In truth, the passenger who could not read this book saw nothing but all manner of pretty pictures in it, painted by the sun and shaded by the clouds, whereas to the trained eye these were not pictures at all, but the grimmest and most dead-earnest of reading-matter.

Now when I had mastered the language of this water, and had come to know every trifling feature that bordered the great river as familiarly as I knew the letters of the alphabet, I had made a valuable acquisition. But I had lost something, too. I had lost something which could never be restored to

The Light of Common Day: Realism in American Fiction (Bloomington: Indiana University Press, 1971), pp. 3–22. Reprinted by permission of Edwin H. Cady.

me while I lived. All the grace, the beauty, the poetry, had gone out of the majestic river!

—Mark Twain, "Old Times on the Mississippi,"
1875.

"But it is the business of the novel—"

"Ah! said the other man.

"It is the business of the novel to picture the daily life in the most exact terms possible, with an absolute and clear sense of proportion. As a usual thing, I think, people have absolutely no sense of proportion. Their noses are tight against life, you see. They perceive mountains where there are no mountains, but frequently a great peak appears no larger than a rat trap. An artist sees a dog down the street—well, his eye instantly relates the dog to its surroundings. The dog is proportioned to the buildings and the trees. Whereas, many people can conceive of that dog's tail resting upon a hill top."

"You have often said that the novel is a perspective," observed the other man.

"A perspective, certainly. It is perspective made for the benefit of people who have no true use of their eyes. The novel, in its real meaning, adjusts the proportions. It preserves the balances."

— W. D. Howells as quoted by Stephen Crane,
"Fears Realists Must Wait. An Interesting talk with
William Dean Howells." New York Times, October
28, 1894.

The house of fiction has in short not one window, but a million—a number of possible windows not to be reckoned, rather; every one of which has been pierced, or is still pierceable, in its vast front, by the need of the individual vision and by the pressure of the individual will. These apertures, of dissimilar shape and size, hang so, all together, over the human scene that we might have expected of them a greater sameness of report than we find. They are but windows at the best, mere holes in a dead wall, disconnected, perched aloft; they are not hinged doors opening straight upon life. But they have this mark of their own that at each of them stands a figure with a pair of eyes, or at least with a field-glass, which forms, again and again, for observations, a unique instrument, insuring to the person making use of it an impression distinct from every other. He and his neighbors are watching the same show, but one seeing more where the other sees less, one seeing black where the other sees white, one seeing big where the other sees small, one seeing coarse where the other sees fine. And so on, and so on; there is fortunately no saying on what, for the particular pair of eyes, the window may not open; "fortunately" by reason, precisely, of this incalculability of range. The spreading field, the human scene, is the "choice of subject"; the pierced aperture, either

*broad or balconied or slit-like and low-browed, is the "literary form";
but they are, singly or together, as nothing without the posted presence of
the watcher—without, in other words, the consciousness of the artist. Tell me
what the artist is, and I will tell you of what he has been conscious.*

— Henry James, Preface to The Portrait of a Lady,
1908.

The concern common to the foregoing statements by principal American realists is concern for vision. They point toward a literature which rests upon a particular theory of vision. In a preliminary way, I should define it as: Realism, a theory of Common Vision. Though it would take a very long time to elaborate the helpful qualifications of that stark phrase, at this point I should like to emphasize the useful ambiguity of "common." It may mean "common" as average, ordinary, normal, democratic. It may also mean "common" as shared, general, normative, perhaps even universal.

The aim here is to make a beginning toward lending content to "realism" and "realistic." The hope is to enrich the vocabulary of literary discussion by adding precision to key terms. By examining a historical moment of self-proclaimed realism, perhaps we can move from the verifiable ideas and attitudes of "a realism" toward more abstract and generally applicable meanings. The realism I know best is that of American literature of roughly 1860–1910, and I shall therefore take my examples from it.

Historically that realism appears to exhibit six major characteristics. It began as a negative movement with (1) the customary features of a literary revolt and (2) a new notion of reality from which to be critical of its past. It developed (3) a positive method and content, and (4) its own ethical outlook. It (5) involved itself in a major, but losing, battle for American public taste. Finally (6), in its latest stages it turned toward the psychologism which was to succeed it.

We have become accustomed in the past two centuries to the general pattern of a literary revolt. First comes ennui with the worn conventions of overpopular fashions. Yearning for newness leads to youthful cries of back to nature, and Young Turks riot in the pages of little magazines. Something like that happened with the brilliant generation of Americans who became more or less thirty years old in 1870. They were fed up with romanticism. They expended magnificent resources of wit and creative energy to burlesque it out of public countenance. They defined their dearest wishes for expression and artistic success in contradiction to it. They welcomed eagerly a newness which promised to set them free.

To say it briefly, intellectual newness came to this generation in that form of nineteenth-century scientism ordinarily associated with the man Robert Frost once called "John L." Darwin. For this middle generation of American Darwinists, exposed in youth to the old idealism, Thomas Huxley's agnosticism seemed the properest response to the newness. It led them toward a vaguely positivistic factualism. And, insofar as they were writers, it reinforced their ennui to create a burningly reductive antiromanticism. This "negative realism" turned easily to the satiric reduction of romantic, Dionysian egoism and glamor. Henry James may, as he perceived to his cha-grin, have "cut the cable" in *The American* and let the balloon of experience float away into the romantic "disconnected and uncontrolled." But in *The Portrait of a Lady* he was soon engaged in the realist's joyous game of shooting down romantic balloons, piercing them through to let the gassy hot air out and drop them back to earth. A like effect was the aim of Mark Twain's unending campaign against "Sir Walter Scottism." Young William Lyon Phelps, interviewing Howells, reported that he never saw a man laugh so consumedly as Howells while numbering the follies of romance. Howells once described the zest of critical warfare as the fun of "banging the Babes of romance about."

The serious side of their antiromantic attitude showed in what became the human-ism of these realists. One can distinguish the realist from the romanticist on the one side and the naturalist on the other by precisely this distinction. The romantic, in the long run, is concerned with the ideal, the transcendent, the superhuman. The natu-ralist is concerned with vast forces, heredity and environment, a world of brute chance, with what we share of animality, with ultimate reduction, the subhuman. As against the romantic, the realist was certainly reductive. There is type significance in the fact that the fathers of Howells and James were Swedenborgians. Both sons had been taught to believe in a double vision according to the doctrine of "correspon-dence": above every physical existence there hovered spiritual significance, an angel, an essence, an eternal destiny. As agnostics, both in time felt compelled to blot tran-scendence out from the realm of intellectual fact. Their vision fell from an upward to a level plane where it focused upon man and his life in the world.

Such humanism produced important technical, that is literary, as well as meta-physical and ethical effects. It led realists to deemphasize plot: for them character, the simple, separate person, came to count; not flashing action or terrific fable. By the same token, literary emotional and sentimental heights, what Howells was to call "ef-fectism," were cut down. Obviously it would seem false to make believe that nonsub-lime people should pretend to superhuman emotions. In realistic hands, the tools of the novelist would be devoted to the main end of bodying forth characters in their habits as they lived. As a corollary there came a shift in their method to what might be called the imploding symbol, to symbols which functioned to intensify inwardly the total effect of a novel, which did not refer outside the novel to general meaning. A second corollary became an emphasis upon contemporaneousness. The historical novel came to be thought a psychological anomaly.

As is already apparent, no serious writer could have rested in mere negations. Bur-lesquing romance went well in a humor-mad age. But serious literature required a "positive realism," methods developed to express and present the new vision of the common man in his world. The realists' favorite positive technique became what they called the "dramatic method." It demanded the suppression of the "author" from his scene in the novel as the playwright was excluded from all drama except that of "ro-mantic irony" with its deliberately suicidal destruction of illusion. It demanded the creation of "transparent" narrators who seemed never to intrude between the reader and his vision of the characters, who spoke, when "scenes" and "pictures" could not simply be presented, in an unobtrusively "middle" voice. It regarded plot as the account of a breaking in upon and subsequent retreat from an instant of that seamless continuity which is life and so, once more, suppressed plot as much as editors and public would permit.

Devotion to the dramatic method affected symbolism and "effectism," as has been said. But perhaps its most fateful impulse was that toward the development of the theory of the novel. At the beginning of the realists' period, novelistic theory was cruder than neoclassical theory of tragedy. By the period's end, the famous prefaces of Henry James had presented a thoroughly sophisticated theory from which a serious young novelist could derive everything he might need. The heart of that contribution, of course, lay in the development (by, incidentally, a whole generation of major practitioners in a huge, international school) of the techniques and theory of control of fictional narrative through control of "point of view." Novelists so preoccupied with problems of vision were peculiarly prepared to contribute to an understanding of point of view.

With their scorn for the romantically unique, intense, or superhuman, and with their humanistic concern for persons, the American realists sympathized with democracy. Realism as democracy became a significant feature of the literary movement. Increasingly, the writers concentrated on the commonness of the lives of common men. They thought the common significant because it was fresh to literature (that is, never really done before), because it was intrinsically real, and because it was uniquely important from the "universal" side of the implication of "common." They were led in turn to reinterpret the American Dream and use the language of Emerson and of Whitman without transcendental reference. The realists dreamed not of "the American Adam" but the superiority of the vulgar. When Matthew Arnold foresaw the ultimate damnation of democracy in the absence of distinction from America, Howells rejoiced. If a nation, he remarked, could produce Emerson and Hawthorne, Lincoln, Grant, and Mark Twain and still escape distinction, there was true hope for it. Precisely the same attitudes Twain immortalized in certain adventures of Huck Finn and of Hank Morgan, the Connecticut Yankee. And, after his fashion; Henry James expressed cognate perceptions in portraits of that most contemptible of men, the Europeanized American.

The evolution of the travel book and of the perceptions of cultural relativity which the practice of travel writing engendered in the writers helped give rise to realism, and thereafter a natural concern of the realist was the international theme. Henry James on the Europeanized American, Howells's exploration of the "conventional unconventional" conflict, and Twain's transmutation of the frontier humorist's war against the Eastern snob all came to the same point. Of necessity, the realist fought snobbery and factitious aristocracy. In doing so he rang every imaginable change upon the theme of the Innocent Abroad. We are far from having exhausted the meaning inherent in the famous opposed curves of the attitudes of James and Twain toward American values, early Twain against early James and late against late. And Howells, sharing with and often anticipating both, arrived at his visions of Tolstoi and Altruria in a fascinating kind of mediation between them.

A fourth characteristic of this American realism was its moral vision. As one may see in the familiar writings of Howells and James—*The Rise of Silas Lapham*, "The Beast in the Jungle"—essential to their moral vision was an active disbelief in the health or safety of romantic individualism, of Dionysian self-assertion. The same sense gives resonance to Huck Finn's famous decision to go to hell for Nigger Jim. Conformity to the code of Tom Sawyer's misshapen "civilization" would have brought Huck the sensations of "salvation" for his "ornery" soul and the comfort of self-respect for his "low-down" and outcast character. He had almost chosen respectable self-identity and the sanction to stand upright in an individualistic culture. Instead, he chose damnation: that is, solidarity (as Edward Bellamy would call his religion beyond egotism) or "complicity," as Howells repeatedly termed it, with Jim—in hell, if necessary. A like self-sacrifice accords Jim his climactic meed of heroism when he steps out of hiding, presumably into bondage again if not death by torture, when the frantic doctor calls for aid to wounded Tom Sawyer.

These were the attitudes, consciously antiromantic, which led Stephen Crane to conclude that, "The final wall of the wise man's thought . . . is Human Kindness of course." Their reduction (at least in nasal altitude) of morality from sublimity to solidarity made the common vision appear essential to a right grasp of life. Therefore Howells announced that a bad novel was a school of crime. And Hjalmar Hjorth Boyesen, with Scandinavian solemnity, backed him up by arguing that "romance" deprives its devotees of "sound standards of judgement," whereas realism reveals "the significance of common facts and events . . . the forces that govern the world . . . and the logic of life."

Their moral vision reinforced the realists' affinities for democracy and contemporaneousness and brought them toward effective insights into the human problems of the historically unique industrial culture forming around them. Those insights stimulated their alliances with the growing sentiment of reform. The preservation and extension of democracy, Populism, Progressivism, Nationalism (Bellamy's, that is), unions and the labor movement, socialism, anti-imperialism, and, perhaps most permanently, a long-continuing critical examination of the American Business Mind, occupied in various ways much of the thought and creative inquiry of the American realists as their movement matured. Even Henry James, most obviously with *The Princess Casamassima* and "The Jolly Corner," took his part.

Of the long and little-understood international critical fight of the era, the Realism War in its American aspect, it is probably not necessary to say a great deal. The realists fought to capture American taste from romanticism, lost, and left romanticism established, dominant as it has been since the foundation of the Republic and, in spite of all resistance, in what appears to be our native mold. The gains of their warfare were a considerable contribution to the theory of the novel and a legacy of modes and of challenge which would substantially affect novelists to come.

Finally, since some sort of change seems to be historically inevitable, it was proper that American realism should develop in such a way as to prepare for its own succession. The writers moved toward an increasingly psychological realism, propelled by two major forces. One of these was the displacement of positivism from its dominance of late nineteenth-century thought. A decade like the nineties, which began with William James's *Psychology* and ended with the unleashing of those electronic factors in physical thought which produced Henry Adams's image of "himself lying in the Gallery of Machines at the Great Exposition of 1900, his historical neck broken by the sudden irruption of forces totally new," was bound to loosen the grip of positivism on the imagination. A second force, however, arose from the practices of realistic fiction itself. The more one confronted the mystery of persons living out their fates and struggling toward death, the more his scrutiny turned from the outward sign to the inward process. Howells noticed in 1903, when he was writing a novel Freudian in everything but specifically Viennese terminology, that all the realists had been turning to psychology. Indeed, many had been flirting with psychic phenomena as far-flung as the claims of spiritualism. What he did not seem to notice was that he himself had been working in psychological realism since he began *The Shadow of a Dream* in 1889.

Obviously, however, the methods and angles of vision of realism could not be finally satisfactory for the exploration of psychology. The more one moved from the seen toward the unseeable, from the common toward the private vision, the more other methods appealed. The movement toward symbolism of the late James was as natural as the movement into stream of consciousness for Joyce. Thus realism prepared the way for its succession.

One must, it goes without saying, be aware that the Americans did not work in isolation. They participated in a huge, though ill-defined, international realistic school. To the best of my knowledge, no one has yet essayed to study the figure of late nineteenth-century international realism, though obviously such names as those of Flaubert, Zola, and Daudet in France; Turgenev, Tolstoi, Dostoevski, Gogol in Russia; Galdós, Palacio Valdés, and Pardo-Bazan in Spain; Bjornson, Ibsen, and Brandes in Scandinavia; Hauptmann in Germany, Verga in Italy, Hardy and then Bennett and Galsworthy in England, stand out. I could not pretend to discuss the grand pattern. But perhaps I can propose certain general considerations, more or less abstracted from the American experience, for clarifying the terms "realism" and "realistic."

As a beginning, I wish to propose two distinctions which I should like to make precise. The first is to distinguish between "realism" as a literary mode and "reality" in every extraliterary sense. The second is to distinguish the literary situation in which apparently realistic means have been employed to secure final, total effects which are not realistic from the work which does finally, in totality, achieve realism. Ultimately, I shall propose a general definition of realism which might survive these distinctions.

Most ordinary, dictionary definitions of realism are circular. Realism, they say, deals with what is real (if not merely with what is unpleasant). The OED is a notorious offender in this respect, and the Webster International says: "In art and literature, fidelity to nature or to real life." Apart from bald circularity, there are several objections to such definitions. They provide no means of distinguishing realistic from other literature. We do not have, and are not likely soon to achieve, general agreement about the nature of reality—the qualities of "nature" and "real life." Furthermore, such questions are metaphysical and philosophical, and we are after a literary definition. We need to discard the notion that realism must rest upon a discarded nineteenth-century and vaguely positivistic factualism—or, indeed, rest upon any philosophical realism—and look further.

Questions of definition in literary studies are customarily (and I think rightly) referred to the effects of literature upon the reader. Consideration of such an essentially psychological question sometimes leads to a definition in which literature is called "realistic" because it is so vivid, powerful, profound, or exact in its effect upon the receiving imagination that it "seems real." But this definition, I think, confuses "realism" with literary success. The essence of literary art is to "seem real" in the sense of captivating the reader's imagination, no matter what the qualities of the experience to which imagination is led in the chains of art. That way, all true literature becomes "realistic." But whatever means everything means nothing. "Realism" as a term is destroyed. If it is to have any viable critical use, the term must distinguish some kind of true, of successful, literature from other kinds. The same dead end is reached by the argument that "realism" should be taken to mean "faithful to the writer's unique and personal sense of reality." Every sound expressive success, regardless of variances among authors' faiths and visions, would become "realistic." We must return to the problem of psychological effect, but for the present let us affirm that literary realism has nothing special to do with "reality" as such.

In the present posture of general knowledge, including that of some fundamental sciences, formidable intellectual difficulties stand in the way of proposing to "imitate nature" or "transcribe reality." As Werner Heisenberg concluded, at the epistemological foundations of modern physics Platonism seems to have reclaimed its power. In the end phenomena elude our grasp. We can know not themselves but only ideas of them, and the very injection of an idea into a natural process for purposes of investigation appears so to alter the process as to make it impossible to be sure what the realities unobserved might be.

To say "process" introduces still more unsettling questions about imitating nature: which nature? In social and psychological as well as physical realms we now see no solid, autonomous "fact." Instead there appear complex, if not, for practical purposes, endlessly receding grades of flowing abstraction. Ancient rational categories melt to flux. The further one follows, the more remote from common human, or even uncommon personal, experience grow the unimaginably complicated processes. And they are always emergent, always "becoming." They "arrive" only wherever we call a halt by arbitrary intellectual fiat. Still worse, when, for purposes of art or knowledge, we call the halt, that arrest is made, that stop occurs, not infrequently past any point at which things remain available to the ways we have of imagining experience. No telling how much "reality" altogether outruns us. The problem of what then to make of what we have imagined, or of what to do with ourselves in relation to it, becomes acute.

It is probably not profitable to spin out illustrations of such problems. They inhere in any consideration of the peeling layers of the means one possesses for understanding the chair he sits in. The work of understanding the chair rises in one direction at last into the mysteries of the psychological origins of form; or in another direction at last to the baffling physical concept of matter as a swirl of energy when energy is not quite definable; or in yet another direction at last toward the uncontrollable question of why, culturally, there should be chairs when nothing biological demands them. One loses, ultimately, all sense of direct connection to experience.

Clearly we are now in the way of developing art which runs likewise "free" of experience. It is not our purpose here to explore such art, however. We are to look toward those kinds of thought and art, together with the problems of understanding which lie behind them, which may help us toward a definition of realism. Realism is obviously a kind of art which does deal with experience, even common and shared, not highly personal or esoteric experience. The question is, how?

Let us turn on to a perhaps useful distinction between "realism" and "verisimilitude." It is my impression that much confusion in the discussion of realism has been caused by failure to attend to the difference between the effect of one part of a work of literature and the effect of the whole. Because, for instance, there are moments of strategic attention to homely detail in *The Faerie Queene* and in *Henry IV*, Part I, it is sometimes said that they are realistic. They are in total effect heroic, chivalric, exotic, rather romantic, and, in the case of *The Faerie Queene*, allegorical-fantastic great works, but not realism.

The same point might be made by examining such very different pieces as the opening pages of *Gulliver's Travels* and Poe's famous tale "The Descent into the Maelstrom." In Swift's opening there is a wonderfully "voiced" and detailed account of the ordinary career of a wilful lad who became a commonplace ship's surgeon. We are led comfortably into an apparently normal memoir of travel and adventure by sea, suspicion at rest, disbelief suspended. And all at once we find ourselves in Lilliput. The tactic is obvious. In Poe's tale we are drawn with the narrator into a scene of horror, hanging with his ship on the wall of a mammoth whirlpool down the sides of which we may slip inexorably to destruction as gravity slowly overcomes centrifugal force. Both the unity and Gothic effect of the tale demand, however, that the narrator shall escape while we, at least through the duration of the tale, shall believe in his escape. How to do this? Poe resorts to a brilliantly precise description of just how it was that objects whirled and swam, sank or stayed up in the maelstrom. We see with the narrator that he *must* lash himself to a barrel and leap into the torrential wall of water, abandoning his fear-paralyzed brother to destruction with the heavy ship. The total effect is one of fantastic horror and release, Gothicism at its best.

If one were to take the moments of what might look like realism in all four works to authorize calling the works realistic, he would have lost, at least to that extent, the grounds for differentiating among them. Yet it is clearly important critically to avoid confounding *The Faerie Queene*, *Henry IV*, Part I, *Gulliver's Travels*, and "The Descent into the Maelstrom." To call them all realistic would be to obscure the essential literary qualities of each; for each has as the essential qualities of its greatness, qualities not realistic. Hence the usefulness of distinguishing local, partial, even fragmentary uses of realistic effects to contribute to what will in the long run and total effect be nonrealistic, from what achieves realism in final effect. The partial or local effects I would call "verisimilitude," reserving the word "realism" for the other.

What, then, to come finally to the point, should be called "realism"? If this were easy to answer, there would have been no excuse for all the prologue. It is certainly not, and especially across patterns of culture or down historical perspectives, easy. By way of attempting an answer, I wish to recur to the earliest pages of this discussion and suggest that literary realism be seen as dependent upon a theory of common vision. That theory rests upon the combination of a theory of literary art with an amateur theory of perception.

First, the theory of common vision assumes that art-technical (the words of the text on the page in their patterns) arouses in the reader art as experience by impelling his imagination to create that experience subjectively. It observes that there is some, presently obscure, relationship between the experience a reader gets (or can make) from "non-art," what we call "life," and the experience he derives from art. It sees that there are many varieties of both orders of experience and that in some meaningful sense art-experiences and non-art experiences can be paired as with A to A-I, B to B-I, etc. The difference between A and A-I arises from the great difference in what occasions each; their likeness arises from their relating to the same category of subjective effect. For instance, one sees a view, sees a painting, reads a poetic description: and "feels" landscape. One "sees" a ghost, he sees *Hamlet*, he reads *Hamlet*. One eats at a cafeteria, he reads of so eating. It is not to be doubted that art as technique will strategically have shaped art-experience. We can apparently not quite know how that non-art experience occurs which may range from foggy undifferentiatedness to something explosive or fateful. The point to be clung to is that there persistently are varietal likenesses between instances of the two orders of experience. That is why one should be loath to deny relationship between literature and "reality" even while observing all the caveats noted earlier.

It might therefore be possible to propose a positive and general definition of realism as representing the art-variety of a "real" order of non-art experience—an order, that is, which even those who held to deeply opposed temperamental and metaphysical notions of ultimate reality might agree to accept as "real" in some useful and common, even though minimal, sense. That variety I should propose to be the socially agreed upon "common vision" which permits ordinary processes of law and social control to succeed, creates the possibility of games, makes most technical, economic, and even educational enterprises possible. That world of the common vision is, indeed, what is ordinarily referred to as "reality." But, of course, it has not been reality for many people of the past as it is not for many—and especially for many artists—today. It could not finally serve, that is, for any true Idealist, or Humean sceptic, or Existentialist, or mystic, Zen, or hippie thinker.

The world of common vision does certainly not in itself encompass all the varieties of "reality" available to art experience. But it certainly is, on the other hand, in fact one sort of reality common to almost everybody. It provides the ground for one kind, a dominant variety, of non-art experience. There must surely be a variety of art-experience cognate to the world of common vision. Regardless, then, of whether it is absolutely so or not, what usually appears to be "reality" is experience which it appears that we share with other people. We check the content and qualities of our experience with the experience of others to see whether ours is "real" or not. With some orders of experience we check so automatically that it never occurs to us to ask whether we ought to, whether it is valid to check with others. When doubt strikes us with regard to the commonness of most experience, we fear we may be retreating from reality into fantasy.

And of course it is in the areas of experience which are most socially verifiable that we feel ourselves most shared and sharing. In a game the ball is either caught or not caught—and the resultant exultation or dejection depends altogether on group-related gambling emotions. The like holds true for the law or politics; they also entirely depend on community of experience, on the experience of reality as common vision.

So it is just upon this question of the possibility of experience socially based upon common vision that the possibility of literary realism hangs. If the novelist can through the illusions of his art induce imaginative experience within his reader consonant with the reader's ordinary communal experience, then intriguing possibilities appear. There can be a literature peculiarly potent in its appeal to some of the sanest and most useful processes of the human mind. From certain practical and moral points of view, that should be a literature uniquely valuable—for, if it were successful as art, done with esthetic force, conceived by the eye of a necessarily supersensitive observer, the illusion of experience, the "sense of life" conveyed could not fail to be deeply instructive. The power of art to create experience more intense, more sharply defined and vivid, more satisfactorily shaped than the experience people can normally create for themselves would be lent to the deepening and enhancement of the common vision. Such literature would make us better citizens, more loyal in our loves, more perceptive in critique, faithful to perspectives clearly seen.

Such a literature would be time and culture bound of course. Especially concerned with persons in their relations with other persons, it would tend to be democratic. In order to preserve its integrity as art rather than essay or sermon, it would have to forswear the vatic anarchies of "organicism" and concentrate hard on problems of form. It would learn to master the arts of creating illusions of objectivity and impartiality, abjuring the cult of artistic personality and the temptation to romantic irony.

All these, and perhaps other, features would go to make a particular kind of literary method and effect. The importance of the kind would, as with all kinds, depend largely on the power of its practitioner to achieve artistic success—the strong command of the reader's imagination—by its method. In this respect the kind would be no different from any other. The whole argument here is to show that the literary art of the common vision deserves recognition as a kind and is, theoretically as well as historically, entitled to the name of realism.

Finally, I should like to suggest that if we meant the foregoing things by "realism" and "reality" we could justify the nineteenth-century realists outside and beyond the conventions of their time and thought—forward into the present and backward as far as we know art. So doing, we could still grasp the relevant patterns and call what seems to conform to these patterns "realism." Admittedly, cross-cultural problems might become very difficult. For us the difficulties of imagining our way into the realisms of cultures which take magic, witchcraft, or mythology as ordinarily operative can be great. So too our difficulties with bygone science and scientism. For instance, astrology, the psychology of humours, phrenology, or even Zolaistic naturalism are hard for us to take as matters of the common vision. They must be defined socially in their proper contexts by mighty efforts of the historical or the cross-cultural imagination.

But there may be valuable rewards for such efforts. The thrill of insight and the power of command through a knowledgeable sympathy with men of other times, other places, may accompany, through the ambiguity of "common" as universal, a new grasp of those human universals which we are told some cultural anthropologists are beginning to find in human nature. Thus we might recover one of the traditional glories of the study of literature.

THIRTY-ONE

FROM DOCUMENT TO SYMBOL

Zola and American Naturalism

Frederick J. Hoffman

Frederick J. Hoffman (1909–67) received his Ph.D. from Ohio State University in 1942. One of the leading critics of twentieth-century American literature during the 1950s and 60s, he taught at the University of Wisconsin and the University of California, Riverside. Among Hoffman's books are *Freudianism and the Literary Mind* (1945), *The Modern Novel in America* (1951), *The Twenties: American Writing in the Postwar Decade* (1955), *William Faulkner* (1961), and *The Mortal No: Death and the Modern Imagination* (1964). After Hoffman's death in 1967, "From Document to Symbol," which he had originally read at a scholarly meeting in 1960, was found among his papers.

—i—

I shall begin with two quotations from Henry James on the subject of Zola. The subject fascinated him, perhaps beyond what he thought its merits to be; and he seemed always to have any uneasy sense that Zola's energy and conscientiousness had a far greater reputation than they really ought to have had. Writing to Robert Louis Stevenson in 1893, James said:

> . . . I met Zola at luncheon the day before he left London and found him very sane and common and inexperienced. Nothing, literally nothing, has ever happened to him but to write the Rougon-Macquart. It makes that series, I admit, still more curious . . . [1]

Revue des Langues Vivantes, U.S. Bicentennial Issue (1976): 203–12. Reprinted by permission of Mary John, Executor of the Estate of Frederick J. Hoffman.

The passage covers a full range of James's estimate of Zola, even of his envy of him. To him, Zola's achievement was and remained a "mystery," a "wonder." In his brilliant essay of 1903, James described the mystery as "the wonder of the scale and energy of Zola's assimilations."

> This wonder besets us above all throughout the three books I have placed first (*L'Assommoir, Germinal, La Débâcle*). How, all sedentary and "scientific," did he get so near? By what art, inscrutable, immeasurable, indefatigable, did he arrange to make of his documents, in these connections, a use so vivified?[2]

These are the important questions, not only for Zola but for modern naturalism: how, if it is so "sedentary" and so "scientific," does it manage to get "*so near?*" And to *what* must it approximate in its energetic concern over representation? James would have his own answer to the second question: to "consciousness," perhaps, to the conventions and forms of art. For he couldn't help feeling that Zola's achievement had been "accidental" and unexpected, a miracle of formal representation in the midst of "slobber" and "waste."[3] Zola did not himself regard his results so disparagingly. Indeed, had he lived to read James's essay (he died a year before it appeared), he would have shrugged off the suggestion that he was "sedentary" at all. No artist showed so much documentary and "scholarly" zeal, or moved about so energetically in quest of accumulations of factual support for his conceptions.

That he was "scientific" Zola never denied. He was caught in a tangle of method, particularly, and discovery, that should have ruined a lesser man. The history of Zola's flirtations with contemporary science and of his attempts to campaign for the "experimental novel" is so well known that they don't need repeating here. Beyond this history, one needs to assert the essential damage and the surviving advantage it caused. For one thing, Zola was too easily gulled by contemporary scientific speculation into planning and forwarding vast and clumsy schemes of representation, noting as he went along, with an unfortunate scrupulousness, the "*tares nerveuses,*" the hereditary causes of specific damages inflicted on successive Rougons and Macquarts— often with no credit to Zola and no enlightenment to the reader.

The Zola who has endured, who occasionally managed to get "*so near,*" survived all of this frenzied documentary concern. He was not so much a victim of method as a sponsor of it; and the essay on "The Experimental Novel" (1880) really impressed his American contemporaries much more than it did himself. The point is that, in such works as *L'Assommoir* and *Germinal*, the values of structure and representation survive and transcend the brief and occasional nods of obeisance to "experimental science." It is not just that science did in this case did not succeed in triumphing over the conventions of art, but that it actually contributed to the act of sustaining them. *L'Assommoir* is a remarkable *genre* piece; its pages reveal Zola's Paris with a convincing veracity and multiplicity.

The details multiply, but they also seem to arrange themselves, and they yield an occasional imagery that (while sometimes superficial and naïve) point to later symbolic uses of the naturalist text. Gervaise, looking out upon the Paris streets at the novel's beginning, becomes aware and frightened of two inevitable conclusions of human appetite and indulgence:

> . . . Elle allait, les regards perdus, des vieux abattoirs noirs de leur massacre et de leur puanteur, à l'hôpital, neuf, blafard, montrant, par les trous encore béants de ses rangées de fenêtres, des salles nues où le mort devait faucher . . . [4]

Later, in her own *blanchisserie*, she senses the beginnings of her decline from prosperity and virtue:

> Elle s'abandonnait, étourdie par le léger vertige qui lui venait du tas de linge, sans dégoût pour l'haleine vineuse de Coupeau. Et le gros baiser qu'ils échangèrent à pleine bouche, au millieu des saletés du métier, était comme une première chute, dans le lent avachissement de leur vie.[5]

These minor details, taken from a multitude of their kind, suggest a transition from document to symbol in naturalist literature. They are not expertly realized beyond their status as "research data," and they do yield in tone to the inherent moralist who always trailed some yards behind Zola as "experimental" novelist. But they are also examples of the kind of exercise in particularity that enabled Zola occasionally to "get so *near*" to the representational and imaginative virtues of his art. More important is the *weight* of his two greatest novels. *Germinal* especially is a triumph of weights and balances; it gains solidity mainly from the essential contrasts, tensions and balances which the massiveness of his subject permits him to maneuver into form. Professor F. W. J. Hemmings, in what is unquestionably the finest close study in English of Zola's work, speaks of the structure of *Germinal* "in terms of cubic capacity, of the balance of weights and counterweights. In *Germinal* Zola constructs, where before he had simply painted."[6]

The tensions exist naturally within the situation; they provide their own ironies, menaces, and pressures. Above all, they are the result of crises of theory and interpretation. Zola has here made of theory, not a vehicle of polemical omniscience, but a part of the narrative dynamics. It is not to Zola's disadvantage, but to Étienne Lantier's, that theory has been too naïvely and too ignorantly accepted and forwarded. The characterization of Étienne is a triumph in the history of "revolutionary" narrative. He rises upon the strength of his awareness of weakness; he falls for reasons of his weakness in appraising his strength.

But his interpretation is only one of several. *Germinal* may be considered a study of the tensions caused by these several attempts to put interpretive pressure upon a specific human crisis. From these pressures of theory, the tragedy, accident, comedy, and irony of the "strike novel" emerge. Within them, we take the measure, not only of Étienne and the local situation, but of the master situation of human distress and its parallels in other literatures and other times. As in *L'Assommoir*, the mass of imagery points both to structure and to symbolic order; the smallest detail may communicate or evoke a major stroke of pathos or meaning:

Une rafale leur coupa la parole. Puis, Étienne demanda, en montrant le tas sombre des constructions, au pied du terri:

—C'est une fosse, n'est-ce pas?

Le Vieux, cette fois, ne put répondre. Un violent accès de toux l'étranglait. Enfin,
il cracha, et son crachat, sur le sol empourpré, laissa une tache noire.

.   .   .

M. Hennebeau ne se fâcha point. II eut même un sourire.

—Ah! dame! cela se complique, du moment où vous n'avez pas confiance en moi
. . . Il faut aller là-bas.

Les delégués avaient suivi son geste vague, sa main tendue vers une des fenêtres.
Où était-ce, là-bas? Paris, sans doute. Mais ils ne le savaient pas au juste, cela se
reculait dans un lointain terrifiant, dans une contrée inaccessible et religieuse, où
tronait le dieu inconnu, accroupi au fond de son tabernacle . . . [7]

—ii—

The career of Zola's novels in America is an eloquent testimony of a very complicated
mixture of Calvinism, scientific pride, and gentility in this country's nineteenth-century history. In the one sense, a fading Calvinism united (or seemed to unite) with a
narrowly conceived deterministic disposition, so that God and nature damned and
doomed alternately and unequivocally. Beyond these exercises of the mind's mistaken
candor, there was a strenuous attempt to preserve the proprieties of the commonplace
in the work of Howells, whose realistic convictions did not prevent his having recourse to verbal and situational euphemisms. The guardians of decorum (Howells
should not be counted among these) were represented at their worst in the translation
of Zola by Mary Neal Sherwood, who hid behind the masculine pseudonym of "John
Stirling" and performed miracles of tonal reduction.[8]

These phenomena are not the important facts of Zola's influence in America. Much
more significant was his having offered the "fait accompli" of a literature presumably
emerging from current scientific deliberations and bearing the marks of its "experimental method." This impact had its several results: a naïve acceptance of Zola's
tongue-in-cheek journalistic crusade on behalf of the "experimental novel," an eager
drive toward the increase of commonplace documentation, an accumulation of
pseudo-scientific vocabularies, above all a search for the excitement and melodrama
of naturalistic situations. Zola had said to his friend Céard: "My characteristic is the
hypertrophy of the accurate detail; I take my leap into the stars from the springboard
of exaggeration. The truth flies up to the skies of symbolism."[9] Frank Norris took
this, or its equivalent, to mean that "Terrible things must happen to the characters
of the naturalistic tale. They must be twisted from the ordinary, wrenched from the
quiet, uneventful round of everyday life and flung into the throes of a vast and terrible drama . . . "[10]

The most important developments in American naturalism have nothing to do with
melodrama or lycanthropy or katastates and anastates, but are distinctly related to

James's original statements concerning representation and what he seemed to think were Zola's successful assimilations of data. It was a question of objective narrative. Superficially, both Zola and James believed in the author's staying scrupulously aloof from their novels; both accepted the hypothesis of "scenic representation" as a means toward form. But, while Zola's scenes were manifold and saturated with detail, James's became more and more attenuated, accessible to a very different conception of what a scene should be and could do.

Mary Colum's remark that the only kind of character Zola would accept is the "physiological man"[11] is very wide of the mark; but it is true that Zola's men were an indispensable consequence of the rhetoric of experimental particularity, and James's were largely selves or consciousnesses dedicated to the task of understanding both environment and the moral conventions that underlie art. The worst kinds of modern literary hero came out of Zola's obsessively diligent attempts to define man phenomenally and to confine him to a limited area of independent decision and action. Étienne is an admirably precise characterization, as is Gervaise, but neither of them helped in their example. The "lessons" of both are admonitory in modern naturalism, but they are instructive and enlightening only in an elementary sense.

—iii—

I think it a mistake to accept naturalist clichés too literally. Pure documentation is as tediously unilluminating as pure symbolism is obscurely unavailable to definition. Yet the naturalist clichés have remained operative in modern American fiction, and its history largely comprehends the stresses and strains affecting their definition. Charles Walcutt, in his significant book on the subject, lists these as *determinism, survival, violence,* and *taboo.*[12] Each of these, as well as the implications of all of them, had undergone radical changes in our literature.

Most significant of all their implications is the problem of symbolic control in the novel. I should suggest three important ways of access to symbolism from the basically documentary sources of naturalism. In the first case, the sheer weight and repetitiveness of fact leads to symbolic suggestion, quite often to symbolic intrusions; that is, when particulars repeat themselves exhaustively, the images which define them form clusters which provoke symbolic inference. Too often in early American naturalism the author was impatient with the slow accretive process and imposed clumsy, overt symbols upon it, thus negating the process itself and making the details something less than effective. But the initial effort, granting that the particulars are in themselves aesthetically sound, is itself a move toward a symbolic ordering.

There are also special kinds of naturalistic commitment, the consequences of new orders of knowledge (psychoanalysis, for example, in its many complex manifestations), which require the invention and use of new structural devices. The so-called "stream-of-consciousness" novel is a symbolic form dominated at least in part by naturalist incentives. Here we have primarily a series of dialogic and monologic situations; and the move from documents to symbol is characterized by recourse to dialogue and monologue. Both restore to document what has often been notoriously missing from it; the self-analytical function, which yields very complex returns.

Early American naturalists are conspicuously weak in their handling of dialogue. The art of dialogue receives its major encouragement in the novels of Henry James; even here, the early novels have far less meaningful dialogue than the later. One may describe the career of modern fiction as a move from basic exposition (Zola) to internal analysis (the early James) to the most complex forms of intellectual exchange (the late James). Beyond these, there is the kind of interior monologue of Joyce, Virginia Woolf, and Faulkner, which demands symbolic ordering on several levels of narrative structure, simply because time and space are so radically revised that exposition *must* take new forms.

A third (and a final) aspect of the development from document to symbol is the "way of technique." That is, assuming the documentary resources of a novel to be massive and abundant, the novelist resorts to symbolic "short cuts," which have the virtues and the risks of a *multum in parvo* representation. Unlike *McTeague*'s gold tooth, the symbolic ordering in *The Great Gatsby* is not just an act of overlaying a symbol upon matter, but an exercise in condensation. The fictional values gain much from an apparent reduction in scope, though they need to be used in a creative art of reconstruction, moving out from the precisely limited center into a much larger area of explication and associative re-ordering. Though interpretations of it are eligible to a great variety of suggestions, the "deepest quality of a work of art" is still, as James said it was, "the quality of the mind of the producer."[13] Within the limits that must be noted as belonging to basic naturalistic history, the terms of Mr. Walcutt's summary remain functional in each of these three stages from documentary to symbolic literature.

Not only has naturalism undergone an immensely complicated revision in twentieth century literature; the terms in which it was originally understood are now radically changed. Primary among them is a shift in ideological ground. The simplistic maneuvers of experimental science described by Zola's favorite mentor, Claude Bernard, are no longer feasible. As Zola himself knew, scientific "method" can no longer be so simply transferred to the laboratory of the novelist. We are less sure of our facts, and especially of their applicability. The modern American novel is now essentially a novel without an ideology, or at least it is one not dominated by a driving ideological purpose.

Philosophical purpose has been strikingly altered. It has become not at all a purpose linked to metaphysics or theology, but one devoted to the analysis of epistemological properties and occasionally to their ontological promise. Zola's purpose in *Germinal* was to present "objectively" a revolutionary situation; he very largely succeeded in producing one. Outside Russia, the revolutionary dynamics of literature have largely disappeared—unless one considers the counter-dynamics of a novelist like Norman Mailer as the beginnings of a new essay in ideological definition.

In his latest novel, there are two important implications: the growth of sophistication with respect to scientific discovery; and an elaborate redistribution of literary energies in terms of *residual* theological and philosophical metaphors, within semi-secular or purely secular contexts. As for the first of these, reader sophistication has made many of the pretenses in early naturalist novels seem quite ridiculous. As Nathalie Sarraute has said, the reader has seen time cease to be the swift stream that carried the plot forward, and become a stagnant pool at the bottom of which a slow, subtle decomposition is in progress; he has seen our actions lose their usual motives and accepted meanings, he has witnessed the appearance of hitherto unknown sentiments and seen those that were most familiar change both in aspect and name.[14]

The second of these is the most important. The activity of secularization ranges widely, from the position that metaphors no longer have the slightest religious significance, to the rather strenuous effort (as in Faulkner's *A Fable*) to "save" religious metaphors (as viable literary and moral elements) by putting them into an intricately contrived system of secular meaning. In a sense we may say that, in recent literature at least, both religious and moral forms of discourse are available to any kind of manipulation. The rise of Jewish literature since the War to a position equal in importance to Southern Protestant is a significant result. The reasons are not hard to find: Jewish culture is inherently both comical and serious; it treats moral situations in terms of a skeptical attitude toward elaborate theological schemata of transcendence; it brings God down to earth and allows ordinary human maneuvers the possible status of a "conversation with Him." It does not, in brief, depend so much upon any and all forms of transcendence; or, rather, the means of transcendence, as its problem, are more humanistically contained.

We may conclude by restating Walcutt's four terms: Zola's novels were described as "shocking" to Americans who first read them; they pictured a world still vitally affected by a naïve view of Darwin's observations of animalistic struggles for survival and the superficial inferences made from them; it was a world of violence, which became more powerfully and more intricately violent in the years following his death; and he wrote at least partly in terms of the consequences of a scientific determinism. All of these characteristics remain in force; each of them has been significantly altered. Modern American fiction has had the curiously paradoxical aspect of a determinism located within the self. Its symbols, therefore, are projections of self-identity in default of eternal verities.

In addition, modern literature has been affected by several different views of the "objectivity" Zola so earnestly and energetically sought. Sophisticated critical minds have been turned upon the literary object and have quite thoroughly redefined its values, both in and out of literature. Modern American novelists (like Willard Motley) who have strived simply to "document" the human condition have written tedious and inchoate novels. Within a limited, inward looking, quite frankly secular consciousness, the American novelist has explored the range of possible self-definition and the relationships of self to "other."

In the light of new circumstances, American naturalism has had to turn from Zola's documentary zeal and his superficially earnest "reforming" morality, toward a more limited, a more sophisticated and skeptical, moral and symbolic order of human events. The tensions of ideological interpretation so skillfully represented in *Germinal* no longer exist; in their place are rudimentary, internal, symbolic tensions, which require a quite different kind of literary representation. Some of the original naïve strength of conviction or doubt still does exist—noticeably in writers like Faulkner who persisted beyond their own generation. But Marx is dead, and Sartre is dying. That is, neither a strongly historical ideology nor a melodramatic vision of choice is any longer sufficient to explain human natures. The modern hero is *"en situation,"* but cannot ideologically explore his situation. His maneuvers are therefore passionately symbolic actions; they are the strategies he uses in the hope of establishing a moral ground of both passion and action.

NOTES

1. *Letters of Henry James*, ed., Percy Lubbock. New York: Scribner's, 1920. Vol. 1, pp. 209–10.

2. "Emile Zola," in *The Art of Fiction and Other Essays*, ed., Morris Roberts. New York: Oxford University Press, 1948. P. 175. Originally in the *Atlantic Monthly*, August, 1903.

3. See his letter of March 3, 1911, to H. G. Wells, in *Henry James and H. G. Wells*, eds., Leon Edel and Gordon Ray. Urbana: University of Illinois Press, 1958. Pp. 127–28.

4. *L'Assommoir* (1877). Paris: Charpentier, 1927. Vol. 1, p. 8.

5. *Ibid.*, I, 182–83.

6. *Emile Zola.* Oxford: The Clarendon Press, 1953. P. 179.

7. *Germinal* (1885). Paris: Charpentier, 1921. Vol. I, pp. 3–4, 248.

8. For example, "Elle ne pleurait plus seulement Maman Coupeau, elle pleurait quelque chose d'abominable, qu'elle n'aurait pu dire, et qui l'étouffait," becomes "She did not weep for Mama Coupeau but rather for herself;" "ces cochonneries" becomes "such pernicious things." See Albert Salvan, *Zola aux Etats-Unis*. Providence: Brown University Studies. Vol. VIII, p. 34.

9. Quoted in Hemmings, p. 213.

10. Quoted by Malcolm Cowley, "A Natural History of American Naturalism." In John Aldridge, ed. *Essays on Modern Fiction*. New York: Ronald Press, 1952. P. 377.

11. *From These Roots.* London: Jonathan Cape, 1938. P. 231.

12. *American Literary Naturalism*. Minneapolis: University of Minnesota Press, 1956. Pp. 20–21.

13. Roberts, p. 21.

14. "The Age of Suspicion," tr. Maria Jolas. In *Noonday*, No. 1 (September, 1958), 94. Originally the title essay of *L'Ere du soupçon; Essais sur le roman*. Paris: Gallimard, 1956, p. 65.

THIRTY-TWO

AMERICAN LITERARY NATURALISM

The Example of Dreiser

Donald Pizer

Donald Pizer (1929–) received his B.A. (1951) and Ph.D. (1955) from the University of California, Los Angeles. He has taught at Tulane University, where he is Pierce Butler Professor of English, since 1957. In addition to book-length studies of Hamlin Garland, Frank Norris, Theodore Dreiser, and John Dos Passos, Pizer has published three volumes of essays on various phases of American realism and naturalism: *Realism and Naturalism in Nineteenth-Century American Literature* (1966; 2nd rev. ed., 1984); *Twentieth-Century American Literary Naturalism: An Interpretation* (1982); and *The Theory and Practice of American Literary Naturalism: Selected Essays and Reviews* (1993).

American literary naturalism has almost always been viewed with hostility. During its early years the movement was associated with Continental licentiousness and impiety and was regarded as a literature foreign to American values and interests. "We must stamp out this breed of Norrises," a reviewer of *McTeague* cried in 1899.[1] In our own time, though antagonism to naturalism is expressed more obliquely, it is as deeply rooted. A typical discussion of the movement is frequently along the following lines.[2] The critic will examine the sources of naturalism in late nineteenth-century scientism, in Zola, and in post-Civil War industrial expansion. He will note that to a

Studies in American Fiction 5 (May 1977): 51–63. Reprinted in *The Theory and Practice of American Literary Naturalism: Selected Essays and Reviews* (Carbondale: Southern Illinois University Press, 1993), pp. 54–68. Text from *The Theory and Practice of American Literary Naturalism: Selected Essays and Reviews*. Reprinted by permission of *Studies in American Fiction*.

generation of American writers coming of age in the 1890s the mechanistic and materialistic foundations of contemporary science appeared to be confirmed by American social conditions and to have been successfully applied to the writing of fiction by Zola. But he will also note that Stephen Crane, Frank Norris, and Theodore Dreiser were often muddled in their thinking and inept in their fiction, and he will attribute these failures to their unfortunate absorption of naturalistic attitudes and beliefs. Our typical critic will then discover a second major flowering of naturalism in the fiction of James T. Farrell, John Steinbeck, and John Dos Passos in the 1930s. He will remark that scientism has been replaced by Marxism and that the thinking of this generation of naturalists is not so much confused as doctrinaire, but his account of their work will still be governed by the assumption that naturalism is a regrettable strain in modern American literary history.

Indeed, the underlying metaphor in most accounts of American fiction is that naturalism is a kind of taint or discoloration, without which the writer would be more of an artist and through which the critic must penetrate if he is to discover the essential nature and worth of the writer. So those writers who most clearly appear to be naturalists, such as Dreiser and Farrell, are almost always praised for qualities that are distinct from their naturalism. We are thus told that Dreiser's greatness is not in his naturalism[3] and that he is most of all an artist when not a philosopher.[4] And so the obvious and powerful thread of naturalism in such major figures as Hemingway, Faulkner, and (closer to our own time) Saul Bellow is almost always dismissed as an irrelevant and distracting characteristic of their work.

This continuing antagonism to naturalism has several root causes. One of the clearest is that many critics find naturalistic belief morally repugnant. But whereas earlier critics stated openly their view that naturalism was invalid because man was as much a creature of divine spirit as animal substance, the more recent critic is apt to express his hostility indirectly by claiming that naturalistic novelists frequently violate the deterministic creed that supposedly informs their work and are therefore inconsistent or incoherent naturalists. On one hand, this concern with philosophical consistency derives from the naturalist writer's interest in ideas and is therefore a justifiable critical interest. On the other, there seems little doubt that many critics delight in seeking out the philosophically inadequate in naturalistic fiction because man is frequently portrayed in this fiction as irredeemably weak and deluded and yet as not responsible for his condition. It is the rare work of fiction of any time in which threads of free will and determinism do not interweave in a complex pattern that can be called incoherent or inconsistent; on strictly logical grounds man either has free will or he does not. Yet it is principally the naturalistic novel that is damned for this quality, which suggests that it is the weighting of this inconsistency toward an amoral determinism—not its mere presence—that is at stake.[5]

Another source of the hostility of modern critics to the naturalistic novel lies in recent American political history. American naturalism of the 1890s was largely apolitical, but in the 1930s the movement was aligned with the left wing in American politics and often specifically with the Communist party. In the revulsion against the party that swept the literary community during the 1940s and 1950s, it was inevitable that naturalistic fiction of the 1930s would be found wanting because the naturalists of that decade, it was now seen, had so naively embraced some form of communist belief. The most influential critical discussions of American naturalism during the 1940s and 1950s—Philip Rahv's "Notes on the Decline of Naturalism," Malcolm Cowley's " 'Not Men': A Natural History of American Naturalism," and Lionel Trilling's "Reality in America"[6]—have as an underlying motive a desire to purge American literature and its historiography of an infatuation with an alien and destructive political ideal.

A final reason for the antagonism toward naturalistic fiction is that several generations of academic critics have been attracted by an increasingly refined view of the aesthetic complexity of fiction. They have believed that a novel must above all be organic—that is, be the product of a romantic imagination—and they have found principally in the work of Hawthorne, Melville, Faulkner, and to a lesser extent James, that enlargement of metaphor into symbol and that interplay of irony and ambivalence that bring fiction close to the complex indirection of a metaphysical lyric. Stephen Crane is the only naturalistic writer whose fiction satisfies these expectations, and his work is generally held to be uncharacteristic of the nonartistry of a movement more adequately represented by Dreiser.[7]

I do not wish to suggest by this brief survey of the critical biases that have led to the inadequate examination of American naturalism that there are not naturalistic novels muddled in conception and inept in execution. But just as we have long known that the mind-set of an early nineteenth-century critic would little prepare him to come to grips with the essential nature and form of a romantic poem, so we are coming to realize that a generation of American critics has approached American literary naturalism with beliefs about man and art that have frequently distorted rather than cast light upon the object before them.

Theodore Dreiser is the author whose work and career most fulfill the received notion of American naturalism; indeed, it is often difficult to determine the demarcation between literary history and critical biography in general discussions of American naturalism, so completely is Dreiser as thinker and writer identified with the movement in America. It would be instructive, therefore, to test the example of Dreiser—to note, initially and briefly, those characteristics of his career and work that lead us to describe him as a naturalist; and then, more fully, to examine some of the naturalistic elements in his fiction. But unlike so much of the criticism of naturalism I have been describing, I do not wish to undertake this test with the assumption that Dreiser's fiction is confused in theme and form because he is not a consistent naturalist or that his work is best when he is least naturalistic. In short, I do not wish to consider his naturalism as an unfortunate excrescence. Rather, I want to see how his naturalistic predispositions work in his fiction and whether or not they work successfully.

Dreiser was born an outsider. His parents were of Catholic, German-speaking immigrant stock and throughout Dreiser's youth the large family was agonizingly poor. As a young man Dreiser sought the success and position that his parents had lacked and also shed the religious and moral beliefs which, he believed, had shackled them.

While a young reporter in Pittsburgh in the early 1890s, he found his deepest responses to life confirmed by his reading of Herbert Spencer and Balzac. There were, he believed, no discernible supernatural agencies in life, and man was not the favored creature of divine guidance but an insignificant unit in a universe of natural forces. Although these forces, whether biological or social, were the source of racial progress, they often crushed the individual within their mechanistic processes. Like many of his generation, Dreiser found that the observed realities of American society supported this theory of existence. The mills and libraries of Pittsburgh were evidence of progress, but the lives of the immigrant foundry workers—to say nothing of the lives of Dreiser's own errant sisters and brothers—appeared dwarfed and ephemeral compared with the grinding and impersonal power of a vast economic system and a great city. Yet the city itself, as Balzac had amply demonstrated, was exciting and alluring, and not all were crushed who sought to gain its wonders. In *Sister Carrie* Dreiser was to write, "Among the forces which sweep and play throughout the universe, untutored man is but a wisp in the wind."[8] But though Hurstwood is swept away by these forces, and though Carrie's career is that of a storm-tossed ship, Carrie survives and indeed grows in understanding by the close of the novel. So accompanying Dreiser's endorsement of an amoral determinism there exists a disconcerting affirmation of the traditionally elevating in life—of Carrie, for example, as a figure of "emotional greatness," that is, of imaginative power. Forty-five years after *Sister Carrie* Dreiser joined the Communist party while celebrating in his last two novels the intuitive mysticism at the heart of Quaker and Hindu belief. Here, in brief, at the two poles of his career and work is the infamous intellectual muddle of Dreiser and, by extension, of naturalism itself. And this muddle appears to be matched by a corresponding lack of control and firmness in fictional technique. Dreiser documents his social scene with a pseudoscientific detachment yet overindulges in personal philosophical disquisitions; he attempts to write a "fine" style but produces journalistic cliché and awkwardness.

So in most important ways Dreiser fulfills the conventional definition of the American naturalist. All the major paradoxes are present: his identification with the "outsider," which was to lead to a contemptuous view of the mainstream of middle-class American life, yet his lifelong worship of "success"; his acceptance of a "scientific" mechanistic theory of natural law as a substitute for traditional views of individual insight and moral responsibility, yet his affirmation of many of these traditional views; and his deep response to a major European novelist, including the form of his fiction, yet his seeming neglect of style and form. I cannot hope to discuss these major characteristics of Dreiser as a naturalist as each appears in his eight novels. But I can pursue the vital naturalistic theme of mechanistic determinism in two of his principal novels, *Jennie Gerhardt* and *An American Tragedy*, and thereby reach toward at least a modest understanding of the example of Dreiser.[9]

Dreiser began *Jennie Gerhardt* in early 1901, soon after the publication of *Sister Carrie*. He wrote most of the novel during the next two years, though he did not complete it until late 1910. Like *Sister Carrie*, *Jennie Gerhardt* is about a girl from a poor family who has several sexual affairs with men of higher station but who emerges from her adventures not only unsullied but also elevated in character and insight. The novel differs from *Sister Carrie* primarily in Dreiser's characterization of Jennie and of Lester Kane, the principal man in Jennie's life. Kane, at least on the surface, is a more powerful, successful, and contemplative figure than Hurstwood, and Jennie differs from Carrie in that she is a warm and generous giver rather than a taker.

In the course of the novel, Jennie is seduced first by Senator Brander, by whom she has a child, Vesta, and then by Lester Kane. She and Kane are attracted to each other by a powerful natural "affinity" and they live together contentedly for several years. But because Lester is gradually forced to accept that a permanent union with Jennie would adversely affect his business career and the comfortable certainties of his social and family life, they do not marry. Eventually they part, Lester marries Letty Gerald, a woman of his own class, and Jennie suffers the death of both her father and Vesta.

One of the major scenes in *Jennie Gerhardt* is Lester's visit to Jennie after the death of Vesta. Deeply depressed by Vesta's death and by his realization that he erred in leaving Jennie, Lester tells her, "it isn't myself that's important in this transaction [that is, life itself] apparently; the individual doesn't count much in the situation. I don't know whether you see what I'm driving at, but all of us are more or less pawns. We're moved about like chessmen by circumstances over which we have no control."[10] This famous pronouncement, which has supplied several generations of literary historians with a ubiquitous image for the philosophical center of American naturalism, requires careful analysis both in its immediate context and in relation to the novel as a whole if it is to be properly understood.

Whatever the general truth of Lester's words, they represent a personal truth. His pawn image expresses both his sense of ineffectuality in the face of the central dilemma of his life and a covert supernaturalism that has characterized his thought throughout the novel despite his overt freethinking. Earlier he had attributed his difficulties merely to bad luck. But by the time he and Jennie separate, he has elevated and generalized "fate" into a specific force that is at once social, supernatural, and (as far as he is concerned) malevolent:

> It was only when the storms set in and the winds of adversity blew and he found himself facing the armed force of convention that he realized he might be mistaken as to the value of his personality, that his private desires and opinions were as nothing in the face of a public conviction; that he was wrong. The race spirit, or social avatar, the "Zeitgeist" as the Germans term it, manifested itself as something having a system in charge, and the organization of society began to show itself to him as something based on possibly a spiritual, or, at least, supernatural counterpart. (373–74)

Lester's speculative statement that men are but pawns in the control of circumstances is thus in part an explanation and a defense of his own conduct. In particular, it is a disguised apology to Jennie for his failure to marry her when he could have done so. But it is also a powerful means of characterizing Lester. Throughout his life he had lived for the moment and had postponed making decisions about the direction of his life. But the decisionless flow of time contained an impetus of events that constituted an implicit and irreversible decision, and when Lester at last awoke to the fact that his life had been decided for him, he bitterly and angrily blamed fate.

Because Lester is a perceptive and on the whole an honest figure, his belief that men are pawns involves more than a rationalization of his own indecisiveness and ineffectuality. His belief also aptly characterizes social reality as that reality has been dramatized in the novel. The pressure of circumstances on Lester in his relationship with Jennie has indeed been intense, from their initial meeting within the convention of a seduction—a convention that appeared to preclude marriage—to the later opposition of Lester's personal, business, and social worlds to the continuation of the relationship. In a passage cut from Chapter XI of the final holograph of the novel, Dreiser himself, as narrator, echoed Lester's attribution of superhuman powers to social force. "The conventions in their way," he wrote, "appear to be as inexorable in their workings as the laws of gravitation and expansion. There is a drift to society as a whole which pushes us on in a certain direction, careless of the individual, concerned only with the general result."[11]

In his final position as one deeply puzzled by the insignificance of the individual, Lester therefore reflects a persistent strain in Dreiser's thought. Before making his pawn speech to Jennie, Lester had "looked down into Dearborn Street, the world of traffic below holding his attention. The great mass of trucks and vehicles, the counter streams of hurrying pedestrians, seemed like a puzzle. So shadows march in a dream" (400). The scene effectively images both Lester's and Dreiser's belief that life is a helter-skelter of activity without meaning either for its observers or for the "shadows" who give it motion. As a man aware of the direction of modern thought, Lester is able to give this view of life an appropriate philosophical framework. In the years that pass after Vesta's death, his response to life, Dreiser tells us, becomes "decidedly critical":

> He could not make out what it was all about. In distant ages a queer thing had come to pass. There had started on its way in the form of evolution a minute cellular organism which had apparently reproduced itself by division, had early learned to combine itself with others, to organize itself into bodies, strange forms of fish, animals, and birds, and had finally learned to organize itself into man. Man, in his part, composed as he was of self-organizing cells, was pushing himself forward into comfort and different aspects of existence by means of union and organization with other men. Why? Heaven only knew. . . . Why should he complain, why worry, why speculate?—the world was going steadily forward of its own volition, whether he would or no. Truly it was. (404–5)

It must not be assumed, however, that Lester's pessimistic response to the "puzzle" of man's role in a mechanistic world is Dreiser's principal and only philosophical theme in *Jennie Gerhardt*. For Jennie, though not Lester's equal in formal knowledge or in experience, is his equal in the "bigness" of her responsiveness to the underlying reality of life, and she discovers not only puzzlement and frustration in life but also an ineradicable beauty. Dreiser therefore follows his comments on Lester's critical outlook with an account of Jennie's final evaluation of life. This evaluation, because of its source and its strategic location, has significance equal to Lester's beliefs. Jennie, Dreiser writes,

> had never grasped the nature and character of specialized knowledge. History, physics, chemistry, botany, geology, and sociology were not fixed departments in her brain as they were in Lester's and Letty's. Instead there was the feeling that the world moved in some strange, unstable way. Apparently no one knew clearly what it was all about. People were born and died. Some believed that the world had been made six thousand years before; some that it was millions of years old. Was it all blind chance or was there some guiding intelligence—a God? Almost in spite of herself she felt that there must be something—a higher power which produced all the beautiful things—the flowers, the stars, the trees, the grass. Nature was so beautiful! If at times life seemed cruel, yet this beauty still persisted. The thought comforted her; she fed upon it in her hours of secret loneliness. (405)

Jennie and Lester's complementary views of life represent Dreiser's own permanent unresolved conception of the paradox of existence. To both figures the world "was going steadily forward of its own volition," apparently guided by some unknowable power. Individuals counted for little in this process, but individuals of different temperaments might respond to the mechanism of life in different ways. One kind of temperament might be bitter and despairing, another might affirm the beauty that was inseparable from the inexplicable mystery of life. It has frequently been noted that Dreiser himself held both views at different stages of his career—that he stressed a cruelly indifferent mechanistic universe in *Hey Rub-a-Dub-Dub* (1920) and a mechanistic world of beauty in *The Bulwark* (1946). It has not been as fully realized that he held the two positions simultaneously as well as consecutively and that he gave each position equal weight and dramatic expression in *Jennie Gerhardt* without resolving their "discrepancy." For to Dreiser there was no true discrepancy; there was only the reality of distinctive temperaments that might find truth in each position or, as in his own case, of a temperament that might find an element of truth in both. Dreiser's infamous philosophical inconsistency is thus frequently a product of his belief that life is a "puzzle" to which one can respond in different ways, depending on one's makeup and experience.

The naturalistic "philosophy" of deterministic mechanism in Dreiser's novels is therefore usually secondary, within the fictional dynamics of each novel, to the role of the concept as a metaphor of life against which various temperaments can define themselves. Or, to put the matter another way, Lester's belief in one kind of mechanistic philosophy and Jennie's in another are less significant fictionally than the depiction of Jennie as a woman of feeling and of Lester as a man of speculative indecision. But it should also be clear that in attributing a secondary fictional role to the mechanistic center of *Jennie Gerhardt* I am not saying that the philosophy muddles the novel or that the novel is successful for reasons other than the philosophy. I am rather saying that the philosophy and the fiction are one and inseparable. As a late nineteenth-century novelist, Dreiser absorbed and used naturalistic ideas. But he did not do so, at his best, in a way that can be distinguished from his absorption of an understanding of character and of experience in general. It is this unity of understanding and of purpose that gives Dreiser's novels their power. At his most successful, Dreiser embodies in his novels the permanent in life not despite the ideas of his own time but because, like most major artists, he uses the ideas of his own time as living vehicles to express the permanent in man's character and in man's vision of his condition and fate.

Most students of American literature are aware that Dreiser derived the central plot and much of the detail of *An American Tragedy* from the Chester Gillette-Grace Brown murder case of 1906. Less commonly known is that although Dreiser's principal source—the reports of Gillette's trial in the *New York World*—presented him with a wealth of detail about Gillette's life in Cortland (the Lycurgus of the novel) leading up to the murder of Grace Brown, it offered only a few hints about Gillette's experiences before his arrival in that city. Thus, Book One of *An American Tragedy*, which deals with Clyde's early life in Kansas City, is in a sense "invented." Such major events of this portion of the novel as Clyde's sister's pregnancy, his job at the Green-Davidson Hotel, his longing for Hortense, and the automobile accident that concludes the book have no source in Gillette's life.

Because Dreiser in Book One is "inventing" a background for Clyde it is possible to view this section of the novel as the application to fiction of a simplistic deterministic ethic in which the author crudely manufactures hereditary and environmental conditions that will irrevocably propel the protagonist toward his fate. So, in Book One, we are offered Clyde's weak and fuzzy-minded father and coldly moralistic mother. We discover that Clyde is a sensitive youth who longs for the material and sensual pleasures of life but lacks the training, strength, and guile necessary to gain them. Ergo: weakness and desire on the one hand and irresistible attraction yet insurmountable barriers on the other will resolve themselves into an American tragedy.

Dreiser in this opening section of the novel is indeed seeking to introduce the deterministic theme that a young man's nature and early experience can solidify into an inflexible quality of mind that will lead to his destruction. Yet once said, this observation is as useless to criticism as the equally true statement that *King Lear* is about the failure and triumph of love. For Dreiser in Book One of *An American Tragedy* is not a simple and simpleminded naturalist applying a philosophical theory to documentary material but rather a subtle fictional craftsman creating out of the imagined concrete details of a life an evocative image of the complex texture of that life.

Clyde's desire for "beauty and pleasure"[12] in Book One is in direct conflict with his parents' religious beliefs and activities, and thus Clyde's dominant impulse from early boyhood is to escape. At fifteen he makes his first major break from his parents' inhospitable mission existence and toward the life he desires when he gets a job as assistant clerk at a drugstore soda fountain. This position, with its accompanying "marvels" of girls, lively talk, and "snappy" dressing, offers a deeply satisfying alternative to the drab religiosity of Clyde's boyhood. He recognizes the appeal of this new world "in a revealing flash": "You bet he would get out of that now. He would work and save his money and be somebody. Decidedly this simple and yet idyllic compound of the commonplace had all the luster and wonder of a spiritual transfiguration, the true mirage of the lost and thirsting and seeking victim of the desert" (I, 26).

Dreiser's summary of Clyde's response to the lively worldliness of the soda fountain introduces a theme, and its imagery and tone, that pervades the entire novel. Clyde's need—his thirst—has the power to transform "spiritually" the tawdry and superficial world of the drugstore into the wondrous and exalted. So frequent and compelling is Dreiser's use of "dream" in connection with Clyde's longing that we sometimes fail to realize that his desires also have a basically religious context in which his "dream" is for a "paradise" of wealth and position ruled by a "goddess" of love. Clyde at this moment of insight at the soda fountain is truly converted. He has rejected the religion of his parents only to find a different kind of heaven to which he pledges his soul with all the fervor and completeness of his parents' belief. Yet like their "cloudy romance" of a heaven above, Clyde's vision of a "paradise" below is a "true mirage." He has thus not really escaped from his parents, and his initiation into life at the soda fountain and later at the Green-Davidson is no true initiation, for he has merely shifted the nebulous and misdirected longings of his family from the unworldly to the worldly. He still has the naïveté, blindness, and absolute faith of his parents' enthusiasm and belief. And because he is, like them, a true believer, he does not learn from experience and he does not change.

Clyde's job as a bellhop at the Green-Davidson is both an extension and an intensification of his conversion experience at the soda fountain. To Clyde, the hotel is "so glorious an institution" (I, 33), a response which at once reflects the religiosity of its sexual attractions and their embodiment in a powerful social form. The Green-Davidson has both an intrinsic and an extrinsic sexuality. So deep and powerful is Clyde's reaction to its beauty and pleasure—to its moral freedom, material splendor, and shower of tips—that he conceives of the hotel as a youth does his first love. The Green-Davidson to Clyde is softness, warmth, and richness; it has a luxuriousness that he associates with sensuality and position—that is, with all that is desirable in life: "The soft brown carpet under his feet; the soft, cream-tinted walls; the snow-white bowl lights set in the ceiling—all seemed to him parts of a perfection and a social superiority which was almost unbelievable" (I, 42). "And there was music always—from somewhere" (I, 33). Clyde thus views the hotel both as "a realization of paradise" and as a miraculous gift from Aladdin's lamp, two images of fulfillment that, in their "spiritualizing" of his desires, appropriately constitute the center of his dream life.

But the hotel has a harsh and cruel sexuality in addition to its soft, warm, and "romantic" sensuality. Older women and homosexuals prey on the bellhops, who themselves frequent whores, and the hotel offers many instances of lascivious parties on the one hand and young girls deserted by their seducers on the other. Clyde, because of his repressed sexuality, cannot help responding to this aspect of sex with "fascination" despite his fears and anxieties. The sexual reality of the hotel is thus profoundly ambivalent. Clyde longs above all for the "romance" of sex and for warmth and a sense of union, but the overt sexuality that he in fact encounters is that of hardness, trickery, and deceit—of use and discarding. Both Clyde's unconscious need and his overt mode of fulfillment join in his response to Hortense. "Your eyes are just like soft, black velvet," he tells her. " 'They're wonderful.' He was thinking of an alcove in the Green-Davidson hung with black velvet." (I, 112). Clyde unconsciously desires "softness" and later finds it in Roberta, but he is also powerfully drawn by the "hardness" of wealth and sexual power that he is to find in Sondra and that he first encounters at the Green-Davidson. Thus he endows Hortense with an image of warm softness that reflects his muddled awareness of his needs. For though Hortense is properly associated in his mind with the Green-Davidson because of their similar sexual "hardness," she is incorrectly associated with an image of softness and warmth.

Clyde's belief that the Green-Davidson is a "glorious . . . institution" also represents his acceptance of the hotel as a microcosm of social reality. So he quickly learns that to get ahead in the world—that is, to ingratiate himself with his superiors and to earn large tips—he must adopt various roles. So he accepts the hierarchy of power present in the elaborate system of sharing tips that functions in the hotel. So he realizes that he must deceive his parents about his earnings if he is to have free use of the large sums available to him as an eager novice in this institution. And because the world of the Green-Davidson—both within the hotel and as hotel life extends out into Clyde's relations with the other bellhops and with Hortense—also contains Clyde's introduction into sexual desire and sexual warfare, he assumes that the ethics of social advance and monetary gain are also those of love. Thus, when in Lycurgus he aspires to the grandeur of Sondra and her set, his actions are conditioned by an ethic derived from the Green-Davidson—that hypocrisy, dishonesty, role-playing, and sexual deceit and cruelty are the ways in which one gains what one desires and that these can and should be applied to his relationship with Roberta.

The major point to be made about Dreiser's rendering of the Green-Davidson Hotel as an important experience in Clyde's life is that we respond to his account not as an exercise in determinism but as a subtle dramatization of the ways in which a distinctive temperament—eager, sensitive, emotional, yet weak and directionless—interacts with a distinctive social setting that supplies that temperament with both its specific goals and its operative ethic. Again, as in *Jennie Gerhardt*, there is a naturalistic center to this fictional excellence. It is correct to say that Clyde's life is determined by his heredity and environment. But, once more, as in *Jennie Gerhardt*, the naturalism and the fictional strength are inseparable. The naturalism is not an obstacle to the excellence but the motive thrust and center of the bedrock fictional portrayal of how people interact with their worlds and why they are what they are.

To sum up. One of the major conventions in the study of American naturalism is that naturalistic belief is both objectionable in its own right and incompatible with fictional quality. But the example of Dreiser reveals that the strength often found in a naturalistic novel rests in the writer's commitment to the distinctive form of his naturalistic beliefs and in his ability to transform these beliefs into acceptable character and event. We are moved by the story of Jennie and Lester and by the account of Clyde's career not because they are independent of Dreiser's deepest beliefs but rather because they are successful narratives of man's impotence in the face of circumstances by a writer whose creative imagination was all of a piece. Until we are willing to accept that the power of a naturalistic writer resides in his naturalism, we will not profit from the example of Dreiser.

NOTES

1. Quoted by Franklin Walker, *Frank Norris: A Biography* (Garden City, NY: Doubleday, Doran, 1932), pp. 222–23.

2. The most characteristic discussions of American naturalism occur in histories of American fiction. See, for example, Harry Hartwick, *The Foreground of American Fiction* (New York: American, 1934), pp. 3–20; George Snell, *The Shapers of American Fiction, 1798–1947* (New York: Dutton, 1947), pp. 223–48; Frederick J. Hoffman, *The Modern Novel in America* (Chicago: Regency, 1951), pp. 28–51; and Edward Wagenknecht, *Cavalcade of the American Novel* (New York: Holt, 1952), pp. 204–29. But see also Oscar Cargill, *Intellectual America* (New York: Macmillan, 1941), pp. 82–175, and Lars Ahnebrink, *The Beginnings of Naturalism in American Fiction* (Cambridge: Harvard Univ. Pr., 1950).

3. Charles C. Walcutt, *American Literary Naturalism: A Divided Stream* (Minneapolis: Univ. of Minnesota Pr., 1956), p. 220.

4. Eliseo Vivas, "Dreiser, An Inconsistent Mechanist," *Ethics* (July 1938); revised version, *The Stature of Theodore Dreiser*, ed. Alfred Kazin and Charles Shapiro (Bloomington: Indiana Univ. Pr., 1955), p. 237.

5. Two extreme examples of this position are Randall Stewart, *American Literature and Christian Doctrine* (Baton Rouge: Louisiana State Univ. Pr., 1958), pp. 114–20, and Floyd Stovall, *American Idealism* (Norman: Univ. of Oklahoma Pr., 1943), pp. 134–36.

6. The essays were published originally in 1942, 1947, and 1950 respectively.

7. See, for example, Charles Thomas Samuels, "Mr. Trilling, Mr. Warren, and *An American Tragedy*," *Yale Review* 53 (Summer 1964): 629–40. Samuels finds *An American Tragedy* inept beyond belief.

8. *Sister Carrie*, ed. Donald Pizer (New York: Norton, 1970), p. 56.

9. Portions of the discussion of *Jennie Gerhardt* and *An American Tragedy* which follows appear in different form in my *Novels of Theodore Dreiser: A Critical Study* (Minneapolis: Univ. of Minnesota Pr., 1976). I do not wish by my emphasis on the deterministic thread in naturalism to appear to be supporting a return to a simplistic definition of naturalism as "pessimistic determinism" or some such formula. I have devoted much effort over two decades in various critical studies of individual naturalists as well as in more general essays on the movement as a whole to the position that naturalism is a complex literary movement in which distinctive writers combine in their works distinctive strains of traditional humanistic values and contemporary deterministic belief. Rather, I seek in this essay to suggest that just as we were long guilty of not recognizing the element of covertly expressed traditional value in most naturalists, so we have also been guilty of an uncritical disparagement of the more readily identifiable deterministic strain in their work.

10. *Jennie Gerhardt* (New York: Harper, 1911), p. 401. Citations appear hereafter in the text.

11. In the Theodore Dreiser Collection, University of Pennsylvania Library; quoted by permission of the University of Pennsylvania Library.

12. *An American Tragedy* (New York: Boni and Liveright, 1925), I, 5. Citations appear hereafter in the text.

THIRTY-THREE

REALISM

Alfred Habegger

Alfred Habegger (1941–) received his Ph.D. from Stanford
University in 1967 and has been a member of the English
Department of the University of Kansas since 1966. In ad-
dition to *Gender, Fantasy, and Realism in American Litera-
ture* (1982), he is the author of *Henry James and the
"Women Business"* (1989) and *The Father: A Life of Henry
James, Sr.* (1994).

What *was* realism, exactly? Up to this point I've assumed that we share a rough sense
of what it was. If the reader has followed my contentions without any uneasiness over
what I understand by realism, then all is well; there is communality. But if there is
only uneasiness, then it is high time I admit that I have adhered all along to René
Wellek's description of realism as "the objective representation of contemporary social reality."[1] Wellek offers this formula as a period concept, strictly appropriate to
nineteenth-century European and American literature. With the proviso that there is
no reason for not generalizing the concept (in order to take in twentieth-century non-
Western literatures, for instance). I find Wellek's formula satisfactory. But it must be
understood that it is only a definition based on a well-informed survey of the subject,
and not anything more. Too many studies of American realism tend to confuse definition, which serves to point out and distinguish a group of objects (in this case, realistic novels) and to classify them by their common denominator, with certain other
activities an intellectual may reasonably undertake to perform with them.[2] In particular, there is no reason why Wellek's concept cannot lead to the sort of analysis that
makes use of the most far-reaching thought on the subject of realism, that of Georg
Lukács.

A definition of a period concept in literature is useful if it opens the way to a fuller
sense of literary and historical processes, cleavages, identities. Wellek's definition is

particularly valuable in enabling one to get past the confusion concerning Mark Twain. If we entertain the idea that this artist was something other than a realist, we find ourselves following an irresistible line of thought. The widespread, though by no means universal, opinion that the *Adventures of Huckleberry Finn* is a realistic book begins to look rather questionable. Not only does this work not deal with contemporary society, it presents a view of antebellum life along the Mississippi that is highly colored. The picture of Pokeville or Brickville may be factual and pointed, but it does not seem realistic. The Grangerford chapters are wonderful, but whatever they are they are not realistic, as one immediately sees in comparing them to De Forest's sensitive exploration of a family feud in *Kate Beaumont*. In none of Mark Twain's "novels" was he "objective" or "contemporary." No doubt a debunking factuality was one of the tricks in his trade, but I doubt whether his trade was realism. He was too close to popular and folk art to enter that line of work. Mark Twain was a preacher, public exhorter, moralist, satirist, prankster, entertainer, yarn-spinner, and public fool, not to mention newspaperman, traveler, pilot, prospector, investor, and writer-businessman. My wife's grandfather, born into a farm family, was named Mark Twain by an enthusiastic parent. Would that baby have been so named if his eponym had been a realist?

Another consequence of Wellek's definition is that the body of writing known as local color, which flourished after the Civil War, can be sharply distinguished from realism. These two forms were born together and remained in close touch, but the difference—local color's adherence to old times rather than the passing scene—cannot be too much emphasized. James, and to a much lesser extent, Howells looked down on local color fiction (though James came to admire Jewett).[3] To some extent they were justified in taking this attitude. Local color's devotion to odd places and speech-ways and curious veins and outcroppings from the past all reflected a deep rejection of the contemporary world. Howells and James knew how important it was for the novel to try to come to terms with modern urban, "middle-class," civilized life. The local colorists were animated by a nostalgia that is easy to sympathize with, even though it disqualifies their literature from the centrality realism aspired to. The local colorists were well aware of their peripheral status, for they invariably dealt with regions, cultures, and vernaculars that were picturesque survivals. Certainly *The Grandissimes* is that rare thing, a good historical novel, Mary E. Wilkins Freeman's stories are wonderfully accurate and moving. Harriet Beecher Stowe's *Oldtown Folks* or *Oldtown Fireside Stories* preserve rural life in fine artistic form, and Sarah Orne Jewett remains one of the best American writers. A story like "The White Heron," where a country girl protects a bird from a city scientist, deals in an indirect but uncompromising way with the destructive tendencies of modern life. But can modern life, no matter how bad, be understood from a position somewhere off the map? Realism, at any rate, insists that it can't be.

The third and most difficult exclusion is within James's own corpus of fiction. James was a realist for a time—roughly 1876 (*Roderick Hudson*) to 1890 (*The Tragic Muse*). But he neither began nor ended as one, and the failure to see this has undermined many investigations of American literary realism. In James's early disdainful reviews of Trollope and Rebecca Harding Davis, or his first disparaging references to Flaubert, his original antipathy to realism seems clear.[4] He later changed his mind on the two male writers and realism, but he never abandoned a certain contempt for lowlife characters, and on the whole his realism remained conservative. It was always modified by a predisposition to picture the world as a high-minded and finely conscious person would picture it. Sometimes James would upset the high-minded view; sometimes he would endorse it. His ambivalence in this matter corresponds to the sort of ambivalence toward Europe that he dramatized in "A Passionate Pilgrim" and analyzed in his memoirs with such tender irony. His 1884 essay, "The Art of Fiction," is by no means a defense of realism (as it makes a case for Robert Louis Stevenson), but a defense of artistic freedom and an attack on all rules, orthodoxies, cliques, and schools, including the realists. The essays James wrote soon after, on Howells and Constance Fenimore Woolson, clearly anticipated his approaching repudiation of realism in the 1890s, when he wrote a number of rich interiorized fictions. These late books offer a fascinating vision of the world rather than an objective representation of it. I do not see how they can be considered realistic.

The exclusion of Mark Twain, the local colorists, and James's later novels limits the field but still leaves a large corpus of realistic fiction by James, Howells, H. H. Boyesen, E. W. Howe, Joseph Kirkland, John Hay, Henry Adams, Alice Wellington Rollins, and Constance Fenimore Woolson (one of the best of the novelists on the border between local color and realism). The most important and productive of these were clearly James and Howells.

With the field properly marked off, we can now move on to a brief analysis of some essential qualities of the American realistic novel. And first, we must supplement Wellek's definition with a more explicit recognition of the dialectical nature of realism. Wellek concluded his chapter by suggesting that "the theory of realism is ultimately bad aesthetics because all art is 'making' and is a world in itself of illusion and symbolic forms."[5] This objection must be reckoned with, for it points out that no art can be defined simply by referring to its subject matter, even if that subject matter is objectively represented. The proper response is to recognize that realism was not an independent genre or independent symbolic form or anything of the sort. It belonged to the mid-nineteenth-century genre of the novel, but bore in part an adversary or corrective relation to a major type of novel, women's fiction. Women's fiction was characterized by an idealized heroine, a strong appeal to the reader's fantasies or daydreams, a great deal of "domestic" social and psychological detail, and a plot based on love interest that led up to a decisive speech—"I love you." As a social institution, this genre was closely tied in to contemporary female roles and definitions of marriage. Once realism is seen as an inevitable reaction *within* the novel genre, the problem brought up by Wellek vanishes. The detailed verisimilitude, close social notation, analysis of motives, and unhappy endings were all part of a strategy of argument, an adversary polemic. These techniques were the only way to tell the truth about, to test, to *get at*, the ideal gender types, daydreams, and lies that were poisoning society and the novel. Realism was an analysis of quiet desperation. Attempting to break out, and to help their readers break out, of a suffocated, half-conscious state, Howells and

James had to be circumstantial. It was the only way to make their case. One of James's early views, which he would never abandon, was that "when once a work of fiction may be classed as a novel, its foremost claim to merit, and indeed the measure of its merit, is its *truth*."[6] The book that made James sound this battle cry was a woman's novel, *Azarian*, by Harriet Prescott Spofford. Several years later, James would see that the only way to tell the truth was by means of realism. And several years after that, when American women's fiction no longer dominated the field, realism, for James, also lost its appeal.

But why would James and Howells be so concerned to oppose popular women's fiction? Why would a high mimetic art go to the trouble to be so aware of, so responsive to, an often cheap fantasy art? John G. Cawelti's excellent study of formula stories, *Adventure, Mystery, and Romance*, points to the answer. As Cawelti shows, most formula stories enable the reader to enjoy the pleasures of escape and entertainment by offering him or her a familiar set of stereotypes, a superior protagonist that takes us out of ourselves "by confirming an idealized self-image" and "an imaginary world that is just sufficiently far from our ordinary reality to make us less inclined to apply our ordinary standards of plausibility and probability to it."[7] It may be hard to imagine a supremely talented writer going to all the bother of resisting such literature. The writer might actually enjoy it. But if we imagine a formula literature that insisted its world was not at all imaginary, that exhibited an unusual richness of verisimilitude and contemporary detail, that stimulated a very emotional identification and then appealed to the most respected ethical and religious ideals, the case is altered. Escape literature characterized by an intensely felt confusion between fantasy and reality might easily arouse the best talents to resistance.

There is thus a noticeably rational element in realistic fiction. Full of sober and comprehensive assessments, Howells and James were very different from the euphoric women's novels that preceded them. These earlier books were full of extreme highs and lows, a passionate brooding over the problem of being female. The male realists tried to deal with this and other problems more dispassionately. But unlike Oliver Wendell Holmes, Sr., and his "medicated" novel about the neurotic Elsie Venner, Howells and James were anything but prying Hawthornesque scientists poking at patients they saw as wholly other. As I have already argued, these two men were themselves strangely feminine and were deeply implicated in their own heroines. The strength of their best realistic work lies in their equilibrium between the passionately felt identity characteristic of women's novels and the detached judgment that was an essential component of realism.

This detachment has misled many later critics, who have been ignorant of the popular fiction against which Howells and James established themselves. One of the serious flaws in many accounts of realism is an extreme emphasis on its rationalistic or scientific component—determinism, environment, heredity, Darwinian evolution, and the evolving technological society in the background.[8] One must not overlook such matters, but they did not so much inspire the realists as authorize them.[9] What inspired them was something much deeper, much more strongly felt. One gains a sense of the real animus in realistic fiction only by considering the society and popular art of the time. In particular, the gender roles that were implied both by the major social institutions and the lineaments of the novel's idealized hero and heroine formed the basic source of realism. How did it happen that some of the major realistic novels in various countries—*Anna Karenina, Madame Bovary, Middlemarch, The Portrait of a Lady,* and *A Modern Instance*—all told the story of a bad marriage? The source of realism lay right on the surface—love interest—and yet ran far deeper than intellectual history can reach.

Of course, one dares not overlook the intellectual currents in Howells and James. To some extent these realists worked to deflate the self-assertive romantic ego. The anti-egotism James got from his father enabled him to study the romantic agony of a Roderick Hudson or the suicidal transcendentalism of the Bostonians. James's strong aversion to the self-culture symbolized by Concord entered deeply into his fiction. Howells attacked romantic egotism in both its overt form and its ironic masks. His adolescent enthusiasm for Heine suggests that his mature realism represented a solution to a malaise not far removed from that in twentieth-century modernism. Yet I think we approach the heart of the matter if we take our cues from the novel as cultural artifact rather than the novel as intellectual history. Essentially, the realists refused to give their readers the sort of satisfaction the novel generally afforded.

Women's novels offered a heroine who the reader could playfully and temporarily become. Popular fiction of all kinds—the sensation novels, Beadle's dime novels, working-girl fiction of the 1880s and 90s, the historical romances of the latter decade—all spotlighted a single leading character, who was of greater intrinsic interest than anyone around her or him. Fiction worked by offering the reader an alternative ego. Thus, the pleasure the reader experienced at the end was an ego-pleasure—a happy embrace, a successful coup, a completed journey, a threat finally averted. This satisfaction, and the fantasies containing it, reflected to some extent the atomization of society, the individual's increasing alienation, and the well-publicized success of a few great achievers. The surge of industrial activity in nineteenth-century America puffed up the ego with dreams of stunning personal success, of inevitably triumphant personal nobility. Realism was a critical response to the simultaneously inflated and privatized ego that was made hungry by contemporary society and fed by the fantasies in popular fiction. That is one of the reasons realism was often "pessimistic"—it insisted that the self was limited and conditioned and not capable of the apotheosis promised by mass fantasy. James told stories in which the protagonist often had to do without his heart's desire. Howells did the same, but he also tried a more radical idea. He prevented the reader from identifying with any one character. James did this in one realistic novel, *The Bostonians.* Howells did it in a dozen.

This particular difference between the two writers is worth noting. While James studied Isabel in great detail so that she became "an easy victim of scientific criticism," he also hoped the reader would feel "an impulse more tender and more purely expectant." That is to say, James still allowed us, though just barely, the old pleasure of "becoming" Isabel and getting some of the traditional shivers of fear, anticipation, anxiety, and so forth. But Howells did not permit the reader to feel much tender expectancy in *A Modern Instance.*[10] Refusing to tell a story that lined up with a major fantasy, he began with a familiar courtship situation that gradually petered out into a naturalistic world devoid of satisfaction or unity and with an inherent centrifugal tendency. Hoping to sever the novel from its rooted daydreams, he wrote time-bound narratives populated by people infinitely richer than those of any other nineteenth-century American writer.[11] Yet the mainspring at times seemed broken. Unlike James, who told a familiar story over and over, Howells told the non-story of people trying to live by false ideals and fantasies and getting tripped up by them. The *point* of the novel was to let us escape into a fully imagined world, one held together by a single thread of narrative movement and thus assimilable by an ego reading in time. Howells insisted that the novel was not dessert but meat and potatoes, for he wanted to use it to represent a people partly ruined by the dream of transcendence.

The strong ethical concern in American realism has often been noted. Ben Halleck, Silas and Penelope Lapham, Isabel Archer, and Hyacinth Robinson all have to make a difficult decision with important consequences for themselves and others. The distinctive contribution of realism in representing ethical choice was to insist on its importance even while hedging it about with enormous material and obligatory compulsions. In realism the self was free, but just barely. All the characters listed here can and must choose, but each of them has only two choices, and only one of these (except for Ben) seems in each case to be correct. Even more striking is the fact that in every case except Penelope's, the correct choice enforces a painful discipline on the self (in Hyacinth's case, death). Here we see a reflection of the massive Victorian content in Howells' and James's realism—but we also see a denial of the faith, dramatized in so many popular novels, that the straight and narrow path leads to warm embraces and valuable stock certificates. American realism was an extremely moral fiction. But its insistence that we live in society rather than in the wonderful fantasy-world of so much popular fiction was sane, practical, and truthful.

Thackeray had pretended that *Vanity Fair* was a novel without a hero, even though it obviously had a heroine, however bad. But in *A Hazard of New Fortunes* and to some extent in *April Hopes, The Minister's Charge*, and *The Quality of Mercy*, Howells succeeded in making novels in which no one person was preeminent. These novels asserted that the essential thing about our lives is the way we are associated, and attempted to counter the exaggerated and dreamy egotism that had been a genre quality of the novel. Henry James was overwhelmed by the richness of *A Hazard of New Fortunes*, yet he thought it lacked form and style. In spite of everything there is to be said for the novel, James may have been right. While *Hazard* does have certain formal principles of order, it also lacks a primitive story unity, which is purposely withheld. What makes the novel all the more significant is its close engagement with the modern world and the egalitarianism implied in its following several independent but linked careers. Howells was our ultimate democratic writer: he refused to tell us what to think about his characters' lives in his own voice; he tried to consider each of them as important as the others; and he managed to enter into almost every one in a magnificent way.

The fact that our first great realist also happens to be our most democratic writer shows that realism was not just a negative force combating the narcissistic ego, or the mystification of marriage, or the falsity of the period's ideal gender roles. The positive side of American realism was its vision of democratic action.[12] Howells was able to achieve what he did partly because he emerged from a people living in a roughly democratic system under conditions of relative ease—a people with some power to direct their own lives. It was because of this power that realism turned to the casual and material world and insisted on the primacy of what ordinary people, living under recognizable pressures, *try to do*. Realism never tells us what is to be done, but it assumes, fundamentally, that choice, regardless of the difficulties, exists.

Because realism reflected a limited but genuine sense of individual power to act in the world, realism occupied, historically and logically, a middle position between mid-Victorian women's fiction, with its powerful wonder-working heroines, and the modernist tradition as represented by James Joyce. What differentiates these three groups of fiction from one another is their varying use of the kind of projected activity we call daydreaming. In Susan Warner and Augusta J. Evans, the daydream was able to triumph over harsh social necessity. In Joyce on the other hand the world triumphs over the daydream in such a way that the most the daydreamer can possibly achieve is a moment of insight into his folly and the world's darkness.[13] "Araby" and "The Dead" end, not in action, but in moments of stunned, immobile understanding in which the protagonist perceives the utter vanity of his dreams. It is because the Joycean epiphany precludes all relevant action that *The Dubliners* and *A Portrait of the Artist as a Young Man* are not, in spite of all their exact historical and psychological detail, finally realistic. Realism minus the potentially effective human will is no longer realism.

The evidence of this claim is to be seen in Joyce's career, with its steady drift from realism toward allegory. Why was Joyce's climactic work a timeless dream (entirely different from daydream) at a wake? Because decent political activity had been excluded from his fiction from the beginning of his career. Joyce the exile became an allegorist for the same fundamental reason Boethius and many others have turned to this form. Unlike realism, the literature of writers with some democratic freedom, allegory is the literature of exiles, prisoners, captives, or others who have no room to act in their society. While realism pays close attention to the facts of the contemporary social scene, corrects some of the current stereotypes, and tries to represent the casual flow of events, allegory offers a timeless scene, a universe of static types and symbols rather than casual change, a view of behavior that sees the actor or hero as the matrix for competing absolutes or abstract types, and facts that require interpretation rather than recognition followed by action. Allegory is the product of mind living under absolutism and hence projects an implacable world of abstract types— precisely the type of world projected by the violated will. Allegory is one of many human artifacts expressing a sense of individual powerlessness.[14] The reason why *The Consolations of Philosophy* begins when the hero is thrown in prison is identical with the reason why *Pilgrim's Progress* begins at the point when the hero learns that his city is to be destroyed and that he can do nothing about it except seek another country. It is the same reason why so many medieval allegories begin as dream, consolation, vision, or escape for the soul that is doomed, helpless, or consumed by hopeless love. The reason is that in allegory, unlike realism, the individual is in chains.

Realism attacked abstract types because abstract types are the mind-forged manacles immobilizing the human will. In 1882 Thomas Sergeant Perry defended Howells' kind of fiction in the way that seems most fitting and true. "Just as the scientific spirit digs the ground from beneath superstition, so does its fellow-worker, realism, tend to prick the bubble of abstract types. Realism is the tool of the democratic spirit, the modern spirit by means of which the truth is elicited."[15] It is not hard to understand why abstract types should seem implacable to a cultivated mandarin living at a time when the *res publica* gets weaker and bullies get stronger, or to a Puritan overwhelmed by an arbitrary sovereign deity and endowed with a depraved will incapable of doing good. It is also possible to understand (though my own sympathies are strained) why early twentieth-century expatriates who felt swamped by the rise of the "vulgar" common man should prefer forms of literature that deny the possibility or importance of ethical-political activity. But I cannot sympathize at all with writers and intellectuals of the post-World War II era who live in the Western democracies (speaking loosely) and yet declare that realism is dead. Realism is far too important to let die, for if it does we do.

NOTES

1. René Wellek, *Concepts of Criticism* (New Haven: Yale University Press, 1963), pp. 240–41. E. B. Greenwood tried to invalidate Wellek's approach in "Reflections on Professor Wellek's Concept of Realism," *Neophilologus* (1962), 46(2): 89–96. For rejoinder, see Wellek, "A Reply to E. B. Greenwood's Reflections," *Ibid.* (3): 194–96.

2. The chief studies of American realism are: Everett Carter, *Howells and the Age of Realism* (Philadelphia: Lippincott, 1954); Robert P. Falk, "The Rise of Realism," Harry Hayden Clark, ed., *Transitions in American Literary History* (Durham: Duke University Press, 1953), pp. 379–442; Warner Berthoff, *The Ferment of Realism* (New York: Free Press, 1965); Donald Pizer, *Realism and Naturalism in Nineteenth Century American Literature* (Carbondale: Southern Illinois University Press, 1966); Harold H. Kolb, Jr., *The Illusion of Life: American Realism as a Literary Form* (Charlottesville: University Press of Virginia, 1969); Edwin H. Cady, *The Light of Common Day: Realism in American Fiction* (Bloomington: Indiana University Press, 1971); Olov W. Fryckstedt's survey of Howells' movement towards realism in *In Quest of America: A Study of Howells' Early Development as a Novelist* (Cambridge: Harvard University Press, 1958), ch. 4; C. Hugh Holman, *Windows on the World: Essays on American Social Fiction* (Knoxville: University of Tennessee Press, 1979).

For broader discussions of realism, see especially the summer 1951 issue of *Comparative Literature*; Damian Grant, *Realism* (London: Methuen, 1970); Erich Auerbach, *Mimesis: The Representation of Reality in Western Literature*, Willard Trask, trans. (Garden City, NY: Doubleday, 1957); and Joseph Peter Stern, *On Realism* (London: Routledge and Kegan Paul, 1973). Wellek, "Auerbach's Special Realism," *Kenyon Review* (Spring 1954), 16: 299–307, has shown that the concept of realism in Auerbach's superb book is somewhat contaminated with existentialism. Stern follows Auerbach in taking realism to be, not a period-concept, but "a perennial mode of representing the world and coming to terms with it" (p. 32). The strength of Stern's book is in its patient teasing out of the nuances of *realism* and its wide-ranging exploration of "the realistic mode" as a timeless quantity. I hope I am not flattering myself in thinking that one main difference between my and Stern's approach is similar to the difference, in biological nomenclature, between splitters and lumpers. I being the splitter. At any rate, Stern's is the best book on realism as a perennial mode of writing.

The Stalinist view of realism may be represented by the assertion in Boris Suchkov, *A History of Realism* (Moscow: Progress, 1973), p. 143: "It was the conflict between the individual and his environment that underlay the action in works of critical realism, and this reflected the process of atomisation of bourgeois society, since the gradual advance of alienation also entailed a widening of the gap between the individual and his environment. The conditions for genuinely epic literature were only created in our own time by socialist realism, the main feature of which is analysis and portrayal of the process of reconciliation of the individual and society as a result of socialist transformation of private ownership social relations." For an excellent analysis of critical realism *cum* Lukács versus socialist realism *cum* Gorky, see George Bisztray, *Marxist Models of Literary Realism* (New York: Columbia University Press, 1978).

Lukács for the most part fought socialist realism. Although I have taken more from this critic than from any other writer on realism, I have essentially reassembled certain fragments of his system for my own constructions. The finest quality of his work is what Bisztray calls its "theoretical-methodological clairvoyance" (*ibid.*, p. 96). I cannot accept his use of certain Marxist categories or the Hegelian concrete universal, or his ignoring folk and popular literature. Certain vital elements in Lukács' thought, such as his grasp of modern bourgeois decay, may be abstracted from their Marxist context and integrated in other systems. In particular, for the concept of the concrete universal as embodied in the historically significant character type, I substitute a particular culture's ideal gender role as embodied in a male or female character-type. See Georg Lukács, *Studies in European Realism: A Sociological Survey of the Writings of Balzac, Stendhal, Zola, Tolstoy, Gorki and Others*, Edith Bone, trans. (London: Hillway, 1950); *The Meaning of Contemporary Realism*, John and Necke Mander, trans. (London: Merlin Press, 1963); *The Historical Novel*, Hannah and Stanley Mitchell, trans. (London: Merlin Press, 1962).

For a recent defense of realism with which I am in full agreement, see Gerald Graff, "The Politics of Anti-Realism," *Salmagundi* (Summer–Fall 1978), no. 42, pp. 4–30.

3. A remark in an 1876 review by James illustrates his patronizing view of local color: "The author has bravely attempted to write a characteristic American novel, which should be a tale of civilization — be void of big-hearted backwoodsmen and of every form of 'dialect.' " Review of Charles Henry Doe's *Buffets* in "Recent Novels," *Nation* (January 13, 1876), 22: 32. Howells was generally more favorable and discriminating. The same year, in accepting "Freedom Wheeler's Controversy with Providence" by Rose Terry Cooke (whom he did not always care for), he wrote: "I am very glad to accept your story which I think extremely well wrought throughout" (unpublished letter, June 6, 1876, owned by Connecticut Historical Society, Hartford). Ten years later he called this story "a masterpiece" — "Editor's Study," *Harper's* (February 1887), 74: 484. Howells' support of various local and local color writers — E. W. Howe, Cable, Murfree, Jewett, Wilkins Freeman, Woolson, etc. — is known. Less well-known is that the four most distinguished writers he singled out in his "Editor's Study" essay on the short story in America were all women local colorists — Cooke, Murfree, Jewett, Woolson. In fact, as Ann Douglas has pointed out, many of the local colorists were the impoverished though more polished heirs of the women novelists of the 1850s; see "The Literature of Impoverishment: The Women Local Colorists in America 1865–1914," *Women's Studies* (1972), 1(1): 3–45. On the other hand, Claude M. Simpson, Jr., traced local color in part to frontier humor in his compre-

hensive introduction to *The Local Colorists: American Short Stories, 1857–1900* (New York: Harper, 1960). Douglas persuades me that the local-color short story was to a large extent a diminished version of the earlier women's novel, muted but better pitched; yet I think she underrates Jewett and Wilkins Freeman.

4. The proof-text here is James's review of *The Schonberg-Cotta Family* in *Nation* (September 14, 1865), 1: 345. At this time James equated realism with local color and scorned both: "It is just now very much the fashion to discuss the so-called principle of realism, and we all know that there exists in France a school of art in which it is associated with great brilliancy and great immorality. The disciples of this school pursue, with an assiduity worthy of a better cause, the research of local colors, with which they have produced a number of curious effects. We believe, however, that the greatest successes in this line are reserved for that branch of the school which contains the most female writers; for if women are unable to draw, they notoriously can at all events paint, and this is what realism requires. For an exhibition of the true realistic *chique* we would accordingly refer that body of artists who are represented in France by MM. Flaubert and Gerôme to that class of works which in our own literature are represented by the 'Daisy Chain' [by Charlotte Yonge] and 'The Wide, Wide World' [by Susan Warner]." The sarcasm of this recommendation reflects Godkin's editorial policies and James's own early hostility to realism. James was saying that the final, absurd consequences of the realists' program could be foreseen in the unspeakably bad "domestic" novelists. One of several critics who take this passage to express *approval* is Henry Nash Smith, "The Scribbling Women and the Cosmic Success Story," *Critical Inquiry* (September 1974), 1: 68.

5. Wellek, *Concepts of Criticism*, p. 255. Stern's analysis of realism offers an alternative, possibly preferable, response to Wellek from my own.

6. *North American Review* (January 1865), 100: 272; italics James's.

7. John G. Cawelti, *Adventure, Mystery, and Romance: Formula Stories as Art and Popular Culture* (Chicago: University of Chicago Press, 1976), pp. 18–19.

8. This is the flaw in Maurice Larkin's generally quite authoritative survey of European realism, *Man and Society in Nineteenth-Century Realism: Determinism and Literature* (London: Macmillan, 1977). An exaggerated view of the influence of science on realism has led an astonishing number of thinkers to declare that the obsolescence of nineteenth-century science has led to the obsolescence of realism.

9. Quoted from Cady, *Light of Common Day*, p. 70.

10. George William Curtis, "Editor's Literary Record," *Harper's Monthly* (January 1883), 66: 314–315, felt the "defects" of the hero and heroine of *Modern Instance* were "so palpable and obtrusive" that the "story fails to awaken genuine sympathy for any one of its actors." The reviewer in "Literature/A Woman's Reason," *Critic* (December 22, 1883), 3: 518–519, regretted that this novel and *Modern Instance* did not "carry our imaginations and hold them long captive in spite of themselves" (Clayton Eichelberger, *Published Comment on William Dean Howells through 1920: A Research Bibliography* [Boston: G. K. Hall, 1975], pp. 46–47).

11. Gary Stephens, "Haunted Americana: The Endurance of American Realism," *Partisan Review*, (1977), 44: 71–84.

12. Cf. Stern, *On Realism*: "the democratic ideology" is "a more natural habitation for the practice of literary realism than any other ideology I know" (p. 57); and realism "cannot help being interested in the political scene" (p. 53).

13. Cf. Robert L. Caserio, *Plot, Story, and the Novel from Dickens and Poe to the Modern Period* (Princeton: Princeton University Press, 1979), p. xiii: "When writers and readers of novels lose interest in plot and story, they appear to lose faith in the meaning and the moral value of acts."

14. Among many modern instances, there is David Caute's *The Illusion: An Essay on Politics, Theatre and the Novel* (London: André Deutsch, 1971). This book attacks a premise of realism and naturalism—the idea that it is possible and okay for art to provide an illusion of life. Caute's essay is pervaded with the familiar hysteria that insists it is "radical," displays a commitment to something that is vague but very sweeping, admires Sartre, Brecht, and Chernyshevsky, but is afraid, finally, that there is nothing to be done after all. The author has a chronic impulse to undercut himself: "Let me offer an assertion which I shall instantly retract" (p. 21). He comes out fighting for the idea that literature must commit itself to social change, but rejects realism's mimesis of imperfect society precisely because this mimesis is a "mirage" (p. 96) that reenters the world and "reshapes" (p. 97) it. He argues for "the dialectical novel," which "must inevitably de-mystify fiction by recognising its fictitious nature" (p. 265). What sort of fiction does Caute like most at the end of his book? "In the political novel," he tells us, more truthfully than I think he realizes, "the allegory is the most commonly employed metaphor of alienation" (p. 259). He cites several modern allegories, singling out Orwell's *Animal Farm* for high marks. Further, he rather unoriginally sees anti-utopia as "the authentic political allegory of our age" (p. 260), with its "singular individual who has not yet succumbed or been crushed or been totally absorbed by the prevailing totalitarianism" (p. 261). I think Caute's book inadvertently supports my contention that allegory—and the praise of allegory—grows out of a desperate sense of helplessness.

15. T. S. Perry, "William Dean Howells," *Century* (March 1882), 23: 683.

THIRTY-FOUR

THE COUNTRY OF THE BLUE

Eric J. Sundquist

Eric J. Sundquist (1952–) received his Ph.D. from Johns Hopkins University in 1978. He has taught at Johns Hopkins, the University of California, Berkeley, and Vanderbilt University, and is presently on the faculty of the University of California, Los Angeles. One of the most prolific and wide-ranging younger scholars in the study of American literature, Sundquist's works include *Home as Found: Authority and Genealogy in Nineteenth-Century American Literature* (1979), *Faulkner: The House Divided* (1983), and *To Wake the Nations: Race in the Making of American Literature* (1993). Sundquist's "The Country of the Blue" served as the Introduction to a collection of essays on American realism by various scholars.

In a short story entitled "The Next Time," which appeared in 1895—the same year in which *The Red Badge of Courage* appeared as a book, in which Norris gave up his first attempts to publish *McTeague* and took off for South Africa, in which Howells recoiled from the previous year's publication of his utopian romance, *A Traveler from Altruria*, and in which Twain wandered aimlessly between *Tom Sawyer Abroad* (1894) and *Tom Sawyer, Detective* (1896)—Henry James's novelist-hero, after failing yet again to become commercially successful because he is too good a writer, simply floats away "into a grand indifference, into a reckless consciousness of art." What happens to Ray Limbert, says James of his admitted fictional double, is that "he had merely waked up one morning again in the country of the blue and had stayed there with a good conscience and a great idea." He dies shortly thereafter.

The country of the blue is, of course, an exceptionally Jamesian territory; and

American Realism: New Essays, ed. Eric J. Sundquist (Baltimore: Copyright © 1982 by The Johns Hopkins University Press), pp. 3–27. Reprinted by permission of The Johns Hopkins University Press.

while one can define the dilemma of American realism by the example of James only through rather calculated effort, I want to suggest that Ray Limbert's career, by a variety of analogies the following essays unfold, is representative of that dilemma. James's story, as R. P. Blackmur points out, is a fable of the writer "who struggles desperately to make society his prey, but fails because he cannot help remaining the harmless, the isolated monarch of his extreme imaginative ardent self."[1] This is not to say that all American authors of the period necessarily had either the fine talents or the crass motives of Ray Limbert, but rather that the gulf between the "real world" and their own isolated, imaginative selves often remained a conspicuous one or, on the contrary, collapsed altogether and left them in the bluest of countries, the country of American romance.

Though few readers completely agree on definitions or examples, the perennial distinction between the "romance" and the realistic "novel" in American fiction remains a useful one. The most familiar and influential argument for this distinction is made by Richard Chase, who emphasizes that the romance rejects verisimilitude, continuity of plot, and the reconciliation of character to society, and embodies instead "the aesthetic possibilities of radical forms of alienation, contradiction, and disorder."[2] While it is not my intention to extend this view in detail—or to promote it as the greatest distinguishing feature of American fiction—I do want to suggest that it is within the framework of these widely accepted terms that the significance of American realism must initially be considered. To cite briefly two examples: what possible relationship is there between Crane's frantically stylized war novel and the Civil War itself? And what outrageous claims must be made about Twain's *Pudd'nhead Wilson* (1894) in order to include it in more classical or traditional definitions of realism? No matter that we know *The Red Badge of Courage* derived factually from a *Century Magazine* series on "Battles and Leaders of the Civil War" and that its action can therefore be anchored rather precisely in the battle of Chancellorsville: to point to this evidence, interesting though it is, may only make its final relevance more disquieting; just as pointing to Twain's interest in a famous case of Siamese twins or in racist evolutionary theories and laws (*Plessy v. Ferguson*, 1896, was just around the corner) or in the development of fingerprinting does not prevent the novel from seeming a bizarre instance of naturalistic farce but guarantees it.

Like James, Crane and Twain also inhabit the country of the blue, not in their case because they failed of popular success (in this respect they were more properly his opposite) but because their reckless, imaginative selves refused to yield to the literalizing demands of a strict realism. One might object that Crane and Twain, for example, are no more representative of the school of realism than James himself is. The point, though, is that American realism virtually has no school; its most dominating and influential advocate, William Dean Howells, often seems to ride along in a strange vacuum, nearly unheeded in his continual insistence on the proprieties of the everyday, stable characterization, and moral certainty, while almost every other important author of the period simply refused, in these terms, to become a realist.

If it has had a definable life at all in America, realism has surely had a life that stretches beyond the boundaries proposed by this collection. To establish a definition by beginning with the writers who made their professional appearances after the Civil War, however, is not particularly difficult to justify, for such a definition can with some freedom even claim the participation of Whitman, the consummate spokesman in both poetry and prose for democratic realism; but to conclude with Dreiser is an act nearly impossible to defend. One might rather say that American realism begins with Dreiser's *Sister Carrie* (1900) and reaches maturity some twenty to thirty years later in the works of Lewis, Dos Passos, Farrell, and Hemingway. But if Dreiser stands at the beginning of such a tradition, the age that made him possible is of particular interest. And it is precisely because the period between the Civil War and the first decades of the twentieth century resists convenient generic classification and satisfactory theoretical containment that it displays most openly the intense struggle of realism in America.

What Alfred Kazin noted of nineteenth-century American realism in 1942—that it "had no true battleground, as it had no intellectual history, few models, virtually no theory, and no unity"—was by implication also true of the twentieth-century literature he proceeded to examine and (by further implication) true as well of the critical thought that sought to characterize those periods. This remains partially true today not at all because of critical disinterest or ineptitude but, rather, because of the utter diversity even among writers who claimed in their own right, or were so acclaimed by their readers, to have certain alliances or affinities with each other. One origin of the problem, as Kazin remarked, lay in the fact that, while various European traditions of realism could more clearly be seen to have grown out of identifiable and logically successive climates of political and philosophical thought, realism in America "grew out of the bewilderment, and thrived on the simple grimness, of a generation suddenly brought face to face with the pervasive materialism of industrial capitalism."[3] To say that American realism had no philosophical or political program, no reliable public spokesmen, and thus no literary "heroes" is to pose a problem requiring further attention, but one that reminds us that the heroes of this age were certainly not novelists and were seldom—with the possible exceptions of Grant and Roosevelt—political leaders. Rather, they were inventors and entrepreneurs, or financial wizards such as Rockefeller and Gould, Carnegie and Yerkes; and their careers, particularly as they verged on and incorporated the mythical, help to reveal the importance of Kazin's claim.

Both the ideals and the public idealizations of the founding fathers seemed at best badly shaken, and at worst impossibly irrelevant, following the Civil War, and a corresponding pressure may be discerned in the literature that at once incorporated that loss in the tribute of muted nostalgia and in part gave way to its consequences. Not Captain Ahab but the Captains of Industry were the new cultural embodiments of heroism. If we only see this clearly in retrospect (just as Ahab has only been seen clearly from the perspective of the twentieth century), it is because we live in the society that they—as forefathers do—made possible and necessary, and therefore feel more fully the psychological implications of the transfiguration of "father" and "family" into "boss" and "corporation." One has only to cite in abbreviated form a modern analyst's description of this transfiguration to sense a concomitant evolution and relocation of one of the prominent concerns of American romance, the validity of patriarchal authority, in the more socially complicated textures of realism:

> The development of a hierarchical system of social labor not only rationalizes domination but also "contains" the rebellion against domination. . . . The guilt of rebellion is thereby intensified. The revolt against the primal father eliminated an individual person who could be (and was) replaced by other persons; but when the dominion of the father has expanded into the dominion of society, no such replacement seems possible, and the guilt becomes fatal. . . . With the rationalization of the productive apparatus, with the multiplication of functions, all domination assumes the form of administration. At its peak, the concentration of economic power seems to turn into anonymity: everyone, even at the top, appears to be powerless before the movements and laws of the apparatus itself. . . . Corporealization of the superego is accompanied by corporealization of the ego, manifest in the frozen traits and gestures, at the appropriate occasions and hours.[4]

Marcuse's argument, so suggestive of Dreiser's position at the climax of one century and the outset of another, also suggests incidentally a secondary subversion of the self's "natural" relationship to the figure of fatherly authority; for the public incorporation of that authority is matched from below and within, as it were, by the location of inherited models of behavior in the physiology of the organism itself. By something of a paradox, it is the interiorization of authority manifest in Darwinian social theories (and later in the rise of psychoanalysis and the professional social sciences) that makes possible, even inevitable, the corporate externalization of authority. While Marcuse's assessment is not by any means the whole story, it is nonetheless an indication of the complex contours of realism in America and of the fact that, as Kazin reminds us, the social and psychological effects of industrial capitalism constitute the place at which one must begin.

The seemingly sudden and demonstrably swift acceleration into being of finance capitalism based on industrial technology following the Civil War underlies the many forms of intellectual reaction that, by twists and turns, by adventurous challenge and imaginative endorsement, followed from it, reaching backward to include strains of motivation prevalent in earlier American thought and writing, and extending forward in ways that render any single definition inadequate. Which is to say again that the life of American realism exists, perhaps, either everywhere or nowhere; like "the real" itself, it resists containment, and for the very good reason that "the real" in America, like the country itself, has always had a notoriously short life. Why then, should the period it entitles be particularly subject to this pressure? I want to suggest, returning to James's parable of the writer, that one conspicuous reason is that the period between the Civil War and World War I is one in which American writers felt most compelled, and tried hardest, to become "realists"—and failed. With imperial relentlessness they sought to master a bewildering society that seemed always, in turn, to be mastering them; under such pressure, they returned ever more feverishly to the imagination—to its shaping and distorting powers—and as a consequence kept waking up in the country of the blue, which of necessity was America itself.

They did not, quite obviously, fail to write important and sometimes great fiction; neither did they fail to explore through documented fact and extrapolated theory the pervasive influence of social Darwinism on the structure and values of the American community, nor did they back away from probing the very real, and therefore enchanting, relationship between the calculations of business and the imaginations of literature. Quite the reverse: precisely because the consequent entanglements of these investigations were so thoroughly felt and so actively represented, American realistic fiction—like the literature of romance that preceded it, and like the ostensibly nonliterary documents of religious and political thought that were the country's first works of the imagination—kept spilling out into the "neutral territory" of romance that Hawthorne had made emblematic of American fiction, "appropriating a lot of land which had no visible owner, and building a house, of materials long in use for constructing castles in the air." Like its preface, *The House of the Seven Gables* (1851) reaches into the past in order to propel itself forward, tying together in a complex network of fully realized symbolic action the dreams of a nation on the brink of portentous social revolution. In this respect and others it contains a wealth of American themes—the simultaneous exhilaration and anxiety felt, and expressed, in the disavowal of tradition; the intense probing of literature's necessary connection to social and commercial realities; the risks of mimetic fidelity; and the constant pressures brought to bear upon the domain of the self by the material world. The actions of Hawthorne's characters, and the action of Hawthorne himself as narrator, constitute the point of transition that the "neutral territory" itself is; and by doing so they anticipate a central activity (to bring the imagination to bear upon reality) and a continuing difficulty (to resist capitulation to that reality) of American realism.

Hawthorne's novel is one example of an earlier work to which predominant themes running through American realism can be traced. The list is long and would surely, for example, have to include Brown's *Arthur Mervyn* (1799–1800), Poe's "The Man of the Crowd" (1840), Lippard's *The Quaker City* (1844), Cooper's *The Crater* (1847), and Davis's *Life in the Iron Mills* (1861). But let us simply add that, by dwelling excessively on the material and technological details of American life, and by measuring the distance between the sovereign territory of the individual self and the powers of social or political community that surround and create individual destiny, *Moby-Dick* (1851) and Whitman's poetry and prose at once define an American tradition that is beyond generic classification and emphatically point toward prominent concerns in the age of realism. If it also seems that Hawthorne, Whitman, and Melville resist the intrusion of the real into the territory of the romance, however, one can bound the age of realism in exactly those terms by noting that, like America itself, the struggle had simply moved west by the end of the century. For the poet-hero of Norris's *The Octopus* (1901), his imaginative vision of the "huge romantic West" is urgently troubled by the imposed mapping of telegraph wires and ranch fences, and is stopped cold by the leviathan railroad, a "note of harsh colour that refused to enter into the great scheme of harmony. It was material, sordid, deadly commonplace." In Presley's vision, as in Norris's own, "the romance seemed complete up to that point. There it broke, there it failed, there it became realism, grim, unlovely, unyielding."

Such a view is certainly not sustained by the end of the novel, where Presley's romance expands dramatically to include the harsh, unyielding forces of technology; and because he insisted that naturalism was indeed a form of romance, and therefore utterly opposed to realism, Norris's case is perhaps a singular one. But his initial insistence on this opposition helps define the remarkable intrusion of romance into the work of nearly every writer of the period. Even Howells, writing from his editorial throne, felt compelled to imagine a way around this difficulty when he ventured in an essay collected in the classic statement on American realism, *Criticism and Fiction* (1891), that there was little significant difference between romanticism and realism, because each sought, in its own day, "to widen the bounds of sympathy, to level every barrier against aesthetic freedom, to escape from the paralysis of tradition." When the romance had "exhausted itself in this impulse," Howells declared, "it remained for realism to assert that fidelity to experience and probability of motive are essential conditions of great imaginative literature." When realism in turn becomes "false to itself" and fails to accomplish this, Howells predicted, it too will perish. There is no room here to do justice to the complexity of Howells's full argument, but one is tempted to note that, for some of the very reasons Howells points to, American realism (including much of his own work) did not achieve a certain and stable force, exhaust that force, and perish; rather, it failed case by case by refusing to renounce romance and by levelling the barriers of aesthetic freedom too completely.

To escape the "paralysis of tradition" is, of course, the typifying American gesture—in religion, in politics, in business, in literature, in life. This is one reason *The House of the Seven Gables* is so instructive a turning point, one whose revolutionary fervor recapitulates earlier American projects in religious and political rebellion (which, like the Pyncheon curse, have a power that can neither die nor be fully implemented) and predicts the threatened paralysis of the commercial or material "real" in the age of capitalism. Like several of Melville's works, Hawthorne's novel precedes the Civil War but in retrospect seems to have comprehended in advance its effects and aftermath. The other side of the coin is Twain, whose whole career exemplifies the agony of retrospect. By merging his own involvement in the paralysis of social (and literary) traditions with the real, bewildering presence of social and economic revolution, Twain demonstrated with considerable power that the Civil War, morally and culturally iconoclastic as it may have been, was not a clean break; instead, it represented a translation of materials and a transfiguration of figures of authority themselves—from the tyranny of the family to the tyranny of the corporation, say—one in which what Whitman in his 1872 preface to *Leaves of Grass* called America's "vast seething mass of materials" became more visibly and vexingly the dominant force in the construction of social reality, but also one in which fiction, as Howells remarked, would make "Reality its Romance."

Let us say, though, that the Civil War is followed by extraordinary progress in the development of communication and transportation, in the spread of education, and in the suddenly increased mobility of people and ideas; that it produces, therefore, a kind of "temporal concentration" that unifies the nation but also

> abrogates or renders powerless the entire social structure of orders and categories previously held valid; the tempo of the changes demands a perpetual and extremely difficult effort toward inner adaptation and produces intense concomitant crises. He who would account to himself for his real life and his place in human society is obliged to do so upon a far wider practical foundation and in a far larger context than before, and to be continually conscious that the social base upon which he lives is not constant for a moment but is perpetually changing through convulsions of the most various kinds.

This apt description of America following the Civil War comes, however, from Erich Auerbach's description of the social aftermath of the French Revolution.[5] It is appropriate not simply because Auerbach is accounting here for the great age of French realism, which America lags slightly behind, but also because it clarifies the way in which the social and economic results of the Civil War can be seen, both figuratively and actually, to extend and recapitulate America's own democratic revolution in 1776, while at the same time threatening to subvert its opulent possibilities of freedom by turning wilderness into mines, ranches, and oil wells; theology into science; men into machines; and founding fathers into executives of the State. Though the frontier, as an imaginative territory, was not closed by the time Frederick Jackson Turner claimed the physical frontier was in 1893, it is nevertheless true that the mapping, filling, containing, and controlling of both territories—the one in theory, the other in practice—that took place between the war and the end of the century was awesome. That romance remained a persistent force in American realism must be ascribed in part to the extraordinary force of the idea of the boundlessness of the country, a wilderness of fancied space that Whitman and Norris, for example, could celebrate even as they saw it cut, calculated, sold, and turned into cities.

The threat to physical space during the period is matched and, at times, fully accommodated by concurrent threats to ideal space—that is, the space of God, the space of beauty, the space of the self—of the kind elaborated in Dreiser's late essay "The Myth of Individuality" (1934), which depicts man as something "lived" by an incomprehensible cosmic force struggling "to express itself." Again, though, one must be careful to note, as Richard Poirier has, that this notion of individuality is not a sudden development in the American tradition, but might be said to "adapt Emerson's idea of the Over-Soul to the metropolis," so that from a social point of view (and the point of view of the novelist) the self becomes "anonymous" and individuality is achieved precisely "by the surrender of those features which define the individual as a social or psychological entity."[6] The transfiguration of Nature into City— or more simply into the one idea of FORCE at once acclaimed and lamented in *The Octopus* and *The Education of Henry Adams* (1907), for example—is an abstract emblem of those pervasive extenuations of the self that may be traced in the intrusion of technology, not simply into the lives of the novel's characters, but more particularly into the dominion of the novel's own enterprise: police surveillance in *The Princess Casamassima* (1886); fingerprinting in *Pudd'nhead Wilson*; dentistry and mining in *McTeague* (1899); the magazine and the elevated railway in *A Hazard of New Fortunes* (1890); the cash register in "The Blue Hotel" (1898); the newspaper and the camera in *An American Tragedy* (1925); the bicycle, baseball, and telephones in *A Connecticut Yankee in King Arthur's Court* (1889).

As it is an age of inventions, so it is an age of ideas—"ideas so passionately held," Jay Martin points out, "that they even seemed adequate substitutes for ideals."[7] In effect, ideas and inventions at times come so nearly to approximate one another that their very production becomes conspicuous; and becoming conspicuous becomes frightening, to the extent that Adams in the *Education* could inaugurate the century of paranoia by declaring that the universe is no longer an absolute but a "medium of exchange" in which personality itself is differentiated into "complex groups, like telephonic centers and systems." The evolutionary theories promoted by and derived from Herbert Spencer and Thomas Henry Huxley could—and did—justify almost any social, economic, or religious program, just as surely as they could—and did—undermine or invalidate any program that failed to "produce." In this atmosphere, the market becomes the measure of man himself; for as the Protestant ethic divides and conquers, the gap between inherent values and their external representations widens until it dissolves altogether: inner values of the spirit are drawn outward until they appear at last to merge with the things from which one cannot be distinguished and without which one cannot constitute, build, or fabricate a self. The self becomes an *image* of the real, and the real becomes an advertisement of and for the self.

The influence of Spencer, Huxley, and their disciples was immense; but an overemphasis on the infiltration of science into philosophy and theology alone might lead us to miss the equally important proliferation of systems of classification in other, more particular fields. William James's *Principles of Psychology* (1890), which stressed an acute connection between the mind and the nervous system and defined them together as an organized habit of adjustment to environment, and Oliver Wendell Holmes's *The Common Law* (1881), one of the first treatises to see laws themselves as evolutionary and adaptive rather than as static ideals, are dignified works of scholarship. But how distinguish them in importance for the world in which we live from Frederick W. Taylor's *The Principles of Scientific Management* (1911), which promoted increased industrial production through minute, systematic improvements of worker efficiency, or Daniel Edward Ryan's influential *Human Proportions in Growth* (1880), which made possible the standardization of measurement in men's and boy's clothing? Cash registers, adding machines, electric lighting, factory mechanization, quality control, mail-order firms and their catalogues, all manner of transportation and communication improvements—machines everywhere reminded man of the mechanism his body was in fact and the machine it threatened to become in action. In an age in love with competing systems and transfixed by the inevitable importance of exact detail, the problems of the novelist and the man in the street alike are dispiriting: How can life be organized, governed, made plausible? in the romance of man among the beasts, what remains of the mystic, the invisible? who, as Dreiser asks in *Sister Carrie*, "shall translate for us the language of the stones?"

The pressure of these disruptive questions may be felt throughout the literature of the period—in such diverse but equally intense investigations of guilt and sanity as *The Damnation of Theron Ware* (1896), *The Turn of the Screw* (1898), *The Red Badge of Courage*, and "The Yellow Wallpaper" (1892); or in the more exact probings of the "fictions of law and custom" that control and define society in *Pudd'nhead Wilson*, *Billy Budd* (1924), and *The Financier* (1912), where Dreiser's miniature essay on "verdicts" assumes a frantically large compass:

> Men in a jury-room, like those scientifically demonstrated atoms of crystal which scientists and philosophers love to speculate upon, like finally to arrange themselves into an orderly and artistic whole, to present a compact, intellectual front, to be whatever they have set out to be, properly and rightly—a compact, sensible jury. One sees this same instinct magnificently displayed in every other phase of nature—in the drifting sea-wood to the Sargasso Sea, in the geometric interrelation of air-bubbles on the surface of still water, in the marvelous unreasoned architecture of so many insects and atomic forms which make up the substance and the texture of this world. It would seem as though the physical substance of life— this apparition of form which the eye detects and calls real—were shot through with some subtlety that loves order, that is order.

In this passage, which centers on the trial of a character (Frank Cowperwood) modelled on one of the financial geniuses of the nineteenth century (Charles T. Yerkes), we find a peculiar convergence of the "forms, measured forms" that haunted Melville's Captain Vere and the quasi-mystical "phase of the Real, lurking behind the Real" that Whitman adumbrated in the 1876 preface to *Leaves of Grass*. What could be more real than the romance of system?

The realistic novel often depends upon translating a sufficiency, even a superfluity, of detail into determined hierarchical but mutually dependent orders—not only in order to correspond to the complicated fabric of contemporary life but also to make of such staggering detail its own ordering technique, one in which the value and scope of the self (and of value itself) is measureable and in which, as a result, the distinction between aspects of the self and its implemented devices becomes increasingly obscure. Such a problem is, again, not entirely new to the age; and the concomitant exhilaration and fear it promotes may be seen to reanimate the unconscious eruption of the gothic into an earlier age of reason. Twain's *Connecticut Yankee*, for example, appears quite literally to comprise a nightmare of contemporary industrial technology; its madman hero is the corporate "Boss" of his own "Republic," and its apocalyptic annihilation of thousands by electric fences seems inarguably modern— until we recall that Benjamin Franklin, in 1773, advocated the convenient and efficacious mass slaughter of animals and fowl by electricity. A more precise index of the reactivation of eighteenth-century concerns can be found in the manifold resemblances between the gothic and naturalism, which in its most extraordinary (and therefore representative) forms envisions a kind of biological sublime. The gothic is the grandfather of naturalism as surely as Erasmus Darwin is the grandfather of Charles Darwin. When Charles Brockden Brown appealed to the elder Darwin's *Zoonomia* in order to validate his theory of "Mania Mutabilis" in *Wieland* (1798), he anticipated by about a century the scientific characterization of abnormal behavior indulged in by Dreiser and Norris—with this difference: in naturalism, the abnormal becomes the barely submerged norm.

In this respect and others Benjamin Franklin Norris quite rightly differentiates the dull, commonplace realism of Howells—"the drama of a broken teacup, the tragedy of a walk down the block"—from the "romance" of naturalism, which takes its theoretical method from Zola's influential essay "The Experimental Novel" (1880) and works, Norris maintains in *Responsibilities of the Novelist* (1903), as a finely tempered, flawless "instrument with which we may go straight through the clothes and tissues and wrappings of flesh down into the red, living heart of things." Revelling in the extraordinary, the excessive, and the grotesque in order to reveal the immutable bestiality of Man in Nature, naturalism dramatizes the loss of individuality at a physiological level by making a Calvinism without God its determining order and violent death its utopia.[8] The ease with which naturalism verges upon parody, especially in Crane and Norris, thus results in part from a gothic *intensification of detail* that approaches the allegorical without finding release into or through it; the characters inhabit alien landscape filled with inflated symbols, and they die not in bed, at home, of old age and natural causes, but in open boats, in Death Valley, in the electric chair, in silos of WHEAT, in the nowhere of the Yukon—in blinding fields of force, sudden traps of mysterious making. And they do so at the level of technique by becoming bloated figures in which the human constantly threatens to detach and deform itself into the bestial (as in Norris) or, at extremity, in which the human disappears completely into the beast (as in London). It is no simple coincidence, therefore, that *The Call of the Wild* (1903) depicts the seemingly inevitable union of naturalism and aestheticism, and vividly endorses—in a Paterian moment of pure *symbol*—the extinction of the social, civilized self in a frenzy of sensation:

> There is an ecstasy that marks the summit of life, and beyond which life cannot rise. And such is the paradox of living, this ecstasy comes when one is most alive, and it comes as a complete forgetfulness that one is alive. This ecstasy, this forgetfulness of living, comes to the artist, caught up and out of himself in a sheet of flame; it comes to the soldier, war-mad on a stricken field and refusing quarter; and it came to Buck, leading the pack, sounding the old wolf-cry. . . . He was sounding the deeps of his nature, and of the parts of nature that were deeper than he, going back into the womb of Time.

Romance, as Norris quite correctly saw, remained the visceral, spiritual essence of the real.

In theoretical terms, Norris's case (and certainly London's) is a peculiar one; but it is worth remembering that, in terms of social dramatization, his definitions distinguish him only from Howells but not necessarily from Twain, Dreiser, and Crane or even, perhaps, from James and Wharton. For them as well, survival in the social world, as in the physical world that may be its model and origin, depends upon the kind of adaption and manipulation Dreiser makes emblematic of both the "constructive genius of nature" and the "creative power" of man's achieved mastery of nature (or the city, or society, or Wall Street) in his fable of the Black Grouper at the conclusion of *The Financier*: "Its great superiority lies in an almost unbelievable power of simulation. . . . An implement of illusion one might readily suspect it to be, a living lie, a creature whose business it is to appear what it is not, to simulate that with which it has nothing in common, to get its living by great subtlety." The obsession with lying as a gesture that at once defines the environment in which one lives and expresses the necessity of masks and disguises in mastering that environment equally illuminates Wharton's and James's dramatizations of a self that is at constant risk of surrendering its powers of will and is therefore willing to perform the many roles necessary to survival in the theater of social manners. And the most elaborate American representations of the lies of which society is constructed — *Adventures of Huckleberry Finn* (1885) and *The Confidence-Man* (1857) — remind us here how Twain and Melville, always enthusiasts of the masquerade, serve to define an age that may be variously limited by *Moby Dick* and *The Gilded Age* (1873) on one side and *Billy Budd* and *The Mysterious Stranger* (1908) on the other.

As these works and others press toward and anticipate modernism, both the absorption of the self in the facade of the material world and the increasingly visible "construction" of social reality become by necessity part of the technical apparatus of the novel, which, like the self and like the landscape, gets filled up and, in the end, used up. "We are no longer a raw-material reservoir, the marvel and despair of less fortunate cultures," remarks Wright Morris of the dilemma of American modernism anticipated by Crane and Dreiser, for "our only inexhaustible resource at the moment is the cliché. An endless flow of clichés, tirelessly processed for mass-media consumption, now give a sheen of vitality to what is either stillborn or secondhand."[9] To qualify this assessment properly, one would have to note the obvious ways in which the production of clichés continues, quite unavoidably, to express the amplitude of American raw material by transforming what is scarce or unattainable into what is evidently abundant. But Morris, for the moment, takes us farther than we can arguably go.

Although the freedoms of action, belief, and imagination that are under pressure in the age of American realism threaten at times to dissolve into marketable clichés, they are nonetheless fully involved with very real political and industrial forces; and the same forces that appear to render the imagination suspect or marginal, or to leave it in unnerving postures of acquiescence and accommodation, also bring literary art more conspicuously into the world of business by making it resemble or become a business itself. This in itself is not a particularly new development: for Emerson, for Hawthorne, for Poe, for Melville, the burdens of having to "stammer out something by way of getting a living" (as Melville put it in *Moby-Dick*) were a subdued but continual theme. But it is in the work of Twain, Howells, James, and Dreiser that the survival of literature in the community of the marketplace becomes more than a minor obsession. That so many writers of the period made a living—both initially and along the way—as magazine and newspaper journalists is a rather accurate measure of stylistic and thematic developments as well as an indication of the changing configurations of literature as a profession.[10]

One should notice in this connection that the professional (and symbolic) role of the central character in *A Hazard of New Fortunes* is that of "editor," a professional position that Howells brilliantly exploits in order to scrutinize, more than slightly autobiographically, the moral hazards of literature's tentative encounter with both the world of business and the world of social oppression for which it may be responsible. As "the missing link between the Arts and the Dollars," the magazine *Every Other Week* occupies the mediating position that the editor himself does; the editor in turn bears the burden, as Basil March does, of balancing aesthetic and social responsibilities, of putting money in service of art without capitulating to it, and therefore of maintaining an integrity that continually risks becoming immobilized in neutrality. When Crane approvingly reported in the *New York Tribune*, 1891, that Hamlin Garland had called *A Hazard of New Fortunes* "the greatest, sanest, truest study of a city in fiction," he paid a deserved compliment (which Howells returned when *Maggie* appeared, first in 1893 and again in 1896) but at the same time, perhaps, began to mark off the glib, ironic stance that his own roles of aesthete and journalist would make possible in his fiction. Howells's novel dramatizes these potentially compromising dangers most vividly in its depiction of the social voyeurism that March and his wife engage in while traveling on New York's elevated railway, where

> the fleeting intimacy you formed with people in second and third-floor interiors, while all the usual street life went on underneath, had a domestic intensity mixed with a perfect repose that was the last effect of good society with all its security and exclusiveness. March said it was better than the theater, of which it reminded him, to see those people through their windows: a family party of workfolk at a late tea, some of the men in their shirt-sleeves; a woman sewing by a lamp; a mother laying her child in its cradle; a man with his head fallen on his hands upon a table; a girl and her lover leaning over the windowsill together. What suggestion! What drama! What infinite interest!

While it is the purpose of the novel to develop the ironies implicit in this scene and in Basil's exultation, this is the Howellsian aesthetic of realism in miniature. And it is also the position of the editor, who is manifestly carried along and above society by the mechanisms of mass transit and quick transition that propel society itself, and who is resolutely caught in the position of an enthused but ineffectual spectator.

As *A Hazard of New Fortunes* makes apparent, the professionalization of literature reflects, both by challenge and by endorsement, the escalating professionalization of thought and life in later nineteenth-century America, which in turn reflects and extends the proliferation of the various modes of mechanization that have made it possible. It is an age in which money, machines, and men become, not exactly interchangeable, but analogous to the extent that distinctions among the values each might seem inherently to possess are broken down on a large scale. The realistic novel, then, depicts not so much the disappearance of value as the transfiguration of value itself into something whose power is a function of the many pressures of the economic and social market. The obsession with material reality that characterizes some definitions of American realism must therefore be understood to encompass the particular powers—of moral commitment, of adaptive roles, of the staging of action—that material reality can make manifest but cannot always fully define or control. In his important essay on "Reality in America," for example, Lionel Trilling complains that "in the American metaphysic, reality is always material reality, hard, resistant, unformed, impenetrable, and unpleasant. And that mind is alone felt to be trustworthy which most resembles this reality by most nearly reproducing the sensations it affords."[11] The crucial shift in emphasis that Trilling's statement contains is likely to go unnoticed unless we recognize the implications of moving from the "material" to "sensations" through the mediating terms "reproducing" and "affords." It is precisely the purpose of industrial capitalism to translate the material into the sensational (and then back again into the material, and so on) both by making it appear to afford something we need and to be itself affordable.

It is worth noting once again that the basis of this translation lies in "reproduction," an idea of virtually limitless importance for the period since, in a psychological sense as well, reproduction is itself entwined in the technology of capitalism with the very possibility of boundless opportunity and possession. A complete appreciation of the figurative centrality of reproduction in the age of realism would clearly have to take account of the ramifying problems of sexuality—the sacrifice of intimacy to public life, the increasing divorce of domestic and business concerns, the endless appetite for sentimental plays and novels—examined with equal apprehension by Howells, Norris, Adams, James, Gilman, and Wharton, but perhaps most melodramatically characterized by Dreiser (ever the armchair Freudian) when he wrote in "Neurotic America and the Sex Impulse" (1920) that out of the "defeated pursuit" of sexual gratification "comes most of all that is most distinguished in art, letters, and our social economy." Though we may judge that Dreiser has the cart before the horse, and though we may certainly object to his maintaining that beneath every "displacement" or "transferal" of sexual impulse into "desires for wealth, preferment, distinction and what not" there lies "a deep and abiding craving for women," there is little gain-saying his characterization of one of the primary psychological effects of capitalistic reproduction, in which the biological becomes mechanized and exteriorized, and the self is turned into a virtual product of its eminently desirable and reproducible products. The "incorporation" of fathers by business (or, on the other hand, the biological internalizing of them by theories of evolution) may in this respect be the most troubling sign of the concomitant suppression and sentimental idealization of women that female authors struggled against and the feminization of the self that many male authors both courted and feared.

The agitation over the breakdown of traditional sexual roles that marks much realistic fiction, as well as the portrayal of domestic spheres of action in forms of imprisonment or landscapes of utopian isolation, may thus be understood to derive from a more pervasive recasting of organic laws; and the systemization of manners and beliefs as evolving forms of habitual response may be seen both to resemble and to produce the models of capitalistic reproduction: everything evolves upward and outward, constantly positing the *desirable* and the *valuable* as something to be strived for. The fact that literature, in its representational capacity, is always implicated in a special mode of reproduction makes it particularly susceptible to the cumulative pressures of such power. As a way of sketching an approach to this problem, we might keep in mind the transfiguration of inherent value that Walter Benjamin has observed to take place in "the work of art" when it is brought to inhabit—and particularly when it is produced in—"the age of mechanical reproduction." What is in jeopardy in this age, Benjamin notes, is the "authority" or "aura" of the object: "the technique of reproduction detaches the reproduced object from the domain of tradition," and by making it eminently reproducible undermines its very claim to authenticity.[12] Benjamin speaks here rather strictly about the extreme consequences for the visual arts brought about by the development of photography; and with respect to any narrow understanding of the authority and reproduction of the work itself, the case of literary art is surely a somewhat different one. But with respect to the authenticity of the experience it seeks to describe by its own representation or reproduction, the realistic novel necessarily includes (as many of its theorists claim) a further documentation of that threat to the aura of tradition depicted in photography's mechanized reproduction of reality and more recently characterized by Daniel Boorstin as the new industrial age's obsession with "making experience repeatable."[13] The camera, the kinetoscope, and the gramophone make leisure a work of mechanical reproduction that is wholly continuous with industrial capitalism; and they quite certainly must be understood to usher in an age of special anxiety for the book—an anxiety, as Wright Morris reminds us, that the twentieth century verifies day by day but that Hawthorne, of course, anticipated: the photograph is evidence of ironic necromancy in *The House of the Seven Gables*, but in *An American Tragedy* it is evidence of cold-blooded murder.

This particular liberation from the paralysis of tradition, while it makes possible the maintenance and further secularization of tradition, also threatens to subvert or trivialize it by making it "like" the techniques of reproduction that bring it into being, and moreover by making those who utilize it "like" the techniques themselves. At extremity, in our century, the media versions of reality upon which we so heavily depend offer a particular danger: overwhelmed by mirror images of itself and unable to distinguish between the authentic and the facade of the copy, the self may ultimately reject the external altogether—and exactly to the degree that it has become its mediated victim. An "overexposure to manufactured illusions," Christopher Lasch warns, "soon destroys their representational power. The illusion of reality dissolves, not in a heightened sense of reality as we might expect, but in a remarkable indifference to reality."[14] This too is the dilemma of modernism—and more obviously of post-modernism—but it is important to see its origins in the late nineteenth century. For to the relatively influential extent that realistic literature began to take a photographic reproduction of life as its model, the novel must be seen as an assault on the "aura" of tradition exemplified, in America at least, by the romance—an economic extenuation of that secularization of Puritan experience which the romance itself embodied.

One way to gauge this extenuation in its manifold results is to note, as George Becker has, that the "slice-of-life approach" taken by many realistic novelists "spells the death of the hero as he has been traditionally presented." Because the hero by definition is "heightened" or "distorted" for effect, and personifies "a center of good or evil force" that demands "our identification to an intense degree," he has no place in the realistic novel, whose exemplary quality is "its typicality."[15] To insist on the singularity of this feature would be a mistake (and in the case of American realism would be patently absurd), but it raises important questions about the character of the hero in realistic fiction with respect to the role he performs, the space he can dominate, and the value or authority he is meant to have as the representative embodiment of certain cultural and social values. To the extent that he has these capacities at all, we might want to say that he is exterior to the novel's realistic scheme. That this is only provisionally true in the case of American realism, and in some respects divorces it from European traditions of the same period, does help to define the continued accommodation—indeed, the embracing—of romance in the age of capitalistic reproduction.

That accommodation can occur precisely because the preponderant and tangible materialism of life is always, in terms of utility, set in motion and mediated by money, a thing at once thoroughly abstract and (as Trina McTeague's ecstatic passion in a bedful of gold demonstrates) potently physical. The age of realism in America is the age of the *romance of money*—money not in any simple sense but in the complex alterations of human value that it brings into being by its own capacities for reproduction. As it defines, by changing, our notions of a self, so too it may define a change in our notions of a novelistic hero. For in the anatomy of American realism, the possible distortions of character that might lead the hero out of a society whose debased values and hypocritical entanglements of virtue he appears to reject are countered by those distortions of character that can make the hero the exemplary figure of power within that society. Such a hero does not reject society but masters it and though the novelist may present in his hero's career a critique of society, he does so by representing the hero not as different from us but rather very much, too much, like us. The hero is democratized not by being swallowed up by the fierce oblivion of materiality (as in the case of Dreiser's Hurstwood or Crane's Maggie) or by being levelled to insignificance (as is often the case in Howells, who adamantly proclaimed that he did "not believe in heroes") but rather by being permitted to incorporate the age's own dream of success, its own special romance.

In this respect, one may very well need to distinguish the American novel of realism from the European, which Leo Bersani has demonstrated in the case of the French novel to be largely ordered by the need of society to provide itself "with strategies for containing (and repressing) its disorder within significantly structured stories about itself." The realistic novel, Bersani argues, permits "psychological complexity" only so long as it does not "threaten an ideology of the self as a fundamentally intelligible structure," and it thus "admits heroes of desire [only] in order to submit them to ceremonies of expulsion. This literary form depends, for its very existence, on the annihilation or, at the very least, the immobilizing containment of anarchic impulses."[16] As it distinguishes the realistic novel from the modernist, and as it defines important dimensions of French realism in particular, this is a very compelling argument. But one must recognize that it is true of the American novel of the period only to a limited extent.

To the greater extent that the novelistic self becomes lost in a seemingly random or tyrannically calculating system of values in the age of industrial capitalism, the most forceful threat to an ideology of the self may appear not in the anarchic impulses of radical characterization but in the psychological complexity produced by society's own manufacture of desire. Though the "hero of desire" who reflects, incorporates, and virtually becomes those values may be expelled, he is expelled not so much because he threatens society as because he is unable to master its intricacies of survival. In an important essay that in part responds to Bersani's theory by noting a crucial difference between the cases of Howells and Dreiser, Walter Michaels has demonstrated a strong alliance between those excesses of sentimentality that Howells abhorred and Dreiser encouraged, and the very production of surplus desire in capitalistic society—an alliance so pervasive that, granting *Sister Carrie* the exemplary status in American realism it seems to merit, we must say "the capitalism of the late nineteenth and early twentieth centuries acted more to subvert the ideology of the autonomous self than to enforce it."[17] To accept this is to accept as well the possibility that "the real" of realism—stable character, coherently static society, the minimizing of excess or surplus in desire—is extraordinarily unstable and constantly veers toward romance through its unavoidable encounter with, and participation in, a system whose ideological essence is the resistance of such qualities.

In an age in which Andrew Carnegie and P. T. Barnum could offer equally popular lectures on "The Gospel of Wealth" and "The Art of Money-Getting," and in which the best of best sellers were Horatio Alger stories and Russell Conwell's *Acres of Diamonds* (1888; originally a sermon and lecture), we must be wary of minimizing society's own desire for more objects of desire. Carrie Meeber's emulation of the desirable—before the looking-glass of store windows, in her bedroom, in the audience and on the stage—depicts a state of desire for possessions in which interior and exterior, stimulus and response, have become thoroughly merged. Unlike Crane's Maggie, whose story would seem underhanded satire of *Sister Carrie* had it not appeared first, Carrie is able in her acting to "reproduce" what she sees until she has and harbors it herself; like money, like the theater, like the journalistic accounts and advertisements of reality the book contains, Carrie herself becomes a *medium* that pathetically, melodramatically reproduces and multiplies a form of desire that is at once sexual and hauntingly dispassionate. In the end (as Carrie Madenda) she embodies the world around her by offering, as Ames tells her, "a natural expression of its longing." As the "representative of all desire," she takes on an earlier role of the now declining and finally insignificant Hurstwood, in whose seductive voice she once heard "instead of his words, the voices of the things which he represented." Carrie is a classic example of the "conspicuous consumption" that Veblen's *The Theory of the Leisure Class* (1899) portrays as the habitual, emulative goal of American society; and she thoroughly dramatizes the mechanism of that desire, which, as René Girard points out, is one of triangulation where "the value of the article consumed is based solely on how it is regarded by the Other."[18] Carrie's easy transformation from consumer to consumed is thus a concise illustration of the character of success in the age of capitalism: the "possession of self" becomes indistinguishable from the "self of possessions," and the hero of desire, rather than diverging from society, totalizes that society by containing and expressing it in an erotic materialism of the self.

Carrie's case may be as melodramatic as she is, but I want to suggest again that it represents, in particular terms, Dreiser's understanding of the resistance of American realism to literal or actualized structures of social containment by demonstrating American society's own resistance of the literal and its continued incorporation of romance as a prevalence of desire, of "the possible," of fantasy, of the Other. The most thorough incorporation, from the standpoint of fictional technique itself, is of course James, whose whole career—particularly after his eccentric but revealing 1886 excursion into more explicit social realism in *The Bostonians* and *The Princess Casamassima*, and even more emphatically after his failure as a dramatist in the early 1890s—is a sustained augmentation of novelistic powers of inspection in order to locate infinitely richer, more luxurious surpluses of character that in the end are out of all proportion to the action in which character is engaged. The "luxury" that James identifies in "The Lesson of Balzac" (1905), "the extraordinary number and length of his radiating and ramifying corridors—the labyrinth in which he finally lost himself," describes rather exactly the endless play of speculation and desire to which so many of James's scenes are subject. And by exaggerating strains one may find throughout the fiction of the period, James's courting of this "hallucination" of value reminds us of Tocqueville's prophetic assertion in *Democracy in America* (1835) that the characteristic and paradoxical "restlessness" of Americans in the midst of their obvious prosperity produces a very "strange melancholy" and often a simple "madness."

At the level of action, Tocqueville's remarks predict most accurately the bestialities of Norris and the urban psychodramas of Dreiser, who remarks in *Jennie Gerhardt* (1911) that "the multiplicity and variety of our social forms, the depth, subtlety, and sophistry of our imaginative impressions, gathered, remultiplied, and disseminated by such agencies as the railroad, the express and the post office, the telephone, the telegraph, and the newspaper," produce by their "dazzling and confusing phantasmagoria of life" a stultification of mental and moral nature, and an "intellectual fatigue through which we see the ranks of the victims of insomnia, melancholia, and insanity constantly recruited." But at the level of technique, Tocqueville's observations bear most upon the case of James, whose impressionistic method, working from within various interiors or "centers" of consciousness, makes a virtue of surplus desire to the point that the self disappears not merely into material possessions (for in James possessions are more conspicuously assumed, rather than consumed) but into the further moral and psychological reverberations that the express resemblance between people and possessions can produce. One may speak of Jamesian "realism," then, only by recognizing how urgently the concentration on the *within* presumes the prior incorporation of magnified and ever-accelerating values derived from *without*, and by noting how completely the moral assessment of character is embodied by the narrative imagination that can reproduce and relocate those values without end, a virtue that James rightly designates in *The Wings of the Dove* (1902) as "the imagination of expenditure."

Such a brief sketch can do James's achievements in the novel no justice, but it is worthwhile remembering that the most impressionistic of the nineteenth-century realists—James and Crane—are also the ones who ultimately seem most modern, in part because their concentration on technique anticipates modernist preoccupations, and in part because they demonstrate an increasing discrepancy between the figurative life of the mind and the literal life of the material. In the case of Crane, such experiments in technique are certainly of variable inspiration, ranging from instances of clear motivation (the pressure of combat in *The Red Badge of Courage*) to inexplicable but explosive moral puzzles ("The Blue Hotel") to Brechtian derangements of the literal landscape (*Maggie*). But the effects very much resemble those James produces, with infinitely richer texture, in his late novels and in *The American Scene* (1907); as technique becomes more clearly a mediating form, mind and material shrink away from one another even as they become wholly dependent and come more explicitly to inhabit the constructed world of language—the world that Crane, with manifold irony, implied in *Maggie* was one of "transcendental realism."

In this respect, however, it is worth remembering also that the psychological realism of James and Crane represents most evidently and most tellingly the continued presence of romance. The writer who assumes such a stance must—as Hawthorne put it in his preface to *The House of the Seven Gables*—"claim a certain latitude" in the management of his "atmospheric medium," and in mingling "the Marvellous" with the "actual substance of the dish offered to the Public" be wary of "bringing his fancy-pictures almost into positive contact with the realities of the moment." The writer insufficiently aware of these risks, or even the one who willingly takes them, may wake up in the country of the blue.

BIBLIOGRAPHICAL NOTE

The critical literature on American realism is diverse, and the following list of books can only be suggestive. Among studies devoted primarily to the period, the most important include: Vernon L. Parrington, *The Beginning of Critical Realism in America*, vol. 3, *Main Currents in American Thought* (New York: Harcourt, Brace, 1930); Maxwell Geismar, *Rebels and Ancestors: The American Novel, 1890–1915* (Boston: Houghton Mifflin, 1953); Kenneth S. Lynn, *The Dream of Success: A Study of the Modern American Imagination* (Boston: Little, Brown, 1955); Charles C. Walcutt, *American Literary Naturalism: A Divided Stream* (Minneapolis: University of Minnesota Press, 1956); Warner Berthoff, *The Ferment of Realism: American Literature,*

1884–1919 (New York: The Free Press, 1965); Donald Pizer, *Realism and Naturalism in Nineteenth-Century American Literature* (Carbondale: Southern Illinois University Press, 1966); Larzer Ziff, *The American 1890s: Life and Times of a Lost Generation* (New York: Viking Press, 1966); Jay Martin, *Harvests of Change: American Literature, 1865–1914* (Englewood Cliffs, NJ: Prentice-Hall, 1967); Harold H. Kolb, Jr., *The Illusion of Life: American Realism as a Literary Form* (Charlottesville: University Press of Virginia, 1969); Gordon O. Taylor, *The Passages of Thought: Psychological Representation in the American Novel, 1870–1900* (New York: Oxford University Press, 1969); Edwin H. Cady, *The Light of Common Day: Realism in American Fiction* (Bloomington: Indiana University Press, 1971); Harold Kaplan, *Power and Order: Henry Adams and the Naturalist Tradition in American Fiction* (Chicago: University of Chicago Press, 1981); and Alan Trachtenberg, *The Incorporation of America: Culture and Society in the Gilded Age* (New York: Hill & Wang, 1982).

Important studies devoted in part to the period include: Alfred Kazin, *On Native Grounds* (1942; reprint ed., New York: Anchor-Doubleday, 1956); James D. Hart, *The Popular Book: A History of America's Literary Taste* (1950; reprint ed., Berkeley and Los Angeles; University of California Press, 1963); Richard Chase, *The American Novel and Its Tradition* (1957; reprint ed., Baltimore: Johns Hopkins University Press, 1980); Wright Morris, *The Territory Ahead* (1957; reprint ed., Lincoln: University of Nebraska Press, 1978); Marius Bewley, *The Eccentric Design: Form in the Classic American Novel* (New York: Columbia University Press, 1958); Leslie Fiedler, *Love and Death in the American Novel* (1960; rev. ed., New York: Dell, 1966); Leo Marx, *The Machine in the Garden: Technology and the Pastoral Ideal in America* (New York: Oxford University Press, 1964); John Cawelti, *Apostles of the Self-Made Man* (Chicago: University of Chicago Press, 1965); Richard Bridgman, *The Colloquial Style in America* (New York: Oxford University Press, 1966); Richard Poirier, *A World Elsewhere: The Place of Style in American Literature* (New York: Oxford University Press, 1966); David Weimer, *The City as Metaphor* (New York: Random House, 1966); Daniel Aaron, *The Unwritten War: American Writers and the Civil War* (New York: Alfred A. Knopf, 1973); Harry B. Henderson III, *Versions of the Past: The Historical Imagination in American Fiction* (New York: Oxford University Press, 1974); Warwick Wadlington, *The Confidence Game in American Literature* (Princeton: Princeton University Press, 1975); and Henry Nash Smith, *Democracy and the Novel: Popular Resistance to Classic Writers* (New York: Oxford University Press, 1978).

NOTES

1. R. P. Blackmur, "In the Country of the Blue," *A Primer of Ignorance* (New York: Harcourt, Brace, 1967), p. 196.

2. Chase, *The American Novel and Its Tradition*, p. 2. See also pp. vii–28. A similar account may be found in Perry Miller, "The Romance and the Novel," in *Nature's Nation* (Cambridge: Harvard University Press, 1967), pp. 241–78.

3. Kazin, *On Native Grounds*, pp. 10, 12.

4. Herbert Marcuse, *Eros and Civilization: A Philosophical Inquiry into Freud* (1955; reprint ed., New York: Vintage-Random, 1962), pp. 82–94.

5. Erich Auerbach, *Mimesis: The Representation of Reality in Western Literature*, trans. Willard R. Trask (Princeton: Princeton University Press, 1953), p. 459.

6. Poirier, *A World Elsewhere*, pp. 214, 248.

7. Martin, *Harvests of Change*, p. 202.

8. See Chase, *The American Novel and Its Tradition*, pp. 198–204.

9. Morris, *The Territory Ahead*, p. 12.

10. See Ziff, *The American 1890s*, pp. 120–65.

11. Lionel Trilling, *The Liberal Imagination: Essays on Literature and Society* (New York: Viking Press, 1950), pp. 10–11.

12. Walter Benjamin, "The Work of Art in the Age of Mechanical Reproduction," in *Illuminations*, trans. Hannah Arendt (New York: Schocken Books, 1969) p. 221.

13. Daniel Boorstin, *The Americans: The National Experience* (New York: Random House, 1973), pp. 370–90.

14. Christopher Lasch, *The Culture of Narcissism: American Life in an Age of Diminishing Expectations* (New York: W. W. Norton, 1979), p. 160.

15. George Becker, ed., *Documents of Modern Literary Realism* (Princeton: Princeton University Press, 1963), p. 29.

16. Leo Bersani, "Realism and the Fear of Desire," in *A Future for Astyanax: Character and Desire in Literature* (New York: Little, Brown, 1976), pp. 51–88.

17. Walter Benn Michaels, "*Sister Carrie*'s Popular Economy" *Critical Inquiry* 7, no. 2 (Winter 1980): 373–90.

18. René Girard, *Deceit, Desire, and the Novel*, trans. Yvonne Freccero (Baltimore: Johns Hopkins University Press, 1965), p. 223.

THIRTY-FIVE

PREFACE AND CASTING OUT THE OUTCAST

Naturalism and the Brute

June Howard

June Howard received her Ph.D. from the University of California, San Diego, in 1979, and teaches at the University of Michigan. She has also edited New Essays on "The Country of the Pointed Firs" (1994).

PREFACE

The present study is a detailed reading of a single literary genre, American literary naturalism, as a distinctive response to its historical moment. As I make that statement its implications clamor for annotation—I may not mean exactly what the reader expects when I speak of genre, of history, or of literary texts as responses to history. The chapters that follow make those discriminations; they proceed more or less inductively, working from within familiar formulations to reconstruct our ideas of genre criticism, of the relation between literary form and history, and of naturalism and American naturalism. Let me here suggest more summarily just where those arguments will lead us.

When Americans of the late nineteenth and early twentieth centuries voiced their thoughts for contemporaries or recorded them for posterity they often reported that they felt themselves living in a perilous time, a period of change and uncertainty, of dislocations and disorders. Naturalism is a literary form that struggles to accommodate that sense of discomfort and danger, a form that unremittingly attends to the large social questions of its period. An investigation of naturalism thus doubly entails an investigation of its historical moment—as the condition of its production and as

Reprinted from Form and History in American Literary Naturalism, by June Howard (Chapel Hill: University of North Carolina Press, 1985), pp. ix–xii, 88–103. Copyright © 1985 by the University of North Carolina Press. Used by permission of the publisher.

the source of discourses embedded within the works. I will sketch a range of historical and cultural reference for the ideas and images we encounter in the pages of American naturalist novels; in this matrix, narrative strategies, literary conventions, and passing references to concepts or stereotypes take on significances unsuspected when one is reading only in terms of a single text. I conceive my task to be reading across the texts not to uncover but to construct an object of study: naturalism as a literary form. My contention will not be that naturalism has an ideology or reflects an ideology, but that the form itself is an immanent ideology. It is a way of imagining the world and the relation of the self to the world, a way of making sense—and making narrative—out of the comforts and discomforts of the historical moment. Those reports of disorder and that narrative sense express, we should note, not "America" but some Americans. Our generalizing habit of speech, embodied in so many discussions of American literature, is itself continuous with the assumption that certain points of view matter more than others, with a systematic forgetfulness organized along the lines of class, race, and gender. To elicit the voices of nonhegemonic groups from the historical record is not the task I have taken on here. But naturalism does bear within itself the memory of that forgetfulness, for silenced (but not silent) masses are one of its most urgent concerns. In today's public language social class is often deeply encoded, even disguised, while the naturalists remind us of a world in which actions and meanings are constantly seen in terms of class, in which omnipresent class conflict is virtually assumed.

Social class is a crucial, although it is certainly not the only, concern focused in American naturalism's notion of the "brute," which I will examine as a conceptual category, a register of characterization, a pressure on plot. The brutal, doomed characters of naturalism have greatly interested literary critics, and the determined world they inhabit is indeed the best-known aspect of the genre. I will argue, however, that one cannot appreciate the significance of naturalism's philosophical determinism without also recognizing the perspective from which those characters are viewed, that of the observant and articulate naturalist in close conference with his reader. That perspective is often revealingly inscribed within the narrative itself in the form of observant and articulate characters who explore and deplore the terrain of cause and effect. The author and reader and the characters who represent them inhabit a privileged location, assuming a kind of control over forces and events through their power to comprehend them. Yet the privilege of the spectator, constructed by contrast, is necessarily vulnerable; fear and desire—sexual passion and violence, the fatal spell of the commodity, the fascination of the Other—constantly disrupt the design of safety. To venture any dealings with the powers that inhabit causality proves hazardous; characters who go slumming in the realm of determinism risk their freedom and expose themselves to the dangers of paralysis and proletarianization. Acting on the assumption of control and attempting to translate knowledge to power, they reveal the crucial difference between omniscience and omnipotence.

The structure I adumbrate here is, I will suggest, characteristic of naturalism, and within literary forms it uniquely distinguishes that genre. But I will also suggest that this immanent ideology shares its imaginative horizons with roughly contemporary formations such as criminal anthropology and political progressivism. And although naturalism can be characterized by this gesture toward control, it cannot be reduced to it. I assume that genres are not static entities or even stable structures but distinctive concatenations of aesthetic imperatives and formal choices that weave, dynamically and unevenly, through literary texts; I will examine the heterogeneous conventions and narrative strategies—melodramatic, sentimental, documentary—to be found in naturalist novels. An understanding of the traces of other genres embedded in these works is indispensable to understanding them, for naturalism is strongly marked by such internal difference.

Naturalism is not a fashionable genre; the efflorescence of critical publication by American academics has produced only a relatively small body of work dealing with this group of writers. I suspect that many critics find naturalist novels somehow scandalous. They fail signally to be well-made novels; they insist tactlessly upon a relation between literature and reality; they traffic brazenly with the formulas of popular literature and journalism; and they are obsessed with class and commodities in a most embarrassing fashion. Aesthetic judgments and generic standards themselves of course embody values and are ideological; the nature and significance of critics' judgments of naturalism will also enter into my analysis. American naturalism was formed in the formative period of our own time, and the questions that absorb the naturalists will prove not so very distant from those of the latter twentieth century.

The naturalists and their contemporaries were scarcely alone in feeling that they lived in a peculiarly difficult period—in every modern period some have voiced this complaint. But to immerse oneself in the documents of the period is gradually to come to recognize the depth of their sense of confusion and danger and to respect the historical specificity of their reported discomfort. The naturalists imagined their situation in genuinely *different* terms from those in which we imagine ours. Whatever we have in common with them, they were not merely people like us wearing different clothes, characters in one of the costume dramas with which the mass media surround us. For the naturalists the world we live in now was not a foregone conclusion; the history they knew did not inevitably lead to the present state of American society. Their choices were real choices. It is my hope that this study will bring my readers, as it has me, to a recognition of the irrevocable openness of any historical moment and an apprehension of naturalism not as an exhibit in a gallery of literary types but as a dynamic solution to the problem of generating narrative out of the particular historical and cultural materials that offered themselves to these writers. This recognition is in some sense the discovery that our own history is contingent, that our world really was not a foregone conclusion. That discovery may perhaps produce not only a renewed sense of historical difference but a renewed sense of historical possibility.

These are ambitious aims for a work of genre criticism. I would suggest not only that genre criticism and historical analysis are compatible, but that they can complete each other in a literary history of unique flexibility and power. I propose this study as a contribution to a revitalized literary history that simultaneously attempts to do justice to the historical specificity of the given moment and attempts to imagine how human history might be one narrative, one adventure in which transformations of both literary and social forms play their parts.

CASTING OUT THE OUTCAST: NATURALISM AND THE BRUTE

The various incarnations of the Other I have explored in these general ideological discourses of the period of naturalism are fluidly but consistently coordinated. We will continue to see them in the analyses that follow, re-produced in narrative form and thus transformed, yet still carrying their ideological messages. Reading naturalism synoptically with this general ideology renders one more acutely aware of how strongly class-marked the oppositions that divide the characters of naturalist novels are. The determined and helpless yet menacing "naturalist" characters are drawn from or drawn into the working class and the underclass. The terrain they inhabit is imagined as squalid, dangerous, but exciting—even exotic, for it is alien territory to the middle-class perspective (sometimes that of a character or characters, generally that of the narrator) from which it is explored. Chapter 4 will examine that apparently safer, more orderly center of perception. Let us here merely sketch the brute and suggest the nature of the contrast, turning to Norris's early sketches for *The Wave*—a journal whose "small and homogeneous" audience clearly shared the perspective of that second category of characters—for the simplest, clearest examples.[1]

We may take a brief piece Frank Norris published in the San Francisco *Wave* in 1897 as a cameo portrait of the image of the laborer as brute—"Brute" is in fact its title—that enters naturalism from the general ideology of the period. I quote the sketch in its entirety:

> He had been working all day in a squalid neighborhood by the gas works and coal yards, surrounded by lifting cranes, pile drivers, dredging machines, engines of colossal, brutal strength, where all about him were immense blocks of granite, tons of pig iron; everything had been enormous, crude, had been huge in weight, tremendous in power, gigantic in size.
>
> By long association with such things he had become like them, huge, hard, brutal, strong with a crude, blind strength, stupid, unreasoning. He was on his way home now, his immense hands dangling half-open at his sides; his head empty of thought. He only desired to be fed and to sleep. At a street crossing he picked up a white violet, very fresh, not yet trampled into the mud. It was a beautiful thing, redolent with the scene of the woods, suggestive of everything pretty and delicate. It was almost like a smile-made flower. It lay very light in the hollow of his immense calloused palm. In some strange way it appealed to him, and blindly he tried to acknowledge his appreciation. He looked at it stupidly, perplexed, not knowing what to do; then instinctively his hand carried it to his mouth; he ground it between his huge teeth and slowly ate it. It was the only way he knew.[2]

Here Norris passes in review a number of the most important elements to be found, in various combinations, in the images of the brute: his strength, his incapacity for self-consciousness and self-control, the coarse nature that is the result of the "squalid" environment of industrial labor and, probably, the heredity that bred those instincts and huge teeth. Confronted by something that is beyond him, he can feel only a glimmer of desire without understanding, and therefore he destroys the object of his desire. The brute's blind strength makes him dangerous even here, at his most stolid and least vicious; the fear that a bloodbath and the destruction of civilization loom on the horizon remains potent.

In another group of sketches for *The Wave* Norris juxtaposes courtship among the middle class and the working class. The first of the group of pieces titled "Man Proposes" (1896) takes place in a resort hotel. The innocent young couple whose quiet walk in the moonlight is the subject of the little tale communicate their feelings with subtlety and restraint; indeed, the exaggerated delicacy of their sentiments is such that the light touch of his arm around her waist becomes immensely significant. In the "proposal" at the end no words are spoken:

> He partially closed the door with his heel, and as she straightened up he put his arm about her neck and drew her head toward him. She turned to him then very sweetly, yielding with an infinite charm, and he kissed her twice.
>
> Then he went out, softly closing the door behind him.
>
> This was how he proposed to her. Not a word of what was greatest in their minds passed between them. But for all that they were no less sure of each other.
>
> *She* rather preferred it that way.[3]

In this sketch Norris does not consider it necessary to write about the physical appearance or background of the characters; everything is taken for granted, common ground—indeed, predictable and clichéd. In the second sketch, in contrast, he gives detailed descriptions:

> He was an enormous man, strong as a dray horse, big-boned, heavily muscled, slow in his movements. His feet and hands were huge and knotted and twisted, and misshapen by hard usage. Through the grime of the coal dust one could but indistinctly make out his face. The eyes were small, the nose flat, and the lower jaw immense, protruding like the jaws of the carnivora, and thrusting the thick lower lip out beyond the upper. His father had been a coal heaver before him, and had worked at that trade until he had been killed in a strike. His mother had drunk herself into an asylum and had died long ago.[4]

This description, it is readily apparent, depends upon meanings generated in the ideological discourses already discussed.

The difference in the terms the two sketches use to represent femininity and sexuality is particularly marked. The object of the coal heaver's affections "was not very young, and she was rather fat; her lips were thick and very red, and her eyes were small, her neck was large and thick and very white, and on the nape the hair grew low and curling" (p. 60). Like the girl in the previous sketch she is engaged in womanly work, but she is doing the wash rather than kissing a child goodnight. As she works, the man takes a frank interest in her body that would be unthinkable in the sentimental idiom of the first piece: "The tips of her bare elbows were red, and he noted with interest how this little red flush came and went as her arms bent and straightened. . . . As her body rose and fell, he watched curiously the wrinkles and folds forming and reforming about her thick corsetless waist" (pp. 60–61). This unrestrained flesh contrasts with the control implied by the "firm, well-laced waist" (p. 56) of the middle-class girl.

The form of the proposal reveals both the man's emotions and his ability to express them as coarse: " 'Say,' he exclaimed at length, with the brutal abruptness of crude, simple natures, 'listen here. I like you better'n anyone else. What's the matter with us two gett'n married, huh?' " (p. 61). Norris's association of sexuality and violence appears in the scene's conclusion:

> She, more and more frightened at his enormous hands, his huge square-cut head, and his enormous brute strength, cried out, "No, no!" shaking her head violently, holding out her hands and shrinking from him. . . .
> Suddenly he took her in his enormous arms, crushing down her struggle with his immense brute strength. Then she gave up all at once, glad to yield to him and to his superior force, willing to be conquered. She turned her head to him, and they kissed each other full on the mouth, brutally, grossly. [pp. 61–62]

The contrast between the two kisses could scarcely be more striking. This is indeed virtually a generic opposition—in the middle class love is a sentimental courtship vignette, in the working class it is a fragment of sordid "naturalism." Parts of this second sketch, in fact, also appear in the proposal scene in *McTeague* (1899). In these brief examples two classes and two worlds are defined by sheer opposition and contained within the frames of their separate texts.[5] As we return to the naturalist novel proper, the task of defining their relation becomes more complex, since the opposition is inscribed in a single narrative and is often complexly displaced or mediated.

The ideology of brutality sometimes carries fairly elaborated systems of explanation for the existence of such degraded beings. We have already seen how Norris links physical, moral, and social degradation in *Vandover and the Brute*. The reference in "Man Proposes" to the coal heaver's parents suggests, in one of the most powerful causal theories invoked by naturalism, that such brutality is encoded in the genes. McTeague's lust for Trina, for example, is (in a passage immediately preceding the proposal scene) directly attributed to his tainted heredity:

> . . . the brute was there. Long dormant, it was now at last alive, awake. From now on he would feel its presence continually; would feel it tugging at its chain, watching its opportunity. Ah, the pity of it! Why could he not always love her purely, cleanly? What was this perverse, vicious thing that lived within him, knitted to his flesh?
> Below the fine fabric of all that was good in him ran the foul stream of hereditary evil, like a sewer. The vices and sins of his father and of his father's father, to the third and fourth and five hundredth generation, tainted him. The evil of an entire race flowed in his veins. Why should it be? He did not desire it. Was he

to blame?

But McTeague could not understand this thing. It had faced him, as sooner or later it faces every child of man; but its significance was not for him. To reason with it was beyond him. He could only oppose to it an instinctive stubborn resistance, blind, inert.[6]

McTeague is doubly, triply condemned to brutality. Like every "child of man" he is acted on by his heredity, but he also comes of a defective line and lacks the distinctively human capacity that could enable effective resistance: reason. The determining force of heredity can produce manly strength as well as bestial vice, however; in Norris's story "Thoroughbred" (1895) the apparently effeminate scion of a prominent, wealthy family shows his true mettle in a crisis and proves that "good blood is what makes all the difference" in men as in dogs.[7] But in naturalism bad blood always proves more fascinating than good.

Norris's account of McTeague's bad blood relies upon the vocabulary of contemporary criminal anthropology. Two more early fictions which draw quite directly on that source demonstrate that the brute inscribed in the gene does not necessarily stay in the outer darkness of the slums. "A Reversion to Type" (1897) focuses on a commonplace, respectable department-store floorwalker. Schuster is described by the first-person narrator as "too damned cheeky" because he flirts with his lady customers and "entertained ideas on culture and refinement"; thus, failing to accept his humble place in society, he mildly endangers class boundaries and begins to reveal himself as potentially disruptive to society. When he indulges in a drinking bout he runs wild and eventually attempts highway robbery—the very crime, we learn at the end of the story, for which his grandfather was sent to San Quentin. It is this unsuspected criminal ancestry that turns a respectable man into a "free-booter":

Schuster, like all the rest of us, was not merely himself. He was his ancestors as well. In him, as in you and me, were generations—countless generations—of forefathers. Schuster had in him the characteristics of his father, the Palace Hotel barber, but also he had the unknown characteristics of his grandfather, of whom he had never heard, and his great-grandfather, likewise ignored. It is a rather serious matter to thrust yourself under the dominion of unknown, unknowable impulses and passions. That is what Schuster did that night. Getting drunk was an impulse belonging to himself, but who knows what "inherited tendencies," until then dormant, the alcohol unleashed within him?[8]

Heredity can conceal a criminal self even within a respectable man.

In "A Reversion to Type" Schuster is able to return to his inconspicuous job and reveals his lapse only on his deathbed. In "A Case for Lombroso" (1897) the consequences of hidden genetic defects are more devastating, and there can be no return. The characters have farther to fall: they are well-born, wealthy, educated. Norris ostentatiously allies his narrator and male protagonist with a readership supposedly belonging to a social elite; of Stayne's achievements in college, for example, he writes that "you others who have been at Harvard will know just what all this means" (p.

35). But Stayne abandons his self-control, yielding to the temptation represented by Cresencia Hromada. Cresencia has an extraordinary, morbid sensitivity that is attributed to the fact that she "had come of a family of unmixed blood, whose stock had never been replenished or strengthened by an alien cross. Her race was almost exhausted, its vitality low. . . . To-day Cresencia might have been called a degenerate" (p. 36). In Norris's version of the fashionable notion of hereditary degeneracy not only interbreeding but any contact between certain people produces disaster for both—the reaction is virtually chemical. Cresencia's uncontrollable passion for Stayne degrades her, and his response to it degrades him. "He realized that she would take anything from him—that she would not, or rather, that she could not, resent any insult, however gross. And the knowledge made the man a brute" (p. 41). The sexual excess and violence implied in their relationship constitute an intolerable eruption of brutality within the elite, and social degradation follows: "Stayne's name has long since been erased from the rolls of his club. Hromada is thoroughly déclassé, and only last month figured in the law courts as the principal figure in a miserable and thoroughly disreputable scandal" (p. 42). If these invasions of the brute into the realm of the human being are possible, civilization and stable identity seem at best provisional privileges, to be guarded at all costs against the most minute disruptions of social order and self-control.

Not only the themes but the very titles of these stories declare their debt to Cesare Lombroso and the widely influential theories of criminal anthropology. In *The Novels of Frank Norris* Donald Pizer has provided an invaluable account of the impact of this and other intellectual movements on Norris's work.[9] What concerns me, however, is not so much questions of influence as the way in which these concepts, incorporated into the novels, continue to emit ideological signals and shape possibilities for meaning. For Norris as for others of his period hereditary determinism offers a satisfying way of understanding individual destiny in terms of biology, social problems in terms of the evolution of the species—in short, the historical as the natural. But its consequences as worked out in the narratives themselves often reinscribe the disturbing social contradictions that the abstract theories claim to resolve.

The idea of the atavism in particular seems to fascinate the naturalists, offering a way of representing disruptive forces as the primitive embedded within civilization and indeed within the individual.[10] London also makes frequent use of the atavism, although he generally takes a more benevolent view of such reversion than Norris does; we have already seen in *White Fang* that the primitive can be vitalizing. Although Vandover and McTeague are consumed and destroyed when the dormant brutes within them awaken, the protagonists of *Before Adam* (1906) and "When the World Was Young" (1910) manage, although not always comfortably, to live double lives. The hero of "When the World Was Young" literally shares his body with an atavistic personality, the two selves alternating in a bizarre circadian rhythm. The narrator of *Before Adam* also has a nocturnal double: through dreams he reexperiences the life of an ancestor of the mid-Pleistocene. He writes that "this other-personality is vestigial in all of us, in some of us it is almost obliterated, while in others of us it is more pronounced. Some of us have stronger and completer race memories than others. . . . My other-personality is almost equal in power with my own personality. And in this matter I am, as I said, a freak—a freak of heredity."[11]

In *Before Adam* as in *White Fang* the themes of naturalism are transmogrified in a nonhuman world. Within that world we find the atavism reinscribed; the narrator's other self also has atavistic dreams that take him still farther back into man's past, "back to the winged reptiles and the clash and the onset of dragons, and beyond that to the scurrying, rodent-like life of the tiny mammals, and far remoter still, to the shore-slime of the primeval sea. I cannot, I dare not, say more. It is all too vague and complicated and awful" (p. 139). And to the denizens of the mid-Pleistocene the most terrifying being is still the "mighty monster, the abysmal brute" Red-Eye (p. 209), who has reverted to a still more primitive stage of evolution. This brute's uncontrollable strength menaces the fragile social order developing among the proto-humans. The obsessive quality of the tale's concern with the atavism is captured—as well as it can be in an excerpt—in its last words, as the creature comes stalking in among the tribe from the outer darkness: "I can see him now, as I write this, scowling, his eyes inflamed, as he peers about him at the circle of the Tree People. And as he peers he crooks one monstrous leg and with his gnarly toes scratches himself on the stomach. He is Red-Eye, the atavism" (p. 242). London, exploring the Other within, meets him again as the Outsider.

The fascination of the atavism persists into our own period.[12] Themes related to those of *Before Adam* are reworked in the time-travel dreaming of Michael Bishop's *No Enemy But Time* and in the exploration of racial memory of Paddy Chayefsky's *Altered States*.[13] The significance of the atavism, the fears and even more strongly now the hopes it evokes, are different. Nature seems in these contemporary works a receding, elusive Other rather than a brute straining at its chain. *No Enemy But Time* retains the inarticulate vulnerability of the brute, *Altered States* the possibility that the Other is not merely a fierce potency but a ravening beast. *Altered States* has perhaps most in common thematically with naturalism: its scientific fascination with the gene, its obsession with the predator, its emphatic suggestion that if the explorer-scientist ventures too far into the unknown he may not be able to return, and its ultimate redemption of the hero through the agency of the woman and the family. In Chapter 5 we will see how an appeal to domestic ideology is incorporated in a number of naturalist novels, just as in *Altered States* the scientist's astonishing reversions lead him, in a resounding anticlimax, to rediscover the family:

"that ultimate moment of terror that is the beginning of life . . . is nothing, simple hideous nothing. . . . It's human life that is real! Truth is the illusion! . . . that moment of terror is . . . a real and living horror living and growing within me now, eating of my flesh, drinking of my blood. It's real because I have made it real. It's not just talk. It's alive. It's in me. It is me. And the only thing that keeps it from devouring me is you." "I think you're trying to tell me you love me," she said.[14]

This is an existential terror that one would want to trace to rather different sources than the naturalist nightmare of class struggle. Yet there is a significant continuity, for the vertiginous view down the evolutionary scale to primordial man and beyond that opens before the hero is astonishingly similar to what we see in *Before Adam*. And as so often in naturalism, the ultimate terror is the loss of stable personal identity, the collapse of self into Other.

We encounter the brute in its far-flung manifestations as a creature perpetually outcast, yet perpetually to be cast out as it inevitably reappears within self and within society. The terror of the brute includes, certainly, the fear of revolution and chaos, of the mob and the criminal, as invoked, for example, in *White Fang* by the prospect of being torn apart by the hungry wolf-pack or attacked by the murderous Jim Hall. It also includes the fear of becoming the outcast through the social degradation and psychological disintegration depicted in *Vandover and the Brute*; the brute can devour one from within, as it does Vandover: "At certain intervals his mania came upon him, the strange hallucination of something four-footed, the persistent fancy that the brute in him had now grown so large, so insatiable, that it had taken everything, even to his very self, his own identity—that he had literally *become the brute*."[15] These fears, powered at least in part by the mechanism of projection, are not ultimately separable. Naturalism's image of the brute is not simply a misrecognition of the actuality of the Other, an inaccurate, ignorant stereotype of the proletariat or lumpenproletariat (although certainly it is that), but a representation of the relation of a relatively privileged class to conditions of existence that produce this range of inconsistent fears. In this system of meanings, at this level, the social and the psychological can no longer usefully be distinguished.

We may call the "persistent fancy," the obsessive fear that haunts naturalism, by the scandalous name of *proletarianization*. It is an anxiety traditionally associated with although certainly not limited to the petty bourgeoisie who, possessing small capitals or professional skills, passionately defend their narrow footholds of economic security. In that structurally vulnerable position, trapped between the working class and the corporation, individuals may well experience themselves as "above" the interests of classes—as in Chapter 4 we will see the naturalist spectator and the progressive reformer proclaim themselves—and yet menaced by both. I call the term scandalous because American public discourse so often strives to efface class division in a rhetoric of equality; indeed, I sometimes suspect that one of the reasons naturalism has proven such as uncomfortable form for contemporary literary critics is its open interest in class. But I do not mean to imply that its representations of class are somehow the truth of the varied material naturalism processes. All the components that enter into the representation of the Other are genuine and irreducible; anxieties about social class have no predetermined priority over, for example, anxieties about masculinity, and each can serve as a way of carrying or managing the other. But the privileges of autonomy, awareness, control that characters and narrator struggle so desperately to establish and maintain are deeply marked as class privileges, and loss of those privileges is figured as the destruction of intellect, humanity, even civilization itself. We might wish for a term that alluded to the criminal and the tramp as well as the laborer—the relation between the categories of "lumpenproletariat" or underclass and "proletariat" is itself, of course, controversial. But proletarianization seems an appropriate rubric under which to explore naturalism's recurrent strategy of sequencing a narrative according to the progress of a character's deterioration.

In the work of Frank Norris, for example, this characteristic plotting can be seen in epitome in the declassing of Stayne and Cresencia Hromada in "A Case for Lombroso," dominates *Vandover and the Brute*, crucially informs *McTeague*, and enters into *The Octopus* (1901) as well. Although I have approached this point through the ideological discourses surrounding genetic determinism, this persistent fancy takes many forms—Dreiser's *Sister Carrie* and Crane's *Maggie* are both structured in part by progressive deteriorations, yet neither is particularly concerned with heredity. *The Octopus* incorporates the racial ideology that is a persistent element of Norris's and London's work as a peripheral concern, for example in the passing comment that at the jackrabbit drive the "Anglo-Saxon spectators roundabout drew back in disgust, but the hot, degenerated blood of Portuguese, Mexican, and mixed Spanish boiled up in excitement at this wholesale slaughter."[16] But the two characters in that novel who decline most precipitously have no such tainted blood. Magnus Derrick is an Anglo-Saxon, a "fine commanding figure, imposing an immediate respect, impressing one with a sense of gravity, of dignity, and a certain pride of race" (1:59). He is educated and articulate, wealthy and powerful: "In whatever circle he moved he was the chief figure. Instinctively other men looked to him as the leader. . . . He even carried the diction and manner of the rostrum into private life. It was said of him that his most colloquial conversation could be taken down in shorthand and read off as an admirable specimen of pure, well-chosen English. He loved to do things upon a grand scale, to preside, to dominate" (1:61). Yet as early as the third chapter, tempted by profit and power but also genuinely seeing no other solution to the wheat ranchers' problems, Derrick listens to arguments for a bribery scheme and allows his son to take part; thus he takes his first steps in corruption and his first steps on the road downward.[17]

Each subsequent step involves Derrick more deeply: "He began to see how perilously far he had gone in this business. He was drifting closer to it every hour. Already he was entangled, already his foot was caught in the mesh that was being spun" (1:181). Soon he is "hopelessly caught in the mesh. . . . He was blinded, dizzied, overwhelmed, caught in the current of events, and hurried along he knew not where. He resigned himself" (2:8). Derrick ceases to exert his will—and we already know the danger of such an abandonment of effort. His deterioration ends only when he has lost his money, his ranch, his sons, his honor, his eloquence, his authority, his belief in himself. He is destroyed as a human being; as the character Presley puts it, he is not only beggared but broken:

> "If it had only killed him, . . . but that is the worst of it. . . . It's broken him; oh, you should see him, you should see him. A shambling, stooping, trembling old man, in his dotage already. He sits all day in the dining room, turning over papers, sorting them, tying them up, opening them again, forgetting them—all fumbling and mumbling and confused. And at table sometimes he forgets to eat. And, listen, you know, from the house we can hear the trains whistling for the

Long Trestle. As often as that happens the Governor seems to be—oh, I don't know, frightened. He will sink his head between his shoulders, as though he were dodging something, and he won't fetch a long breath again till the train is out of hearing. He seems to have conceived an abject, unreasoned terror of the Railroad." [2:272–73]

Finally, Derrick has sunk so low that he is willing to accept a menial position with the railroad that has destroyed him. He is brutalized and, quite literally, proletarianized.

Dyke begins as an employee of the railroad. Fired from his job, his hopes for a profitable farm destroyed by the railroad's freight charges, he too joins battle with the Pacific and Southwestern and is devoured. Like Derrick, he makes choices early in the novel that from the reader's perspective inevitably lead him to ruin, although their catastrophic consequences astonish him. Other characters, too, see where Dyke is heading; Annixter exclaims at one point, " 'Drinking at Caraher's. . . . I can see *his* finish.' . . . [They] contemplated the slow sinking, the inevitable collapse and submerging of one of their companions, the wreck of a career, the ruin of an individual; an honest man, strong, fearless, upright, struck down by a colossal power, perverted by an evil influence, go reeling to his ruin" (2:73). Dyke becomes a train robber, a murderer, a hunted man; his "finish" is a life sentence to the penitentiary:

Jailed for life! No outlook. No hope for the future. Day after day, year after year, to tread the rounds of the same gloomy monotony. He saw the grey stone walls, the iron doors; the flagging of the "yard" bare of grass or trees—the cell, narrow, bald, cheerless; the prison garb, the prison fare, and round all the grim granite of insuperable barriers, shutting out the world, shutting in the man with outcasts, with the pariah dogs of society, thieves, murderers, men below the beasts, lost to all decency, drugged with opium, utter reprobates. To this, Dyke had been brought. Dyke than whom no man had been more honest, more courageous, more jovial. This was the end of him, a prison; this was his final estate, a criminal. [2:329]

Criminal Dyke and weak-minded Derrick have joined the ranks of the defective, a fate that appears in its full horror when set against contemporary treatments of the "unfit" like Henry Boies's. Dyke and Derrick have "become the brute."

The Octopus is a novel woven of many diverse elements, and I will analyze it more fully in Chapter 4. But the plot of decline provides one of the novel's important organizational structures, a strategy that generates narrative and enables closure. The sequence of a deterioration plays an even more important role in a novel like Stephen Crane's *Maggie: A Girl of the Streets* (1893), which is otherwise virtually without plot. *Maggie* seems Crane's most "naturalist" work, yet its relation to the form is still somewhat oblique.[18] Certainly, Crane evokes images of brutality; the slum world he creates is pervaded by an uncouth cruelty exemplified by the battling urchins of the first chapter, "the whirling mob of Devil's Row children [in whose yells] there were notes of joy like songs of triumphant savagery," and by the monstrous apparition of

Maggie's mother: "Her face was inflamed and swollen from drinking. Her yellow brows shaded eye-lids that had grown blue. Her tangled hair tossed in waves over her forehead. Her mouth was set in the same lines of vindictive hatred that it had, perhaps, borne during the fight. Her bare, red arms were thrown out above her head in an attitude of exhaustion, something, mayhap, like that of a sated villain." At this moment in the novel the perspective from which this apparition is viewed is embodied in the little boy bending over her, "fearful lest she should open her eyes, and the dread within him . . . so strong, that he could not forbear to stare, but hung as if fascinated over the woman's grim face."[19] This dread and fascination are to a considerable degree shared by the narrator and reader; Crane's slum is part of the exotic terrain of the naturalist novel.

Yet the purposes to which the novelist turns these images are very different from those we have seen so far. I take the exposure of the artificiality and inadequacy of human representations and precepts to be central to Crane's project in *Maggie*; the novel is, as Alan Trachtenberg calls it, "a complicated piece of parody written with a serious regard for the task of rendering a false tale truly."[20] Crane's stylized prose can revitalize perceptions, can defamiliarize and transform the very process of reading in a fashion more familiar in the twentieth century than in the period of realism and naturalism. The fictions reveal a skepticism about their own tourist's point of view on the slums in the works themselves, as in the frame story of the sketch "An Experiment in Misery." When the narrator's friend asks him if he has discovered the tramp's point of view by his experiment, he replies, "I don't know that I did . . . but at any rate I think mine own has undergone a considerable alteration."[21] This sophistication, however, has not prevented Crane from sometimes being read as unself-consciously representational nor his images of slum-dwellers from being taken as simple contributions to the ideology of brutality.

I think it is true that, as Walcutt contends in his reading of the novel, none of the characters in *Maggie* is "free." But I would argue that this is less because Crane is a determinist than because he is a fatalist. He is not concerned with tracing the sources of individual and social pathology with the implicit or explicit hope of eventually bringing them under control: Crane is in fact utterly uninterested in causality. We have little information about the specific determinants of Maggie's character and choices, no direct analysis of the causes of her despair, but rather a series of almost disconnected scenes unified by style, by defamiliarization, above all by the plot of fatality. Like the flower found and devoured by the "Brute" of Norris's sketch, Maggie appears from nowhere, uncaused; she makes no resistance and understands nothing about why she is destroyed. All that Maggie sees, and virtually all that the reader knows, is that she cannot survive in this brutal world. The very subtitle of the novel—*A Girl of the Streets*—preconcludes its outcome; the fact that Maggie grows up in the streets of New York is figured in the same words and is essentially *the same* as her doom as a girl of the streets, a prostitute.

Hurstwood's story in *Sister Carrie* is also organized according to the plot of fatality, as the thematic analysis of Chapter 2 suggests. Let us retrace the already familiar stages of his slow but gradually accelerating deterioration. In retrospect we may look back at choices Hurstwood makes in Chicago and see how they lead to his downfall, as he increasingly neglects his home for unlawful pleasures. The turning point, of course, comes when he steals his employers' money and flees Chicago. In New York Hurstwood is excluded from his former pleasures and sources of self-esteem, and although there is no apparent decline, the narrator writes that "psychologically there was a change, which was marked enough to suggest the future very distinctly indeed. This was in the mere matter of the halt his career had received when he departed Chicago. A man's fortune or material progress is very much the same as his bodily growth. Either he is growing stronger, healthier, wiser, as the youth approaching manhood, or he is growing weaker, older, less incisive mentally, as the man approaching old age." From this point he is irretrievably committed to "the road downward." Here Dreiser invokes an explicitly determinist, even biological explanation for Hurstwood's decline—the passage on the pernicious influence of the katastates produced by remorse, for example, occurs in this chapter.[22]

Yet throughout *Sister Carrie* also offers detailed accounts of more delicately balanced social forces that could also help to explain Hurstwood's decline. Hurstwood has become an outsider to the prosperous world he once inhabited; it is like "a city with a wall about it. Men were posted at the gates. You could not get in. Those inside did not care to come out to see who you were. They were so merry inside there that all those outside were forgotten, and he was on the outside" (chap. 33, p. 241). Like Dyke, he is walled away from the respectable world, the world of warmth, humanity, satisfied desire. Dreiser constantly reports a complex interaction between Hurstwood's self-image, others' reactions to him, and his reaction to their reactions. Carrie in particular, that "apt student of fortune's ways" (chap. 11, p. 75), is exquisitely responsive to his successive losses of status and self-esteem. *Sister Carrie* is above all, as we have seen, a novel of the image and the code of commodities, and Dreiser carefully describes the gradual deterioration of Hurstwood's wardrobe and grooming. When a potential employer takes him for a prosperous man Hurstwood cannot bear to undeceive him; when Mrs. Vance sees him shabby and unshaven he is deeply shaken. As carefully as any ethnomethodologist, Dreiser studies the intersubjective processes that construct identity, for oneself and for others; again, the psychological and the social are inseparable.

Hurstwood finds his new identity as a failure intolerable, and increasingly withdraws from interactive, intersubjective connections into a private world of fantasy and an impersonal, public world of journalistic spectacle: "He was getting in the frame of mind where he wanted principally to be alone and to be allowed to think. The disease of brooding was beginning to claim him as a victim. Only the newspapers and his own thoughts were worth while" (chap. 33, pp. 243–44). Both his capital and his capacity for self-exertion slip away, and as the process of proletarianization progresses Hurstwood drifts into menial work and then into begging. He becomes a pitiable figure: "An old, thin coat was turned up about his red ears—his cracked derby hat was pulled down until it turned them outward. His hands were in his pockets. . . . People turned to look after him, so uncouth was his shambling figure" (chap. 47, pp. 361–62). Hurstwood's degradation is at once social, moral, and intellectual, for he has also become incapable of coherent thought: "Hopelessly he turned back into Broadway again and slopped onward and away, begging, crying, losing track of his thoughts, one after another, as a mind decayed and disjointed is wont to do" (chap. 47, p. 363). Mindlessly, he seeks only food and warmth. Hurstwood has been utterly brutalized.

Hurstwood has lost not only his place in the world but himself. He is no longer capable of realizing how he appears to others or comprehending what is happening to him; the brute has no understanding, cannot regard himself or explain himself. It falls to Presley to observe and describe the fates of Derrick and Dyke, to the modern narrator of *Before Adam* to tell the story of his atavistic dream-self. The self is always human, the brute always Other; thus when Hurstwood is plunged into the world of determinism he cannot recognize himself in it. Working as a motorman during a streetcar strike, he holds himself apart from the other men: "he felt a little superior to these two—a little better off. To him these were ignorant and commonplace, poor sheep in a driver's hand. 'Poor devils,' he thought, speaking out of the thoughts and feelings of a bygone period of success" (chap. 41, p. 302). But that driven Other is—most explicitly in *Vandover and the Brute*—a nightmarish double of the self.

The narrative of proletarianization, demonstrating that one can tumble down as well as climb up the social ladder, implicitly proposes a frightening question to the reader: is anyone safe? Dreiser especially gives us an outcast with whom we must empathize, and as we follow Hurstwood down into his abyss the distinction between self and Other seems fearfully precarious. The gesture of exclusion reinforces the antinomy between human and brute without rendering the image of the brute any less potent, and the assertion of superiority always inscribes a doubt: "that isn't me (is it?)—that couldn't happen to me (could it?)." The sympathetic emotion provoked in the reader by Hurstwood's misfortunes itself contains this fear, as the naturalists' cynical contemporary Ambrose Bierce suggests when he defines "pity" as "a failing sense of exemption, inspired by contrast."[23]

But the trajectory of his fall tends to carry Hurstwood beyond the reach of empathy. We see him, still sympathetically, but more and more from outside as his point of view enables an exploration of "The Curious Shifts of the Poor"—the world of mission meals, flophouses, charity hospitals which is the same alien ground within the civilized city that Crane explores in "An Experiment in Misery." We can never quite see him, as other people do, simply as "a chronic type of bum and beggar" (chap. 47, p. 360), but he begins to merge into the mass of pitiable, helpless drifters who are portrayed in a version of the familiar imagery of the brute—they have "ox-like stares" (chap. 45, p. 346), wait patiently "like cattle" (chap. 47, p. 358). As Hurstwood waits to be admitted to a cheap lodging house, he is not only among but has become one of the unfit who bear on their bodies and in their minds the marks of degradation:

There was a face in the thick of the collection which was as white as drained veal. There was another red as brick. Some came with thin, rounded shoulders, others with wooden legs, still others with frames so lean that clothes only flapped about them. There were great ears, swollen noses, thick lips, and above all, red, blood-shot eyes. Not a normal, healthy face in the whole mass; not a straight figure; not a straightforward, steady glance. [chap. 47, p. 366]

These damaged men stand passively in the cold, looking at the door "as dumb brutes look, as dogs paw and whine and study the knob" (chap. 47, p. 367). It was to this, to the inevitable catastrophe of his brutalization and suicide that Hurstwood's road was, all along, leading him. Unlike the reader, who in the act of reading experiences himself as free, Hurstwood is and always was the doomed victim of forces beyond his comprehension and control. The disturbing question, "Could it happen to me?," can never be abolished. But the very *fatality* of the narrative of proletarianization works to contain its threat.

Dreiser's typical image of the brute is not Norris's vicious, violent beast but a weak, pitiable animal. Certainly, his brutal characters are dangerous and can harm others; yet even when, as in the play *The Hand of the Potter* or the early story "Nigger Jeff," Dreiser writes about a rapist, it is the criminal's vulnerability that concerns him. (The purple prose such a criminal evokes from Norris is recorded in passages from *The Octopus* discussed in Chapter 4). In *The Hand of the Potter* Isadore cries, expressing the sentiments implicit in the title, " 'I couldn't help it, could I? I didn't make myself, did I?,' " and the implication of the play as a whole bears out his appeal.[24] Jeff begs, " 'I didn't go to do it. I didn't mean to dis time. I was just drunk, boss.' " It is not lust or rage but his fear of the lynch mob that reduces him to complete brutality: "He was by now a groveling, foaming brute. The last gleam of intelligence was that which notified him of the set eyes of his pursuers."[25] Even when Dreiser deals with outright political violence during the streetcar strike, the anger he depicts is understandable human anger, not the rage of the brute. But imbecility and incomprehension can consume the self as surely as savagery. It is the helpless submission to the brutal world of toil that is the terrifying possibility in Dreiser's work, for if these characters are not unspeakable horrors neither are they fully human. Working with complex materials in the general ideology of the period, the naturalists invent an Other that is revealingly consistent but also significantly variable; thus, Dreiser's characteristic image of the brute is the ox, while Norris's is the wolfish monstrosity, and London's is the dangerous but potent and therefore glamorous wolf.[26]

The ritual act of casting out the obsessively recurrent apparition of the brute is dramatized in naturalism in the narrative strategy I have called the plot of decline. This plot provides a powerful ordering force in naturalist storytelling (we will encounter other such narrative strategies in Chapter 5). It is enacted under the sign of philosophical determinism, but carries its own conviction and carries naturalism well beyond that realistic program. The inexorable process of Hurstwood's deterioration is assigned a cause, indeed several causes, yet it belongs to the realm of fatality rather than that of causality. Nor are the ends of Maggie and Vandover, for example, ever really in doubt—from the beginning they are clearly no match for the forces arrayed against them. In "A Case for Lombroso," too, the reason cited for the protagonists' fatal effect on one another is not remotely adequate to its result: "had they never met,

Miss Hromada and young Stayne would yet have been as fine specimens of woman-hood and manhood as you could wish to know. Once having met, they ruined each other" (pp. 41–42). Determinism and fatality alike tend to reduce brutality to victimization, yet without rendering it any less threatening. Whatever form it may take, whatever effort may be made to capture and control it in webs of causality or plot, the brutal Other signifies danger. It inescapably inscribes in the represented social and psychological order and in the order of the text an anxiety that ultimately has its source not in antinomies nor in narratives but in the historical moment of naturalism.

NOTES

1. Robert A. Morace, "The Writer and His Middle Class Audience: Frank Norris, A Case in Point," *Critical Essays on Frank Norris*, ed. Don Graham (Boston: G. K. Hall, 1980), p. 53. Morace also notes that *The Wave*, ironically in view of Norris's later *Octopus*, was founded as a publicity organ for a hotel owned by the Southern Pacific.

2. Frank Norris, "Suggestions: III. Brute" (1897), in vol. 10 of *The Complete Edition of Frank Norris* (Garden City, N.Y.: Doubleday, Doran & Co., 1928), pp. 80–81.

3. Frank Norris, "Man Proposes—No. 1" (1896), in vol. 10 of *The Complete Edition of Frank Norris*, p. 58.

4. Frank Norris, "Man Proposes—No. II" (1896), in vol. 10 of *The Complete Edition of Frank Norris*, p. 59.

5. There are five sketches in this series; I analyze only the first two, but the others can easily be placed. The third sketch deals with the danger incurred by a man who does not observe class boundaries carefully enough and gets entangled with a sexually aggressive girl of lower social class although he is really in love with someone else. Norris describes the situation in a familiar idiom: "There was something in him, some sensual second self, that the girl evoked at moments such as this; something that was of the animal and would not be gainsaid" (p. 68). The fourth is similar to the first; again the proposal is already set in a domestic scene and the girl's love is implied rather than stated directly (clearly Norris sees open consent as putting female purity in doubt). The fifth also deals with the world of the privileged but shows the proposal resulting in a misunderstanding because a catastrophic event (a shipwreck—and the significance of that image will be discussed elsewhere) intervenes. Only the second of these pieces can be considered naturalist; the third and fifth, however, show elements of the naturalist realm disrupting the middle-class domesticity that is unchallenged in the first and fourth.

6. Frank Norris, *McTeague: A Story of San Francisco* (1899), vol. 8 of *The Complete Edition of Frank Norris*, pp. 27–28.

7. Frank Norris, "Outward and Visible Signs: V. Thoroughbred" (1895), in vol. 10 of *The Complete Edition of Frank Norris*, p. 208.

8. Frank Norris, in *The Complete Edition of Frank Norris*, vol. 4. The first two quoted phrases are from p. 43, the third from p. 46, and the long passage from p. 45.

9. Donald Pizer, *The Novels of Frank Norris* (Bloomington: Indiana University Press, 1966). On this point see especially pp. 56–63.

10. See James Richard Giles, "A Study of the Concept of Atavism in the Writings of Rudyard Kipling, Frank Norris, and Jack London" (Ph.D. diss., University of Texas, 1967).

11. Jack London, *Before Adam* (New York: Macmillan, 1907), p. 18.

12. For example, see Stephen Jay Gould, "Fascinating Tails," *Discover* 3, no. 9 (1982): 40–41, for an account of a small contemporary furore over a human infant born with a tail.

13. This analysis suggests a connection between naturalism and a genre to which some of London's fiction has retrospectively been attributed: science fiction. The last chapter provides a model for discussing the way in which different generic strands coexist in a single text.

14. Paddy Chayefsky, *Altered States: A Novel* (1978; reprint, New York: Bantam, 1979), p. 200.

15. Frank Norris, *Vandover and the Brute* (1914), vol. 5 of *The Complete Edition of Frank Norris*, p. 278.

16. Frank Norris, *The Octopus: A Story of California* (1901), vols. 1 and 2 of *The Complete Edition of Frank Norris*, 2: 214.

17. This portrait of Derrick as admirable and ethical is not wholly consistent; witness the remark that shocks Presley that he is indifferent to long-term freight rates because "by then we will, all of us, have made our fortunes" (ibid., 2:14). This element of the gambler in Derrick's character manifests a dissonance in Norris's treatment of the profit-seeking rancher.

18. This is not, I should note, a question of whether or not Crane's work "belongs" to naturalism, but a question of a different articulation of materials in different novels. Crane's work is also of course somewhat earlier than the "moment" of naturalism I have taken as my topic.

19. Stephen Crane, *Maggie: A Girl of the Streets* (1893), reprinted in *Bowery Tales*, vol. 1 of *The Works of Stephen Crane*, ed. Fredson Bowers (Charlottesville: University Press of Virginia, 1969), pp. 8, 18.

20. Alan Trachtenberg, "Experiments in Another Country: Stephen Crane's City Sketches," *Southern Review* 10 (1974): 265–85, reprinted in *American Realism: New Essays*, ed. Eric J. Sundquist (Baltimore: Johns Hopkins University Press, 1982), p. 145.

21. Stephen Crane, "An Experiment in Misery" (1894), in *The New York City Sketches of Stephen Crane and Related Pieces*, ed. R. W. Stallman and E. R. Hagemann (New York: New York University Press, 1966), p. 43.

22. Theodore Dreiser, *Sister Carrie*, ed. Donald Pizer (New York: W. W. Norton, 1970), chap. 33, pp. 239 and 244.

23. Ambrose Bierce, *The Devil's Dictionary* (1911; reprint, New York: Albert & Charles Boni, 1925), p. 255. The contents of this volume appeared in newspapers from 1881 to 1906 and were first collected as *The Cynic's Word Book* in 1906.

24. Theodore Dreiser, *The Hand of the Potter* (New York: Boni and Liveright, 1918), p. 169.

25. Theodore Dreiser, *Free and Other Stories* (New York: Boni and Liveright, 1918), p. 101.

26. Although I derive this analysis from the study of naturalist novels themselves, evidence that an opposition between privilege and Otherness fascinated each of these writers is not difficult to find. Robert H. Elias in his biography of Dreiser takes the tension between Dreiser's sense of himself as a spectator and as a vulnerable participant as fundamental to the novelist's character (*Theodore Dreiser: Apostle of Nature*, emended edition [Ithaca, N.Y.: Cornell University Press, 1970]). Warren French finds a similar ambivalence in Norris's college experiences, attributing his "attitude of inherent superiority" and "racial and class snobbery" to the social atmosphere of Norris's fraternity, and his "terrifying self-doubts" to his failure as a student (*Frank Norris* [New York: Twayne, 1962], pp. 20–21). Andrew Sinclair discusses the idiosyncratic determinants of London's fear of the Other: "Jack always said that he had lost his boyhood, but he had never lost his primitive terror of *Them*—the unknown people beating carpets in the yard, the Chinese gamblers of his drunken deliria, the Greek poachers of the Bay and the Italian scabs of the slums who had robbed him of his birthright as a pioneer American, the true heir of the land of California" (*Jack: A Biography of Jack London* [New York: Harper and Row, 1977], p. 220). Each author is different, of course; an analysis of the authorial ideology in each case would be a useful although sizable undertaking.

THIRTY-SIX

REALISM AND "ABSENT THINGS IN AMERICAN LIFE"

Amy Kaplan

Amy Kaplan received her Ph.D. from Johns Hopkins in 1982 and teaches at Mount Holyoke College. In addition to *The Social Construction of American Realism* (1988), she is co-editor (with Donald Pease) of *Cultures of United States Imperialism* (1993).

The fate of realism in American literary history has undergone dramatic reversals on theoretical, political, and historical grounds. From an objective reflection of contemporary social life, realism has become a fictional conceit, or deceit, packaging and naturalizing an official version of the ordinary. From a style valued for its plain-speaking vernacular, realism has adopted a rhetorical sophistication that now subverts its own claims to referentiality. From a progressive force exposing the conditions of industrial society, realism has turned into a conservative force whose very act of exposure reveals its complicity with structures of power. These reversals accompany changes in the historical understanding of American capitalism, from a class-based system structured by relations of production to a culture of consumption and surveillance which sweeps all social relations into a vortex of the commodity and the spectacle. Pivotal in the changing fate of realism is the enduring dominance of the romance thesis that makes realism by necessity a failure. Whereas for critics in the forties and fifties, realism failed to represent contemporary society because of the absence of a dense social fabric, for literary historians of the sixties the realists' perception of the presence of complex social changes marred their achievement of literary

The Social Construction of American Realism, by Amy Kaplan (Chicago: University of Chicago Press, 1988), pp. 1–14. © 1988 by The University of Chicago. Reprinted by permission of Amy Kaplan and The University of Chicago Press. Pp. 2–7 appeared originally in *The Yale Review* 74 (1984): 126–31. Reprinted by permission of Blackwell Publishers.

form. For a more recent generation of critics, realism fails because of a linguistic absence which makes referentiality impossible. Common to all these approaches is the assumption of an inadequate relation between American fiction and American society, though the blame—or credit—can be attributed to either side.

I

"One might enumerate the items of high civilization, as it exists in other countries, which are absent from the texture of American life, until it should become a wonder to know what was left."[1] So begins Henry James's famous list of the "absent things in American life" in his early book on Hawthorne. Part lament, part boast, it set the tone for the study of American fiction over half a century later, when critics sought to explain why American novelists apparently were not interested in writing about society. Whereas James points to the lack of a "complex social machinery to set a writer in motion"[2] as the major difference between Hawthorne's antebellum world and his own vastly more complicated age, literary critics of the post-World War II era turned this deficiency into the distinguishing feature of an American literary tradition. In other words, the supposedly impoverished soil of American culture has proved most fertile for the American imagination.

This view underlies the now familiar and currently disputed distinction between the European novel and the American romance, which was drawn most fully a generation ago by Richard Chase in *The American Novel and Its Tradition*.[3] In the richly textured social world of the European novel, Chase argued, characters develop in relation to entrenched institutions and the struggle between classes. The isolated hero of the American romance, in contrast, embarks on a melodramatic quest through a symbolic universe, unformed by networks of social relations and unfettered by the pressure of social restraints. As his title suggests, Chase was deliberately establishing a national alternative to F. R. Leavis's *The Great Tradition* of English novelists from Jane Austen to George Eliot, Henry James, and Joseph Conrad. Where the "great tradition" seeks order through the reconciliation of the individual and society, the American tradition, from *Wieland* to *The Sound and the Fury*, explores the open-ended states of individual alienation and cosmic disorder. Chase founds his tradition on the profoundly ahistorical thesis that, in the absence of a settled, class-bound society, Americans do not write social fiction. Despite subsequent criticism, Chase's romance thesis has in effect shaped the canon of American fiction that we still read, teach, and write about today—a canon that was initiated by Brown and Cooper, developed by Hawthorne and Melville, and reached its apotheosis in James and Faulkner, with detours through Twain, Norris, and Fitzgerald.[4]

Of course the boundary of any literary canon defines what it precludes as well as what it includes. The purpose of opening this book on American realism with the seemingly worn-out romance thesis is not to beat a dead horse by recovering a suppressed tradition or to turn the romance/realism dichotomy on its head. Rather it is to show how the dominance of the romance in framing an American canon has done more than merely exclude realistic novels; more importantly, the assumptions underlying the romance thesis have determined the study of American realism from the forties to the present, and have limited the range of critical inquiry. The association of the romance with a uniquely American culture has displaced realism to an anomalous and distinctly un-American margin of literary criticism, which has necessarily viewed its literary mode as a failure. Reproducing James's "absent things" in different theoretical guises, studies of American realism have repeatedly reinforced the ahistorical assumption of an impossible or flawed relationship between American literature and society.[5]

Although Chase traces his theory to the "lesson of the master," James, he in fact was indebted to two contemporary trends in postwar literary criticism: the New Critics' regard for the lyric as the highest literary form and, most important, his colleague Lionel Trilling's antiliberal polemics. Even though he rejects the New Critics' myopic attention to poetic technique, Chase values the romance precisely for those poetic qualities—symbolism, for example—that raise fiction above the historical contingencies of narrative into the realm of "universal human significance." Toward a similar end but through different means, Chase codifies many of the reflections in Trilling's *The Liberal Imagination*, where to James's list of the "absent things," Trilling adds the category of "manners": "a culture's hum and buzz of implication . . . the whole evanescent context in which its explicit statements are made . . . the things that for good or bad draw the people of a culture together."[6] Turning this loss into a gain, Chase finds writers in the "New World" liberated from "the momentarily settled conditions involving contrasting classes with contrasting manners," conditions which enabled the realistic novel of the "Old World."[7]

Although the romance thesis—like the texts it privileges—seems to grow full-blown out of the American soil to define the exceptional nature of American culture, in fact it emerges victorious from an implicit political attack on alternative forms of fiction and criticism. In his influential essay "Reality in America," Trilling berates historian V. L. Parrington, whom he lumps together with critics as different as Granville Hicks and F. O. Matthiessen; he faults such critics for their deterministic view of "material reality, hard, resistant, unformed, impenetrable, and unpleasant" and for their naive expectation that literature should mechanically reflect this "reality," unrefined by the intervention of the "mind."[8] Trilling's quarrel with what might be called the aesthetics of liberalism issued in the toppling of Theodore Dreiser from the American pantheon for his crude style and lack of intellect, and the replacement of Dreiser by Henry James for the latter's belief in the creative power of the mind to shape its own reality within the limits of moral ambiguity rather than the field of social relations. While the need to value James over Dreiser may sound ludicrous today, for Trilling this exchange amounted to a political choice: "Dreiser and James: with that juxtaposition we are immediately at the dark bloody crossroads where literature and politics meet."[9] The liberal praise of Dreiser's realism for its "great brooding pity" for the victims of capitalism, ran the risk, in Trilling's eyes, of endorsing Stalinism, for, according to another essay, "some paradox of our natures leads us, when once we have made our fellow men the objects of our enlightened interest, to go on to make them the objects of our pity, then of our wisdom, ultimately of our coercion."[10] To represent class difference in America, implied Trilling, is to impose a politically dangerous and aesthetically disingenous literary mode. The only stand against these threats, for Trilling, is "moral realism which is the product of the free play of the moral imagination," i.e., the qualities for which he valued James.[11]

Thus Trilling's and Chase's vision of the American novel must be understood in the context of their times. They were recasting a literary tradition to echo their own generation's disillusionment with oppositional politics and their disbelief in the efficacy of human agency in what Trilling called the "social field," the province of the novel itself. This tradition contributed to the broader intellectual consensus which held that America was a classless society without internal ideological conflicts. Yet the legacy of these critics extended beyond their own time to frame an American canon which equates the romance with the exceptional nature of American culture and which makes realism an anomaly in American fiction; as an inherently flawed imitation of a European convention, realism is, in effect, un-American. If the "thinness" of American culture cannot nurture social fiction, then those novelists who do confront contemporary social issues must be imaginatively handicapped, inorganically related to that culture.

In the 1960s critics reclaimed what Larzer Ziff called "the lost generation" of American realists, writers never lost to literary historians, such as Alfred Kazin.[12] This rediscovery, however, reproduced Trilling's distinction between "mind" and "reality" in the form of two distinct critical approaches: the definition of realism primarily on formalist grounds and the use of realism to designate a literary historical period between the Civil War and World War I. Critics such as Donald Pizer, Harold Kolb, and Charles Walcutt delineated the formal characteristics, the recurring imagery, and the philosophical dimensions that could define realism and naturalism as coherent and serious literary genres.[13] But by and large these critics divorced the texts they analyzed from the social context embedded in those forms. The second set of critics, in contrast, grouped diverse texts together according to an extra-literary category, the historical background of social change—an approach reflected in the titles of such works as Warner Berthoff's *The Ferment of Realism* and Jay Martin's *Harvests of Change*.[14] Although these critics viewed realistic writing as a response to the upheavals of urban-industrial capitalism, they judged texts either by their mimetic accuracy, which usually missed the mark, or by New Critical measures, which found them lacking in organic form and narrative unity. The treatment of texts as responses to social change implicitly situates literature outside the arena of social history, looking down and commenting upon it, and thereby reinforces the rigid split between social structures and literary structures. Reproducing Trilling's distinction between "mind" and "reality," those critics who valued the realists for their commitment to the representation of contemporary American social life often devalued the realists as unsophisticated literary craftsmen. Stylistic inconsistencies and problematic endings were usually treated as internal formal flaws rather than as narrative articulations of ideological problems. The period from *The Adventures of Huckleberry Finn* to *Sister Carrie* is rich in examples of that peculiarly American category, the failed masterpiece.

Contemporary literary theory has effectively broken down the dichotomy between social context and literary form implicit in the concept of realism as empirical reflection and in the assumption that American novelists who turn their gaze on society write flawed prose. The influence of theory can be found in Eric Sundquist's *American Realism: New Essays*, an anthology which reflects two distinct trends in literary criticism: poststructuralism and the renewed interest in history.[15] The antimimetic assumption of postructuralist theory which holds that reality is not reflected by language but that language in fact produces the reality we know has opened the realistic narrative to sophisticated interpretive scrutiny. These approaches, however, tend to locate the power of realistic texts precisely in their ability to deconstruct their own claims to referentiality. Through the lenses of contemporary theories, those characteristics once considered realistic are revalued for exposing their own fictionality. The spokesman for American realism, William Dean Howells, for example, operates under the anxiety of Hawthorne's influence, a pressure which at key points disrupts the realistic trajectory of his novels, swerving them into the realm of romance.[16] Edith Wharton, once considered the rare American novelist of manners, writes a "romance of identity" in *The House of Mirth*, whose heroine's magnetic appeal is explained by the psychoanalytic theory of narcissism.[17] Thus new theories tend to support an old thesis—that American novelists escape from or fail to represent their society; the concept of realism disappears in the current critical discourse as the romance continues to subvert realistic representation.[18]

In his introduction to *American Realism*, Sundquist revoices Chase's thesis in arguing that American realism "did not achieve a certain and stable force, exhaust that force and perish; rather it failed case by case by refusing to renounce romance completely and by levelling the barriers of aesthetic freedom too completely."[19] On the one hand, Trilling's contest between the free mind and obdurate reality returns in Sundquist's conclusion, which privileges James and Crane both for the "continued presence of the romance" in their writing and for their modernity, "because they demonstrate the increasing discrepancy between the figurative life of the mind and the literal life of the material."[20] On the other hand, Sundquist revives the literary-historical approach to realism which ties together the diversity of literary forms generated by writers between the Civil War and World War I in response to the bewildering social transformations of industrial capitalism. Yet instead of trying to confront or represent those changes, American writers "returned ever more feverishly to the imagination."[21] Thus the history of realism in America is once again the history of failure.

Yet the perceived failure or impossibility of mimesis has led recent critics to chart a more dynamic relation between social and literary structures, one that does not place the text outside society as an imaginative escape, a static window for observation, or a reflecting mirror. Historical perspectives hold that the textual production of reality does not occur in a linguistic vacuum; neither is it politically innocent, of course, but always charged by ideology—those unspoken collective understandings, conventions, stories, and cultural practices that uphold systems of social power. These approaches situate realistic texts within a wider field of what has been called "discursive practices." Thus we now understand, for example, the strange amalgam of romance and realism in Dreiser and Norris, not as a failure of form, but in relation to the unstable language of financial speculation which informs both the content and the narrative strategies of their novels.[22] We see realism in the *Princess Casamassima* not as the free play of the moral imagination but as the enactment and exposure of the discourse of surveillance which polices the urban social system.[23] June Howard has recently reinterpreted the genre of naturalism as a literary form with an "immanent ideology" that "struggles to accommodate that sense of discomfort and danger" of its period.[24] As they begin to treat literary form as a social practice, these historical approaches reclaim the American novelist's engagement with society. Realists do more than passively record the world outside; they actively create and criticize the meanings, representations, and ideologies of their own changing culture.

The renewed interest in history, however, has reconstructed a new social context for realism as well. Realism is now related primarily to the rise of consumer culture in the late nineteenth century, in which the process of commodification makes all forms of the quotidian perform in what Guy Debord has called the "society of the spectacle." In this context, the novelist's attempt to represent everyday life is understood either as a way of staging a "series of acts of exhibition"[25] for public consumption, or as a means of engaging in one of the most common activities of modern urban life: "just looking."[26] Realism is similarly related to the culture of surveillance, in which the realist participates in the panoptic forces which both control and produce the real world by seeing it without being seen in turn.[27] In these historical revisions everyone is either a performer or a spectator, an inspector or a specimen. These studies have succeeded in resituating the realistic project as cultural practice within society rather than placing the realist outside society as a neutral observer. Yet by viewing realism as the staging of spectacles or the enforcement of power, these approaches do not view the production of the real as an arena in which the novelist struggles to represent reality against contradictory representations. By treating realism as an expression of consumer culture or a form of social incorporation, these studies tend to overlook the profound social disturbances that inform realistic narratives.[28]

Changes in the historical understanding of realism have accompanied the reevaluation of realism's political stance, from a progressive force exposing social conditions to a conservative force complicit with capitalist relations. This change is once more dramatized by the critical stature of Theodore Dreiser.[29] No longer notorious for their exposure of a brutal, class-ridden urban society, his novels heroically enact the ceaseless theatricality of modern urban life and the externalization of the self onto evanescent social roles. No longer valued or scorned for his depiction of social facts, he is lauded for his sentimentalism, which embraces rather than criticizes the logic of capitalism.[30] Freed from the strictures of both Parrington and Trilling, Dreiser has been reinstalled in the literary pantheon to embody the romance of American capitalism.

II

If, as successive generations of literary critics have asserted, realism repeatedly fails in its claims to represent American society, then the realistic enterprise must be redefined to ask *what* realistic novels do accomplish and *how* they work as a cultural practice.

My project is not to rewrite the history of American realism as a history of success but to move beyond that dichotomous judgment to explore the dynamic relationship between changing fictional and social forms in realistic representation. If realism is a fiction, we can root this fiction in its historical context to examine its ideological force. Why does the fiction of the referent become a powerful rallying cry for some, a point of contention for others, and an assumption taken for granted by still other writers at the particular historical juncture of the 1880s and 1890s? How do literary texts produce a social reality that can be recognized as "the way things are"? And what counterforces threaten to disrupt this process of recognition? How does "reality" come to be associated with depictions of brutality, sordidness, and lower-class life, and how are the same realms often cordoned off as "unreal"? Is realism part of a broader cultural effort to fix and control a coherent representation of a social reality that seems increasingly inaccessible, fragmented, and beyond control?

This book explores these questions by reexamining realism's relation to three interrelated contexts which have remained central to the study of realism but whose complexity has been obscured by the dominance of the romance thesis: realism's relation to social change, to the representation of class difference, and to the emergence of a mass culture. These broad contexts are given historical specificity through close analysis of the theory and practice of realism in the works of William Dean Howells, Edith Wharton, and Theodore Dreiser, authors who, each in a different way, have become critical touchstones in the debate about the viability of realism in American fiction.

This study opens with the premise that the urban-industrial transformation of nineteenth-century society did not provide a ready-made setting which the realistic novel reflects, but that these changes radically challenged the accessibility of an emergent modern world to literary representation. Realism simultaneously becomes an imperative and a problem in American fiction. It neither compensates for the absence of a complex social fabric nor records a naive belief in the correspondence between language and the intractable material world; rather it explores and bridges the perceived gap between the social world and literary representation. Realists show a surprising lack of confidence in the capacity of fiction to reflect a solid world "out there," not because of the inherent slipperiness of signification but because of their distrust in the significance of the social. They often assume a world which lacks solidity, and the weightiness of descriptive detail—one of the most common characteristics of the realistic text—often appears in inverse proportion to a sense of insubstantiality, as though description could pin down the objects of an unfamiliar world to make it real. The realists inhabit a world in which, according to historian Jackson Lears, "reality itself began to seem problematic, something to be sought rather than merely lived."[31] Realistic narratives enact this search not by fleeing into the imagination or into nostalgia for a lost past but by actively constructing the coherent social world they represent; and they do this not in a vacuum of fictionality but in direct confrontation with the elusive process of social change.

This realism that develops in American fiction in the 1880s and 1890s is not a seamless package of a triumphant bourgeois mythology but an anxious and contradictory mode which both articulates and combats the growing sense of unreality at the heart of middle-class life. This unreal quality comes from two major sources for the novelists in this study: intense and often violent class conflicts which produced fragmented and competing social realities, and the simultaneous development of a mass culture which dictated an equally threatening homogeneous reality. Attempting to steer a precarious course between these two developments, realists contribute to the construction of a cohesive public sphere while they at once resist and participate in the domination of a mass market as the arbiter of America's national idiom.

This study attempts to recuperate realism's relation to social change not as a static background which novels either naively record or heroically evade, but as the foreground of the narrative structure of each novel. For it is the sense of the world changing under the realists' pens that makes the social world so elusive to representation. Henry James articulates this dual sense of urgency and evasiveness when he writes of his return to New York in *The American Scene* in 1904. The enigma of the tall buildings supplants the "absent things" with the "terrible things in America," terrible by virtue of being "impudently new and still more impudently 'novel.' "[32] Restating the impossibility of realism in America, James notes the lack of a New York Zola, with "his love of the human aggregation" and more importantly the "huge reflector" of his novelistic tradition.[33] In contrast to James's earlier view of Hawthorne's New England, however, here it is not the absence of a complex social machine but the sense he has, while watching the skyscrapers dwarf Trinity Church, that the enormity of this machine and the rapidity of its changes had outstripped the literary forms available for representing it: "the monstrous phenomena themselves, meanwhile, strike me as having, with their immense momentum, got the start, got ahead of, in proper parlance, any possibility of poetic, of dramatic capture."[34] James articulates both a fear and a challenge underlying many realistic novels, that social "material" as he calls it is not an absence but something monstrous and threatening, and that the novelist is not in the role of reflecting but capturing, wrestling, and controlling a process of change which seems to defy representation.

Thus realism will be examined as a strategy for imagining and managing the threats of social change—not just to assert a dominant power but often to assuage fears of powerlessness. The threats of social change surface double-faced in the realistic novel: they appear as the potential for revolutionary upheaval, which the narrative of *A Hazard of New Fortunes*, for example, works to quell; or as the corporate imposition of novelty as the status quo, the "impudently new" which *The House of Mirth* both counters and enacts in its narrative structure. In *Sister Carrie* the threat of and desire for revolutionary change are pitted against the monotony of change as the quotidian, in an unresolved conflict. American realism will be treated in these analyses in part as what Fredric Jameson has called a "strategy of containment," but realism does not totally repudiate revolutionary change by seeking to "fold everything which is not-being, desire, hope and transformational praxis, back into the status of nature."[35] The realists do not naturalize the social world to make it seem immutable and organic, but, like contemporary social reformers, they engage in an enormous act of construction to organize, re-form, and control the social world. This act of construction makes the social world at once mechanical and improvised, locked in place and tentative. Furthermore, by containing the threats of social change, realistic narratives also register those desires which undermine the closure of that containment.[36]

For realists, the problem of representing social change is inseparable from the problem of representing social classes, a link made by James in his own use of the word "alien" in *The American Scene*. There he labels as "monstrous," like the skyscrapers, the working-class immigrants crowding the streets in New York City. The immigrants' "monstrous presumptuous interest" does not just impose itself from without, it makes the narrator's "most intimate relation" to society seem alien and threatening: "the idea of the country itself underwent some profane overhauling through which it appears to suffer the indignity of change."[37] Class difference and class conflict have long been viewed as the social medium which either enables or cripples the realistic novel. Whereas for some the apparent absence of a class-based society in America makes realism impossible, for others the proliferation of classes in urban industrial society produces the raw material for realism. While critics have continually faulted realists for their "inaccurate" portrayal of working-class and immigrant life, Howard has more productively analyzed this "inaccuracy" as an ideological strategy for imposing class hierarchies through representation.[38]

Class difference struck the realists less as a problem of social justice than as a problem of representation. They were less concerned with the accuracy of portraying "the other half" than with the problem of representing an interdependent society composed of competing and seemingly mutually exclusive realities. The novels in this study are filled with crowds and mobs which must be "sifted and strained" into what James calls the "germ of a public" and what Howells calls a "vision of solidarity." The novels construct a vision of a social whole, not just as nostalgia for lost unity or as a report of new social diversity, but as an attempt to mediate and negotiate competing claims to social reality by making alternative realities visible while managing their explosive qualities. In contrast to Howard's argument that the main naturalist strategy is to reinscribe class power-relations as formal narrative divisions between the spectator and the brute, I will argue that realistic strategies tend less to regulate conflict by formalizing otherness than to negotiate conflict in the narrative construction of common ground among classes both to efface and reinscribe social hierarchies.

Both Howells and Wharton have been criticized for their lack of realism, for their inability to portray those classes outside their immediate purview. One, however, portrays middle-class life and the other upper-class society in relation to the pressure of other classes lurking at their boundaries. In fact the realist participates in drawing such boundaries in a way that exposes their tenuous yet ideological necessity. To present a coherent view of a society as a whole, realists draw boundaries and explore their limits. The social world of each novel is constituted as much by those outside the immediate range of representation as by those at the center. In *A Hazard of New Fortunes*, the claims of a shadowy urban working class continually threaten to explode into the middle-class community, whose representation is shaped by this pressure. In *The House of Mirth*, viewed as one of the few American novels of manners to portray the claustrophobic setting of the upper class, the representation of high society depends as much on attracting the spectatorship of crowds as it does on excluding those crowds. Dreiser's novels, alternately praised for their depiction of working-class life and their spectacle of consumer culture, construct a world in which consumption is offered as a problematic solution to the power relations of a class society. All three authors focus on class difference to forge the bonds of a public world that subsumes those differences. Where Howells imagines a community based on work and character, Wharton seeks community in the exchange of intimacy and Dreiser posits a community of anonymous consumers and spectators with shared desires. Realistic novels often share an impulse with their utopian counterparts to project into the narrative present a harmonic vision of community that can paradoxically put an end to social change. Realistic novels have utopian moments that imagine resolutions to contemporary social conflicts by reconstructing society as it might be.

Those urban spaces often treated as the unproblematic setting of the realistic novel prove, on closer scrutiny, to be a threatening repository of the unreal which must be brought into the realm of representation and tamed: the streets of *A Hazard of New Fortunes*, the ballrooms of *The House of Mirth*, the workplaces of *Sister Carrie*. Not only does the social space populated by these novels extend to the crowded city streets, but this expansion of representation renders domestic space a conflicted and problematic realm for representation. The realists are preoccupied with the problem of inhabiting and representing rented space, from the middle-class apartment of the Marches, to Lily Bart's boardinghouse and Hurstwood's rented beds, to the hotel rooms of Norma Hatch and Carrie. Rented spaces constitute a world filled with things neither known nor valued through well-worn contact, but cluttered instead with mass-produced furnishings and the unknown lives of strangers and their abandoned possessions, and valued through the measure of time and space as money. The project of the realistic novels is to make these rented spaces inhabitable and representable. While realistic narratives chart the homelessness of their characters, they thereby construct a world in which their readers can feel at home.

In constructing a cohesive social world to contain the threats of social change, realists had to draw from and compete with other cultural practices that had the same goal. If class conflict posed fragmented realities that challenged the cohesion of any public sphere, the growing dominance of a mass culture—in the form of newspapers, magazines, advertising, and book publishing—created a national market which constructed for consumers a shared reality of both information and desire. The new media promised a coherent and a cohesive world in place of older forms of cultural authority. In asserting their own authority to represent reality, novelists wrote out of this newly developing mass culture against which they attempted to define their work. Realism cannot be understood only in relation to the world it represents; it is also a debate, within the novel form, with competing modes of representation. Howells, both in his criticism and his novels, asserts realism's truth value not only in its fidelity to real life but in its contest with popular fiction and mass journalism. Wharton, who wrote best-sellers in an age that coined this term, defined her own writing against the popular women's fiction that preceded her and the society novelist, with whom she was often identified. Dreiser, whose apprenticeship included journalism and the editorship of a short-lived ladies magazine, both incorporated these popular modes and dissociated his realism from them.

To understand realism's struggle with other modes of representation is to restore to realism its dynamic literary qualities. The development of realism has traditionally been explained in terms of its parody of older conventions of the romance, as in the case of *Don Quixote*. Alfred Habegger has shown how realism in the fiction of Howells and James engages in an internalized polemic against the early maternal tradition of the sentimental novel.[39] Yet realism can also be understood as an argument, not only with older residual conventions, but with emergent forms of mass media from which it gains its power and against which it asserts itself. Realistic novels do more than juggle competing visions of social reality; they encompass conflicting forms and narratives which shape that reality.

In this competition with other cultural practices, realism also becomes a strategy for defining the social position of the author. To call oneself a realist means to make a claim not only for the cognitive value of fiction but for one's own cultural authority both to possess and to dispense access to the real. Indeed realists implicitly upheld the contradictory claim that they had the expertise to represent the commonplace and the ordinary, at a time when such knowledge no longer seemed available to common sense. If the realists engaged in the construction of a new kind of public sphere, they were also formulating a new public role for the author in the mass market. Realists are often seen to take the self-effacing stance of the neutral observer. Yet by writing so often about writers, realists explore both the social construction of their own roles and their implication in constructing the reality their novels represent.

NOTES

1. Henry James, *Nathaniel Hawthorne* (1879), reprinted in *Literary Criticism: Essays on Literature, American Writers, English Writers*, ed. Leon Edel and Mark Wilson (New York: Library of America, 1984), p. 351.

2. Ibid., p. 320.

3. Richard Chase, *The American Novel and Its Tradition* (New York: Doubleday, 1957). Versions of the romance thesis, which holds that American writers characteristically escape from society and history, have informed a variety of studies, from D. H. Lawrence, *Studies in Classic American Literature* (New York: Penguin, 1923), to Richard Poirier, *A World Elsewhere* (New York: Oxford, 1966). Another statement can be found in R. W. B. Lewis, *The American Adam* (Chicago: University of Chicago Press, 1955).

4. No area of American literature is more contested today than that of the canon. But testimony to the power of the romance thesis is the fact that feminist criticism of American literature has focused predominantly on the sentimental novelists of the mid-nineteenth century as the countertradition of American fiction. See, for example, Ann Douglas, *The Feminization of American Culture* (New York: Avon, 1977); Nina Baym, *Woman's Fiction: A Guide to Novels by and about Women in America, 1820–1870* (Ithaca, N.Y.: Cornell University Press, 1978); Jane Tompkins, *Sensational Designs: The Cultural Work of American Fiction, 1790–1860* (New

York: Oxford University Press, 1985). Although excellent studies have been done of individual women writers in the late nineteenth century, few full-length synthetic studies comparable to those of the earlier period have focused on the generation of American women writers—contemporary with the male American realists—as a group or coherent "tradition" or movement.

5. Another sign of the power of the romance can be seen in the fact that the most powerful critiques of the ahistorical nature of American criticism still focus on the same sacred American texts that constitute Chase's "tradition." See Myra Jehlen, "New World Epics: The Middle-Class Novel in America," *Salmagundi* 36 (Winter 1977): 49–68; and Carolyn Porter, *Seeing and Being: The Plight of the Participant Observer in Emerson, James, Adams, and Faulkner* (Middletown, Conn.: Wesleyan University Press: 1981).

6. Lionel Trilling, "Manners, Morals, and the Novel," in *The Liberal Imagination* (New York: Viking Press, 1950), pp. 206–7.

7. Chase, *The American Novel*, p. 158.

8. Trilling, "Reality in America," in *The Liberal Imagination*, p. 13. It is important to note that Trilling conflates critics with very different political and aesthetic theories. Parrington considered "critical realism" as the culmination of an American progressive tradition with roots in the eighteenth century; by portraying objective conditions, critical realism "questioned the excellence of the industrial system." Vernon Louis Parrington, *The Beginnings of Critical Realism*, vol. 3 of *Main Currents in American Thought* (New York: Harcourt, Brace, 1930), p. 238. For Marxists in the thirties, such as Granville Hicks and Bernard Smith, the goal of realism was to expose underlying forces of the capitalist system. Matthiessen, in contrast, placed Dreiser's "picture of conditions" squarely in an American democratic tradition by comparing him to Whitman, in *Theodore Dreiser* (New York: William Sloane, 1951), pp. 59–60. Yet even these critics tend to treat realism as a goal never fully achieved in American fiction. While to explore these theories of realism in detail would require another study, my argument is based on the claim that Trilling and Chase in effect won the argument and shaped the consequent study of American realism.

9. Trilling, "Reality," p. 11.

10. Trilling, "Manners, Morals, and the Novel," p. 221.

11. Ibid., p. 222. On Trilling's conception of "moral realism," and his attack on liberalism as thinly veiled Stalinism, see Mark Krupnick, *Lionel Trilling and the Fate of Cultural Criticism* (Evanston, Ill.: Northwestern University Press, 1986), pp. 57–75. Krupnick, however, naively accepts Trilling's characterizations of Parrington, liberalism, and popular-front politics as accurate historical description.

12. Larzer Ziff, *The American 1890s: Life and Times of a Lost Generation* (Lincoln: University of Nebraska Press, 1966), Alfred Kazin, *On Native Grounds: An Interpretation of Modern American Prose Literature* (1942; rpt., New York: Anchor Books, 1956).

13. Although many studies combine both literary history and formalist criticism, those primarily formalist include Charles C. Walcutt, *American Literary Naturalism: A Divided Stream* (Minneapolis: University of Minnesota Press, 1956); Donald Pizer, *Realism and Naturalism in Nineteenth-Century American Literature* (Carbondale: Southern Illinois University Press, 1966); Harold Kolb, *The Illusion of Life: American Realism as Literary Form* (Charlottesville: University Press of Virginia, 1969). The New Critical discovery of Dreiser might be marked by Robert Penn Warren's essay on *An American Tragedy* in the *Yale Review* 52 (October 1962): 1–15.

14. Warner Berthoff, *The Ferment of Realism: American Literature, 1884–1919* (New York: Macmillan, 1965); Jay Martin, *Harvests of Change: American Literature, 1865–1914* (Englewood Cliffs, N.J.: Prentice-Hall, 1967); see also Kazin, *Native Grounds*, and Ziff, *1890s*.

15. Eric Sundquist, *American Realism: New Essays* (Baltimore: The Johns Hopkins University Press, 1982).

16. Richard Brodhead, "Hawthorne Among the Realists: The Case of Howells," in Sundquist, *American Realism*, pp. 25–41. In his book *The School of Hawthorne* (New York: Oxford University Press, 1986), chap. 5, Brodhead revises his argument to situate Howells's realism in a social context, but he still concludes that realism is subverted by Howells's moral preoccupations with fiction as a source of cultural value.

17. Joan Lidoff, "Another Sleeping Beauty: Narcissism in *The House of Mirth*," in Sundquist, *American Realism*, pp. 238–58.

18. See also essays in Sundquist, *American Realism*, by Laurence Holland and Evan Carton, who argue that Mark Twain's novels, long noted for their fresh use of the vernacular, self-consciously expose a fictionality that informs their linguistic and moral structure; and Donald Pease, who claims that *The Red Badge of Courage*, once viewed as the major realistic portrayal of the Civil War, undermines the very possibility of representation.

19. Sundquist, *American Realism*, p. 9.

20. Ibid., p. 23.

21. Ibid., p. 7.

22. Howard Horwitz, " 'To Find the Value of X': *The Pit* as a Renunciation of Romance," in ibid., pp. 215–37; Walter Benn Michaels, "Dreiser's *Financier*: The Man of Business as a Man of Letters," in ibid., pp. 278–96 (reprinted in Walter Benn Michaels, *The Gold Standard and the Logic of Naturalism* [Berkeley: University of California Press, 1987]).

23. Mark Seltzer, "*The Princess Casamassima*: Realism and the Fantasy of Surveillance," in Sundquist, *American Realism*, pp. 95–119.

24. June Howard, *Form and History in American Literary Naturalism* (Chapel Hill: University of North Carolina Press, 1985), p. ix.

25. Philip Fisher, "Appearing and Disappearing in Public: Social Space in Late Nineteenth-Century Literature and Culture," in Sacvan Bercovitch, ed., *Reconstructing American Literary History* (Cambridge, Mass.: Harvard University Press, 1986), p. 177.

26. Rachel Bowlby, *Just Looking: Consumer Culture in Dreiser, Gissing, and Zola* (New York: Methuen, 1985).

27. Mark Seltzer, *Henry James and the Art of Power* (Ithaca, N.Y.: Cornell University Press, 1984).

28. Alan Trachtenberg and June Howard are exceptions to this tendency to conflate capitalism with a culture of consumption and to ignore the underlying anxieties about social change. In *The Incorporation of America: Culture and Society in the Gilded Age* (New York: Hill and Wang, 1982) chap. 6, Trachtenberg views realism, especially on the part of Howells, as an expression of those democratic tendencies which ultimately support a middle-class effort to impose homogeneous genteel standards. Howard focuses on naturalism as a genre rather than on realism.

29. Philip Fisher, *Hard Facts: Setting and Form in the American Novel* (New York: Oxford University Press, 1985), chap. 3.

30. Walter Benn Michaels, "*Sister Carrie*'s Popular Economy," *Critical Inquiry* 7 (1980): 373–90 (reprinted in Michaels, *The Gold Standard*).

31. T. J. Jackson Lears, "From Salvation to Self-Realization: Advertising and the Therapeutic Roots of the Consumer Culture, 1880–1920," in Richard Wight Fox and T. J. Jackson Lears, eds., *The Culture of Consumption: Critical Essays in American History, 1880–1980* (New York: Pantheon, 1983), p. 6.

32. Henry James, *The American Scene* (Bloomington: Indiana University Press, 1968), p. 76.

33. Ibid., p. 82.

34. Ibid., p. 83.

35. Fredric Jameson, *The Political Unconscious* (Ithaca, N.Y.: Cornell University Press, 1981), p. 193.

36. Though my use of the concept "social construction" is indebted in the broadest sense to Peter L. Berger and Thomas Luckmann, *The Social Construction of Reality: A Treatise in the Sociology of Knowledge* (New York: Doubleday, 1966), I am not directly applying their theory to American realism. While Berger and Luckmann see the construction of reality maintaining stability against the threat of competing definitions of the real (*Social Construction*, pp. 147–49), I aim to relate realism to the struggle for social power (which is not central to their argument) and see the construction of reality as an unstable process that confronts and incorporates competing definitions of the real in the form of each novel.

This is not intended as a thorough consideration of the theory of Berger and Luckmann; instead I am drawing on their basic insight in order to intervene in the literary critical debate that treats realistic representation either as a reflection of an external social world that literature cannot act upon, or as an artistic convention or linguistic fiction which can only undermine its own claims to referentiality. To conceive of a more dialectical relationship between literature and society, I approach realism as social construction in a double sense: realistic novels construct the social reality they present as "the way things are"; yet this process does not take place in a linguistic vacuum because realism as a theory and a practice is itself constructed and reconstructed by society, as it was at the end of the nineteenth century and in each subsequent generation of novelists and literary critics.

Some scholars have called for the direct application of Berger's and Luckmann's theory to the methodology of American studies. See R. Gordon Kelly, "*The Social Construction of Reality*: Implications for Future Directions in American Studies," *Prospects* 8 (1983): 49–48; Kay Mussell, "*The Social Construction of Reality* and American Studies: Notes toward Consensus," *Prospects* 9 (1984): 1–16.

37. James, *American Scene*, p. 86.

38. Howard, *Form and History*, chap. 4, analyzes the portrayal of working-class characters as brutes in naturalistic representations as a form of class control.

39. Alfred Habegger, *Gender, Fantasy, and Realism in American Literature* (New York: Columbia University Press, 1982).

THIRTY-SEVEN

BLACK AND WHITE STRANGERS

Kenneth W. Warren

Kenneth W. Warren (1957–) received his Ph.D. from Stanford University in 1988; he is a member of the English faculty of the University of Chicago.

I

While in the eyes of many white observers, the nation's endorsement of Jim Crow laws, especially in regard to public and private conveyances in the South, should have solved its major and social problem, Henry James's *The American Scene* suggested otherwise. Chronicling the writer's impressions of his native land upon his return in 1904, the book severely censures American society. Encapsulating James's indictment of the United States was an embittered and extended apostrophe to the Pullman in which he had made his journey to the Southern states. The railroad exemplified for James the failure of American society to fulfill its promise of civilization. Haste, vulgarity, and ugliness were the legacy of a society that had impressed James more with what it had left undone than with what it had done. Focusing his ire not on the locomotive but on the Pullman, which was a place of habitation as well as transportation, James made these cars representative of the civilization of which America was boasting. The Pullman was "the great symbolic agent" in which were carried, "if not Caesar and his fortune, at least almost *all* facets of American life."[1] On the whole, the people that it did carry were too much like one another for James's taste—too steeped in trade to be little more than exemplars of the triumph of vulgarity and lowness and the absence of social distinction.

Had he been so inclined, James's search for "that part of the national energy that is not calculable in terms of mere arithmetic" (*A*, 389), might have led him to a prolonged encounter with the literature of black America. Despite the fact that the

Black and White Strangers: Race and American Literary Realism, by Kenneth W. Warren (Chicago: University of Chicago Press, 1993), pp. 109–30. © 1993 by The University of Chicago. Reprinted by permission of Kenneth W. Warren and The University of Chicago Press.

Gilded Age's gospel of progress and prosperity had found endorsements from Frederick Douglass, until his death in 1895, and from Booker T. Washington, whose address to the Atlanta Cotton Exposition later that same year sought to secure black economic participation in the new industrial South, some black American intellectuals had been voicing criticisms of the Gilded Age, at least as early as 1892 with the publication of Frances Harper's *Iola Leroy*. The closing decades of the nineteenth century may have been known for producing an unprecedented number of millionaires, but Harper's heroine had a ready answer to the query whether " 'the world [was] most indebted . . . to its millionaires or to its martyrs. . . . To be,' continued Iola, 'the leader of a race to higher planes of thought and action, to teach men clearer views of life and duty, and to inspire their souls with loftier aims, is a far greater privilege than it is to open the gates of material prosperity and fill every home with sensuous enjoyment.' "[2] The American home, as Iola shrewdly observed, had become a place of conspicuous consumption. He or she who could help fulfill these newly created desires could profit handsomely. Untold riches were at hand, but racial service and leadership mandated that black elites forego the new paths to economic success. The higher calling was the way of renunciation and sacrifice. Harper's novel, however, was making a virtue of necessity. In the words of Professor Langhorne, a scholar from Georgia who speaks at a council on the welfare of black Americans: "How many of us to-day . . . would be teaching in the South, if every field of labor in the North was as accessible to us as to the whites?" (*I*, 248). The path of racial service was the only one available; few of those favored by the creation of new avenues to prosperity happened to be black.

In recompense, however, there were the virtues of black solidarity and black identity. Again, to quote Professor Langhorne, "this prejudice, by impacting us together, gives us common cause and brings our intellect in contact with the less favored of our race" (*I*, 248). Additionally this recompense was not merely compensation but reward beyond measure. It was the key to avoiding self-estrangement. "Masquerading as a white man" was a sure path to becoming a "moral cripple" (*I*, 203,266). While white identity promised "a life of careless ease and pleasure," life as a black American would have "a much grander significance" (*I*, 274).

The economic liabilities of black racial identity could be inflected differently, as illustrated by Albion Tourgée. In his brief on behalf of Homer Plessy, Tourgée had asked whether, in a society premised upon the denial of basic civil and economic rights to African Americans, it is "possible to conclude that the reputation of being white is not property? Indeed, is it not the most valuable sort of property, being the master-key that unlocks the golden door of opportunity?"[3] Harper's novel concurred on this point, asserting that "to be born white in this country is to be born to an inheritance of privileges, to hold in your hands the keys that open before you the doors of every occupation, advantage, opportunity, and achievement" (*I*, 265–66). In the race to riches, being black was a decided handicap. But where Tourgée's brief sought to secure for Plessy the rights of property that racial distinctions were denying him, Harper treated such opportunities as incipient Faustian bargains.[4] Correspondingly in *Iola Leroy* the plot repeatedly calls upon its light-skinned African-American characters to choose between material prosperity—embodied in a white identity—and moral duty—embodied in a black one. Iola, her uncle Robert, her brother Harry, and her eventual husband, Dr. Latimer, each refuse opportunities to suppress the fact of their partial black ancestry in favor of material benefits. We are told, for example, that Dr. Latimer's wealthy paternal grandmother had "made overtures to receive him as her grandson and heir" if he would "forsake his mother's people" (I, 238). Moved by Latimer's striking "resemblance to her dear departed son," the grieving woman declares herself willing to overlook her grandson's mixed racial heritage if he will agree to overlook it as well. The reader is assured, however, that the young physician had "nobly" declined the offer. In the story he ultimately comes to displace the white Dr. Gresham as Iola's suitor. The two eventually marry and then embark jointly on a life of service to the race—in effect turning their backs upon the values of the Gilded Age.

As far as James was concerned, however, there was no reason that he should have been aware of Harper's novel, which was published twelve years before he returned to the United States, and which was not reviewed in major white journals. Harper's voice could have easily been lost in the disconcerting din that confronted James on his homecoming. And had he heard it, its sentimental overtones, its use of dialect, and its didactic moralism would not, despite its dissent from the doctrine of material wealth, have identified it as a potential ally for the "restless analyst" of *The American Scene* (A, 25).

William James, however, had made sure that his brother would not miss entirely the notes sounded by black America. As Henry prepared for his Atlantic crossing, William mailed him a copy of the newly published *The Souls of Black Folk*, telling him, "I am sending you a decidedly moving book by a mulatto ex-student of mine, Du Bois, professor of history at Atlanta (Georgia) negro College. Read Chapter VII to XI for local color, etc."[5] It is easy to imagine how Henry James's reading of *The Souls of Black Folk* could have been one of the signal moments in American literary history, bringing together the novelist who was redefining the contours of American fiction and the scholar/novelist/activist who was articulating a new vision of African Americanness. As part of James's reintroduction to his native land, *The Souls of Black Folk* might have suggested an alternate trajectory for *The American Scene* such that its criticism of a society scored by commercialism might have also become a powerful brief against American racism. William, as we have seen, had inveighed publicly against lynching on two separate occasions, impressing on his readers the urgency of putting a halt to the violence against African Americans. Henry, as he traveled South, saw evidence to confirm the pervasiveness of the lynching spirit. Accompanied through Richmond by an unreconstructed young Southerner, Henry is made to understand that though his companion "wouldn't have hurt a Northern fly, there were things (ah, we had touched on some of these!) that, all fair, engaging, smiling, as he stood there, he would have done to a Southern negro" (A, 389). The benign aspect that Southern whites turned to their Northern counterparts did not bother to conceal the virulence of their enmity toward blacks. Despite this conversation, James elsewhere in *The American Scene* discounts the influence that his voice or any other might have in ameliorating the racial situation in the South. Whatever the available wisdom about improving race relations, "the lips of the non-resident were, at all events, not the lips to utter this wisdom." "Silence," James avers, is a preferable policy (A, 376).

One need only turn to "The After-Thought" of *The Souls of Black Folk* to see how disappointing this silence would necessarily have been to Du Bois. Leaving his reader with the plea to *"vouchsafe that this my book fall not still-born into the world-wilderness,"* Du Bois had invested the success of his project in the willingness of his readers to respond with "thought" and "thoughtful deed."[6] *The American Scene* is nothing if not thoughtful, but its handling of the race problem falls dreadfully short of the clear denunciations of lynching and mob violence that prevailing conditions called for. In addition, the voice of *The Souls of Black Folk* would have been somewhat critical of James's methods. Du Bois had warned his reader that the truth about the black South would likely elude the casual observer. He cautioned that "to the car-window sociologist, to the man who seeks to understand and know the South by devoting the few leisure hours of a holiday trip to unravel the snarl of centuries,—to such men very often the whole trouble with the black fieldhand may be summed up by Aunt Ophelia's word 'shiftless' " (S, 469). Du Bois's invocation of Stowe's Aunt Ophelia from *Uncle Tom's Cabin* points up the problem of the North's critical stance toward African Americans. A woman of principle and duty, Miss Ophelia cannot at first bear to touch Topsy, and until she learns from the example of Little Eva, she is unable to have any effect on Topsy's behavior. If one gets closer one will see a truer picture. The apparent shiftlessness of black laborers (Du Bois describes two young men who present "a happy-go-lucky, careless picture of irresponsibility"), is simply apparent: "they are not lazy; to-morrow they'll be up with the sun; they work hard when they do work, and they work willingly. They have no sordid, selfish, money-getting ways, but rather a fine disdain for mere cash" (S, 469). What looks from a distance like shiftlessness is an effect of specific economic conditions. Du Bois elaborates his description of these two fellows by delineating the problems of the crop lien and sharecropping systems, and by noting the ill effects upon the populace of "absentee landlordism" and drastic declines in cotton prices (S, 471). Poverty and apparent laziness are the result of deep structural problems. Moreover, in their own way, the two black workers were critics of the Gilded Age, refusing to rouse themselves merely for the purpose of material profit.

In *The American Scene*, however, Du Bois's warning and explanations, which appear in one of the chapters that William singled out for Henry's attention, seem to fall on deaf if not rebellious ears. Traveling through an impoverished Southern landscape on his way to Charleston, James, from his relatively comfortable Pullman, asserts contra Du Bois that "the social scene might be sufficiently penetrated, no doubt from the car window" (A, 397). Having eschewed the statistical methods of social scientists and having wedded himself to an impressionistic analysis, James might have assumed, if he assumed anything at all, that Du Bois's censure of "car-window sociologists" was not meant for his "restless analyst." The writer of *The American Scene* is certainly not a sociologist; "reports, surveys and blue-books" are insufficient to capture the qualities that James wishes to record. But whatever the reason, James, in somewhat uneasy disregard of Du Bois's warning, works his rather distant impressions assiduously, and the theme that emerges from these observations is the carelessness of Southern society: "I seem to remember . . . the number of things not cared for" (A, 397).

Seeking to account for these "things," James embarks on an analysis that, unlike Du Bois's, attempts to downplay economic analysis. Instead James begins by comparing the scene to a " 'short story' in one of the slangy dialects promoted by the illustrated monthly magazines" (A, 397), arraigning the Charleston landscape on its lack of taste and aesthetic appeal. When James seeks to figure in his own point of view, however, economic differences return with a vengeance. Commenting on all of the interests that were missing from the Southern story, James remarks that

> the grimness with which, as by a hard inexorable fate, so many things were ruled out, fixed itself most perhaps as the impression of the spectator enjoying from his supreme seat of ease his extraordinary, his awful modern privilege of this detached yet concentrated stare at the misery of subject populations. (Subject, I mean, to this superiority of his bought convenience—subject even as never, of old, to the sway of satraps or proconsuls.) If the subject populations on the road to Charleston, seemingly weak indeed in numbers and in energy, had to be viewed, at all events, so vividly, as not "caring," one made out quite with eagerness that it was because they naturally couldn't. The negroes were more numerous than the whites, but still there *were* whites—of aspect so forlorn and depressed for the most part as to deprecate, though not cynically, only quite tragically, any imputation of value. It was a monstrous thing, doubtless, to sit there in a cushioned and kitchened Pullman and deny to so many groups of one's fellow-creatures any claim to a "personality" but this was in truth what one was perpetually doing. The negroes, though superficially and doubtless not at all intendingly sinister, were the lustier race; but how could they care (to insist on my point) for such equivocal embodiments of the right complexion? Yet these were, practically, within the picture the only affirmations of life except themselves; and they obviously, they notoriously, didn't care for themselves. (A, 397–98)

In this lengthy and convoluted passage James tracks the path from subjection to subject for the Southern populations within his view and not only finds the way blocked but also finds that he and the Pullman in which he is seated are among the major obstacles. The contrast between the privilege of the Pullman and the poverty of the countryside is so marked that the social distance between James and the people he criticizes appears to be greater than that separating the ruler from the ruled in ancient despotisms. As a passenger on the train—as someone who can pay his way—James is not merely a spectator but an actor who creates or imputes the values of the scene. In the words of Carolyn Porter, James's acknowledgement of "the seer's complicity without sacrificing his contemplative stance is a concept of action which derives from the identity of the capitalist and the artist."[7] The necessary aesthetic detachment can be had for the right price, and James can redeem his trip South only be profiting on his investments.

In addition, having already decided in the chapter on Richmond that the black presence has contributed to the "prison of the Southern spirit," James cannot but view the numerical dominance of blacks on the landscape as an impediment to contemplative ease. The African Americans on the scene are not candidates for subjectivity in their own right but problems to be overcome or solved. They are not "intendingly sinister" but presumably sinister nonetheless—"like some beast that had sprung from the jungle" (A, 375). On the other hand, what prevents James from imputing value—the value of subjectivity—to the comparatively few whites that he sees is their impoverished aspect. They look depressed—as if they do not care for themselves—and their indifference compounds the problem of black subjectivity. Such subjectivity or caring by African Americans is, for James, theoretically possible; blacks as servants could care for the whites in their midst. But since the impoverished whites are such "equivocal embodiments" of their race, even this mediated path to black caring is interdicted (A, 398).

All, however, is not lost for James's restless analyst. Having denied others a personality, having decided that his position is part of the problem, James asserts that he "can make up for other deficiencies" by caring enough for all. The aesthetic possibilities of the South might be lost on its natives, but such possibilities will not be lost on James. His receptiveness to impressions will make up the difference.

James's solution is not peculiar to his Southern journey but to his travels taken as a whole. The logic of *The American Scene* dictates that text and author have to make up for what is lacking in the United States. There is, James suggests, an "aesthetic need, in the country, for much greater values, of certain sorts, than the country and its manners, its aspects and arrangements, its past and present, and perhaps even future, really supply" (A, 457). James must provide the nation's inhabitants that which they cannot provide themselves. Accordingly, though he seeks those domestic institutions—country clubs, libraries, universities, etc.—that defy the nation's rampant commercialism, he must also deprecate their efficacy, if only to make plain the logic of, and the need for, *The American Scene*. This imputation of national need, perhaps as much as any other factor, may help explain James's treatment of *The Souls of Black Folk* in his text.

Looking upon the extraordinary "vacancy" that comes to characterize Southern life for him, James is brought to wonder, "How can everything so have gone that the only 'Southern' book of any distinction published for many a year is *The Souls of Black Folk*, by that most accomplished of members of the negro race, Mr. W. E. B. Du Bois?" (A, 418). With a remarkable backhanded compliment that measures Du Bois's stature against the abnormally stunted growth of the surrounding Southern culture, James attributes Du Bois's prominence as much to the lack of any real competition from other "Southern" writers as to features of the text itself. In doing so, James conveniently overlooks Du Bois's "Northern" upbringing and the possibility that *The Souls of Black Folk* is more a competitor with James's book than with other

"Southern" texts. The salience of *The Souls of Black Folk* attests, for James, to the absence of anything else in the American South.

The Souls of Black Folk, of course, was as deeply committed to a critique of the excesses of the Gilded Age as was *The American Scene*. Noting that "all in all, we black men seem the sole oasis of simple faith and reverence in a dusty desert of dollars and smartness" (*S*, 370), Du Bois insisted that the nation could resist the ravages of capitalism only if black Americans embraced ideals rather than wealth. In an extended conceit that amounted to a restaging of Booker T. Washington's Atlanta Exposition speech, which offered a blueprint for black economic growth, Du Bois looked upon the city of Atlanta and wrote, "Here stands this black young Atalanta, girding herself for the race that must be run; and if her eyes be still toward the hills and sky as in the days of old, then we may look for noble running" (*S*, 419). As Robert Stepto has noted, "Atlanta serves in *The Souls* as . . . a battleground wherein Du Bois can struggle with the language and influence of a predecessor."[8] Washington had used the occasion of his speech to reiterate his criticism of basing black colleges on the liberal arts model. In his view those black students who "knew more about Latin and Greek when they left school . . . seemed to know less about life and its conditions." These men and women, he told his auditors, had overlooked "the fact that the masses of us are to live by the production of our hands."[9]

In response Du Bois deliberately employed a classical image to represent the city that was showcased as the apotheosis of the new, industrial, prosperous South. Of course, Du Bois had included in *The Souls of Black Folk* a direct criticism of Washington in the chapter "Of Booker T. Washington and Others," which was one of the few chapters that Du Bois wrote specifically for *The Souls of Black Folk*. This chapter, however, merely made more explicit what was evident elsewhere in the volume: the path of Booker T. Washington was not the proper path for black America.

The derivation of Atlanta from the mythical maiden Atalanta was admittedly forced, but in Du Bois's eyes, "if Atlanta be not named for Atalanta, she ought to have been" (*S*, 416). The story of the maiden, who though capable of outrunning even the fastest young man is captured by Hippomenes because she allows herself to be distracted by the three golden apples that he rolls before her, provided for Du Bois an apt image of the potential of black America if it pursued political and intellectual equality and of the dangers it faced if black folk accepted the program of Washington. In addition, Du Bois's formulation may have been autobiographically tinged. So dazzling was the afterglow of Washington's success at Atlanta that Du Bois had initially become part of the chorus of praise that greeted the Wizard of Tuskegee, penning a note to Washington saying, "Let me heartily congratulate you upon your phenomenal success, at Atlanta — it was a word fitly spoken."[10] And Du Bois was also not entirely above the glitter of the Gilded Age. In his *Dusk of Dawn* autobiography, he conjectured that "had it not been for the race problem early thrust upon me and enveloping me, I should have probably been an unquestioning worshiper at the shrine of the social order and economic development into which I was born."[11] "Race," or at least "the race problem," provided a platform for social heterodoxy. Rather than being simply an accident of birth, race becomes a central player in underwriting Du Bois's critique of America. Similar to expatriation, racial alienation provided blacks with the critical distance that made them, to use James's words, simultaneously "as 'fresh' as an inquiring stranger" and "as acute as an initiated native" (*A*, n.p.). The virtues of racial difference in both *The Souls of Black Folk* and *Dusk of Dawn*, however, seemed to issue not only from the specific social and historical conditions of African Americans but also from romantic racial notions of the special qualities possessed by black people. If blacks were to "save" America they would as a group have to cultivate those unique qualities that only they could contribute to the world.

Du Bois worried, though, that even within the black world the "question of cash and a lust for gold" had already largely displaced the values of faith and reverence, and that America would be the worse for that loss. He asked aloud, "What if to the Mammonism of America be added the rising Mammonism of the reborn South, and the Mammonism of this South be reinforced by the budding Mammonism of its half-awakened black millions? Whither, then, is the new-world quest of Goodness and Beauty and Truth gone glimmering?" (*S*, 419). Rather than a dissent from the dominant values of the age, black American life was on the way to becoming an endorsement of the gospel of greed.

Within Du Bois's various reflections on black Americans at the turn of the century, then, were shifting perspectives which were shared by some of his contemporaries. On the one hand, blackness entailed a posture of dissent from or resistance to Gilded Age America; the souls of black folk were a potential remedy for those ills. Howells's Dr. Olney, in *An Imperative Duty*, stood among those articulating this view. Olney saw in blacks a natural "bulwark against the proletarianization of the lower classes" and a counterpoint to what he saw as the public licentiousness of Irish and other immigrants.[12] Somewhat carried away on a wave of racial goodwill, Olney speculates at one point that "if the negroes ever have their turn—and if the meek are to inherit the earth they must come to it—we shall have a civilization of such sweetness and goodwill as the world has never known yet. Perhaps we shall have to wait their turn for any real Christian civilization."[13] This romanticized picture of black Americans was as much a product of white misgivings about the changing industrial order as anything else. Although there is some irony in Howells's presentation of Olney's sentiments, the novel does attempt to make Olney's views compatible with a liberal progressive view of race relations. American society could profit from a more general integration of African Americans.

Romanticized views of blacks, however, could also serve the needs of political and social conservatives who wished to discredit or roll back civil rights gains. The happy-go-lucky darky images of the antebellum South could be contrasted favorably to the images of impoverished, potentially dangerous blacks of post-Reconstruction. Such contrasts were staples of plantation fiction and minstrelsy, both of which were going strong through the 1890s. The needs fulfilled by these images were not solely racial: "For many white audiences the black African was the creature of a pre-industrial life style with a pre-industrial appetite,"[14] allowing whites to indulge their nostalgia for a lifestyle that was no longer available to them as they congregated in urban centers. The promise of black America was an assurance that old ways and old pleasures were recuperable.

Of course the old ways were beyond recovery. The solace embodied in popular representations of black Americans could only clash with reality in such a way that the contemporary condition of black folk seemed to be a betrayal of vanishing ideals as well as an index and intensification of the ills of American society. In the black world, Du Bois observed, "changes so curiously parallel to that of the Other-world" were occurring so that "well-paid porters and artisans" were displacing the preachers and teachers who once advocated black ideals (S, 418). African America was as vulnerable to the new commercial industrial order as was the rest of America. Because the emancipation of black Americans and the acceleration of capitalist transformation were roughly coincident it was also possible to see black Americans as somehow responsible for undesirable changes, which accounts in part for the unflattering picture of black America that James drew in *The American Scene*.

II

In many respects, James's preconceptions on his southward journey were all but indistinguishable from plantation romances or minstrel shows—in fact they probably derived from the latter. "One had remembered," James recalled in *The American Scene*, "the old Southern tradition, the house alive with the scramble of young darkies for the honour of fetching and carrying" (A, 423), and it was this image that he had hoped to find. What perhaps had made this memory concrete was the combination of the minstrel shows and afterpieces that James had no doubt seen as a child and his brief experience with the young slave boy, Davy, who had come North with his Aunt Sylvia as servants for the Norcom family, and who subsequently escaped. The boy and his mother, in James's words, "had been born and kept in slavery of the most approved pattern and such as this intensity of their condition made them a joy, a joy to the curious mind, to consort with." Davy, for James, stood out because "servitude in the absolute thus did more for him socially than we had ever seen done, above stairs or below, for victims of its lighter forms."[15] Although the escape of Sylvia and Davy should have served as a critique of his romanticizations, the picturesque memory of Davy and of the Old South seemed to help keep alive in James the possibility of an alternative to the raw and slovenly society that he excoriated on his Northern and Southern travels.

In *The American Scene* this preferred alternative was not initially the slave South per se. Slavery, James recognized, had been a "monomania" (A, 419) and was responsible for all the South's current ills. It was the "interest" that had banished all other interests. Instead of the slave South, the southern past in which James sought "to take refuge" was "the larger, the less vitiated past that had closed a quarter of a century or so before the War, before the fatal time when the South, monomaniacal at the parting of the ways, 'elected' for extension and conquest" (A, 418). Though the historical period to which James refers is one that had already fixed itself along lines of white racial dominance, it was, for James a period when other points of view, even the possibility of abolition, could find expression in the South. This South puts in a momentary appearance in Charleston when an "elderly mulatress," whom James takes to be a servant, responds to his knock on the door of an old house, and exposes to him a momentary glimpse "of the vanished order" in the faded, yet picturesque interior (*A*, 403). In the short interval between the woman's opening and closing the door there is a notably brief but conscious interaction between her and James. She knows, or at least James imputes to her, the knowledge that he is seeking some vision of that distant Southern past. Aware that the scene behind her is but a shabby reminder of what had been, she cares enough to feel embarrassed, and, as James says, "before I could see more, and that I might not sound the secret of shy misfortune, of faded pretension, to shut the door in my face" (*A*, 403).

This brief encounter, coupled with his inadvertent entry into a walled garden, having a "finer feeling for the enclosure," a sense of privacy, effects for a time a transfer of James's allegiances from North to South. "One sacrificed the North" in favor of a South where "those aspects in which the consequences of the great folly [slavery] were, for extent and gravity, still traceable; I was coldbloodedly to prefer them" (*A*, 404). Contrary to his initial impressions, slavery seems not to have banished all interests but to have permitted the possibility of caring. Though James admits that such a change on his part is "monstrous," he cannot help but prefer the picturesque remnant of a slave past to the depressing vacancy he saw on the road to Charleston. Faced with choosing between the two contrasting visions, he wonders, "What in the world was one candidly to do?" (*A*, 405). Thus compelled to choose the slave past, James then entertains the prospect of seeing more of the favorable vision he had met in Charleston. This anticipation attends his journey further South, but it is an anticipation that is not to be fulfilled. He finds during his subsequent encounters with Southern blacks no incident of personal service equal to that quick shutting of the door by the woman in Charleston.

Du Bois, in *The Souls of Black Folk*, had warned his reader not to expect to find "the faithful, courteous slave of other days, with his incorruptible honesty and dignified humility . . . [who] is passing away just as surely as the old type of Southern gentleman is passing" (*S*, 418). The South of the plantation school, if it had ever existed, was no longer to be found.[16] Du Bois had also warned that the confrontation with black Southern poverty could be disconcerting; "One can easily see how a person who saw slavery thus from his father's parlors, and sees freedom on the streets of a great city, fails to grasp or comprehend the whole of the new picture" (*S*, 477). Despite this warning, James nonetheless expresses surprise at what he terms "the apparently deep-seated inaptitude of the negro race at large for any alertness of personal service" (*A*, 423). What prompts James to disparage black servants is an incident in which a "negro porter . . . put straight down into the mud of the road the dressing-bag I was obliged, a few minutes later . . . to nurse on my knees" (*A*, 423). Thus discomfited by his muddy trousers, James proceeds to revise his recent transfer of allegiance to the slave order:

One had counted, with some eagerness, in moving southward, on the virtual opposite—on finding this deficiency [of alert personal service], encountered right
and left at the North, beautifully corrected; one had remembered the old Southern tradition, the house alive with the scramble of young darkies for the honour
of fetching and carrying; and one was to recognize, no doubt, at the worst, its
melancholy ghost. Its very ghost, however, by my impression had ceased to walk;
or, if this be not the case the old planters, the cotton gentry, were the people in
the world the worst ministered to. I could have shed tears for them at moments,
reflecting that it was for *this* that they had fought and fallen. (*A*, 423)

As Donna Przybylowicz observes, James's reading of the scene made him "blind to the
possible resentment of the blacks whose reluctance to place themselves in a subservient position is deliberate and not due to any particular lack."[17] The potential politics
of these servants' actions is hidden from his view. But James's blindness is not surprising because the path to black subjectivity in *The American Scene* runs through their
capacity for personal service. While James can imagine and articulate appeals for understanding from the Southern "drummer" and the American girl, he makes no similar attempt on behalf of black servants. From his point of view, the interpretive options for reading the behavior of black servants are limited: Either the comforting
past which he thought he had glimpsed in Charleston has been thoroughly obliterated, or quite possibly, it had never existed. If the latter is true, then the Southern
planters are confirmed in their folly, for the order they fought to preserve was no different, at least in its aesthetic appeal, from the industrial North.

As he lay to rest the ghost of the plantation "darky," James was busy constructing
another black phantasm to take its place. As an index of a South that never was, and
an earlier American sense of ease that never really had a chance, figures in black became for James one of the symbols of America's failure to develop any real critical or
aesthetic sense. If blacks had not given the Southern planter any sense of aesthetic
ease, they gave the current scene its air of disease. James continues his disparagement
of black servants by observing that

the negro waiter at the hotel is in general, by an oddity of his disposition, so zealous to break for you two or three eggs into a tumbler, or to drop for you three or
four lumps of sugar into a coffee-cup, that he scarce waits, in either case, for your
leave; but these struck me everywhere as the limit of his accomplishment. He
lends himself sufficiently to the rough, gregarious bustle of crowded feeding-
places, but seemed to fall below the occasion on any appeal to his individual
promptitude. (*A*, 423–24)

Somewhat reminiscent of Louis Leverett in "The Point of View," James finds African
Americans ideally suited for, and perhaps emblems of the vulgarity of, American public life. While this view is a direct result of his Southern experience, it seems in the
text to start well back of it. James's slightly patronizing but on the whole laudatory
view of the old society at Newport, Rhode Island, turns on a black/white dichotomy
that, while not explicitly racial, helps underwrite a racial logic. Newport is fondly

remembered in *Notes of a Son and Brother* for its leisure, its aesthetic intensity, and its role as a sort of way station for repatriated Americans.[18] In *The American Scene* James celebrated this "handful of mild, oh delightfully mild, cosmopolites" for similar reasons: "their having for the most part more or less lived in Europe, that of their sacrificing openly to the ivory idol whose name is leisure, and that, not least of a formed critical habit" (A, 222). Europe, leisure, and criticism had marked the members of this society as different from those Americans for whom travel was merely tourism, a brief respite from commercial pursuits. Though his tone in describing the old Newport types is slightly deprecatory—they "move about, vaguely and helplessly, with the shaft [of Europe] still in [their] side" (A, 223)—James cannot dismiss them because they stand out as "excrescences on the American surface, where nobody ever criticized, especially after the grand tour, and where *the great black ebony god* of business was the only one recognized" (A, 222; emphasis added).

Opposing Newport to the rest of America, spiritual expatriation to tourism, and criticism to bland acceptance, James figures these oppositions in any ivory/ebony contrast. Certainly the concentration of African Americans within the ranks of domestics, particularly the use of blacks as Pullman porters, in conjunction with James's dissatisfaction with American servants, and his hostility to modern travel in general, would have made this association understandable. Du Bois and Washington each, albeit in slightly different ways, link railroad porters to the vitiation of black life. Moreover, the connection of blacks to the vulgarization of civilized behavior had occurred in James's fiction at least since "The Point of View." But the dynamic of *The American Scene* is as much compositional as it is sociological, and the questions of black against white or text against margin were provisional strategies for trying to organize his American impressions—impressions which, detractors of *The American Scene* might insist, were not coherently organized until James wrote "The Jolly Corner," which was published in 1908.

James's lengthy short story, which appeared first in the *English Review* and was quickly revised for the New York Edition of James's work, relates the experiences of fifty-six-year-old Spencer Brydon, whose return to New York after a lengthy absence mirrors James's own. His return, like his creator's, confronts him with a homeland he no longer knows, and which challenges him to give forth his impressions. But rather than have his protagonist focus on giving an account of the confusing changes in his homeland, James has Brydon admit that his " 'thoughts would still be almost altogether about something that concerns only myself.' " Recognizing, perhaps that the subject of *The American Scene* was not so much America but himself, James, through Brydon, allows that subject to center his tale so that the focus becomes "what he might have been, how he might have led his life, and 'turned out,' if he had not so, at the outset, given [New York] up." Fueling these speculations for Brydon is his discovery, while supervising the conversion of one of his houses into apartment units, that despite having opted for an aesthetic life three decades ago, he has "a capacity for business and a sense for construction."[19] This belated discovery becomes so powerful as a possible missed opportunity that Brydon's desire to envision himself as he might have been takes palpable shape. The story finds Brydon, in the house of his birth, the house on the "jolly corner," stalking this alter ego, a figure his friend Alice Staverton claims has appeared in a dream.

James's story exhibits the various oppositions discussed earlier—for example, the "dollars" of New York are counterpointed by an incalculable aesthetic experience, represented by Miss Staverton. Though residing in New York throughout Brydon's absence, Alice nonetheless embodies for Brydon *their* common, their quite faraway and antediluvian social period and order" (J, 439). The quiet of private life she is able to preserve is played off New York's "public concussions"; and Brydon, who has been away "worshipping strange gods" (J, 450) now speculates about what he would have become had he offered a sacrifice at some domestic shrine. Brydon's private speculations share, in many respects, the depth and dimension of the copious travel narrative James had already composed. This being said, however, what is also intrinsic to "The Jolly Corner" is its patent absurdity and ridiculousness. Investing his search for his alter ego with all the emotional edge of a big-game hunt, Brydon must nonetheless admit that "he might, for a spectator, have figured some solemn simpleton playing at hide-and-seek" (J, 459). His "jungle," the servants' rooms; his prey, the fearful imaginings of his Irish housekeeper—Brydon's drama could be played out on some comic stage. In fact, when after "a calculated absence of three nights" from his stalkings he feels himself being followed, he adopts a strategy of turning around abruptly to see if his alter ego might betray itself:

> He wheeled about, retracing his steps, as if he might so catch in his face at least the stirred air of some other quick revolution. It was indeed true that his fully dislocalised thought of these manoeuveres recalled to him Pantaloon, at the Christmas farce, buffeted and tricked from behind by ubiquitous Harlequin; but it left intact the influence of the conditions themselves each time he was re-exposed to them, so that in fact this association, had he suffered it to become constant, would on a certain side have had ministered to his intenser gravity. (J, 460)

Similar to the American stage of the period where high drama and farce cohabited in a way that did not appear incongruous, Brydon's reflections on his antics do not entirely banish the farcical interpretation. On the contrary, inasmuch as his more serious interpretation of his action persists despite the absurd overtones, Brydon remains convinced of the gravity of his quest.

As a youthful devotee of American theater, James had ample experience counterbalancing seriousness and farce as part of his aesthetic. "Young Henry was taken to all the leading New York theatres of the mid-century—Burton's, the Broadway, and the National, Wallack's Lyceum, Niblo's Gardens and Barnum's 'Lecture Room' attached to the Great American Museum."[20] Harlequinades were a staple of the stage—farces and burlesques, which often featured blackface characters. At one point "Negro specialties were featured on almost every playbill"[21] as afterpieces, and Christmas traditions included visits to minstrel shows like "Harlequin Jim Crow" and "The Magic Mustard Pot."[22] In *A Small Boy and Others* James specifically recalls attending in London "a Christmas production preluding to the immemorial harlequinade," an experience that had been presaged by his many visits to Niblo's Gardens in New York, where, like other New York theaters, minstrel afterpieces were regularly staged, and where, James recalled, "we had . . . harlequin and columbine, albeit of less pure a tradition."[23] In addition, James's *Autobiography* indicates that the figure of the harlequin provided him an apt metaphor for presenting the elder Henry James's attitudes towards his sons' search for a vocation. James's father's willingness to tolerate meanderings and changes of mind struck his son as a "happy harlequinade."[24]

In alluding to harlequins (whose traditional costume includes black and white mask and clothing) in "The Jolly Corner," which is staged appropriately on the "black-and-white squares" of the floor of Brydon's ancestral home, James casts the aesthetic/commercial dichotomy on which the story turns in a slightly different light than is commonly assumed. Brydon's facility at handling his business concerns and the renovation of his other house lead Alice Staverton to conjecture that "if he had but stayed at home he would have anticipated the inventor of the sky scraper. If he had but stayed at home he would have discovered his genius in time really to start some new variety of awful architectural hare and run it till it burrowed in a goldmine" (J, 440–41). Brydon's alter ego's lack of taste and his pursuit of money would have been figured in his designing of architectural grotesques. But the surprise and shock that attend Brydon's confrontation with the figure he confronts downstairs indicate that what he finds is not what he expects. The face he sees "was unknown, inconceivable, awful, disconnected from any possibility" (J, 474). What he finds is "a black stranger" with white hands on which two fingers are missing.

Brydon is convinced of and appalled by the lack of identity between himself and the black stranger—"Such an identity fitted his at *no* point" (J, 477)—and the shock leads to what he asserts is his death: "Yes—I can only have died" (J, 480). As to the lack of identity between Spencer and the phantom he confronts, however, Alice Staverton, asserts the opposite. Not only is the stranger in some way Spencer, but according to Alice, Spencer himself had, on the morning of the latter's adventure, appeared to her as "a black stranger" (J, 484)—a figure perhaps in blackface. But instead of precipitating a death, whether figurative or literal, this figure performs the office of a cupid, bringing together Alice and Spencer so that the story ends with a mutual declaration of love.

Spencer's alter ego does correspond to Brydon's expectations in terms of wealth (Brydon surmises that his alter ego has a "million a year"), cementing again the connection between black figures on the one hand and public vulgarity and commercial interests on the other. Perhaps undergirding this story is not so much a contrast between aesthetics and business but the unsettling territory in which the two meet. Not only is Brydon's European freedom, as Alice astutely notes, made possible by the income derived from his American rents, but James in invoking images from the popular theater also seems to point up another disturbing possibility. The aesthetic alternative for a figure like Brydon or James would not have been to construct monstrous but impressive skyscrapers but to become a participant in the production of " 'intellectual' pabulum" to fulfill the democratic demand—a demand so great that "the journalist, the novelist, the dramatist, the genealogist, the historian, are pressed as well, for dear life, into the service" (*A*, 458). Among the available options was participation on the minstrel stage. As Alexander Saxton points out, "typical purveyors of minstrelsy, then, were northern and urban; they were neither New Englanders nor Southerners (although their parents may have been); and if of rural or small town origin, were most likely to have come from upper New York State." Like James they were "eager to break into the exclusive and inhospitable precincts of big city theater."[25]

James clearly associated writing for the theater with the "thought of fabulous fortunes," worldly success, and aesthetic disfigurement—his plays were, in his words, "mutilated" and "massacred," not unlike the maimed figure Brydon meets in "The Jolly Corner." Writing for the theater was a form of devil worship, "a most unholy trade." And though James's major theatrical debacle, the production of *Guy Domville*, took place on the British stage, his desire for success as a dramatist, was quite possibly a species of "the strong American impulse that he no doubt possessed . . . to elbow one's way to achievement by solid worldly enterprise!"[26] In a possible pun on *Guy Domville*, Spencer describes his unfitness to play his alter ego's role by saying that he couldn't have worn his monocle in the stranger's environment: "I couldn't have sported mine 'downtown.' They'd have guyed me there" (J, 485). Moreover, inasmuch as minstrelsy continued to appear on the British stage through the turn of the century, the market in which James would have imagined himself a competitor would have featured blackface performers as well.

The remedy for James's problem was not a purge of the theater so to speak, but a habit of critical distinction. As we saw earlier, James's recollections of his childhood visits to the theater stressed his growth as a young critic, as someone who could make the proper distinctions. In "The Jolly Corner," where the possibility of seeing Spencer Brydon as a ridiculous figure, where the possibility of "guying" him is openly acknowledged, Alice Staverton, whose "imagination would still do him justice," provides the necessary discerning audience. Unlike the London audience which mercilessly condemned James's enactment of the conflict between two contradictory modes of life, Staverton's ironic comments and criticisms are "not, like the cheap sarcasms with which one heard most people, about the world of 'society,' bid for the reputation of cleverness, from nobody's really having any" (J, 444). She can appreciate both the black stranger and Brydon's difference from him; she can accept and appreciate both.

The point here, however, is not so much that "The Jolly Corner" is directly about James's thwarted theatrical desires. Rather I want to stress that over the course of the 1880s, 1890s, and through the turn of the century, popular representations of black/white racial difference exert a constant pressure on the work of an author like James such that in thinking through the possibility of aesthetic redemption, it seemed almost necessary to distance oneself from black strangers. By masking Brydon's other self in black, "The Jolly Corner," like black minstrelsy, simultaneously acknowledged the power of, while establishing the means of control over, the Other.

The pity and acceptance that Alice Staverton feels towards the black stranger dissipate in her relief that Brydon and not the stranger is the figure whose head rests on her lap. After having asserted an identity between Spencer and the black stranger, she

recants and assures Brydon in the story's final sentence that "he isn't—no, he isn't—
you!" (J, 485)—thus distancing Brydon and herself from the vulgarities of a New
York in which the house on the jolly corner will seemingly function as an ironic oasis.

Alice Staverton's assurance to Brydon that he is not a part of the ravaged life that
surrounds them is an assurance that many realists, confronted with the unsettling social changes brought about by immigration, economic upheaval, conservative back-
lash against progressive reform, as well as their own attacks on convention and tradition, could not themselves feel. Americans at the close of the nineteenth century
found themselves in what Lawrence Levine calls "a universe of strangers," strangers
who "spilled over into the public spaces that characterized nineteenth-century America and that included theaters, music halls, opera houses, museums, parks, fairs, and
the rich public cultural life that took place daily on the streets of American cities."
For elites like James, culture, in the sense of high culture, became a place of refuge,
a place of "retreat."[27] Despite the fact that African-American access to these places,
and to "culture" itself was often limited by statutory, economic, and even aesthetic
factors, the black presence was never entirely absent. As attested to by the minstrel
echoes in "The Jolly Corner," in the American context, "culture" could never be a
comfortable refuge. Writers like Henry James were always confronting and seeking
to contain their own participation in and complicity with the aspects of their society
they deplored. It is within these efforts to define and distinguish among the values of
American cultural life that it becomes possible to trace the racial dimensions of the
American literary imagination.

NOTES

1. James, *The American Scene* (Bloomington: Indiana University Press, 1968), pp. 465,
406; hereafter abbreviated *A*.

2. Harper, *Iola Leroy* (New York: Oxford University Press, 1988), p. 219; hereafter abbreviated *I*.

3. Tourgée, quoted in William Boelhower, *The Thin Disguise: Ethnic Semiosis in American
Literature* (Venice: Edizioni Helvetia, 1984), p. 83.

4. I am indebted to Mark Goble for pointing out the employment of the Faust myth in tales
of "passing" like James Weldon Johnson's *Autobiography of an Ex-Colored Man*.

5. William James, letter to Henry James, 6 June 1903, *Letters of William James*, ed. Henry
James, 2 vols. (Boston: Atlantic Monthly Press, 1920), 2: 196.

6. Du Bois, *The Souls of Black Folk*, in *Writings* (New York: Library of America, 1986), p.
547; hereafter abbreviated *S*.

7. Porter, *Seeing and Believing: The Plight of the Participant Observer in Emerson, James,
Adams, and Faulkner* (Middletown, Conn.: Wesleyan University Press, 1984), p. 133.

8. Robert Stepto, *From Behind the Veil: A Study of Afro-American Narrative* (Urbana: University of Illinois Press, 1979), p. 59. See also pp. 82–91 for further charting of Du Bois's revisions of Washington.

9. Washington, *Up from Slavery*, in *Three Negro Classics* (New York: Avon, 1965), p. 76.

10. Du Bois, *Writings*, p. 1286.

11. Du Bois, *Dusk of Dawn*, in *Writings*, p. 1286.

12. See Kenneth W. Warren, "Possessing the Common Ground in William Dean Howells's *An Imperative Duty*," *American Literary Realism, 1870–1910* 20 (1988): 27.

13. Howells, *An Imperative Duty*, vol. 17 of *A Selected Edition of William Dean Howells*, ed. Ronald Gottesman (Bloomington: Indiana University Press, 1970), p. 7.

14. Berndt Ostendorf, *Black Literature in White America* (New York: Barnes and Noble Press, 1982), p. 78.

15. James, *A Small Boy and Others*, in *Autobiography*, ed. Frederick W. Dupee (New York: Criterion Books, 1956), p. 142.

16. See Stepto, *From Behind the Veil*, pp. 78–79, on Du Bois's criticism of the plantation school.

17. Donna Przybylowicz, *Desire and Repression: The Dialectic of Self and Other in the Late Works of Henry James* (University: University of Alabama Press, 1986), p. 266.

18. See James, *Notes of a Son and Brother*, in *Autobiography*, esp. pp. 274–300.

19. Henry James, "The Jolly Corner," *The Novels and Tales of Henry James*, vol. 17 of the New York Edition (1909), pp. 435, 448, 438; hereafter abbreviated J.

20. Leon Edel, "Henry James: The Dramatic Years," in *The Complete Plays of Henry James* (Philadelphia: Lippincott, 1949), p. 23.

21. Carl Wittke, *Tambo and Bones: A History of the American Minstrel Stage* (Westport, Conn.: Greenwood Press, 1968), p. 37. On the ubiquity of minstrel performances on the American stage, see also George C. D. O'Dell, vol. 4 of *Annals of the New York Stage* (New York: Columbia University Press, 1931).

22. See Harry Reynolds, *Minstrel Memories: The Story of Burnt Cork Minstrelry in Great Britain from 1836 to 1937* (London: Alston Rivers Ltd., 1928), pp. 77–78. On the Christmas tradition of minstrelry, see the excerpt from the diary of Charles DeLong in Alexander Saxton, *The Rise and Fall of the White Republic: Class Politics and Mass Culture in Nineteenth-Century America* (New York: Verso, 1990), p. 172. Also particularly helpful here is Henry Louis Gates's discussion of black harlequin in *Figures in Black: Words, Signs, and the "Racial" Self* (New York: Oxford University Press, 1987), pp. 51–53.

23. James, *A Small Boy and Others*, pp. 181, 98.

24. Ibid., p. 302.

25. Saxton, *The Rise and Fall of the White Republic*, p. 168.

26. Edel, "The Dramatic Years," pp. 51, 52, 52, 51.

27. Lawrence W. Levine, *Highbrow/Lowbrow: The Emergence of Cultural Hierarchy in America* (Cambridge, Mass.: Harvard University Press, 1988), p. 177.

THIRTY-EIGHT

EXPANDING THE CANON OF AMERICAN REALISM

Elizabeth Ammons

Elizabeth Ammons received her Ph.D. from the University of Illinois in 1974. She is currently Professor of English and Dean of Humanities and Arts at Tufts University. Ammons's books include *Edith Wharton's Argument with America* (1980) and *Conflicting Stories: American Women Writers at the Turn into the Twentieth Century* (1991). She is a coeditor of the *Oxford Companion to Women's Writing in the United States* (1995).

Iktomi surprised me, particularly as a part of this course, because the Sioux realism—a markedly *different* realism—is, first, not at all what I might define as "realism" and, second, it *must* be accepted as the reality of whoever subscribes to it.

Joseph Pelletier

These three books—*The Rise of Silas Lapham, Old Indian Legends, The Conjure Woman*—taught me to see that my idea of realism is not everyone's.

Emma Lockwood

Being able to write is a healing, an act that speaks to one's tangible existence and worth as one whose voice not only roars, but is given attention to.

Lucy Park

The Cambridge Companion to American Realism and Naturalism: From Howells to London, ed. Donald Pizer (Cambridge: © Cambridge University Press 1995), pp. 95–114. Reprinted with the permission of Cambridge University Press and Elizabeth Ammons.

How does an artist of color express anger in a way that will not alienate a mainstream white audience predisposed to hostility?

Lisa Hom

When we say American realism, two immediate questions are: Whose reality? And: Whose America? To suggest those questions, I have opened with statements written by four of my students. Also, I begin with my students' words to anticipate two other core ideas. First, the whole issue of canonicity is at heart an issue of the classroom; what is at stake is which books get taught and which do not, which voices get heard. Second, I will be arguing in favor of a reconceptualization of American realism that holds at its center the principle of multiculturalism.

An excellent place to begin any discussion of canonicity and American realism is Amy Kaplan's overview of modern scholarship in *The Social Construction of American Realism* (1988). As Kaplan explains, post-Second World War opinion tended to go in two directions. Charles C. Walcutt's *American Literary Naturalism: A Divided Stream* (1956), Donald Pizer's *Realism and Naturalism in Nineteenth-Century American Literature* (1966), and Harold Kolb's *The Illusion of Life: American Realism as Literary Form* (1969) consider texts apart from their social contexts in order to offer close New Critical analyses. In contrast, Warner Berthoff's *The Ferment of Realism: American Literature, 1884–1919* (1965) and Jay Martin's *Harvests of Change: American Literature, 1865–1914* (1967) situate texts in their social contexts in order to see how they reflect those contexts. Challenging the premises that govern both of those approaches, more recent studies such as Eric Sundquist's *American Realism: New Essays* (1982), June Howard's *Form and History in American Literary Naturalism* (1985), and Kaplan's book respond to postmodern theoretical concerns. They raise questions about what is "real," what is knowable, and what is involved in the acts of creating, reading, interpreting, discussing, and writing about texts.

Kaplan cuts to the quick of postmodernism's impact on the concept of realism when she points to the "antimimetic assumption of poststructuralist theory which holds that reality is not reflected by language but that language in fact produces the reality we know."[1] This philosophical position leads to exciting new interpretive perspectives. But it can also, as Kaplan points out in her description of the Sundquist collection, deconstruct the whole idea of realism. If language does not reflect, but instead *creates*, reality, then what reality, or what knowable, communicable one, can realist texts logically be said to stand in relation to? Hence, as Kaplan says, postmodernist critics frequently "locate the power of realistic texts precisely in their ability to deconstruct their own claims to referentiality. Through the lenses of contemporary theories, those characteristics once considered realistic are revalued for exposing their own fictionality" (5). The outcome, too often but predictably, is pronouncement of realism's failure, extinction, or nonexistence and the concomitant reassertion of romance as America's best, only, and truest form.[2]

Scholars such as June Howard and Amy Kaplan deal with the challenge of poststructuralist theory by arguing, in Kaplan's words, that "Realists do more than passively record the world outside; they actively create and criticize the meanings, representations, and ideologies of their own changing culture" (7). Thus realism can be said simultaneously to reflect *and* to be part of, to be enmeshed in and produced by, its social context. What this accomplishes is a crucial complication of the idea that texts simply "reflect" their society. As Carl R. Kropf and R. Barton Palmer observe at the beginning of a special issue of *Studies in the Literary Imagination* devoted to narrative theory, when "issues relating to interpretation and the connection between texts and the 'real world' . . . figure prominently on the critical agenda" of contemporary scholarship, "such criticism today avoids both a naive reflectionism and the pseudo-Leavisite view that novels speak directly to readers, unmediated by the structural or technical aspects of storytelling."[3] Consequently, as Kaplan notes, recent critics have tended to reevaluate "realism's political stance, from a progressive force exposing social conditions to a conservative force complicit with capitalist relations" (7). (Dreiser is most frequently used to illustrate this argument.) Charting her own course, Kaplan builds on the historian T. J. Jackson Lears's contention that at the turn of the century "reality itself began to seem problematic, something to be sought rather than merely lived." Kaplan argues that realistic narratives enact this search— "not by fleeing into the imagination or into nostalgia for a lost past but by actively constructing the coherent social world they represent; they do this not in a vacuum of fictionality but in direct confrontation with the elusive process of social change" (9). Realists, in this view, "show a surprising lack of confidence in the capacity of fiction to reflect a solid world 'out there,' not because of the inherent slipperiness of signification but because of their distrust in the significance of the social" (9). Hence their art, which is "anxious and contradictory," simultaneously "articulates and combats the growing sense of unreality at the heart of middle-class life" (9).

The problem with this approach lies in the narrowness of the field of writers to which such a definition of realism applies. A Learsian, postmodernist perspective does illuminate works by Henry James, Theodore Dreiser, and Edith Wharton, the three authors Kaplan studies; and no doubt it can profitably be applied to work by other authors as well. Also, the way in which such a perspective engages important theoretical issues, particularly the question of how realism functions as social reflector even as it is social participant and product, is clear and useful. But how well does such a theory help us understand Zitkala-Ša, Pauline Hopkins, Charles Chesnutt, or Charlotte Perkins Gilman? Or Sui Sin Far, W. E. B. Du Bois, Alice Dunbar-Nelson, Anzia Yezierska, Simon Pokagon, María Cristina Mena, Frances Ellen Harper, Upton Sinclair, James Weldon Johnson? Can we really claim that floating feelings of personal disorientation—individualistic anxiety about the "elusive process of social change" and "a growing sense of unreality at the heart of middle-class life"—were the important issues facing writers who were people of color, feminist, working-class, or poor? Confronted with lynching, rape, Jim Crow laws, land dispossession, cultural erasure, domestic violence, deportation, anti-Semitism, economic oppression, racist immigration laws, and widespread disenfranchisement—to name only some obvious "realities" that, despite postmodernism's claims, were hardly linguistic fictions—many turn-of-the-century authors struggled with problems ignored (in some instances actively denied and suppressed—even caused) by privileged white writers such as James and Wharton. To reconceptualize the period so that a full range of authors can come into view, and to do so in a way that allows us not simply to introduce them as tokens but, rather, to place on an even footing Henry James and Sui Sin Far, Charles Chesnutt and Edith Wharton, I am proposing multiculturalism. It is a paradigm for canon-formation that is intellectually provocative, inclusive, historically sound, and pedagogically flexible.

I

In "Canonicity and Textuality," Robert Scholes explains that the curriculum—what students are told to read—stands at the center of all of our debates about literary canons, which is to say, the texts agreed upon as constituting the "best" or most important works one should read in order to be educated about a given period, author, genre, literary movement, or tradition. With the professionalization of literary studies in the United States early in the twentieth century, "the canon supported the literary curriculum and the curriculum supported the canon. The curriculum, in literary studies, represented the point of application, where canonical choices were tested in the crucible of student response. Works that proved highly teachable (like Shakespeare) remained central in the canon as well as in the curriculum." Professors added other writers they found especially "teachable," such as John Donne, whose poetry was particularly well suited to New Criticism's investment in complex, tight, textual explication by experts. At the same time, formerly admired but less "teachable," because more obvious, authors such as Oliver Goldsmith fell out of canonical favor.[4] Perhaps the most important thing about this process, Scholes observes, is how unconscious it was. Until the last twenty years or so, decisions about canonicity—who's in and who's out—

> were seen as "natural"—or even as not occurring at all. What has happened to literary studies in those decades is a part of larger cultural happenings that can be described (and deplored, if you like) as the politicization of American life. Once upon a time we believed that if the best men (yes) were appointed to the bench, we would get the best judicial decisions. Now, we know that one set of appointments to the Supreme Court will give us one set of laws and another set of appointments will give us others. What is happening is part of the evolution of a democratic society. With respect to the literary canon, [Northrop] Frye's statement about [Matthew] Arnold's touchstones was a political bombshell: "We begin to suspect that the literary judgments are projections of social ones." Which is to say that the literary canon is a social, and therefore a political, object, the result of a political process, like so much else in our world. (147)

Canonicity is a human, not a divine or "natural," phenomenon. Professors decide what the "best" and most important books are on the basis of what they want to teach and write about. Those decisions, in turn, are grounded in social and political values that do not exist in a vacuum, but in the context of faculty members' histories, training, and biases, which are, in their turn, inseparable from consideration of class, gender, race, ethnicity, sexual orientation, nationality, religion, and culture—among other things.

For the canon-making professoriat, then, the questions are not all that obscure. To which texts and authors is it important to expose the young and why? When I construct my syllabus for, say, American realism in the way that it was constructed for me by my professors ten, twenty, or thirty years ago, what social and political values am I perpetuating and endorsing? What version of America am I presenting? Even more specifically, if I make my reading list all white, or all white plus one lonely black as a token to "diversity," what story of "our" (whose?) national past am I creating? Likewise, if I say I have to make my list consist of 80 percent elite white writers because otherwise I will disserve my students, who will come away not having read the canonical authors they "need" to know, whose definitions of disservice, canonicity, and need am I employing?

The obvious point here is that syllabi and, behind them, canons, are all composed of choices. As Robert Hemenway observes, "Although it sounds immodest to say so, English professors largely define the literary canon by choosing to teach certain works. . . . No writer, no book, is likely to be accepted into the canon without the sanction of the university curriculum."[5] Even in English departments where freedom to design syllabi is denied, the design of syllabi is still recognized, at some level, as simply that: a design, a made-up construct. Departmental politics may make argument pointless, but that does not mean that argument about whether a book should or should not be on a syllabus actually *is* irrational—as opposed, for example, to arguing about whether to eat rocks. In short, every time we teach from a syllabus, whether we have designed it or it has been given to us, we participate in a canonical argument. We assert that this list of texts and authors, as opposed to all the lists we are not teaching, is the important one to engage at this time, in this place, and for these reasons, stated or unstated.

Given the constructed character of the canon, what construction shall we choose? My own position is that, if American realism means anything, it means attention to the multiple realities figured in the work of the broadest possible range of authors writing in the late nineteenth and early twentieth centuries. We are educating the young in a world where—to use my own city, Medford, Massachusetts, as an example—the high school was closed as I was writing this essay in 1992 because of a racial "brawl." Although 16 percent of the 1,250 students were black or Hispanic, there were only two black teachers. White teachers interviewed in the newspaper said they saw nothing offensive about white students dressing in Ku Klux Klan regalia for a Halloween party and having pictures of themselves in those costumes published in the yearbook. When the overwhelmingly white local and state police forces descended on the school, they arrested twelve black, two Hispanic, and one white male student. A story I have now heard several times repeats how an African American girl in a history course raised her hand to ask which black people the class would be studying, only to be told, none. In answer to her question, why, she was told because there were none.

None of us needs to look far to find this world. I could, instead of my town, refer to my university—Tufts—which, like any other, contains behind-the-scene rapes, swastikas scrawled on a dormitory door, suicides, racist complaints about the bad English of "foreign" teaching assistants, and on and on—all in a community that is committed to confronting and dealing with issues of discrimination, hatred, and fear. How shall I proceed in this world? It makes no sense to me to teach American realism as a middle- to upper-class white, male, literary period preoccupied with ways of preserving privilege when, in fact, literary production in the period can be shown to have been more various and more contested by people traditionally denied access to publication than at any preceding time in United States history. My choice is to focus on the presence of diversity, conflict, and turbulence—as well as exuberance, idealism, and celebration—that a genuinely multicultural representation of authors and texts makes possible.[6] To illustrate, my most recent syllabus for American realism (1992) consisted of: Henry James, *Daisy Miller*; William Dean Howells, *The Rise of Silas Lapham*; W. E. B. Du Bois, *The Souls of Black Folk*; Charlotte Perkins Gilman, "The Yellow Wallpaper"; Zitkala-Ša, *Old Indian Legends*; Kate Chopin, *The Awakening*; Charles Chesnutt, *The Conjure Woman*; Pauline Hopkins, *Of One Blood*; Sui Sin Far, selections from *Mrs. Spring Fragrance*; Upton Sinclair, *The Jungle*; Edith Wharton, *Ethan Frome*; María Cristina Mena, "The Vine-Leaf"; Willa Cather, *O Pioneers!*; and selected stories from Anzia Yezierska, *Hungry Hearts*.

Typically, arguments in favor of multiculturalism as an organizing principle for curricula begin with the self-evident truth that the world is, and the United States has always been, multicultural. Henry Louis Gates, Jr., states: "Whatever the outcome of the cultural wars in the academy, the world we live in is multicultural already. Mixing and hybridity are the rule, not the exception."[7] John Brenkman explains:

> As multiculturalism has begun to impinge on education and on contemporary cultural and literary criticism, neoconservative commentators like to blame an imaginary cabal of leftists who have surreptitiously (and unbeknownst to ourselves) taken over academia, hellbent on stirring racial and ethnic animosities. The neoconservatives, ever mindful of tradition and neglectful of history, will not own up to the real reasons multiculturalism has entered the scene so forcefully, namely, because the United States is rife with unsolved social and political problems whose history reaches all the way back to Columbus.[8]

For Gates, who provides thoughtful comments about weak arguments sometimes invoked in its defense, multiculturalism's imperative lies in its power to increase knowledge and tolerance. To those who worry about exacerbating divisions, he responds: "Ours is a world that already is fissured by nationality, ethnicity, race, and gender. And the only way to transcend those divisions—to forge, for once, a civic culture that respects both differences and commonalities—is through education that seeks to comprehend the diversity of human culture. Beyond the hype and the high-flown rhetoric is a pretty homely truth: there is no tolerance without respect—and no respect without knowledge."[9] For Brenkman, the goal is similar. "A democracy in the contemporary world cannot create a monocultural citizenry. . . . We must define and defend the equality, not the homogeneity, of citizens in the context of multiculturalism."[10]

Multiculturalism should not be confused, however, with simplistic white-oriented feel-good diversity. Paula Gunn Allen speaks with passion about the absence of real change in the academy. Native people, along with women, men, and gay people of color are "labeled as 'marginal,' the 'poor,' the 'victims,' or we are seen as exotica. Our 'allies' adamantly cast us in the role of helpless, hopeless, inadequate, incompetent, much in need of white champions and saviors, dependent upon an uncaring State for every shred of personal and community dignity we might hope to enjoy. Right, left, and center see us as their shadows, the part they disown, reject, repress, or romanticize."[11] White people's magnanimous decisions to "include" writers of color on undeconstructed white reading lists; descriptions of human beings as "marginal" or "Other"; arrogant projections of elite western theory onto cultural expressions of people writing outside western frameworks; patronizing assumptions that all art created by people of color is obsessed with nothing but subverting dominant-culture forms, as if no referent could possibly exist except the master narrative[12]—all of these are just the new colonialism. They are simply new ways of asserting the hegemony of a western, Eurocentric perspective. They are not part of any genuinely *multi*cultural perspective.

Allen especially attacks elite western academic assumptions that philosophical and literary theories invented by privileged white patriarchs can. be applied, willy-nilly, around the globe.[13] She rejects what many would argue are the three basic propositions of fancy contemporary theory in the West. To the notion that "gender (or sex) is a metaphor, a social construct," she responds, "In other systems—systems not so bound in a self-referencing, nearly psychotic death dance—meaning is derived and ascribed along different lines" (307). On the academy's obsession with language, she points out that "western minds have supposed (wrongly) for some time that language is culture and that without a separate language a culture is defunct" (308). On the alleged politicalness of all human reality, she states: "In the world of the patriarchs everything is about politics; for much of the rest of the world, politics occupies little if any part of our preoccupations" (310).

As Paula Gunn Allen's challenges make clear, multiculturalism does not consist of simply gathering various cultural expressions together under the interpretive control of dominant-cultural paradigms. Multiculturalism, approached in the spirit of genuinely wishing to understand how different people define, create, accept, and inhabit different cultural realities, is a difficult and often threatening—even painful—undertaking that involves opening ourselves intellectually and emotionally to various and frequently conflicting cultural premises, practices, and values. How to do so in a way that does not reproduce the existing power structure and yet deals with the ways in which that power structure affects all of us is a basic question. The task requires not only a new canon but also substantial new knowledge and a significantly new pedagogy, both in theory and in practice.

When I apply these concerns to the question of how to expand the canon of American realism, five models for the new construction of literary study—suggested by Paula Gunn Allen, Henry Louis Gates, Jr., Paul Lauter, Annette Kolodny, and Renato Rosaldo—strike me as particularly useful.

Allen advocates the obvious—starting over.

> Perhaps the best course is to begin anew, to examine the literary output of American writers of whatever stripe and derive critical principles based on what is actually being rendered by the true experts, the writers themselves. While we're at it, we might take a look at the real America that most of us inhabit—the one seldom approached by denizens of the hallowed (or is it hollow?) groves of academe—so that we can discover what is being referenced beyond abstractions familiar to establishment types but foreign to those who live in real time. I am suggesting a critical system that is founded on the principle of inclusion rather than on that of exclusion, on actual human society and relationships rather than on textual relations alone, a system that is soundly based on aesthetics that pertain to the literatures we wish to examine. (309)

Allen's advice, for me, means building a definition of American realism not simply on William Dean Howells's famous prescriptions for realists, grounded as they are in white, middle-class ideas about what is ordinary, common, and representative of the lives of actual men and women in the United States, but also on Charles Chesnutt's articulations of what it means as an African American writer to try to render "reality"; Zitkala-Ša's definition of Sioux reality in *Old Indian Legends*, as well as her representation of mixed cultural realities in her autobiographical writing; and Sui Sin Far's fictional and autobiographical definitions of the "real" from her particular Chinese American point of view. In other words, to follow Allen's advice and start over with a truly heterogeneous set of writers, works, and life conditions is to arrive at a new conceptualization of American realism as a multiple rather than a unitary phenomenon, American realism as American realisms.

Allen's concept of foregrounding writers rather than preconceived inherited theories about American literature is echoed in Henry Louis Gates's recommendation that we think of American literature as a conversation among authors; Paul Lauter's suggestion that we construct American literary study on a comparativist model; and Annette Kolodny's proposal that we relocate American literary inquiry onto what she identifies as frontiers, borderland sites.[14] Gates, recognizing that debates about canonicity and American literature are really about "the twin problematic of canon formation and nation formation," says, "it is time for scholars to think of a comparative American culture as a conversation among different voices—even if it is a conversation that some of us were not able to join until very recently" (300). Lauter, referring to the metaphorical use of "mainstream" as "the Great River theory of American letters," argues that the model itself is the problem. It "presents variations from the mainstream as abnormal, deviant, lesser, perhaps ultimately unimportant. That kind of standard is no more helpful in the study of culture than is a model, in the study of gender differences, in which the male is considered the norm, or than paradigms, in the study of minority or ethnic social organization and behavior, based on Anglo-American society. What we need, rather, is to pose a comparative model for the study of American literature" (1). Kolodny, inviting us to think of the ways in which cultural differences meet, retain their separateness, and yet engage in exchange at those human boundaries we call frontiers, focuses on Hispanic and Anglo-American encounters but also invokes an imagined moment in turn-of-the-century United States history: "the crush of languages and cultures on a single day at Ellis Island in 1905." She says: "The texts that attempt to delineate these frontier moments—like the literary histories generated to accommodate them—will tell many different stories. . . . The singular identities and unswerving continuities that Americanists have regularly claimed for our literary history are no longer credible" (13).

Each of these models posits multiplicity of perspective as the premise—the governing idea—for the study of American literature. Also, all these scholars—Allen, Gates, Lauter, Kolodny—caution against reinscribing a patriarchal white model by talking in terms of centers, margins, others, subversions, and re-visions, as if, again, all cultural expression finally can do nothing but revolve around the great white western Center.

An undeniable difficulty in adopting such models is the threat that radical change poses to us as teachers. Who can possibly know everything that needs to be known if we have to become Americanist comparativists? One answer, Renato Rosaldo suggests, speaking of cultural studies in general, is that we *won't* know everything. Our authority as professors will change, and with it the character of our pedagogy and the dynamic of the classroom. As Rosaldo puts it, we already teach in a world classroom, which means that our authority as teachers is not what it was even a decade ago. Who among us can be Asian, African, lesbian, European, working-class, male, female, and of mixed blood, all on different days of the week or different parts of the hour? The question is how to teach when we cannot know, either through experience or training, everything—cannot be the complete authority.[15]

Obviously, multiculturalism means that faculty members have to commit themselves to lifelong continuing education in cultures other than their own—a situation different only in focus, not kind, from what is expected now. Also, it is already the case that graduate education is changing and that a younger generation, as has always been true, will be more skillful at performing what the emerging new project requires than their elders. But another part of the answer lies in a changed classroom, one where group exploration, team teaching, admission of the limits of one's own current knowledge, and encouragement of targeted serious research at the undergraduate level will represent the norm rather than the exception. Creating this kind of classroom without abrogating responsibility as the person paid and trusted to be knowledgeable and in charge *and* without exploiting students who happen to be members of culture groups to which the professor does not belong are key issues.

II

For a glimpse of the kind of canon that a multicultural construction of American realism opens up, let me juxtapose four of the texts on my syllabus: *Mrs. Spring Fragrance* (1912), "The Yellow Wallpaper" (1892), *The Conjure Woman* (1899), and *Old Indian Legends* (1901).[16] Others could be used, but these four work well in providing a broad range of cultural perspectives within a short time frame. (Although the book was published in 1912, many of the stories in Sui Sin Far's volume were written and published in the 1890s.) Since some of these texts and their authors may be unfamiliar, I will give brief biographies.

Sui Sin Far was the first Chinese American writer to publish serious fiction in the United States about Chinese American life. Born in 1865 and also known as Edith Eaton, she was one of fourteen children. Her father was English and her mother Chinese. She grew up in Canada and then, as an adult, supported herself as a single woman by working as a stenographer, reporter, and magazine-fiction writer, traveling and living in Canada, the Caribbean, and the United States, where she settled in Seattle for ten years. Because her appearance was not obviously Asian, she could have "passed" for white. She chose, however, to identify herself as Chinese American, despite the racist persecution consequent upon that choice, as she explains in her autobiographical essay, "Leaves from the Mental Portfolio of a Eurasian" (1909). Her only published book, *Mrs. Spring Fragrance*, appeared two years before her death in 1914; it is a collection of thirty-seven stores divided into two sections, the second of which is intended for children. The stories for adults take place in Chinese American communities and display a wide array of plots, issues, and characters, ranging from fictions that dramatize interactions between white Americans and Chinese Americans to fictions solely about relationships and issues within the Asian American community.[17]

Charlotte Perkins Gilman, born in 1860 and descended from the famous Beecher family, grew up in a repressive, white Protestant, middle-class household in New England. Her father abandoned his wife and children while Charlotte was young, leaving her mother bitter and impoverished; and, as an adult, Gilman found her own first marriage and experience of motherhood psychologically devastating. She suffered such severe, incapacitating mental breakdowns that she underwent treatment by the renowned rest-cure physician Dr. S. Weir Mitchell, which nearly drove her permanently insane. After divorcing and giving up her daughter to the child's father, she remarried, but had no more children and devoted her life to writing and speaking about women's rights. Best known for her short story "The Yellow Wallpaper," her book-length feminist analysis *Women and Economics* (1898), and her feminist utopia *Herland* (1915), Gilman, who died in 1935, dedicated her life to the cause of white middle-class feminism and became one of the leading theorists of the era. She published more than a thousand essays, in addition to writing poetry, novels, and short stories.[18]

Charles Waddell Chesnutt was born in 1858 in Cleveland, Ohio, to free black parents who had moved north from Fayetteville, North Carolina. Although the family returned to Fayetteville when Charles was eight, as an adult he moved his own family back to Cleveland in 1884. A member of the bar, Chesnutt's real ambition was to make his living as a writer, and with his short story "The Goophered Grapevine" in 1887 he became the first African American author to be published in the *Atlantic Monthly*. In 1899, by invitation of the publisher, he collected seven of his stories in *The Conjure Woman*, his first book. It was followed that same year by *The Wife of His Youth and Other Stories of the Color Line* and then three novels, *The House Behind the Cedars* (1900), *The Marrow of Tradition* (1901), and *The Colonel's Dream* (1905). Chesnutt's books sold poorly, which meant that, although he continued to publish occasionally, he could not make a living as a writer. In 1928, four years before his death, he was honored by the National Association for the Advancement of Colored People with the prestigious Spingarn Medal.[19]

Zitkala-Ša, also known by her English name, Gertrude Bonnin, was born on the Pine Ridge Indian Reservation in 1876. Her mother was Yankton Sioux; her father, a white man, left the family. When she was eight, Zitkala-Ša persuaded her mother to let her go away to a missionary school for Indians in Wabash, Indiana, a traumatic experience that she chronicled in her autobiographical piece for the *Atlantic Monthly* in 1900, "Impressions of an Indian Childhood." Yet when she returned to the reservation from Indiana, Zitkala-Ša found herself so changed that she was unable to resume the life she had left; after a few years, she departed again, this time for Earlham College in Indiana, and then, because she was an accomplished violinist, the Boston Conservatory of Music. Zitkala-Ša published two books, *Old Indian Legends* (1901) and *American Indian Stories* (1921). Her primary dedication was to Indian rights activism, however, and she devoted her life to public speaking, lobbying, and political advocacy. In 1926 she founded the National Council of American Indians; also, her labor contributed to the passage of the Indian Citizenship Bill. When she died in 1938, she was buried in Arlington National Cemetery in Washington, D.C.[20]

To group Sui Sin Far's *Mrs. Spring Fragrance*, Charlotte Perkins Gilman's "The Yellow Wallpaper," Charles Chesnutt's *The Conjure Woman*, and Zitkala-Ša's *Old Indian Legends* is to interrogate the very category "American realism." Although produced at about the same time and for much the same purpose—namely, to reach and affect the thinking of a hostile (or at the very least ignorant), conventional, white, educated readership, a readership such as that served by the *Atlantic Monthly*—each of these texts constitutes and employs realism in radically different ways from the others.

Mrs. Spring Fragrance, like many other texts at the turn of the century—W. E. B. Du Bois's *The Souls of Black Folk* (1903), Sarah Orne Jewett's *The Country of the Pointed Firs* (1896), Alice Dunbar-Nelson's *The Goodness of St. Rocque* (1899), Hamlin Garland's *Main-Travelled Roads* (1891)—is a communally focused, coherent, long narrative composed of collected stories. They can be read randomly as individual short stories, but the book can also be read straight through as a composite long fiction. Thus the effect of the work as a whole, even simply at this mechanical formal level, is to send a complex message about the relationship between individual and collective identity. Each individual's story is important; yet by the end no one individual's story can be said to be more important than another's. The emergent group focus, in addition to showing that the book's stories were written at different times for different magazines, implies an aesthetic and a definition of realism that privilege community and place the issue of culture itself at the center of narrative.

Filled with characters who embody distinctly diverse cultural perspectives—immigrant Chinese, native-born white American, many versions of Chinese American—Mrs. *Spring Fragrance* explores life in North America from a range of Asian American perspectives. The book is organized by no single protagonist's experience or point of view. We are asked to think about immigration, deportation, detention centers, feminism, marriage, art, love, language, clothing, social class, child-rearing, education, nationality, and internationalism from multiple perspectives, seeing how an issue looks to a new immigrant in contrast to an "Americanized" inhabitant of Chinatown as opposed to a Caucasian American, all the time with age and gender entering the equation as well. Indeed, this is an ideal text to which to bring Kolodny's concept of interpretive "frontiers," for it is composed of constantly shifting and frequently interfacing cultural perspectives, often in conflict with each other. Multiplicity of viewpoint drives Mrs. *Spring Fragrance*, whose very subject is cultural relations. As Sui Sin Far has Mrs. Spring Fragrance announce early in the book: " 'Many American women wrote books. Why should not a Chinese? She would write a book about Americans for her Chinese women friends. The American people were so interesting and mysterious.' " Lest we miss the flipped stereotype, Sui Sin Far has Mrs. Spring Fragrance repeat, " 'Ah, these Americans! These mysterious, inscrutable, incomprehensible Americans! Had I the divine right of learning I would put them into an immortal book!' "[21] Attacking—and sometimes reinforcing—stereotypes, Mrs. *Spring Fragrance* enacts cultural clash in the United States. It is about the pain and struggle—and occasional joy—of dealing with generational, racial, sexual, and cultural conflicts, all within a dominant power structure set up to discriminate against people who are not of European descent.

In contrast, "The Yellow Wallpaper," which Horace Scudder of the *Atlantic Monthly* rejected as too horrible and depressing to print, focuses narrowly on white upper-middle-class, feminine reality, which it locates—appropriately—deep within one single, locked, hyperdomestic room. Gilman's setting is the exaggeratedly privatized world of the genteel Victorian family. This environment is insular and male-dominated; literally cut off from the public, commercial realm of open social exchange; scientifically rationalized (the authority figure is literally a physician); secretly and sadistically violent (the paraphernalia of torture and imprisonment masquerade as nursery trappings); and organized by a bourgeois division of labor based on formal servitude (there are two women in the story, one a privileged wife, the other her servant). As with Mrs. *Spring Fragrance*, here too the narrative form beautifully reflects and is the product of the cultural values it examines. Whereas Sui Sin Far's book is multiple and diverse both conceptually and structurally, Gilman's story is very tightly aimed and unified. Its form stages the private, secret, individual consciousness of its female narrator/protagonist. As readers we enter this single mind, which is, at bottom, what the story is about: experiencing the inside of one person's mind, the interior life of one representative but highly individualistic, privileged, white woman who is being forcibly held and reindoctrinated into a suffocating Victorian ethic of decorous, dependent femininity. The aesthetic employed and enjoyed, like the cultural reality the story reflects but is also produced by, locates pleasure and meaning in the exercise of individual, isolated, autonomous intellect. That is, Gilman's story about cultural oppression—about white patriarchal subjugation of women—attacks western patriarchal values at the same time that it endorses a modern, patriarchal, Eurocentric definition of mental health and creative genius which places a premium on the solitary, individualistic expression of human intelligence.

The Conjure Woman, in contrast, reflects and is generated by an emphatically *un*-unitary but instead complexly dual cultural consciousness, similar to that expressed by Chesnutt's famous compatriot W. E. B. Du Bois in his metaphor of the Veil in *The Souls of Black Folk* (1903). The seven tales comprising Chesnutt's book perform the clash between European American and African American cultures in the United States. Every tale begins with a frame story which, almost to the letter, reproduces the patriarchal white Anglo-Saxon Protestant culture pictured by Gilman, right down to centrally figuring a "sick" privileged wife, Annie, who is cared for by her ultra-rational, successful, power-focused husband, John. Interacting with these two is Julius, an old rural Southern black man who bonds with and heals Annie and skillfully manipulates John, managing to keep for himself a healthy measure of economic and narrative control despite the white man's power. These envelope-narratives detailing the power struggle between Julius and John with Annie on the sidelines frame the book's seven conjure tales, which are inherited, oral, African American stories. Told by Julius, they constitute a significantly different realism from that contained in the frame stories.

In Julius's inner tales people change into animals and back again into people; a person can inhabit a tree, and then the wood sawn from it; a man can grow young and old with the seasons year after year. The power to make such things happen belongs to conjure women and men, powerful black people whose cultural heritage is African. For John, a successful white man, these tales are nonsense. For Annie, in contrast, they are compelling; she responds to the way Julius's stories define slavery from an African American perspective, and she is tempted to believe in their "magic." For us as readers able to hear all three characters, Julius, John, and Annie, there is yet a third rhetorical situation. The book's inner and outer tales set up a constant, complex, cultural dialogue—literally a conversation, to recall Gates's term—about the cultural construction of realism. The frame stories, we have no doubt, are "realism." After all, they mimic the economic, psychological, sociological, and historical "facts" of race relations, racism, and racial resistance in the United States as they are often represented. But what about the inner tales? Is conjure "realism"? Obviously, modern western wisdom—witness Chesnutt's white man, John—says no. But African and African American wisdom—the wisdom at work in the traditional tales—says otherwise. Conjure exists; it happens. Mysterious metaphysical powers that defy western reason inhabit the universe; and certain people have access to those powers, whether white people can accept it or not.[22] As Julius observes: " 'I don't know if you believes in conjure or not. Some of the white folks don't.' "[23] Camouflaged in downhome, nonthreatening, black dialect designed to make Chesnutt's tales appear no different from white Plantation School ditties, *The Conjure Woman* is a radical text. It asserts that an Afrocentric cultural reality not only exists in the United States but has actual power. In the final (Afrocentric) analysis, it is Julius's conjure, not modern science's medicine, that heals Annie.

Old Indian Legends makes an equally radical choice. It presents a single cultural reality, which is Sioux. Although the book exists in print and is written in English, it claims a place in Anglo-derived United State literature for a Native American, which is to say, a nonwestern, work of art. And Zitkala-Ša makes that claim in full awareness of her narratives' prior and prime identity on the North American continent. As she states in her preface: "I have tried to transplant the native spirit of these tales—root and all—into the English language, since America in the last few centuries has acquired a second tongue."[24]

Everything about *Old Indian Legends* challenges standard academic notions about American realism. Its announced, intended audience of children says that it cannot be "serious" literature (even though *Huckleberry Finn*, of course, is); and this announcement is reinforced by Zitkala-Ša's simplicity of language and presentation, her main characters' embodiment as animals, and the protagonist's identity as trickster—all of which distance and confuse the reader taught to expect and admire Henry James. Most disorienting, perhaps, is the complete, uncommented-upon absence of white people in *Old Indian Legends*—and with them the complete absence of any Judeo-Christian frame of reference. How do western-trained readers read this book? As Arnold Krupat, addressing the issue of academic critical methodology and Native American texts, points out, "Native American cultural production is based upon a profound wisdom that is most certainly different from a Western, rationalistic, scientistic, secular perspective."[25] This leads me (despite Krupat's argument to the contrary) to try different ways of proceeding, ways that bring into the classroom oral and communal experiences of literature in addition to individual, analytic thinking.

Certainly, it is important to contextualize *Old Indian Legends* by providing conventional academic lectures and discussions that focus on Sioux culture and history, including, in particular, information about the Massacre at Wounded Knee, which occurred just eleven years before Zitkala-Ša's book and must have exerted a major influence on her decision to issue a collection of traditional tales. Also, because the subject has been so neglected, in most United States classrooms some formal lecturing is necessary to introduce students to the activity of thinking seriously about Native American literary traditions, values, and aesthetic principles.[26] Still, a text such as *Old Indian Legends* demands more than just intellectualizing. Without falling into sentimental, bogus attempts to "be" Indian, the approach to this text needs, in some way, to stretch students' awareness. In representing Sioux reality independent of European presence, *Old Indian Legends* asserts a cultural integrity and strength—an indestructableness—which stands at the very core of this book's realism. Iktomi the trickster constantly changes shapes, plans, plots, roles, locations, faces, bodies, jokes, schemes, fates, and futures. But all of this contradictoriness coheres in one created principle within one complex universe that embraces—weblike—all worlds, visible and invisible. Artistic principles of repetition, laughter, silence, orality, and cyclicness reinforce Zitkala-Ša's realism of multivocal creational wholeness and continuity, a realism both reflected in and productive of this book. To try to open ourselves to some of this fullness, I have my class read a tale out loud, and then I ask all the students to commit one story to memory, using their own words but sticking close to Zitkala-Ša's telling. We then spend time in class storytelling—*not* a high-status activity in the academy—which leads us to reflect on which details got lost, why we are poor storytellers, the relation between oral and printed forms, the structure of education in the modern West, the reality embodied by Iktomi, and the realism of animals and human beings exchanging form. Also, it might be worth mentioning, before we start the book I give a quiz. The first question is: As you look at the door in our room, what direction on the earth are you facing? The second is: What time did the sun rise this morning?

To close by returning to Paul Lauter's recommendation that we use a comparativist approach to American literature: What is gained and what is lost in adopting a multicultural definition of American realism? Lost is the high degree of security and even comfort, not to mention tidiness, that a traditionally constructed Anglo-oriented canon offered many of us. I no longer can present my students with a relatively uncomplicated, coherent, linear story about United States prose fiction in the second half of the nineteenth and the beginning of the twentieth centuries. The cultural line I once taught, running unbroken from Henry James and Mark Twain through William Dean Howells, Stephen Crane, Frank Norris, Charlotte Perkins Gilman, Kate Chopin, Theodore Dreiser, Edith Wharton, Upton Sinclair, Willa Cather, and Sherwood Anderson (with, perhaps, James Weldon Johnson thrown in for diversity), had the virtue of being very manageable and teachable. Except for trying to get students to think historically, the class could move smoothly through the semester, tracing variations on repeated themes.

Such a monocultural canon, however, does not begin to capture the multiplicity of cultural perspectives that literary production of the period—evincing what Warner Berthoff wisely called a ferment—brought into being. A multicultural canon yields no unified story about realism. Philosophically and artistically, the realism of *Old Indian Legends* clashes with the realism of "The Yellow Wallpaper" or *Mrs. Spring Fragrance*, two works that, in turn, contrast strongly (though not entirely) with each other. At the same time, *Old Indian Legends* shares some strong affinities with *The Conjure Woman*, both of which, for example, insist on the reality of conjure and interspecies transformations. In short, a multicultural construction of American realism does reveal sharp, fundamental disjunctions: Henry James and Anzia Yezierska, Edith Wharton and Sui Sin Far, Pauline Hopkins and Frank Norris. But it also generates provocative new links and connections: *Daisy Miller, Of One Blood,* and *The Autobiography of an Ex-Colored Man,* on the "international theme"; *Mrs. Spring Fragrance, O Pioneers!* and *Hungry Hearts,* on immigrant experience; *Old Indian Legends, The Conjure Woman,* and *The Custom of the Country,* on tricksters; *Iola*

Leroy, *The Awakening*, and "The Vine-Leaf," on women's liberation. Most important, as Martha Banta eloquently argues in "Melting the Snows of Yesteryear; or, All Those Years of a White Girl Trying to Get it Right," an expanded canon looks, little by little, more like America.[27] A multicultural canon contains the cultural range, complexity, conflict, and contradictions of the nation itself. As Jules Chametzky has pointed out, the melting-pot theory of the United States was contested from its very beginning late in the nineteenth century. There has never been "an" American culture. "There *is* only . . . now as 'then' only *contention*, struggle, unmaking and making, discovery and invention, loss and gain."[28] Expanding the canon of American realism creates a canon that represents that contention.

NOTES

1. Amy Kaplan, *The Social Construction of American Realism* (Chicago: University of Chicago Press, 1988), p. 5.

2. Ibid., p. 6.

3. "Editors' Comment," *Studies in the Literary Imagination* 25 (1992): 1.

4. Robert Scholes, "Canonicity and Textuality," *Introduction to Scholarship in Modern Languages and Literatures*, ed. Joseph Gibaldi (New York: Modern Language Association of America, 1992), p. 147.

5. Robert Hemenway, "In the American Canon," *Redefining American Literary History*, ed. A. LaVonne Brown Ruoff and Jerry W. Ward, Jr. (New York: Modern Language Association of America, 1990), p. 63.

6. For a similar argument, see Hemenway, who advocates incorporation of African American literature into all literature classes (pp. 63–72).

7. Henry Louis Gates, Jr., "Pluralism and Its Discontents," *Profession 92*, ed. Phyllis Franklin (New York: Modern Language Association of America, 1992), p. 38.

8. John Brenkman, "Multiculturalism and Criticism," *English Inside and Out: The Place of Literary Criticism; Essays from the 50th Anniversary of the English Institute*, ed. Susan Gubar and Jonathan Kamholtz (New York: Routledge, 1993), p. 88.

9. Gates, "Pluralism", p. 37.

10. Brenkman, "Multicultualism," pp. 94, 96.

11. Paula Gunn Allen, " 'Border' Studies: The Intersection of Gender and Color," *Introduction to Scholarship*, p. 304.

12. I take the concept "master narrative," of course, from Frederic Jameson, *The Political Unconscious: Narrative as a Socially Symbolic Act* (Ithaca, N.Y.: Cornell University Press, 1981).

13. The Latin Americanist Francine Masiello similarly argues against the global application of western high theory, with its presumption that abstract, translatable constructs exist that can validly be employed anywhere. In Masiello's view, the academy must attend to and learn from the theory of local people (in her case, people living in Latin America), which is in her opinion embedded irretrievably in particular histories, languages, and local contexts. Untitled paper, Modern Language Association Convention, New York, 1992.

14. Henry Louis Gates, Jr., " 'Ethnic and Minority' Studies," *Introduction to Scholarship*, pp. 288–302; Paul Lauter, "The Literatures of America: A Comparative Discipline," *Redefining American Literary History*, pp. 9–34 (also see Lauter, *Canons and Contexts* [New York: Oxford

University Press, 1991]); Annette Kolodny, "Letting Go Our Grand Obsessions: Notes Toward a New Literary History of the American Frontiers," *American Literature*, 64 (1992): 1–18.

15. Renato Rosaldo, untitled paper, Modern Language Association Convention, New York, 1992.

16. For other discussions that proceed similarly, see Lauter's comparativist treatment of Henry James and Charles Chesnutt in "The Literatures of America"; or, broadening the field of vision dramatically, Marilyn Sanders Mobley's excellent study, *Folk Roots and Mythic Wings in Sarah Orne Jewett and Toni Morrison: The Cultural Function of Narrative* (Baton Rouge: Louisiana State University Press, 1991); or my book, *Conflicting Stories: American Women Writers at the Turn into the Twentieth Century* (New York: Oxford University Press, 1991).

17. For extended discussion, see Amy Ling, *Between Worlds: Women Writers of Chinese Ancestry* (New York: Pergamon, 1990); also, I discuss Sui Sin Far in *Conflicting Stories* and in "The New Woman as Cultural Symbol and Social Reality: Six Women Writers' Perspectives," *1915, The Cultural Moment*, ed. Adele Heller and Lois Rudnick (New Brunswick, N.J.: Rutgers University Press, 1991), pp. 82–97. Although *Mrs. Spring Fragrance* does not exist in paperback, the University of Illinois Press is issuing one, along with a book-length critical biography of Sui Sin Far by Annette White-Parks. Until then, individual stories and the autobiographical essay, "Leaves," can be found in two accessible paperback anthologies: *The Heath Anthology of American Literature*, vol. 2, ed. Paul Lauter et al. (Lexington, Mass.: D. C. Heath, 1990), and *American Women Regionalists, 1850–1910*, ed. Judith Fetterley and Marjorie Pryse (New York: W. W. Norton, 1992).

18. For representative discussions of Gilman, see Ann Lane, *To Herland and Beyond: The Life and Work of Charlotte Perkins Gilman* (New York: Pantheon Books, 1990); Susan S. Lanser, "Feminist Criticism, 'The Yellow Wallpaper,' and the Politics of Color in America," *Feminist Studies 15* (1989): 415–41; and my chapter on Gilman in *Conflicting Stories*.

19. Excellent discussions of Chesnutt can be found in William L. Andrews, *The Literary Career of Charles W. Chesnutt* (Baton Rouge: Louisiana State University Press, 1980); and Houston A. Baker, Jr., *Modernism and the Harlem Renaissance* (Chicago: University of Chicago Press, 1987). Also, the biography written by Chesnutt's daughter, Helen M. Chesnutt, remains an important source: *Charles Waddell Chesnutt: Pioneer of the Color Line* (Chapel Hill: University of North Carolina Press, 1952).

20. Little scholarship on Zitkala-Ša exists. See Dexter Fisher, "Zitkala-Ša; The Evolution of a Writer," *American Indian Quarterly 5* (1979): 229–38.

21. Sui Sin Far, *Mrs. Spring Fragrance* (Chicago: A. C. McClurg & Co., 1912), pp. 22, 31.

22. For two excellent relevant studies, see Henry Louis Gates, Jr., *The Signifying Monkey: A Theory of Afro-American Literary Criticism* (New York: Oxford University Press, 1988), and Lawrence W. Levine, *Black Culture and Black Consciousness: Afro-American Folk Thought from Slavery to Freedom* (New York: Oxford University press, 1977).

23. Charles Chesnutt, *The Conjure Woman* (1899; rpt. Ann Arbor: University of Michigan Press, 1969), p. 11.

24. Zitkala-Ša, *Old Indian Legends* (1901; rpt. Lincoln: University of Nebraska Press, 1985), p. vi.

25. Arnold Krupat, *The Voice in the Margin: Native American Literature and the Canon* (Berkeley and Los Angeles: University of California Press, 1989), p. 14.

26. Among the many useful books on the subject designed for teachers are Houston A. Baker, Jr., ed., *Three American Literatures: Essays in Chicano, Native American, and Asian-American Literature for Teachers of American Literature* (New York: Modern Language Association of America, 1982); Paula Gunn Allen, ed., *Studies in American Indian Literature: Criti-*

cal Essays and Course Designs (New York: Modern Language Association of America, 1983); and A. LaVonne Brown Ruoff, *American Indian Literatures: An Introduction, Bibliographic Review, and Selected Bibliography* (New York: Modern Language Association of America, 1990).

27. Martha Banta, unpublished paper, Modern Language Association Convention, New York, 1992.

28. Jules Chametzky, "Beyond Melting Pots, Cultural Pluralism, Ethnicity—or, *Deja Vu* All Over Again," *MELUS* 16 (1989–90): 13.

Bibliography
Index

BIBLIOGRAPHY

This list is confined to twentieth-century studies of late nineteenth- and early twentieth-century American realism and naturalism. Works devoted to one author are not included.

Ahnebrink, Lars. *The Beginnings of Naturalism in American Fiction . . . 1891–1903*. Cambridge: Harvard University Press, 1950.

Becker, George J., ed. *Documents of Modern Literary Realism*. Princeton: Princeton University Press, 1963.

Bell, Michael Davitt. *The Problem of American Realism: Studies in the Cultural History of a Literary Idea*. Chicago: University of Chicago Press, 1993.

Berthoff, Warner. *The Ferment of Realism: American Literature, 1884–1919*. New York: Free Press, 1965.

Block, Haskell M. *Naturalistic Triptych: The Fictive and the Real in Zola, Mann, and Dreiser*. New York: Random House, 1970.

Borus, Daniel H. *Writing Realism: Howells, James, and Norris in the Mass Market*. Chapel Hill: University of North Carolina Press, 1989.

Bowron, Bernard R., Jr. "Realism Is America." *Comparative Literature* 3 (1951): 268–85.

Cady, Edwin H. *The Light of Common Day: Realism in American Fiction*. Bloomington: Indiana University Press, 1971.

Cargill, Oscar. *Intellectual America: Ideas on the March*. New York: Macmillan, 1941.

Carter, Everett. *Howells and the Age of Realism*. Philadelphia: Lippincott, 1954.

Chase, Richard. *The American Novel and Its Tradition*. Garden City, NY: Doubleday Anchor, 1957.

Conder, John J. *Naturalism in American Fiction: The Classic Phase*. Lexington: University Press of Kentucky, 1984.

Corkin, Stanley. *Realism and the Birth of the Modern United States: Cinema, Literature, and Culture*. Athens: University of Georgia Press, 1996.

Cowley, Malcolm. " 'Not Men': A Natural History of American Naturalism." *Kenyon Review* 9 (1947): 414–35.

Dike, Donald A. "Notes on Local Color and Its Relation to Realism." *College English* 14 (1952): 81–88.

Ellmann, Richard, and Charles Feidelson, Jr., eds. *The Modern Tradition: Backgrounds of Modern Literature*. New York: Oxford University Press, 1965.

Falk, Robert. "The Literary Criticism of the Genteel Decades: 1870–1900." In *The Development of American Literary Criticism*, ed. Floyd Stovall. Chapel Hill: University of North Carolina Press, 1955.

———. "The Rise of Realism, 1871–1891." In *Transitions in American Literary History*, ed. Harry H. Clark. Durham, N.C.: Duke University Press, 1953.

———. *The Victorian Mode in American Fiction, 1865–1885*. East Lansing: Michigan State University Press, 1965.

Farrell, James T. "Some Observations on Naturalism, So Called, in Fiction." In *Reflections at Fifty*. New York: Vanguard, 1950.

Figg, Robert M., III. "Naturalism as a Literary Form," *Georgia Review* 18 (1964): 308–16.

Frierson, William C., and Herbert Edwards. "Impact of French Naturalism on American Critical Opinion, 1877-1892." *PMLA* 63 (1948): 1007-16.

Furst, Lilian R., and Peter N. Skrine. *Naturalism*. London: Methuen, 1971.

Geismar, Maxwell. *Rebels and Ancestors: The American Novel, 1890-1915*. Boston: Houghton Mifflin, 1953.

Giles, James R. *The Naturalistic Inner-City Novel in America: Encounters with the Fat Man*. Columbia: University of South Carolina Press, 1995.

Graham, Don. "Naturalism in American Fiction: A Status Report." *Studies in American Fiction* 10 (1982): 1-16.

Habegger, Alfred. *Gender, Fantasy, and Realism in American Literature*. New York: Columbia University Press, 1982.

Hakutani, Yoshinobu, and Lewis Fried, eds. *American Literary Naturalism: A Reassessment*. Heidelberg: Carl Winter, 1975.

Hicks, Granville. *The Great Tradition: An Interpretation of American Literature Since the Civil War*. New York: Macmillan, 1933.

Hoffman, Frederick J. "From Document to Symbol: Zola and American Naturalism." *Revue des Langues Vivantes*, U.S. Bicentennial Issue (1976): 203-12.

Hook, Andrew. *American Literature in Context III, 1865-1900*. London: Methuen, 1983.

Howard, June. *Form and History in American Literary Naturalism*. Chapel Hill: University of North Carolina Press, 1985.

Kaplan, Amy. *The Social Construction of American Realism*. Chicago: University of Chicago Press, 1981.

Kaplan, Harold. *Power and Order: Henry Adams and the Naturalist Tradition in American Fiction*. Chicago: University of Chicago Press, 1988.

Kazin, Alfred. "American Naturalism: Reflections from Another Era." In *The American Writer and the European Tradition*, ed. Margaret Denny and William H. Gilman. Minneapolis: University of Minnesota Press, 1950.

——. *On Native Grounds: An Interpretation of Modern American Prose*. New York: Harcourt, Brace, 1942.

Kolb, Harold H., Jr. *The Illusion of Life: American Realism as a Literary Form*. Charlottesville: University Press of Virginia, 1969.

Lehan, Richard. "American Literary Naturalism: The French Connection." *Nineteenth-Century Fiction* 38 (1984): 529-57.

Lutwack, Leonard. "The Iron Madonna and American Criticism in the Genteel Era." *Modern Language Quarterly* 15 (1954): 343-48.

Martin, Jay. *Harvests of Change: American Literature, 1865-1914*. Englewood Cliffs, NJ: Prentice-Hall, 1967.

Martin, Ronald E. *American Literature and the Universe of Force*. Durham, NC: Duke University Press, 1981.

McKay, Janet H. *Narration and Discourse in American Realistic Fiction*. Philadelphia: University of Pennsylvania Press, 1982.

Michaels, Walter Benn. *The Gold Standard and the Logic of Naturalism: American Literature at the Turn of the Century*. Berkeley: University of California Press, 1987.

Mitchell, Lee Clark. *Determined Fictions: American Literary Naturalism*. New York: Columbia University Press, 1989.

Parrington, Vernon Louis. *The Beginnings of Critical Realism in America, 1860-1920*. Vol. 3 of *Main Currents in American Thought*. New York: Harcourt, Brace, 1930.

Perosa, Sergio. *American Theories of the Novel, 1793-1903*. New York: New York University Press, 1983.

Pizer, Donald. *Realism and Naturalism in Nineteenth-Century American Literature*. Rev. ed. Carbondale: Southern Illinois University Press, 1984.

——. *The Theory and Practice of American Literary Naturalism: Selected Essays and Reviews*. Carbondale: Southern Illinois University Press, 1993.

Pizer, Donald, ed. *The Cambridge Companion to American Realism and Naturalism: Howells to London*. New York: Cambridge University Press, 1995.

Pizer, Donald, and Earl N. Harbert, eds. *American Realists and Naturalists*. Vol. 12 of *Dictionary of Literary Biography*. Detroit: Gale Research, 1982.

Quirk, Tom, and Gary Schornhorst, eds. *American Realism and the Canon*. Newark: University of Delaware Press, 1994.

Rahv, Philip. "On the Decline of Naturalism." *Partisan Review* 9 (1942): 483-93.

Rathbun, John W., and Harry H. Clark. *Ameri-*

can Literary Criticism, 1860–1905. Boston: Twayne, 1979.

Salomen, Roger. "Realism as Disinheritance: Twain, Howells and James." American Quarterly 16 (1964): 531–44.

Seaman, Roger. "Naturalist Narratives and Their Ideational Context: A Theory of American Naturalist Fiction." Canadian Review of American Studies 19 (1988): 47–64.

Seltzer, Mark. Bodies and Machines. New York: Routledge, 1992.

Shi, David. Facing Facts: Realism in American Thought and Culture, 1850–1920. New York: Oxford University Press, 1995.

Spencer, Benjamin T. "The New Realism and a National Literature." PMLA 56 (1941): 1116–32.

Sundquist, Eric J., ed. American Realism: New Essays. Baltimore: Johns Hopkins University Press, 1982.

Taylor, Gordon O. The Passages of Thought: Psychological Representation in the American Novel, 1870–1900. New York: Oxford University Press, 1969.

Thorp, Willard. American Writing in the Twentieth Century. Cambridge: Harvard Univesity Press, 1960.

Trachtenberg, Alan. The Incorporation of America: Culture and Society in the Gilded Age. New York: Hill and Wang, 1982.

Trilling, Lionel. "Reality in America." In The Liberal Imagination. New York: Viking, 1950.

Walcutt, Charles C. American Literary Naturalism, A Divided Stream. Minneapolis: University of Minnesota Press, 1956.

Wilson, Christopher P. The Labor of Words: Literary Professionalism in the Progressive Era. Athens: University of Georgia Press, 1985.

Ziff, Larzer. The American 1890s. New York: Viking, 1966.

INDEX

DONALD PIZER is Pierce Butler Professor of English at Tulane University. A specialist in late nineteenth- and early twentieth-century American literature, he has published widely in this area. Among his books are full-length studies of Frank Norris, Theodore Dreiser, and John Dos Passos as well as *Realism and Naturalism in Nineteenth-Century American Literature* (1966; 2nd rev. ed., 1984) and *The Theory and Practice of American Literary Naturalism: Selected Essays and Reviews* (1993). He has held fellowships from the Guggenheim Foundation, the National Endowment for the Humanities, and the American Council of Learned Societies.